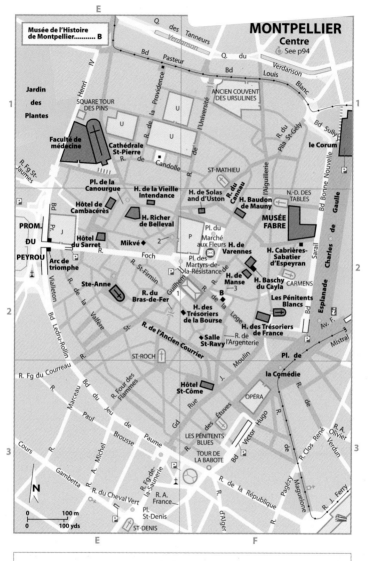

Musée de l'Histoire de Montpellier........... B

MONTPELLIER
Centre
See p94

Q. des Tanneurs

Verdanson

Q. du Verdanson

Bd Pasteur

Bd Louis Blanc

Jardin des Plantes

SQUARE TOUR DES PINS

Henri IV

Bd

R. de la Providence

de l'Université

ANCIEN COUVENT DES URSULINES

R. du Pila St-Gély

Bd Sully

le Corum

Faculté de médecine

Cathédrale St-Pierre

R. de Candolle

ST-MATHIEU

R. de l'Aiguillerie

N.-D. DES TABLES

Bd Bonne Nouvelle

R. Fg St-Jaumes

Pl. de la Canourgue

H. de la Vieille Intendance

H. de Solas and d'Uston

R. du Cannau

H. Baudon de Mauny

MUSÉE FABRE

Gaulle

de

Charles

Hôtel de Cambacérès

H. Richer de Belleval

PROM.

Bd

J

Pre.

Hôtel du Sarret

Mikvé ♦

Foch

Pl. du Marché aux Fleurs

H. de Varennes

H. Cabrières-Sabatier d'Espeyran

Sarail

DU

R.

2

CARMENS

PEYROU

Arc de triomphe

R. St-Firmin

Pl. des Martyrs-de-la-Résistance

R. de

H. de Manse

3

H. Baschy du Cayla

Esplanade

Av. F.

Vialleton

Ste-Anne

R. du Bras-de-Fer

Guilhem

1

H. des Trésoriers de la Bourse

R. de la Loge

Les Pénitents Blancs

Bd Ledru-Rollin

R. de la Valfère

R. St-

R. de l'Ancien Courrier

♦ Salle St-Ravy

H. des Trésoriers de France

R. de l'Argenterie

Mistral

ST-ROCH

J. Moullin

Pl. de

la Comédie

R. Fg du Courreau

R. Four des Flammes

Hôtel St-Côme

OPÉRA

R. A. Olivier

Marceau

Bd du Jeu de Paume

Rue

des Étuves

R. Clos René

Verdun

Paul Brousse

Gd

LES PÉNITENTS BLEUS

Bd Victor Hugo

R. de

Cours Gambetta

R. A. Michel

R. du Cheval Vert

R. Fg de la Saunerie

TOUR DE LA BABOTE

R. de la République

Pagézy

Maguelone

R. J. Ferry

N

0   100 m

0   100 yds

R. A. France

Pl. St-Denis

ST-DENIS

R. d'Alger

E   F

STREET INDEX   Castellane (Pl.)............... 1   Chabaneau (Pl.)............... 2   Petite Loge (R. de la)............... 3

THE**GREEN**GUIDE
Languedoc Roussillon Tarn Gorges

Tarn gorges, Lozère © Jean-Paul Azam/hemis.fr

MICHELIN

THE GREEN GUIDE LANGUEDOC ROUSSILLON TARN GORGES

Editorial Director	Cynthia Ochterbeck
Principal Writer	Terry Marsh
Production Manager	Natasha George
Cartography	John Dear
Photo Editor	Yoshimi Kanazawa
Interior Design	Chris Bell
Layout	Natasha George
Cover Design	Chris Bell, Christelle Le Déan

Contact Us
Michelin Travel and Lifestyle North America
One Parkway South
Greenville, SC 29615
USA
travel.lifestyle@us.michelin.com

Michelin Travel Partner
Hannay House
39 Clarendon Road
Watford, Herts WD17 1JA
UK
℘01923 205240
travelpubsales@uk.michelin.com
www.ViaMichelin.com

Special Sales
For information regarding bulk sales, customized editions and premium sales, please contact us at:
travel.lifestyle@us.michelin.com

Note to the reader Addresses, phone numbers, opening hours and prices published in this guide are accurate at the time of press. We welcome corrections and suggestions that may assist us in preparing the next edition. While every effort is made to ensure that all information printed in this guide is correct and up-to-date, Michelin Travel Partner accepts no liability for any direct, indirect or consequential losses howsoever caused so far as such can be excluded by law.

HOW TO USE THIS GUIDE

PLANNING YOUR TRIP

The blue-tabbed PLANNING YOUR TRIP section at the front of the guide gives you **ideas for your trip** and **practical information** to help you organise it. You'll find tours, practical information, a host of outdoor activities, a calendar of events, information on shopping, sightseeing, kids' activities and more.

INTRODUCTION

The orange-tabbed INTRODUCTION section explores the Languedoc-Roussillon's **Nature** and geology. The **History** section spans from the Paleolithic to the Cathars. The **Art and Culture** section covers architecture, art, literature and music, while the **Region Today** delves into modern Languedoc Roussillon Tarn Gorges.

DISCOVERING

The green-tabbed DISCOVERING section features Principal Sights by region, featuring the most interesting local **Sights**, **Walking Tours**, nearby **Excursions**, and detailed **Driving Tours**. Admission prices shown are normally for a single adult.

ADDRESSES

We've selected some of the best hotels, restaurants, cafés, shops, nightlife and entertainment to fit all budgets. See the Legend on the cover flap for an explanation of the price categories. See the back of the guide for an index of where to find hotels and restaurants.

Sidebars

Throughout the guide you will find blue, orange and green-coloured text boxes with lively anecdotes, detailed history and background information.

😊 A Bit of Advice 😊

Green advice boxes found in this guide contain practical tips and handy information relevant to your visit or to a sight in the Discovering section.

STAR RATINGS★★★

Michelin has given star ratings for more than 100 years. If you're pressed for time, we recommend you visit the ★★★, or ★★ sights first:

★★★ **Highly recommended**
★★ **Recommended**
★ **Interesting**

MAPS

- 🕲 Country map
- 🕲 Principal Sights map
- 🕲 Region maps
- 🕲 Maps for major cities and villages
- 🕲 Local tour maps

All maps in this guide are oriented north, unless otherwise indicated by a directional arrow. The term "Local Map" refers to a map within the chapter or Tourism Region. A complete list of the maps found in the guide appears at the back of this book.

PLANNING YOUR TRIP

INTRODUCTION TO LANGUEDOC ROUSSILLON TARN GORGES

DISCOVERING LANGUEDOC ROUSSILLON TARN GORGES

Languedoc-Roussillon

CONTENTS

Welcome to Languedoc Roussillon Tarn Gorges

High, wide and handsome, the Languedoc-Roussillon's mountains, valleys, vineyards and towns and villages are a perfect companion to an identical landscape of neighbouring Tarn and Aveyron.

Languedoc-Roussillon

MONTPELLIER AND ITS REGION
(pp90–120)

There is a great intimacy about the Montpellier region; a vibrant, buzzing, bustling friendliness and captivating atmosphere, fanned by the warm breezes of the Mediterranean that raise the soft thyme, rosemary, broom and rock rose scents of the *garrigue*.

LE GARD: THE COAST TO THE CÉVENNES *(pp121–145)*

This department, named after the river Gard, is a place of many contrasts and great variety, with the blessing of fine landscapes: the Cévennes, the Camargue, the Cévenol foothills, the Cèze and Rhone valleys, all creating a leading tourist destination.

LA LOZÈRE AND LE PAYS CÉVENOL *(pp146–169)*

La Lozère covers four mountain ranges. In the northwest lies the basalt plateau of Aubrac. The north and northeast of the department embrace the Margeride mountains, formed of granite, and with peaks reaching more than 1 500m. The *causses* are in the southwest, while the southeastern corner contains the Cévennes.

LES CAUSSES AND THE TARN GORGES *(pp170–197)*

Between the Causse Méjean and the Causse de Sauveterre, the Gorges du Tarn form a canyon fashioned by the River Tarn. The so-called *causses* are part of a vast, wild and beautiful limestone plateau, Les Grandes Causses.

PAYS HAUTE-LANGUEDOC AND THE VINEYARDS *(pp198–231)*

Wine production in Haute-Languedoc is marked by the choice of grape varieties. The diversity of the soil produces varied wines. Haute-Languedoc is also blessed with a scattering of stunning Gallo-Roman settlements.

CARCASSONNE AND PAYS CATHARE *(pp232–264)*

The history of the Cathar believers permeates France, but is nowhere more focused than in the great citadels among the mountains to the south. The story continues in the city of Carcassonne, both in the *bastide* lower town south of the Canal du Midi, and in the ancient walled citadel.

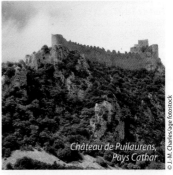

Château de Puilaurens, Pays Cathar

© J.-M. Charles/age fotostock

PERPIGNAN, CÔTE VERMEILLE AND THE ROUSSILLON PLAIN
(pp265–285)

The eastern end of the Pyrenees, where the mountains tumble down to the sea is neither France nor Spain. This is Catalonia, a culture with deep and ancient roots; passionate, with a vibrancy that attracts artists.

PYRÉNÉES ORIENTALES AND ANDORRA *(pp286–313)*

With the Roussillon Plain to the north and the mountain of Canigou to the south, the Pyrénées-Orientales are a region of great contrast. Attractive villages dot a verdant and peaceful landscape of great natural beauty. Popular skiing and walking territory.

Midi Toulousain

TOULOUSE AND AROUND
(pp316–339)

Nicknamed the 'Pink City' for its red-brick buildings, Toulouse is a mildly frenetic, hugely entertaining and vibrant place. This capital of France's largest region (Midi-Pyrénées) very much has its own glorious identity. A lively student population brings an added and colourful dynamic.

ALBIGEOIS AND THE BLACK MOUNTAIN (pp340–368)

Albi may lend its name to an horrific episode in the history of France, but its villages are delightful, decorating the Tarn river, Montagne Noire, and south-western tip of the Massif Central, and a broad ridge of densely forested upland separating Tarn from Aude.

L'ARIÈGE (pp369–390)

The Ariège is renowned as a frontier between Gascony and Languedoc, France and Spain. It is also a region of a considerable prehistoric interest that manifests itself in caves, decorated with fine paintings, and artefacts.

SAINT-GAUDENS AND AROUND
(pp391–410)

The region of Comminges, a province of the ancient kingdom of Gascony, lies at the centre of the Pyrenees. Archaeological remains found near Aurignac have given their name to one of the continent's earliest prehistoric cultures from more than 30 000 years ago.

LA BIGORRE (pp411–438)

Far from being the preserve of the *alpinistes*, the Hautes-Pyrénées offer endless space and fresh air, with a range of signposted walks from easy

Grotte de Niaux, l'Ariège

to strenuous. There are many beautiful places to visit – the mountains have lakes and waterfalls in abundance – but outstanding visits are the Cirque de Gavarnie, the Pont d'Espagne and the splendid Gave de Marcadau that lies beyond.

THE GERS REGION (pp439–455)

Characterised by charming villages and with the Pyrenees to the south, Le Gers is renowned for its gastronomic specialities, including Armagnac brandy, Côtes de Gascogne wines, Floc de Gascogne and foie gras.

MONTAUBAN AND AROUND
(pp456–470)

The area north of the city of Toulouse is a peaceful haven of scenery, teeming with wildlife and dotted with attractive medieval villages. There is a strong historical heritage here, but the area has a low profile. The principal town is Montauban, on the boundary between Bas Quercy and the alluvial plains of the Garonne.

L'AVEYRON AND THE LOT VALLEY (pp471–493)

In the west of Aveyron lie a group of fortified medieval bastides. In the southeast there are strong links with the Knights Templar. In the centre, lies the city of Rodez from which roads splay out like the spokes of a wheel. The Lot valley is lush and green and sparsely populated.

9

Transhumance in Cévennes
© Didier Zylberyng/Travel Pictures

Michelin Driving Tours

LOCAL DRIVES

The following is a selection of the driving tours in the Discovering section. Allow ample time to enjoy scenery and to make unplanned stops.

Le Lodèvois Rouge

65km/40mi from Lodève.
See LODÈVE.
This corner of the Mediterranean backcountry is called 'the red' because of the colour of its sandstone. After skirting the Lake Salagou the route reaches the highlight of the tour: the extraordinary geological spectacle of the Cirque de Mourèze, a gigantic natural amphitheatre strewn with enormous blocks of rock.

Bassin de Thau

74km/46mi from Sète.
See BASSIN DE THAU.
The coast of the Languedoc is formed by a string of lagoons. This tour visits one of them to see the oyster and mussel beds for which it is renowned. It also stops at a dinosaur museum.

The Coast Road

33km/20mi from Cerbère.
See CÔTE VERMEILLE.
An easy touring route goes along this beautiful indented stretch of coast close to the Spanish border, passing through the picturesque anchovy-fishing town of Collioure. Alternatively, there's a mountain route (37km/23mi) inland, also giving views of the 'Vermilion Coast'.

The Sidobre

53km/33mi from Castres.
See CASTRES.
Not far from the town of Castres in the Tarn *département* is a cluster of granite rocks sculpted by the elements into extraordinary forms and shrouded in woods.

Lake Salagou and the village of Celles

© Jean du Boisberranger/hemis.fr

Tarn Gorges Road

Two tours: 30km/18mi from Florac and 60km/37mi from Ste-Énimie.
See GORGES DU TARN.
The immensely deep canyon of the Gorges du Tarn is a must-see sight of France. These two tours can be driven separately or joined up to explore the bottom of the gorge and climb high above it for unbeatable views.

Lot valley

50km/30mi from Rodez.
See LOT VALLEY.
The valley of the slow moving river Lot makes for a pleasant short tour, with stops at a string of pretty towns including Montrozier, Bouzouls, Saint-Geniez d'Olt, and St-Côme d'Olt.

Vallée des Cauterets

12km/7.5mi from Cauterets.
See CAUTERETS.
Of the picturesque tours in the Pyrenees, this is one of most rewarding. The route leaves the spa of Cauterets and climbs past a series of waterfalls to reach the beauty spot of Pont d'Espagne. Here a chair lift takes you up to the beautiful Lac de Gaube higher in the mountains, or you can walk into the beautiful Gave de Marcadau valley.

Route du Tourmalet
30km/19mi from Barèges.
See LUZ-ST-SAUVEUR.
The Pyrenees are famed for their high mountain passes and this is one of the best. The route twists up to the pass, which provides a test of endurance for the riders of the Tour de France. From La Mongie, you can take a cable car up to the observatory on the summit of the Pic du Midi de Bigorre for an even better view.

Vallee de l'Ossé and Vallée d'Auzoue
40km/25mi from Condom.
See CONDOM.
The Gers is a great region for backroads touring and this route brings together many interesting sights: the Roman villa of Séviac, the circular village of Fourcès, the fortified village of Larresingle and the abbey of Flaren. It includes a stop to sample Armagnac brandy on the way.

THEMED TOURS
Montpellier "Follies"
Two tours: 9km/6mi east and 22km/14mi west, both from Montpellier.
See MONTPELLIER.
As a break from urban sightseeing, these two short tours take you into the outskirts of the city to visit 30 aristocratic residences built by wealthy citizens in the 18C.

Templars and Hospitallers
166km/103mi from Millau.
See CAUSSE DU LARZAC.
In the 12C the Knights Templar established themselves on the Causse du Larzac. They, and the Knights Hospitallers, left behind commanderies and fortified towns, notably the well-preserved Le Couvertoirade. The tour also visits the caves where Roquefort cheese is matured.

Les Corbières Cathares: Round Trip from Duilhac-sous-Peyrepertuse
117km/73mi from Duilhac-sous-Peyrepertuse. See LES CORBIÈRES.
The last Cathars (dissenters of the Middle Ages) took refuge from persecution in the dramatically sited castles of Peyrepertuse, Queribus and Montsegur.

Dyer's Woad Country
80km/50mi from Saint-Félix-Lauragais.
See SAINT-FÉLIX-LAURAGAIS.
In the 14C and 15C fortunes were made in Toulouse by merchants trading in woad, which was used to make a blue dye. The story of this economic boom is traced by this tour through the city's hinterland.

The Canal du Midi
Three tours: 50km/31mi from Seuil de Naurouze to Carcassonne, 120km/75mi from Carcassonne to Béziers (see CARCASSONNE); 114km/71mi from the Prise d'Alzeau to the Seuil de Naurouze (see La MONTAIGNE NOIR SOUTH).
An extraordinary feat of 17C aquatic engineering, the Canal du Midi connects Toulouse with the Mediterranean. Three tours visit the attractions along the canal, especially the flight of eight locks near Béziers (*Les Bateaux du Soleil; ℰ04 67 94 08 79; www.bateaux-du-soleil.fr*).

Le Chemin des Verriers
44km/27mi from Sommières.
See SOMMIÈRES.
Glassmaking thrived around Sommières from the Middle Ages to the 18C, as can be seen in a museum and glassmaker's workshop, both stops on the route.

Bastides and Castelnaux
77km/48mi from Marciac.
See MARCIAC.
Bastides are new towns built in the Middle Ages; Castelnau towns that sprang up in the shelter of a castle. This tour through Gascony visits both.

Vallée du Louron
46km/28mi from Arreau. See ARREAU.
Several charming villages, and churches with ornately painted interiors.

When and Where to Go

WHEN TO GO
CLIMATE

Although much of this region is predominantly Mediterranean in climate, it is open to oceanic influences from the Atlantic and, in its northern part, to the harsher climatic conditions of the Massif Central. As for the Pyrenees mountain range, its valleys are under the influence of several weather systems determined by the altitude and the direction the slopes are facing.

Late **winter** and **early spring** offer plenty of snow for cross-country skiing in the Aubrac, and Alpine skiing in the Pyrenees.

Spring is the ideal season for walking and riding tours and for discovering the region in general.

Summer is dry and hot with luminous skies, particularly along the Mediterranean. Sudden, violent storms bring relief from the scorching heat from time to time but the sun rarely admits defeat for more than a few hours.

In **autumn**, rainfall is often abundant particularly in the Toulouse and Albi areas, while warm southwest winds blowing over the whole region bring alternating periods of dry and wet weather.

WEATHER FORECAST

Information about the weather in France is available on www.meteofrance.com, and this is by far the best option since it gives a wide range of data.

Other options are:

National forecast: ☎ 32 50
Local forecast: ☎ 08 92 68 02 XX, where XX is the number of the *département* (e.g. for the Nord – ☎ 08 92 68 02 59).

WHERE TO GO
ONE WEEK

Most of the unmissable sights in this guide fall roughly in a broad diagonal line southwest to northeast, from the Pyrenees to the Cévennes with Toulouse as the natural fulcrum. Start in Bigorre, in the central Pyrenees, and devote two days to seeing the beauty spots of the mountains, especially the Cirque de Gavarnie and the Pic du Midi. It is an easy trip from here to Toulouse, ancient capital of the Languedoc, which is worth a day's sightseeing. The city makes a good base for two essential day trips: one to the red-brick city of Albi and the medieval town of Cordes-sur-Ciel; the other to the walled citadel of Carcassonne. Spend the last three days getting to and exploring the sights around the Cévennes and in Lozère, especially the great canyon of the Gorges du Tarn, the caves of Aven Armand, the rock formations of Montpellier-le-Vieux, the Millau viaduct and the immense bowl in the landscape, the Cirque de Navacelles.

TWO WEEKS

With two weeks, there's more time to see the Pyrenees thoroughly, both the heights and the foothills. The shrine of Lourdes and the cathedral of Saint-Bertrand-de-Comminges can be included in your itinerary as can French Catalonia inland from Perpignan (Mount Canigou and its abbey, the Prieuré de Serrabone, and the abbey of St-Michel-de-Cuxa) and along the coast (Elne, Collioure and the Côte Vermeille). Other additions can be Andorra and the Cathar castles of the Ariège and Aude, notably Montségur and Peyrepertuse. The Ariège also has two extraordinary caves, the Mas d'Azil and Niaux. The abbey of Moissac can be added as an excursion from Toulouse and a detour north can be made to see Conques and the upper Lot valley. After touring the Cévennes and Gorges du Tarn, descend to the coast via the caves of Les Demoiselles and the abbey of St-Guilhem-le-Desert to visit Montpellier, Pézenas and Narbonne.

SIGNPOSTED ITINERARIES

Tourist authorities and heritage organisations in France have helpfully mapped out travel itineraries to help you discover particular regions or traditions. You will find brochures in tourist offices, and the routes are generally well marked and easy to follow (*signs posted along the roads*).

HISTORY

Some of these itineraries are managed by the **Fédération Nationale des Routes Historiques** (*21 Rue Victor Hugo 18003 Bourges. 02 48 65 31 55. www.routes-historiques.com*). Apply to local tourist offices for leaflets with mapped itineraries. The list below includes a local contact when appropriate:

♦ **Route historique du pastel en pays de cocagne** (dyer's woad country between Toulouse and Albi. Château-Musée du Pastel, 81220 St-Paul-Cap-de-Joux, 05 63 70 63 82).

♦ **Route historique en Languedoc-Roussillon** (Château de Flaugergues, 1744 avenue Albert-Einstein, 34000 Montpellier, 04 99 52 66 46).

♦ **Route historique en Terre Catalane: de l'Homme de Tautavel à Picasso** (Réseau culturel Terre catalane, 110 rue du Théâtre, BP 60244, 66002 Perpignan Cedex, 04 68 64 93 54).

LE CHEMIN DE SAINT JACQUES

The most popular long distance routes across southwestern France are the various branches of the pilgrimage towards Santiago de Compostela in Spain (The Way of St James, *see p59*). Almost every stop along the way has some point of architectural interest. These routes are mostly used by walkers and cyclists, but can also be followed in a car with judicious use of the road network. In many towns the path of the Chemin de Saint Jacques is marked by the saint's symbol of a scallop shell. Hoteliers and restaurateurs on the routes are proud of their associations with the pilgrimage. There are four main routes through France which converge in the western Pyrenees before cross over into Spain. Two of them are within the area of this guide:

The **Via Podiensis** is synonymous with the GR 65 long-distance footpath. It passes through Aubrac, Saint-Come-d'Olt, Espalion, Estaing, Conques, Decazeville, Moissac, Auvillar, Lectoure, Condom, Flaran and Nogaro.

The **Chemin d'Arles**, or Via Tolosane, was used in the past by pilgrims from Provence and Italy. It goes through Montpellier, Murat-sur-Vebre, La Salvetat-sur-Agout, Brassac, Ferrières, Castres, Revel, Toulouse (where the great church of St Sernin was built for the benefit of pilgrims), L'Isle-Jourdain, Gimont, Auch, Montesquiou, Bassoues, Marciac and Maubourguet before continuing into the Béarn region.

DO-IT-YOURSELF ITINERARIES

France is extremely good at showing off its heritage and certain organisations exist to draw tourists' attention to what is on offer. The following organisations all offer a select list of towns, villages and monuments fulfilling certain criteria that can be put together to make an itinerary:

♦ **Les Plus Beaux Villages** www.les-plus-beaux-villages-de-france.org/en.

♦ **Villes et Pays d'Art et de l'Histoire** www.vpah.culture.fr.

♦ **Villes et Villages Fleuries** www.villes-et-villages-fleuris.com.

♦ **Les Plus Beaux Detours de France** www.plusbeauxdetours.com.

Of course, notwithstanding the 'status' conferred by recognition by these organisations, you will find countless equally charming places that are not included.

15

What to See and Do

OUTDOOR FUN
WATER SPORTS

Swimming, water-skiing, sailing
Beaches – The Languedoc coast has vast sandy beaches which stretch invitingly for miles, often sandwiched between the sea and lagoons. The best are to be found between La Grande-Motte and Palavas-les-Flots, from Sète to Cap-d'Agde, and around Cap-d'Agde and Valras. Bathing conditions are indicated by flags on beaches which are surveyed by lifeguards (no flags means no lifeguards): green indicates it is safe to bathe and lifeguards are on duty; yellow warns that conditions are not that good, but lifeguards are still in attendance; red means bathing is forbidden as conditions are too dangerous.

Lakes and reservoirs – The main lakes and reservoirs with facilities for swimming and various water sports, including sailing and windsurfing, and where it is possible to go for walks or picnic on the lake shore, include: Bages, Sigean, Leucate, Ganguise, Jouarre (**Aude**); Pareloup, Pont-de-Salars, Villefranche-de-Panat (**Aveyron**); Les Camboux (**Gard**); La Ravière, Thau, Salagou (**Hérault**); Naussac, Villefort (**Lozère**), Matemale (**Pyrénées-Orientales**).

Useful addresses
- **Fédération française de Voile**
  17 Rue Henri-Bocquillon, 75015 Paris Cedex 16. ℘01 40 60 37 00; www.ffvoile.fr.
- **Ligue de voile du Languedoc-Roussillon** – Patio Santa Monica, 1815 Ave Marcel Pagnol, 34470 Pérols. ℘04 67 50 48 30. www.ffvoilelr.net.
- **France Stations Nautique** – 17 Rue Henri-Bocquillon, 75015 Paris. ℘01 44 05 96 55. www.station-nautique.com.

- **Fédération française de ski nautique et de Wakeboard**
  9–11 rue du Borrego, 75020 Paris. ℘01 53 20 19 19. www.ffsnw.fr.

Marinas – The numerous marinas dotted along the coast offer pleasure craft over 100 000 moorings. Information is available from the various harbour master's offices or from the **Association des ports de plaisance du Languedoc-Roussillon**, Mairie, www.upvlr.com.

Canoeing, kayaking and rafting
Canoeing is a popular family pastime on the peaceful waters of the region. **Kayaking** is practised on the lakes and, for more experienced paddlers, rapid sections of the rivers. The upper and middle valley of the Tarn, and the valleys of the Dourbie, the Orb, the Hérault and the Garonne among others are wonderful places to explore by canoe, with their beautiful scenery, stretches of rapids and tiny beaches ideal as picnic spots. Centres for canoeing have been set up in the Parc régional du Haut-Languedoc.
Various canoeing guides and a map, *France canoe-kayak et sports d'eau,* are on sale from the **Fédération française de canoë-kayak**, 87 quai de la Marne, 94344 Joinville-le-Pont, ℘01 45 11 08 50; www.ffck.org.
Rafting is the easiest of these fresh-water sports, since it involves going down rivers in inflatable craft steered by an instructor; special equipment is provided.

Other useful addresses
- **Comité départemental de canoe-kayak de l'Ariège**
  Complexe sportif de l'Ayroule, 09000 Foix.
  ℘06 82 28 39 90.
  www.ariegepyrenees-outdoor.com.
- **L'Échappée Verte** organises trips throughout the region.
  ℘06 13 07 04 03.
  www.echappeeverte.com.

CANYONING, HYDROSPEED AND DIVING

Canyoning is a technique for body-surfing down narrow gorges and over falls, as though on a giant water slide, whereas **hydrospeed** involves swimming down rapids with a kickboard and flippers. These sports require protection: wear a wet suit and a helmet.

Information: **Fédération Française de la Montagne et de l'Escalade**, 8-10 Quai de la Marne, 75019 Paris. 01 40 18 75 50; www.ffme.fr.
The list of **diving** clubs in the region is available from the **Fédération Française d'Études et de Sports Sous-marins**, 24 quai de Rive-Neuve, 13284 Marseille Cedex 07; 04 91 33 99 31; www.ffessm.fr.

FRESHWATER FISHING

Information about fishing is available from the **Conseil Supérieur de la Pêche**, Delegation du Sud-Ouest; 05 62 73 76 80; www.csp.ecologie. gouv.fr, or from the **Fédération Nationale de la Pêche en France**, 17 rue Bergére, 75009 Paris; 01 48 24 96 00; www.federationpeche. fr (which has branch offices at Albi, Carcassonne, Mende, Montpellier, Nîmes, Perpignan, Rodez, Tarbes and Toulouse).
Mountain lakes and streams of the Pyrenees region are ideal for trout fishing. Two-week holiday fishing permits are available in some areas – contact the local federation for details (or try local fishing tackle shops or tourist offices). For information on fishing regulations in the 20 or so lakes in the Bouillouses area, contact the tourist office in Font-Romeu.

SEA FISHING

Salt-water fishing can be practised on foot, from a boat or underwater with diving gear along the coast and in the lagoons where fish abound. Half and full-day sea fishing trips are organised at locations like the rocky coast around Grau d'Agde and offshore from Banyuls-sur-Mer: www.agde-croisiere-peche.com.

♦ **Fédération Française des Pêcheurs en Mer** can provide information about marinas, and fishing clubs and schools along the coast. Résidence Alliance, Centre Jorlis, 64600 Anglet; 05 59 31 00 73; www.ffpm-national.com.

WALKING

There is an extensive network of well-marked footpaths in France which make walking (la randonnée) easy. Several **Grande Randonnée (GR)** trails – recognisable by the red and white horizontal marks on trees, rocks and in town on walls, signposts etc – go through the region, the

© Christian Guy/hemis.fr

Walking the Cirque d'Estaubé at Gèdre, Parc national des Pyrénées

Horse-riding on the Étang des Baronnets, Le Grau du Roi

© Franck Guiziou/hemis.fr

most famous being, no doubt, the Santiago de Compostela trail from Moissac to St-Jean-Pied-de-Port (GR 65). Along with the GR trails are the **Petite Randonnée (PR)** paths, which are usually blazed with blue (2h walk), yellow (2h15–3h45) or green (4–6h) marks. Of course, with appropriate maps, you can combine walks to suit your desires.

To use these trails, obtain the 'Topo-Guide' for the area published by the **Fédération Française de la Randonnée Pédestre**, 64 rue du Dessous des Berges, 75013 Paris; 01 44 89 93 90; www.ffrandonnee.fr. Some English-language editions are available as well as the magazine 'Passion Rando', which includes ideas for overnight itineraries and places to stay, together with information on the difficulty and accessibility of trails. Another source of maps and guides for excursions on foot is the **Institut Géographique National (IGN)**, which has a boutique at 50 rue de la Verrerie, 75004 Paris; 01 43 98 85 10; to order from abroad, visit www.ign.fr, for addresses of wholesalers in your country. In the region, you can find many of the publications in bookstores, at sports centres or equipment shops, and in some of the country inns and hotels which cater to the sporting crowd.

Stanfords (12–14 Long Acre, Covent Garden, London WC2E 9LP; 020 7836 1321; www.stanfords.co.uk) has a wide selection of books and maps for travellers, which you can also buy online.

Suggestions and useful addresses
The **Parc National des Pyrénées** is perfect for walkers, whether your expedition is planned for half a day or includes overnight stops.

From July to the end of September mountain refuges under park surveillance are open to accommodate 30–40 people a night; there are also smaller, year-round refuges which are not guarded. In the summer, it is imperative to reserve in advance. One- or two-night stays are generally the rule; some refuges may provide meals prepared by the guardian (see PARC NATIONAL DES PYRÉNÉES).

♦ **La Balaguère**
48 route du Val d'Azun, 65400 Arrens-Marsous. 05 62 97 46 46. www.labalaguere.com. Organises walking trips in the Pyrenees, sometimes round a theme (history, flora, fauna…).
♦ **Chamina Voyages**
Naussac, 48300 Langogne. 04 66 69 00 44. www.chamina-voyages.com. Organises walks with or without guide in the southern part of the Massif Central and in the Pyrenees.

It is also possible to follow **herds** on their way to summer pastures in the Aubrac region (apply to the tourist office in St-Chély-d'Aubrac, ☎05 65 44 21 15) or to take a **donkey** with you contact the **Fédération nationale ânes et randonnées**, Check the website – http://en.ane-et-rando.com – for a list of organisers, or the **Association 'Sur le chemin de R.L. Stevenson**', 48220 Le Pont-de-Montvert; ☎04 66 45 86 31; www.chemin-stevenson.org, provides a list of B&B, hotels, restaurants, places where donkeys can be hired and tourist offices along the itinerary followed by Stevenson in 1878 and described in his *Travels With a Donkey in the Cévennes*.

CYCLING AND MOUNTAIN BIKING

Many GR and GRP footpaths are accessible to mountain bikers. However, in areas particularly suitable for cycling, there are special trails waymarked by the **Fédération Française de Cyclisme** (1 rue Laurent Fignon, CS 40 100, 78180 Montigny le Bretonneux; ☎08 11 04 05 55; www.ffc.fr); these are graded in difficulty (*green is easy; blue is fairly easy; red is difficult; black is very difficult*); ask for the '*Guide officel des sites VTT*', which supply itineraries and brochures as well as information on where to stay and where to call for urgent repairs. The **Office National des Forêts'** website – www.onf.fr – publishes cycling maps and guides for adults and children, focusing on ways to actively discover forests.
For additional information about cycling clubs, rental etc, contact the **Fédération Française de Cyclotourisme** (12 rue Louis-Bertrand, 94207 Ivry-sur-Seine; ☎01 56 20 88 88; www.ffct.org), the **Ligue Languedoc-Roussillon de Cyclotourisme** (Maison Régionale des Sports, 1039 Rue Georges Meliés, CS 37093, 34967 Montpellier; http://languedoc-roussillon.ffct.org), as well as local tourist offices.

RIDING TOURS

The **Fédération Française d' Équitation** (☎02 54 94 46 00; www.ffe.com), publishes a monthly brochure listing horse-riding leisure activities throughout France. In addition, this organisation will give you the address of the nearest Comité Départemental du Tourisme Équestre (CDTE) who can provide maps and brochures and lists of riding centres in your area. It is also possible to contact regional associations directly:

♦ **Comité Régional d'Equitation Languedoc Roussillon** Immeuble Emeline 1, 315 av, Saint Sauveur du Pin, 34980 St-Clement de Rivière. ☎06 27 73 89 40. www.crelr.fr.
♦ **Comité Régional de Tourisme Equestre de Midi-Pyrénées** Maison des Sports, 190 Rue Isatis, 31670 Labège. ☎05 62 24 18 14. www.crte-midi-pyrenees.com.

EXPLORING CAVES

Some of the numerous caves and chasms in the region, such as the avens (swallow-holes) of the limestone plateaux, are among the most famous in France. Exploring caves can be a dangerous pastime; it is therefore essential to have the right equipment and be accompanied by a qualified guide – many local clubs can provide both. For more information contact:

♦ **Fédération Française de Spéléologie** 28 rue Delandine, 69002 Lyon ☎04 72 56 09 63. www.ffspeleo.fr.
♦ **École Française de Spéléologie** As above.
♦ **Comité Régional de Spéléologie Midi-Pyrénées** 7 rue André-Citroën, 31130 Balma. ☎05 34 30 77 45. www.comite-speleo-midipy.com.

Leave only footprints; take only memories

Choosing the right equipment for a walking expedition is essential: flexible walking shoes with non-slip soles, a waterproof jacket or poncho, an extra sweater, sun protection (hat, glasses, lotion), drinking water (1–2l per person), high energy snacks (chocolate, cereal bars, bananas), and a first aid kit. Of course, you'll need a good map (and a compass if you plan to leave the main trails). Plan your itinerary well, keeping in mind that while the average walking speed for an adult is 4kph/2.5mph, you will need time to eat and rest, and children will not keep up the same pace. Leave details of your itinerary with someone before setting out (innkeeper or fellow camper).

Respect for nature is a cardinal rule and includes the following precautions: don't smoke or light fires in forests, which are particularly susceptible in the dry summer months; always carry your rubbish out; leave wild flowers as they are; walk around, not through, farmers' fields; close gates behind you.

In the dry, rocky scrubland of the *garrigues* and the *causses*, walkers may come across snakes, so it is important to wear stout footwear, preferably with some protection around the ankle. Most of the time the snakes will make themselves scarce as soon as they hear someone coming, so make plenty of noise, and avoid lifting up rocks to avoid disturbing any snakes resting beneath them.

GOLF

The Michelin map *Golf, les parcours français* (French golf courses) will help you locate golf courses in the region covered by this guide.

For further information, contact the **Fédération Française de Golf**, 68 rue Anatole-France, 92309 Levallois-Perret Cedex. ℘01 41 49 77 00; www.ffg.org. The **Ligue de Golf Languedoc-Roussillon** (*ch du Golf, Vacquerolles, 30900 Nîmes; ℘04 66 68 22 62; www. liguegolflanguedocroussillon.org*) publishes a guide of golf courses in the region.

MOUNTAIN SPORTS

Safety first is the rule for beginners and old hands alike. The risk associated with avalanches, mud slides, falling rocks, bad weather, fog, glacially cold waters, the dangers of becoming lost or miscalculating distances, should not be underestimated.

Avalanches occur naturally when the upper layer of snow is unstable, in particular after heavy snowfalls, and may be set off by the passage of numerous skiers or walkers over a precise spot. A scale of risk, from 1 to 5, has been developed and is posted daily at resorts and bases for walking trails. It is important to consult this *Bulletin Neige et Avalanche* (BNA) before setting off on any expeditions cross-country or off-piste. You can also check conditions on www. meteofrance.com, or on the mobile app Météo-France.

Lightning storms are often preceded by sudden gusts of wind, and put climbers and walkers in danger. In the event, avoid high ground, and do not move along a ridge top; do not seek shelter under overhanging rocks, isolated trees in otherwise open areas, at the entrance to caves or other openings in the rocks, or in the proximity of metal fences or gates. For general information on mountain sports in the Pyrenees, apply to: **Hautes-Pyrénées Tourist Office** 11 rue Gaston Manent, 65950 Tarbes; ℘05 62 56 70 00; www.tourisme-hautes-pyrenees.com.

Mountain guides suggest a choice of guided activities.

♦ **Bureau des guides de Luchon** 66 allée d'Étigny, 31110 Luchon. ℘05 61 79 56 08. www.bureau-guides-luchon.com.

© Pierre Jacques/hemis.fr

Via ferrata on the cliffs of the Causse de Sauveterre above the Tarn gorges at Liaucous

- **Bureau des guides de la vallée de Cauterets**
  2 rue de la Raillère, 65110 Cauterets. ✆06 42 06 33 82. www.guides-cauterets.com.
- **Bureau des guides d'Argelès-Gazost** ✆06 84 59 86 38. http://guidesargeles.blogspot.co.uk.
- **Bureau des guides de Luz Saint Sauveur** ✆05 62 92 87 28. www.guides-luz.com.
- **Bureau des guides de Saint Lary** 65170 St-Lary-Soulan. ✆05 62 40 02 58. www.guides-saintlary.com.
- **Bureau des guides Ariège-Pyrénées**, Gare Aval Téléporté, Camp de Granaou, 09110 Ax-les-Thermes. ✆05 61 01 90 62. www.guides-ariege.com.

ROCK CLIMBING

The Pyrenees, the Cévennes, and even the deep Tarn Gorges provide excellent conditions for rock climbing with the assistance of local guides (⏏ *see above and www.guides-montagne.org*). Beginners should take advantage of the numerous courses available to learn a few basic techniques. For additional information, contact this federation which provides the location of all the rock-climbing sites in France:

- **Fédération Française de la Montagne et de l'Escalade**, 8-10 quai de la Marne, 75019 Paris; ✆01 40 18 75 50; www.ffme.fr.

SKIING

When it comes to snow adventure, the resorts in the south of France have long been regarded as the poor relation to the Alps. Yet there is excellent downhill and cross-country skiing, snowboarding and snow-shoeing to be enjoyed here, not least among the **Pyrenees**, which remain largely under-valued by winter sports enthusiasts, and are a prized location, offering fresh, varied pistes – as well as some highly regarded off-piste runs – enjoyed mainly by locals. Indeed,

Useful Contacts for Skiers

Comprehensive information about skiing localities in Languedoc-Roussillon is listed on **www. destinationsuddefrance.com**. The principal organisation in the UK for skiing is the **Ski Club of Great Britain** (The White House, 57–63 Church Road, Wimbledon, London SW19 5SB. ✆020 8410 2000. www.skiclub.co.uk). But a number of other website-based organisations maintain accurate, up-to-date information, e.g. www.snowheads.com, and the **Eagle Ski Club,** the UK's largest and most active ski-touring and ski-mountaineering club (www.eagleskiclub.org.uk).

Snowboarding in the Pyrenees

©Cédric VILLEGIER/Fotolia.com

Skiing in the Languedoc-Roussillon is remarkably cheap compared with the Alps, but they are just as well equipped, and offer downhill skiing, cross-country skiing, tobogganing and sledging, country snow hiking, and even treks with dog sleighs for the very fit. The station at Mas de la Barque specialises in cross-country. Among the Pyrenees in particular, there is remarkably little evidence of the overcrowding experienced in the Alps (except at weekends), and so these dramatic mountains offer a carefree skiing experience amid scenery every bit as dramatic and inspiring as the Alps. Because development to accommodate skiers has been gradual, most Pyrenean resorts have avoided descending into unsightly, charmless places, and many retain an atmosphere of village identity and beauty. Significant investment in lift systems and the improved quality of the accommodation means the gap between the Alps and the Pyrenees is closing all the time.

In the **Pyrenees** there are over 50 skiing resorts to choose from, most notably Tourmalet and La Mongie, the biggest linked resort with more than 100km/62mi of slopes and a 1 000m off-piste descent from the Pic du Midi observatory. Font-Romeu is one of the oldest ski resorts not only in the Pyrenees but in Europe, dating back to the 1920s, and it remains a justly popular destination today. For *après ski* try the lively towns of Cauterets, Saint Lary-Soulan, Luz-Ardiden, Luchon or Les Angles. Gentler slopes are also being used above Gavarnie, making the most of the 'alpine' pastures that are lush with flowers in the summer months.

The principality of **Andorra** has long been a popular goal for skiers originally drawn by the duty-free status looking for cheap *après ski* and budget holiday destinations. Andorran ski schools have an excellent reputation for English-speaking instructors, and the result

the whole range of the Pyrenees and the mountain uplands of the **Aubrac**, **Lozère** and the **Cévennes** to the north, lend themselves perfectly to all forms of winter snow activities. The **Cévennes** are not as high or as developed as the Pyrenean resorts, but still offer excellent cross-country skiing and down-hill runs.

The most convenient **Lozère** ski station is Prat Peyrot on Mount Aigoual, which, at 1 500m above sea level, enjoys claims that from the summit you can see the Mediterranean on one side and the Atlantic on the other.

The **Aubrac** is mainly a domain for cross-country skiing, with 200km/124mi of signposted trails linking Brameloup, Nasbinals, Aubrac, Saint-Urcize and Laguiole.

☺ Useful tips ☺

Always bear ski-slope etiquette in mind when out on the piste: never set off without checking that the way uphill and downhill is clear; never ignore signposts; beware of the danger of avalanches on loosely packed snow (especially skiing off-piste). If in any doubt, check the rules at the ski resort before setting off.

of continuing investment in the facilities and infrastructure has been to provide Andorra with some of the most modern, efficient lift systems in Europe.

Grand Valira is the linked ski area of Pas de la Casa and Soldeu el Tarter, and has expanded into France. The other linked area is Vallnord, which includes Pal-Arinsal, Ordino-Arcalis and La Massana. You can also try cross-country skiing at La Rabassa.

HANG-GLIDING, PARAGLIDING AND KITE-FLYING

On **hang-gliders** *(deltaplanes)*, fliers skillfully suspend themselves from what is little more than a rudimentary, kite-like wing.

Almost anyone with the willpower to jump off a cliff can give **paragliding** *(parapente)* a try (with the assistance of trained professionals, of course). A number of centres offer instruction and rent equipment, particularly around Millau, in the Grands Causses, around Marvejols and Mende and in the Pyrenees (Barèges, Campan, Peyragudes, Superbagnères, Moulis near St-Girons, Prat d'Albi near Foix).

Kite-flying is a popular activity in the region, particularly on the beaches. General information (hang-gliding, paragliding and kite-flying) is available from: **Fédération Française de Vol Libre**, 4 rue de Suisse, 06000 Nice; ℘04 97 03 82 82; http://federation.ffvl.fr.

SPECTATOR SPORT – RUGBY

Rugby is big in the southwest. Every town and village has its team, and passions run high as enthusiastic supporters follow their team's progress in the weekly Sunday matches that take place from October to May. More information is available from the **Fédération Française de Rugby**, 3–5 rue Jean de Montaigu, 91463 Marcoussis; ℘01 69 63 64 65; www.ffr.fr.

SPAS

France has long been renowned for its health spas, a popular retreat for many, who would often be granted spa treatment on the French national health service. The Pyrenees are home to numerous mineral and thermal springs, which have brought fame to the area for their health restoring qualities since Antiquity. Pyrenean spas fall into two categories: sulphurated or salt water springs.

Sulphurated springs – Waters can reach temperatures up to 80°C. The main spa resorts in this category are Cauterets, Bagnères-de-Luchon, Saint-Sauveur, Ax-les-Thermes, Amélie-les-Bains, Bagnols-les-Bains and Balaruc-les-Bains.

Salt water springs – The main spa resorts in this category are Ussat-les-Bains, Alet-les-Bains, Le Boulou, Lamalou-les-Bains, and the water in Avène-les-Bains makes it particularly suitable for treatment of skin diseases.

USEFUL ADDRESSES

◆ **Chaîne Thermale du Soleil/ Maison du Thermalisme**
32 avenue de l'Opéra, 75002 Paris. ℘08 00 05 05 32. www.chainethermale.fr.

◆ **Union Nationale des Établissements Thermaux**
1 rue Cels, 75014 Paris. ℘01 53 91 05 75. www.medecinethermale.fr.

SEA-WATER THERAPY

Known as *thalassothérapie* in French, this kind of cure has increased in popularity in recent years. The main centres in Languedoc-Roussillon are at **La Grande-Motte**, **Cap-d'Agde**, **Port-Barcarès** and **Banyuls-sur-Mer**. **France Thalasso**, 57 rue d'Amsterdam, 75008 Paris; ℘05 59 51 35 03; www.france-thalasso.com has a list of sea-water therapy centres.

ACTIVITIES FOR KIDS 👪

In this guide, sights of particular interest to children are indicated with a FAMILY symbol (👪). This region of France has a lot to offer children, from swimming and playing in the sand along the sunny Mediterranean coast to having fun in amusement parks or visiting zoos, safari parks, aquariums, museums and sights of special interest.

Aqualand at Cap d'Agde (👜*see Le CAP d'AGDE*) will fascinate children with a liking for all things that swim in the sea, while underground adventure can be had in the **Grotte de Clamouse** (👜*see SAINT-GUILHEM-LE-DÉSERT, Excursion*), and the **Grotte des Demoiselles** (👜*see GROTTE DES DEMOISELLES*), where they can also enjoy a simple train ride. Staying on the underground theme, the **Labouiche underground river** (👜*see FOIX*) near Foix is quite an experience revealing superb examples of stalagmites and stalactites.
In Carcassonne, children will enjoy an evening stroll or dinner in the medieval city, especially later in the day as the sun goes down and the lights of the modern city below cast an eerie glow into the sky. During the day, take a ride on the **Canal du Midi**, if only to amaze at its ingenuity.
In Mont-Louis the **solar furnace** (👜*see MONT-LOUIS*) is always popular with children, while a chance to see the **wolves** at Gévaudan (👜*see MARVEJOLS*) should not be missed; arrive before feeding time. The **Réserve Africaine de Sigean** (👜*see RÉSERVE AFRICAINE DE SIGEAN*), south of Narbonne, is a perfect place to get up close with the wild animals of Africa. Animals of a less fiercesome nature can be hired in Gavarnie, for a simple **pony trek** (👜*see CIRQUE DE GAVARNIE*) up to see the magnificent waterfall. On the Parc de la Plaine, just outside Toulouse the **Cité de l'Espace** will entertain children all day.

SHOPPING

Major shopping malls are few and far between, Montpellier and Toulouse being the exceptions. Elsewhere there are numerous shopping opportunities in the narrow streets of Narbonne, Perpignan and Carcassonne. But the best shopping experience comes from the countless local and regional markets held every week in virtually every town and village, and which range from small stalls offering produce grown by the man selling it to you, to some of the finest, freshest food and drink produce available. Just walking round the markets, especially that in La Capitole in Toulouse, is a memorable and aromatic experience. Traditional markets known as *marchés au gras* were previously held in winter months only for the sale of ducks and geese, prepared and raw livers. The most picturesque of these markets are now held in Samatan (Gers) on Mondays year-round and in Mirande (Gers) on Mondays from November through to March.
You can view a full list of market days at www.jours-de-marche.fr.

LOCAL SPECIALITIES

Gastronomy – Apart from foie gras and confit, the region is rich in gastronomic products: cassoulet from the Toulouse region (tinned), honey from the Cévennes, nougat from Limoux, cured ham and varied charcuterie from the mountainous areas, not forgetting cheeses such as Roquefort and Fourme de Laguiole. The region also offers a choice of red, rosé and white wines, natural sweet wines and stronger tipple such as Armagnac.
Handicraft – Glazed pottery adds a touch of colour to most local markets in the Cévennes and Languedoc regions, whereas the Cerdagne specialises in rope-soled shoes. The Pyrenees are famous for the softness of their woollen blankets and pullovers.

Cooking Courses

A number of farmhouse-inns offer sessions which include lessons on preparing foie gras, confits, cou farci and other delights, as well as lodging and board. For information, contact:

- **Loisirs-Accueil du Gers**
  ℰ05 62 61 79 00.
  www.gers-tourisme.fr.

Wine-Tasting

The Languedoc-Roussillon AOC appellation covers 50 000ha of vines on the slopes of the garrigue from Narbonne to Nîmes, an area that covers 156 communes, of which 5 are in Aude, 14 in Gard and the rest in Hérault. All sizeable vineyards offer the chance of a *dégustation*, or tasting, and while there is no obligation to buy, it's proper to do so.

Information on visiting wine-growing establishments and wine cooperatives can be obtained from the following address:

- **Vins de pays d'Oc**
  Addresses of wine-growers and co-operatives are available from the Syndicat des Producteurs de Vin de Pays d'Oc, Domaine de Manse, avenue Paysagère, Maurin, 34970 Lattes. ℰ04 67 13 84 30. www.paysdoc-wines.com.

Wine tasting and **guided tours** of vineyards are organised by the:

- **Maison des Vins**, 1 avenue de la Promenade, 34360 St-Chinian.
  ℰ04 67 38 11 69; www.saint-chinian.com *(Tasting of St-Chinian wine Mon–Fri 9am–7pm, Sat 10am–1pm, 2.30–6.30pm, Sun 10am–1pm; wine festival on 3rd Sunday in July)*.
- **Minervois**, Syndicat du cru Minervois, 35 quai des Tonneliers 11200 Homps. ℰ04 68 27 80 00. www.leminervois.com.
- **Vin d' Estaing AOC**, Maison de la Vigne, du Vin et des Paysages d'Estaing, D920 - L'Escaillou - Coubisou, 12190 Estaing. ℰ05 65 44 04 42; www.vivreaupays.pro.

- **Blanquette de Limoux**
  Contact the Syndicat des vins AOC de Limoux. ℰ04 68 31 12 83, www.limoux-aoc.com.
- **Fitou AOC**, Les Cabanes, 11480 La Palme. ℰ04 68 40 42 70. www.fitouaoc.com.
- **Vins de Gaillac**, Maison des Vins, Abbaye St-Michel, 81600 Gaillac.
  ℰ05 63 57 15 40.
  www.vins-gaillac.com.
- **Madiran and Pacherenc du Vic-Bilh**
  Maison des vins de Madiran et Pacherenc du Vic-Bilh, 4 place de l'Église, 65700 Madiran.
  ℰ05 62 31 90 67.
- **Armagnac and Floc de Gascogne**
  Bureau national interprofessionnel de l'Armagnac AOC, 11 pl de la Liberté, 32800 Eauze. ℰ05 62 08 11 00.
  www.armagnac.fr.
  Comité interprofessionnel du Floc de Gascogne, rue des Vignerons, 32800 Eauze.
  ℰ05 62 09 85 41.
  www.floc-de-gascogne.fr.

SIGHTSEEING
TOURIST TRAINS

These are a pleasant and original way of exploring the region. In the Cévennes, a little steam train runs between Anduze and St-Jean-du-Gard, via Prafrance bamboo plantation and following the Gardon rivers.
The **Train à Vapeur des Cévennes** is a steam train that travels through the Gardon Valley, from St-Jean-du-Gard to Andouze, stopping at La Bambouseraie bamboo plantation. www.trainvapeur.com.
The **Petit Train Jaune** (Little Yellow Train) offers a picturesque journey through the Cerdagne and Conflent regions; it runs between Latour-de-Carol and Villefranche-de-Conflent, once a day each way. www.ter-sncf.com.
The **Train du Pays Cathar et de Fenouilledes** is a red train travelling from Saint Paul to Axat, in the Eastern Pyrenees. www.tpcf.fr.

FROM ABOVE

For an aerial view of the region either as passenger or pilot, apply to flying clubs usually located within the perimeter of airports:

- **Fédération Française de Planeur Ultra-léger Motorisé**, 96 bis rue Marc-Sangnier, 94709 Maisons-Alfort. ✆01 49 81 74 43. www.ffplum.com.

RIVER AND CANAL CRUISING

Take a boat trip of a few hours or more on the lakes of the Narbonne region, down the River Tarn, along the Canal du Midi or along the coast from Sète. Rivers, canals and lakes offer numerous possibilities to enjoy pleasant boat trips, thus slowing down the pace and alleviating the stress of a busy touring holiday.

- **Trips aboard a passenger barge**, *see CASTRES*.
- **Trips on the Garonne and Canal du Midi**, Péniche Baladine and Le Capitole, *see TOULOUSE*.
- **Trips on the Canal du Midi**, **Bateau Lucie**, *see Canal du MIDI*.

- **Trips on the River Baïse**, **Gascogne-Navigation**, *see CONDOM*.
- **Trips down the River Tarn**, *see Gorges du TARN*.
- **Sea trips**, *see SÈTE*.

Houseboats

Houseboats with a capacity for six to eight people enable visitors to get a different perspective on the canals of the region.

- **Le Canal du Midi**
  Information about boat trips along the Canal du Midi, and a map-guide is available from www.plan-canal-du-midi.com. You can order guides to the canal network of France from www.guide-fluvial.fr.

Companies from which houseboats can be **hired** (or contact local tourist offices for information):

- **Adnavis**, La Maison du Canal, 80 Grand'rue, 34290 Servian. ✆04 67 90 95 51. www.adnavis.com.
- **Les Canalogs**, Chemin Départamental 62, 34280 Carnon. ✆03 85 53 76 74. www.canalous-canaldumidi.com.

Canal du Midi at Toulouse

©Thieury/Fotolia.com

- **Le Boat,** Le grand bassin, BP 1201, 11492 Castelnaudry.
  𝒞04 68 94 42 80; www.leboat.fr (In the UK, 𝒞023 9222 2177; www.leboat.co.uk).
- **Locaboat Plaisance**
  Port au Bois, 89303 Joigny.
  𝒞03 86 91 72 72.
  www.locaboat.com.
- **Nicols:** Route du Puy St Bonnet, 49300 Cholet (reservations 𝒞02 41 56 46 56).
  www.nicols.com.

NATIONAL AND REGIONAL NATURE PARKS

For information on the **Parc national des Cévennes**, visit the reception and information centre at Château de Florac (*6 bis place du Palais, 48400 Florac; 𝒞04 66 49 53 00; www. cevennes-parcnational.fr*). Useful information on the park includes the Institut Géographique National (IGN) maps at a scale of 1:100,000 or 1:25 000, *'Topo-guides'* of the long-distance footpaths which cross the region and the tourist guide *'Parc national des Cévennes'* (🖐 see FLORAC). For information on the **Parc national des Pyrénées**, apply to 2 rue IV Septembre, 65007 Tarbes; 𝒞05 62 54 16 40; www.parc-pyrenees.com. Several Maisons du Parc throughout the park provide information on the park's flora and fauna and on rambling opportunities in this mountainous area (🖐 see Parc national des PYRÉNÉES). The information centre of the **Parc Naturel Régional du Haut-Languedoc**, Maison du tourisme du Parc, place fu Foirail, 34220 St-Pons-de-Thomières; 𝒞04 67 97 38 22; www.parc-haut-languedoc.fr. (🖐 see SAINT-PONS-DE-THOMIÈRES). The **Parc Naturel Régional des Grands Causses**, 71, bvd de l'Ayrolle, 12101 Millau Cedex; 𝒞05 65 61 35 50; www.parc-grands-causses.fr. (🖐 see MILLAU).

BOOKS

Travels with a Donkey in the Cévenne - Robert Louis Stevenson, 1879.
One of the classic travel books. Penned by Stevenson while still in his 20s, it tells of his epic 12-day 120-mile hike with a donkey through the mountains of the Cévennes.
French Leaves: Letters from the Languedoc - Christopher Campbell Howes, 2002. Retired headmaster from Scotland evokes the scents, sights and sounds, the vibrant colours and earthy vitality of the area with British detachment.
Notes from the Languedoc - Rupert Wright, 2003. A beautifully crafted collection of anecdotes about Languedoc, originally written as letters to the author's grandmother. A gem!
Rick Stein's French Odyssey - Rick Stein, 2005. The TV chef's account of his sedate journey at 4mph on a canal barge called 'The Anjodi' through the Languedoc-Roussillon along the Canal du Midi. Stein focuses on country food prepared from ingredients found in local markets.
In the High Pyrenees: A new life in a mountain village - Bernard Loughlin, 2003. A loving and hilarious account of the sensations and intrigues of a mountain village.
Virgile's Vineyard - Patrick Moon, 2013. The story of a year in the Languedoc wine country; enthusiastic, informative, and above all throughly entertaining.
The Wines of the Languedoc-Roussillon - Wendy Gedney, 2014. A fresh approach, bursting with information about the wines and food of the region.

FILM

Bernadette, 1988. Actress Sydney Penny gives a poignant performance as the teenager Bernadette Soubirous, who has visions of the Virgin Mary in a cave at Lourdes. Shot in and around the pilgrimage site and the local Pyrenean villages in winter.

Calendar of Events

Many Regional Tourist Offices publish brochures listing local fêtes, fairs and festivals. Most places hold festivities for France's National Day (14 July) and 15 August, a public holiday, but the French need little excuse to drop everything and have a party. Enquire locally, and get involved.

FEBRUARY
Toulouse
'Fête de la Violette' (violet festival). ✆08 92 18 01 80.
Limoux
Traditional carnival every weekend (and Shrove Tuesday). All-night 'Blanquette' party follows. ✆04 68 31 11 82. www.limoux.fr.
Prats-de-Mollo, St-Laurent-de-Cerdans, Arles-sur-Tech
Traditional carnival. ✆04 68 39 70 83. www.pratsdemollolapreste.com.

MARCH–APRIL
Toulouse
Laughter in springtime. ✆05 62 21 23 24. www.printempsdurire.com.

APRIL (TO OCTOBER)
Parc national des Cévennes
Nature festival: themed walks, exhibitions, shows, markets. ✆04 66 49 53 00. www.cevennes-parcnational.fr.

MAY
Aubrac
'Fête de la transhumance': Seasonal shepherd's festival held on the weekend nearest to the 25 May. ✆ 05 65 44 20 78. www.traditionsenaubrac.fr.

JUNE
Maguelone
Festival of ancient and baroque music (1st two weeks). ✆04 67 60 69 92. www.musiqueanciennea maguelone.com.
Perpignan
Saint-Jean Festa Major (with mid-summer bonfires around 21 June). ✆04 68 66 30 30. www.perpignantourisme.com.
Toulouse
Festival Rio Loco: rock, jazz, pop, tango dancing. ✆05 61 22 99 00. www.rio-loco.org.

JUNE-JULY
Montpellier
International Festival of Dance. ✆0 800 600 740 (tickets). www.montpellierdanse.com.

Fête de la transhumance, Aubrac

© Stephan Zabel/iStockphoto.com

Festival du Muscat, Frontignan

© Jean-Pierre Degas/hemis.fr

JULY
Bastille Day
There are celebrations everywhere for France's national holiday, 14 July.

Carcassonne
Festival of the City: Medieval Cité is 'set alight' by an evening firework display; classical music concerts, theatre, opera, dance, jazz (14 July). ☎04 68 11 59 15. www.festivaldecarcassonne.com.

Céret
International Sardana festival 400 dancers in costume (2nd fortnight). ☎04 68 87 46 49. www.ot-ceret.fr.

Cordes-sur-Ciel
'Fête médiévale du Grand Fauconnnier' (historical pageant and entertainments (mid July). ☎05 63 56 34 63. www.grandfauconnier.com.

Cap d'Agde
'Fête de la Mer' sea festival (last weekend). ☎04 67 01 04 04. www.capdagde.com.

Frontignan
'Festival du Muscat' (mid month). ☎04 67 18 31 60. www.frontignan-tourisme.com.

Luz-St-Sauveur
'Jazz à Luz' (early July) ☎05 62 92 38 30. www.jazzaluz.com.

Montauban
Jazz festival (2nd fortnight) ☎05 63 63 56 56. www.jazzmontauban.com.

Montpellier
'Festival de Radio-France et de Montpellier Languedoc-Roussillon' opera, symphonies, chamber music, jazz (2nd fortnight). ☎04 67 61 66 81. www.festivalradiofrancemont pellier.com.

St-Guilhem-le-Désert
Musical season at the abbey (1st fortnight). ☎04 67 57 44 33. www.saintguilhem-valleeherault.fr.

Tour de France
The famous cycle race passes through the region. It always includes a hill climb to at least one of the passes of the Pyrenees.

JULY–AUGUST
Lastours
Son et lumière show at the chateau. ☎04 68 77 56 02.

Moissac
'Festival de la Voix' ☎05 63 05 08 08. www.moissac-culture.fr.

Sète
Festival Fiest'A Sète – music of the world. ☎04 67 74 48 44. www.fiestasete.com.

Poster of the Féria in Béziers

S. Quillon/MICHELIN

Prades: St-Michel-de-Cuxa
Pablo Casals festival. Concerts in the abbey (mid-July to mid-August). ☏04 68 96 33 07. www.prades-festival-casals.com.

St-Bertrand-de-Comminges, St-Just-de-Valcabrère, St-Gaudens, Martres-Tolosane.
'Festival du Comminges', classical music, chamber music. ☏05 61 95 44 44. www.festival-du-comminges.com.

Vic-Fezensac
Tempo Latino. Latino music festival. ☏05 62 06 34 90. www.vic-fezensac-tourisme.com.

AUGUST
Bagnères-de-Luchon
Flower festival (last Sunday). ☏05 61 79 21 21. www.luchon.com.

Banyuls-sur-Mer
Sardana festival (2nd weekend). ☏04 68 88 00 62. www.banyuls-sur-mer.com.

Béziers
'Féria' (around 15 August). ☏04 67 76 84 00. www.ville-beziers.fr.

Bouzigues
Oyster fair (1st or 2nd weekend in the month). ☏04 67 78 30 12. www.bouzigues.fr.

Marciac
International jazz festival. ☏08 92 69 02 77. www.jazzinmarciac.com.

Mirepoix
Puppet festival (1st weekend). ☏05 61 68 20 72. www.mima.artsdelamarionnette.com.

Palavas-les-Flots
Jousting by night on canal (15 Aug). ☏04 67 07 73 00. www.palavaslesflots.com.

Pont de Salers and other villages
International folklore festival (5th–12th). ☏05 65 46 80 67. www.festival-rouergue.com.

Vic-Fezensac
'Feria' (bullfighting). ☏05 62 06 34 90.

SEPTEMBER
Toulouse
Piano recitals at Les Jacobins. ☏05 61 22 21 92. www.pianojacobins.com.

Journées du Patrimoine
Historic monuments and heritage sites open day.

Perpignan
Festival Jazzèbre (Jazz festival). ☏04 68 51 13 14. www.jazzebre.com.

OCTOBER
Montpellier
International fair. ☏04 67 61 67 88. www.foire-montpellier.com.

Know Before You Go

USEFUL WEBSITES

www.destinationsuddefrance.com
A dedicated, multi-language website for Languedoc-Roussillon. All the practical information you might need for a stay in the region.

uk.rendezvousenfrance.com
The French Government Tourist Office site is packed with practical information, advice and tips for those travelling to France, including choosing package tours and even buying a property. The homepage has a number of links to more specific guidance, for American or Canadian travellers for example, or to the FGTO's London pages.

www.ViaMichelin.com
This site has maps, tourist information, travel features, suggestions on hotels and restaurants, and a route planner for numerous locations in Europe. In addition, you can look up weather forecasts, traffic reports and service station location, particularly useful if you will be driving in France.

www.franceguide.com
The French Government Tourist Office site is packed with practical information and tips for those travelling to France.

www.france-travel-guide.net
A practical and developing France-wide website for the traveller, written by a Francophile travel writer. Includes essential information, as well as a wide range of regional and local content to help plan and inspire a stay in France.

www.thegoodlifefrance.com
A comprehensive and well-established website covering the whole of France, living in France, things to do, culture and language and gastronomy. Publishes an online magazine and regular newsletter produced by ex-pat Brit living in France.

www.drive-france.com
This detailed and well-maintained website tells you everything you need to know about driving in France, including all the latest changes to French driving law. Also has an online shop for essential supplies.

www.ambafrance-uk.org and www.ambafrance-us.org
The French Embassies in the UK and the USA have a website providing basic information (geography, demographics, history), a news digest and business-related information. It offers special pages for children and pages devoted to culture, language study and travel, as well as links to other selected French sites (regions, cities, ministries).

www.pyrenees-online.fr
This regional site has a mine of information about accommodation, ski resorts and activities in the Pyrenees mountains.

www.ariegepyrenees.com
This site focuses on walking in the Ariège, offering pages of different itineraries in the area.

www.geoportail.fr
An impressive French government mapping system. Zoom in on any part of France that takes your fancy. It even shows up hamlets and fields.

DriveEuropeNews (https://driveeuropenews.com/france)
A guide to real time traffic, travel and weather information in France, also including tolls (or not), the auto toll tag, traffic forecasts, emergency contacts and news sources in English.

TOURIST OFFICES ABROAD

Australia
French Tourist Bureau, 25 Bligh Street,
Sydney, NSW 2000, Australia
📞(0)292 31 62 77.
au.rendezvousenfrance.com

Canada
Maison de la France, 1800 av. McGill
College, Bureau 1010, Montreal,
Quebec H3A 3J6, Canada
📞(514) 288 20 26.
ca.rendezvousenfrance.com

South Africa
Block C, Morningside Close
222 Rivonia Road, MORNINGSIDE 2196
– JOHANNESBURG
📞00 27 (0)10 205 0201

UK and Ireland
Lincoln House, 300 High Holborn,
London WC1V 7JH. 📞0207 061 66 00.
uk.rendezvousenfrance.com

USA
825 Third Avenue, New York, NY
10022, USA 📞(212) 838 78 00.
us.rendezvousenfrance.com

TOURIST OFFICES
Visitors may also contact local tourist
offices for more precise information,
and to receive brochures and maps.
The addresses and telephone numbers
of tourist offices in the larger towns
are listed after the symbol 🎫.

Below, the addresses are given for local
tourist offices of the *départements* and
régions covered in this guide.

- ◆ **Ariège**
  Agence de Développement
  Touristique d'Ariège Pyrénées,
  BP 30143, 09000 Foix.
  📞05 61 02 30 70.
  www.ariegepyrenees.com

- ◆ **Aude**
  Agence de Développement
  Touristique de l'Aude, Allée
  Raymond Courrière, 11855
  Carcassonne Cedex 9

📞04 68 11 66 00.
www.audetourisme.com

- ◆ **Aveyron**
  Comité Départemental du Tourisme
  de l'Aveyron, 17 rue Aristide-Briand,
  BP 831, 12008 Rodez.
  📞05 65 75 40 12.
  www.tourisme-aveyron.com

- ◆ **Gard**
  Agence de Développement et de
  Réservation Touristiques (ADRT)
  du Gard, 3 rue Cité Foule, BP 122,
  30010 Nîmes Cedex 4.
  📞04 66 36 96 30.
  www.tourismegard.com

- ◆ **Gers**
  Comité Départemental du
  Tourisme du Gers, 3 boulevard
  Roquelaure, BP 50106,
  32002 Auch Cedex.
  📞05 62 05 95 95.
  www.tourisme-gers.com

- ◆ **Haute-Garonne**
  Comité Départemental du
  Tourisme de la Haute-Garonne,
  14 rue Bayard, CS 71509,
  31015 Toulouse Cedex 6
  📞05 61 99 44 00.
  tourisme.haute-garonne.fr

- ◆ **Hautes-Pyrénées**
  Hautes-Pyrénées Tourisme
  Environnement, 11 rue Gaston-
  Manent, BP 9502, 65950 Tarbes
  Cedex 9
  📞05 62 56 70 05.
  www.tourisme-hautes-
  pyrenees.com

- ◆ **Hérault**
  Agence de Développement
  Touristique de l'Hérault,
  avenue des Moulins,
  34184 Montpellier Cedex 4.
  📞04 67 67 71 71.
  www.herault-tourisme.com

- ◆ **Lozère**
  Comité Départemental du
  Tourisme de la Lozère,

14 boulevard Henri-Bourillon, 48000 Mende.
☎ 04 66 65 60 00.
www.lozere-tourisme.com

◆ **Pyrénées-Orientales**
Agence de Développement Touristique des Pyrénées-Orientales, 2. Boulevard des Pyrénées, 66000 Perpignan
☎ 04 68 51 52 53.
www.tourisme-pyrenees orientales.com.

◆ **Tarn**
Comité Départemental du Tourisme du Tarn, 41 rue Porta, BP 225, 81006 Albi Cedex.
☎ 05 63 77 32 10.
www.tourisme-tarn.com

◆ **Tarn-et-Garonne**
Agence de Développement Touristique du Tarn-et-Garonne, 100 boulevard Hubert Gouze, CS 90534, 82005 Montauban Cedex
☎ 05 63 21 79 65.
www.tourisme82.com

Regional tourist offices
◆ **Languedoc-Roussillon:**
Sud de France Développement, Maison Sud de France, 3840 Avenue Georges Frêch, CS 10012, 34477 Pérols Cedex.
☎ 04 99 64 29 29.
en.destinationsuddefrance.com

◆ **Midi-Pyrénées:**
Comité Régional du Tourisme Midi-Pyrénées, 15 rue Rivals, CS 78543, 31685 Toulouse Cedex 6.
☎ 05 61 13 55 55.
www.tourism-midi-pyrenees.com

♽ See the Principal Sights in the *Discovering the Region* section for the addresses and telephone numbers of the local tourist offices *(Syndicats d'Initiative)*. Eight towns and areas, labelled **Villes et Pays d'Art et d'Histoire** by the Ministry of Culture, are mentioned in this guide (Lectoure, Mende, Montauban, Narbonne, Perpignan, Pézenas, Toulouse and the Têt valley).
More information is available from local tourist offices and from www.vpah.culture.fr.

INTERNATIONAL VISITORS
EMBASSIES AND CONSULATES
Australia Embassy
4 rue Jean-Rey, 75015 Paris Cedex.
☎ 01 40 59 33 00
www.france.embassy.gov.au.

Canada Embassy
37 avenue Montaigne, 75008 Paris.
☎ 01 44 43 29 00.
www.international.gc.ca

Eire Embassy
12 ave Foch, 75116 Paris.
☎ 01 44 17 67 00.
www.embassyofireland.fr

New Zealand Embassy
103, rue de Grenelle, 75007 Paris.
☎ 01 45 01 43 43.
www.nzembassy.com/france

UK Embassy
35 rue du Faubourg St-Honoré, 75008 Paris Cedex 08.
☎ 01 44 51 31 88.
www.ukinfrance.fco.gov.uk/en

UK Consulate
16 bis, rue d'Anjou, 75008 Paris.
☎ 01 44 51 31 00.
www.ukinfrance.fco.gov.uk

USA Embassy
2 avenue Gabriel, 75008 Paris Cedex.
☎ 01 43 12 22 22.
france.usembassy.gov

USA Consulate
2 rue St-Florentin, 75001 Paris.
☎ 01 43 12 22 22.
france.usembassy.gov

ENTRY REQUIREMENTS
Passport
Passport – Nationals of countries within the European Union entering France need only a national identity

card or, in the case of the British, a valid passport or ID for the whole length of your stay in France.Nationals of other countries must be in possession of a valid national passport.

👁 In case of loss or theft, report to your embassy or consulate and the local police.

👁 *You must carry your documents with you at all times; they can be checked anywhere.*

Visa – No entry visa is required for Australian, Canadian, New Zealand and US citizens travelling as tourists and staying less than 90 days, except for students planning to study in France. If in doubt, apply to your local French Consulate.

US citizens – General passport information is available by phone toll-free from the Federal Information Center (item 5 on the automated menu), 📞800-688-9889. US passport forms can be downloaded from http://travel. state.gov.

CUSTOMS REGULATIONS

The UK Customs website (www.hmrc. gov.uk) contains information on allowances, travel safety tips, and to consult and download documents and guides. There are no limits on the amount of duty and/or tax paid alcohol and tobacco that you can bring back into the UK as long as they are for your own use or gifts and are transported by you. If you are bringing in alcohol or tobacco goods and UK Customs have reason to suspect they may be for a commercial purpose, an officer may ask you questions and make checks. There are no customs formalities when bringing caravans, pleasure-boats and outboard motors into France for a stay of less than six months, but a boat's registration certificate should be kept on board.

HEALTH

It is advisable to take out comprehensive travel insurance cover, as tourists receiving medical treatment in French hospitals or clinics have to pay for it themselves. Nationals of non-EU countries should check with their insurance companies about policy limitations. Keep all receipts.

British and Irish citizens, if not already in possession of an EHIC (European Health Insurance Card), should apply for one before travelling. The card entitles UK residents to reduced-cost medical treatment. Apply online at www.ehic.org.uk. The card is not an alternative to travel insurance. It will not cover any private medical healthcare or costs, such as mountain rescue in ski resorts, being flown back to the UK, or lost or stolen property.

Details of the healthcare available in France and how to claim reimbursement are published in the leaflet Health Advice for Travellers, available from post offices. All prescription drugs taken into France should be clearly labelled; it is recommended to carry a copy of prescriptions.

ACCESSIBILITY

Sights with good accessibility are indicated in this guide with a ♿. On French TGV and Corail trains there are wheelchair spaces in 1st-class carriages available to holders of 2nd-class tickets. On Eurostar and Thalys, special rates are available for accompanying adults. All airports offer good accessibility. Disabled drivers may use their EU blue card for parking entitlements.

Information about accessibility is available from **Association des Paralysés de France** (17 bd Auguste Blanqui, 75013 Paris. 📞01 40 78 69 00; www.apf.asso.fr), which also has a nationwide network of branches.

The **Michelin Guide France** and the **Michelin Camping Caravaning France**: Revised every year, these guides indicate where to find facilities accessible to the disabled.

The French railway (SNCF) gives information on travel at www. voyages-sncf.com, as does Air France at www.airfrance.fr.

Getting There and Getting Around

BY PLANE

Various international and other independent airlines operate services to **Paris** (Roissy-Charles de Gaulle and Orly airports), **Montpellier** and **Toulouse**. Check with your travel agent, however, before booking direct flights, as it may be cheaper to travel via Paris. Air France (℘09 69 39 02 15; www.airfrance.fr), links Paris to Montpellier, Béziers-Agde and Toulouse several times a day. Other airlines offering flights to several towns in the region include British Airways, Flybe, easyJet and Ryanair. Contact airline companies and travel agents for details of package tour flights with a rail or coach link-up as well as fly-drive schemes.

- **Aéroports de Paris**
  ℘3950 from France (€0.35 per min) www.adp.fr.
- **Air France**
  Air France Call Centre: ℘3654 from France (€0.35 per min); ℘+33 (0)892 702 654 from abroad. www.airfrance.com.
- **British Airways**
  ℘0825 825 400 from France (€0.18 per min). ℘0844 493 0787 option 2 from UK (7p/min plus your phone company's access charge). www.britishairways.com.

☺ *Since 1 March 2016, children aged 12–15 no longer pay Air Passenger Duty (APD) when travelling in economy. This encompasses all British Airways flights departing from a UK airport. Some affected customers may be charged the adult APD and be eligible for a refund.*

PRACTICAL ADVICE

Practical advice for travelling by plane, specifically as regards carrying liquids, gels, creams, aerosols, medicines and food for babies is provided on www.franceguide.com. Some countries impose restrictions on liquids bought in duty-free shops when transferring to a connecting flight.
Since the 1st April 2015, all UK ports and airports are required by the UK government to carry out **Exit Checks** to collect the passport or identity card details from every person leaving the country, at their point of departure, and pass this information to UK Border Force.

BY SHIP

There are numerous **cross-Channel services** from the United Kingdom and Ireland. To choose the most suitable route between your port of departure and your destination use the **Michelin Tourist and Motoring Atlas France, Michelin map 726** (which gives travel times and mileage) or **Michelin Local Maps** from 1:200 000 series.

- **Brittany Ferries** ℘0330 159 7000 (UK). www.brittanyferries.com. Services from Portsmouth, Poole and Plymouth.
- **Condor Ferries** ℘0345 609 1024. www.condorferries.co.uk. Services from Weymouth, Poole and Portsmouth.
- **DFDS Seaways** operate routes between Dover and Calais, Dover-Dunkerque Portsmouth-Le Havre and Newhaven-Dieppe. ℘(UK) 0871 574 7235 and 0800 917 1201. www.dfdsseaways.co.uk.
- **P&O Ferries** ℘0800 130 0030 (UK). www.poferries.com. Service between Dover and Calais.

BY TRAIN

All services throughout France can be arranged through **Voyages-SNCF** in the UK: Personal callers are welcome to drop into Voyages-SNCF Travel Centre, 193 Piccadilly, LONDON W1J 9EU. ℘0844 848 5 848. www.voyages-sncf.com.
Eurostar runs from London (St Pancras) to Paris (Gare du Nord) in 2h15 (up to 20 times daily). ℘03432 186 186 (from UK); ℘+44 (0)1233 617 575 (from outside UK).

© Franck Guiziou/hemis.fr

Train Jaune running through Parc naturel régional des Pyrénées Catalanes

www.eurostar.com. Or contact the French national railways www.voyages-sncf.com.
SNCF operates a telephone information, reservation and prepayment service in English from 8am to 7pm (French time). In France call ☏36 35 (Client Service Hotline).
Citizens of non-European Economic Area countries will need to complete a landing card before arriving at Eurostar check-in. These landing cards can be found at dedicated desks in front of the check-in area and from Eurostar staff. Once you have filled in the card please hand it to UK immigration staff.
France Rail Pass and **Eurail Pass** are travel passes that may be purchased by residents of countries outside the European Union. Contact: www.voyages-sncf.com.
At the SNCF (French railways) site, **www.sncf.fr**, you can book ahead, pay with a credit card, and receive your ticket in the mail at home.
There are numerous discounts available when you purchase your tickets in France, from 25–50% below the regular rate. These include **discounts** for using senior cards and youth cards (which must be purchased, showing your name and a photograph), and lower rates for 2–9 people travelling together (advance purchase necessary). There is a limited

number of discount seats available during peak travel times, and the best discounts are available during off-peak periods.
Tickets for rail travel in France must be validated (*composter*) by using the (usually) automatic date-stamping machines at the platform entrance (failure to do so may result in a fine). The French railway company **SNCF** operates a telephone information, reservation and prepayment service in English from 7am to 10pm (French time). To buy train tickets in France call ☏36 35. More useful advice on rail travel in France is available at www.seat61.com.

BY COACH/BUS
www.eurolines.com is the international website with information about travelling all over Europe by coach (bus).
Eurolines (UK). ☏08717 8177.
Eurolines France. From France: ☏0892 89 90 91 (€0.34/min); International: ☏+33 1 41 86 24 21.

BY CAR
ROUTE PLANNING
The area covered in this guide is easily reached by main motorways and national routes. **Michelin map 726** indicates the main itineraries as well as alternate routes for avoiding heavy traffic during busy holiday periods, and gives estimated travel

times. **Michelin map 723** is a detailed atlas of French motorways, indicating tolls, rest areas and services along the route; it includes a table for calculating distances and times. The Michelin route-planning service is available at **www.viamichelin.com**. Travellers can calculate a precise route using such options as shortest route, route avoiding toll roads, Michelin-recommended route and gain access to tourist information (hotels, restaurants, attractions).

The roads are very busy during the holiday period (particularly weekends in July and August) and, to avoid traffic congestion it is advisable to follow the recommended secondary routes (signposted as *Bison Futé – itinéraires bis*). The motorway network includes rest areas *(aires de repos)* and petrol stations *(stations-service)*, with restaurant and shopping complexes attached, about every 40km/25mi. For information about **real time traffic conditions** look at www.autoroutes.fr, and France at a Glance: https://driveeuropenews.com/france.

DOCUMENTS
Driving Licence
Travellers from other European Union countries and North America can drive in France with a valid national or home-state **driving licence**. An **international driving licence** is useful because the information on it appears in nine languages.

Registration papers
For the vehicle, it is necessary to have the registration papers (logbook) and an approved nationality plate.

INSURANCE
Many motoring organisations offer accident insurance and breakdown service schemes for members. Check with your insurance company with regard to coverage while abroad. Because French autoroutes are privately owned, European Breakdown Cover service does not extend to breakdowns on the autoroute or

its service areas – you must use the emergency telephones, or drive off the autoroute before calling your breakdown service..

ROAD REGULATIONS
The minimum driving age is 18.
Traffic drives on the right.
All passengers must wear **seat belts**. Children under the age of 10 must ride in the back seat. Headlights must be switched on in poor visibility and at night; dipped headlights should be used at all times outside built up areas. Use side-lights only when the vehicle is stationary. In the case of a **breakdown**, a red warning triangle or hazard warning lights are obligatory as are reflective safety jackets.
In the absence of stop signs at intersections, cars must **give way to the right**.
Traffic on main roads outside built-up areas (priority indicated by a yellow diamond sign) and on roundabouts has right of way. Vehicles must stop when the lights turn red at road junctions and may filter to the right only when indicated by an amber arrow. The regulations on **drinking and driving** (limited to 0.50g/l) and **speeding** are strictly enforced – usually by an on-the-spot fine and/or confiscation of the vehicle.
All cars must carry a compulsory portable alcohol **breathalyser kit**, and **high visibility vests** for all passengers.

Speed limits
Although liable to modification, these are as follows:

♦ **toll motorways** (autoroutes) 130kph/80mph (110kph/68mph when raining);
♦ **dual carriageways and motorways without tolls** 110kph/68mph (100kph/62mph when raining);
♦ **other roads 90kph/56mph** (80kph/50mph when raining) and in towns 50kph/31mph;
♦ **outside lane on motorways** during daylight, on level

RENTAL CARS – CENTRAL RESERVATIONS		
Avis	✆ 0808 284 0014 (UK)	www.avis.fr
Europcar	✆ 08 25 35 83 58	www.europcar.fr
Budget France	✆ 08 00 00 35 64	www.budget.fr
Hertz France	✆ 01 39 38 38 38	www.hertz.fr
SIXT- Eurorent	✆ 08 20 00 74 98	www.sixt.fr
Enterprise	✆ 0 825 16 12 12	www.enterprise.fr

ground and with good visibility – minimum speed limit of 80kph/50mph.

♦ **built-up areas** (50kph/30mph)

CAR RENTAL

There are car rental agencies at airports, railway stations and in all large towns throughout France. European cars have manual transmission; automatic cars are available only if an advance reservation is made. Drivers must be over 21; between ages 21 and 25, drivers are required to pay an extra daily fee; some companies allow drivers under 23 only if the reservation has been made through a travel agent. It is relatively expensive to hire a car in France.

Car hire and holders of UK driving licences

In 2015, changes to the UK Driving License came into force which mean that details of fines, penalty points and restrictions are now only held electronically.

This change will affect you if you turn up at French airport, for example, to pick up a hire car, because you are going to have to make arrangements for the hire company to be able to access your online driving record by means of a DVLA-issued pass code.

The pass code number, however, can be used only once; so if this isn't set up before you get to the hire company desk you may face delays. Moreover, the code is valid for 21 days only and then lapses, so you will need internet access if trying to hire a car while already in France.

The new system allows you to download a summary of your licence record, which can be printed or shared. To log into the system you will need to know your National Insurance number and postcode, so take them with you in case you need to log in to the DVLA website while abroad. To access your online driver record you need the last eight digits of your driving licence, plus the special pass code. You can view your licence at www.gov.uk/view-driving-licence. You will also be able to call the DVLA and give permission for your driving record to be checked verbally.

PETROL/GASOLINE

French service stations dispense:

♦ *sans plomb 98*
  (super unleaded 98)
♦ *sans plomb 95*
  (super unleaded 95)
♦ *diesel/gazole* (diesel)
♦ *GPL* (LPG).

Prices are listed on signboards on the motorways; fill up off the motorway for better prices; check hypermarkets on the outskirts of towns.
The website www.prix-carburants.gouv.fr collects information on current fuel prices around the country.

Where to Stay and Eat

Hotel & Restaurant listings fall within the Address Books within the Discovering section of the guide.

WHERE TO STAY

The Green Guide is pleased to offer descriptions of selected lodgings for this region. The Address Books in the *Discovering* section of the guide give descriptions and prices *(based on double ocupancy)* of typical places to stay with local flair. The Legend on the cover flap explains the symbols and prices used in the Address Books. Use the **map of Places to Stay** on the inside cover to identify recommended places for overnight stops. For an even greater selection, use the **Michelin Guide France**, with its famously reliable star-rating system and hundreds of establishments all over France. Book ahead to ensure that you get the accommodation you want. Some places require an advance deposit or a reconfirmation. Reconfirming is especially important if you plan to arrive after 6pm. For further assistance, **Loisirs Accueil**, (www.loisirsaccueilfrance.com), is a booking service that has offices in some French *départements* – contact the tourist offices listed above for further information. A guide to good-value, family-run hotels, **Logis et Auberges de France**, (www.logishotels.com/en), is available from the French Tourist Office, as are lists of other kinds of accommodation such as hotel-châteaux, bed-and-breakfasts, etc. **Relais et châteaux** ($\mathcal{C}$01 76 49 39 39; www.relaischateaux.com), provides information on booking in luxury hotels with character.

ECONOMY CHAIN HOTELS

IIf you need a place to stop en route, these can be useful, as they are inexpensive (€50 for a double room) and generally located near the main road. There may not be a restaurant; rooms are small, with a television and private bathroom.
Here are some modestly priced chains:

- ♦ **Akena** $\mathcal{C}$01 69 84 85 17 www.hotels-akena.com
- ♦ **B&B** $\mathcal{C}$02 98 33 75 29 www.hotel-bb.com
- ♦ **Ibis Budget Hôtel** $\mathcal{C}$08 92 68 89 00. www.ibis.com
- ♦ **Premiére Classe Hôtel** $\mathcal{C}$0 207 519 50 45 www.premiereclasse.com

The hotels listed below are slightly more expensive (below €65), and offer a few more amenities and services. Central reservation numbers:

- ♦ **Campanile** $\mathcal{C}$0 207 519 50 45. www.campanile.com
- ♦ **Kyriad** $\mathcal{C}$0 207 519 50 45. www.kyriad.com
- ♦ **Ibis** $\mathcal{C}$08 92 68 66 86 www.ibishotel.com

Hotel booking websites

There is a growing number of hotel booking agencies and user-review companies operating online these days, all of them offering hotel rooms at discounted and competitive prices from high-end hotels to budget and economy establishments. It is always worth checking websites such as these to find good value discounts.
However, the general ease of booking hotel rooms online sometimes makes it worthwhile dealing with the hotels direct, since these can often offer the best rates available at the time of booking.

COTTAGES, BED & BREAKFASTS

Gîtes de France publishes a selection of bed and breakfast addresses on its website, which lists establishments throughout France offering a room and breakfast at a reasonable price. Book online at www.gites-de-france.com. The **Fédération nationale Clévacances** *(54 bd. de l'Embouchure, BP 2166, 31022 Toulouse Cedex 09. www.clevacances.com)* offers a wide choice of accommodation (rooms, flats, chalets and villas) throughout France.

The **Fédération des stations vertes de vacances et villages de neige** (6 r. Ranfer-de-Bretenières, BP 71698, 21016 Dijon Cedex. ℘03 80 54 10 50, www.stationsvertes.com) is a non-profit organisation that promotes almost 600 rural locations throughout France, selected for the quality of their environment, accommodation and available leisure activities.

FARM HOLIDAYS

The *Bienvenue à la Ferme* website (www.bienvenue-a-la-ferme.com) lists the addresses of farms renting out rooms or other types of accommodation to tourists, or which offer fresh farm produce, lunch or dinner, and other activities. Local tourist offices also keep lists of farm accommodation.

HOSTELS, CAMPING

Youth hostels *(auberges de jeunesse)* offer simple, inexpensive and often convivial accommodation.
The international youth hostels movement, International Youth Hostel Federation or Hostelling International, has dozens of hostels in France. There is an online booking service on www.hihostels.com, which you may use to reserve rooms as far as six months in advance. To stay in hostels, you may need a membership card.
To obtain an IYHF or HI card (there is no age requirement) contact the IYHF or HI in your own country for information and membership applications (in the UK ℘01707 324170. There are two main youth hostel associations (auberges de jeunesse) in France, the **Ligue Française pour les Auberges de la Jeunesse** (67 r. Vergniaud, 75013 Paris. ℘01 44 16 78 78; www.auberges-de-jeunesse.com) and the **Fédération Unie des Auberges de Jeunesse** (27 r. Pajol, 75018 Paris. ℘01 44 89 87 27. www.fuaj.org).
The **Michelin Camping France** guide lists a selection of campsites. This region is very popular with campers in the summer months, so it is wise to book in advance.

WALKERS

Walkers can consult the guide, *Gîtes d'Étapes et Refuges* by A and S Mouraret, which can be ordered from: www.gites-refuges.com.
This guide, which lists 4 000 places to stay, also contains much information to help with planning itineraries and is intended for those who enjoy walking, cycling, climbing, skiing and canoeing-kayaking holidays.

WHERE TO EAT

The Green Guide is pleased to offer a selection of restaurants for this region. The Address Books in the *Discovering* section of the guide give descriptions and prices of typical places to eat with local flair. The Legend on the cover flap explains the symbols and prices used in the Address Books.
Use the red-cover **Michelin Guide France**, with its famously reliable star-rating system and descriptions of hundreds of establishments all over France, for an even greater choice.
In the countryside, restaurants usually serve lunch between noon and 2pm and the evening meal between 7.30 and 10pm. The 'non-stop' restaurant is still a rarity in small towns in the provinces.

⌣ *For information on local specialities, see the Introduction.*
⌣ *For assistance in ordering a meal in France, see the Menu Reader, under Useful Words and Phrases.*

Gourmet guide

The Languedoc region boasts some spots which appeal to the gourmet tourist interested in discovering local specialities. Among the places which have been awarded the *Site remarquable du goût* (for 'remarkable taste sensations') distinction are the Aubrac area for its Laguiole and Fourme cheeses, the Rocher de Combalou for its Roquefort cheese, the Étangs de Thau for their production of oysters, and mussels, Banyuls for its sweet wine, and Collioure for its anchovies.

MENU READER

La Càrte	The Menu
ENTRÉES	**STARTERS**
Crudités	Raw vegetable salad
Terrine de lapin	Rabbit terrine (pâté)
Frisée aux lardons	Curly lettuce with bacon bits
Escargots	Snails
Cuisses de grenouille	Frog's legs
Salade au crottin	Goat cheese on a bed of lettuce
PLATS (VIANDES)	**MAIN COURSES (MEAT)**
Bavette à l'échalote	Flank steak with shallots
Faux filet au poivre	Sirloin with pepper sauce
Côtes d'agneau	Lamb chops
Filet mignon de porc	Pork fillet
Blanquette de veau	Veal in cream sauce
Nos viandes sont garnies	Our meat dishes are served with vegetables
PLATS (POISSONS, VOILAILLE)	**MAIN COURSES (FISH, FOWL)**
Filets de sole	Sole fillets
Dorade aux herbes	Sea bream with herbs
Saumon grillé	Grilled salmon
Coq au vin	Chicken in red wine sauce
Poulet de Bresse rôti	Free-range roast chicken from the Bresse
Omelette aux morilles	Wild-mushroom omelette
PLATEAU DE FROMAGES	**SELECTION OF CHEESES**
DESSERTS	**DESSERTS**
Tarte aux pommes	Apple tart
Crème caramel	Cooled baked custard with caramel sauce
Sorbet: trois parfums	Sorbet: choice of three flavours
BOISSONS	**BEVERAGES**
Bière	Beer
Eau minérale (gazeuse)	(Sparkling) mineral water
Une carafe d'eau	Tap water (no charge)
Vin rouge, vin blanc, rosé	Red wine, white wine, rosé
Jus de fruit	Fruit juice
MENU ENFANT	**CHILDREN'S MENU**
Jambon	Ham
Steak haché	Ground beef
Frites	French fried potatoes

Well-done, medium, rare, raw = *bien cuit, à point, saignant, cru*

©Andrew Johnson/iStockphoto.com

Basic Information

BUSINESS HOURS

In the provinces the banks open from 10am–12.30pm and 2.30–4.30 Tue–Sat. (They often close early the day before a Public Holiday). Most of the larger shops are open Mondays to Saturdays from 9am to 6.30 or 7.30pm. Smaller, individual shops may close during the lunch hour. Hypermarkets usually stay open non-stop from 9am until 9pm or later.

COMMUNICATIONS

All towns and many villages have at least one public call box, mostly used for emergencies. These use prepaid phone cards *(télécartes),* rather than coins. *Télécartes* can be bought in post offices, branches of France Télécom, *bureaux de tabac* (cafés that sell cigarettes) and newsagents.

NATIONAL CALLS

French telephone numbers have 10 digits. Paris and Paris region numbers begin with 01; 02 in northwest France; 03 in northeast France; 04 in southeast France and Corsica; 05 in southwest France.

INTERNATIONAL CALLS

To call France from abroad, dial the country code 33, omit the initial zero of the French number, and dial the remaining nine-digit number. When calling abroad from France dial 00, followed by the country code, followed by the local area code (usually without any initial zero), and the number of your correspondent.

INTERNATIONAL DIALLING CODES			
℘ (00 + code)			
Australia	61	New Zealand	64
Canada	1	United Kingdom	44
Eire	353	United States	1

Toll-free numbers in France begin with 0800.

MOBILE PHONES

While in France, all visitors from other European countries should be able to use their mobile phone just as normal. Visitors from some other countries, notably the USA, need to ensure before departure that their phone and service contract are compatible with the European system (GSM).

The three main mobile phone operators in France are SFR, Orange and Bouygues.

If you do not have your mobile phone with you, or you discovered it would not be compatible with the European system, depending on the length of your visit and on how often you plan on using the phone, it may be wise to consider buying or hiring one with a coverage plan that fits your needs. There are a variety of options you can choose from, making it less expensive than you might imagine.

Bouygues www.bouyguestelecom.fr.
Orange www.orange.fr.
SFR www.sfr.fr.

You can now also buy a prepaid EuroSIM card (www.lefrenchmobile. com) to use in France, and some providers have a European traveller service that allows you to use up your home allowances rather than pay roaming charges.

MAIL/POST

Main post offices open Monday to Friday 8am to 7pm, Saturday 8am to noon. Smaller branch post offices generally close at lunchtime between noon and 2pm and at 4pm.

Postage via airmail:
- **UK:** letter (20g) €1.
- **North America:** letter (20g) €1.25.
- **Australia, NZ:** letter (20g) €1.25.

Stamps are also available from newsagents and *bureaux de tabac.* Stamp collectors should ask for *timbres de collection* in any post office.

DISCOUNTS

Significant discounts are available for senior citizens, students, young people under the age of 25, teachers, and groups for public transportation, museums and monuments and for some leisure activities such as the cinema (at certain times of day). Bring student or senior cards with you, and bring along some extra passport-size photos for discount travel cards.

The **International Student Travel Confederation** (www.isic.org), global administrator of the International Student and Teacher Identity Cards, is an association of student travel organisations. ISTC members collectively negotiate benefits with airlines, governments, and providers of other goods and services for the student and teacher community. The corporate headquarters address is Keizersgracht 174-176, 1016 DW Amsterdam, The Netherlands; ☎31 20 421 28 00.

Pass Inter-sites, Reseau Culturel Terre Catalane – This 'passport' is available at many sites in the area where the Catalonia culture and traditions are still strongly felt. The network has different routes organised by themes (Prehistory, Baroque, Medieval churches, chateaux, Natural and Scientific Heritage, Ethnic and Ethnological Heritage and Modern Art). Some of the routes are geared up for children and the price of the pass varies according to the sites. See *www. reseauculturel.fr*.

Carte Intersites Pays Cathare – This is a similar offer covering 16 sites of Cathar heritage: the châteaux of Lastours, Arques, Quéribus, Puilaurens, Termes, Villerouge-Termenès, Saissac, Peyrepertuse and Usson; the château Comtal de Carcassonne; the abbeys of Caunes-Minervois, Saint-Papoul, Saint-Hilaire, Lagrasse and Fontfroide; and the Musée du Quercorb in Puivert. It also gives free admission for one child. www.payscathare.org.

ELECTRICITY

The electric current is 220 volts. Circular two-pin plugs are the rule. Adapters should be bought before you leave home; they are on sale in most airports.

EMERGENCIES

International emergency number 112
Police (Gendarme) 17
Fire (Pompiers) 18
Ambulance (SAMU) 15

First aid, medical advice and chemists' night-service rotas are available from chemists/drugstores (*pharmacie*, identified by a green cross sign).

MONEY
CURRENCY

There are no restrictions on the amount of currency visitors can take into France. Visitors carrying a lot of cash are advised to complete a currency declaration form on arrival, because there are restrictions on currency export.

Since January 2002, the euro has been the official currency of France. One euro is divided into 100 cents or *centimes d'euro*.

BANKS

Banks are open from 9am to noon and 2pm to 4pm and branches are closed either on Monday or Saturday. Banks close early on the day before a bank holiday. A passport is necessary as identification when cashing traveller's cheques in banks. Commission charges vary and hotels usually charge more than banks for cashing cheques. One of the most economical ways to use your money in France is by using **ATM/cash machines** to get cash directly from your bank account or to use your credit cards to get cash advances. Before you leave home, check with the bank that issued your card about emergency replacement procedures, and ask them to note that your credit card is likely to be used abroad for a while.

Be sure to remember your 4-digit PIN, you will need it to use cash dispensers and to pay with your card in most shops, restaurants, etc. ATM code pads are numeric; use a telephone pad to translate a letter code into numbers. Visa is the most widely accepted credit card, followed by MasterCard; other cards (Diners Club, Plus, Cirrus) are also accepted in most cash machines. Most places post signs indicating the cards they accept; if you don't see such a sign, and want to pay with a card, ask before ordering or making a selection.

Cards are widely accepted in shops, hypermarkets, hotels and restaurants, at tollbooths and in petrol stations. *If your card is lost or stolen* call the appropriate 24-hr hotlines listed on www.totallymoney.com/guides/lost-stolen-credit-card. Better still: always carry with you the correct number to call for your particular credit cards. You must report any loss or theft of credit cards or traveller's cheques to the local police who will issue you with a certificate (useful proof to show the issuing company).

TAXES

In France a sales tax (TVA or Value Added Tax ranging from 5.5 percent to 19.6 percent) is added to almost all retail goods – it can be worth your while to recover it. VAT refunds are available to visitors from outside the EU only if purchases exceed €175 per store.

PUBLIC AND SCHOOL HOLIDAYS

Public services, museums and other monuments may be closed or may vary their hours of admission on public holidays.

National museums and art galleries are closed on Tuesdays; municipal museums are generally closed on Mondays. In addition to school holidays at Christmas and in spring and summer, there are long mid-term breaks in February and early November.

1 January	New Year's Day (Jour de l'An)
	Easter Day and Easter Monday (Pâques)
1 May	May Day (Fête du Travail)
8 May	VE Day (Fête de la Libération)
Thurs 40 days after Easter	Ascension Day (Ascension)
7th Sun–Mon after Easter	Whit Sunday and Monday (Pentecôte)
14 July	France's National Day (Fête de la Bastille)
15 August	Assumption (Assomption)
1 November	All Saint's Day (Toussaint)
11 November	Armistice Day (Fête de la Victoire)
25 December	Christmas Day (Noël)

French schools close for vacations five times a year: one week at the end of October, two weeks at Christmas, two weeks in February, two weeks in Spring and the whole of July and August. In these periods, all tourist site and attractions, hotels, restaurants and roads are busier than usual.

SMOKING

Smoking has been banned inside all public spaces, including hotel rooms, bars and clubs since January 2008. It is still permitted on outdoor café terraces and in specially-built fumoirs.

WHEN IT IS NOON IN FRANCE, IT IS	
3am	in Los Angeles
6am	in New York
11am	in Dublin
11am	in London
7pm	in Perth
9pm	in Sydney
11pm	in Auckland

In France 'am' and 'pm' are not used but the 24-hour clock is widely applied.

TIME

France is 1hr ahead of Greenwich Mean Time (GMT). France goes on daylight-saving time from the last Sunday in March to the last Sunday in October.

TIPPING

Since a service charge is automatically included in the price of meals and accommodation in France, any additional tipping is up to the visitor, usually small change, and generally not more than 5%. Hairdressers are usually tipped 10–15%.

As a rule, prices for hotels and restaurants as well as for other goods and services are significantly less expensive in the French regions than in Paris.

Restaurants usually charge for meals in two ways: a *forfait* or *menu*, that is, a fixed price menu with two to three courses, sometimes a small pitcher of wine, all for a set price, or *à la carte*, the more expensive way, with each course ordered separately. It is important to tell the waiting staff that you are ordering from the fixed price menu, otherwise they may charge you separately for each dish.

Cafés have very different prices, depending on where they are located. The price of a drink or a coffee is cheaper if you stand at the counter *(comptoir)* than if you sit down *(salle)* and sometimes it is even more expensive if you sit outdoors *(terrace)*. In some big cities, prices go up after 10pm in the evening.

Useful Words and Phrases

Sights

	Translation
Abbaye	Abbey
Beffroi	Belfry
Chapelle	Chapel
Château	Castle
Cimetière	Cemetery
Cloître	Cloisters
Cour	Courtyard
Couvent	Convent
Écluse	Lock (Canal)
Église	Church
Fontaine	Fountain
Halle	Covered Market
Jardin	Garden
Mairie	Town Hall
Maison	House
Marché	Market
Monastère	Monastery
Moulin	Windmill
Musée	Museum
Parc	Park
Place	Square
Pont	Bridge
Port	Port/harbour
Porte	Gate/gateway
Quai	Quay
Remparts	Ramparts
Rue	Street
Statue	Statue
Tour	Tower

On The Road

	Translation
Car Park	Parking
Diesel	Gazole
Driving Licence	Permis De Conduire
East	Est
Garage (For Repairs)	Garage
Left	Gauche
Motorway/highway	Autoroute
North	Nord
Parking Meter	Horodateur
Petrol/gas	Essence
Petrol/gas Station	Station Essence
Right	Droite
South	Sud
Toll	Péage
Traffic Lights	Feu Tricolore
Tyre	Pneu
Unleaded fuel	Sans Plomb
West	Ouest
Wheel Clamp	Sabot
Zebra Crossing	Passage Clouté

Time

	Translation
Today	Aujourd'hui
Tomorrow	Demain
Yesterday	Hier
Winter	Hiver
Spring	Printemps
Summer	Été
Autumn/fall	Automne
Week	Semaine
Monday	Lundi
Tuesday	Mardi
Wednesday	Mercredi
Thursday	Jeudi
Friday	Vendredi
Saturday	Samedi
Sunday	Dimanche

Numbers

	Translation
0	zéro
1	un
2	deux
3	trois
4	quatre
5	cinq
6	six
7	sept
8	huit
9	neuf
10	dix
11	onze
12	douze
13	treize
14	quatorze
15	quinze
16	seize
17	dix-sept
18	dix-huit
19	dix-neuf
20	vingt
30	trente
40	quarante
50	cinquante
60	soixante
70	soixante-dix
80	quatre-vingt
90	quatre-vingt-dix
100	cent
1000	mille

Food and Drink

	Translation
Beef	Bœuf
Beer	Bière
Bread	Pain
Breakfast	Petit-déjeuner
Butter	Beurre
Cheese	Fromage
Chicken	Poulet
Dessert	Dessert
Dinner	Dîner
Fish	Poisson
Fork	Fourchette
Fruit	Fruits
Glass	Verre
Ham	Jambon
Ice Cream	Glace
Ice Cubes	Glaçons
Knife	Couteau
Lamb	Agneau
Lettuce Salad	Salade
Lunch	Déjeuner
Meat	Viande
Mineral Water	Eau Minérale
Mixed Salad	Salade Composée
Orange Juice	Jus D'orange
Plate	Assiette
Pork	Porc
Red Wine	Vin Rouge
Restaurant	Restaurant
Salt	Sel
Spoon	Cuillère
Sugar	Sucre
Vegetables	Légumes
Water	De l'eau
White Wine	Vin Blanc
Yoghurt	Yaourt

Useful Phrases

	Translation
The bill, please	L'addition, s'il vous plaît
Goodbye	Au Revoir
Hello/good morning	Bonjour
How...?	Comment...?
Excuse me	Excusez-moi
Thank you	Merci
Yes/No	Oui/Non
I'm sorry	Pardon
Why?	Pourquoi?
When?	Quand?
Please	S'il vous plaît

CONVERSION TABLES

Weights and Measures

		![UK]	
1 kilogram (kg) 6.35 kilograms 0.45 kilograms	**2.2 pounds (lb)** 14 pounds 16 ounces (oz)	**2.2 pounds** 1 stone (st) 16 ounces	*To convert kilograms to pounds, multiply by 2.2*
1 metric ton (tn)	**1.1 tons**	**1.1 tons**	
1 litre (l) 3.79 litres 4.55 litres	**2.11 pints (pt)** 1 gallon (gal) 1.20 gallon	**1.76 pints** 0.83 gallon 1 gallon	*To convert litres to gallons, multiply by 0.26 (US) or 0.22 (UK)*
1 hectare (ha) **1 sq kilometre (km²)**	**2.47 acres** **0.38 sq. miles (sq mi)**	**2.47 acres** **0.38 sq. miles**	*To convert hectares to acres, multiply by 2.4*
1 centimetre (cm)	**0.39 inches (in)**	**0.39 inches**	*To convert metres to feet, multiply by 3.28; for kilometres to miles, multiply by 0.6*
1 metre (m)	**3.28 feet (ft) or 39.37 inches or 1.09 yards (yd)**		
1 kilometre (km)	**0.62 miles (mi)**	**0.62 miles**	

Clothing

Women	EU	US	UK		Men	EU	US	UK
	35	4	2½			40	7½	7
	36	5	3½			41	8½	8
	37	6	4½			42	9½	9
Shoes	38	7	5½		Shoes	43	10½	10
	39	8	6½			44	11½	11
	40	9	7½			45	12½	12
	41	10	8½			46	13½	13
	36	6	8			46	36	36
	38	8	10			48	38	38
Dresses	40	10	12		Suits	50	40	40
& suits	42	12	14			52	42	42
	44	14	16			54	44	44
	46	16	18			56	46	48
	36	6	30			37	14½	14½
	38	8	32			38	15	15
Blouses &	40	10	34		Shirts	39	15½	15½
sweaters	42	12	36			40	15¾	15¾
	44	14	38			41	16	16
	46	16	40			42	16½	16½

Sizes often vary depending on the designer. These equivalents are given for guidance only.

Speed

KPH	10	30	50	70	80	90	100	110	120	130
MPH	6	19	31	43	50	56	62	68	75	81

Temperature

Celsius (°C)	0°	5°	10°	15°	20°	25°	30°	40°	60°	80°	100°
Fahrenheit (°F)	32°	41°	50°	59°	68°	77°	86°	104°	140°	176°	212°

To convert Celsius into Fahrenheit, multiply °C by 9, divide by 5, and add 32.
To convert Fahrenheit into Celsius, subtract 32 from °F, multiply by 5, and divide by 9.
NB: Conversion factors on this page are approximate.

Hôtel de Ville, Place du Capitole, Toulouse
© Jean-Marc Barrère/hemis.fr

The Region Today

This guide covers two of France's former 21 mainland regions, Languedoc-Roussillon (capital Montpellier) and Midi-Pyrénées (capital Toulouse). They cover almost 73 000 sq km/28 000 sq mi of southwest France broken down into 13 departments.

THE PEOPLE

Languedoc-Roussilllon and Midi-Pyrénées are already home to over 5 million people; but they are also the fastest growing regions in France as migrants from the north and from other countries increasingly move south in search of a better climate and lifestyle. The demographic trend, however is not homogeneous. While the cities are expanding, many villages have experienced depopulation. In recent decades there has been a new trend in the opposite direction. As the road network improves, much of the countryside has been converted into a dormitory for urban workers or a weekend refuge for second home owners.

The region's booming demographics pose a challenge for the provision of cost-effective health, education and other services, and for the protection and management of the environment.

ECONOMY

The economy of the region is similarly in flux. Unlike the north of France the southwest has never had much heavy industry, being traditionally reliant on agriculture and its ancilliary trades. The closure of such mines and factories as there were has forced the region towards hi-tech manufacturing (symbolised by the Airbus assembly plant outside Toulouse) and, above all, the service sector.

TOURISM

Particularly important is tourism. This is the fourth most visited area of France after Paris, Provence and the Alps, receiving some 28 million visitors a year, one-third from outside France. A sizeable number come for the beaches of the Mediterranean coast. Others come to explore wine regions, relax in spas, go boating on the Canal du Midi or, in winter, ski in the Pyrenees.

Between them, Languedoc-Roussillon and Midi-Pyrénées have two of France's mainland national parks (the Cévennes and the Pyrenees), seven of the 42 UNESCO World Heritage Sites plus a share in two more and 11 of the 37 *Grands Sites* (outstanding natural or manmade attractions) of France.

For almost all visitors the relaxed lifestyle, friendly nature of the people and excellent cuisine are also a major draw.

FOOD AND DRINK

Every small corner of the country has its speciality product or dish and asking about it will be a way to understand the culture and folk history of the region.

AVEYRON AND LOZÈRE

The region stretching from the Aveyron *département* to the Cévennes has a delectable local cuisine, based on livestock bred on the *causses*. Local cheeses include: Fourme de Laguiole, a type of Cantal used to make the local dish *aligot*; Bleu de Causses, a blue cheese made from cow's milk; Pérail and the well-known Roquefort, both from ewe's milk; and Cabécou or Cévennes *pélardons* from goat's milk. Lamb from the causses is a delicious, but pricey, main course. Many local recipes feature mutton or pork, common in traditional cooking. Offal such as tripe also features widely on local menus: *tripoux de Naucelles* (tripe stewed in white wine with ham and garlic); charcuterie from Entraygues; sausages from St-Affrique and Langogne; *trénels de Millau* (sheep's tripe stuffed with ham, garlic, parsley and egg); *alicuit* from Villefranche-en-Rouergue (stewed chicken livers).

Fresh fish is hard to come by, apart from river trout, but recipes featuring salted or dried fish are common, such as *estofinado* (stockfish stew). Chestnuts are traditionally used in soups and stews, or roasted and eaten whole with a glass of cider. For those with a sweet tooth, there are *soleils* from Rodez (round yellow cookies flavoured with almonds and orange blossom), fouaces from Najac (*brioches* flavoured with angelica), Cévennes *croquants* (hard almond cookies) and nènes (small aniseed biscuits) from St-Affrique.

THE MEDITERRANEAN

On and near the coast, the cuisine makes rich use of herbs from the *garrigues* (rosemary, thyme, juniper, sage, fennel), garlic and olive oil, and fresh aubergines, tomatoes, courgettes and peppers. A local garlic soup called *aigo boulido* is made with garlic, olive oil and thyme. Some dishes include snails, delicious wild mushrooms (*cèpes, morilles*) or even – as a special treat – truffles, found growing at the foot of the holm-oaks on the slopes of the Hérault and the Gard.

Common meat dishes feature mutton or pork, and occasionally veal. Local game raised on fragrant wild herbs, juniper berries and thyme, has a remarkable flavour, as do the lambs and sheep raised on the *causses*. They are used in pies or stews. Regional cheeses are mainly from goat's milk, very tasty when heated and served on a bed of lettuce. Menus near the coast are based on a variety of seafood: oysters and mussels from Bouzigues, *bourride sètoise* (fish stew from Sète), gigot de mer de Palavas (fish baked with garlic and vegetables) and seafood pasties. In Montpellier, fish dishes are accompanied by *beurre de Montpellier*, a sauce of mixed herbs, watercress, spinach, anchovies, yolks of hard-boiled eggs, butter and spices. Sweets include *oreillettes* (orange biscuits fried in olive oil), eaten in Montpellier at Epiphany and on Shrove Tuesday, or *grisettes* (candy made from honey, wild herbs and liquorice).

Catalan cuisine

The cooking of Roussillon, the Catalan corner of France is worth singling out. Its specialities include **Bouillinade**, the Catalan version of *bouillabaisse* (fish soup), and *civet de langouste au Banyuls* – spiny lobster stewed in dry Banyuls wine. The small port of Collioure lands anchovies. These are either pickled in brine and then packed in jars of oil or used to make *anchoïade*, a savoury paste of anchovies, olive oil and garlic.

In Les Aspres, **escalade** is a fragrant soup made with thyme, garlic, oil and egg. Mushrooms fried in oil with an olive sauce are eaten with game (partridge and hare). Catalan charcuterie includes such delicacies as black pudding (boutifare or boudin), pig's liver sausage, and cured hams and salami from the Cerdagne mountain. **Cargolade**, snails from the garrigue grilled over burning vine cuttings, frequently feature in the open-air meals which follow prayer retreats at the hermitages. Sweets include crème *catalane* (crème brûlée with caramel), *bunyettes* (orange-flavoured doughnuts), *rousquilles* from Amélie-les-Bains (small almond biscuits) and fresh fruit from Roussillon's many orchards (peaches, pears, and melons).

TOULOUSE, TARN, GERS AND PYRÉNÉES

Toulouse's signature dish is cassoulet, a thick stew of haricot beans, sausage, pork, mutton and preserved goose.

The Gers, to the west of the city is renowned for its goose and duck, either preserved as *confits* or as foie gras, or in stews. This region is also said to produce the finest garlic in France.

Visitors to the Tarn should not miss charcuterie from the Montagne Noire, *bougnettes* from Castres (small, flat pork sausages) and cured hams and sausages from Lacaune.

The Pyrenees produce a tasty ewe's milk cheese called brebis. On the plains north of the range, white beans are a speciality, notably, around Tarbes where the higly prized *haricots tarbais* are grown.

WINE

Coteaux du Languedoc

The wine growing region of Languedoc is blessed with a Mediterranean climate and a variety of soil types (layers of schist, pebble terraces and red clay). It is the main producer of French table wine (*vins de table and vins de pays*), but today wine-growers here are concentrating on improving local grape varieties and the way they are blended. Their efforts have been rewarded with an increase in the number of designated AOCs (Appellations d'Origine Contrôlée) in the region. Promoted to AOC in 1985, the **Coteaux du Languedoc** appellation includes red, rosé and white wines produced in the Hérault, Gard and Aveyron *départements*. Besides Faugères and St-Chinian, whose heady, powerful wines have won these areas their own AOC designations, the AOC has been awarded to particular vintages. For red and rosé wines, these are: Cabrières, La Clape, La Méjanelle, Montpeyroux, Pic-St-Loup, St-Christol, St-Drézéry, St-Georges-d'Orques, St-Saturnin and Vérargues, and for white wines: Picpoul-de-Pinet, aged in oak casks. The Carignan grape is the main grape variety cultivated in the region. The Cabrières region also produces **Clairette du Languedoc**, a dry white wine made from the Clairette grape, an AOC winner. Local table wine is sold under the label 'Vins de pays d'Oc' or 'Vin de Pays' followed by its *département* of origin. Notable vins doux naturels from the Coteaux du Languedoc include Muscat de Frontignan, Muscat de Mireval and Muscat de Lunel.

Corbières and Roussillon
The **Fitou** AOC is reserved for a red wine from a specific area in the Corbières. Its alcohol content must be at least 12 percent, output is limited to 30hl per hectare, and the wine must have been aged in a cellar for at least nine months. Fitou wines, produced from high quality grapes, are strong and full-bodied.
The **Corbières** AOC covers an area with a mixture of soil types, producing a variety of wines. Besides red wines with a fine bouquet, production includes fruity rosés and some dry white wines.
The Roussillon vineyards are noted for their high quality *vins doux naturels* (dessert wines), the **Côtes du Roussillon** and **Côtes du Roussillon Village** wines classified as AOC, and their robust, earthy local wines. Just north of Agde,

the tiny village of Pinet produces a dry white wine called Picpoul de Pinet (from the Picpoul grape). It makes the perfect accompaniment to oysters from the nearby Bassin de Thau. This region's *vins doux naturels* represent the majority of French production of wines of this type. The grape varieties – Grenache, Maccabeu, Carignan, Malvoisie, among others – add warmth and bouquet to these wines. The warm local climate and the sunny vineyards make these wines mature perfectly with a high natural sugar content. The most famous examples are **Banyuls**, **Maury**, **Muscat de Rivesaltes** and **Rivesaltes**.

Minervois
The Minervois region is reputed for its fine, fruity robust red wines which are well balanced and have a deep, rich red colour. The St-Jean-du-Minervois vineyard, covering the limestone *garrigues* on the uplands in the northwest, produces a fragrant muscat dessert wine.

Blanquette de Limoux
This sparkling white wine, much in demand for its fine quality, is made from the Mauzac and Clairette grapes ripened on the slopes around Limoux.

Gaillac and Fronton
The wines of the Gaillac vineyards, to the west of Albi, are classified as *Appellation d'Origine Contrôlée*. Dry white wines with a fragrant bouquet are made using local grape varieties Mauzac, Len de Lel and Ondec. There are three types of Gaillac white: sweet (*moelleux*), very slightly sparkling (*perlé*) and sparkling (*mousseux*). Gaillac red is made from traditional grapes such as Gamay, Syrah, Merlot and Cabernet, mixed with local varieties like Braucol or Duras for a robust wine, or Négrette.
Slightly farther west, just north of Toulouse, **Côtes du Frontonnais** wines are produced from a very old grape variety, the Négrette, mixed with Cabernet, Syrah, Fer Servadou and Cot, to give supple fruity wines which are best drunk young. There are two AOCs around Carcassonne: Cabardès, well balanced with

Roussillon vineyards with the massif du Canigou in the background

© Jean-Paul Azam/hemis.fr

plenty of body, and Malepère, a fruity red wine. Both of these wines are perfect complements to game and red meat.

Gascony

The Gers has four main wine areas. **Côtes de Gascogne** is a vin de pays region covering a broad swathe of the northwest of the department and is known for its whites more than its reds and rosés. Roughly the same area is used to produce Armagnac brandy.

Next door, to the east, is the **Côtes du Condomois**, another vin de pays area centred on the town of Condom.

In the west are two areas of interest. One is **Saint-Mont** a relatively small area of vineyards classed as VDQS (*Vin Délimité de Qualité Supérieure* – one step down from AOC), but with a growing reputation for its reds.

The vineyards of **Madiran** AOC cross over into the departments of Hautes-Pyrénées and Pyrénées-Atlantiques. They are renowned for their unmistakeable thick, dark red wines made principally from the tannat grape. Madiran's white wines are called Pacherenc d Vic Bilh and are mainly sweet.

The Gers also has a speciality aperitif, **Floc de Gascogne,** produced in red and white versions by mixing Armagnac with grape juice according to a 16C recipe.

Aveyron

The Aveyron vineyards were once a source of great wealth to the region, thanks to the work of the monks from Conques. Covering steep slopes, these vineyards stand out from the surrounding mountain landscape. The well balanced red wines of **Marcillac** (AOC), with a hint of raspberry, go well with the tripe dishes of the Rouergue region. The red wines from **Entraygues** and **Fel**, classified as VDQS have substance and a nice fruity flavour. The whites from these designations are lighter with more finesse. In the Lot valley, the **Estaing** VDQS vineyards are cultivated on the valley sides up to an altitude of 450m and produce pleasant dry whites and subtle, fragrant reds. The Tarn valley between Peyreleau and Broquiès is home to the **Côtes de Millau** VDQS vineyards, which produce mainly red and rosé wine. **Cerno** is a local aperitif made from Côtes de Millau wine and herbal extracts.

Organic Wine

Almost every region has at least one producer of organic or natural wines who reject artficial and industrialised processes reliant on chemicals. Organic wines are also available from whole food shops which are located in cities.

History

The southwest of France has been occupied by human beings almost as long as anywhere on the European continent. It grew to be an important place during the Gallo-Roman period but reached its apogée in the Middle Ages when its civilisation was the envy of northern Europe. Subsequently the southwest was largely eclipsed from the great movements of history as power in France became concentrated in the crown and the country's centre of gravity shifted north.

PREHISTORY

During the Quaternary Era some two million years ago, glaciers spread over the highest mountains and humans began to populate Europe, particularly the Pyrenees.

THE STONE AGE					
PERIOD	HOMINID EVOLUTION	STAGE OF CIVILISATION	SITES	FAUNA	CLIMATE
1 500 MEGALITH AGE **NEOLITHIC**		Dolmens and tumulus			
		Points and arrows Polished stone choppers			Warm
7 500 **MESOLITHIC** AZILIAN 10 000		Painted stones Carved Venus figures Needles Burins			
MAGDALENIAN SOLUTREAN **UPPER PALEOLITHIC** AURIGNACIAN PERIGORDIAN	Cro-Magnon **Homo sapiens**	Harpoons Convex side scrapers Spears Bone tools Cave paintings and engravings	Lespugue Brassempouy Gargas Aurignac	Reindeer Mammoths, Bears, Cave Hyena, Woolly Rhinoceros, Hippopotamus	Würm Glacial Period
35 000 MOUSTERIAN **MIDDLE PALEOLITHIC** LEVALOISIAN 150 000		Oval flints Blades, Disks, Arrows, Scrapers, Biface flint tools		Mammoth Elephant	Warm
TAYACIAN ACHEULIAN	**Neanderthal Man**	Handaxes in flint or quartzite Awls Scrapers Saws		Appearance of Mammoth Ox, Lion	Riss Glacial Period
LOWER PALEOLITHIC				Aurochs/Bison, Rhinoceros, Tiger	Warm
CLACTONIAN	Montmaurin Man	Handaxes, shaped on both sides ("bifaces")	Montmaurin	Hippopotamus, Rhinoceros Big Bear	Mindel Glacial Period
ABBEVILLIAN	Java Man *Pithecanthropus erectus*				Warm Günz Glacial Period
2 million					
	Lucy (Ethiopia) *Australopithecus afarensis* **Homo erectus**				
3 million years ago					

R. Corbel

LOWER PALEOLITHIC

The Lower Paleolithic (Old Stone Age 530 000–250 000 years ago) is represented by Tautavel man, a 'Homo erectus' who inhabited Roussillon 450 000 years ago. He was 20–25 years old, 1.65m tall and stood upright. He had a flat receding forehead, prominent cheekbones and rectangular eye sockets beneath a thick projecting brow. No trace of any hearth has been found, so it is assumed that this intrepid hunter probably ate his meat raw. He used caves as look-outs to track animal movements, as temporary places to camp, to dismember prey, and as workshops for manufacturing tools.

MIDDLE PALEOLITHIC

The presence of numerous Mousterian deposits is evidence that Neanderthal man lived in what is now southwest France. Taller than 'homo erectus,' he had a well-developed skull (1 700cm^3), constructed vast dwelling and burial places, and produced more sophisticated, specialised tools such as double-sided implements, stone knives with curved edges, chisels, scrapers, pointed tools and various notched implements. With 'homo sapiens' a significant human presence developed. During the Aurignacian period (named after the town of Aurignac), stone implements were supplemented with tools made of bone and horn. With them they sculpted human figures like the Aurignacian 'Venuses'.

Cave Artists

During the Solutrean and Magdalenian periods, technical evolution progressed even further. Towards the end of the last Glacial Period, boar and deer inhabited the changing landscape. Humans hunted and fished, yet their greatest innovation was the birth of art. Some of the best prehistoric cave paintings can be seen in the Pyrenees at Niaux in the Ariège and Gargas in the Comminges, both open to the public. The meaning of this art is still puzzled over by experts.

NEOLITHIC

The Neolithic Age (New Stone Age, approximately 9 500–3 500 years ago) brought polished stone tools and earthenware. Cattle-rearing and wheat and barley cultivation had become a means of subsistence by the fourth millennium, and dwellings more elaborate, with supporting structures, flat hearths for cooking and silos for storage. In the Narbonne region communities developed specialised activities and began bartering and trading with one other. Inhabitants of the densely populated middle mountain slopes raised stock and developed weapons (arrows, axes and knives), jewellery and earthenware.

THE DOLMEN BUILDERS

The Aveyron *département* has the greatest concentration of dolmens, in France. These and other megalithc structures are thought to date from the end of the Neolithic just before the Bronze Age, around 2500–1500 BCE.
Dolmens consist of horizontal slabs supported by vertical stones and are believed to have been tombs.
In the south of the Aveyron and north of the Tarn there are some even more curious prehistoric remains: statue-menhirs depict a human figure, perhaps a protective goddess. The figure has arms, hands, short lower limbs, a face tattooed in patterns, neck adorned with jewellery, eyes, nose, but strangely, no mouth.

ROMANISATION

Because of its strategic position on the trade route (the Via Domitia) along the coast between Spain and Italy, the Languedoc was conquered in around 121 BCE long before the rest of Gaul (51–58 BCE). The largest city en route was Narbonne, founded in 118 BCE as the first Roman colony outside Italy. The Gallo-Roman civilisation left a few monumental signs of its greatness but also some lesser but more revealing ones, such as the potteries at Montans in the Tarn. Gaul only fell to the invading barbarians in the 4C.

TIME LINE
ANTIQUITY
BC

1800-700 Bronze Age. End of Pyrenean Megalithic culture.

1000-600 End of Bronze Age and first Iron Age. Arrival of continental, then Mediterranean influences.

600-50 Development of metallurgy in ancient Catalonia (Catalan forges).

6C The Celts invade Gaul.

214 **Hannibal** crosses the Pyrenees into Roussillon.

2C Roman Conquest. The **Romans** occupy the region later known as Bas Languedoc.

118 Foundation of Narbonne, capital of **Gallia Narbonensis**, at the crossing of the Via Domitia and the road to Aquitaine.

58-52 **Caesar** conquers Gaul.

27 Bas Languedoc becomes part of Gallia Narbonensis, marking the beginning of a long period of prosperity.

3C and 4C Christianity arrives in the region. Decline of Narbonne and Toulouse.

313 **Edict of Milan**. Emperor Constantine grants Christians freedom of worship.

356 **Council of Béziers**, Arian heresy.

INVASIONS, THE MIDDLE AGES

3C-5C **Invasions** by the Alemanni, the Vandals, then the Visigoths. Toulouse becomes the capital of the Visigothic kingdom.

507 Battle of Vouillé: **Clovis** defeats the Visigoths, and restricts their kingdom to seven cities (Carcassonne, Narbonne, Béziers, Agde, Nîmes, Elne and Maguelone).

719 The **Saracens** capture Narbonne.

732 **Charles Martel** defeats the Saracens at Poitiers.

737 Charles Martel recaptures the seven cities from the Visigoths.

759 Pépin the Short recaptures Narbonne.

801 **Charlemagne** marches into Spain and integrates Catalonia into his Empire, allowing it to remain autonomous.

843 The **Treaty of Verdun** divides Charlemagne's Empire: territories west of the Rhône to the Atlantic Ocean are given to Charles the Bald.

877 **Charles the Bald** dies and most of the great princely houses that will rule the south of France until the 13C are established.
The counts of Toulouse own the old kingdom of seven cities and the Rouergue; the Gévaudan belongs to the Auvergne family.

10C Religious revival and **pilgrimages to St James's** shrine in Santiago de Compostela, Spain.

987 Hugues Capet is crowned king of France.

11C Renewed economic and demographic growth in the West. The counts of Toulouse assert their power. Wave of construction of ecclesiastical buildings. Tour of Languedoc by Pope Urban II.

1095 **First Crusade**.

1112 The count of Barcelona becomes viscount of Béziers, Agde, Gévaudan and Millau.

UNION WITH THE FRENCH CROWN

12C-13C Flowering of the art and culture of the troubadours. **First bastides** (fortified towns) are constructed.

1140-1200 The **Cathar** doctrine spreads.
1152 Henry II Plantagenet marries Eleanor of Aquitaine.
1204 The king of Aragon gains sovereignty of Montpellier, Gévaudan and Millau.
1207 Raymond VI, count of Toulouse is excommunicated.
1208 Pierre de Castelnau, legate to Pope Innocent III, is assassinated.
1209 **Albigensian Crusade** *(details below in the section on the Cathars).* Simon de Montfort captures Béziers and Carcassonne.
1213 Battle of Muret.
1226 A new crusade: **Louis VIII** seizes Languedoc.
1229 The **Treaty of Paris** ends the war against the Albigensians. St Louis annexes the whole of Bas Languedoc. Toulouse University is founded.
1250-1320 The **Inquisition** quells the last strongholds of the Cathars.
1270 St Louis dies.
1276-1344 Perpignan is capital of the **kingdom of Majorca** and the Balearic Islands, which was founded by Jaime I of Aragon and includes the Cerdagne, Roussillon and Montpellier.
1278-88 the 'Pariatges' establish the co-sovereignty of the Bishop of Urgell and the Count of Foix over Andorra
1290 The counts of Foix inherit the Béarn.
1292 Annexation of Pézenas, the Rouergue and the Gévaudan.
1312 **Philip the Fair** dissolves the Order of the Templars, and their considerable estates in the Causses are given to the Knights Hospitallers of St John of Jerusalem (or of Malta).

1331-91 Life of Gaston Fébus.
1337 Beginning of the **Hundred Years War** lasting until 1453.
1348 The **Black Death** kills one third of the population of Languedoc.
1349 The king of Majorca sells the seigneury of Montpellier to Philip of Valois.
1350-1450 The Pyrenees and Languedoc suffer a long period of war, unrest, epidemics and famine.
1360 **Treaty of Bretigny**: end of the first part of the Hundred Years War. Rouergue is ceded to the king of England. Languedoc is divided into three seneschalsies: Toulouse, Carcassonne and Beaucaire.
1361 Outlaws plunder the countryside.
1420 Charles VII enters Toulouse.
1462 Intervention of Louis XI in Roussillon.

WARS OF RELIGION AND UNION WITH FRANCE

1484 The **princes of Albret**, 'kings of Navarre,' gain ascendancy in the Gascon Pyrenees (Foix, Béarn, Bigorre).
1512 Ferdinand, the Catholic monarch, divests the Albrets of their territory.
1539 The edict of **Villers-Cotteret** decrees French the legal language of France.
1560-98 Protestants and Roman Catholics engage in **Wars of Religion**.
1589 Henry IV ascends to the throne and his right of co-sovereignty over Andorra passes to the French crown.
1598 The **Edict of Nantes** gives Protestants freedom of worship and guaranteed strongholds (Puylaurens, Montauban).

1607 Henri IV unites his own royal estates (including the fiefs of Foix and Béarn) to the French Crown.

1610 **Henri IV is assassinated** and religious strife is renewed.

1629 Under the **Treaty of Alès**, Protestants keep their religious freedoms but lose their strongholds.

1643-1715 Reign of Louis XIV.

1659 The **Treaty of the Pyrenees** unites Roussillon and the Cerdagne with the French Crown. The definitive frontier between France and Spain is agreed.

1666-80 Riquet constructs the **Canal du Midi**.

1685 **Revocation** of the Edict of Nantes. Numerous Protestants flee the country.

1702-04 **War of the Camisards**.

FROM FIRST SPA RESORT TO MODERN TIMES

1746 De Bordeu's thesis on mineral springs promotes the creation of **spa resorts** and the popularity of 'taking cures'.

1787 Ramond de Carbonnières, first enthusiast of the Pyrenees, stays in Barèges.

1790 France is divided into new administrative districts (*départements*).

1804-15 First **Empire**. New thermal springs are discovered in the Pyrenees.

1852-1914 Second Empire and Third Republic. Development of spa resorts, rock climbing and scientific studies of the Pyrenees.

1858 The Virgin Mary appears to 14-year-old Bernadette Soubirous sparking the Lourdes pilgrimages

1875 **Phylloxera** destroys Languedoc's vineyards.

1901 First **hydroelectric** schemes implemented.

1907 Wine-growers in Bas Languedoc join a protest (*'Mouvement des gueux'*) against overproduction, competition from imported Algerian wines and falling prices.

1914-1918 First World War.

1939 When the Spanish Civil War ends, refugees from the defeated Republicans pour over the border.

1940-44 On the fall of France, Nazi Germany occupies the north and west of the country, leaving the rest to be controlled by the Vichy government. The Pyrenees prove to be of vital importance to the **French Résistance**. The Massif de l'Aigoual is a major headquarters for the maquis.

1958 Fifth republic is inaugurated.

1963 Plans are made to develop the Languedoc-Roussillon coastline.

1967 The Pyrenees national park is created.

1969 Maiden flight of '**Concorde** 001.'

1970 Designation of the **Parc National des Cévennes**. Founding of Airbus Industrie.

1972 The regions of Languedoc-Roussillon and Midi-Pyrénées come into being.

1973 Designation of the **Parc naturel régional du Haut Languedoc**.

1992-97 The new motorway (A 75) linking Clermont-Ferrand with Béziers opens in progressive sections.

1993 Toulouse underground railway (**métro**) begins operation. Andorra gets a written constitution and becomes a de jure independent state.

1994 **Puymorens tunnel** opens in the Pyrenees.

Way of St James

According to legend, the apostle St James travelled from Palestine to Spain to Christianise the country, but was beheaded. Two of his disciples carrying his body were stranded on the coast of Galicia and buried St. James' remains there. The site of the grave was unknown until around 813 when a shower of stars falling over an earth mound drew a hermit's attention to the grave. The spot became known as *Campus stellae* (Compostela) and a chapel was erected here. St James became the patron saint of all Christians as well as the symbol of the Spaniards' struggle to regain their land from the Moors. After the first French pilgrimage in 951, Compostela grew as famous as Rome and Jerusalem, attracting pilgrims from all over Europe.

In 1130, the French monk Aymeri Picaud wrote a tourist guide for pilgrims, the Codex Calixtinus, which included a layout of the routes leading to Santiago de Compostela. Included in this guide are St-Jean-Pied-de-Port in the foothills of the Pyrenees, part of the *camino frances* (the French way): the **via Podiensis** which links the Aubrac mountains and Condom, the **via Tolosane** (coming from Arles and traversing Toulouse and Auch) and the **Caussade** (via Conques, Rodez, Foix and Lourdes). Over the centuries, the pilgrimage tradition enhanced the region's cultural heritage, particularly in Conques, Rocamadour, Saint-Sernin de Toulouse and St-Bertrand-de-Comminges. In recent decades there has been a revival of interest in the various routes of the pilgrimage for modern travellers.

1995	Designation of the **Parc naturel régional des Grands Causses**.
1996	The **Canal du Midi** joins the UNESCO World Heritage List.
1997	The medieval city of **Carcassonne** and the Cirque de Gavarnie join the UNESCO World Heritage List.
1999	Massive December storms slam the southwest coast of France.

THE NEW MILLENNIUM

2001	Explosion rocks the AZF chemical plant near Toulouse, killing 29 and wounding 2 400.
2002	The euro replaces the franc as France's official currency.
2004	The Millau viaduct becomes the world's tallest bridge. The last native Pyrenean brown bear, a female named Cannelle, is shot by a hunter.
March 2005	The maiden flight of **Airbus 380**, a 555-seat superjumbo jet assembled in Toulouse.
2007	**Nicolas Sarkozy** is elected President of France. The southwest mainly votes for the losing Socialist candidate, Ségolène Royal.
2008	France ratifies the **Lisbon Treaty** on EU reform. EU governments **pledge up to 1.8 trillion euros** to shore up their financial sectors following economic crisis.
2009	Govermment unveils **$33.1bn economy stimulus** package.
2010	The Government introduces an austerity programme, with the aim of reducing the public sector wage and retirement bill.
2011	Perpignan is linked to Figueras in Spain by a high-speed TGV railway line through Le Perthus tunnel.
2012	François Hollande elected 7th President of the French Fifth Republic.
2015	Paris is subject to terrorist attacks both in January and November.

THE CATHARS

The 13C repression of the Cathar sect profoundly affected the history of the Languedoc, which then became linked with that of the French kingdom.

THE CATHAR DOCTRINE

The Cathar doctrine originated in a labyrinth of Eastern influences prevalent in Europe during the 11C and 12C, and focused on the opposition of 'Good' and 'Evil.' Obsessed with a fear of evil, the Cathars (from the Greek *kathari* or 'pure ones') sought to free man from the material world, restoring him to divine purity. Their interpretation of biblical texts collided head-on with Christian orthodoxy. They strove to emulate Christ but denied Christ's divinity.

THE CATHAR CHURCH

Four bishops from Albi, Toulouse, Carcassonne and Agen headed this breakaway church which came to be called 'Albigensian.' The Cathar church comprised a hierarchy of vocations which distinguished between **Parfaits** ('Perfect ones') and **Croyants** ('Believers'). Reacting against the decadent laxity of the Roman Catholic clergy, the austere Parfaits embraced poverty, chastity, patience and humility. The Cathar church administered only one sacrament, the **Consolamentum**, used at the ordination of a Parfait, or to bless a dying Croyant. The Cathars rejected the traditional sacraments of baptism and marriage, and tolerated different customs and attitudes. Their beliefs, way of life and religious rituals challenged Roman Catholic thought, causing violent disputes.

A FAVOURABLE ENVIRONMENT

The Cathar heresy spread to the towns, centres of culture and trade, and then into the Languedoc lowlands. It was probably no coincidence that the Cathar church flourished between Carcassonne and Toulouse, Foix and Limoux, areas dominated by the Languedoc cloth industry. The **'Bonhommes'** (Parfaits) were often textile manufacturers or merchants. Powerful lords such as Roger Trencavel, viscount of Béziers and Carcassonne, and Raymond, count of Foix, supported the heresy.

THE FIRST WAR AGAINST THE CATHARS

In 1150, St Bernard arrived in the Albigeois region to convert the Cathar heretics, but met with minimal success. In 1179 the Third Lateran Council drew up plans to counter the spread of the heretical sect. In 1204, Pope Innocent III sent three legates to preach against the Cathars and persuade the Count of Toulouse, **Raymond VI**, to withdraw his protection of them. The count refused and was excommunicated in 1207. In January 1208, the papal legate Pierre de Castlenau was assassinated and Raymond VI was immediately accused of his murder. This sparked the **First Albigensian Crusade** in March 1208, preached by Pope Innocent III. Knights from the Paris region, Normandy, Picardy, Flanders, Champagne and Burgundy, and noblemen from the Rhineland, Friesland, Bavaria and even Austria rallied forces under the command of Abbot Arnaud-Amaury of Cîteaux, and then under **Simon de Montfort**. The 'Holy War' was to last over 20 years. In 1209, 30 000 residents of Béziers were massacred. Carcassonne was besieged and fell in 1209. Viscount Raymond-Roger de Trencavel was taken prisoner and was replaced by Simon de Montfort, who captured one Cathar fortress after another: Lastours, Minerve, Termes and Puivert (1210). By 1215, the whole of the Count of Toulouse's territory was in the hands of Montfort. Raymond VII avenged his father by waging a war of liberation for eight years. Simon de Montfort died in 1218 and was succeeded by his son, Amaury.

THE SECOND CRUSADE

Strongholds might fall, but the Cathar doctrine was not easily quashed. In 1226, a **Second Albigensian Crusade** was preached, lead by the King of France himself, Louis VIII. The Holy War evolved into a political struggle. In the Treaty of Meaux-Paris in 1229, Blanche of Castille annexed a vast territory to the French Royal estate. A century later, it became the Languedoc. The battle against heresy was not over; it was continued by the **Inquisition**. Pope Gregory IX entrusted the **Inquisition** to the Dominican Order in 1231. In 1240, the Crusaders captured Peyrepertuse. Pierre-Roger de Mirepoix, the governor of the main Cathar stronghold at Montségur, undertook an expedition to Avignonet in 1242, killing members of an Inquisition tribunal. Six thousand Crusaders installed themselves at the foot of his castle, and their siege lasted ten months.

In March 1244, the fortress capitulated to the besieging Crusaders, and they built an enormous pyre on which they burned alive 220 unrepentant Cathars. Other Cathars took refuge in the fortress at Puilaurens, where they were butchered after the fall of Montségur. The war against the Cathars reached its end in 1255 with the siege and fall of Quéribus, the last remaining Cathar stronghold.

Architecture

Languedoc-Roussillon and Midi-Pyrénées has a wealth of architecture of all periods from the Roman occupation. It is especially noted for its canon of Romanesque churches which were followed by Gothic creations in a distinctly southern variant of the style.

ROMAN ARCHITECTURE

The earliest buildings in the southwest of France date from the Gallo-Roman period: the amphitheatre and Maison Carée in Nimes, and the Pont du Gard aqueduct. The ground plans of more modest villas can be seen in several places, notably Montmaurin in the Comminges and Seviac in the Gers.

MILITARY ARCHITECTURE IN THE MIDDLE AGES

The intense military activity of the Middle Ages left many traces throughout the Languedoc. The Albigensian Crusade, the pillaging bands of outlaws during the Hundred Years War, and the proximity of Guyenne, under English rule until 1453, all prompted feudal lords to build strong defences. Castles were erected at the mouths of canyons and on rocky pinnacles. Now reduced to ruins, the numerous fortresses on the Montagne Noire lend a austere grandeur to the landscape.

In the 10C and 11C, the collapse of public power and the crumbling authority of the princes and counts led to a increased number of fortified strongholds. During the 12C and 13C, the castles were once again in the hands of the king and great feudal lords, and were a source of frequent rivalry in Languedoc, constantly seething with border disputes.

CASTLES

Cities could be defended by the Gallo-Roman city walls like those of Carcassonne. But outside the city limits, fortresses were always built on high ground. In the 10C, crude **mounds**, either natural or man-made hillocks large enough for a simple shelter, multiplied rapidly on flat land. Over the centuries they evolved into impregnable citadels, like Cathar castles.

The end of the 11C marked the advent of stone **keeps** or donjons, either rectangular (Peyrepertuse) or rounded with thick walls and narrow window slits. The only means of access was on the first floor, via a ladder or a retractable gangway. The interior was divided into several storeys. The dark and vaulted ground floor was a store room; the upper floors could be used as reception or living rooms. As residences, most keeps had limited facilities. Many were merely defensive towers housing a garrison. The lords preferred to live in a larger building in the **lower courtyard**, either adjacent to or detached from the keep. During the 13C and 14C, the main cas-

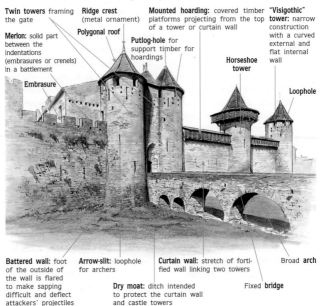

CARCASSONNE – East gateway of the Château Comtal (12C)

Twin towers framing the gate

Merlon: solid part between the indentations (embrasures or crenels) in a battlement

Embrasure

Ridge crest (metal ornament)

Polygonal roof

Putlog-hole for support timber for hoardings

Mounted hoarding: covered timber platforms projecting from the top of a tower or curtain wall

"Visigothic" tower: narrow construction with a curved external and flat internal wall

Horseshoe tower

Loophole

Battered wall: foot of the outside of the wall is flared to make sapping difficult and deflect attackers' projectiles

Arrow-slit: loophole for archers

Dry moat: ditch intended to protect the curtain wall and castle towers

Curtain wall: stretch of fortified wall linking two towers

Fixed bridge

Broad **arch**

R. Corbel/MICHELIN

tle building was extended and made more comfortable as a residence. The keep then became incorporated with the other buildings and acquired one or several enclosing walls, interrupted at intervals by towers. **Puilaurens Castle**, with its fortified wall and four corner towers, is a fine example of this new trend, whereas the keep at **Arques** is a remarkable specimen of 13C military construction.

Siege warfare

When a castle couldn't be taken by surprise attack, long sieges often ensued. Perched on rocky outcrops and surrounded by steep rock faces, Cathar fortresses confounded conventional techniques of siege warfare. In 1210, thirst and disease forced the fortress of **Termes** to succumb, and in 1255 the fall of **Quéribus**, last bastion of the Cathars, was achieved by treacherous means.

When laying a siege, the attackers surrounded the stronghold and built trenches, stockades, towers, blockhouses etc. to counter attacks by relief armies and to prevent those under siege from making a possible sortie. Lengthy

sieges could go on for months if not years, so an entire fortified town would be built round the besieged fortress. To break through the stronghold's curtain wall, sappers dug tunnels into the foot of it, shoring up the cavity with wooden props. They set these props alight so the tunnel and part of the curtain wall above collapsed. They employed slings, mobile siege towers and battering rams. Military engineers supervised the construction of the various siege devices, about which they had learned much during the Crusades.

WATCHTOWERS

These are a common feature in the Corbières, Fenouillèdes, Vallespir and Albères. They transmitted signals using fire by night and smoke by day, and a specific code to convey the nature or gravity of the danger. These visual communications links in the Catalan mountains sent information from the far reaches to **Castelnou Castle** in Les Aspres during the Catalan earldoms of the early Middle Ages, and to Perpignan during the reign of the kings of Aragon.

FORTIFIED CHURCHES

Towards the end of the 10C, churches in southern France became fortified. The church's robust architecture and bell-tower suited for keeping watch, gave the local inhabitants a refuge in times of warfare. The church was traditionally a place of asylum: the Truce of God defined the areas of immunity as extending as far as 30 paces all around the building.

Machicolations, either mounted on corbels or supported on arches between buttresses, as in Beaumont-de-Lomagne appeared in France at the end of the 12C on Languedoc churches. Also known as murder-holes, they allowed stones and lethally hot liquids to be dropped on attackers at the base of a defensive wall. Strict regulations on the fortification of churches were prescribed at the time of the Albigensian Crusade. The count of Toulouse and his vassals were accused of abusing their privilege in this regard, so the bishops regained a monopoly which had long eluded them.

For Languedoc the 13C marked the union with the French crown and the triumph of orthodoxy over heresy. Large brick churches in the Gothic style of Toulouse were constructed, with a layout and height appropriate for fortifications. The cathedral of Ste-Cécile in Albi, with its severe 40m high walls, looks like a massive fortress at the heart of the subjugated Cathar country. Bernard de Castanet, Bishop of Albi, laid its first stone in 1282. Fortified churches and villages still scatter the upper valleys of the Pyrenees. In Prats-de-Mollo, the church of Stes-Juste-et-Ruffine is a curious blend of roofs and fortifications. One of the finest sights is Villefranche-de-Conflent with its ramparts refurbished by Vauban. The Aveyron has two superb fortified churches, Sainte-Radegonde and Inières from the 13 and 14C large enough to house the local populace in times of attack. Other examples of fortified churches in the Languedoc are the cathedral at Maguelone, the church of St-Étienne in Agde, the cathedral of

Fort de SALSES (15-17C)

Salses fortress is a typical example of a half-buried fortification.

Curtain wall

Barracks

Horseshoe-shaped **demi-lune** (projecting outwork)

Drill ground

Barbican: outer defence work to protect an important part of the castle

Counterscarp: outside wall of the moat

Moat

Keep

Battered wall

Bastion

Scarp: inside wall of the moat

Parados: wall behind the firing positions

Horseshoe-shaped **redoubt** (fortification detached from main fort complex)

Rounded top of curtain wall: the parapet protects the firing positions from overhead

R. Corbel/MICHELIN

Notre-Dame in Rodez and the cathedral of St-Nazaire in Béziers.

BASTIDES

In 1152, Eleanor of Aquitaine took as her second husband Henry Plantagenet, count of Anjou and lord of Maine, Touraine and Normandy. Their joint estates equalled those of the King of France. Two years later, Henry Plantagenet inherited the throne of England, ruling as Henry II. The Franco-English wars that followed lasted for over 300 years. In the 13C the kings of France and England built *bastides*, or fortified 'new' towns, to secure their territorial claims. The *bastides* had grid layouts with straight streets intersecting at right angles. At the town's centre was a square surrounded by covered arcades, called *couverts* (Mirepoix). Carcassonne's 'Ville Basse,' Montauban and Villefranche-de-Rouergue are particularly fine examples of these 'new towns' (13C and 14C).

The Half-Timbered House

The characteristic bastide house – indeed the medieval common man's dwelling par excellence – was half-timbered. Where stone was to hand, it was usually the material of choice for medieval house builders. However, if it was unavailable or unaffordable, the usual alternative was to construct a half-timbered house (*maison à colombages* or *maison à pans de bois*). The principle is simple: a skeleton of hardwood with cheap infill (such as brick and clay and straw) packed between the post and beams. The result is a quick and relatively easy house to build that is supple enough to resist earth tremors although susceptible to fire.

There are many excellent surviving examples from the 15C to the 17C in the inland towns and villages of the southwest, especially in the Ariège, the Gers (where the streets of bastides are typically lined with them), Tarn, Aveyron and Lozère. They can also be seen in the old part of Toulouse.

MEDIEVAL RELIGIOUS ARCHITECTURE
ROMANESQUE ARCHITECTURE

Languedoc, crossroads of many civilisations, has enjoyed various architectural influences: from Auvergne, the church of Ste-Foy in Conques; from Provence, the abbey of St-Victor in Marseille, from Aquitaine, the basilica of St-Sernin in Toulouse and the church of St-Pierre in Moissac. Red or grey sandstone was used in the Rouergue region and farther south, brick and stone were combined harmoniously .

Early Romanesque churches

At the beginning of the 11C, Church prosperity promoted an ecclesiasti-

Covered arcades of Mirepoix

© Philippe Michel/age fotostock

ELNE – Cloisters of the cathedral of Ste-Eulalie-et-Ste-Julie (12-14C)

The cloisters are a set of four roofed galleries around a central quadrangle, enabling monks to walk under cover from the conventual buildings to the church.

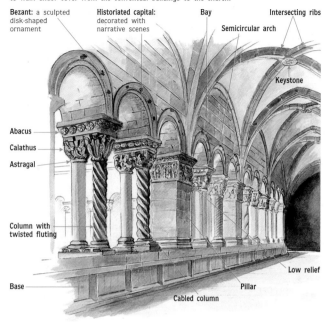

Bezant: a sculpted disk-shaped ornament

Historiated capital: decorated with narrative scenes

Bay

Intersecting ribs

Semicircular arch

Keystone

Abacus

Calathus

Astragal

Column with twisted fluting

Base

Cabled column

Pillar

Low relief

R. Corbel/MICHELIN

cal construction boom. Austere rustic buildings were erected of rough-hewn stones mixed with mortar, having only a few narrow deeply splayed windows. The walls around the outside of the apse were often adorned with Lombard bands, vertical pilasters projecting only slightly from the apse wall and linked at the top by small arcades. Inside, naves were roofed with barrel vaulting and ended in an oven-vaulted apse (quarter sphere).

The heavy stone vaulting put a heavy load on the supporting walls, so windows were reduced to a minimum, and side aisles were built to buttress the nave. The abbey church at St-Guilhem-le-Désert dates from this period.

Catalan architecture

Towards the mid-10C an original architectural style combining Mozarabic and Carolingian influences appeared in the Catalan Pyrenees. The abbey church of **St-Michel-de-Cuxa** in Conflent is a good example, with its low, narrow transept, elongated chancel with an apse, side aisles, and barrel vaulting throughout, lending it an Early Romanesque complexity. The simpler style of **St-Martin-du-Canigou**, with vaulted nave supported by pillars, was widely copied during the 11C.

Following this, church construction evolved with barrel vaulting supported by transverse arches (Arles-sur-Tech, **Elne**) and the use of richer decorative motifs. The introduction of domes on pendentives was one of the most remarkable achievements of Catalan architecture.

Crudely made from roughly hewn rock, remote mountain sanctuaries are notable for their fine square towers decorated with small arcades and their Lombard bands, constructed down to the 13C. The beautiful grey or pink marble from the Conflent and Roussillon quarries was used for sculptural elements, and Pyrenean craftsmen produced more and more altar tables. **Serrabone** priory's 12C decoration of is one of Roussillon's finest examples of Romanesque art. Painted murals are an

ST-MICHEL-DE-CUXA – Bell-tower of the abbey church (11C)

The Romanesque churches in Roussillon and Catalonia nearly all feature one or two Lombard bell-towers. This style was probably imported from Italy in the 11C, making its earliest appearance at St-Michel-de-Cuxa, and later became typical of the architecture of this region. The bell-tower at Cuxa stands at the far south end of the transept (originally, there was a matching tower at the far north end).

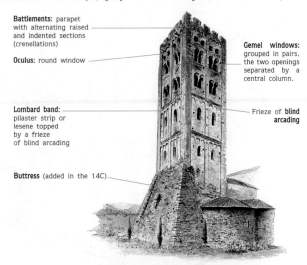

Battlements: parapet with alternating raised and indented sections (crenellations)

Oculus: round window

Lombard band: pilaster strip or lesene topped by a frieze of blind arcading

Buttress (added in the 14C)

Gemel windows: grouped in pairs, the two openings separated by a central column.

Frieze of **blind arcading**

TOULOUSE – Cross section of the basilica of St-Sernin (11-14C)

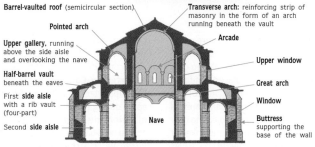

Barrel-vaulted roof (semicircular section)

Pointed arch

Upper gallery, running above the side aisle and overlooking the nave

Half-barrel vault beneath the eaves

First side aisle with a rib vault (four-part)

Second side aisle

Transverse arch: reinforcing strip of masonry in the form of an arch running beneath the vault

Arcade

Upper window

Great arch

Window

Buttress supporting the base of the wall

Nave

Beneath the chancel lies the **crypt,** an underground chapel designed to house holy relics

CONQUES – Dome of the abbey church of Ste-Foy (12-14C)

The dome supported on squinches above the transept crossing was built in the 12C. Eight supporting ribs were added in the 14C.

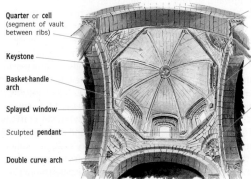

Quarter or **cell** (segment of vault between ribs)

Keystone

Basket-handle arch

Splayed window

Sculpted **pendant**

Double curve arch

Ogive: diagonal rib following or supporting the pointed arch of the vault

Drum: cylindrical (or polygonal) wall supporting a dome

Squinch: small series of corbelled arches bridging the gaps at the corners between a square plan structure, such as a tower, and a circular or polygonal superstructure (dome etc). In this case it is decorated by figures sculpted in **high relief.**

R. Corbel/MICHELIN

NARBONNE – Cathedral of St-Just-et-St-Pasteur (13-14C)

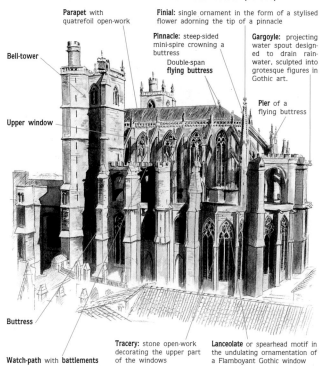

Parapet with quatrefoil open-work

Finial: single ornament in the form of a stylised flower adorning the tip of a pinnacle

Pinnacle: steep-sided mini-spire crowning a buttress

Double-span **flying buttress**

Gargoyle: projecting water spout designed to drain rain-water, sculpted into grotesque figures in Gothic art.

Bell-tower

Pier of a flying buttress

Upper window

Buttress

Watch-path with **battlements**

Tracery: stone open-work decorating the upper part of the windows

Lanceolate or spearhead motif in the undulating ornamentation of a Flamboyant Gothic window

R. Corbel/MICHELIN

important feature of the architecture of this period; apses were painted with the image of Christ in Majesty, or of the Apocalypse or the Last Judgement. Andorra has some magnificent Romanesque churches in its own variant of the Catalan style.

Moissac and Conques

Moissac Abbey on the road to Santiago de Compostela, was important throughout Languedoc in the 11C and the 12C. Its doorway and cloisters are masterpieces of Romanesque art. The **tympanum**, a stone rendering of a book illumination, represents Christ in Majesty surrounded by the symbols of the four Evangelists. It suggests a latent Eastern influence via Spain. The trefoil and polylobed arcades are reminiscent of Mozarabic art. The decorative style at Moissac bears some relation to that of Toulouse, another cradle of medieval Romanesque sculpture.

Another pilgrimage Romanesque church with a magnificent carved tympanum is Ste-Foy in Conques.

St-Sernin in Toulouse

Toulouse flourished as the centre of the Languedoc Romanesque School in the peak of its glory. The largest Romanesque basilica in western Europe, and a major pilgrimage church, the basilica of **St-Sernin** is grandiose.

This subtle blend of stone and brick is vaulted throughout, and features several typical Romanesque techniques: semicircular barrel vaulting on transverse arches in the main nave; half-barrel vaulting in the galleries; ribbed vaulting in the side aisles; and a dome over the transept crossing. Bernard Gilduin's workshop completed the sculpted decoration in less than 40 years (1080–1118). The **Porte Miègeville** was completed in 1100 and reflects Spanish influences from the workshops of Jaca and Com-

TOULOUSE – Interior of the church of Les Jacobins (13-14C)

Quarter or cell

Lierne: auxiliary rib in a ribbed vault

Tierceron: subdivision of a lierne

Formeret, or wall rib

Lancet: a narrow window with a sharply pointed arch like a spearhead

Column: cylindrical support composed of three parts – the base, the shaft and the capital

Plinth

Torus

Keystone

Rib

Lanceolate upper window

Engaged column

Pier: rectangular support projecting from wall, into which an engaged pilaster or column is built.

Large pointed arch

R. Corbel/MICHELIN

postela. The shape of the capitals is influenced by the classical Corinthian order, to which decorative motifs of animals or narrative scenes have been added. The cloisters of St-Sernin abbey, La Daurade Monastery and St-Étienne Cathedral were destroyed in the 19C, but architectural fragments are exhibited in the Musée des Augustins.

SOUTHERN FRENCH GOTHIC

The south of France did not adopt the principles of Gothic architecture used in the north, but developed its own style inspired by Romanesque. The chancel of Narbonne Cathedral is virtually the only French Gothic style construction.

Languedoc Gothic

In the 13C, a specifically southern Languedoc Gothic style developed, characterised by the use of brick, interior painted walls, and a belfry wall or a bell-tower decorated with mitre-shaped arched openings, (as in the church of Notre-Dame-du-Taur or the upper storeys of the bell-tower of the

basilica of St-Sernin, both in Toulouse). Massive buttresses interspersed with chapels supported the roof vault. The light weight of brick made it possible to build vaulted roofs instead of the earlier timber roofing. Its vast size accommodated the large congregations desired by preachers in the wake of the Albigensian Crusade.

Albi Cathedral

Albi's Ste-Cécile Cathedral, begun in 1282 and completed two centuries later, demonstrates southern French Gothic at its best. The cathedral's single nave, lit through very narrow window openings, is 100m long and 30m high and has 12 bays supported by massive buttresses. The absence of side aisles, transept or ambulatory results in a better structural balance. In 1500, the Flamboyant Gothic style expressed itself in the shape of the choir screen and **rood screen**, and in the last three storeys of the bell-tower. The ornate canopy porch was added in 1533.

Rood screen, Cathédrale Ste-Cécile, Albi

© Aurelie1/iStockphoto.com

The mendicant orders

The Dominican friars, known as 'Jacobins' in France, built their first monastery in Toulouse in 1216, but sadly, it was destroyed by fire in 1871. In 1222, during the lifetime of their founder St Francis of Assisi, it was occupied by the Franciscan Order. The vaulting of the church of **Les Jacobins**, with its 'palm-tree' ribbing and twin colonnettes of the cloisters, contribute to the grace of the structure.

The bastide churches

The *bastides*, or 'new towns', inspired the construction of churches accessible to the central market place. The southern French Gothic style was particularly suitable to the building of small churches in confined spaces, Although it has been modified over the centuries, Montauban's church of St-Jacques is a good example of the Languedoc School, with its single nave and octagonal brick bell-tower.

LATER STYLES
RENAISSANCE

Renaissance ideas were first introduced to France following the Italian wars at the end of the 15C. The arrival of Neapolitan artists brought from Italy by Charles VIII at the end of 1495 brought new life to French architecture. In the southwest the Renaissance style was applied to country chateaux and to stately urban mansions built by the newly wealthy as can be seen in particular in Toulouse (the Hôtel d'Assezat is a fine example), Montpellier and Pezenas.

CLASSICISM

The accession of the Bourbon dynasty in 1589, following the era of stagnation that characterised French art and architecture towards the end of the Renaissance, heralded a radical shift in direction: the period of material prosperity that coincided with the reign of Henri IV fired architects eager for change with new ideas and new interpretations of classical, antique themes.

A new worldy, mercantile power was replacing the old feudal order of aristocracy and church. Wealthy burghers wanted private chateaux that spoke of their economic prowess and public buildings that demonstrated their political power. The facade of the Capitole (1759), Toulouses city hall, is a fine example of the assertion of municipal and regional by business-minded burghers. Classical architecture held sway until long after 1789.

Castles in the age of the cannon

Medieval fortresses may have been falling into ruins in the 17C, but new fortresses were built and they had to withstand a new weapon. Methods of bombardment had evolved over the

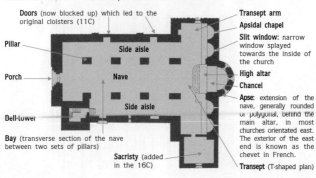

CORNEILLA-DE-CONFLENT – Ground plan of the church of Ste-Marie (11-12C)

This church originally had a basilical ground plan with three aisles, a very common layout in Roussillon in the 11C. The transept was added in the 12C.

Doors (now blocked up) which led to the original cloisters (11C)

Pillar

Porch

Bell-tower

Bay (transverse section of the nave between two sets of pillars)

Sacristy (added in the 16C)

Side aisle

Nave

Side aisle

Transept arm

Apsidal chapel

Slit window: narrow window splayed towards the inside of the church

High altar

Chancel

Apse: extension of the nave, generally rounded or polygonal, behind the main altar, in most churches orientated east. The exterior of the east end is known as the chevet in French.

Transept (T-shaped plan)

R. Corbel/MICHELIN

centuries. Towards the mid-15C the inventions of two talented gunners, the Bureau brothers, placed the French royal artillery on top of the world. No feudal fortress could withstand French attacks and in one year, Charles VII recaptured 60 positions from the English. Military architecture was transformed to meet this new threat. Low thick bastions replaced towers and curtain walls were built lower and up to 12m thick. In the 17C, these new defence systems were perfected by Sébastien Le Prestre de **Vauban** (1633–1707), resulting in defences like the **Fort de Salses**. It is half-buried and protected with curtain walls with rounded tops to shield it from bullets and attackers scaling the walls. Developing the ideas of his predecessors – military engineers employed by the King – Vauban evolved a system based on the use of massive bastions complemented by ravelins or demilunes, the whole being protected by very deep defensive ditches. Vauban's designs are notable for the way he made use of natural obstacles, used only local materials and added aesthetic value to the functional works he produced, incorporating monumental stone entrance gates, often adorned with sculpture.

ECLECTICISM

In the 19C, French architecture, as elsewhere in Europe, was characterised by a penchant for eclecticism: bringing styles from the past (Antique, Romanesque, Gothic, Renaissance and Classical) back into fashion, and borrowing foreign architectural styles, especially those of the Far East. The spa towns of the Pyrénées, such as Luz-St-Sauveur and Cauterets have examples of eclectic buildings. Later, under the Third Republic, towns and villages built themselves town halls and schools – often combined in one building – in eclectic styles.

MODERN ARCHITECTURE

Southwest France is not the obvious place to look for cutting-edge contemporary architecture but it has sometimes attracted attention to itself. The development of the Languedoc coast provided a blank canvas for large-scale thinking and one result was La Grande Motte, a new city of pyramids entirely for the pursuit of pleasure. it was built under the direction of Jean Balladur from 1967 onwards. The Antigone district in Montpellier, which is by the Catalan architect Ricardo Bofill, meanwhile, has been much admired.

Since the 19C architects have worked with engineers to create some splendid functional constructions, most of which go unnoticed. The Millau motorway viaduct, however, is not just a bridge you drive across but one you go out of your way to see. It is the result of a collaboration between the British architect Norman Foster and the French engineer Michel Virlogeux.

Secular architecture

TOULOUSE – Hôtel d'Assézat (16C)

The Hôtel d'Assézat, designed by Nicolas Bachelier, is the earliest example of Palladian style architecture in Toulouse, with its characteristic superposition of the Classical decorative orders – Doric, Ionic and Corinthian.

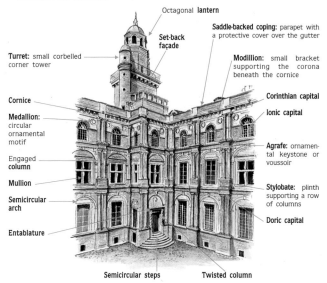

Octagonal **lantern**

Saddle-backed coping: parapet with a protective cover over the gutter

Set-back façade

Modillion: small bracket supporting the corona beneath the cornice

Turret: small corbelled corner tower

Cornice

Corinthian capital

Ionic capital

Medallion: circular ornamental motif

Agrafe: ornamental keystone or voussoir

Engaged **column**

Mullion

Stylobate: plinth supporting a row of columns

Semicircular arch

Doric capital

Entablature

Semicircular steps

Twisted column

MONTPELLIER – Rotunda of the Hôtel St-Côme (17C)

This octagonal rotunda houses an amphitheatre which was used for dissections.

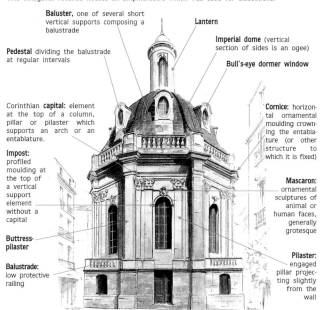

Baluster, one of several short vertical supports composing a balustrade

Lantern

Pedestal dividing the balustrade at regular intervals

Imperial dome (vertical section of sides is an ogee)

Bull's-eye dormer window

Corinthian **capital:** element at the top of a column, pillar or pilaster which supports an arch or an entablature.

Cornice: horizontal ornamental moulding crowning the entablature (or other structure to which it is fixed)

Impost: profiled moulding at the top of a vertical support element without a capital

Mascaron: ornamental sculptures of animal or human faces, generally grotesque

Buttress-pilaster

Pilaster: engaged pillar projecting slightly from the wall

Balustrade: low protective railing

R. Corbel/MICHELIN

Mountain house
in the Cévennes

House on the Causses

Buron in the Aubrac

Barn thatched with broom,
Monts de l'Espinouse

Farmhouse with balcony
in the Rouergue

Wine-grower's houses in the Hérault

R. Corbel/MICHELIN

RURAL ARCHITECTURE

The design and construction of rural houses derives from the needs of their inhabitants. In the stock raising regions of Causses, the Cévennes and the Aubrac, sheepfolds are a common architectural feature; in the plains of Bas Languedoc, it is the wine cellar (chai). Construction materials derive from local sources. In the Cévennes, roofs may be of volcanic lava, slate and schist slabs, and in the Causses, limestone slabs.

Today's rural houses employ new construction methods, often because craftsmen skilled in traditional techniques are hard to find. Evolving agricultural practices have also changed the style of traditional rural cottages.

CAUSSES

On the causses houses are robust, thick-walled and covered in dry white limestone. The ground floor comprises a cellar and tool room, and the first floor provides living quarters. An outside staircase leads to the upper floor, and a cistern near the kitchen collects rain water. Where timber is scarce, roofs are replaced by a stone vault.

The sheepfold, usually a low-lying rectangular building of rough-hewn stone, may be quite distant from the house.

CÉVENNES

Solid mountain houses designed to withstand the rigorous climate are typical here. Walls and roofs are built of schist, and windows are small. Lintels, window frames and corner stones may be sandstone or limestone. Chestnut trees provide structural timber. If the house is built on sloping ground, the stone steps leading to the first floor living quarters sometimes look like a bridge. The stable and barn are on the ground floor. Roofs are covered with rough schist slabs (lauzes).

BAS LANGUEDOC

The curved terracotta pantile is the trademark of this region. The main façades of houses often have a triangular pediment. Living quarters are separated from the stable and barn. The rectangular wine cellar (chai) occupies the ground floor. There are two doors in the façade: a large round-arched doorway leading into the cellar, and a smaller entrance to the first-floor living quarters. The houses of wine-growers have tiny windows to keep out the strong Mediterranean sun. Small drystone huts, known as **capitelles** or **cazelles**, dot the vineyards. These served as shelters for shepherds or to store farming implements. The generally circular walls are built of schist or limestone, and the corbelled roof vault is formed by overlapping layers of lauzes like fish scales.

HAUT LANGUEDOC

In the Castres region, as in the region around Albi, walls are built entirely of brick, whereas in the eastern parts of Haut Languedoc brick is used only for framing doors and windows, sometimes decoratively. Many farms in Haut Languedoc boast a **dovecot**, either attached to the main farmhouse, or close by. In centuries past, pigeons were used to fertilise poor soils, and were therefore a sign of wealth or privilege.

AVEYRON

In Rouergue, walls are of schist or granite rubble masonry. On the roof, covered with schist or slate lauzes, are dormer windows which make the main façade look as if it has pediments. On the ground floor, are the wine cellar and tool room; on the first floor, the living quarters and the attic serves for drying chestnuts. The houses of well-to-do farmers comprise several buildings (living quarters, stable, barn and a turret serving as a dovecot) and a courtyard. In the fields, small, round conical-roofed drystone huts which resemble the bories of Haute Provence serve as shelters, barns or tool-sheds. The **buron** is typical of the Aubrac pleateau. This solid one-room hut of lava and granite, used by cowherds as living quarters from May to October, is usually built in pastureland on sloping ground near a spring. The single room serves for accommodation and for cheesemaking, and the cellar for maturing the cheese.

Folklore and Religious Festivals ★★

Local legends: The Languedoc countryside is scattered with megalithic monuments, and their names reflect local superstitions: Planted Stone, Giant's Tomb, Fairies' Dwellings etc. The fantastic shapes of these rock formations have also inspired folk tales of their origins. Common are tales of animals that have been bewitched – cows which no longer give milk, dogs which lose their sense of smell. Local people have traditions to guard against malevolent spirits, like wearing clothes back to front or throwing salt on the fire. Myths like the Bête du Gévaudan abound in regions where wild beasts have preyed upon livestock and even people. Wild animals like the Pyrenean bears have had festivals dedicated to them, the Fête de l'Ours held in the Vallespir region (Arles-sur-Tech, Prats-de-Mollo and St-Laurent-de-Cerdans) in late February–early March, and again during the summer tourist season.

Carnaval de Limoux

© arenysam/iStockphoto.com

Carnival time: Carnival time in the Aude traditionally begins with the winter slaughtering of the pig. Children with masked or blackened faces go from house to house asking for food, and adults join the fun by dressing back-to-front, cross-dressing, or dressing up as babies or old people. A straw dummy is paraded round the village and made the scapegoat for all the misfortunes which have befallen the villagers. The dummy is sentenced before a mock court held in the local *patois* slang, before it is hanged or burnt and children dance around the fire.

At the famous carnival in Limoux (Sundays from January to March, as well as Shrove Tuesday and Ash Wednesday) people dressed as Pierrot figures dance around place de la République, beating time with sticks decorated with ribbons. They are pursued by revellers in various disguises all acting the clown. The festivities last until nightfall, when resin torches light the square. The carnival ends with the Nuit de la Blanquette.

Sardana: This Catalan dance is accompanied by a **cobla**, an orchestra with a dozen or so brass, wind and percussion instruments which evoke a range of emotions from gentle to passionate. The sight of the whirling dancers flourishing garlands at festivals and local competitions is exciting, and the sardana festival at Céret is the most famous.

Religious festivals: The most common religious festivals are in honour of local patron saints. St Peter, patron saint of fishermen, is honoured in Gruissan on 29 June. Mass is celebrated for local fishermen at the parish church, then a procession winds to the harbour where a wreath is cast into the water to commemorate those lost at sea.

On Good Friday in Perpignan, a procession is held by the Pénitents de la Sanch, a religious brotherhood founded in the 15C and dedicated to the Holy Blood. Penitents dress in long black or red robes with pointed hoods and walk through Perpignan's streets to the cathedral, carrying *misteris* – painted or sculpted images of Scenes of the Passion of Christ.

Traditions

LANGUAGE
THE 'LANGUE D'OC'

The fusion of Vulgar Latin with the old Gallic language gave rise to a group of 'Romance' languages, with the 'Langue d'Oïl' in the north of France and the 'Langue d'Oc' in the south. The languages were distinguised by the way the word *oui* was pronounced in each region, and the border between the two lay north of the Massif Central. Today the term **Occitan** has replaced the term Langue d'Oc and comprises several major dialects spoken in Languedoc, Gascony, Limousin, Auvergne and Provence.

Street sign in Occitan, St-Côme-d'Olt

S. Sauvignier/MICHELIN

LANGUAGE OF THE TROUBADOURS

The language of Oc is the language of the troubadours, poets who composed plaintive songs of unrequited love and travelled around southern France entertaining the nobility during the 11C to 13C. Their poetry of 'courtly love' replaced the earthy, vaguely erotic sensibilities of the 12C with a purely spiritual celebration of love, often embellished with references to the Virgin Mary. Famous troubadours include Bernard de Ventadour from the Limousin, who sang at the court of Raymond V of Toulouse; Peire Vidal, whose reputation stretched from Provence to the Holy Land; Jaufré Rudel and Guiraut Riquier. Political satire against Rome and the clergy held a special place in Occitan literature. The troubadours' influence spread to Germany and Italy, where it was said that Dante, when writing his *Divine Comedy*, hesitated between Provençal and Tuscan.

In the destructive wake of the Albigensian Crusade, the Occitan tongue declined. A group of Toulouse poets tried to revive it in the early 14C, by initiating the Jeux Floraux medieval poetry competition. But Occitan was dealt a heavy blow with the 1539 Edict of Villers-Cotterêts, which made Parisian French the official national language. Reforms introduced for Provençal by Frédéric Mistral and the Félibrige gave renewed impetus to the revival of Occitan. The Escola Occitana was founded in 1919 and the Institut d'Études Occitanes in Toulouse in 1945, with the aim of disseminating and standardising Occitan. A 1951 law allowed Occitan to be taught in schools, and in 1969 it became a language for examination at *baccalauréat* level.

CATALAN

The Catalan language is very close to Occitan, spoken from Salses in Roussillon to Valencia in Spain, and Andorra and Capcir to the west. Catalan is the national language of Andorra.

Catalan reached its height during the 13C, through the writings of poet and philosopher Ramon Llull. Like the language of Oc, it declined in the 16C when Philip II imposed Castilian Spanish over other regional dialects. Catalan is still spoken in everyday life, and the literary renaissance begun in the 19C is enhancing Roussillon's cultural identity.

English words derived from Catalan include 'aubergine' (*albergínia*) and barracks (*barraca* – meaning hut).

SPORT
RUGBY

The game of rugby was born in 1823 in Rugby, England when William Webb Ellis broke the rules during a football game at Rugby College by grabbing the football with both hands. Rugby came to France in the early 20C and caught on in the southwest, where it is said to suit the robust Occitan temperament. It is now played and followed with huge enthusiasm in every town and village throughout the Pyrenees. Despite the rough physical nature of the game, played in true Occitan 'jusqu'au bout' spirit, smaller teams lay rivalry aside after the game, and players share a lavish meal to round off the event.

At the top level, however, competition is fierce, especially for the French national rugby championships. Top teams include Toulouse, Béziers, Perpignan and Narbonne.

HUNTING

Hunters are a common sight in the countryside in the autumn. The National Hunters' Federation estimates that they number over 1.4 million.

Strict rules are laid down for hunting and these are displayed outside town halls. A hunter must be in possession of a valid licence for the territory. Only certain animals – those known to have stable or growing populations – may be hunted during stipulated seasons and for some species quotas are enforced. Some animals are classed as pests and can be killed without restriction. Favourite larger prey include wild boar and deer.

TRADITIONAL CRAFTS

The enchanting settings and traditional ways of small isolated villages in the Cévennes, Rouergue, Causses and Languedoc, have long been an attraction for crafts workers. **Revel** has been famous for its fine furniture and marquetry ever since the cabinet-maker Alexandre Monoury arrived from Versailles in 1889. It is also home to weavers, gilders, lacquerers, wood sculptors, bronzesmiths and blacksmiths. Wool-making and its related crafts have centred around **Mazamet** since the mid-19C. From the late Middle Ages, **Durfort** specialised in beaten copper traditionally used to make pots and cauldrons. **Laguiole** is renowned for its elegant pocket

knives with curved handles made of horn. Fine kid gloves are made in and around **Millau**, and since the revival of silk farming in the region, the **Cévennes** has evolved as a silk making centre. The wood of the nettle tree is used in making pitchforks at **Sauve** (Gard). The glazed vases of **Anduze**, which adorn many a garden, have been renowned since the 17C. Sheep bells are produced in village workshops at Castanet-le-Bas or Hérépian, in the Hérault valley. Brickworks abound on the Garonne river plain and on the Roussillon coast where red clay is plentiful.

In the Albi region are several tanning workshops and others related to shoemaking. **Graulhet** produces leather for lining shoes, Dyer's woad (Isatis tinctoria) is still cultivated around **Magrin** and the blue dye is used to colour clothes and textiles. Stone has been cut and polished in the Ariège region since the end of the 19C and **Saurat** has the last sandstone quarry in operation, and the last millstone producer in France.

The **Bethmale valley** is a production centre for traditional wooden sabots. They are made from locally grown beech or birch and marked with a heart shape, recalling the local legend of a shepherd betrayed by his fiancée. High-quality, luxurious horn combs are made in **Lavelanet**, near Foix, In French **Catalonia**, typical crafts include whips made from nettle tree wood of Sorède in the Lower Tech valley, corks from Roussillon cork oak, espadrilles at St-Laurent-de-Cerdans, the red and yellow Catalan textiles in geometric designs, and garnets cut and set at Perpignan.

TRANSHUMANCE

The traditional pastoral life of mountain areas involves moving herds of cattle or flocks of sheep from the lowlands to the uplands for summer grazing. Modernity has somewhat undermined the hard work of transhumance – there are easier ways to make a living – but it is still practised in the Pyrenees and on the Aubrac plateau in the Aveyron.

Nature

This region offers varied natural surprises – from the generous slopes of the Pyrénées, the fresh, rolling vineyards, all the way through to the chalky plateaux of Cévennes.

LANDSCAPES

The regions described in this guide encompass a wealth of spectacular landscapes. To the northeast lie the rounded hills of the Auvergne and the rolling green pastures of the Aubrac. The cattle fairs of Laissac and Nasbinals really enliven the region. Winter snows intensify the peacefulness of the landscape, a haven for cross-country skiers seeking silence and pure air. Farther east the undulating plateaux of the Margeride are chequered with pastureland and forests, vital resources for the local economy.

To the south the countryside around the River Lot changes dramatically, with limestone plateaux, sheer cliffs and deep river gorges. These arid rocky limestone plateaux are known as the **Causses**. Cutting between them are spectacular river gorges or canyons carved by eons of water erosion. Although today this river may seem like an innocent trickle, during a flash flood it becomes a raging torrent.

To the east of this breathtaking landscape of causses and river gorges rise the rugged **Cévennes** mountains with their complex network of ridges and gullies crowned by impressive fortifications. The **Cévennes** was impenetrable for centuries, and today its mystery and utter remoteness gives modern travellers the thrilling sense of treading where no-one has gone before.

To the west the harsh landscape of the Grands Causses gives way to the **ségalas** – 'rye fields'- where gentle hills shelter fertile valleys. The sun-scorched limestone hills of the **garrigues** form the geographical transition between the Causses and the Cévennes, and the fertile wine-growing plains of the Bas Languedoc. The *garrigues* bristle with white rocks and clumps of holm-oak, broom and aromatic wild thyme and rosemary, and with the olive trees, mulberry bushes and vines cultivated here, create a truly Mediterranean landscape. Between the *garrigues* and the long straight Languedoc coast glittering with lagoons, vineyards seem to stretch forever over the plains and hillsides. Summer enlivens this landscape with colourful crowds of holidaymakers, and autumn brings the cheerful bustle of the grape harvest.

Moving farther south, the Pyrenees make a formidable natural frontier between France and Spain. The steep slopes on the French side drop sharply down into France. They are scored by valleys separated by high ridges, which

Causses landscape of Mont-Lozère at Finiels, Parc National des Cévennes

© Christian Guy/hemis.fr

link the Pyrenees to the inland plains and the coast. From the Montcalm summit (3 078m) to the Albères massif (1 256m at the Neulos peak), the mountains gradually descend into the Mediterranean.

THE CAUSSES, THE CÉVENNES AND THE TARN GORGES

The Aubrac and the Margeride

The **Aubrac** mountains run northwest to southeast between the Truyère and Lot valleys. Produced by volcanic activity in the Tertiary Era, these formidable streams of solidified basalt several hundred metres thick cover a granite core. The asymmetric mountain range slopes gently down to the Truyère in the northeast, where it remains about 1 000m above sea level. Ravines score the steeper south-western slopes.

Above 850m, the Aubrac is a vast pasture with daffodils and narcissi blooming in the spring, and beech woods, moorland and lakes in the west. Crops do not thrive in this sparsely populated region of only 14 inhabitants per sq km, compared to the national average of 96 per sq km. Long arduous winters bury the plateau under inches of snow. The region's inhabitants live principally by stock rearing. One or two local cheesemakers still produce *fourme de Laguiole* in their drystone huts. The spring and autumn livestock fairs of Laissac and Nasbinals are major events rich in local colour. The **Margeride**, a granite massif running parallel to the volcanic mountains of the Velay to the north, stretches between the Allier, to the east, and the high volcanic plateaux of the Aubrac, to the west. Its highest point at the Randon beacon (signal) is 1 551m above sea level.

The high-lying ground of the **Montagne** averages 1 400m in altitude. Vast stretches of pastureland and occasional forests of pine, fir and birch cover its undulating plateaux. North of Mende, the plateaux (Palais du Roi, La Boulaine) are littered with granite rocks eroded into fascinating columns, obelisks or rounded blocks, sometimes piled precariously on top of one another.

Below the Montagne lie rolling plains (the **Plaines**) scattered with numerous rocky outcrops, where people live in large farmhouses either isolated or grouped into small hamlets. The Margeride's local economy is based on timber, livestock and uranium.

West of the mountain range lies the **Gévaudan**, a lower-lying plateau (alt 1 000m–1 200m) in the shadow of the Aubrac.

The Causses

South of the Massif Central, the vast limestone plateaux of the Causses constitute one of France's most unusual natural regions. The Causses are bordered by the Cévennes to the east, by the Lot Valley to the north and by the plains of the Hérault and Bas Languedoc to the south. To the west they stretch as far as the Lévézou and Ségala plateaux, and beyond to the *causses* of Quercy which form the eastern limit of the Aquitaine basin.

The limestone rock creates a landscape rich in contrasts: the arid tablelands of the *causses*, the colossally deep river gorges, and the curious natural wells formed by swallow-holes. The white drystone dwellings in villages and hamlets accentuate the rugged surroundings. In 1995 the *causses* became part of the Parc naturel régional des Grands Causses, conserving the unique natural, architectural and cultural heritage of this region.

Contrasting with the deep green ravines, the *causses* seem an endless expanse of grey, rocky semi-desert. The dry ground formed of limestone rock soaks up rainwater like a sponge, yet beneath this arid surface is a hive of aquatic activity. The plateaux, some 1,000m/3,280ft above sea level, have dry scorching summers and long cold winters, with deep snows and violent sweeping gales.

To the west, at the edge of the cliffs beside new plantations of black Austrian pine, the groves of beech, oak and Scots pine show all that remain of the ancient forest destroyed by grazing flocks during the Middle Ages. To the east, thistles and tufts of lavender splash

Rocks of Roquesaltes, Saint-André-de-Vézines, Causse Noir,
Parc naturel régional des Grands Causses

© Pierre Jacques/hemis.fr

the moorland with radiant blues, and clumps of juniper grow on rocky outcrops as stunted bushes or small trees up to 10m high. Their leaves are sharp and spiny, and their small blueish-black berries enhance local game dishes.

The *causses* have traditionally been the preserve of sheep, which thrive easily on the sparse local vegetation. Traditionally, sheep supplied wool for the local textile industries in the towns (serge and caddis). Today sheep are reared for their ewe's milk (*lait des brebis*) for the famous cheese matured underground in caves. The Roquefort area has about 500,000 head. Lambskin is processed in Millau, and *Bleu des Causses*, a blue cheese from cows' milk, is produced nearby.

Eroded rock formations

Here and there spectral landscapes of bizarrely shaped rocks haunt the skyline. The protruding ledges and sheer sides of the huge rock strata resemble abandoned cities with streets, monumental doorways, ramparts and strongholds all falling into ruin. They are created by **dolomite**, composed of soluble carbonate of lime, and rather insoluble carbonate of magnesium. Water streaming down the rocks erodes them into rounded crests up to 10m high, which then morph into pillars, arcades, towers, and unworldly beasts inspiring the imagination. The eroded rock forms clay residues which nourish vegetation that

enhances the scenic beauty of Montpellier-le-Vieux, Nîmes-le-Vieux, Mourèze, Les Arcs de St-Pierre, Roquesaltes and Le Rajol.

The river gorges

Known also as *canyons*, from the Spanish *cañon*, the Tarn gorges between Les Vignes and Le Rozier, and the Jonte and Dourbie gorges are magnificent examples. Here the sweeping horizons give way to a vertiginous vertical landscape of cliff faces which may drop 500m or more. The cliff walls are pocked with caves called baumes, from the local word 'balma' in use before the Romans arrived. Many local villages and hamlets are named after baumes, including Cirque des Baumes and Les Baumes-Hautes in the Tarn gorges, Baume-Oriol on the Causse du Larzac and St-Jean-de-Balmes on the Causse Noir.

Caves and chasms

The caves *(grottes)* and chasms *(avens)* on the surface of the causses or in the hollow of a valley shelter strange watery subterranean worlds contrasting with the aridity of the plateaux. Rainwater does not flow over the limestone plateaux of the Causses here, but percolates down into fissures, dissolving the limestone to produce natural chasms called **avens** or **igues**, which gradually increase in size and widen into caves.

Tarn gorges at Laval-du-Tarn

© Franck Charton/hemis.fr

A water course that disappears into a chasm in the causses may create a network of underground rivers spanning several hundred miles. These water courses join up with larger rivers, widen their course and gush along as cascades. Slow flowing underground rivers form small lakes above natural dams known as **gours**. The Grotte de Dargilan contains many examples of gours. Although underground rivers are not easy to access, speleologists believe they are quite numerous. On the Causse du Larzac, the underground river Sorgues was discovered through the **Aven du Mas Raynal**. On the Causse du Comtal north of Rodez, the Salles-la-Source stream is accessed via the **Gouffre du Tindoul de la Vayssière**. The Bonheur, gushing into the open air at the Bramabiau 'Alcôve,' is another underground river.

M. Janvier/MICHELIN

Chestnut tree

The Cévennes

Lying to the southeast of the Massif Central and stretching from the Tarnague to the Aigoual, the schist and granite peaks of the Cévennes appear as a succession of almost flat plateaux clad in peat bogs – the *Aigoual Pelouse* (or 'lawn') and the Mont Lozère Plat ('dish'). The Mediterranean side is very steep and the Atlantic side slopes more gently on either side of a watershed at the eastern end of Mont Lozère, at the Col de Jacreste *(pass on N 106, east of Florac)* and the Col du Minier.

The crests

The Cévennes are not very high; Mont Lozère, with its long granite ridges, has an altitude of 1 699m. Mont Aigoual, which offers a fine panorama, does not exceed 1 567m. The crests are covered by meagre pastureland and grazing sheep. Pastoral hamlets dot the landscape, with houses made from granite blocks built low to resist the wind. Lower slopes shelter small villages and holm-oaks, heather and *châtaigneraies* (chestnut groves).

The upper valleys

Numerous streams flow along deep, steep-sided ravines created by erosion of granite and schist relief. Some streams, surging with trout and scented by grassy slopes covered with apple trees, are reminiscent of the Alps.

The lower valleys

These all face south and mark the transition between the Cévennes and Mediterranean country. The sun is intense here, where green meadows adjoin terraced slopes cultivated with vines, olive trees and mulberry bushes. Lavender is distilled throughout the region. You can still find traces of the silkworm breeding which once flourished in the region: large three-storey buildings with narrow windows and spinning mills of old silkworm farms *(magnaneries)*.

The Cévennes landscape

The upper valleys of the Cévennes have dwindling populations, and crops are sparse and meagre. Alongside small streams, meadows planted with apple trees intersperse with fields. The sweet chestnut tree covers most of the slopes, leaving little room for the vines trained to grow on trees, vegetable gardens and fruit trees growing near water sources at the base of the valleys. In certain villages on the periphery of Mont Lozère and in the Margeride, sheep owners gather their sheep into a communal flock led by a single shepherd to graze by day on the mountain, and to return at night to their enclosures to fertilize the soil.

The Ségalas and the Lévézou

The Grands Causses are separated from the Quercy Causses by the Lévézou massif and a group of plateaux named the Ségalas, after the rye *(seigle)* cultivated here.

The Lévézou

This large rugged massif of crystalline rock in the central Aveyron between Millau and Rodez rises to 1 155m at the Puech del Pal, its peak. The uplands around Vezins, with clumps of undergrowth and moorland populated by sheep, are bleak compared to the lowlands, with their woodlands, meadows and large lakes. The Lévézou has stimulated its economic activity by developing its rivers for hydroelectric power, and its lakes of Pont-de-Salars, Bage, Pareloup and Villefranche-de-Panat for tourism. During the 19C the Ségalas began to prosper by producing lime

> And still it was perhaps the wildest view of all my journey. Peak upon peak, chain upon chain of hills ran surging southward, channelled and sculptured by the winter streams, feathered from head to foot with chestnuts, and here and there breaking out into a coronal of cliffs. The sun, which was still far from setting, sent a drift of misty gold across the hilltops, but the valleys were already plunged into a profound and quiet shadow.
> **Robert Louis Stevenson:** *Travels With a Donkey in the Cévennes*

from the Carmaux coal basin and the Aquitaine's limestone rocks.

The Carmaux-Rodez, Capdenac-Rodez railway lines facilitated the transport of this precious soil conditioner, which enabled moorland and rye fields to grow clover, wheat, maize and barley. Stock rearing also developed: cattle and pigs in the west, and sheep in the east and southeast, particularly around Roquefort. Today the gently undulating landscape of the Ségalas is covered with green pastures, copses and meadows hedged with hawthorn, topped by chapels on the hilltops *(puechs)*.

The rich red soil coloured by iron oxide sediments, particularly in the Camarès or Marcillac regions. This extremely fertile soil is ideal for growing fruit. Rodez is the principle town in the Ségalas, followed by Villefranche-de-Rouergue on the boundary of the Ségalas and the Quercy Causses.

LANGUEDOC

Bas Languedoc

The Languedoc region stretches from the Rhône to the Garonne. Toulouse is the capital of Haut Languedoc and Montpellier is the capital of Bas (Mediterranean) Languedoc. Bas Languedoc covers a 40km/25mi wide strip along the Mediterranean coast. South of the Cévennes, the Garrigues rise 200m–400m above sea level. Below the Garrigues stretches a sandy plain covered with vineyards, and a necklace of lagoons which ornament the coast. The flat of the plain is broken by limestone outcrops like La Gardiole mountain at Montpellier, Mont St-Clair at Sète, La Clape mountain at Narbonne, and the mountains of Agde (Pic St-Loup). Bas Languedoc lies between mountains of the Massif Central, from the Cévennes, the Espinouse, Minervois and Lacaune mountain ranges, as far as the Montagne Noire, and the first limestone foothills of the Pyrenees, the Corbières.

The Garrigues

The name Garrigues derives from the Occitan garric: kermes oak. This region of mountain and limestone plateaux is watered by the Hérault, the Vidourle and the Gard rivers. The mountains of St-Loup and Hortus loom over the flat landscape. Like the *causses*, the Garrigues were formed by marine deposits from the Secondary Era. Pastures scorched by the sun, and stunted vegetation like dwarf kermes oaks, rockroses and tufts of thyme and lavender cover the region. In spring this arid countryside is a carpet of brilliant wildflowers.

The coast

Languedoc's Mediterranean coast is lined with lagoons separated from the sea by sand bars created by waves and currents. These salt water lagoons teem with eels, grey mullet, sea perch, sea bream and clams. The Aude and the Orb did not form such lagoons, nor did they create deltas, because coastal currents constantly swept away their alluvial deposits.

The invasive sand left the old ports of Maguelone and Agde stranded inland. The Thau lagoon, virtually an inland sea, is the only navigable lagoon. The Thau is noted for its oyster and mussel farms, and the small fishing ports of Marseillan and Mèze which have developed marinas. Sète, built in the 17C, is now the second largest French port on the Mediterranean.

Haut Languedoc

The prospering agricultural Toulouse and Lauragais regions are the 'granary' of the south of France. The alluvial plains of the Garonne and the Tarn brim with strawberry beds, and apple, pear and peach orchards. Market gardening and poultry farming are big here. Vineyards grow around Carcassonne and Limoux and on the Gaillac slopes to the west.

THE PYRENEES

The Pyrenees stretch 400km/248mi from the Atlantic to the Mediterranean in a relatively narrow (30km/19mi to 40km/25mi on the French side of the frontier) yet also continuous barrier: the average height of the Pyrenees is

Harvesting mussels from the Étang de Thau at Bouzigues

Aure valley and the summit of Lustou with the village of Azet, Haute-Pyrénées

© Jean-Paul Azam/hemis.fr

1 008m and there are few major routes of communication across the mountains.

Valleys

The Pyrenees chain has no lateral (east to west) valleys to connect its deep north south valleys, and so internal communication has always difficult, especially when mountain passes are impassable in winter. Some valleys were therefore isolated for much of the time, and this led to a survival of socially autonomous lifestyles of the kind still to be found in such petit pays districts as the Couserans, the Quatre Vallées (Four Valleys) region, and the Pays Toy. The principality of Andorra developed its own identity for similar reasons.

Formation of the range

Approximately 250 million years ago a Hercynian (Palaeozoic) mountain mass similar to the Massif Central or the Ardennes stood on the site occupied by the Pyrénées today; however, whereas the central and northern heights experienced a relatively tranquil existence, this chain between the Atlantic and the Mediterranean was sited in a particularly unstable zone. Already vigorously folded, and then partially levelled by erosion, the Hercynian block was submerged about 200 million years ago beneath a continental sea and covered by Secondary Era sedimentary deposits,before being totally resurrected – and literally shaken from top

to bottom – by the Alpine folding, the earliest spasms of which occurred here. Under the enormous pressure of this mountain-building movement the most recent beds, still comparatively pliant, folded without breaking but the rigid ancient platform cracked, broke up and became dislocated. Hot springs burst through near the fractures; mineral deposits formed and metal-bearing ores appeared. During the geological eons that passed while this was occurring, the mountain mass, now tortured and misshapen, was worn down by erosion, and the material torn from it washed out by rivers across the plains below.

The Central Pyrenees

The overall structure of the Pyrénéan region is characterised by the juxtaposition of large geological masses arranged longitudinally. Starting from the Upper Garonne, the relief encompasses: The rises known as the Petites Pyrénées, of only medium height but remarkable for the alignment of limestone crests pleated in a fashion typical; the real foothills, formations of the Secondary Era (either Cretaceous or Jurassic), with folded beds more violently distorted; The Axial Zone, the true spine of the Pyrénées along which granitic extrusions, recognisable by sharply defined peaks chiselled by glacial erosion, thrust through the Primary sediments; the Balaïtous; the Néouvielle and Maladetta massifs; the Luchon Pyrénées.

The summits however are not made up entirely of granite, since patches of extremely hard schist and limestone exist which are even more resistant to erosion; the southern Secondary Era sediments, under-thrust to a height of more than 3 000m at Monte Perdido, (on the Spanish side of the frontier). One masterpiece stands out among this limestone relief in France: the lower part of the Gavarnie amphitheatre, with its gigantic platforms of horizontal strata piled one upon the other.

Glaciers

A thousand years ago the ancient glaciers thrust their abrasive tongues across the mountain landscape, gouging out the terrain as far as the present sites of Lourdes and Montréjeau. Since then these giant ice rivers have shrunk to negligible proportions (less than 10sq km/4sq mi in the Pyrénées). There is only one whole glacier, complete with tongue and terminal moraine, in the entire range: the Ossoue, on the eastern slopes of the Vignemale.

Many of the most dramatic a features to be found at the heart of the Pyrénées were formed by the old glaciers: hanging valleys, amphitheatres, canyons transformed into pastoral sweeps, jagged crests and scatters of huge boulders, lakes (over 500 in the French Pyrénées), cascades, bluffs, sudden morainic platforms and powerful waterfalls, some of which are harnessed for the production of hydroelectric power.

Mediterranean Pyrenees

The eastern, Mediterranean Pyrenees, more open to the outside world, connect with the Corbières massif to the north. This stretches as far as the Montagne Noire, the furthest southern outpost of the Massif Central, and separates the Aquitaine basin from the plains of Mediterranean Languedoc.

The limestone foothills between the Corbières and the axial ridge of the Pyrenees differ from the northern sedimentary surface of the Central Pyrenees. **The Plateau de Sault** gives way to rows of jagged crests towering over the **Fenouillèdes'** deep furrow. The River Aude cuts through this crust in a burst of breathtaking gorges. The eastern Pyrenees were the first peaks to emerge from the earth's crust, pushed upwards to staggering heights by the earth's ancient folding movements. Over the geologic eons, they have been worn down to a lower altitude than the Central Pyrenees. The valleys of the **Cerdagne** and the **Capcir** (1 200m and 1 600m above sea level) shelter villages and cultivated land. These valleys were formed by erosion in the flanks of the Pyrenees, and filled up with clay, marl and gravel accumulated towards the end of the Tertiary Era. East of Canigou (alt 2 784m), the Pyrenean range drops into the trench occupied by the Mediterranean. The **Albères**, the chain's final set of peaks cut between the Roussillon, to the north, and the Ampurdan, to the south (in Spain).

The parallel valleys of the Têt and the Tech allow Mediterranean influences to penetrate to the heart of the mountain range. Renowned for their brilliant sunlight, dry climate, orange trees and pink oleander, these valleys have very attractive resorts.

The Roussillon plain, stretching for 40km/24mi, was originally a gulf which was filled in with debris from the mountain range at the end of the Tertiary/beginning of the Quaternary Era. Arid rocky terraces (**Les Aspres**) are cultivated with fruit trees and vines. An offshore sand bar separates the sea from the **salanques** marshes, where alluvial deposits from the Têt and the Agly are several hundred metres deep.

GASCONY AND THE GARONNE

The Aquitaine basin is part of a series of French sedimentary beds, which resulted from the silting up of an ancient ocean depth; what distinguishes Gascogne (Gascony), the region lying between the Pyrénées (in the south), the Adour river (in the west) and the River Garonne (east and north), is the upper covering provided by enormous masses of debris washed down by the rivers after the erosion of the mountains during the Tertiary Era. The most common formation in Gascony is known as the molasse – layers of sand frequently cemented into a soft yellow sandstone penetrated by discontinuous marl and limestone beds. This geological structure has resulted in a hilly landscape of mixed topography.

From an agricultural point of view the soils here vary between terreforts, which are clayey and heavy to work, and boul- bènes – lighter and slightly muddy, but less fertile and more suitable for grazing and cattle breeding.

The rivers, all tributaries of the Garonne, fan out northwards from the foothills of the mountains and cut through the hills of Armagnac in thin swathes.

The Garonne corridor

The Garonne river and its tributaries cut a vast aquatic corridor linking Aquitaine and Languedoc. At the edges of this corridor, the relief becomes undulating: to the south, tiny beaches at the foot of the Pyrenees are shored up by gravel; to the north, the ancient plateau merges with the sedimentary hills of the Tarn region.

THE EVOLVING LANDSCAPE

While some of scenery of southwest France may still be in its pristine natural condition, most landscapes are as we see them today because of human intervention and rather than being in a steady state they are in constant evolution as old ways of life give way to new.

Farming

Wherever a living can be made from the land, farming is practised. Crops and livestock vary according to the relief and the soil. The lowlands and gentle hills are generally given over to profitable crops such as maize and sunflowers. Anywhere that can be intensively cultivated, such as the Roussillon plain and parts of the Garonne valley are used for orchards and market gardens. Intensive farming can have a huge impact on the landscape. Subsidies favour monoculture which makes great use of fertiliser and pesticides which reduce biodiversity.

Livestock are generally less widely spread than they were fifty years ago when every farm would keep pigs and chickens. The fields of the Gers are used to raise ducks and geese. Sheep are reared in the Pyrénées and cows on the Aubrac plateau of the Aveyron.

Grazing animals keep down the resurging natural vegetation and where animals were once grazed but are no longer, the natural vegetation returns. In the Cirque de Moureze, for example, centuries of livestock grazing stripped back the forest cover to reveal dolomitic limestone formations sculpted by into towers and stacks by the elements.

Cattle farming in the Aubrac

When local people abandoned farming in the area in search of easier ways of life, the vegetation began to grow back.

Vineyards

The vine is more than just another crop; a whole culture surrounds its cultivation and the making of wine. However, the French drink less wine than they used to and as demand falls, the area of vineyards is shrinking.

Forestry

France has huge areas of woodland, much of it broadleaf, much of it actively managed in order to supply building timber or firewood. The total forested area is increasing as trees move on to land which has become unprofitable for farming and hence abandoned.

In some places, however, deforestation is the problem. In prime arable areas trees and hedgerows are hacked down to increase field size with a consequent detriment to wildlife.

The loss of tree cover is particularly marked in the Cévennes where it can prevent the ground absorbing precipitation in a region prone to violent storms. In September 1900, 98cm of rain fell in Valleraugue in 48 hours – about 40cm more than the average rainfall in Paris in a whole year. The sparse plant cover cannot contain the rain, so it gushes down into the valleys, becoming 18m–20m high flood waves which destroy everything in their path.

The National Forestry Commission undertakes re-afforestation programmes.

Industry

Southwest France has never been industrialised on any large scale but like the rest of the country it is in an era of post industrialisation. The former mines at Carmaux and Decazeville have been put to the uses of recreation and tourism. Some industrialisation continues, however, particularly quarrying in the Pyrenees. Inevitably, perhaps, local politicians tend to put any scheme which will provide employment before the need to conserve the countryside and its wild inhabitants.

Both the Pyrenees and the Aveyron also have extensive infrastructure (dams, pipes and power stations) for the production of hydroelectric power.

A relatively new form of renewable energy, meanwhile, is also affecting the landscape. The first modern grid-connected wind turbine was installed at Port-la-Nouvelle on the Languedoc coast in 1993. Since then, France has invested heavily in windpower in line with its commitments to the EU. The department of the Aude has particularly

Shepherd and his herd at the Route de Garin in the Comminges

© Jean-Pierre Degas/hemis.fr

Mountain rains meet Mediterranean sun

The Languedoc **climate** is basically Mediterranean, with summer temperatures soaring towards 30°C in Perpignan – one of the hottest places in France in season. The region has its own version of the Provençal mistral, the **tramontane**, which periodically whistles through the Languedoc corridor from the northwest. July and August are hot and, as elsewhere in France, may be crowded, especially towards the coast. (Although the Languedoc coast is never as busy as the Côte d'Azur at this time of year.) Those seeking respite from the coastal plain's blistering heat should head up to the mountains… or down into some of the region's numerous caves. June and September are good months to visit, as the weather is fine and warm, apart from the odd shower of rain.

Autumn on the Mediterranean coast remains relatively mild, making it a good season for a tour of the Corbières vineyards and neighbouring ruined Cathar strongholds. Rainfall in the Pyrenees and over Mont Aigoual is heavy, particularly in the autumn. But this is the harvest season, which adds a splash of colour to the Cévennes and the Montagne Noire.

The first snow falls from late October, and by Christmas the resorts are alive with keen skiers, both downhill and cross-country in the Pyrenees, Andorra, and the Capcir and Cerdagne mountain plateaux, and predominantly cross-country in the Aubrac, Mont Lozère and Aigoual massif.

The coming of milder spring weather brings a burst of colour to the Pyrenees, with mountain wildflowers in bloom, and a show of petals in Roussillon's many orchards. Spring and summer are the best seasons to visit the *Causses*, as temperatures are rarely oppressively hot. It is the ideal time of year for exploring the gorges by canoe, or for pot-holing, rock-climbing and hiking.

good resources of wind and its hillsides are dotted with large windfarms.

Urban areas

The cities are expanding. Particularly urban fringes: vast out of town shopping centres and light industrial estates. A new phenomenon is 'rurbanisation': the merging of the suburbs into the countryside making the latter an extension of the urban area. On the coast, tourism has a huge impact as the number of villas and apartments proliferates.

Communications

More people with more reasons to move about for business or leisure demand more and faster communications. Motorways and other roads are proliferating, taking up space and stimulating economic development wherever they reach to. There are plans to build new TGV high speed railway lines along the Mediterranean coast and down the Garonne valley. The southwest would be unimaginable without the Canal du Midi

and the Millau Viaduct has become an unofficial wonder of the modern world.

Protected areas

To counteract some of the worst effects of modernity on the landscape certain areas are protected to a greater or lesser measure. The greatest protection is afforded by the two national parks, the Cévennes and the Pyrenees where human interfernce is strictly controlled. The only people allowed to sleep within the precinct of the Pyrenees park are shepherds, refuge wardens and (temporarily) hikers and climbers.

The designation parque naturel régional is less stringent. It covers a large inhabited area which has an irreplaceable way of life and its aim is to balance conservation with development. Languedoc-Roussillon and Midi Pyrenees have 5 of France's 49 parques naturels régionaux: Grands Causses, Haut-Languedoc, Pyrénées-Arigéoises, Pyrénées-Catalanes and Narbonnaise-Méditerranée.

La Grande Motte
©Yann Guichaoua/Travel Pictures

MONTPELLIER AND AROUND

The city of Montpellier has improved dramatically in the last 25 years. It is a worthy 'capital' of a region that contrasts the lush countryside of the Vallée de l'Hérault, wherein lie delightful retreats like St Guilhem-le-Désert and the limestone cave system at Clamouse; with coastal resorts like La Grande Motte, with its pyramid buildings; the ancient fishing port of Sète; and picturesque old **villages** like Mourèze, with narrow streets and small houses, so characteristic of the heady-scented *garrigue* hinterland.

Highlights

1 The main starting point for any tour is the **Place de la Comédie** (p94)

2 The oldest botanical garden in France: the **Jardin des plantes** (p100)

3 Enjoy the view from the **promenade du Peyrou** (p100)

4 The **Antigone district**'s outstanding architecture (p100)

Introducing Hérault

In this luxurious sun-soaked region you find long, golden sand beaches, oyster-growing lagoons, monasteries, castles and wild inland spaces, the *garrigue*, where olives are grown, and the vineyards yield some of the finest wines in France. The rugged landscape ripples south-eastwards from the craggy fringes of the Central Massif to form a more restrained amphitheatre bordering the Mediterranean. The region has seen it all, from Romans to builder monks, from crusades to an Age of Enlightenment.

The Envy of France

No European city can match the growth of Montpellier. In the last 40 years, its population, 25% of which is student, has risen tenfold. Montpellier is today France's eighth city by population; it used to be the twenty-fifth. It was founded in 985 at an advantageous position at the crossroads of the Roman 'Via Domitia', the salt road a little to the south, and the 'Cami Roumieu' taken by the pilgrims bound for Compostella. Cultures from far and wide have contributed to the city's growth.

Montpellier is envied throughout France as a centre for intellectual excellence, and at the Faculty of Medicine, Rabelais is said to have found the inspiration for the scenes of drunkenness that fill the lives of the students in his Pantagruel... hard to imagine, of course.

Saint-Guilhem-le-Désert

© Pierre Jacques/hemis.fr

Egg shaped

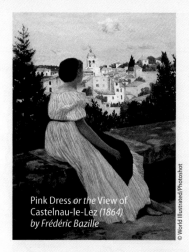

Pink Dress *or the* View of Castelnau-le-Lez *(1864) by Frédéric Bazille*

Twenty years ago, with traffic tearing round it, the place de la Comédie was oval shaped and known as the place de l'Oeuf. Today, the oval is still there, but as a pattern of embedded marble lost in the middle of a huge plateau flanked on one side by elegant 19C buildings and on the other by the sleek new blue trams that criss-cross the city and are set for considerable expansion.

Bistrots, brasséries and cafés spill out into the square, which at night is often a stage setting for impromptu student dance sessions. More professional displays take place in the 19C theatre, which serves as a backdrop to a statue of the Three Graces. In the Grand Rue Jean Moulin is the Hotel Perier – not so much a hotel as a *maison particulière*, or mansion house. It was the birthplace of **Frédéric Bazille** (1841–1870), an impressionist painter of some distinction. The image of Bazille crops up in a few places throughout Montpellier, notably his head, which appears on a number of the statues of other distinguished people, in particular Saint Roch. The sculptor of these statues was **Auguste Baussan**, a good friend of Bazille, who saw nothing extraordinary in using his friend's head, not literally of course, in place of the real thing.

The private mansions are rather more numerous in the centre of Montpellier than is generally evident. They lie tucked away behind huge doorways, beyond which intimate courtyards give into opulent houses of some evident wealth. The 15C **Hôtel des Trésoriers de la Bourse** is one, and the house at the top of the rue des Soeurs Noires, built by the celebrated Marquis de Montcalm, another. Many are not open to the public, but guided tours from the tourist office can often get you in for a glimpse into an altogether different world.

Place de la Comédie

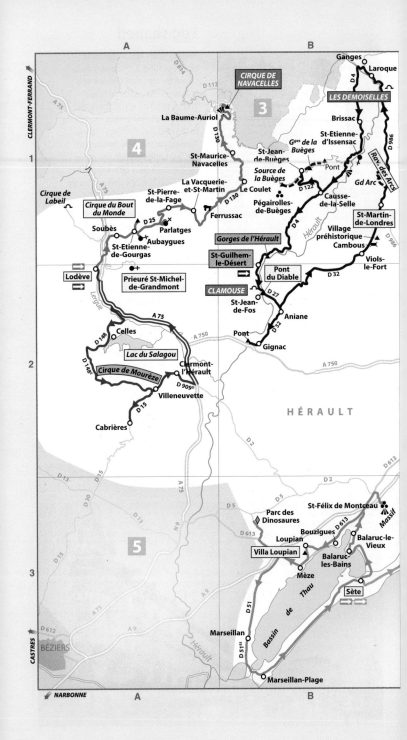

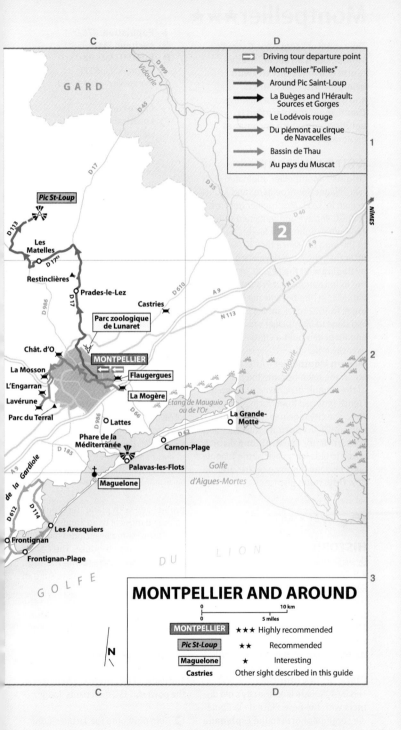

MONTPELLIER AND AROUND

MONTPELLIER	★★★	Highly recommended
Pic St-Loup	★★	Recommended
Maguelone	★	Interesting
Castries		Other sight described in this guide

Driving tour departure point

Montpellier "Follies"

Around Pic Saint-Loup

La Bùeges and l'Hérault:
Sources et Gorges

Le Lodévois rouge

Du piémont au cirque
de Navacelles

Bassin de Thau

Au pays du Muscat

0   10 km
0   5 miles

N

Montpellier★★★

The capital of Languedoc-Roussillon, Montpellier is an administrative centre and university city with beautiful historical districts and gardens. There is a bustling charm about the place that is uplifting, and which encourages exploration.

A BIT OF HISTORY

Origins – Montpellier originated with two villages: Montpellieret and Montpellier. In 1204, Montpellier became a Spanish enclave and remained so until 1349 when John III of Majorca sold it to the king of France for 120 000 *écus*. After that, the town developed quickly by trading with the Levant. In the 16C, the Reformation, and Protestants and Catholics in turn became masters of the town. In 1622 royal armies of Louis XIII laid siege to Montpellier's fortifications and Richelieu built a citadel to watch over the rebel city.

Modern Montpellier – After the Revolution the town became the *préfecture* of the Hérault *département*. When the French returned from North Africa after 1962, the city regained its dynamism – reflected in the **Corum** conference and concert centre, the **Antigone** district, linked to old Montpellier by the Triangle and Polygone shopping centres and the new **Odysseum** district.

- ▶ **Population:** 276 054.
- **Michelin Map:** 339: I-7.
- **Info:** 30 place de la Comédie, 34000 Montpellier. ☏04 67 60 60 60. www.montpellier-france.com.
- ▶ **Location:** 170km/106mi west of Marseille. The tourist office (🕐open 9am–6pm) organises guided tours that include access to many areas usually closed to the public.
- **Don't Miss:** Place de la Comédie; a walk in the Old Town; the view from the promenade du Peyrou; the neo-Classical architecture of the Antigone district.
- **Kids:** The Lunaret Zoo; Mare Nostrum Aquarium.

TRANSPORTATION
TRAMWAY
Transports de l'Agglomération de Montpellier. ☏04 67 22 87 87. *www.tam-voyages.com.* A new Montpellier tram allows passengers to go just about anywhere within the city and beyond in minutes.

🐾 WALKING TOUR

HISTORIC MONPELLIER★★
🕐*3h. See map II.*
Between place de la Comédie and the Peyrou Arc de Triomphe are Montpellier's historic districts, last vestiges of the original medieval town. Superb 17C and 18C private mansions, *hôtels*, line the streets, with their remarkable staircases hidden in inner courtyards.

Place de la Comédie
This lively square links the city's old districts with the new. Place de la Comédie continues north to the **Esplanade** promenade with plane trees, outdoor cafés and musical bandstands.
The **Corum** complex includes the 2 000 seat Berlioz opera house. The Corum terrace overlooks the town's rooftops, St-Pierre cathedral and white spire of Ste-Anne's church.
To the east lie the **Triangle** and the **Polygone** complex (shopping centre and administrative buildings).

▶ Take rue de la Loge.

The name of this street is a reminder of the powerful 15C merchants' lodge.

▶ Turn right onto rue Jacques-Cœur.

Old town

© Hans Georg Eiben/Getty Images

Hôtel des Trésoriers de France

No 7. This private mansion housing the Musée Languedocien was the Hôtel Jacques-Cœur when the king's treasurer lived here in the 15C. In the 17C, it became the Hôtel des Trésoriers de France, occupied by senior magistrates administering the royal estates in Languedoc. Finally, it was named "Lunaret" in memory of Henri de Lunaret who bequeathed it to the Société Archéologique de Montpellier.

Turn left onto rue Valedeau and right onto rue Embouque-d'Or.

On the left is the **Hôtel de Manse** (*4 rue Embouque-d'Or*). The count of Manse, treasurer to the king of France, had Italian artists design this interior façade with its double colonnade and beautiful staircase called the "Manse's Steps."
Opposite is the **Hôtel Baschy du Cayla**, with its Louis XV façade.

Hôtel de Varennes★

2 place Pétrarque. Information at the tourist office. ☎04 67 60 60 60.
Gothic rooms contain Romanesque columns and capitals from the original church of Notre-Dame-des-Tables. Gemel windows and castle doors have been incorporated into the walls. The city of Montpellier uses the 14C **Salle Pétrarque** for receptions. The mansion houses two museums.

Musée du Vieux Montpellier

Hôtel de Varennes, first floor.
🕐*Open Tue–Sun 10.30am–12.30pm, 1.30–6pm.* ⬤€3. ☎04 67 66 02 94.
This local history museum contains old maps, religious objects and documents from the Revolution.

Musée Fougau

Hôtel de Varennes, second floor.
🕐*Open Wed and Thu 3–6pm.*
⬤*No charge.* ☎04 67 84 31 58.
The museum derives its name from the Languedoc expression *lou fougau* (the hearth). Objects, furniture and decors represent popular 19C local arts and traditions.

Turn right onto rue de l'Aiguillerie.

As this street's name ('needle factory') suggests, it was the town's street for arts and crafts in the Middle Ages. Some shops still retain their beautiful 14C and 15C vaulted roofs.

Take rue Glaize on the right and continue along rue Montpellieret.

Musée Fabre★★

37 bd Sarrail; enter through 39 bd Bonne-Nouvelle. ♿🕐*Open Tue–Sun 10am–6pm.* ⬤€7. ☎04 67 14 83 00.
The museum, founded in 1825 with the generosity of the Montpellier painter **François-Xavier Fabre** (1766–1837),

95

Musée Fabre

D. Chapuis/MICHELIN

displays Greek and European ceramic ware, and paintings from the Spanish, Italian, Dutch and Flemish schools. Early 19C French painting features works by the *luminophiles* (light-lovers), Languedoc painters who captured the region's superb light on canvas.

Hôtel de Cabrières-Sabatier d'Espeyran

A Second Empire mansion. Visit by applying to the Musée Fabre.

▶ Return to rue de l'Aiguillerie going N around the Musée Fabre, then turn left onto rue de la Carbonnerie.

Hôtel Baudon de Mauny

1 rue de la Carbonnerie.
This house features an elegant Louis XVI façade decorated with flower garlands.

Rue du Cannau

This street is lined with classical town houses: at No. 1, **Hôtel de Roque-maure**; at No. 3, **Hôtel d'Avèze**; at No. 6, **Hôtel de Beaulac**; and at No. 8, **Hôtel Deydé**.

▶ Turn back and take rue de Girone on the right, then rue Fournarié.

Hôtel de Solas

1 rue Fournarié. This 17C town house features a Louis XIII door. Note the plasterwork on the porch ceiling.

Hôtel d'Uston

3 rue Fournarié.
This house dates from the early 18C.

▶ Follow rue de la Vieille-Intendance.

At No. 9 is the **Hôtel de la Vieille Intendance**, whose former residents include philosopher Auguste Comte and writer Paul Valéry.

Place de la Canourgue★

In the 17C, this square was the centre of Montpellier, and numerous *hôtels* remain around the garden with its Unicorn fountain. From here enjoy a view onto the cathedral of St-Pierre.
Hôtel Richer de Bellevue (*annex of the law courts*) once housed the town hall. The square courtyard is decorated with busts and balustrades typical of the late 18C. The façade of **Hôtel de Cambacérès**, by Giral, includes elegant 18C ornamentation and wrought-iron work.
On the southwest corner of the square, **Hôtel du Sarret** is named the Maison de la Coquille ('shell house'), so called because of its squinches, a real architectural feat in which part of the building is supported on part of the vault.

▶ Take rue Astruc and cross rue Foch.

The **Ancien Courrier district** is the oldest part of Montpellier, its narrow pedestrian streets are lined with luxury boutiques.

▶ From rue Foch, take rue du Petit-Scel.

The 19C **church of Ste-Anne** houses temporary exhibitions. Opposite the church porch are the remains of a small building whose early 17C decor is in Antique style.

▶ Take rue St-Anne and rue St-Guilhem to rue de la Friperie, then turn left onto rue du Bras-de-Fer and right onto rue des Trésoriers-de-la-Bourse.

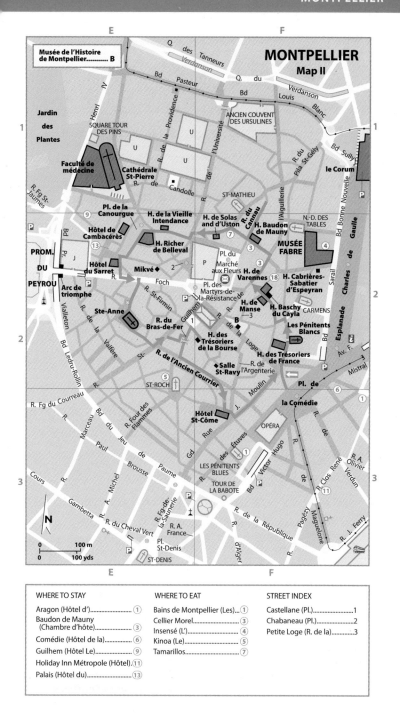

MONTPELLIER
Map II

Musée de l'Histoire
de Montpellier........... B

Jardin
des
Plantes

Q. des Tanneurs
Verdanson
Bd Pasteur
Q. du
Bd
Verdanson
Louis
Blanc

SQUARE TOUR
DES PINS

ANCIEN COUVENT
DES URSULINES

le Corum

Faculté de
médecine

Cathédrale
St-Pierre

Candolle

ST-MATHIEU

N.-D. DES
TABLES

MUSÉE
FABRE

Pl. de la
Canourgue

H. de la Vieille
Intendance

H. de Solas
and d'Uston

H. Baudon
de Mauny

Hôtel de
Cambacérès

H. Richer
de Belleval

Hôtel
du Sarret

Mikvé ◆

Pl. du
Marché
aux Fleurs

H. de
Varennes

H. Cabrières-
Sabatier
d'Espeyran

PROM.
DU
PEYROU

Arc de
triomphe

Foch

Pl. des
Martyrs-
de-la-Résistance

H. de
Manse

H. Baschy
du Cayla

CARMENS

Ste-Anne

R. St-Firmin

R. du
Bras-de-Fer

B

Les Pénitents
Blancs

Esplanade

H. des
Trésoriers
de la Bourse

H. des Trésoriers
de France

Av. F.
Mistral

R. de l'Ancien Courrier

Salle
St-Ravy

R. de
l'Argenterie

ST-ROCH

Pl. de
la Comédie

R. Fg du Courreau

Hôtel
St-Côme

OPÉRA

LES PÉNITENTS
BLUES

TOUR DE
LA BABOTE

R. A.
Olivier
Verdun

Cours
Gambetta

Pl.
St-Denis

ST-DENIS

N

0   100 m
0   100 yds

97

WHERE TO STAY

Aragon (Hôtel d')........................ ①
Baudon de Mauny
  (Chambre d'hôte)..................... ③
Comédie (Hôtel de la)............... ⑥
Guilhem (Hôtel Le).................... ⑨
Holiday Inn Métropole (Hôtel). ⑪
Palais (Hôtel du)......................... ⑬

WHERE TO EAT

Bains de Montpellier (Les)... ①
Cellier Morel............................ ③
Insensé (L')............................... ④
Kinoa (Le)................................. ⑤
Tamarillos................................

STREET INDEX

Castellane (Pl.)......................... 1
Chabaneau (Pl.)....................... 2
Petite Loge (R. de la)............. 3

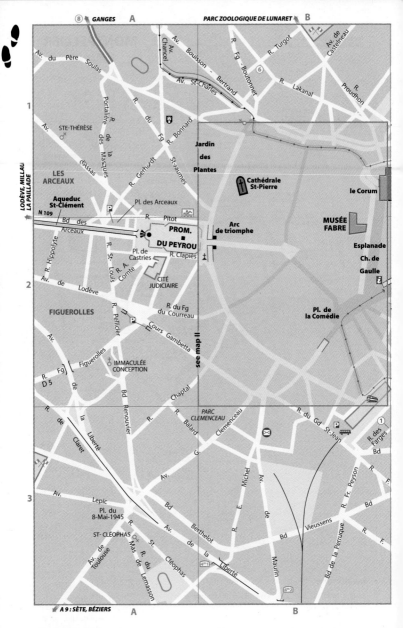

Hôtel des Trésoriers de la Bourse★

4 rue des Trésoriers-de-la-Bourse.
Also called Hôtel Rodez-Benavent, this town house by architect Jean Giral features an impressive open staircase and courtyard whose rear wall is decorated with flame ornaments.

▶ Return to rue du Bras-de-Fer.

The medieval **rue du Bras-de-Fer** leads to **rue de l'Ancien-Courrier★**, lined with art galleries and boutiques.

▶ Turn left onto rue Joubert which leads to place St-Ravy.

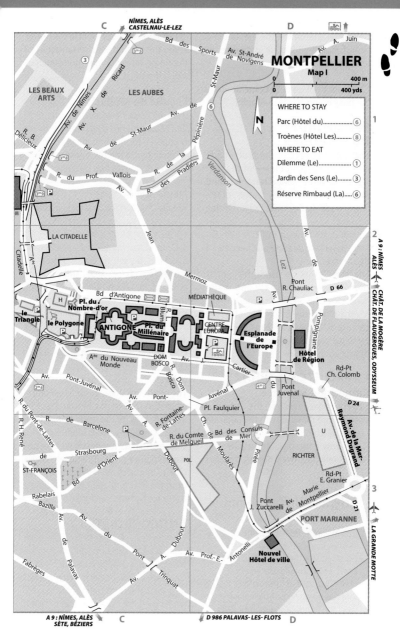

NÎMES, ALÈS
CASTELNAU-LE-LEZ

C

D

MONTPELLIER
Map I

400 m
400 yds

N

WHERE TO STAY

Parc (Hôtel du)................. ⑥
Troènes (Hôtel Les).......... ⑧

WHERE TO EAT

Dilemme (Le)..................... ①
Jardin des Sens (Le).......... ③
Réserve Rimbaud (La)..... ⑥

A 9 : NÎMES, ALÈS
SÈTE, BÉZIERS
C

D 986 PALAVAS- LES- FLOTS
D

Place St-Ravy retains the Gothic windows of the Palace of the Kings of Majorca. The **Salle St-Ravy**, housing temporary exhibitions, has beautiful vaulting decorated with keystones.

▶ Return to rue de l'Ancien-Courrier and take rue Jacques-d'Aragon.

Hôtel St-Côme

Free access to the inner courtyard. Guided tours of the amphitheatre as part of the theme tours organised by the tourist office. ℘04 67 60 60 60.
This town house which is now the Chamber of Commerce was built in the 18C by Jean-Antoine Giral. The famous

polygonal anatomical theatre, under a superb dome with oculi and lanterns, lets in a flood of light.

▶ Return to place de la Comédie via the busy grand-rue Jean-Moulin.

PROMENADE DU PEYROU★★

The upper terrace of the promenade affords a sweeping **view★** of the Garrigues, Cévennes, Mediterranean and Mont Canigou. The key feature of the Promenade du Peyrou is the ensemble of the *château d'eau* and St-Clément aqueduct, 880m long and 22m high. On Saturday, Place des Arceaux becomes a flea market.

The late-17C **Arc de Triomphe** depicts the victories of Louis XIV and major events from his reign: the Canal du Midi, revocation of the Edict of Nantes, the capture of Namur in 1692 and the United Provinces of the Netherlands kneeling before Louis XIV.

LA FACULTÉ DISTRICT
Cathédrale St-Pierre

Towering like a fortress, the cathedral seems more massive with the adjacent façade of the Faculty of Medicine. It is the only church in Montpellier not completely destroyed during the Wars

of Religion. Although built in the Gothic style, the cathedral is reminiscent of the single-nave Romanesque churches along the coast.

Faculté de Médecine
2 rue de l'École-de-Médecine.
The Montpellier Faculty of Medicine occupies a former Benedictine monastery founded in the 14C by order of Pope Urban V. It houses two museums.

Musée Atger★
Faculté de Médecine, first floor, access (signposted) via the Houdan staircase.
🕐*Open Sep–Jul Mon, Wed, Fri 1.30–5.45pm.* No charge. ℘04 34 43 35 80.
Contains drawings bequeathed by Xavier Atger (1758–1833) and works by artists of the 17C and 18C French School, the 16C, 17C and 18C Italian School, and the 17C and 18C Flemish School.

Jardin des Plantes
🕐*Open Jun–Sep Tue–Sun noon–8pm; Oct–May Tue–Sun noon–6pm.*
No charge. ℘04 67 63 43 22.
The oldest botanical gardens in France, created in 1593 for the Montpellier Faculty of Botany for the study of medicinal plants, contains various Mediterranean species such as the nettle tree, holm-oak and mock privet (phillyrea). A large ginkgo biloba planted in 1795 is a graft from the first ginkgo plant introduced to France by Antoine Gouan.

ANTIGONE DISTRICT★
Starting from place de la Comédie (east side), walk to the Antigone district via the Polygone shopping centre.
Catalan architect **Ricardo Bofill** designed the bold new Antigone district. This vast neo-Classical housing project combines prefab technology with harmonious design. Behind a profusion of entablatures, pediments, pilasters and columns are low-income housing, public facilities and local shops, arranged around squares and patios. **Place du Nombre-d'Or** continues with the cypress-lined **place du Millénaire**, place de Thessalie then place du Péloponnèse. The vista stretches from the

History Underground
The crypt of the first Église Notre-Dame-des-Tables, one of Montpellier's oldest churches, destroyed for the last time in 1794, hosts a multimedia presentation of the history and future of a city that has no qualms about calling itself the "surdouée" (exceptionally talented): provided with headphones, you will experience a real immersion in the city's past via 3D reconstructions and slide shows. **Musée de l'histoire de Montpellier** – *Place Jean-Jaurès (via rue de la Loge).* 🕐*Open Tue–Sun 10am–1pm, 2–6pm.* €3. ℘04 67 34 87 50.

"Échelles de la Ville" past the crescent-shaped buildings of **esplanade de l'Europe**, to the **Hôtel de Région**, converted into a dock for Port Juvénal. Beyond, around **avenue Raymond-Dugrand**, dubbed the "Rambla of Montpellier" and honouring the urban planner who was partly responsible for planning the modern city, a brand new district is emerging: architects Michel Macary, Jean Nouvel and Rudy Riccioti, among others, are participating in the design of this place that will house a new city hall as well as a large contemporary arts centre.

ODYSSEUM DISTRICT
Tramway line 1 from the city centre.
The Odysseum complex is a world apart, devoted to leisure, culture and shopping. What began with a multiscreen cinema in 1998, now contains, among other leisure facilities, restaurants, a skating rink, an aquarium and large shopping centre.

Aquarium Mare Nostrum – *Allée Ulysse.* Open Jul–Aug daily 10am–8pm; Sep–Jun daily 10am–7pm. €15.50 (child 5–12, €10.50). 04 67 13 05 50. www.aquariummarenostrum.fr.

Planetarium Galilée – *100 allée Ulysse.* Open: check website for variable opening hours and shows. Closed first two weeks of Sep. €6.30 (child 4–12, €5.30). 04 67 13 26 26. www.planetarium-galilee.com.

LUNARET DISTRICT
Parc zoologique de Lunaret★
50 avenue Agropolis, 6km/4mi N of the Hôpitaux-Facultés district. Leave town on rue Proudhon and take the road to Mende. Open daily except Mon: Apr–Sept 9.30am–6.30pm; Oct and Feb–Mar 10am–6pm; Nov–Jan 10am–5pm. Zoo, no charge: conservatory €6.50 (child 6–18, €3). 04 67 54 45 23. www.zoo.montpellier.fr.

In this vast park bequeathed to the town by Henri de Lunaret, animals seem at liberty in a setting of garrigues and undergrowth. Stroll and observe zebras, bison, alpacas, mouflons, wolves and exotic birds.

Amazonian conservatory★
The planet's largest natural ecosystem presented in a mere 2 500 sq m. Spectacled caimans greet you to this humid and lush environment, a paradise of strange animals such as giant eaters, anaconda, piranhas and howler monkeys. To see these animals at their best, you will need to be patient and alert. The visit ends outside with the large aviary of scarlet ibis. There is also an educational area.

EXCURSIONS
Château de Castries
12km/7mi NE of Montpellier.
(Not open to the public).
The 16C Renaissance château built by Pierre de Castries is still owned by the Castries family. Sadly, one of the wings was destroyed during the Wars of Religion and its stones were used for terraces designed by Le Nôtre. After visiting the château, take D 26 to Guzargues, off N 110, for an interesting **view** of the **aqueduct** built by Riquet to supply water to the château.

Parc du Terral at Saint-Jean-de-Védas
7km/10.5mi SW of Montpellier via the D 613. Open 8.30am–noon, 2–5pm. No charge. 04 67 07 83 00; http://saintjeandevedas.fr.
This is one of the oldest estates in the Montpellier region, mentioned in records dating from the 9C as a summer residence of the bishops of Maguelone. Following multiple sackings and subsequent restorations, it today covers an area of just 3ha, and includes a bamboo garden, a scented garden and a stone and water garden.

🚗 DRIVING TOURS

MONTPELLIER "FOLLIES"

On the outskirts of Montpellier are some thirty 18C aristocratic summer residences with acres of vineyards and pretty gardens with lakes and fountains.

1 SOUTHEAST OF MONTPELLIER
9km/6mi.

From the city centre, follow the signs to the 'Montpellier-Méditerranée' airport. After the bridge over the Lez, take the road to Mauguio (D 24). The Château de Flaugergues is about 2km/1mi down the road, in the Millénaire district.

Château de Flaugergues ★
Open: Park, gardens and cellar daily except Sun and public holidays 9.30am–6pm, Sat 2.30–6pm; Chateau Jun–Jul and Sept daily except Mon 2.30–7pm. Château: €9.50; Park and gardens: €7. ℘04 99 52 66 37. www.flaugergues.com.
This château purchased by Étienne de Flaugergues, Montpellier financier, is the oldest of the Montpellier 'follies'. The tour ends with a tasting of wine produced on the estate.

▶ Return to the road to Mauguio, heading right, and drive past the Château de Flaugergues and under the motorway to get to the Château de la Mogère.

Château de la Mogère★
Open Jun–Sept daily 2.30–6.30pm; Oct–May Sat–Sun and public holidays by appointment. €7. ℘04 67 65 72 01. www.lamogere.fr.
This elegant early 18C château designed by Jean Giral has a harmonious façade surmounted by a pediment. Inside are 18C paintings by Brueghel, Hyacinthe Rigaud, Louis David, Jouvenet.

▶ Return to the city centre on D 172E.

2 WEST OF MONTPELLIER
Round tour of 22km/14mi.

From the city centre take the road to Ganges (D 986) for 6km/4mi, then turn left towards Celleneuve, and then right onto D 127. A little further on, two lion-topped pillars indicate the turn-off to Château d'O.

Château d'O
The 18C château has a beautiful park with statues from Château de La Mosson. Owned by the Conseil Général de l'Hérault, it is used as a theatre during the Printemps des Comédiens festival held every summer.

▶ Carry on to Celleneuve. Follow signs to Juvignac, then turn left onto the road leading to the Château de La Mosson.

Château de La Mosson
The most sumptuous residence in the Montpellier area was built from 1723 to 1729 by a rich banker, Joseph Bonnier, Baron de La Mosson. The Baroque fountain is a reminder of the original lavish decoration of Bonnier's estate, now a public park.

▶ Return to N 109 and take the first road on the left towards Lavérune.

Before long, the road passes through vineyard country.

Château de l'Engarran
Beyond the superb wrought-iron entrance gate from the Château de La Mosson is a Louis XV style building.

▶ Carry on towards Lavérune. The Château de Lavérune is on the far west side of the village.

Château de Lavérune
This imposing 17C–18C residence once belonged to the bishops of Montpellier. The first-floor **Musée Hofer-Bury** (*open Sat–Sun 3–6pm. €2 (child 10–18, €1). ℘04 99 51 20 25*) displays paintings and sculptures by contemporary artists, including Henri de Jordan, Gérard and Bernard Calvet, Roger Bonafé, Vincent Bioulès and Wang Wei-Xin.

▶ Take D 5 back to the city centre.

3 AROUND PIC SAINT-LOUP
Leave Montpellier heading north on the D 17 (direction Quissac), which feeds into the D 65 near Clapiers. 1km/0.6mi

Pic Saint-Loup and vineyards

© Bertrand Rieger/hemis.fr

after Prades-le-Lez, turn left onto a signposted lane.

Domaine départmental de Restinclieres (Prades-le-Lez)

This 215ha estate houses the departmental house of the environment and its exhibitions. From the terrace of the château (17C), you can admire the French-style garden and the managed garrigue. Two rivers, the Lirou and the Lez (which has its source here) cross the estate. This agroforestry experiementation site contains 54 tree species (bald cyprus, gingko, pedunculate oak, magnolia). Informative signs help you identify the fauna and flora.

▶ Rejoin the D 17 to Triadou (5.5km/ 3.4mi); on the left, the D 17-E3 leads to Matelles, 4.5km/2.8mi further on.

Les Matelles

Capital of the "Montferrand Republic" (the small community, created by the bishop of Maguelone in 1276, benefited from fiscal privileges and was governed by elected trustees), the fortified village has retained its charming cobblestone streets and small flower-filled squares. Some houses, built on the rock, have outdoor staircases. The belltower of the Romanesque church was built in the 18C over one of the gates of the ramparts.

▶ 8.9km/5.9mi N along D 986 then D 113 to Cazevielle. Park to E of the village and follow directions to Pic St-Loup.

Pic Saint-Loup★★

▶ *The wide stone path leads up to a calvary. From there, take a little winding footpath that climbs up to the chapel and observatory. Allow 3h there and back.*

St-Loup peak is the highest point of a long ridge above the Montpellier Garrigues.

The summit offers a **panorama★★** of Hortus mountain, the Cévennes, the Nîmes plain and Mont Ventoux, the Alpilles and the Luberon, the Camargue, the Montpellier plain and the Mediterranean string of coastal lagoons.

ADDRESSES

🍴 STAY

🛏🛏 **Hôtel de la Comédie** – *1 bis r.Baudin. ☎04 67 58 43 64. www.hotel-montpellier-comedie.com. 20 rooms.* Located just off of La Place de la Comédie, this budget hotel with 19C façade offers modern bedrooms. Its lively neighbourhood makes an excellent base for exploring.

Hotel du Parc – *8 r. Achille-Bège.* *04 67 41 16 49. www.hotelduparc-montpellier.com.* ☐. *Closed Dec–Feb.* *19 rooms.* A former stately 18C residence, close to the historic centre; former home of the Count Vivier and his family.

Hotel les Troènes – *17 av. Emile-Bertin-Sans.* *04 67 04 07 76. www.hotel-les-troenes.fr. Closed Dec–Feb. 14 rooms.* This family run 1960s hotel is located next to the Montpellier tramway in the university district.

Hôtel Le Guilhem – *18 r. Jean-Jacques Rousseau.* *04 67 52 90 90. www.leguilhem.com. 36 roo*ms. Two 16C and 17C houses. Top-floor rooms offer a lovely view of the nearby cathedral.

Hôtel du Palais – *3 r. du Palais-des-Guilhem.* *04 67 60 47 38. www.hotel dupalais-montpellier.fr. 26 rooms.* This family hotel near the Peyrou gardens and the Place de la Canourgue has small stylish and well-kept rooms.

Hôtel d'Aragon – *10 r. Baudin.* *04 67 10 70 00. www.hotel-aragon.fr. 12 rooms.* A charming little hotel, with well-kept and pleasantly decorated rooms. Breakfast is served on a sunny veranda.

Hôtel Oceania Le Métropole – *3 r. du Clos-René.* *04 67 12 32 32. www. oceaniahotels.com. 80 roo*ms. Formerly the Holiday Inn, this modern hotel, completely renovated during 2016, has managed to preserve its Belle Epoque charm. Rooms are spacious. There is a pool and garden.

Baudon de Mauny – *1 r. de la Carbonnerie.* *04 67 02 21 77. www. baudondemauny.com. 8 rooms.* In the heart of old Montpellier, this hotel has been in the same family for seven generations. Halfway between a B&B and a boutique hotel, this long-established residence marries old and new in a stylish and luxurious setting.

Mercure Antigone – *285 bvd. Aéroport-International.* *04 67 20 63 63. www.accorhotels.com. 114 rooms.* In the heart of Antigone, opposite the Olympic swimming pool; functional rooms, ideal for both business and tourist use.

♈ EAT

L'Insensé – *Musée Fabre, 39 bd. Bonne-Nouvelle.* *04 67 58 97 78. Open Tue–Sun lunch and evenings.* When the Pourcel brothers took over an art museum, the results were ultramodern decor and cuisine worthy of the famous mother restaurant, *Le Jardin des Sens (now closed).*

La Réserve Rimbaud – *820 av. Saint-Maur.* *04 67 72 52 53. http://reserve-rimbaud.com. Open Tue–Sun, closed Sat lunch, Sun eve.* A place of great charm, with an extraordinary terrace overlooking the Lez, a sunny interior with large bay windows and light and authentic cuisine.

Les Bains de Montpellier – *6 r. Richelieu.* *04 67 60 70 87. http://les-bains-de-montpellier.com. Open Mon–Sat. Reservation recommended.* Dine in the shade of the courtyard palm trees or in one of the drawing rooms in these wonderfully restored old 'Parisian baths'. Cuisine uses fresh market produce.

Cellier Morel – *La Maison de la Lozère, 27, r. de l'Aiguillerie.* *04 67 66 46 36. www.celliermorel.com. Closed Sun; Mon lunch and Wed lunch.* Cuisine inspired by dishes of the Lozère, served in an opulent 13C vaulted room or in a charming 18C courtyard garden.

Tamarillos – *2 pl. du Marché-aux-Fleurs.* *04 67 60 06 00. www. tamarillos.biz. Open Tue–Sat, closed Mon and Wed lunch. Reservation recommended.* A style of cooking much of which is based on flowers and fruit. The beautiful interior is contemporary and based on colour, reflection and transparency. One of the best restaurants in Montpellier, serving gastronomic food at reasonable prices.

La Diligence – *2 place Pétrarque.* *04 67 66 12 21. www.la-diligence.com. Closed Sun; Mon lunch and Sat lunch. Reservation recommended.* La Diligence, housed in a 14C vaulted room, was established more than 40 years ago, and has long been a veritable institution of the finest French cooking. Reservations advised.

MIA Restaurant – *609 avenue Raymond Dugrand, RBC Design Centre.* *04 67 73 14 26. www.miarestaurant.fr/ en. Closed Sun. Reservation essential.* With a well-deserved Michelin star, Mia, at the heart of the Design Centre, has been open since 2012 and successfully blends the influences of France, Italy and Spain – all the flavours of the Mediterranean, in fact.

TAKING A BREAK

L'Heure Bleue – *1 r. de la Carbonnerie.* ☏*04 67 66 41 05. Tue–Sat noon–7pm.* This literary tearoom in an 18C mansion is also an art gallery and second-hand shop with a lavish collection of sculptures and curios. Home-baked pastries and some 30 varieties of tea.

Grand Café Riche – *8 Pl. de la Comédie.* ☏*04 67 54 71 44. http://cafe-riche.com. Open daily 7am–midnight.* This century-old café is an institution. Its terrace is a front-row seat for street entertainment on the Place de la Comédie. Exhibitions are held here.

SHOPPING

Markets – Food markets open every morning in the centre city halles (covered markets): Castellane and Arceaux, on the Esplanade Charles-de-Gaulle, the halles Laissac, the new halles Jacques-Cœur in the Antigone district and on the Plan Cabannes. There is also the Sunday morning **farmers' market** in the Antigone district (avenue Samuel-Champlain), and the Saturday morning **organic market** in the place des Arceaux. On the 4th Saturday of every month, **secondhand booksellers** gather on the rue des Étuves. A **flea market** is held on Sunday mornings on the esplanade de la Mosson (stadium car park).

Au Panier Gourmand – *9 r. Boussairolles. Open daily 7am–8pm.* All producers are regional, offering vinegar, wine, syrups, beer (Larzac), fruit, pastis and cheese.

Aux Gourmets – *2 r. Clos-René.* Run by the Fournier family for more than 45 years, this shop close to Place de la Comedie offers a wide variety of sweets and cakes.

Dragées et réglisses Auzier – *3 r. du Courreau.* ☏*04 67 92 63 35. Open Tue–Sat 9am–noon, 2–6pm.* Here, pure, liquorice is transformed into sticks and sweets. Those who aren't fond of this very southern plant can choose between sugared almonds, marshmallows and multicoloured sweets.

Maison régionale des vins et produits du terroir – *34 R. St-Guilhem.* ☏*04 67 60 40 41. Open daily (except Sun in Dec) 9.30am–8pm.* All the finest produce of the region is represented here.

Shops in the Ancien Courrier district

D. Chapuis/MICHELIN

ON THE TOWN

As a student city, Montpellier's cultural landscape is quite diverse, with its jazz enthusiasts, accordion fans and lovers of salsa or classical music. Bars and music cafés cater to new trends.

EVENTS

Montpellier and the surrounding area are rich in all manner of festivals

Festival international Montpellier danse – ☏*0 800 600 740 (free call). www.montpellierdanse.com. Late Jun–early Jul.* Traditional music and dance.

Festival de Radio France et Montpellier Languedoc-Roussillon – ☏*04 67 02 02 01. www.festivalradiofrancemontpellier.com. First 3 wks of Jul.* Concerts, chamber music, jazz, world music.

Festival international cinéma méditerranéen – ☏*04 99 13 73 73. www.cinemed.tm.fr. Late Oct.* Film festival.

Pèlerinage St-Roch – Roch (14C) was born in Montpellier, in rue de la Loge. Today, an important pilgrimage, made by many Italians, takes place on his saint's day of 16 August in Montpellier, with processions, displays of his relics and staff, street entertainment and a guided tour of the city following in his footsteps (organised by the tourist office: ☏*04 67 60 60 60).*

Le Printemps des comédiens – In June and July, the château d'O serves as the setting for the festival's plays. ☏*04 67 63 66 66. www.printempsdescomediens.com.*

Palavas-les-Flots

After the railway line opened in 1872, Palavas became a popular seaside resort. Palavas was the only beach on this coastal stretch until the Languedoc-Roussillon shoreline was developed for tourism.

▶ **Population:** 6 292.
▲ **Michelin Map:** 339 17.
▯ **Info:** Place de la Méditerranée. ☎04 67 07 73 34. www.ot-palavas lesflots.com.
◐ **Location:** 12km/7.5mi S of Montpellier.

SIGHTS
Musée Albert-Dubout
Access on foot from the east bank along quai des Arènes or by boat. ◐*Open Jul–Aug 10am–1pm, 4–6pm; Apr–Jun and Sep–Nov Tue–Sun 2–6pm; Dec–Feb Sat–Sun and school and public holidays (except Mon) 2–6pm.* ☞€5. ☎04 67 68 56 41 *(afternoons only). www.dubout.fr.*
This museum occupies the Ballestras redoubt, a reconstruction of an 18C fortified tower built in the middle of Levant lagoon. It commemorates cartoonist **Albert Dubout**, who drew amusing renderings of Montpellier holidaymakers and numerous scenes of bullfighting. Enjoy terrace views from Mont St-Clair to the gulf of Aigues-Mortes.

Musée du Petit Train
Parc du Levanr, near the Musée Dubout. ♿◐*Opening hours as Musée Albert Dubout.*
Dubout fans and those nostalgic for an era that ended in 1968 will be pleased to discover the locomotive and a carriage of the famous little beach train, surrounded by photographs retracing its history and drawings by the artist.

Phare de la Méditerranée
Information from the tourist office.
From a promenade deck (reached by a lift) at the top of this former water tower, there is a remarkable **view★** of Aigues-Mortes Gulf, from Sète the pointe de l'Espiguette, and, upcountry, of the marshes, Montpellier and the bluish mountains dominated by the sharp silhouette of the pic St-Loup. There is also a fine dining **restaurant** (*www.restaurantlephare.fr*).

EXCURSIONS
Maguelone★
▯ *Parking du Pilou (via the footbridge).* ☎04 67 69 75 87.
This cathedral on an island, hidden among the marshes, is a picture of beauty as unusual as it is serene.
Old cathedral – ◐*Open Jun–Sep 9am–9pm; Oct–May 9am–10am.* ☎04 67 50 63 63.

Lattes
6km/4mi N.
In 1963, the Lattes rediscovered the archaeological site of Lattara, which from 6C BCE to the 3C CE was a thriving port, but was abandoned when increased rainfall silted up the port. Lattara comes to life at the **Musée archéologique Henri-Prades** (*leave Lattes SE on D 132 towards Pérols;* ♿◐*open daily except Tue 10am–noon, 1–5.30pm, Sat–Sun 2–6pm;* ☞€3.50, *no charge 1st Sun in the month;* ☎04 67 99 77 20), sited in the old farmhouse of the painter Bazille. You can learn about the urbanisation of the site during the second Iron Age, the creation of the port and daily life in Lattara. Another section presents the 3C and 4C necropolis of St-Michel where 76 tombs were discovered.

Carnon-Plage
6km/4mi E.
This lido-style beach on the Golfe du Lion is popular with locals. The marina links to the Rhône–Sète canal. The actual beach is separated from the nearby road by sand dunes, which offer protection from the occasional breeze.

La Grande-Motte

La Grande-Motte is a Mediterranean seaside resort enjoying a fine sandy beach and a proximity to Nîmes and Montpellier. Its tall eye-catching pyramids create an original skyline and its Palais des Congrès (conference centre) overlooks a marina accommodating 1 410 yachts.

THE RESORT

The resort's modern design has honeycomb **pyramids**, **buildings shaped like seashells** and Provençal style **villas**. La Grande-Motte is known as a child-friendly resort and was awarded the Pavillon bleu d'Europe for the quality of its sea water –

The beach – The vast sandy beach stretches over 6km/3.7mi and has toilets and showers. Dogs are prohibited.

The port and lakes – Framed by the pyramids, the port can accommodate more than 1 400 boats. Visitors enjoy water sports on Ponant lake and angling in Or lake.

👥 Espace Grand Bleu – ℘04 67 56 28 23. End Jun–Aug 10am–7pm (out of season, check with tourist office). 🎫€10.90 (under 12s, €8.65). Water sports leisure park with giant slide, river with rubber rings, pool with wave machine (open from mid-Jun), Jacuzzi, sauna and aquagym.

ADDRESSES

🏠 STAY

🛏🛏🛏 **Golf Hotel** – 1920 Ave. du Golf. ℘04 67 29 72 00. www.golfhotel34.com. 🅿. 45 rooms. Rooms with balconies that overlook the golf course or Ponant lake.

🛏🛏🛏 **Hôtel de la Plage** – 52, allée du Levant (on the side of Le Grau-du-Roi, near the mouth of the Vidourle). ℘04 67 29 93 00. www.hp-lagrandemotte.fr. Mar–Oct and Dec. 39 rooms. As its name indicates, this hotel faces the beach. All the rooms, which are completely refurbished, are spacious and sunny and benefit from

- **Population:** 8 624.
- **Michelin Map:** 339: J-7.
- **Info:** Ave Jean-Bene and All de Pins, 34280 La Grande-Motte. ℘04 67 56 42 00. www.lagrandemotte.com.
- **Location:** 23km/14.3mi SE of Montpellier.
- **Don't Miss:** The huge fine sandy beach.

a loggia facing the Mediterranean. The restaurant (open in the evenings) has a veranda and specialises in seafood dishes.

🍽 EAT

🍴 **L'Amiral** – 117 av. du Casino. ℘04 67 56 65 53. www.restaurant-lamiral-lagrandemotte.fr. ♿. Near the casino, this brasserie has a baroque style. Friendly and comfortable. Specialises in seafood, with good grilled fish. Friendly, efficient staff.

🍴🍴 **L'Estrambord** – 8 quai Georges-Pompidou. ℘04 67 56 50 50. Open Tue–Sun 10am–1pm. La Grande Motte's oldest restaurant still has its original, rather kitsch decor, enlived by very colourful paintings by Nîmes artist **Michel Gilles** (1943–2008). Serves ice creams, fruit juice cocktails, tapas, salads and grilled dishes and provides a great view of the port.

🍴🍴🍴 **L'Alexandre** – Espl. Maurice-Justin ℘04 67 56 63 63. www.alexandre-restaurant.com. Open Apr–Sep daily (closed Sun eve except Jul and Aug), Oct–Mar Wed–Sun. Discover all the tastes of the Mediterranean in a stylish port setting. Good selection of local wines.

ACTIVITIES

This seaside resort offers a wide range of sport and leisure activities. Take diving lessons at **Blue Dolphin** (71 av. Robert Fages; ℘04 67 56 03 69; www.bluedolphin.fr), learn to sail at the **Centre nautique** (Espl. Jean-Baumel; ℘04 67 56 62 64), take a cruise or go on a fishing excursion with **Étrave croisière** (quai d'Honneur; ℘04 67 29 10 87), or take it easy at the spa of **Thalasso Méditerranée La Grande-Motte (centre Les Corallines)** – Le Point Zéro (on the side of Le Grau-du-Roi); ℘04 67 29 13 13; www.thalasso-grandemotte.com).

Saint-Guilhem-le-Désert★★

This pretty little village is built around an old abbey, in a delightful site at the mouth of untamed river gorges, where the Verdus flows into the Hérault. It owes much of the story of its origins to legend, related in a 12C "Chanson de geste".

> ▶ **Population:** 266.
> ⚲ **Michelin Map:** 339: G-6.
> ⧉ **Info:** ℘ 04 67 56 41 97. www.saintguilhem-valleeherault.fr.
> ◉ **Location:** 47km/29mi NW of Montpellier and 52km/32.5mi E of Lodève.

A BIT OF HISTORY

Childhood friends – Guilhem, the grandson of Charles Martel, was born in about 755. He was brought up with Pépin the Short's sons and was soon noted for his skilful handling of weapons, his intelligence and his piety. The young princes were very attached to him; his friendship with one of them, Charles, the future Charlemagne, was to last until his death.

Guilhem was one of Charlemagne's most valiant officers. Military victories against the Saracens at Nîmes, Orange and Narbonne earned him the title of Prince of Orange. He retuned home, but on finding that his wife had died while he had been away, he decided on a life of solitude and delegated the government of Orange to his son. During a visit to the Lodève region he discovered the Gellone valley and had a monastery built there. Despite being recalled by Charlemagne, Guilhem finally took leave of his king, who gave him the relic of the Cross. Guilhem returned to his monastery and a year later he retreated to his cell until he died in 812.

The abbey of St-Guilhem – After Guilhem's death, the monastery of Gellone became an important place of pilgrimage. By the 12C and 13C, the monastery was home to more than 100 monks and the village of Gellone was renamed St-Guilhem-le-Désert.

THE VILLAGE★

Winding streets cross St-Guilhem to join up in the place de la Liberté where stands the abbey church. You can see some fine **Medieval façades** with twin bays or triangular arches. To the west and north of the square, rue du Bout-du-Monde and rue du Font-du-Portal also have some fine houses.

Abbey church★

All that remains of the abbey founded in 804 by Guilhem is the abbey church, which was built in the 11C and deconsecrated during the Revolution, when the monastic buildings were demolished.

Apse★ – *To see this, walk round the church to the left.* From the alley lined with old houses, the rich decoration of the apse can really be appreciated. Flanked by two apsidal chapels, it features three windows and a series of tiny arched openings.

Interior – The 11C nave is austere in design. The oven-vaulted apse is decorated with seven great arches. On either side are niches in the walls, displaying on the left the reliquary of St Guilhem and on the right the fragment of the True Cross given by Charlemagne.

Cloisters – *Entrance through the door in the south arm of the transept.* Only the north and west galleries on the ground floor remain of the two-storey cloisters.

EXCURSION

👥 Grotte de Clamouse★★★

Temperature: 17°C. ⏰*Open daily: guided tours (1hr). Jul and Aug 10.30am–6.20pm; Jun and Sep 10.30am–5.20pm; Feb–May, Oct and Nov 10.30am–4.20pm.* ✆€10.20 (child 3–15, €5.70; child 15–18, €8.70). ℘ 04 67 57 71 05. www.clamouse.com.

The Clamouse dolomitic limestone cave in the Causse du Sud Larzac was explored in 1945 and opened to tourists in 1964. The Clamouse cave is hollowed out of the Causse du Sud Larzac, near where the gorge of the River Hérault opens onto the Aniane plain.

The cave takes its name from the resurgent spring that bubbles out below the road, cascading noisily into the Hérault after heavy rain, justifying its dialect name of Clamouse ("howler").

The guided tour goes through various natural galleries to the Gabriel Vila chamber, called the sand chamber for the layers of sand deposited by the Hérault river when it floods. The route follows the old river bed through fossilised galleries with chiselled, jagged rock forming a ghostly backdrop. Here are classic calcite stalagmites, stalactites, columns, discs and draperies coloured by mineral deposits; sparkling white **crystallisations** and rarer aragonite "**flowers**"; **crystalline dams** transforming subterranean lakes into jewellery caskets filled with "**cave pearls**" (pisolites). The Grande Finale is a huge translucent concretion known as the "Méduse" (jellyfish).

🚗 DRIVING TOUR

LA BUÈGES AND L'HÉRAULT
112km/70mi. Allow a full day.

▶ Leave St-Guilhem-le-Desert via the D4 then the D27 southeast to Aniane.

Aniane
Aniane is a quiet wine-growing town where St Benedict founded a prosperous abbey in the 8C. Stroll its narrow streets to see the church of St-Jean-Baptiste-des-Pénitents (housing temporary exhibitions), the 17C French Classical church of St-Sauveur and the 18C town hall.

▶ Take the D 42 southwest, heading towards Gignac.

Gignac
The 17C towering **Chapelle Notre-Dame-de-Grâce** has an unusual Italian-style west front. The N 109 crosses the Hérault over **Pont de Gignac**, considered the finest 18C bridge in France.

▶ Return to Aniane and follow D 32 to St-Martin-de-Londres.

Viols-le-Fort
Built on a hill, this fortified village (its ramparts are 14C) is a maze of winding streets lined with old houses.

Village préhistorique de Cambou – *Park in the Cambous car park and walk to the prehistoric village.* ⊙*Open Jul–Aug Tue–Sun 2–7pm; Apr–Jun, Sep–Oct Sat–Sun and public holidays 2–6pm.* ⊛€5.50. ☎04 67 86 34 37.

👥 Remains of 2800–2300 BCE stone dwellings with 2.5m thick drystone walls and corridors were discovered here in 1967. One has been reconstructed.

St-Martin-de-Londres★
This charming village retains traces of its 14C defensive wall and parish close fortified in the 12C. The 11C early Romanesque **church★** has an oven-vaulted semicircular east end.

▶ Follow D 986 N towards Ganges.

Ravin des Arcs★
Park the car by the bridge spanning the Lamalou.

🚶 *Take a path on the left leading to the Ravin des Arcs. It rises as far as a wall then veers to the left. From that point the path is clearly waymarked in red and white (GR 60). Allow 2h round-trip.*

The path goes through scrubland dotted with holm-oaks then descends to the Ravin des Arcs, a narrow canyon 200m deep in places.

Grotte des Demoiselles★★★
ⓒ*See GROTTE DES DEMOISELLES.*

▶ The road traverses a sheer-sided gorge gouged by the River Hérault.

Laroque
Discover the belfry topped by a campanile, the castle and the old silkworm farm overlooking the river.

Ganges

This small industrial town at the confluence of the Hérault and Rieutord rivers makes a good base for exploring.

▷ Leave Ganges SW along D 4.

St-Jean-de-Buèges

Its high golden-stone houses have fine rounded doors and small windows.

Gorges de la Buèges

2.5h circular walk leaving from St-Jean. From the main square, cross the village. The path beginning beneath the castle leads down the gorges to the 15C bridge over the Buèges, before Vareilles.

▷ Retrace your steps; immediately after the bridge, turn right onto the D 122.

The source of the Buèges

*Just before **Pégairolles-de-Buèges**, dominated by the ruins of a castle, take the Méjanel road, which crosses the Coudoulières. After a bridge, a road on the right leads to the source of the river, which refreshes the valley between the Séranne mountain and the Causse de la Selle.

▷ Return to Causse-de-la-Selle and continue on the D 4.

Gorges de l'Herault

The river gorge narrows to the Pont du Diable. The Hérault cuts through sheer rock faces adorned with scrubby trees and vines and olive trees cling to hillsides.
Pont du Diable – Neither the devil nor the Hérault seem to have disturbed this 11C bridge, built by Benedictine monks, which crosses the river and the centuries. There is a beach below.
You cross the Hérault on a modern bridge with views of the gorges and the aquaduct that irrigates the region's vineyards.
St-Jean-de-Fos – Benefiting from its location at the exit of the gorges, the village developed from the 11C, winding its houses 'en circulade' beneath the ramparts. It owed its prosperity to pottery from the 14C–mid-19C. A subsequent decline was halted thanks to tourism, with the return of **potters**, winemakers and olive growers.

▷ From here, you are just 4km/2.5mi from Aniane (to the SE). Continue NW for 2.5mi/4km to return to St-Guilhem.

Grotte des Demoiselles ★★★

At St-Bauzille-de-Putois, take the hairpin road (one-way) up to two terraces (parking facilities) near the entrance to the cave. From the terraces there is an attractive view of Séranne mountain and Hérault valley.

Michelin Map: 339: H-5.
Info: ℘04 67 73 70 02. www.demoiselles.fr.
Location: Saint Bauzille de Putois, 5km/3mi S of Ganges, 38km/24 N of Montpellier.

VISIT

Allow 1h20; temperature: 14°C.
Check website for a wide range of visiting times. ◷*Closed 25 Dec–early Feb.* *€10.80 (child €1.50–€8).*
Located at the heart of Languedoc, these limestone caves host a wide variety of unique mineral formations and are a perfect year-round place to visit. The cave was discovered in 1770, and according to locals, was home to fairies. Martel explored it in 1884, 1889 and 1897, revealing it to be an old swallow-hole opening onto the **Plateau de Thaurac**. The most striking thing about the cave is the number and size of the concretions thickly covering its walls. Narrow corridors lead to a platform overlook-

Grotte des Demoiselles

© Demid/iStockphoto.com

What maidens?

The story goes that one of the first explorers, a man named Jean, tumbled into the great hall of the caves. On his arrival, somewhat knocked about, he saw not '36 candles' but a thousand and one maidens, small fairies dancing all around him… The rest is legend.

ADDRESSES

☞ EAT

☞ **Restaurant des Grottes** – *237 Grand Rue, 34190 St-Bauzille-de-Putois. 2.5km/1.5 W of the Grotte des Demoiselles. ☏04 67 73 70 28. Lunchtimes only Oct–Jun.* ☷. Sit down on this terrace, in the shade of the ancient chestnut tree and hackberry. Inside, time seems to have stood still since 1951. Good value for money.

EVENT

Midnight mass is held in the caves every year on Christmas Eve. Occasional concerts are also held here.

---

ing an immense chamber, 120m long, 80m wide and 50m high. The awesome silence and hanging mist give the impression of being in a gigantic cathedral.

Walkways lead all round this spectacular chamber to the stalagmite resembling a Virgin and Child. Admire the fantastic set of 'organ pipes' adorning the north wall of the cave.

Lodève★

Surrounded by graceful hills, Lodève is close to the mountainous areas of Causse du Larzac and Monts de l'Orb as well as to the Hérault valley and Lac du Salagou. The look-out on the N 9 diversion from Millau offers a sweeping **view** of the site.

A BIT OF HISTORY

At Lodève, Nero minted the coins needed to pay the Roman legions. Bishops ruled the fortified town and diocese during the Middle Ages and in the 10C Bishop Fulcran was noted for giving food to the poor, caring for the sick and defending the town against brigands. In the 12C, one of his successors founded one of the first mills to make paper from rags. The cloth trade developed in the

- ▶ **Population:** 7 733.
- ⊙ **Michelin Map:** 339: E-6.
- ▯ **Info:** 7 Pl. de la République, 34700 Lodève. ☏04 67 88 86 44. www.tourisme-lodevois-larzac.com.
- ◐ **Location:** 60km/37.5mi S of Millau and 58km/36.25mi NW of Montpellier via A75.
- ⊙ **Don't Miss:** Musée Fleury's contemporary art.
- ♟♙ **Kids:** Grotte de Labeil.

13C, and in the 18C Lodève had a monopoly on producing soldiers' uniforms.

The Gothic **Pont de Montifort** spans the Soulondres river and has a very pronounced arch. It was built in the 14C to provide access to the Tines Quarter, where the workshops of the leather workers were located.

SIGHTS
Ancienne Cathédrale St-Fulcran★
Place de l'Hotel de Ville.
The original cathedral is now the crypt. The church was rebuilt in the 10C by St Fulcran, and again in the 13C and 14C. The buttressing and the two watchtowers framing the façade show its defensive function. Eighty-four bishops of Lodève are buried in the first chapel. The third chapel leading to the cloisters (14C–17C) has latticed vaulting characteristic of Late Gothic.

Musée Fleury★
Sq. Georges-Auric. Closed for renovation until 2018; check the website for current status. ☎04 67 88 86 10; www.museedelodeve.fr.
The following original text will be updated once the museum re-opens.
Housed in the former mansion of the cardinal of Fleury (17C–18C), it contains both a fine **contemporary art collection** and numerous historical records of the Lodève area. On the ground floor, sculptures by **Paul Dardé** (1888–1963), a native of Lodève, are displayed beside some 40 pictures representative of the history of painting over the first half of the 20C. **Courbet**, **Braque**, Camoin, **Dufy**, **Caillebotte**, Vlaminck, **Léger**, Soutine and **Poliakoff** are among the artists exhibited. The first floor is reserved for temporary monographic exhibitions, which, every year, attract art-lovers from all over the region.
The second part of the museum is devoted to the town and its region: prehistoric remains and a presentation of local history, from Roman times to the present day. A fine collection of plant **fossils** and impressions left by reptiles, amphibians and large dinosaurs is visible on the second floor. The visit finishes with the **disc-shaped steles** of Usclas-du-Bosc (12C–15C).

National Carpet Factory
Impasse des Liciers, ave. du Gén.-de-Gaulle (in the south, Montpellier road).
Guided tours: ask at the tourist office for details. ☎04 67 88 86 44.
This is the only annex of the Gobelins factory in Paris. Here copies of old patterns are woven for the Mobilier national (national furniture collection). You can visit the weaving workshop.

EXCURSIONS
Prieuré St-Michel-de-Grandmont★
8km/5mi E. Leave on N 9 towards Millau and turn right onto D 153 towards Privat. Open daily 10am–7pm.
Guided tours daily May–Sep 10.30am–7pm; Oct–Apr daily except Sun 10am–6pm. €6.50. ☎04 67 44 09 31. www.prieure-grandmont.fr.
This priory was founded in the 12C by monks of the Grandmont order and is one of the remaining examples of the 150 Grandmont monasteries. The grounds contain fascinating dolmens.

Cirque et Grotte de Labeil
12km/8mi N. Leave on N 9 towards Millau. Turn off W at the junction for Lauroux and take D 151 to Labeil. Open daily Jul and Aug 10am–6pm; mid-Mar–Oct. Guided tours (1h) at 11am, 2pm, 3pm and 4pm (plus 5pm on Sun and public holidays). €9.50 (child 3–12, €5.50). ☎04 67 96 49 47. www.grotte-de-labeil.com.
The **Cirque de Labeil** comprises the southern foothills of Larzac plateau. The cave entrance offers a good view of Lauroux valley. The main features of this damp cave once used for producing Roquefort cheese, are stalactites, stalagmites and frozen falls.

Avène-les-Bains
30km/18.5mi W of Lodève.
Nestling in the a meander of the Orb, this circular-plan village has retained its authenticity. Its narrow streets with their magnificent porches are overlooked by the church of St-Martin, built in 1835 on the former site of a castle, of which little

now remains. It was here, in 1736, that the source of Ste-Odile was discovered. Its waters full of trace elements are used to heal skin diseases and the spa has given its name to a brand of dermatological products.

🚗 DRIVING TOURS

LE LODÈVOIS ROUGE
65km/40mi. Allow half a day.

▷ Leave Lodève heading S on the A 75. Turn off at exit 54 after 5km/3mi.

The banks of **Lake Salagou★** have been developed for fishing, camping, water sports and beaches. Drive around the lake on the D148 for some superb views. Continue on the D148, through Octon and Salasc, then turn left onto the D8 to reach the **Cirque de Mourèze★★** (*☝see CIRQUE DE MOURÈZE*). Take the D8F1 for 500m, turn left onto the D908, then right onto the D15. At **Cabrières**, turn left following the signs to the **Mine de cuivre de Pioch-Farrus** (*♿guided tours Apr–Oct; ☎06 14 91 46 02*), to discover the different methods of extraction used here from 3 000 BCE to the 19C.
Rejoin the D908 and head towards Clermont-l'Hérault. At **Villeneuvette** there is a former royal clothmaking factory, founded in the 17C.
Take the D909 to **Clermont-l'Herault**, where the narrow streets of the old town climb a hill crowned with the ruins of a 12C castle, from which there is a lovely view over the town and surrounding area. The **church of St-Paul★** provides an interesting example of the Gothic architecture of the Hérault.

▷ Return to Lodève via the D609/A75.

DU PIÉMONT AU CIRQUE DE NAVACELLES
45km/28mi, ☝see regional map (p92). Allow half a day.
Leave Lodève via the D151, then follow the D25 to **Soubès**, an old fortified village dominated by its 12C tower.

To explore on foot, follow the chemin des Capitelles (*from place du Terral, 1.5km/0.9mi*) or the sentier botanique de Font d'Amas (*from place du Terral, 2km/1mi loop on the GR71*). Drive 4.3km/2.7mi on the D25, then bear right onto the D25E1 to reach the **Cirque du Bout du Monde★**, an exceptional landscape at the heart of which is a fortified farm.

▷ Rejoin the D25 1km/0.6mi S.

St-Etienne-de-Gourgas, once on an important trade route, today houses the remains of a 14C castle. 1.2km/0.75mi south on the D25E is the 12C **Chappelle St-Michel d'Aubaygues**.

▷ Follow the D25 for 5km/3mi towards St-Pierre-de-la-Fage and bear right onto the D25E.

Parlatges, on the edge of a superb pine forest, is a hamlet with a chapel that was once a pilgrimage site for those seeking healing of speech impediments. Follow the D25 for 5km/3mi to **St-Pierre-de-la-Fage** whose church is a fine example of local architecture.

▷ Continue for 3km/2mi on the D25 then the D9.

At **La Vacquerie-et-Saint-Martin** note the 17C 'Railly' house and Brésilliers windmill.
To reach the **Cirque de Navacelles★★★** (*☝see CIRQUE DE NAVACELLES*), continue on the D9 to La Trivalle, then turn left onto the D130. En route, you will cross a vast plateau rich in megalithic monuments. Information panels nearby will tell you more about these dolmens of Ferrussac and menhirs of Coulet. As you approach **St-Maurice-Navacelles**, enjoy the view of the gorges de la Vis, which stretches as far as the Cevennes. The belvedere of **La Baume-Auriol** offers a splendid view of the cirque de Navacelles as well as an information point and a shop selling local produce.

Cirque de
Mourèze★★

The Cirque de Mourèze hides between the Orb and Hérault valleys, on the south side of Liausson mountain. This vast jumble of dolomitic rocks criss-crossed by footpaths forms a magnificent natural amphitheatre covering over 340ha.

VISIT

The picturesque **village** of Mourèze, with its narrow streets, little houses with outside staircases and its red-marble fountain, lies at the foot of a sheer rock face, at the top of which is a castle. **The cirque★★** is surrounded by enormous boulders, and a number of waymarked footpaths lead through fresh, green nooks and crannies between rocks eroded into strange shapes. From the viewpoint, enjoy a panorama of the dolomitic cirque.

♣♣ Parc des Courtinals

◷ *Open Jul–Aug daily 9.30am–7.30pm; rst of year 10am–6pm.* ♒€4 (child 5–14, €2). ♪04 67 96 08 42. *www.courtinals.com.*

Courtinals park is an ancient Gallic settlement, inhabited from the Middle Neo-lithic Age until about 450 BCE. It is almost surrounded by a high barrier of rocks; at their foot there are natural cavities which once contained flints and pottery.

⚅ **Michelin Map:** 339: F-7.
▮ **Info:** Office du tourisme le Clermontais, Place Jean Jaures, 34800 Clermont-l'Hérault. ♪04 67 96 23 86. www.clermontais-tourisme.fr.
▶ **Location:** 31km/19.3 S of Lodève via the A 75, and 53km/33.1 W of Montpellier via the N 109.
☻ **Don't Miss:** The village streets and view over Cour-tinals park from the cirque.
♣♣ **Kids:** Reconstructed cabin in the Parc des Courtinals.

Dolomitic rocks, Cirque de Mourèze

© Diane White Rosier/iStockphoto.com

Bassin de Thau

The Bassin de Thau covers a massive area of 8 000ha, the largest lagoon on the Languedoc coast. It is separated from the sea by the isthmus of Onglous (Sète beach). To the east is a busy industrial complex; to the south, the offshore sand bar is a beach; whereas on the north shore several villages, such as Bouzigues and Mèze, specialise in oyster and mussel farming.

⚅ **Michelin Map:** 339: F-7.
▮ **Info:** Chateau de Girard, 34140 Mèze. ♪04 67 43 93 08.
▶ **Location:** 30km/18.6mi SW of Montpellier via the D 613 and 31km/19.2mi SE of Bésiers via the D 612.
☻ **Don't miss:** The view from the old abbey of St-Félix-de-Montceau, the mosaics in the villa Loupian, sampling oysters in Bouzigues.

🚗 DRIVING TOUR

74km/46mi, see regional map (p92). Allow about 4h.

▶ Leave Sète (☝ see SÈTE), driving along the eastern shore of the bassin de Thau and head for Balaruc-les-Bains.

Balaruc-les-Bains

Built on flat land on the shores of the Bassin de Thau the third most popular spa resort in France, has many amenities to offer.

Balaruc-le-Vieux

On a hill overlooking the lake, the village has retained its characteristic *'en circulade'* plan. Some houses still have their distinctive grand arched doorways.

▶ Take the the D 2, then the D 613 until you reach Gigean. From there, follow the signs to St-Félix-de-Montceau.

Old abbey of St-Félix-de Montceau

Marvellously situated on a hill with a vast **view★** over the plain and bassin de Thau, the remains of this former Benedictine abbey, built between the 11C and 13C, show the co-existence of a Romanesque chapel and a Gothic church, whose seven-sided apse was lit by three twin bays. A group of volunteers have reconstructed a small Medieval monastic garden, laying out a vegetable garden, scented garden, square physic garden and orchard-cemetery.

Bouzigues

The principal place shellfish farming and fishing, this peaceful village presents its main occupation in its **musée de l'Étang de Thau** (on the dock of the fishing port). Here you can follow the evolution of the fishing and shellfish breeding (a shellfish mas of the 1950s, aquariums filled with species, video). *⏰Open Jul–Aug 10am–12.30pm, 2.30–7pm; Mar–Jun, Sep–Oct 10am–noon, 2–6pm; Nov–Feb 10am–noon, 2–5pm.*

€5 (child 7–12, €3.50). ☎04 67 78 33 57. www.bouzigues.fr/musee.

▶ Return to the D 613 and turn right.

Loupian

Situated on a former Roman estate, this wine-producing village still conserves some remains of its Medieval ramparts (14C fortified gate) as well as its castle, built in the 16C. The **church of St-Hippolyte** (12C, Romanesque) is the former bailey chapel, fortified and inserted into the ramparts in the 14C. In the apse, the stones of the arch, laid out in chevrons, are retained by a faux rib vault.
The church of Ste-Cécile (14C Gothic) is quite majestic with its fine yellow stone bond. Its prominent buttresses are a characteristic feature of Gothic art of the Languedoc, as is the single large nave arched over rib vaults that ends in an elegant polygonal apse.

▶ Join the D 158 E4.

Musée de site gallo-romain Villa-Loupian★

⏰Open Jul and Aug daily 1–7pm; guided tour at 11am; Sept–Jun daily except Tue 1.30–6pm Sat–Sun additional guided tour at 11am. ⏰Closed 3 wks in Jan. €5 (under-12 yrs, €3.50). ☎04 67 18 68 18. www.ccnbt.fr.
This was a vast agricultural estate (villa) from 50 BCE until the 6C. Visit the museum to learn about the daily life of its occupants, their resources (cereals, wine, livestock, oyster-farming) through the interpretations of archeological excavations here. You will discover the luxurious residence of the owners, the function of the different rooms and above all, remarkable polychrome **mosaics★** from the early 5C. Note the trompe-l'œil in the apse of the reception room. The tour is vivid and informative.

▶ Rejoin the D 613 and head to Mèze.

Vineyards in front of the Étang de Thau at Mèze, Mont St-Clair in the background

© Jean-Pierre Degas/hemis.fr

Mèze

An important shellfish centre, this town attracts many tourists to its port and its narrow streets. 15C Gothic church.

▷ Take the D 613 heading towards Montagnac. After 4km/2.5mi, turn right onto a road that crosses the vineyards.

Musée-parc des Dinosaures

🕐 *Open Jul and Aug daily 10am–7pm; Feb–Jun and Sep–Oct daily 2–6pm; Noc–Dec daily 2–5pm; Jan 2–5pm.* 🕐 *Closed 1 and 6–31 Jan, 24–25 and 31 Dec.* €9.80 (child 3–4, €5.40; child 5–11, €8.50). ℘04 67 43 02 80. www.musee-parc-dinosaures.com.

👫 A large deposit of dinosaurs eggs and bones dating back 65 million years were discovered on this site. You can see the skeleton of a 24m long, 12m brachio-saurus and life-size reconstructions of creatures such as the deinonychus and the terrifying tyrannosaurus (6m high and 15m long). A few nests with eggs have been left in situ. For children, there is a mini-excavation site where the fossils of strange animals are hidden.

Musée-parc Préhistoire Origine Évolution

🕐 *As above.* ℘04 67 43 02 80.

👫 Under the shade of pine trees, the visit leads you to discover a series of life-size reconstructions, from the earliest hominids to Homo sapiens, all displayed in a natural setting. Made by anatomist sculptors, the figures are impressive. With its sound environment, 120 sq m floor area and 300 sq m of animal skins, the Paleolithic hut is the highlight of the visit, taking visitors several thousand years back in time.

▷ Return to the D 613 heading toward Mèze then turn right onto the D 51.

Marseillan

Founded in around 6C BCE by Massaliot sailors, Marseillan is a fishing village, but also the birthplace of **Noilly-Prat,** whose warehouses you can visit *(near the port; guided tours May–Sep 10–11am, 2.30–6pm, Mar–Apr, Oct–Nov 10–11am, 2.30–4.30pm;* 🕐 *closed Dec–Feb;* ℘04 67 77 20 15; www.noillyprat. com).* The development of *dry vermouth* (invented in 1813 by Joseph Noilly using herbs, the secret of which is jealously guarded) and natural sweet wines is explained here. One of the characteristic phases of production is the open-air ageing of the mixture of picpoul and clairette grape varieties in 600-litre barrels.

At **Marseillan-Plage,** 6km/3.7mi further on, are miles of sandy beaches.

▷ Return to Sète following the coast.

Sète★

Sète was built on the slopes and at the foot of Mont St-Clair, a limestone outcrop 175m high, on the edge of the Thau lagoon. Once an island, it is linked to the mainland by two narrow sand spits. The new town, east and northeast of Mont St-Clair, runs right up to the sea itself and is divided up by several canals. Sète is the scene of the famous *joutes nautiques*, jousting tournaments, particularly well attended on the day of St-Louis in August.

A BIT OF HISTORY

Birthplace of poets – **Paul Valéry** (1871–1945) wrote to Sète town council, which had congratulated him on his election to the Académie Française, "It seems to me that all my work reflects my roots." In *Charmes*, published in 1922, the poet celebrated the marine cemetery where he was to be buried in July 1945. At the foot of this peaceful setting, the sea can be seen spreading away to the horizon like a vast flat roof.

Another famous native of Sète, the singer-songwriter **Georges Brassens** (1921–81) sang about his place of birth in his "Supplique pour être enterré à la plage de Sète" ("Request to be buried on Sète beach").

The town developed in the 17C when Colbert decided to have a port constructed, making Sète the outlet on the Mediterranean for the Canal des Deux-

▶ **Population:** 44 830.
⚭ **Michelin Map:** 339: H-8.
▯ **Info:** 60 Grand'Rue Mario-Roustan, 34200 Sète. ✆04 67 74 71 71. www.tourisme-sete.com.
◖ **Location:** 36km/22.5mi SW of Montpellier. The main strolling and shopping streets are found on the east side of the 'island'; beaches to the west.
P **Parking:** You'll find lots near the canal fringing Sète on the east.
⚘ **Don't Miss:** The trip up Mont St-Clair, for memorable views of the surrounding area.
◕ **Timing:** Stroll about the town before heading up to Mont St-Clair. Head for the beach or take a cruise on the lagoon.

Mers. The foundation stone was laid in 1666 by **Pierre-Paul Riquet**, architect of the Canal du Midi. To stimulate expansion, in 1673 Louis XIV gave permission for "everyone to build houses, sell and produce any goods with exemption from tax duty." Before very long the town had become a thriving commercial and industrial centre.

Nevertheless, it was not until the 19C that Sète embarked upon its golden age. The harbour and the maritime

Vieux port

TOURS

Tours of Sète and its port:

A number of 'Promenades Touristiques' are available through the tourist office, from the familiar Train Touristique to mini-bus tours and even using Tuk-Tuk vehicles.

Sète Croisières, Quai de la Marine (*Ticket office: 3, quai Aspirant Herber.* ℘*04 67 46 00 46. www.sete-croisieres. com*) offer boat tours around the port, across the Etang de Thau and along the Grand Canal.

---

canal were developed, while the railway companies linked Sète to the PLM network and to the Midi network. By about 1840 Sète was the fifth most important French port. After the conquest of Algeria, Sète found its main outlets in North Africa.

Today, the three main areas of its activity are the handling of bulk goods, passenger and container traffic to North and West Africa, South America, the French Caribbean and Australia, and storage.

MONT ST-CLAIR★

From promenade Maréchal-Leclerc, carry on along avenue du Tennis and take the right fork on to montée des Pierres Blanches. A trip to Mont St-Clair will leave visitors with one of the best of their memories of Sète. This hill rises 175m above sea level.

Parc Panoramique des Pierres Blanches

This park is well covered by waymarked footpaths and makes a pleasant place for a stroll exploring the area. From the viewing table, there is a wide **view**★ over the west end of the Thau lagoon, the lower Hérault plains, the open sea, the Corniche Promenade and beach.

Chapelle Notre-Dame-de-la-Salette

Mont St-Clair is named after a saint who was venerated here as early as the Middle Ages. In the 17C, a hermitage still existed near the small fort of 'La Montmorencette' built by the Duke of Montmorency. When the duke rebelled, the king had the fort dismantled and a former blockhouse transformed into an expiatory chapel. In 1864, it was dedicated to Notre-Dame-de-la-Salette.

Viewpoints

From the esplanade opposite the chapel, where a large cross is lit up every night, there is a splendid **view**★ of Sète, the east end of the Thau lagoon, the Garrigues, the Cévennes, St-Loup peak, the Gardiole mountain and the coast itself, with its necklace of lagoons and small towns. A viewing tower on the presbytery terrace provides a marvellous **panorama**★★. On a clear day, the view extends over the lagoons and the sea as far as the Pyrenees, to the southwest, and the Alpilles, to the east.

▷ Carry on along chemin de St-Clair, which drops steeply downhill.

On the right lies the cliff-top **cemetery**★ celebrated by Paul Valéry and the museum dedicated to him (see below).

▷ Return along Grande-Rue-Haute.

Musée Paul-Valéry

🕐*Open Apr–mid-Nov daily 9.30am–7pm; mid-Nov–Mar Tue–Sun 10am–6pm.* ☞*During exhibition periods €9, at other times €5.50 (10–18 yrs €4.50/€3; under 10 yrs no charge).* ℘*04 67 46 20 98. www.museepaulvalery-sete.fr.*

Facing the sea and close to the **cimetière marin** where Paul Valéry and Jean Vilar are buried, the museum contains many documents on the history of Sète.

SEA FRONT

Vieux port★

The old harbour is the most interesting part of Sète port. **Quai de la Marine** is lined with fish and seafood restaurants, with terraces overlooking the Sète canal. It is the departure point for various **boat** trips (🔊 *see opposite*) around the coast-line and harbour. A little farther down, fishermen and bystanders are summoned by the '**criée électronique**' (electronic auction) when the boats come in at around 3.30pm. It is worth taking a stroll round the other basins and the canals as well.

Promenade de la Corniche – This busy road, leading to the Plage de la Corniche, situated 2km/1mi from the centre of town, cuts around the foot of Mont St-Clair with its slopes covered by villas.

Plage de la Corniche – This 12km/7.5mi-long sandy beach stretches across a conservation area.

👥 Musée international des Arts modestes (MIAM)

23 quai Maréchal de Lattre de Tassigny, along the Grand Canal. 🕐*Open Apr–Sep daily 9.30am–7pm; Oct–Mar Tue–Sun 10am–noon, 2–6pm.* 🕐*Closed 1 Jan, 1 May, 1 Nov, 25 Dec.* 💶*€5.50 (child 10–18, €2.50; under 10 yrs no charge). No charge 1st Sun of the month.* 📞*04 99 04 76 44. www.miam.org.* This entertaining museum is devoted to daily life objects and publicity dating back to the mid-20C.

Centre régional d'art contemporain

26 quai Aspirant-Héber (on the bank opposite the pont de la Savonnerie). 🕐*Open Mon, Wed–Fri 12.30–7pm, Sat–Sun 3–8pm.* 💶*No charge.* 📞*04 67 74 94 37. http://crac.languedocroussillon.fr.* A surprising conversion, this former fish-freezing centre hosts temporary exhibitions. This vast multi-purpose structure has become a place of exchange and teaching around the arts scene.

ADDITIONAL SIGHT
Espace Brassens

67 boulevard Camille-Blanc. 🕐*Open Jun–Sep daily 10am–6pm; Oct–May Tue–Sun 10am–noon, 2–6pm.* ♿📞*04 99 04 76 26. www.espace-brassens.fr.* This museum traces the life and work of the singer-songwriter from Sète, Georges Brassens, in an interesting and

original exhibition combining audio-visual input with visual displays. Brassens is buried in the Le Py cemetery, opposite the museum.

🚗 DRIVING TOUR

AU PAYS DU MUSCAT
28km/17.4mi, see regional map (p93). Allow about 2h (plus time for a swim)

▷ Leave Sète via the D 612, in the direction of Montpellier.

Frontignan-Plage
This small seaside resort has a marina with 600 places. Take the D60, a narrow coastal road between sea and lake.

Les Aresquiers
On this pebble beach enjoyed by naturists, little restaurants serving *bouillabaiise* sometimes hold concerts in the evening (rock and reggae).

▷ Via Vic-la-Gardiole and Mireval, rejoin the D 612 heading towards Frontignan.

Massif de la Gardiole
This massif, to the north, is criss-crossed with signposted paths used by mountain-biking, walking and horseriding enthusiasts.

Frontignan
This small industrial town has given its name to a well-known muscat, whose vineyards spread over nearly 800ha on the edge of the étang d'Ingril.

Eglise St-Paul – In the 14C, this 12C church was rebuilt in the southern Gothic style. Note its door, the frieze of fish and boats and the nave ceiling.

Musée d'histoire locale – Housed in the former chapelle des Pénitents blancs are prehistoric and subaquatic archeological collections and Napoleonic memorabilia.

▷ Return to Sète via the D612.

ADDRESSES

🛏 STAY

🛏 **Camping Les Tamaris** – *140 ave. d'Ingril, 34110 Frontignan, NE on the D 60, direction Les Aresquiers. ℘04 11 32 90 00. www.sandaya.fr/tam. Open Apr–Sep.* 👍. *Reservation recommended. 250 sites.* You can make the most of the beach at this seaside campsite. You'll have only a few metres to walk to dive into the waves! Lovely pool, bar, restaurant and shop.

🛏 **Hôtel Les Tritons** – *Bd Joliot-Curie. ℘09 67 19 43 88. www.lestritons-sete.com.* 👍🅿. *50 rooms.* An ochre-coloured building sited on the corniche. Some of the spacious and colourful rooms face onto the sea, but the others are quieter.

🛏 **Grand Hôtel** – *17 quai du Mar.-de-Lattre-de-Tassigny. ℘04 67 74 71 77. www.legrandhotelsete.com. Closed 18 Dec–2 Jan. 43 rooms.* This fine 1882 edifice on the quays is a local institution. Visitors will be charmed by the vast patio topped by a Belle Époque-style glass roof, cosy bedrooms, period furniture and chic bar.

🛏 **Hôtellerie de Balajan** – *41 rte de Montpellier, 34110 Vic-la-Gardiole. ℘04 67 48 13 99. www.hotel-balajan. com. Closed 24 Dec–4 Jan, Feb and Sun eve (Nov–Mar). 18 rooms.* Some rooms in this welcoming hotel enjoy a view of vineyards and the massif de la Gardiole. The warm atmosphere of the restaurant owes much to the flowers on the tables.

🛏 **Hôtel Port Marine** – *30, Promenade J-B Marty. ℘04 67 74 92 34. http://en.hotel-port-marine.com. 55 rooms. Restaurant* 🍽. A modern hotel located near the marina and pier. The functional rooms are reminiscent of a boat's cabin.

🍴 EAT

🍴 **Good to know** – Part of Sète's population is descended from Italian fishermen, who influenced the local cuisine. You will discover these specialities in the seaside restaurants, often run by fishermen.

🍽 **Chez François** – *8 quai Gal-Durand. ℘04 67 74 59 69. Open Apr–Dec Wed–Mon, Jan–Mar Wed–Mon lunchtimes and Fri and Sat evenings.* Rather wedged in between the outdoor tables of neighbouring restaurants, François provides a benchmark.

🍽 **Les Binocles** – *25 r. Pierre-Semard. ℘04 99 04 98 35. Closed Mon and Tue.* The cuisine is welcoming, like the restaurant's owner. It's here that you'll find the real fisherman's *salad à la sétoise.*

🍽 **Les Demoiselles Dupuy** – *4 quai Maximin-Licciardi. ℘04 67 74 03 46.* Oysters and mussels from the étang de Thau are accompanied by an assortment of fish and shellfish bought at the morning auction. Charming warm welcome.

🍽 **The Marcel** – *5 R. Lazare-Carnot. ℘04 67 74 20 89. Open Mon–Fri 10am–3pm and 6–10pm, Sat 10am–midnight.* Much appreciated by locals, this restaurant in a quiet street in the old part of Sète is a pleasant place to meet. The eclectic decor happily blends Art Deco with velvet armchairs, bistro furniture, etc. It is also used as an art gallery by locals.

DRINK

Ô Dit-Vin – *12 quai Rhin-et-Danube. ℘04 67 46 94 35. http://oditvinsete.e-monsite.com. Open 6pm–1am.* A trendy place makes use of red velvet and intimate corners. Excellent wines accompanied by good tapas.

SHOPPING

Les Halles – *6am–1pm.* This big, lively market lacks charm, but you will find many oyster farmers.

Marché aux Puces – *Pl. de la République. Sun 6am–1pm.* Flea market.

Paradiso – *11 quai de la Résistance. ℘04 67 74 26 48. Open 8.30am–7pm. Closed Mon.* The octopus and tomato sauce pasty, created in 1937, is a local gastronomic speciality.

Biscuiterie Pouget – *47 quai de Bosc. ℘04 67 74 72 38. 9am–noon, plus Wed, Thu and Sat 3–7pm.* This cookie maker has been making 'navettes cettoises' – hard biscuits flavoured with aniseed, lemon, vanilla or orange flower – by hand since 1913. You can also find them at the market.

Cave coopérative du Muscat de Frontignan – *14 Ave. Muscat, 34110 Frontignan. ℘04 67 48 93 20. www. frontignanmuscat.fr.* **Shop**: *open daily Jul and Aug 9.30am–7.30pm; Apr–Jun and Sep 9.30am–12.30pm, 2.30–7pm; Oct–Mar 9.30am–12.30pm, 2–6.30pm;* **guided tours** *(20min): contact for details.*

LE GARD: *The Coast to the Cévennes*

Gard is one of the original 83 departments formed during the French Revolution in 1790. It was created from the ancient province of Languedoc. The area was settled by the Romans in classical times, and was crossed by the strategically important Via Dominitia, constructed over 100 years BCE. The area has traditionally been a prosperous centre of commerce, particularly textiles, and it was one of the main beneficiaries of the development of railways – it is still an important railway junction. The department, named after the river Gard, is a place of many contrasts and great variety, with the blessing of fine landscapes: the Cévennes, the Camargue, the Cévenol foothills, the Cèze and Rhone valleys, all contributing to making Gard a leading tourist destination. The department has a significant wealth of history, culture and tradition: the Pont du Gard, the arena in Nîmes and the Aigues Mortes salt marshes.

History of Denim

The name of Nîmes may not instantly be connected with the manufacture of jeans – bullfighting, yes, but probably not jeans. But denim – de Nîmes – a cotton twill textile was first manufactured in the city's mills, and exported to America in the 19C primarily to clothe slaves. The word comes from the name of a sturdy fabric called serge, originally made in Nîmes by the André family. Originally called serge de Nîmes, the name was soon shortened to denim, and was coloured blue with indigo dye.

Highlights

1 Step back in time in the amphitheatre in **Nîmes** (p124)

2 Visit the **Tour Magne** to get a fine view of Nîmes city (p127)

3 Touring the ramparts in **Aigues-Mortes** (p133)

4 **Pont du Gard**, a wonder of ancient engineering (p137)

5 Wandering the old town of **Uzès** (p139)

Bullfighting in Nîmes

The great passion in Nîmes, although not for everyone, is bullfighting, or ferias as they are known locally. They have been organised in Nîmes since the second half of 19C. The wildest and most renowned is the *Feria de Pentecôte*, which has been run for many years for five days over the Whitsun weekend. Two other ferias take place: one at carnival time in February, when the roof of the Arènes is pulled over for protection from the weather; the other in the third week of September at grape-harvest time, the *Feria des Vendanges*.

Arène, Nîmes

© Günter Lenz/imageBROKER/age fotostock

LE GARD: *The Coast to the Cévennes*

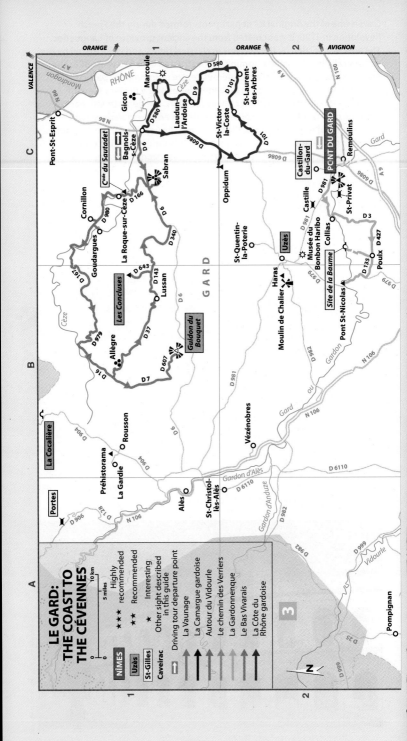

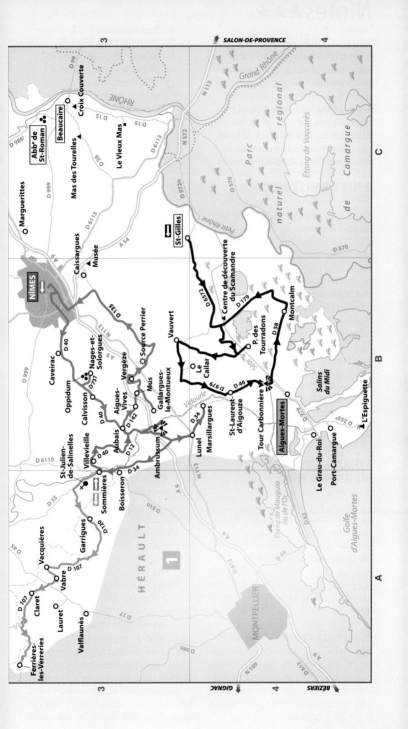

SALON-DE-PROVENCE

Grand Rhône

Parc

Étang de Vaccarès

naturel

de Camargue

Croix Couverte

Beaucaire

Abbᵉ de St-Roman

Mas des Tourelles

Le Vieux Mas

RHÔNE

Marguerittes

Caissargues

Musée

NÎMES

Petit Rhône

St-Gilles

Centre de découverte du Scamandre

Source Perrier

Vauvert

P. des Tourradons

Montcalm

Caveirac

Oppidum

Nages-et-Solorgues

Vergèze

Mus

Le Caillar

Sète

Calvisson

Aigues-Vives

Gallargues-le-Montueux

Vidourle

St-Laurent-d'Aigouze

Salins du Midi

Villevieille

Aubais

Ambrussum

Lunel

Marsillargues

Tour Carbonnière

Aigues-Mortes

L'Espiguette

St-Julien-de-Salinelles

Sommières

Boisseron

HÉRAULT

Le Grau-du-Roi

Port-Camargue

Golfe d'Aigues-Mortes

Vacquières

Garrigues

Étang de Mauguio ou de l'Or

Vabre

MONTPELLIER

Lauret

Claret

Valflaunès

Ferrières-les-Verreries

GIGNAC

BÉZIERS

123

Nîmes★★★

For some, a little bit of Rome in France; for others the similarities are with Madrid and Spain. Whatever your viewpoint, Nîmes has a distinct character of its own lying between the limestone hills of the Garrigue and the plain of Costière to the south. This is a place of busy boulevards shaded by plane trees, renowned for its Roman influences.

A BIT OF HISTORY

The Roman soldiers who came to command Nîmes were veterans of the campaign in Egypt and accustomed to a life of plenty. The building of fortifications here was sanctioned by Emperor Augustus, and the town, located on the strategic Via Domitia, soon began to prosper and build splendid buildings: the Maison Carrée, an amphitheatre capable of seating 24 000 people, a circus, and baths fed by the imposing Pont du Gard (&see Pont du Gard). In the 2C, Nîmes found favour with the Emperors Hadrian and Antoninus Pius (whose wife's family came from Nîmes), and, as a result it continued to flourish.

WALKING TOUR

ROMAN AND MEDIEVAL NÎMES

&See map II opposite.

This walk enables you to discover the principal monuments and buildings of the Roman city, and the area known as 'Écusson', a maze of narrow alleyways in the medieval quarter. Enjoy the shaded boulevards flanked by beautiful mansions, and, if time allows, stop at a street café for a coffee or refreshing Perrier menthe.

Esplanade Charles-de-Gaulle

This vast square, bordered on one side by the columns of the Palais de Justice and street cafés, opens on the other side onto the avenue Feuchères with its fine aristocratic façades: at its centre stands the Pradier fountain, built in 1848.

▶ **Population:** 154 013.
  Michelin Map: 339: L-5.
⊞ **Info:** 6 r. Auguste. ℘04 66 58 38 00. www.ot-nimes.fr.
◐ **Location:** Nîmes is 32km/20mi NW of Arles.
◔ **Timing:** Allow a whole day to wander around the city; but avoid August, which can be far too hot.
℗ **Parking:** Entering the city along the Canal de la Fontaine and boulevard Victor-Hugo, drive around the amphitheatre to get to an underground car park beneath the Esplanade.
◉ **Don't Miss:** A visit to the amphitheatre.

◐ Walk along the boulevard de la Libération into the place des Arènes.

In the place des Arènes, note the statue of El Nimeño, a celebrated Nîmois bullfighter, who tragically met his match in September 1989.

Arènes ★★★

41 r. Fresque. ◔Open daily Jan–Feb, Nov–Dec 9.30am–5pm; Mar and Oct 9am–6pm; Apr–May and Sep 9am–6.30pm; Jun 9am–7pm; Jul–Aug 9am–8pm. ◔Closed during events. ⊛€10 includes audioguide. ℘04 66 21 82 56. www.arenes-nimes.com.
◉ You can also download the audio guide commentary onto a smartphone or mp3 player through the website.
The magnificent amphitheatre is a splendid illustration of the perfection in design achieved by Roman engineers. This amazing structure was built in the reign of Augustus, 80 years before the corresponding structure at Arles. The scale and concept is hugely impressive demonstrating perfect symmetry. In Roman times the monument could hold 24 000 spectators over 34 rows of terraces divided into four separate areas, and the design allowed an unrestricted view of the whole arena. The stone used

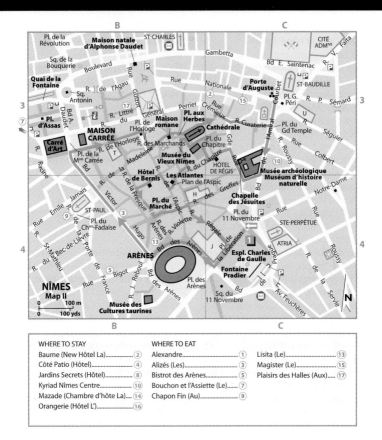

comes from quarries at Roquemaillère and Baruthel, near Nîmes. There are certainly bigger Roman amphitheatres, but this is the best preserved of them all.

▶ Go up the boulevard Victor-Hugo to locate the Maison Carrée.

Maison Carrée

© Romain Cintract/hemis.fr

Maison Carrée★★★

🕐Open daily Jan–Feb, Nov–Dec 10am–1pm, 2–4.30pm; Mar and Oct 10am–6pm (closed 1–2pm in Oct); Apr–May and Sep 10am–6.30pm; Jun 10am–7pm; Jul–Aug 9.30am–8pm. 🕐Closed during events. Visit with audioguide €6. ℘04 66 21 82 56. www.arenes-nimes.com. 🎧 You can also download the audio guide commentary onto a smartphone or mp3 player through the website.

Inspired by the temples of Apollo and Mars Ultor in Rome, the Maison Carrée charms visitors with its harmonious proportions. Set in the centre of an elegant paved square separated from the Carré d'Art by the boulevard Victor-Hugo, it is the only ancient temple to be completely preserved. It is by far the best preserved and purest of all Roman temples, and was built during the time of Augustus (1C BCE). The Maison Carrée owes its exceptional state of preservation to the fact that it was constantly in use from the 11C, and has served as a consular house, stables, apartments and even as a church. After the French Revolution, it became the headquarters for the first prefecture of the Gard region.

Carré d'Art★

16 pl. de la Maison Carrée. 🕐Open daily except Mon 10am–6pm. ☞€5. ℘04 66 76 35 70. www.carreartmusee.com.

Established in 1993 in a beautiful building designed by Norman Foster, the collection covers contemporary art from the period between 1960 to the present day, with nearly 400 works on display.

▷ Walk along the rue de l'Horloge to the place de l'Horloge, and turn right and then left into the Rue de la Madeleine.

Rue de la Madeleine is the principal business street of the city. The **Maison Romane** is the oldest house in Nîmes. The street opens out into the place aux Herbes opposite the **Cathédrale**. Turn into a narrow street to the right of the cathedral, and continue to reach Porte d'Auguste, where the Via Domitia enters the city. Retrace your steps to pass the **Chapelle des Jésuites**, today used for staging concerts. The same building houses the **Musée d'histoire naturelle** which comprises displays of artefacts from Asia, Africa and Oceania.

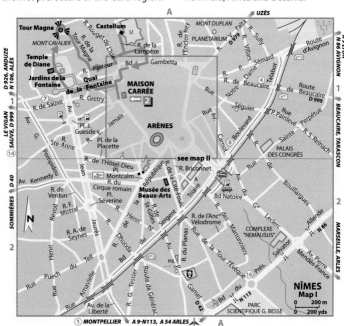

▷ Walk along the rue du Chapitre.

Musée du Vieux Nîmes

pl aux Herbes. 🕐*Open daily except Mon
10am–6pm.* 🕐*Closed 1 Jan, 1 May,
1 Nov, 25 Dec.* ☎*04 66 76 73 70.*
Housed in the former Bishop's Palace
(17C), near the cathedral, this museum
was founded in 1920, and presents a collection of artefacts that evoke the traditional life of Nîmes and its inhabitants.

▷ Walk along the rue des Marchands,
and then by a covered passageway.
Turn right into rue de la Trésorie, and
then right into the plan de l'Aspic.
Continue until a left turn onto the rue
de Bernis.

The **Rue de Bernis** is especially blessed
with properties that have elegant
façades dating from 15C and the 17C.
In the **Hotel de Ville**, you will find four
crocodiles suspended from the ceiling!

▷ Take the rue de l'Hotel-de-Ville, and
then turn right along the rue Régale.

RETOUR AUX SOURCES

♿*See the map I opposite.*

▷ From the Maison Carrée go up
boulevard Alphonse-Daudet as far as
place d'Assas: this vast expanse, was
redesigned by Raysse. To the right, it
leads to the Quai de la Fontaine, an
aristocratic thoroughfare lined with
beautiful mansions.

Jardins de la Fontaine★★

ave Jean-Jaurès.
In Roman times this was the site of a
spring, a theatre, a temple and baths.
Today, these shaded gardens exemplify
the subtle use of water in the landscapes
of Languedoc. They were laid out in the
characteristic manner of the 18C, with
pools leading into a channel, balustraded walls and porticos.
To the left of the fountain stands the
Temple of Diane, ruined in 1577 at
the time of the Wars of Religion. It
dates from the 2C, and rather than
being a temple may well have been a

brothel. Nevertheless, it is worth a visit
before heading for the beautiful green
surroundings of Mont Cavalier, from
which emerges the emblem of the city,
Tour Magne.

Tour Magne★

The Tour Magne, the Great Tower, is the
only remnant of the ancient Augustan
fortifications. It stands at the highest
point of the city, Mont Cavalier. Not surprisingly, it is a focal point for all means
of communication.
Pre-dating the Roman occupation, the
three-storey tower was originally a drystone oval tower, with a maximum height
of 18m, and already part of the city ramparts. A structure both prestigious and
strategic, it represented sanctuary and
protected the central oppidum. By doubling its height and incorporating it into
the town walls, Augustus demonstrated
the new power of the colony of Nîmes
over the 'City'.
When the town's population abandoned
the higher ground, the Tour Magne continued to play a military role, and was
used to defend against the English during the Hundred Years' War.
From a **viewing platform★★** there is a
splendid panorama across the pink roofs
of Nîmes, set against the backdrop of
Mont Ventoux and the Alpilles.

▷ Descend towards the canal de la
Fontaine by the rue de la tour-Magne,
then turn left into rue Pasteur.

Castellum

This circular basin was the culmination
of the aqueduct. Rediscovered in 1844, it
is one of the few to have survived.

▷ Return to the Maison Carrée by
place Antonin and rue Auguste.

ADDITIONAL SIGHTS
Musée de Beaux Arts★

R. Cité-Foulc. 🕐*Open daily except Mon
10am–6pm.* 🕐*Closed 1 Jan, 1 May,
1 Nov and 25 Dec.* ☎*04 66 28 18 32.*
www.ot-nimes.fr.
Refurbished in 1986 around a Roman
mosaic discovered in 1883, the museum

houses works from the 15C to 19C from the Italian, Dutch and French schools. Among the 3,600 works is a fine collection of Italian art from the 16C–17C, and a beautiful ensemble of French art from the 19C.

Musée des Cultures taurines

6 r. Alexandre-Ducros. ⓁOpen *May–Oct daily except Mon 10am-6pm.* ⓁClosed 1 Jan, 1 May. ⓢ€5.50 (free 1st Sun of month). ☎04 66 36 83 77.
Close to the amphitheatre, this museum takes an ethnographic look at the topic of bullfighting.
More than 35 000 objects include documents, posters, costumes and equipment all presented in an airy space.
This is the first museum in France dedicated to the forms of bullfighting.

EXCURSIONS
Aire de Caissargues

Between the interchange for Nîmes-Centre and that for Garons, on the A 54 (direction Arles).
At the end of a tree-lined walkway stands the rebuilt colonnades of the old neo-Classical theatre of Nîmes which formerly stood on the sight of the Carré d'Art. The colonnades are the only remaining vestige of the theatre, destroyed by fire in 1952, and sparked a controversy between supporters of modernity and those with nostalgia for the old building.

Marguerittes

10km/6mi to the E, by the D 6086.
🚶 The trail of the Capitelles is a pleasant route through a group of restored drystone buildings.

🚗 DRIVING TOUR

LA VAUNAGE

44 km/27.5mi. 🕐See region map. 1hr.

▷ Leave Nîmes on the route de Sommières: from the station, take the viaduct in the direction of Montpellier, then turn right into the rue Dhuoda

(direction Alès); cross avenue J-Jaurès and then follow the av. G.-Pompidou, taking a left into the av. Kennedy (D 40).

Caveirac

The town hall of this village occupies an imposing 17C château, with a porch large enough to accommodate the D 103.

▷ Follow the D 40, then take the D 737 towards Nages-and-Solorgues. At the entrance to the village, the first road on the left leads to the Roman fountain.

Nages-et-Solorgues

Located on the first floor of the town hall, the **Musée archéologique** houses various artefacts that evoke the daily life of the inhabitants.

▷ Return to the D 40, and turn left.

Calvisson

At the heart of the Vaunage, this peaceful wine-producing village is renowned for its Easter parade. The **Maison du Boutis** is dedicated to quilting (☎04 66 01 63 75; www.la-maison-du-boutis.fr).

▷ In the village, take the D 107 towards Fontanès; at the exit from the village, turn left onto the route du Roc de Gachone. Rejoin the D 142 and drive to Aigues-Vives. After passing under the autoroute, reach Mus, which, like its neighbour **Gallargues-le-Montueux**, is worth a quick visit.

Vergèze

The **Tonnellerie animée** presents a display of the tools and work methods of coopers (☜guided visits Mon–Fri 9–11.30am, 3–5.30pm, Sat 9–11.30am; ☎04 66 35 45 92).

Source Perrier

The underground spring of the water holding therapeutic properties (☎04 66 87 61 01; www.perrier.com).

▷ Return to Nîmes by the D 135, then the D 613.

ADDRESSES

STAY

Be sure to book well ahead if you intend to stay during the ferias.

Hôtel Côté Patio – *31 r. de Beaucaire. 04 66 67 60 17. www.hotel-cote-patio.com. 17 rooms.* Close to old Nîmes and the Arènes.

L'Orangerie – *755 r. Tour-de-l'Évêque. 04 66 84 50 57. www.orangerie.fr. 37 rooms.* Charming Provençal-style rooms; regional cooking.

Kyriad Nîmes Centre – *10 r. Roussy. 04 66 76 16 20. www.hotel-kyriad-nimes.com. 28 rooms.* Close to Écusson, an agreeable hotel in the centre.

Chambre d'hôte La Mazade – *Dans le village, 30730 St-Mamert-du-Gard. 04 66 81 17 56. www.bbfrance.com/couston.html. 3 rooms.* Colourful and fun, a true family home; al fresco dinner on the terrace.

Hotel Marquis de la Baume – *21 r. Nationale. 04 66 76 28 42. www.new-hotel.com. 34 rooms.* Former mansion, now a delightful hotel.

Jardins Secrets – *3 r. Gaston-Maruéjols. 04 66 84 82 64. www.jardins secrets.net. 12 rooms.* A rare and secret moment in the heart of the city.

EAT

Le Chapon Fin – *3 rue Château-Fadaise. 04 66 67 34 73. www.chaponfin-restaurant-nimes.com. Closed Sun.* Pleasant, air-conditioned restaurant behind the church; local produce.

Bistrot des Arènes – *11 r. Bigot 04 66 21 40 18. Closed evenings on Mon-Wed.* Efficient bistro, close to the amphitheatre.

Les Alizés – *26 bd Victor-Hugo. 04 66 67 08 17. www.restaurant-les-alizes.com.* There's a buzzing atmosphere at this friendly restaurant that serves various local specialities and has a pretty tree-shaded street terrace.

Aux Plaisirs des Halles – *4 r. Littré. 04 66 36 01 02. www.auxplaisirs deshalles.com. Closed Sun, Mon.* Fine dining room; generous servings, and regional wine list.

Le Bouchon et l'Assiette – *5 bis r. de Sauve. 04 66 62 02 93. Closed Tue, Wed.* Decorated with paintings and antiques; seasonal cuisine.

Le Magister – *5 r. Nationale. 04 66 76 11 00.* Paintings brighten weathered-wooden walls; regional cuisine.

Le Lisita – *2 bd des Arènes. 04 66 67 29 15. www.lelisita.com. Closed Sun–Mon.* Opposite the amphitheatre; a beautiful dining room and garden, and arguably the best place in the city centre.

Alexandre – *2 r. Xavier-Tronc (rte de l'aéroport), 30128 Garons (9km/5.5mi SW on the road to Arles, D 42). 04 66 70 08 09. www.michelkayser.com. Closed Sun eve and Mon, Tue (Sep–Jun) Sun–Mon (Jul–Aug).* Two-starred restaurant under the watchful eye of chef/patron Michel Kayser makes this a favourite place with gourmets and gourmands alike.

EVENTS

Bullfights – *Box office: 4 rue de la Violette. 0891 701 401. www.arenesdenimes.com.* There are two main events: the most famous, the *Feria de Pentecôte* is linked to various events in the city. The other is at the time of the grape harvest, and takes place over the third weekend in September (Thu–Sun).

Apart from the ferias, the arena hosts numerous performances and concerts.

Festival de flamenco – *10 days in January. www.theatredenimes.com.*

SHOPPING

Markets

Monday: Flower market: Stade des Costières; flea market: bd J-Jaurès Sud.

Saturday: Food market: pl. du Griffe-St-Césaire.

Tuesday: Farmer's market: Chemin-Bas-d'Avignon.

Friday: Farmer's market: bd J-Jaurès Sud.

Sunday: Flea market: parking de la gare.

3rd Saturday of month: book fair: espl. Charles-de-Gaulle.

Saint-Gilles★

At the gateway to the Carmargue gardoise, this important agricultural city produces fruit and wine, but is especially renowned for its ancient abbey-church, the façade of which is one of the most beautiful examples of Romanesque Provençal statuary, and listed by UNESCO as of World Heritage importance.

- ▶ **Population:** 13,234.
- **Michelin Map:** 339: L-6.
- **Info:** 1 place Frédéric Mistral. 04 66 87 33 75. www.saint-gilles.fr.
- **Location:** 19km/12mi S of Nîmes, and 11km/7mi W of Arles.
- **Timing:** Divide your time between morning and lunch in the town, and an afternoon visit to the edges of the Camargue.
- **Parking:** Use the signed car parks (coming in from Nîmes), and then get about on foot.
- **Don't Miss:** The Camargue gardoise.

A BIT OF HISTORY

Saint-Gilles is a Romanesque city, an important place of pilgrimage on the route of Saint Jacques de Compostela, and, in the other direction, to St Peter's in Rome.

The plateau on which Saint-Gilles is founded, has been occupied since antiquity, and probably since prehistoric times. Numerous archaeological finds attest to its occupation during the Roman era, while from the 5C to 9C the area attracted the attentions of the Goths and Saracens, neither of whom brought peace and settlement to the region. That was left to the hermit, Saint Gilles, who, at the end of 7C, founded a Benedictine monastery here, and a church under the dedication of St Peter. In the 9C, the abbey made history, enjoying a reputation for the miracles allegedly performed by its founder. In the following centuries, pilgrims flocked to the village, as it then was, and started a boom that saw the village rise to become the capital of Mediterranean France.

But the pilgrims were not the only reason for the city's prosperity: the presence of four ports enabled the expansion of trade with the rest of Europe, while the protection of the Counts of Toulouse refined the development and culture of the city. But in the early 13C, Saint-Gilles became implicated in the crusade against the Cathars when the Papal legate, Pierre de Castelnau was assassinated.

The tranquility of the city was also disturbed by the Wars of Religion, while the Reformation made its impact on the city in the middle of the 15C. A century of struggle followed, which proved to be very damaging to to architectural heritage of the city. Ruined by wars and the Revolution, Saint-Gilles gradually declined, but today sees growing prosperity thanks to the pulling power of its abbey-church.

THE TOWN
Église St-Gilles

Open Jul–Aug 9am-12.30pm, 3–7pm; Apr–Jun and Sep–Oct 9am–12.30pm, 2–6pm; rest of year 8.30am–noon, 1.30–5.30pm (Sat 10am–noon, 2–4pm; 5pm Nov and Mar). Closed Sun and public holidays. 4€. 04 66 87 33 75. www.ot-saint-gilles.fr.

It is difficult today to get an impression of the abbey at its peak. To get an idea, you need to mentally reconstruct the choir of the old abbey beyhond the present choir, with, to the right of the church, a cloister with its centre surrounded by a chapter room, a refectory, kitchens and a pantry in the basement. The abbey, like its occupants, was the victim of the Wars of Religion. In 1562, Protestants, not content to throw the incumbents into the crypt, set fire to the monastery. The roof of the church collapsed. In 1622, they demolished the great tower.

Façade★★ – This is one of the finest Romanesque sculptings in the south of France, executed in the 12C by several sculptors (there are five distinct styles indentifiable) who were inspired by Antiquity as evidenced by their love of high-relief.

Old choir – Outside the present church, the foundations of the pillars and walls show perfectly the plan of the old choir and its ambulatory and five radiating chapels.

Crypte★ – Here, around the tomb of Saint Gilles, one of the most important pilgrimages took place: over just three days a crowd of more than 50 000 visited the sanctuary.

Musée de la Maison Romane

℘04 66 87 40 42. Call for hours and charges.

Dating from the end of the 12C, the house belonged to the Roman family of Guy Foulques, a soldier, lawyer and Pope from 1265 to 1268 under the name of Clement IV. The house was restored in the 19C, and is today classed as an historical monument.

🚗 DRIVING TOUR

LA CAMARGUE GARDOISE

73km/45.5mi. See map p123. Allow up to 2 hrs to allow for stops.

Between Costières and the Petit Rhône, Saint-Gilles and Aigues-Mortes, the Camargue gardoise, a land of marshes and reed beds, is a landscape more severe than the Rhône delta.

▷ Leave Saint-Gilles to the SW on the D 6572 (direction Montpellier).

The road crosses the Costières wine region, where there are numerous cellars inviting you to taste and buy.

▷ After 12km/7.5mi, turn left onto the D 779, and on reaching the town turn right on the D 38, then left onto the D 104 as far as the canal du Rhône at Sète.

Pont des Tourradons

From this bridge, lost amid the marshlands, there is an interesting **view★** over the typical landscapes of the Petite Camargue.

▷ Go back to the D 104, then right (Mas Roubaud) onto the D 352.

Vauvert

This large wine village, now part of the suburbs of Nîmes, has kept its old centre, with its halls converted into exhibition spaces. The village was formerly known as Posquières before taking the name of a place of pilgrimage near the Vallis Viridis.

▷ Take the D 6572 towards Aimargues.

Le Cailar

At the entrance to the village is the tomb of a famous Camargue bull 'Le Sanglier'. The **Cercle d'art contemporain** (*9 bd Baroncelli; ℘04 66 88 94 61*), presents displays of contemporary works on the theme of the bull.

Saint-Laurent-d'Aigouze

Another wine-producing village, where the vestry is used as a bull pen during the Camargue races.

▷ Take the D 46 to join the D 58, passing Tour Carbonnière (see AIGUES-MORTES, Exursion). After 9.5km/6mi, turn left onto the D 179.

In **Montcalm**, there are the remains of a large house where the Marquis de Montcalm stayed before leaving for Canada. The road runs along the canal as far as mas des Iscles, where there is parking for the **Centre du Scamandre** (*℘04 66 73 52 05; www.camarguegardoise. com*) dedicated to the protection and management of wetlands.

▷ The D 779 runs alongside the canal des Capettes. After crossing the canal du Rhône at Sète, go back to Saint-Gilles on the D 6572.

Aigues-Mortes★★

Few places evoke the spirit of the Middle Ages as vividly as Aigues-Mortes, sheltering behind its sturdy ramparts amid a landscape of marshland, lakes and salt pans. Today, while tourism plays a major part in the town's economic well-being, wine, asparagus and sea salt are also important staple products. In the surrounding countryside, bulls and the magnificent Camargue horses are bred.

A BIT OF HISTORY

The foundation of the city is attributed to Gaius Marius, around 102 BCE, but the first document mentioning a place called 'Ayga Mortas' (Dead waters) dates from the 10C. Certainly, the salt marshes have attracted fishermen and salt workers since ancient times, including the Benedictine monks of the abbaye de Psalmodi.

Louis IX of France (Saint Louis) rebuilt the port in the 13C as France's only Mediterranean port at that time. As a result, it was the embarkation point of the Seventh and Eighth Crusades (1248 and 1270).

The city walls were built in two phases: first during the reign of Philippe III (the Bold) and then in the time of Philippe IV (the Fair). The Constance Tower, completed in 1248, is all that remains of the castle built in Louis IX's time, although it was designed to be impregnable with six-metre-thick walls. Like other towers in the town, from 1686 onwards, the tower was used as a prison for the Huguenots who refused to convert to Roman Catholicism.

From 1575 to 1622, Aigues-Mortes was one of eight safe havens granted to the Protestants. But the revocation of the Edict of Nantes in 1685 caused severe repression of Protestantism, which was especially marked in Languedoc and the Cévennes in the early 18C giving rise to the 'Camisard War'.

▶ **Population:** 7,115.
Michelin Map: 339: K-7.
Info: Pl. St-Louis, 30220 Aigues-Mortes. ℘04 66 53 73 00. www.ot-aiguesmortes.fr
Location: 41km/25mi S of Nîmes, and 47km/29mi W of Arles.
Kids: Take a ride on the Train touristique, or on a barge.
Timing: 1hr just to stroll around; another 1hr if you visit the ramparts.
Parking: Plenty of parking areas outside the walls.
Don't miss: The Constance tower.

THE CENTRE

The town was built in the bastide format of a regular, squared pattern of streets around a central square. Protected by its walls, the town seems to have escaped the ravages of time, and is today a genial place of cafés, craft shops, department stores and art galleries.

▶ Enter by the porte de la Gardette, and turn left into the rue de la République.

Pass the Baroque **Chapel of the Pénitents Blancs** (*Pl. Saint-Louis*), and keep forward into the rue Baudin, then turn right into rue Rouget de-l'Isle before going left into rue Paul-Bert to locate the **Chapel of Pénitents Gris**, also Baroque.

▶ Retrace your steps and go into rue Pasteur and on to the place Saint-Louis.

The **Église N.-D.-des-Sablons** (*Grand-Rue-Jean-Jaurès*) is Gothic in style and built during the time of Saint Louis, and has suffered numerous misfortunes, even being used as a salt warehouse. Pretty **Place Saint-Louis** is sheltered by plane trees, and is the animated heart of

*Ramparts by the canal,
Tour de Constance in the background*

© Gérard Labriet/Photononstop

the city. In one corner, a covered walk-way shelters a number of **art galleries**.

THE FORTIFICATIONS
Tour de Constance★★
Access by place Anatole-France.
&. ◷*Open May–Aug 10am–7pm; rest of the year 10am–1pm, 2–5.30pm.*
◷*Closed 1 Jan, 1 May, 1 and 11 Nov, 25 Dec.* ⊙*7€.* ℘*04 66 53 61 55. www.monuments-nationaux.fr.*
The tower (1241–49) rests on wooden piles, and was intended to be a symbol of Royal power as much as a purely military installation. The layout of its elaborate internal defences (staircases, winding passageways, portcullises) is typical of the Capetian dynasty, and its fine walls of Beaucaire limestone stand out boldly against the surrounding sandy landscape. Its turret originally served as a lighthouse, the sea, at that time, being only 3km/2mi away.

Ramparts★★
A tour of the ramparts allows you to get an aerial perspective on the town, and the fine view over the marina and the salt pans of Aigues-Mortes.
The ramparts were never seen by Saint Louis. They were begun in 1272 on the orders of Philippe le Hardi, and their completion led to Aigues-Mortes becoming the Capetian kingdom's prin-cipal Mediterranean harbour.
At the end of the 13C, Philippe le Bel improved the port and completed the

defences, adding 20 massive towers to protect the gateways and providing per-fect positions from which to fire along the walls themselves in times of need. Imaginative visitors might visualise themselves as the soldiers charged with defending the city; all that's missing is the moat, now filled in.

EXCURSIONS
Tour Carbonnière
3km/2mi N towards St-Laurent-d'Aigouze.
Built on a dyke among ponds and reedbeds, and on the only land access to Aigues-Mortes, this 14C tower was built to defend against unwanted visi-tors. In 1409, a toll gate was stationed here. From the tower there is an exten-sive view over the lagoons.

Salins du Midi
3km/2mi S along rte du Grau-du-Roi.
◣ *Guided tours on the Petit Train Mar–Oct 10.30am, 11am, 2.30pm, 3pm and 4pm.* ⊙*8.50€ (children 4–13, 6€).* ℘*04 66 73 40 24. www.salins.fr.*
Salt has always been a precious com-modity. Roman legionnaries were paid partly in salt, hence the French word 'salary'. This tour will help you under-stand about the extraction of salt and its conversion to the seasoning found on the dinner table. ⊙*Anyone likely to be affected by insect bites would do well to avoid this visit, or prepare for the avid attention of mosquitoes.*

Le Grau-du-Roi

Built in 1570 on both sides of a breach ('grau') in the coastal defences, between the mouth of the Rhone and the Vidourle, this resort has 18km/11.25mi of beaches. Formerly, it was a humble port used by fishermen living in simple huts. But the railway has put it within striking distances of many cities.

▶ **Population:** 7,892.
◉ **Michelin Map:** 339: J-7.
▤ **Info:** 30 r. Michel-Rédarès, 30240 Le Grau-du-Roi. ✆04 66 51 67 70. ville-legrauduroi.fr.
◉ **Location:** 6.5km/4mi SW of Aigues-Mortes.
◔ **Timing:** It's not a question of time; you're here to relax.
▲▲ **Kids:** Seaquarium.

VISIT

This is a typical grid pattern of streets lined with mainly one-storey houses, that comes alive in the summer seasons, invaded by sun worshippers that bring a host of seasonal craft and tourist shops to life.

The centre, such as it is, is the canal and its swing bridge spanning the 'grau', the docks and the old lantern tower, a symbol of the village. Fishing boats are moored along the quayside, which is lined with restaurants serving mainly sea food of the freshest variety.

From the end of the pier there is a fine view (especially so at sunset) overlooking the Gulf of Aigues-Mortes with, to the left, the tip of the Espiguette (and Port Camargue), and to the right, La Grande-Motte, which seems to over-hang the Pic Saint-Loup, the mountain of Gardiole and Mount St. Clair overlooking Sète.

The beach is the main attraction, with the Boucanet beach extending from the residential and commercial centres. The north beach has a pedestrian promenade, while to the south, the Espiguette beach is the wildest part of the coast.

Seaquarium★

Av. du Palais-de-la-Mer. ♿◔*Open Jul–Aug 9.30am–11.30pm; Apr–Jun and Sep 10am–7.30pm; rest of the year 10am–6.30pm.* ▦*11.50€ (children under 15, 8.50€). ✆04 66 51 57 57. www.seaquarium.fr.*

A fabulous place for children, with both Mediterranean and tropical fish.

Sommières

Built at the foot of a castle with a beautiful square tower, the town has retained much of its medieval character, as evidenced by its fortified gates, its streets crossed by archways, and squares decorated with arcades. Flowing beneath the bridge the Vidourle adds to the charm of the town, once famous for the manufacture of leather and wool. Sommières was annexed into the French kingdom by King Louis X in 1248, following the crusade against the Cathars, and became a Protestant stronghold.

▶ **Population:** 4,505.
◉ **Michelin Map:** 339: J-6.
▤ **Info:** 5 quai Frédéric-Gaussorgues. ✆04 66 80 99 30. www.ot-sommieres.fr
◉ **Location:** 19km/12mi NE of Montpellier, and 46km/29mi S of Alès.
◔ **Timing:** At least 1 hour.
◉ **Don't Miss:** The Roman bridge, and the markets.

THE TOWN
Pont romain

The original bridge was destroyed and thrown into the Vidourle by Tiberius at the start of 1C. It was restored in the 18C, and lies in the lower part of the town.

Marché-Bas
Access by the Reilhe stairway.
The place is surrounded by arcaded houses, and was bordered on the south by the Roman bridge.

Marché-Haut
This market place links with the Marché-Bas by a curious vaulted alley. Also known as the place Jean-Jaurès, this is the former corn market of Sommières. In one corner, a covered passageway leaves the la rue de la Taillade, a former Roman road giving access to the bridge.

Ancien château
Access by car via the rue du Château-Fort or on foot by the Régordanes steps.
The castle provides a beautiful view over the red-tiled roofs of Sommières to the scrubland beyond, and the Cévennes.

🚗 DRIVING TOURS

1 AUTOUR DU VIDOURLE
See region map. Allow 2h.

▷ Leave Sommières by the D 610 and turn right onto the D 40.

Villevielle – This village dominates Sommières with its **chateau** (*℘04 66 80 01 62; www.chateau-de-villevieille.fr*). Its drystone houses seem to be keeping watch over the valley of the Vidourle.

▷ Rejoin the D 40 then turn right onto the D 105, towards Junas.

The village of **Aubais** is where the artist **Claude Viallat** practised his trade. Artists welcome visitors to their studios.

▷ Follow the road to Villetelle on the D 142 and D 12, heading for Ambrussum.

Ambrussum is an archaeological site that has been occupied since the Neolithic era.

▷ Take the D 110E and D 34 for Lunel.

Renowned for its muscat, the small town of **Lunel** is proud of its bullfighting traditions. The 18C building in the Place des Martyrs de la Resistance is home to the **library** endowed by Louis Medard (1768–1841): a collection of nearly 5,000 works dating from the 12C.

▷ Follow the D 34 to Marsillargues.

Marsillargues, birthplace of **Gaston Defferre** (1910–1986), and surrounded by boulevards lined with plane trees. The **castle** was built for Guillaume de Nogaret in 1305, profoundly altered in 16C and destroyed by fire in 1936.

▷ Go back to Sommières on the D 34.

2 LE CHEMIN DES VERRIERS★
See region map. Allow 3h, as far as Ferrières-les-Verreries.

Plague and famine in the Middle Ages on the plateau of Orthus allowed scrubland to invade, and this in turn became a viable fuel resource in the production of glass, giving rise to many workshops in the area, hence the 'Glassmakers Way'.

▷ Leave Sommières on the D 35 (direction Quissac), turn left before entering St-Julien-de-Salinelles with its 11C Romanesque chapel. Go back on the D 35, then after 2.5km/1.5mi turn left onto a narrow lane for Aspères, and in the village take the direction Vacquières. After 11.5km/7mi turn right to the D 109.

Vacquières, with its medieval bridge, is the first of the glass-making villages you come to. At **Claret** on the D 107 towards Sauteyrargues there's a fascinating glass museum (**Halle de Verre**, *av. du Nouveau-Monde; ℘04 67 59 06 39; www.cc-orthus.fr*).

▷ Leave Claret and take the D 107.

At the entrance to the tiny village **Ferrières-les-Verreries**, turn right and descend in zigzags towards the restored Couloubrine glassmaker's **workshop**.

Beaucaire★

The ancient name 'Ugernum' was gradually supplanted by Castrum Bellicadri, which in Occitan became bèu caire, the 'caire' signifying stone. Once famous across Europe for its fairs which for centuries drew in crowds of visitors, this citadel of the counts of Toulouse has today become a quiet and peaceful place.

THE CENTRE
Hôtel de ville
This fine Classical building, built in the late 17C, is not lacking in nobility. The courtyard has a double-columned portico that is worth a look.

Église N.-D.-des-Pommiers
Built with a curved façade, in the Jesuit style that was in vogue in the 18C. Check out the Classical façade of the **hôtel des Clausonnettes** (18C). At No. 23, the **hôtel des Margailliers**, has a beautiful sculpted façade. A little further, the **hôtel de Roys de St-Michel** (18C), is quite attractive. The street leads to the place de la République, where the archways are home to several artisans.

Château★
Montée du Château. Guided *visits on request, bookable at the tourist office.* Closed public holidays. €4.50. 04 66 59 71 34.
Built in the 11C on the site of a Roman castrum, and rebuilt in the 13C following

- **Population:** 15,099.
- **Michelin Map:** 339: M-6.
- **Info:** 24 cours Gambetta, 30301 Beaucaire. 04 66 59 26 57. www.ot-beaucaire.fr.
- **Location:** 14km/9mi N of Arles, and 24km/15mi S of Avignon.
- **Parking:** Along both banks of the canal.
- **Timing:** At least 1hr, but more on market days (Thu, Sun).
- **Don't miss:** The castle and old Beaucaire.

a siege in 1216 by Raimond VII, the castle was eventually dismantled by Richelieu. The castle stood on top of a hill, protected by an enclosure with a curious polygonal tower.

Musée Auguste-Jacquet
Open daily except Tue Apr–Oct 10am –noon, 2–5.15pm. Closed public *holidays, 25 Dec–2 Jan.* €5. 04 66 59 90 07. www.beaucaire.fr.
Housed in the castle, the museum has a fine archaeological section that brings together pieces from prehistoric times to the Gallo-Roman period.It also includes an interesting evocation of old Beaucaire, and documents relating to the ancient fairs.

Château de Beaucaire

© gkuna/Bigstockphoto.com

Pont du Gard★★★

A wonder of the ancient world, the grandiose 1C structure that spans the Gardon Valley is so stunning that it alone justifies a visit.

SIGHTS

The Pont du Gard was built shortly before the Christian era to allow the aqueduct of Nîmes (which is almost 50km/31mi long) to cross the Gard river. The Roman architects and hydraulic engineers who designed this bridge, which stands almost 50m high and is on three levels – the longest measuring 275m – created a technical as well as an artistic masterpiece.

Built of colossal blocks weighing as much as 8 tonnes, that have been hoisted more than 40m, the bridge spans the Gardon valley. With its three tiers of arched arcades and the aqueduct right at the very top, the vast structure's visual impact is spectacular, and time should be taken to view it from as many different angles as possible, for only then will you fully appreciate the ingenuity and skill that brought it into being.

Point d'accueil

Open daily at 9am–8pm (Jul–Aug); 7pm (May–Jun, Sep–Oct); 6pm (Mar–Apr); 5pm (Nov–Feb). €15 (up to 5 persons); year pass €25.

This vast semi-underground building is located between the parking areas on the left bank and the bridge. It contains a museum, 'Ludo', an educational experience for children, cinema, temporary exhibitions and a library.

Museum – A full range of museum displays has been used to help visitors explore and understand the monument: models, full scale replicas, maps, multi-screen images, video and sound archives and all with a common denominator: water.

Ludo – is a fun educational experience for 5–12 year olds. Children are able to explore a number of adventure and games activities at their own pace. The approach is based on learning through enjoyment.

Cinema – A 25 minute film 'Le Vaisseau du Gardon' (Vessel on the Gardon) by Robert Pansard-Besson celebrates the Pont du Gard through a blend of documentary and fiction.

Media library – This resource centre is an area for information, reading and consultation with an equal accent on both the pleasure of learning and also deepening understanding.

Mémoires de garrigue

1.5km (Allow 1–2h).

This trail winds through the typical Mediterranean garrigue landscape. The land surrounding the site was for long neglected, but has been brought back into cultivation with olive trees, vines, mulberry trees, fruits and cereals. This pleasant amble allows you to better

Michelin Map: 339: M-5.

Info: 0 820 903 330. www.pontdugard.fr.

Location: From Remoulins use either the D 19, or the D 981.

Timing: Allow 1hr to a whole day. Come when the bridge is illuminated.

Kids: Spend time in the Ludo.

Pont du Gard

© Matthieu Colin/hemis.fr

understand the natural environment of the *garrigue*, as well as the traditional agrarian activities of the region.

EXCURSIONS
Jardins du château de St-Privat
Park on the right bank of the pont du Gard. ○*Open May–Jun and mid Aug-mid Nov, Sat, Sun and public holidays, 3pm (Meeting point café des Terrasses).* ⊛€7.

On a most romantic site, the castle, simultaneously a palace and a fortress, was built on the site of a Templar commandery, which itself succeeded a Gallo-Roman villa. Among the famed guests at the castle where Catherine de Medici accompanied by the future Henri III and IV, Louis XIII and Cardinal Richelieu.

Castillon-du-Gard★
3km/2mi to the N on the D 981, then left on the D 238.
Medieval perched village of red stone houses; it is the only village from which you can actually see the Pont du Gard.

Remoulins
4.5km/3mi E along the D 981.
This large town has retained some vestige of its ramparts, along with a Romanesque church with bell tower.

Château de Castille
5km/3mi to NW along the D 981.
After a Romanesque chapel and a mausoleum surrounded by columns, a yew-lined drive leads to the castle (⊙*not open to the public*), rebuilt in the 18C by Joseph de Froment of Argilliers, Baron de Castille, who professed an immoderate love for the columns.

🚗 DRIVING TOUR

LA GARDONNENQUE
43km/27mi . ⌚See region map. Allow between 1h and 4h.

It is around the Pont du Gard that the Gardon valley is at its most spectacular, a setting of sculpted rocks shaped by the weather, and the heady scented plants of the *garrigue*.

▷ On leaving the Pont du Gard, take the road to Uzès on the left (D 981), then, after about 2.5km/1.5mi, that for Collias.

Collias
A centre for canoeing and horse riding, and crossed by the GR 63, which here follows the course of the Gardon; the cliffs are also popular with rock climbers.

▷ Having crossed the Gardon, follow the D 3. The road crosses an expanse of garrigue covered in vine and olive trees. In the village of Cabrières, turn right onto the D 427 (direction Poulx).

Poulx
Basically a residential suburb of Nîmes, the village has a small Roman church.

▷ In the village turn right on the D 127.

Film buffs may recognise the road as that used to film scenes from 'Salaire de la Peur', featuring Charles Vanel and Yves Montand.

Site de la Baume★
Leave your car after the final zigzag, and walk along the path that leads to the bottom of the gorge. 🚶 *1h.*
After having passed through the remains of buildings, you reach the Gardon, a picturesque spot, popular with swimmers, naturist and otherwise. On the opposite bank, you can see the cave entrance in the cliff.

▷ Return to Poulx and turn right onto the D 135, then the D 979 (direction Uzès).

The road offers beautiful **views★** of the Gardon, and the series of gorges.

Pont St-Nicolas
This nine-arch bridge was built in the 13C by monks.

Uzès★★

This, the first duchy of France, is set amid a landscape of garrigue and austere charm that dazzles whatever the season. With its shaded boulevards, medieval streets and russet-faced mansions, built mainly in the 17C–18C, when the production of cloth, serge and silk made the city wealthy, Uzès exudes a quiet but radiant beauty.

WALKING TOUR

THE OLD TOWN★

There is something oddly but delightfully bewitching about Uzès, as if a calm sometimes settles on the streets and squares, and then suddenly erupts into a busy world of markets and colour. It is certainly a place where time ticks by without you noticing it, a place that is a subtle balance between the present and the past.

▶ From the avenue de la Libération, turn right into the boulevard des Alliés.

Église St-Étienne

The church is designed with a curved façade in the Jesuit style that was in vogue in the 18C, and built on the site of a 13C church destroyed during the

- ▶ **Population:** 7,935.
- **Michelin Map:** 339: L-4.
- **Info:** Chapelle des Capucins, pl. Albert-ler, 30700 Uzès. ☎04 66 22 68 88. www.uzes-tourisme.com
- **Location:** 38km/24mi W of Avignon, and 25km/16mi N of Nîmes.
- **Timing:** Uzès has a knack of waylaying time; give it half a day or more.
- **Don't miss:** A stroll through the Old Town.

Wars of Religion. On the square is the birthplace of **Charles Gide**, economist and advocate of the co-operative system (1847–1932).

▶ Turn into rue St-Etienne, and head for the place aux Herbes.

Notice at **No. 1**, an imposing Louis XIII diamond-pointed doorway, and, a little further, down a dead end, a beautiful Renaissance façade.

Place aux Herbes★

Pleasant shops and restaurants, flanked by plane trees are the hallmark of this square at the heart of the city, which comes alive on market days. Among the

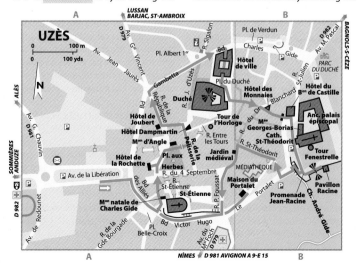

mansions that line the square the Hotel de la Rochette (17C) and, to the north, a corner house flanked by a turret, are quite remarkable.

▶ A narrow alleyway leads to the rue Pélisserie, on the left. Then, on the right, take the rue Entre-les-Tours.

The **Tour de l'Horloge** (12C) has a wrought-iron campanile and was a symbol of the bishop's power over the city.

▶ Go back to the rue Pélisserie, cross the place Dampmartin (Rennaisance façade in the hotel Dampmartin), cross the square and go into the rue de la République. Follow the street, and then turn right into the bvd Gambetta, and then head for the place du Duché.

Duché★

1 pl du Duché. ◷*Open Jul–Aug 10am–12.30pm, 2–6.30pm; rest of year 10am–noon, 2–6pm.*
This fine fortress was never attacked, and is today much as it was during its time. The 12C Romanesque **Tour Fenestrelle★★** is probably the most famous icon of the city. Spend time exploring the grounds of the fortress, including the beautiful **Jardin Médiéval**.

EXCURSIONS
Haras national d'Uzès
3.5km/2mi. Leave Uzès to the N of the D 981). After 2km/1mi, turn left onto the D 407. ⚅◷*Open for unaccompanied visits daily except Sun and public holidays 2–5pm.* 📷*Guided visits Jul–Aug Tue and Thu 10am, 3pm; mid–end Jun and 1–mid-Sep Tue and Thu, 3pm.* ◉€8. ☎04 66 22 38 21.*
Well equipped with modern facilities, including a riding school.

👥 Musée du Bonbon Haribo
Au Pont-des-Charrettes (rte de Remoulins) 2.5km/1.5mi S. ⚅◷*Open Aug 10am–8pm; Jul 10am–7pm; rest of year daily except Mon 10am–1pm, 2–6pm.* ◷*Closed 3rd week in Jan, 25 Dec.* ◉€6 (child 5–15, €3).* ☎04 66 22 74 39. www.haribo.com.*

All about the history and making of sweets, especially those made from jelly. ⓘ*Addresses of local dentists at the entrance!*

👥 Moulin de Chalier à Arpaillargues
3km/2mi. Leave Uzès to the W on the D 982 (direction Anduze). Just before Arpaillargues, take a narrow road descending on the right. ⚅◷*Open Jul–Aug 10am–7pm; Feb–Jun and Sep daily except Mon 10am–noon, 2–6pm; rest of year call for information.* ◷*Closed Jan, 25 Dec.* ◉€7 (child 4–12, €5). ☎04 66 22 58 64.*
www.moulin-de-chalier.fr.*
Housed in an 18C stone building, this museum contains 1 900 vehicles, posters and objects evoking everyday life during the Belle Epoque, including means of transport from 1870 to the 1950s, magic lanterns, Lumirère brothers' cinema, crystal sets and agricultural activities. The 👥 **Train and Toy Train museum** includes a model railway from 1923.

St-Quentin-la-Poterie
5km/3mi. Leave Uzès to the NE on the D 982 (route de Bagnols). After 2km/1mi, turn left onto D 5, then D 23.
The excellent quality of the local clay made a fortune for St-Quentin in the 14C, producing more than 120 000 glazed tiles for decorating the halls of the palaces of the Popes in Avignon. This prosperity continued into the 20C, but declined in the early 1970s. Since 1983, the village has found new prosperity with the arrival of potters and ceramists. Housed in a former olive mill (*14 Rue de la Fontaine*), the **Museum of Mediterranean pottery** houses a collection of 250 pieces, utilitarian or festive, from Spain, Crete, Morocco and Tunisia (◷*open Jun–Aug 10am–1pm, 3–7pm; Sep 10am–noon, 2–6pm; Feb–May and Oct 2–6pm;* ◷*closed Mon–Tue except Jul–Aug, Dec 25;* ◉€3; ☎04 66 03 65 86; www.musee-pottery-mediterranee.com). In addition, the **galerie Terra Viva** provides displays of contemporary ceramics. ⚅◷*Open 10am–7pm.* ◷*Closed Jan–Mar, 25 Dec.* ☎04 66 22 48 78. www.terraviva.fr.*

Bagnols-sur-Cèze

Old Bagnols proves to be quite a charming place surrounded by a ring of boulevards, with its old houses, and Musem of Modern Art. Nature lovers will find much to entertain and delay them in the beautiful Cèze valley. This is a small regional centre, and almost certainly a Roman town before the main part was built in the 13C around a central arcaded square is still preserved today and conveys an ancient historic ambiance.

THE TOWN
Musée d'Art Moderne Albert-André ★

pl. Mallet. ⏱*Open daily except Mon Jul–Aug 3–7pm; rest of year 10am–noon, 2–6pm.* ℘*04 66 50 50 56.*
This beautiful 17C building contains figurative collections of modern art assembled by the artist Albert André, curator from 1918 to 1954. Friends of painters such as Monet, Marquet, Signac, Bonnard and Renoir enriched the Besson donation; a very fine collection of paintings, watercolours, drawings and sculptures signed Renoir, Valadon, Matisse and Van Dongen.

Musée d'archéologie Léon-Alègre

Maison Jourdan, 24 av. Paul-Langevin. ⏱*Open Jul–Aug 3-7pm; rest of year Thu–Sat 10am–noon, 2–6pm.* ⏱*Closed Feb and public holidays.* ℘*04 66 89 74 00.*
Original Rhône collection illustrating the different periods of Antiquity, notably the Celtic-Ligurian civilisation and its relation ship with the Greeks of Marseille (6C–1C BCE), particularly evoked by pottery and bronze objects, ceramics, amphorae, glassware and everyday objects, as well as touching upon the development of the local vineyards. One room is devoted to the oppidum of St. Vincent de Gaujac with a reconstruction of a corner of the hot baths.

▶ **Population:** 18 545.
Michelin Map: 339: M-4.
Info: Espace St-Gilles, 30200 Bagnols-sur-Cèze. ℘04 66 89 54 61. www.tourisme bagnolssurceze.com.
Location: 32km/20mi N of the Pont du Gard, and 25km/15.5mi S of the Ardèche.
Timing: At least 1h–2h to effect a walking tour of old Bagnols, but half a day or more if you start visiting museums.
Don't Miss: The Museum of Modern Art.

🚗 DRIVING TOURS

LE BAS VIVARAIS
See region map. Allow one day.

▶ Leave Bagnols to the W on the D 6 (route d'Alès), turn left onto the D 166.

Sabran is a charming perched village, with a superb panorama. A plumed crest of cypress seems to rise above the village of **La Roquesur-Cèze**, giving it an appearance of serene beauty.
Well worth a visit is the **Cascade du Sautadet★**, although care is needed to approach the watercourse safely. There is a pleasant walk along the ramparts of **Cornillon**, and from its castle a superb **view★** over the valley of the Cèze. The **Guidon du Bouquet★★** commands a vast horizon between the Gard and the Ardèche, and with a fine **view★★** over the Cévenne causses. No less spectacular are **Les Concluses de Lussan★★**, formed in the torrent of Aiguillon. It is remarkably is dry in summer which is the only time you can walk its course.

LA CÔTE DU RHÔNE GARDOISE
See region map – Allow about 3h.

▶ Leave Bagnols by the D 6086 to the S (direction Remoulins) as far as Gaujac; turn right onto the D 310.

The **Oppidum de St-Vincent-de-Gaujac**, high in the forest, has been occupied since the 6C and intermittently over the following centuries. In Roman times, it was a rural sanctuary with temples and baths. At the edge of the *garrigue* scrubland and vineyards, the old stone village of **St-Victor-la-Coste** nestles at the foot of its ruined castle. Formerly the property of the bishops of Avignon, **St-Laurent-des-Arbres** retains several interesting remains of its medieval period, including a Romanesque church, rebuilt in the 14C.

Well worth seeking out, the **Visiatome de Marcoule** (&🕐👥 *open 10am–6pm (Mon and Sat 1–6pm); ℘04 66 39 78 78;* *www.visiatome.fr*) hosts an exhibition on the theme of energy in general and radioactivity in particular. Space is dedicated solely to radioactive waste. The latest set design (screens, animated, interactive games, etc.) makes the visit more fun.

EXCURSION
Pont St-Esprit
11km/7mi to the N.
An audacious and magnificent bridge spanning the Rhone, and built between 1265 and 1309, with 19 of its original 25 arches intact. Allow half a day to visit the town (*℘04 66 39 44 45. www.ot-pont-saint-esprit.fr*).

Alès

Alès is a typical town of the Cévennes plain, with broad bustling streets and esplanades, and a great many summer festivals.

A BIT OF HISTORY
Peace Treaty of Alès – In the 16C, Alès was an important Huguenot centre. The Edict of Grace between Louis XIII and the Protestants was signed here in 1629. Under the **treaty** terms, Protestants lost their political rights and their *places de Sureté* (garrison towns), and other priviliges, but retained their freedom of worship. A bishopric was established here in 1694 but was suppressed a hundred years later.

Louis Pasteur at Alès – In 1847, an epidemic attacked the region's traditional source of income – silkworms. By 1865, 3 500 silkworm breeders were in despair and Louis Pasteur was recruited to find a remedy. By 1868 Pasteur found a method of prevention and a **statue** to honour him was erected in the Bosquet gardens.

Industrial development – From the 12C, Alès prospered from textile manufacturing and the cloth trade. In the 19C, the town became a major industrial centre with mining for coal, iron, lead, zinc and asphalt. Today, Alès specialises in metallurgy, chemistry and mechanical engineering.

▶ **Population:** 39,943.
 Michelin Map: 339: J-4.
 Info: Pl. de l'Hôtel-de-Ville, 30100 Alès. ℘04 66 52 32 15. www.ville-ales.fr.
 Location: 96km/60mi N of Montpellier. The town named after an obscure Roman citizen, Allectus, was called 'Alais' until 1926. An oppidum once stood on the Colline de l'Ermitage. Enjoy a panorama of Alès from the chapel.
 Don't Miss: The view from the château de Portes.

SIGHTS
Cathédrale St-Jean-Baptiste
The cathedral's Romanesque west front has a Gothic porch dating from the 15C. The vaulted neo-Gothic nave dates from the 17C and the great choir from the 18C. Next to the cathedral, in rue Lafare-Alès, is the 18C bishops' palace, **Ancien Évêché**.

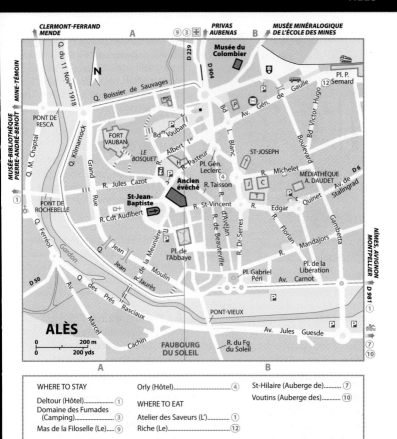

Musée du Colombier

Parc du Colombier. Open Jul–Aug 2–7pm; Sep–Jun daily except Mon 2–6pm. Closed 1 Jan, 1 May, 1 Nov, 25 Dec. 04 66 86 30 40.
This museum in the 18C **Château du Colombier** contains art spanning the 16C–20C, with an early 16C triptych of the Holy Trinity by Jean Bellegambe, and paintings by Van Loo, Mieris, Bassano, Velvet Brueghel, Masereel, Mayodon, Marinot, Benn and others.

Musée-Bibliothèque Pierre-André Benoît★

Take the Rochebelle bridge over the Gardon and follow the signposted route. Montée des Lauriers, Rochebelle. Open Jul–Aug 2–7pm; Sep–Jun daily except Mon 2–6pm. Closed Feb, 1 Jan, 1 May, 1 Nov, 25 Dec. 04 66 86 98 69.

The 18C **Château de Rochebelle** was once the residence of the bishops of Alès. Now restored, it contains the bequeathed collections of Pierre-André Benoît (1921–93) printer, publisher, writer, painter and draughtsman. Benoît collected works of art and books by his friends, who included Char, Claudel, Tzara, Seuphor, Braque, Picasso, Miró, Jean Hugo, Villon, Camille Bryen, Picabia, Braque, and Léopold Survage.

Musée minéralogique de l'École des Mines★

6 avenue de Clavières, in the Chantilly district. Leave the centre via ave de Lattre-de-Tassigny and ave Pierre-Coiras. Open mid Jun–mid-Sep daily except Sat–Sun and public holidays 2–5pm; mid-Sep–mid-Jun by request. €4. 04 66 78 51 69. www.mines-ales.fr.

Château de Portes

©Melvin DUPONT/Fotolia.com

This museum showcases more than 1 000 minerals from around the world, including Australian opal, Moroccan chalcedony, morion quartz and black cairngorm from Aveyron. A 3-D audiovisual show highlights the stones' diversity of shapes and colours.

EXCURSIONS

Mine-témoin★

3km/2mi W. Take the Rochebelle bridge over the Gardon and continue north on rue du Faubourg-de Rochebelle. Turn left onto chemin de St-Raby, then right onto chemin de la Cité-Ste-Marie.
Guided tours: Jul–Aug 10am–7pm; Mar–Jun and Sep–mid Nov 9.30am–12.30pm, 2–6pm. €7. 04 66 30 45 15. www.mine-temoin.fr.

The museum presents the history of mining in the Cévennes from the Industrial Revolution to the present, and comprises 650m of shafts, which Benedictine monks used to extract coal in the 13C.

Château de Portes★

20km/12.5mi NW. Leave Alès on D 904 towards Aubenas, then turn left onto D 906. Park the car at the pass to explore the castle ruins on foot. Open Jul–Aug 10am–7pm (Mon 1–7pm); May–Jun Wed–Sun 2–6pm; Sep daily except Mon 2–6pm; rest of year call for information. €5. 04 66 54 92 05. www.chateau-portes.org.

The now ruined castle of Portes, which provides a **panorama★★** the Chamborigaud valley, Mont Lozère and the Tanargue foothills, once offered protection for pilgrims travelling to St-Gilles. The castle belonged to the lords of Budos from 1320 to the 17C.

Château de Rousson

9km/5.6mi N. Leave Alès on D 904 towards Aubenas then take the third road on the right after Les Rosiers (D 131). Guided tours Jul–Aug 2–7pm. €5. 04 66 85 60 31.

This robust castle overlooking the Aigoual and Ventoux ranges has barely been modified since its construction between 1600–15. Its main façade features mullioned windows and an impressive Louis XIII door with bosses.

Préhistorama

11km/6.8mi N. Leave Alès along D 904, towards Aubenas. Turn left onto a path signposted 'Préhistorama'. Open Jun–Aug 10am–7pm; Feb–May and Sep–Nov 2–6pm. Closed Dec and Jan. €5. 04 66 85 86 96.

This centre retraces the origins of life on earth and the evolution of the human species.

Jardins ethnobotaniques de la Gardie

400m,1,300ft after the Préhistorama. Open Jul–Aug daily except Mon 10am–noon, 3–6pm; May–Jun and Sep weekends 3–6pm. Closed rest of year. 04 66 85 66 90. www.lesjardinsethno.org.

Discover the rich natural environment of the Cévennes.

St-Christol-lès-Alès, Musée du Scribe

2km/1.2mi S towards Anduze and Montpellier; follow the signposting on the right before reaching the 'Pyramid' where the two roads separate. 42 rue du Clocher. Guided tours: Jul–Aug 10am–7pm; Jun and 1–mid Sep daily 2–6pm; Feb–May and mid Sep–Dec Sat–Sun 2.30–7pm. €5. 04 66 60 88 10. www.museeduscribe.com.

This tastefully restored village house with a reconstruction of a 19C classroom celebrates the history of writing materials through the ages – from papyrus and parchment to paper. Exhibits of writing instruments include quills, nibs, penholders and unusual inkwells.

Vézénobres

11km/7mi S. Leave Alès on N 106.
Old medieval Vézénobres perches on a hillside overlooking the Gardon d'Alès and the Gardon d'Anduze. Several houses date from the 12C, 14C or 15C and further evidence of the medieval town is the Sabran gateway, old ramparts and fortress ruins. Stroll through picturesque alleyways and enjoy the view from the top of the village.

ADDRESSES

🛏 STAY

🛌 **Camping Domaine des Fumades** – *30500 Allègre-les-Fumades.17km/10.5mi NE of Alès on D 16 then D 241. ℘04 66 24 80 78. www.domaine.des.fumades.com. Open 17 May–7 Sep. Reservations required. 230 sites.* On the outskirts of Alauzène, this campsite's natural surroundings are well preserved and a magnificent patio, restaurants, shops, three swimming pools and a Children's club add to the enjoyment.

🛌 **Hotel Deltour** – *Chemin des Trespeaux. ℘04 66 54 98 10. www.ales. deltourhotel.com.* 🅿. *30 rooms.* With rooms at reasonable prices, this hotel offers all modern conveniences, including internet connections.

🛌 **Hôtel Orly** – *10 r. d'Avéjan, 30100 Alès. ℘04 66 91 30 00. www.orly-hotel.com. 28 rooms.* At the heart of a large pedestriansied street and shopping centre, a modern and functional hotel.

🛌 **Maison d'Hôtes Mas de la Filoselle** – *344 r. du 19, Mars, 1962, Saint-Martin de Valgalgues. ℘06 61 23 19 95. http://filoselle.free.fr. 4 rms* At the highest point of the village on the outskirts of Alès, an 18C silk farm with themed rooms. *Table d'hôte* in the evening.

🛌 **Le Riche** – *42 pl. Semard. ℘04 66 86 00 33. www.leriche.fr.* This hotel-restaurant opposite the station has an art noveau

dining room and a high quality classic menu. Rooms are modern and functional.

🍴 EAT

🍽 **L'Atelier des Savuers** – *16 fg de Rochebelle. ℘04 66 86 27 77. www.latelierdessaveurs.net. Closed Sat lunch, Sun eve and Mon.* This small restaurant offers a taste of the countryside as well as of regional produce.

🍽 **Auberge de St-Hilaire** – *30560 St-Hilaire-de-Brethmas, 3km/2mi SE of Alès on N 106. ℘04 66 30 11 42. www. aubergesainthilaire.com. Closed Sun eve and Mon.* This inn has a pleasant garden courtyard, warm Mediterranean colours and attractive modern cuisine.

🍽 **Auberge des Voutins** – *409 Route des Écoles, 30340 Méjannes-les-Alès. ℘04 66 61 38 03. Closed Sun eve and Mon except public holidays.* This country dwelling offers traditional cuisine by the fireside or on a shady terrace.

SHOPPING

La Brûlerie – *185 Grand'Rue. ℘04 66 52 14 14. www.labrulerie.com.* Renée Rédarès hs two outstanding qualities: kindness and a talent for coffee...you can enjoy tea, too.

ACTIVITES

HORSERIDING

Centre équestre du Galeizon – *Rte du Pont-des-Camisards, hameau de Labaume, 30480 Cendras. ℘04 66 78 77 98. www.centreequestredugaleizon.com.* Accompanied rides through the beautiful valley of Galeizon.

GOLD PANNING

Jean-Luc Billard – *21 r. de la Montagnade, 11km/6.6mi S of Alès, 30720 Ribaute-les-Tavernes. ℘04 66 83 67 35. www.orpailleur. com.* This 'gold-digger' promises to find gold by panning in the river Gard.

EVENTS

Festival de cinéma Itinérances à Alès – *℘04 66 30 24 26. www.itinerances.org.* Annual film festival held in mid–end March. Information at the tourist office.

Feria – Five days of bodegas, bull runs, concerts and various other festivities following Ascension Day (usually in May).

Fous chantants – Last week of July. www.fouschantants.com. Each year 1 000 singers pay homage to some variety artist (Ferrat, Moustaki, Goldman, Sheller…).

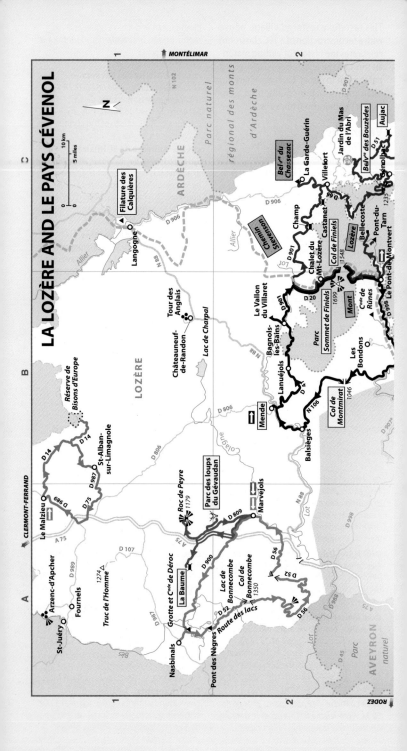

LA LOZÈRE AND LE PAYS CÉVENOL

MONTÉLIMAR

N 102

Parc naturel

régional des monts

d'Ardèche

ARDÈCHE

N

10 km
5 miles

Filature des
Calquières

Langogne

D 906

Allier

N 88

Allier

Lot

Chemin
Stevenson

Bel.re du
Chassezac

La Garde-Guérin

Villefort

Jardin du Mas
de l'Abri

Bel.re des Bouzèdes

Aujac

D 901

Génolhac

D 51

Champ

D 901

Chalet du
Mt-Lozère

Castanet

Col de Finiels
1548

Lozère

Bellecoste

D 906

Pont-du-
Tarn

1235

Tour des
Anglais

Le Vallon
du Villaret

D 901

D 20

Sommet de Finiels
1699

Mont

C.re de
Rûnes

Le Pont-de-Montvert

D 998

Châteauneuf-
de-Randon

Lac de Charpal

Bagnols-
les-Bains

Parc

Les
Bondons

LOZÈRE

Réserve de
Bisons d'Europe

D 14

D 14

St-Alban-
sur-Limagnole

D 987

D 73

D 989

Lanuéjols

D 806

Mende

Olagne

D 806

D 4

Col de
Montmirat
1046

N 106

Balsièges

Lot

D 907

CLERMONT-FERRAND

Le Malzieu

A 75

Roc de Peyre
1179

Parc des loups
du Gévaudan

Marvejols

N 88

D 809

D 998

Arzenc-d'Apcher

Fournels

D 989

Truc de l'Homme
1274

D 107

Grotte et C.re de Déroc

La Baume

D 900

Lac de
Bonnecombe

Col de
Bonnecombe
1350

D 56

D 52

D 56

A 75

St-Juéry

Nasbinals

D 987

D 52

Pont des Nègres

Route des lacs

Bès

Lot

D 45

Parc

naturel

AVEYRON

RODEZ

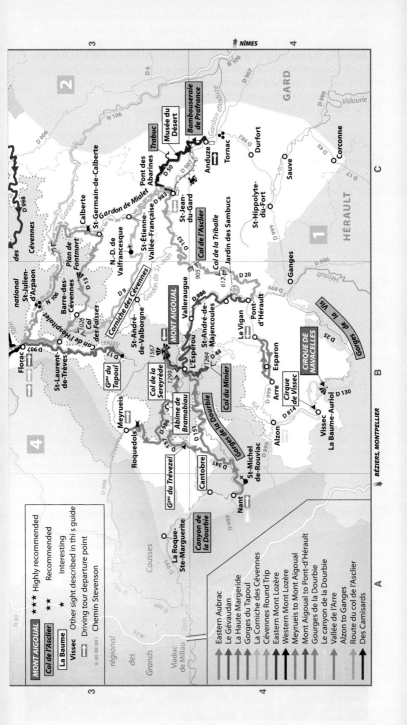

MONT AIGOUAL ★★★ Highly recommended
Col de l'Ascler ★★ Recommended
La Baume ★ Interesting
Vissec Other sight described in this guide
▢▢ Driving tour departure point
┄┄ Chemin Stevenson

Eastern Aubrac
Le Gévaudan
La Haute Margeride
Gorges du Tapoul
La Corniche des Cévennes
Cévennes Round Trip
Eastern Mont Lozère
Western Mont Aigoual
Meyrueis to Mont Aigoual
Mont Aigoual to Pont-d'Hérault
Gorges de la Dourbie
Le canyon de la Dourbie
Vallée de l'Arre
Alzon to Ganges
Route du col de l'Ascler
Des Camisards

national *des* Cévennes

régional *des* Grands Causses

Viaduc de Millau

La Roque-Ste-Marguerite

Canyon de la Dourbie

Florac
St-Laurent-de-Trèves
St-Julien-d'Arpaon
Barre-des-Cévennes
Plan de Fontmort
Col des Faïsses
N.-D. de Valfrancesque
Calberte
St-Germain-de-Calberte
St-Étienne-Vallée-Française
St-Jean-du-Gard
Pont des Abarines
Trabuc
Musée du Désert
Bambouseraie de Prafrance
Anduze
Tornac
Durfort
Sauve
Corconne

Corniche des Cévennes
MONT AIGOUAL
St-André-de-Valborgne
Col de la Sereyrède
L'Espérou
Valleraugue
St-André-de-Majencoules
Le Vigan
Pont-d'Hérault
Col de la Triballe
Jardin des Sambucs
St-Hippolyte-du-Fort
Ganges

Meyrueis
Roquedols
Abîme de Bramabiau
Gres du Tapoul
Col du Minier
Espéron
Arre
Alzon
Esparon
Cirque de Navacelles
Cirque de Vissec
Vissec
La Baume-Auriol

Gorges de la Dourbie
St-Michel-de-Rouviac
Cantobre
Nant
Gres du Trévezel

GARD
Vidourle
HÉRAULT
Hérault
Vis

↑ NÎMES

▶ BÉZIERS, MONTPELLIER

147

LA LOZÈRE AND LE PAYS CÉVENOL

The geography of Lozère is amazingly complex, and covers four mountain ranges. In the northwest lies the basalt plateau of Aubrac, famed as much as anything else for it cattle. The north and northeast of the department embraces the Margeride mountains, formed of granite, and with peaks reaching more than 1 500m. The *causses* are a series of limestone plateaux in the southwest, while the southeastern corner contains the renowned Cévennes, which include the highest point in the department, Mont Lozère. The main activities are farming and tourism, although there is very little arable farming due to poor soil quality. The Cévennes form a huge mountain range covering four departments, part of the Massif Central, a labyrinth of deep, steep-sided and winding valleys, extending from Montagne Noir in the southwest to the Monts du Vivarais in the northeast.

Highlights

1. Take a leisurely stroll around **Marvejols**, a Royal city (p150)
2. Don't miss a visit to see the **wolves of Gévaudan** (p151)
3. Explore the **Le Parc National des Cévennes** (p154)
4. Take a drive around **Mont Lozère** (p157)
5. Visit the **silk museum** in Saint-Hippolyte-du-Fort (p169)

Travels with a Donkey

Scottish author, Robert Louis Stevenson, crossed the Cévennes in 1878, accompanied by his donkey, Modestine. He took a route that today has become the GR 70. The journey, from Monastier-sur-Gazeilles to St-Jean-du-Gard, was recounted in his book *Travels with a donkey in the Cévennes*. The consequence was to bring the beauties of the region to the attention of a wide and readily appreciative audience.

Aubrac Cattle

The cattle of Aubrac are renowned far more widely than the region. They are most evident in the area north of Lozère, and have soft brown coats on muscled bodies, their heads topped by long, lyre-like horns.

This is a very old breed of cattle, with more than 150 years of breeding history originally in the care of Benedictine monks. Cows spend the winters within the confines of the farm and give birth to calves that come easily and muscle up quickly. At the end of spring, the cows and calves head up into the Aubrac mountains to feed on lush grass and flowers that help them to produce the best milk.

Cattle in Aubrac adorned for transhumance

©B. Piccoli/Fotolia.com

Mende★

The capital of the Lozère, the least populated French *département*, is a market town with an imposing cathedral. Its narrow winding streets are lined with lovely old houses with timber doors, portals and oratories.

▶ **Population:** 12 688.
- **Michelin Map:** Map 330: J-7.
- **Info:** Pl. du Forail, 48000 Mende. ℘04 66 94 00 23. www.ot-mende.fr.
- **Location:** 95km/59.3mi NE of Millau via the A 75.
- **Don't Miss:** The Aubusson tapestries at the cathedral.

●●WALKING TOUR

Cathedral★
Most of this cathedral (restored in the early 17C) was built in the 14C under Pope Urban V. The belfries date from the 16C. When Captain Merle seized Mende in 1579, he blew up the cathedral pillars and left only the belfries, walls and chapels.
Mende Cathedral once had the largest bell in Christendom, the 'Non Pareille' ('Unequalled'), weighing 20t. Broken by Merle's men in 1579, all that remains is the enormous clapper, 2.15m long.

▶ Take rue de l'Arjal, to the right of the cathedral.

The street leads to **place Griffon** and the fountain once used to clean the streets.

▶ Turn left onto rue du Soubeyran then right onto rue de la Jarretière leading to place au Blé.

Tour des Penitents
The tower is all that remains of the 12C walls, that have now given way to boulevards.

▶ Go back to place au Blé and turn right into rue Charlier-Hugonnet. Then turn left into rue Basse.

At the junction of two streets, note the **lavoir de la Calquière**, which in times past was used by tanners to clean skins.

▶ Go back up rue Basse. Beyond place du Mazel, turn right into rue du Chou-Vert. Cross the boulevard and go into rue de Chanteronne opposite.

Pont Notre-Dame★
Built in the 13C, this narrow humpback bridge has withstood the force of the Lot on many occasions; its shape is typical of the Lot valley.

▶ Turn around, and at the bottom of rue du Chou-Vert, turn right into rue du Collège, then go left into rue Notre-Dame. At place René-Estoup, turn right into rue d'Aigues-Passes.

No. 7 is a 17C house, where Mandrin, a celebrated brigan of the 18C hid a fabulous treasure.

ADDRESSES

🛏STAY

⊜⊜ **Hôtel de France** – *9 Bd. L.-Arnault. ℘04 66 65 00 04. www.hoteldefrance-mende.com. 31 rooms.* This former coaching inn is in the heart of town; popular and comfortable.

🍽EAT

⊜⊜ **Les Voûtes** – *13 r. Aigues-Passes. ℘04 66 49 00 05. www.les-voutes.com.* Located in a pedestriansed street close to the cathedrale; this popular restaurant specialises in regional cuisine.

⊜⊜ **La Safranière** – *In Chabrits, 5km/3mi north of Mende on the D42. ℘04 66 49 31 54. Closed Sun and Mon. Reservations required.* An energetic young chef plays host to the region's well informed foodies.

Marvejols

The Aubrac and Gévaudan

Marvejols benefits from a favourable climate and setting which has inspired the founding of several medical and pedagogical centres. This 'Royal City' played an important role in 14C wars, and eventually became a Protestant fortress town. It was destroyed in 1586 by Admiral Joyeuse; its fortified gatehouses are reminiscent of its war-torn past.

▶ **Population:** 5 210.
& **Michelin Map:** 330: H-7.
▯ **Info:** Pl. du Soubeyran, 48100. ℘04 66 32 02 14. www.ville-marvejols.fr.
▶ **Location:** 180km/112.50mi NW of Montpellier and 69km/43mi N of Millau.
☺ **Don't Miss:** Château de la Baume.
👥 **Kids:** Wolves of Gévaudan.

VISIT

Fortified gatehouses command the three entrances to the old town. The **Porte du Soubeyran★** records how the town was rebuilt by Henri IV and the other two gatehouses, the **Porte du Théron** and **Porte de Chanelles**, also bear inscriptions recounting the good deeds of Henri IV. Once within the gateways, narrow streets ripple away past shops, cafés and restaurants, with little to betray its bloody history.

🚗 DRIVING TOURS

EASTERN AUBRAC

Round tour NW of Marvejols. 97km/60mi – allow 4h. Leave Marvejols NW along D 900. ☺ Bonnecombe Pass is snowbound from Dec–Apr.

As it climbs, D 900 offers a broad view of Marvejols, La Margeride, Mont Lozère, the Causses and the Cévennes before passing through forests, fields, meadows and pastureland before reaching Nasbinals.

Nasbinals

Nasbinals, which has several lively agricultural **fairs** throughout the year, is also a resort for alpine and cross-country ski and snowshoeing.

▶ Turn back along D 900 to Montgrousset, then take D 52 to the right.

Grotte et Cascade de Déroc

Park by D 52 and take a rough path lined with drystone walls towards a farm.

▣ *The path follows the bank of a stream, to a magical waterfall and a cave with a ceiling vault made of rock prisms.*

The D 52 skirts the shores of Lake Salhiens before cutting across pastureland to the **Col de Bonnecombe**. Beyond the pass, the road drops down through Les Hermaux to St-Pierre-de-Nogaret, then follows a scenic route through the Doulou Valley to St-Germain-du-Teil.

▶ Take D 52 to the left to the Col du Trébatut. Turn right at the crossroads onto D 56, which leads to the Colagne valley. In Le Monastier, take N 9 back to Marvejols.

Route des Lacs

The D 52 climbs into a wild area of lakes and swamps, and skirts Salhiens lake, passing close to that of Souveyrois.

Lac de Bonnecombe

This small lake is one of few in Aubrac that are landscaped, with gateways giving access to its banks.

LE GÉVAUDAN

52km/32mi – about 3h30. From Marvejols drive to the A 75 motorway and follow it towards Clermont-Ferrand. Leave at Exit 37, take the bridge across the motorway and follow signs to Château de la Baume.

Château de la Baume★

🕐🚶 *Jul and Aug: guided tours daily 10am–noon, 2–6pm; Sep–Jun daily except Tue by arrangement.* ⊙€7. ℘04 66 32 51 59.

www.chateaudelabaume.org.
This 17C granite residence boasts a main staircase with Louis XIV balusters and large fireplaces made of chestnut wood soaked in Aubrac peatbogs to impart a dark brown luster and make them rot-proof.

▷ Return to the motorway and take the bridge across it. At the second roundabout, take the third road to the right, then turn right onto D 53 towards St-Sauveur-de-Peyre.

Roc de Peyre

⚐ The top of the rock affords a remarkable panorama of the Aubrac, the Plomb du Cantal, the Margeride, Mont Lozère, Mont Aigoual and the Causses. It is hard to imagine that a fortress once occupied this rocky pinnacle, yet Admiral Joyeuse used 2 500 cannonballs to destroy the keep of this Protestant fief in 1586. Time destroyed the rest.

▷ Turn back and take N 9 to the left then a road on the left towards Ste-Lucie, then turn right onto a road going uphill.

⚐ Parc des loups du Gévaudan★

🕐*Open Jul–Aug 9.30am–7pm; Apr–Jun, Sep–Oct: 10am–5.30pm; Feb–Mar, Nov–Dec 10am–5pm.* 🕐*Closed Jan, 25 Dec.* ⚏€8 (child 3–11, €5). ℘04 66 32 09 22. www.loupsdugevaudan.com.
This **wild animal reserve** shelters some 100 wolves from Europe, Canada and Mongolia. A documentary shot in the park can be viewed on request. Take a guided tour in summer, as wolves are less visible than in autumn/winter.

▷ N 9 leads back to Marvejols.

Le Malzieu

The 'pearl' of the Truyère valley is how locals see Le Malzieu, at the heart of Margeride, about 860m above sea level. There are some remains of the 14C walls, and old houses with tiled roofs. This is a wonderful 'green' resort.

👣 WALKING TOUR

THE TOWN
The town walls, 8–10m high, of which there are a few remnants, were flanked by massive towers and surrounded by ditches, which, in the 14C, formed a hexagon that sheltered up to 2 000 people. Charming streets let you discover the houses with corner turrets, as well as several doorways designed by Italian masons. Take a look at the Saugues gateway and its defensive structure, the clock tower, a former dungeon of the long-since destroyed castle, the Rozières square with its ancient monastery and private buildings lining the streets. At the corner of the square is the Trou de Merle through which a Huguenot captain of that name came to put the town to fire and sword in 1573.

- ▶ **Population:** 769.
- 🖝 **Michelin Map:** 5267: M2.
- 🅸 **Info:** Tour de Bodon, 48140 Le Malzieu-Ville. ℘04 66 31 82 73. www.gevaudan.com.
- ▷ **Location:** 50km/31mi N of Mende by the D 806, then right at St-Chély-d'Apcher on the D 989.
- ⚐ **Kids:** The Bison Reserve at La Haute Margeride.
- 🕐 **Timing:** One hour; half a day for the area.
- 👁 **Don't miss:** A walk through the town's historic streets.

Church
Unlike most churches in the region, the church has no bell comb. The scallop shells that signify and decorate the route of St Jacques de Compostela are visible on the outside of the walls of the south transept.

Town hall

A former chapel houses a small exhibition about the animals of the Gévaudan.

⬤ DRIVING TOUR

LA HAUTE MARGERIDE

45km28mi. Allow 2h.

▷ Leave Le Malzieu on the D 4 to the east, then turn left onto the D 14, then the D 587 towards St-Alban, rejoining the D 14 as far as Ste-Eulaliie; finally take the D 7 on the right for 2km/1.5mi towards Le Chayla.

👥 Réserve des Bisons d'Europe★

Ste-Eulalie. ⏱*Open all year 10am–6pm (5pm according to season).* 💰*€16 (child 3–11, €8.50).* ⏱*Closed mid-Nov–mid-Dec.* ☏*04 66 31 40 40. www.bisoneurope.com.*

Check out this semi-free herd of European bison from Poland, the only country in which the species remains in the wild. Visits are in carriages, and a tour takes about 1hr.

St-Alban-sur-Limagnole

Lying on the route of St James of Compostela, St Alban takes its name from the first English martyr. The chateau, constructed in 1245, has a fine gateway and beautiful galleries in the inner courtyard in local pink sandstone.

St-Chély-d'Apcher

This industrial town is the site of an iron foundry. Steel is produced here. Visit the **Musée de la Métallurgie**, which outlines the town's metalworking history.

▷ Return to Le Malzieu via the D 989.

Châteauneuf-de-Randon

Perched atop a granite hill in the very picturesque southeastern part of Margeride, the village is an agreeable place at any time of year; woodlands and heathery open spaces are great for walking, riding or a little winter skiing – a great place to be at one with the landscape.

THE VILLAGE

At the top of the village, the ruins of the English tower are the only traces of an ancient castle, the name 'Randon' denoting a medieval fortification. After having protected the local populace from the attentions of bandits during the 15C–16C, the castle, in spite of being strategically dominant throughout the region, was dismantled during the reign of Louis XIII (around 1632).

▸ **Population:** 568.
◈ **Michelin Map:** 5267: NO4.
▯ **Info:** Maison Cantonale, Ave Adrien Durand. ☏04 66 47 99 52. www.ot-chateauneufderandon.fr.
▷ **Location:** 171km/107mi to the N of Montpellier, and 30km/19mi NE of Mende.
◔ **Timing:** This isn't a big place; an hour should be more than enough.
◉ **Don't Miss:** The view from the panorama at the top of the village.

EXCURSION

Lac de Charpal

20km/112.5mi to the W by the D 1. 🥾 *8km/5mi. Allow 3h.* Supplying water to Mende, the marked trails around this lake at the heart of the plateau du Roi are popular and enjoyable.

Langogne

In this remarkable place, different eras exist side-by-side, from the Middle Ages to the present day.

THE TOWN
Halle
Built in 1742 as a shelter for livestock, it has since become a corn exchange, supported by 14 granite columns.

Église St-Gervais-et-St-Protais
This 10C building was rebuilt in the 15C and 17C, using sandstone mixed with volcanic material.

Filature des Calquières★
Open Jul–Sep 9am–noon, 1.30–6.30pm; May–Jun 9am–noon, 2–5.30pm; Oct–Apr 9am–noon, 2–5pm. Closed mid-Dec–mid-Jan. €8.50 (child under 16, €5.50). 04 66 69 25 56. http://musee-lozere.com.
This outstanding museum demonstrates the various processes involved in the production of wool. The highlight of the visit is the ancient spinning jenny.

- **Population:** 3 156.
- **Michelin Map:** 5267: P3.
- **Info:** 15, Boulevard des Capucins. 04 66 69 01 38. www.ot-langogne.com.
- **Location:** In the N of the Lozère, 100km/62.5mi N of Alès, and 50km/31mi NE of Mende.
- **Timing:** Allow 1–2 hours.
- **Don't miss:** The musée de la Filature des Calquières, and its spinning jenny – a trip to the heart of the industrial revolution.

EXCURSION
Le Chemin de Stevenson★★
Follow in the footsteps of Robert Louis Stevenson in this 10-day walk (GR 70) through the Cévennes, which is becoming increasingly popular. Donkeys optional!

Florac

On the edge of the Causse Méjean, the Cévennes and Mont Lozère, Florac contains the head office of the Parc national des Cévennes. Florac survived a turbulent history, subjected to a tough feudal regime in the pays du Gévaudan, pays de tyrans (Gévaudan, land of tyrants) and then the Wars of Religion. Today this peaceful town is famous for its good food and outdoor leisure activities.

THE TOWN
Every summer sees *24 heures de Florac*, with riders completing a 160km/99mi circuit on horseback around Monts Lozère and Aigoual and Causse Méjean. The town is quite small, but has a couple of large open squares with restaurants and a few shops – the 'esplanade' is the larger of the two.

- **Population:** 2 014.
- **Info:** 33 Ave. Jean-Monestier, 48400 Florac. 04 66 45 01 14. www.vacances-cevennes.com.
- **Location:** In the Tarnon valley at Tarn gorges entrance.
- **Don't miss:** The 150 menhirs along the Sentier des menhirs de la cham des Bondons.
- **Kids:** The dinosaurs of St-Laurent-de-Trèves.

Château
Open Jul–Aug 9am–6.30pm; Apr–Jun and Sep–Oct 9.30am–noon, 1.30–5.30pm; Nov–Mar daily except Sat-Sun 9.30am–noon, 1.30–5.30pm. Closed 1 Jan, 25 Dec. 04 66 49 53 01.

This 17C building displays exhibits on the landscape, flora, fauna and activities in the Parc National des Cévennes. The **Information Centre** has information on park walks, guided tours, open-air museums (*écomusées*) and overnight accommodation. The nearby 'Spring Trail' (*Sentier de la Source*) is signposted with information on the natural environment of the river Pêcher.

Couvent de la Présentation
This convent was a commandery of the Knights Templar. The façade and monumental doorway date from 1583.

Source du Pêcher
Situated at the foot of the Rochefort rock, this is one of the main resurgent springs on the Causse Méjean. The river bubbles and froths up from the spring during heavy rain or melting snows.

EXCURSIONS
Les Bondons
12 km/7.5mi to N. Leave Florac on the N 106 (direction Mende) then turn right onto D 998 (for Pont-de-Montvert). At Cocurès, turn left onto the route des Bondons.

🚶 Two circuits (2h or 6h) invite you to discover this exceptional gathering of 150 menhirs.

Cascade de Rûnes
15km/9mi to the E. Leave Florac as above, but just after Cocurès, turn right towards Ruas, which you go through to reach Rûnes.
This route, bordered by ash trees, offers pleasant views of the Tarn valley.

🚶 To the S of Rûnes, a footpath leads to a beautiful 58m cascade on the Mirals.

LE PARC NATIONAL DES CÉVENNES
The Cévennes National Park covers an area of 91 500ha, surrounded by a peripheral zone of 237 000ha. It was founded in September 1970 and is the largest of the seven French national parks.

Le Pont-de-Montvert
21 km/13m west of Florac on the D998.

The tall grey houses of Le Pont-de-Montvert stand on either bank of the Tarn, which is spanned by a 17C humpback bridge surmounted by a toll tower. The **Abbot of Chayla**, in charge of Roman Catholic operations in the Cévennes, stayed in Le Pont-de-Montvert and held Protestants prisoner there. On 24 July 1702, two members of the Protestant movement rescued their colleagues and caused the death of the abbot, sparking off the so-called Camisard uprising.

Maison du Mont Lozère
♿🕑*Open Apr and Oct daily except Tue and Wed 3–6pm; May–Jun daily except Tue 10am–12.30pm, 3–6.30pm; Jul–Sept daily 10am–12.30pm, 3–6.30pm.* ✆€3.50. ☎04 66 45 80 73.
This centre is the headquarters of the Écomusée du Mont Lozère, an open-air museum set up by the Parc National des Cévennes. A large polygonal building houses an exhibition on the natural and human history of Mont Lozère, and an overnight shelter (*gîte*) for walkers.

Sentier de l'Hermet
6km/4mi from the Tour de l'Horloge, the clock tower in the centre of Le Pont-de-Montvert; allow 3h there and back.

🚶 This footpath, which includes 12 observation points, reveals the landscapes, flora and fauna of the Tarn gorge, the traditional architecture of L'Hermet hamlet, various types of shepherds' huts and a panorama of the south face of Mont Lozère.

Écomusée de la Cévenne
Created by the Cévennes National Park authority to preserve the history of the Cévennes and to enhance the natural and cultural heritage, this 'eco' museum links many different sites and locations, some developed within others, e.g. the paleontological site of St-Laurent-de-Trier, the path through the landscape of Barre des Cévennes, the Musée des Vallées Cévennes in St-Jean-du-Gard (*see SAINT-JEAN-DU-GARD*), the Musée de la Soie in St-Hippolyte-du-Fort (*see SAINT-HIPPOLYTE-DU-FORT*).

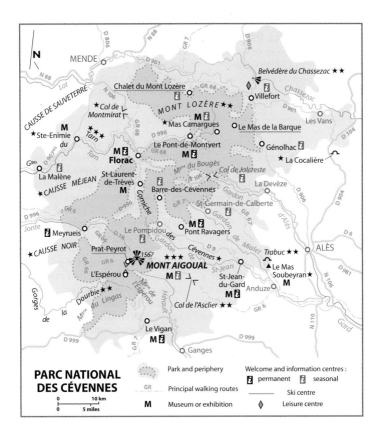

PARC NATIONAL DES CÉVENNES

0   10 km
0   5 miles

Park and periphery

GR   Principal walking routes

M   Museum or exhibition

Welcome and information centres :
🛈 permanent   🛈 seasonal

Ski centre

◆ Leisure centre

Working together or acting individually, the inhabitants of the canton of Pont-de-Montvert restored their traditional heritage.

🚗 DRIVING TOURS

GORGES DU TAPOUL
See regional map – 25km/15.5mi.

▶ Leave Florac to the S on the D 907, then turn right onto the D 996 (direction Meyrueis). At Les Vanels, turn left onto the D 907 as far as Rousses. There, turn right onto the D 119.

The road through the gorges du Tapoul can be obstructed by snow from mid December until mid March between Massevaques and Cabrillac.

The little Trépalous stream descends from the Aigoual, carving through the pink granite. Follow the ravine to find beautiful waterfalls.

▶ Beyond Cabrillac, you reach Mont Aigoual by the D 18 on the left.

LA CORNICHE DES CÉVENNES★
See regional map 58km/36mi from Florac to St-Jean-du-Gard – allow 2h.
This scenic trip is best in late afternoon, when the low-lying sun's rays throw the jagged outline of the ridges and the depth of the valleys into vivid relief.

▶ Leave Florac heading S on D 907. The road hugs the Tarnon valley and Causse Méjean escarpments, before climbing to St-Laurent-de-Trèves.

THE PRACTICAL PARK

Gentiâne – *Castagnols-Vialas.*
℘04 66 41 04 16. Closed mid-Nov–mid-Mar. Donkey hire for family walks (a donkey can carry luggage and a child).

St-Laurent-de-Trèves

On a limestone promontory overlooking this village, 190 million-year-old remains indicate the area was covered by a lagoon inhabited by two-legged, 4m tall **dinosaurs**.

The **Corniche des Cévennes**★ starts from the Col du Rey and continues through the windswept limestone plateau of the **Can de l'Hospitalet**, a Camisard assembly point in the 18C. The road then follows the edge of the plateau overlooking the Vallée Française watered by the Gardon de Ste-Croix. From **Col des Faïsses** (*faïsse*: a bank of cultivated land) the mountain drops away steeply on either side, providing a good view of the Cévennes. The road crosses the bare and rocky Can de l'Hospitalet plateau with stunning views of Mont Lozère, Barre-des-Cévennes, the Vallée Française and the Aigoual massif. At Le Pompidou, the road winds through chestnut groves and sparse daffodil meadows.

▶ Before St-Roman-de-Tousque, turn left onto D 140, then right onto D 983.

The road enters the **Vallée Française** travelled by Robert Louis Stevenson and his donkey Modestine (*℘p148*). The name Vallée Française dates from premedieval times when it was a Frankish enclave within Visigoth territory.

Notre-Dame de Valfrancesque

This charming 11C Romanesque sanctuary is now a Protestant church. The road runs down to St-Jean-du-Gard along the Gardon de Mialet riverbed, past the Marouls farm, a handy stopover for walkers.

Cévennes round trip

75km/47mi. 3h trip. ℐSee regional map.
This trip explores the Cévennes, crisscrossed by deep valleys containing houses roofed with schist slabs, roads lined with chestnut trees, and villages steeped in memories of the Camisard uprising.

▶ Head S from Florac on D 907 and N 106 towards Alès. The road follows the Mimente Valley flanked by schist cliffs. Beyond the ruins of the Château de St-Julien-d'Arpaon is a view of Le Bougès, rising to an altitude of 1 421m. At the Col de Jalcreste, turn right onto D 984 to St-Germain-de-Calberte.

Enjoy views of the Gardon de St-Germain valley. Beyond the pass, the road to **St-Germain-de-Calberte** is graced by chestnut trees, holm-oaks and broom, and then Cévennes-style houses with stone-slab roofs and decorative chimneys. The Château de Calberte, perched on a spur of rock, comes into view in a bend of the road.

▶ Beyond St-Germain-de-Calberte, turn right onto D 13.

Plan de Fontmort

In the Fontmort forest an 1887 obelisk celebrates the Edict of Tolerance signed by Louis XVI, and commemorates battles between Camisard rebels and the Maréchal de Villars.

Barre-des-Cévennes

This small village with its tall bare house fronts was a major defensive position during the Camisard uprising. See remains of entrenchments on the Colline du Castelas. Walk along the Barre-des-Cévennes footpath to discover the village's history and natural environment.

▶ Join the Corniche des Cévennes at the Col du Rey and turn right onto D 983. There are views of the Mont Aigoual range to the left and the Mont Lozère ridge to the right. Return to Florac via St-Laurent-de-Trèves and the Tarnon valley.

Mont Lozère★★

Between Florac, Génolhac and Villefort, this powerful granite massif rises majestically above the Cévennes countryside. Criss-crossed by numerous GR footpaths, including the six-day walk round Mont Lozère detailed in the GR 68 topoguide, this is perfect walking country.

- ⚙ **Michelin Map:** 330: J-8.
- 🛈 **Info:** Génolhac ✆ 04 66 61 18 32. Gagnières ✆ 04 66 25 40 65. www.cevennes-montlozere.com.
- ▶ **Location:** Mont Lozère is NE of Florac and SE of Mende.
- 👫 **Kids:** The Château d'Aujac and the Vallon du Villaret.
- ⚐ **Don't Miss:** The panoramas from pic Cassini and Montmirat, and the château d'Aujac's medieval village.

🚗 DRIVING TOURS

EASTERN MONT LOZÈRE★
Round tour from Le Pont-de-Montvert. 150km/93mi. Allow one day.

▶ Follow D 20 and turn right immediately after leaving Le Pont-de-Montvert.

The narrow road *(heavy summer traffic)* crosses barren pastures and heathland dotted with rocks.

Hôpital
Some old granite buildings in this hamlet have been bought and restored and the Écomusée has re-thatched the roofs of the watermill and old grange.

▶ The GR 7 footpath which crosses L'Hôpital leads to Pont-du-Tarn.

Pont-du-Tarn
🚶 *1h on foot there and back from L'Hôpital.*
The GR 7 follows the old Margeride sheep trail. A pretty bridge spans the river as it threads its way through polished rocks at the foot of the Commandeur woods.

Mas Camargues★
🕐 *Open Jul–Aug daily except Sat–Sun 10.30am–12.30pm, 2.30–6.30pm.* ✆ *04 66 45 80 73.*
This family mansion has been restored by the Parc national des Cévennes. An **observation trail** winds through a sheepfold, mill, small canal, reservoir and countryside.

🚶 Continue the walk to **Bellecoste** *(1km/0.6mi)* to see a communal oven and thatched shepherd's house.

▶ Return to D 20 and turn right.

The road climbs towards Finiels Pass and crosses deserted countryside marked with granite boulders. See Bougès mountain to the south and the hilly outline of the Causse Méjean.

'Mont Chauve'
Mont Lozère is called 'Bald Mountain' for its 35km/22mi of bare, high-lying plateaux. The mountain's Finiels summit (alt 1 699m) is the highest non-volcanic peak in the Massif Central. Its eroded granite has weathered into curious boulders amid heathland and remnants of ancient beech forest. Architecture is robust: some houses have granite boulders in their walls. Life is harsh on these exposed plateaux and most villages are deserted, yet storm bells once used to guide travellers during blizzards are still found here. In the 19C, 100 000 sheep grazed the hillside pastures during the summer.

Col de Finiels★

Alt 1 548m.

From the pass the **view★** encompasses Mont Aigoual and the Causses. Starting the descent, see the Tanargue massif ahead and to the right.

Chalet du Mont Lozère

Here are a refuge chalet, hotel, **information centre** for the Cévennes park and a large UCPA building (for the French open-air sports centres association) welcoming ramblers and horse-riders in summer. From December to April, it becomes a cross-country skiing centre.

Sommet de Finiels★

🚶 *3h on foot there and back.*

From Mont Lozère chalet, take the way-marked path to the top of the ridge. Turn right towards the remains of a stone hut. From here, a sweeping **view★★** takes in high plateaux peaks as far as Pic Cassini and the granite plateau of La Margeride. Follow the ridge to the 1 685m marker and the 'Route des Chômeurs' leads back to the departure point.

▷ Continue on the D 20 to Le Bleymard. Turn right onto D 901 towards Villefort.

The scenery turns bleak and rugged. The road leaves the Lot valley to follow the winding, wooded Altier valley, for a view of the towers of the 15C **Château de Champ**. Past Altier the road winds to Lake Villefort and the ruins of the Renaissance **Château de Castanet**.

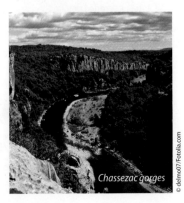
Chassezac gorges
© delmo07/Fotolia.com

Villefort reservoir and dam

The 190m long dam rises to a height of 70m above the river bed. The reservoir supplies the Pied-de-Borne plant downstream. On the road to Langogne are a water sports centre and beach. **Villefort** attracts water sports enthusiasts and makes an ideal base for trips into the Cévennes, Bas Vivarais and Mont Lozère. The Villefort Syndicat d'Initiative runs a seasonal **information centre** on the Parc national des Cévennes.

▷ 8km/5mi to the N by the D 906 (direction Langogne.)

La Garde-Guérin★

An impressive tower pinpoints this old fortified village on the plateau of the Lozère. Surrounded by a multitude of bubbling streams, La Garde-Guérin is on the geological boundary between the granite of Mont Lozère, and the schist of the Ardèche.

The village – All the houses in this village, largely inhabited by people raising livestock, are built of granite, accentuating the mountain characteristics of the area. Many of the houses have mullioned windows.

Donjon – Access by a porch to the left of the church. This is the last significant remains of a primitive castle, where the local lords established a toll of the road to Régordane.

Belvédère du Chassezac★★

🚶 *Park near the sign for the 'Belvédère', to the left of the D 906. A footpath leads to a narrow platform.*

The sight is especially striking, the eye plunging steeply down the gorges of the Chassezac to the foaming water, and the chaotic, jagged rocks.

▷ Return to Villefort. At the exit to the N of Villefort, take the D 66 towards Génolhac.

Mas de la Barque

The road rises above a ravine shaded by chestnut trees, and providing great **views** of Villefort and its valley. It passes through the hamlets of Paillère and

Costeilades. Shortly after the Pré de la Dame, you reach the Mas de la Barque. This forester's house, a welcome place for walkers, surrounded by meadows and tickets, is a popular ski resort in winter.

🥾 The two-hour return path to **Pic Cassini** offers a splendid **panorama**★★ of the Alps and Mont Ventoux.

▷ Return to Pré de la Dame and carry on towards Génolhac.

Belvédère des Bouzèdes ★
The road here makes a loop across the flanks of a hill dropping steeply to the Génolhac, 800m below.

Génolhac
The Maison de l'Arceau in this charming medieval Gardonnette valley town is an information centre on the Parc national des Cévennes and offers overnight accommodation.

▷ Go back towards Villefort on the D 906. At the turning for Génolhac head for Concoules for 2km/1.2mi; keep an eye open for signs indicating a path (800m) to the right.

Jardin du Tomple at Concoules
🕐*Open May–Aug daily 10am–8pm; Sept–Oct Tue, Thu, Sat–Sun 1–7pm. ⊗€5. ℘04 66 61 11 31. www.jardinslanguedoc.com.*
Nestled at the bottom of the valley, a tent marks the entrance to the garden where roses, perennials and shrubs bloom on the terraces.

▷ After Concoules, turn right on the D 451, then right again onto the D 51 before turning left onto the D 313 (direction Ponteils-Village). Take the first track on the left.

Jardin du Mas de l'Abri at Ponteils-et-Brésis
🕐*Open May–Oct 10am–7pm. ⊗€6. ℘04 66 61 17 61. www.jardinslanguedoc.com.*
On the sides of a beautiful valley traversed by a stream, the gardens are

laid out with trails, intimate corners and inviting benches.

▷ Go back to the D 51 and turn left.

The road comes out to **Brésis**, dominated by its medieval castle.

▷ Continue on the D 51 as far as Aujac.

👥 Château du Cheylard d'Aujac
🕐*Open Jul–Aug guided tours daily except Mon 2–7pm; rest of year Sun and public holidays 2–6pm. ⊗€5. ℘04 66 61 19 94. www.chateau-aujac.org.*
The 11C castle over the Cèze valley is one of the best-preserved in the area.

▷ Follow D 134 W towards Génolhac, turn left onto the road to Alès, then right onto D 998 towards Florac.

The road along the Luech valley is particularly scenic as far as St-Maurice-de-Ventalon.

▷ Continue 2km/1mi after Les Bastides, a road on the right leads to Troubat farm-house.

Ferme-fortifiée de l'Aubaret
The pink-granite walls of this fortified farm on the Margeride sheep trail have mullioned windows.

▷ Rejoin D 998 and turn right to return to Le Pont-de-Montvert.

WESTERN MONT LOZÈRE★★
100km/62mi – allow half a day. Leave Mende on D 25 heading SE towards the airport. In Langlade, turn left onto D 41.

Lanuéjols
The **Roman mausoleum** was erected by wealthy Roman citizens to the memory of their two young sons.

▷ Continue along D 41.

Bagnols-les-Bains
The mineral waters of this spa resort were first exploited by the Romans.

Bagnols' altitude and nearby forests contribute to its healthy mountain air.

▷ *From Bagnols drive N along a road leading to Le Villaret.*

👥 Le Vallon du Villaret
🕐 *Open Jul–Aug 10am–6.45pm; Apr–Jun 10.30am–6.45pm; Sep–Oct weekends 11am–6pm.* ⊜*€11.50– €12.50.* ✆*04 66 47 63 76. www.levallon.fr.*
This leisure park has a nature theme and village with artist studios, exhibitions and concert venues.

▷ Return to Bagnols and turn left to Le Bleymard.

The valley sides become steep rocky gorges and in the distance Tournel Castle ruins perch on a rocky spur.

▷ Turn right onto D 20.

Le Pont-de-Montvert
🚻*See FLORAC; Le Pont-de-Montvert.*

▷ Turn right onto D 998 to Florac.

The upper Tarn valley narrows into rugged gorges, and the ruined 14C Miral Castle perches on a promontory.

Florac 🚻*See FLORAC.*

▷ Drive N along N 106 towards Mende.

Beyond the intersection with the road to Ispagnac along the **Tarn gorge★★★** is a spectacular cliff-edge passage overlooks Florac.

Col de Montmirat★
The pass slices between the granite of Mont Lozère and the limestone of the Causse de Sauveterre. Enjoy the **Panorama★**: looming Causse Méjean cliffs, Cévennes ridges and Mont Aigoual. The road descends into the Bramon valley with views of the 'Truc de Balduc' and Mont Lozère foothills.

Balsièges
To the south of this village tower the cliffs of the Causse de Sauveterre. N 88 follows the Lot between the Causses de Mende and de Changefège.

Massif de l'Aigoual★★★

A region of the Aigoual mountain massif falls within the Parc National des Cévennes. Breathtaking river gorges like the Dourbie, the Jonte and the Trévezel carve through the massif, and scenic roads wind through forests and skirt spellbinding ridges, all the way to the panoramic summit.

A BIT OF HISTORY
From July 1944 onwards, the Aigoual massif was the centre of the important 'Aigoual-Cévennes' resistance movement, headquartered at L'Espérou.

🚻 **Michelin Map:** 339: G-4.
▷ **Location:** 70km/45mi E of Millau. The route covers the whole Aigoual massif and leads to the summit. Follow it from Meyrueis to Le Vigan to see the particularly spectacular stretch of road across the Minier Pass and down to the Arre valley.

GEOGRAPHIC NOTES
A gigantic water tower – The Aigoual is one of the major water catchment areas in the Massif Central, as clouds rolling in from the chilly Atlantic converge with warm Mediterranean air over the

Reforestation on the Aigoual

A century ago, **Aigoual**'s mountain massif was devoid of trees and vegetation. A reforestation scheme was launched in 1875 by **Georges Fabre**, head warden of the French Rivers Authority and Forestry Commission. He obtained the rights to purchase communal and privately owned land, and planted large stands of trees along the river banks to prevent soil erosion. Some towns and villages were hostile and refused to part with their pastureland, but over time Fabre restored the Aigoual to its forested glory. He also developed the network of roads and footpaths which covers the Aigoual, restored foresters' lodges, set up arboretums and built an observatory for meteorological research.

summit. Called 'Aiqualis' or 'the watery one,' the mountain's average annual rainfall can be 2.25m.

🚗 DRIVING TOURS

😊 *Driving: between November and May roads may be blocked by snow.*
🚶 *Walking: the GR 6 (Alps-Atlantic) and GR 7 (Vosges-Pyrenees) footpaths meet in the Aigoual massif, with subsidiary walks like GR 66, described in the topoguide Tour du Mont Aigoual. In summer the Parc national des Cévennes organises guided walks.*

MEYRUEIS TO MONT AIGOUAL
32km/20mi. Allow 3h.

▶ 2km/1.25mi to the S on the D 986 to a little road on the left.

Château de Roquedols
Leave your car in the car park, and walk to the castle on a forest trail.
This 15C–16C castle takes the form of a large square flanked by four round towers. From Meyrueis, the climb to the col de Montjardin sets off through forest at first and then along the left bank of the Bétuzon. From the col there is an extensive view of the Larzac plateau, and, soon after, of the mountains of Aigoual and Espérou. Running along the escarpment edge, the road provides beautiful glimpses of the old silver and lead mines of Villemagne.

Abîme de Bramabiau★
Temperature: 8°C. 🚶 *2km/1.25mi there and back.* 👁☀Jul and Aug 10am–6.30pm; Apr–Jun and Sep 10am–5.30pm; Oct 11.30am–5.45pm. ⚅€9. ✆04 67 82 60 78. *www.abime-de-bramabiau.com.*
The river Bonheur bursts into a rocky cirque called the 'Alcôve' as a glorious waterfall. When the river is in spate, the deafening waterfall is like the bellowing of a bull – hence the river's name 'Bramabiau' (*Brame-Biâou*: singing bull). You enter the underground world at the point where the Bramabiau river re-emerges. After crossing the Bramabiau between the first waterfall and the second (underground), the path leads to the 'Salle du Havre' (harbour chamber). At the **'Grand Aven'** swallow-hole, you can admire the cave paintings of Jean Truel. A path along a ledge above the river leads back up the Martel gallery overlooking the 'Pas de Diable' (devil's footprint). Here some 200m of the cavern's length are dug out of a whitish barite seam, which opens into the 'Petit Labyrinthe', leading to the **'Salle de l'Étoile'** (star chamber).

▶ A few hundred yards beyond the Abîme de Bramabiau is the junction with D 157, which leads to the Gorges du Trévezela

Col de la Sereyrède★
This pass straddles the Atlantic-Mediterranean watershed. The road from the Col de la Sereyrède to the Aigoual summit offers **views** over the Hérault valley.

Sentier des Botanistes

1.5km/1mi below the summit, a signpost indicates the trail. 20min walk.

This trail loops round the Trépaloup Peak for 1km/0.6mi and overlooks the arboretum **Hort-de-Dieu**, 'God's garden'. The footpath affords fine views of the craggy ridges of the Aigoual's south face, the Cévennes peaks and forest-covered eastern slopes of the Aigoual.

Mont Aigoual★★★

The French meteorological office *(Météo France)* now occupies this **meteorological observatory** built on the summit in 1887 by the French Rivers Authority and Forestry Commission. Overlooking the Gard, Hérault and Tarn valleys, this site is ideal for testing sophisticated equipment under extreme conditions. An interesting exhibition, **Exposition Météo-France** covers weather forecasting past and present, and the French Météotel system.

From the tower, the **panorama★★★** encompasses the Causses and the Cévennes, the Cantal range, Mont Ventoux, the Alps, the Languedoc plain, the Mediterranean and the Pyrenees. In January you can see both Mont Blanc (Alps) and Maladetta (Pyrenees). In July and August, a heat haze often blurs the landscape and it's best to avoid the summit during the heat of the day. Climb by

The Great 'Draille du Languedoc'

The Col de la Sereyrède was once part of the great 'draille du Languedoc', or wide sheep trail used for transferring flocks from summer to winter pastures. *(Follow the path of the old 'draille' north along D 18, and south along the GR 7 to the town of L'Espérou, where the track turns off towards Valleraugue.)* Sheep tracks are recognisable by the deep channels they cut into the Cévennes ridges. Herds are still driven up to L'Espérou on foot during the Fête de la Transhumance in mid-June.

night to reach the summit at daybreak, when visibility is excellent.

MONT AIGOUAL TO PONT D'HÉRAULT

39km/24mi. Allow 1h30.

From the summit of Mont Aigoual, return to the Col de la Sereyrède. On the left before the pass, look for the waterfall formed by the sprightly young Hérault tumbling through in a ravine on the far side of the valley.

L'Espérou

This small town's picturesque mountain setting and the ski slopes at **Prat-Peyrot** make it a popular summer and winter holiday destination.

Col du Minier★★

This pass offers views of the Mediterranean in fine weather. A memorial stone commemorates Général Huntziger (Commander of the French II Armée in Sedan) and his colleagues killed in an air crash in November 1941.

Lac des Pises – *At the col du Minier, take the forest trail towards the col de l'Homme Mort.*

A nature trail allows visitors to tour this artificial lake, a relic of a tourist project that the national park later abandoned.The walk takes you into relatively unknown landscapes, with a good chance of seeing migrating birds. At the start of the long descent, the road overlooks the Souls ravine, and provides a splendid view of the Montdardier plateau and the Séranne.

Return to l'Espérou and take the D 986 towards Pont d'Hérault.

Arboretum de Puechagut

Created at the end of the 19C by Georges Fabre, the arboretum was intended as a place to experiment with exotic trees.

Belvédère de la Cravate

Lower down, this viewpoint provides a fine panorama over the Arve basin, the Larzac plateau, the mountains of Séranne and Pic St-Loup.

Col du Minier viewed from the meteorological observatory on Mont Aigoual

© Denis Caviglia/hemis.fr

Sentier des 4 000 marches
21km/13mi. Allow one day.
This is for experienced walkers, and starts from the Hort-de-Dieu arboretum.
This stony footpath winds through the Hort-de-Dieu arboretum and across wilder heathland dotted with broom. Winding down the chestnut-covered slopes, the trail offers fine views of Valleraugue and the upper Hérault valley. From **Valleraugue**, return along the same path or follow a more varied but longer itinerary via Aire-de-Côte *(leave Valleraugue along D 10 to Berthézène).*

Jardin des Sambucs
Le Villaret, 30570 St-André-de-Majencoules. Open mid-Apr–mid-May Sat–Sun and public holidays 10am–6pm; mid-May–mid-Sept daily 10am–7pm. €7. ℘04 67 82 46 47. www.jardinsambucs.com.
This garden, with its many perennials, lotus and water lilies, flourishes in a setting of fountains and pools.

Continue on D 986 to Pont d'Hérault.

Gorges de la Dourbie★★

The old market town of Nant lies on the banks of the Dourbie at the mouth of the river gorge. A 7C monastic community transformed this swamp into a fertile valley with vineyards and meadows.

- **Population:** 955.
- **Michelin Map:** 338: L-6.
- **Info:** Nant, Pl. du Claux, 12230. ℘05 65 62 24 21. www.ot-nant.fr.
- **Location:** 34km/21mi SW of Millau.

NANT
The original monastery destroyed by Saracens in the 8C was rebuilt two centuries later. The Benedictine monastery prospered and in 1135 was promoted to the status of abbey. The fortified town that grew up around it became a Roman Catholic bastion during the Wars of Religion. The college founded at Nant in 1662 specialised in literature and philosophy.

The austere abbey church (**Église abbatiale St-Pierre**) has a central arch with a Gothic doorway and trefoil arch moulding. Inside, note the decoration on the **capitals★**.
The old covered market (**vieille halle**), once part of the monastery, has a squat, sturdy gallery with five arcades (14C). From the Chapelle du Claux (Wars of Religion memorial) there is a good view of the 14C bridge (**Pont de la Prade**).

🚗 DRIVING TOURS

GORGES DE LA DOURBIE★★

▷ Leave Nant SE on D 999. From Nant to L'Espérou 35km/22mi.

About 1h. 👁 There are numerous sharp bends and difficult road junctions.

Between St-Jean and Nant, the Dourbie valley is wide and cultivated. On the left are the four towers of Castelnau Castle, now a farm. Leave the car at the 'St-Michel' signpost to the left of the road and climb the narrow path to the chapel.

St-Michel-de-Rouviac
In the 12C, this Romanesque chapel was a priory and a daughter-house of Nant abbey. Both buildings have similar capitals with knotwork and palmettes.

St-Jean-du-Bruel
This summer holiday resort opening onto the Dourbie gorge, makes a base for various walks. A 15C **humpback bridge** spans the Dourbie, and near the new bridge is an attractive 18C covered market.

👥 Noria – Maison de l'Eau★
👟🕐 *Open Jul–Aug daily 10am–7pm; Apr–Jun daily 2–6pm; Sep–Oct daily except Mon 2–6pm.* 🕐*Closed Nov–Mar.* ✆€6. 𝒫05 65 62 20 32. *www.noria-espacedeleau.com.*
On the banks of the Dourbie, this ancient mill has seen flood damage on many occasions, and undergone many changes since the 13C.
Today, it is at the heart of a fascinating learning space that illustrates the interaction between man and water, whether on the surrounding plateaux or elsewhere. Among the many attractions is an interesting presentation of the valley's hydroelectric system.

▷ Take the D 341.

Col de la Pierre Plantée
A view from the pass overlooks the Dourbie valley, Lingas mountain range and Causse du Larzac.

▷ Turn left onto D 47.

Gorges du Trévezel★
The Trévezel river flows between the Aigoual range and the Dourbie valley, over a bed strewn with boulders. The valley gradually narrows to become a ravine and the narrowest part is known as the *Pas de l'Ase* ('Donkey's Step').

▷ Return to Col de la Pierre Plantée and turn right onto D 151.

The narrow winding road runs high above the **Gorges de la Dourbie★★** all the way to Dourbies.

L'Espérou
🕮*See Massif de l'AIGOUAL.*

LE CANYON DE LA DOURBIE★★
From Nant to La Roque-Ste-Marguerite 17.9/11.1mi. Allow 1h. Downstream from Nant, the valley narrows again between the limestone rocks of the Grands Causses.

▷ Leave Nant on the D 991 SE.

Cantobre★
This picturesque village at the confluence of the Trévezel and Dourbie Rivers deserves its name: *quant obra*, meaning 'what a masterpiece'.

Canyon de la Dourbie★★
The road offers a superb **view★** of the village and remains of the old castle of the **Marquis de Montcalm** (1712–59) who died on the Plains of Abraham in Quebec City, Canada, defending the town against the English. The road continues past **Moulin de Corps**, a water-mill powered by a resurgent spring.

La Roque-Ste-Marguerite
This village lies in the shadow of the ruin-shaped rocks of Le Rajol and Mont-pellier-le-Vieux and a 17C castle tower.

Le Vigan

This little town in the Cévennes lies on the southern slope of Mont Aigoual in the fertile Arre valley. An old bridge dating from before the 13C spans the Arre. There is a good view of it from a platform on the riverbank, upstream of the bridge.

> ▶ **Population:** 4 085.
> ◔ **Michelin Map:** 526 N7-8.
> ▯ **Info:** Pl. du Marché. ✆04 67 81 01 72. www.cevennes-meridionales.com.
> ◑ **Location:** 70km/44mi SW of Alès, and 65km/41mi N of Montpellier.

THE TOWN

Among the most agreeable places in this town, the promenade des Châtaigniers, created in the 18C, crosses a former fairground, and, as its name suggests, is amply shaded by chestnut trees.

The heart of Vigan, however, is the grand place du Quai, which used to be a halt on the royal route between Aix and Montauban. Spanning the Arre, the Vieux Pont, is earlier than the 13C. There is a good view of it from upstream.

🚗 DRIVING TOUR

VALLÉE DE L'ARRE

The route follows the valley and offers a lovely contrast between its southern slopes of arid limestone that forms the cliffs of the Blandas plateau, the north, where slate and oak predominate, forming the foothills of the Lingas mountain range. The village of **Arre** has long specialised in dyeing textiles.

Cirque de Navacelles★★★

The Cirque de Navacelles is the most impressive natural feature of the Vis valley, which cuts between the causses of Blandas to the north and Larzac to the south. The cirque is formed by an immense, magnificent meander, deeply embedded in almost vertical walls of rock. The meander, which once encircled a little promontory, was abandoned by the river Vis, which broke through the neck of a loop, just where the village of Navacelles had established itself.

> ▯ **Info:** Point Info belvédère de la Baume-Auriol. ✆04 67 44 63 10.
> ◑ **Location:** 72km/45mi NW of Montpellier, 34km/21m NE of Lodève and SE of Ganges by the D25 & D130.
> ◈ **Don't Miss:** The Belvédère Nord, the Cirque de Vissec and the Gorges of the Vis.
> ◔ **Timing:** Allow two hours.

🚗 DRIVING TOUR

ALZON TO GANGES
57km/35mi. Allow 2h.

Downstream from Alzon, the road (D 814) drops to the floor of the valley, then crosses the river which makes wider and wider meanders on the flat valley floor. D 113 runs along the floor of the

Cirque de Navacelles

© Pierre Jacques/hemis.fr

valley to Vissec and crosses a bridge over the river, which is frequently dried up at this point.

Vissec
The village, squatting deep down inside the canyon, consists of two districts, each on an outcrop, one of which is almost completely encircled by the Vis.

Cirque de Vissec★
During the climb up to Blandas (*gradient 9 percent*), there is a view of the gorge with its bare cliff walls.

Belvédère Nord
From this viewpoint on the north edge of the plateau there is an interesting view over the **Cirque de Navacelles** and the Vis canyon. The clearly marked road winds down one or two hairpin bends at the top of the cliff, then forms a large loop round the Combe du Four, before dropping steeply down to the floor of the cirque and onto Navacelles.

Navacelles
This village has a pretty single-arched bridge over the Vis. 🏃 A path from Navacelles leads to the resurgence of the Vis and the Virenque near three watermills.

> **Cliff Hanger**
> Roads in this region tend to be poorly maintained and can often be wide enough only for a single vehicle. The road down into the valley is sheer, clinging to the cliff face; a dramatic drive.

La Baume-Auriol
From north of the farm, there is a magnificent view of the cirque. Beyond La Baume-Auriol, the road continues to St-Maurice-Navacelles, where you should turn left towards Ganges. Farther along, the road plunges downhill in a series of hairpin bends.

Gorges de la Vis★★
Beyond Madières, the road sticks closely to the banks of the Vis, which cuts between the tall dolomitic cliffs of the Causse de Blandas and the slopes of Séranne mountain. After Gorniès, a bridge spans the Vis. Look out for a lovely view of **Beauquiniès**, a pretty terraced village, and then of the **Roc de Senescal**, which juts out like a ship's prow from the slope on the left. The valley becomes narrow and rugged, before running into the Hérault gorge. Carry on along the banks of the Hérault to Le Pont and Ganges.

Saint-Jean-du-Gard

The narrow high street of this ancient town, lying on the banks of the Gardon, is lined with austere houses. An old humpback cutwater bridge spanning the river, which was partially destroyed by flooding in 1958, adds a picturesque note to the scenery.

SIGHTS
Château
First mentioned in 1314, the château (⊶ *not open to the public*) was damaged during the Wars of Religion, an episode that the owners illustrated in an exhibition of paintings and old books.

▶ **Population:** 2 871.

⚅ **Michelin Map:** 339: I-4.

🄸 **Info:** Pl. Rabaut-St-Étienne, 30270 St-Jean-du-Gard. ℘04 66 85 31 11.

◗ **Location:** 30km/19mi W of Alès by the N110, then the D910A and 88km/55mi from Montpellier by the A9 and the N110. Follow the D907 to St Jean du Gard.

🅿 **Parking:** Difficult especially on Tuesday (Market).

◉ **Don't Miss:** The view from the Col d'Asclier.

🕔 **Timing:** Allow one hour for the town – more if you visit the market.

🚗 DRIVING TOUR

ROUTE DU COL DE L'ASCLIER★★

44km/27mi from St-Jean-du-Gard to Pont-d'Hérault. Allow 1h30.

😊 *The pass is usually blocked by snow from December to March.*

This itinerary leads from the Gardon valley to the Hérault valley across a typical Cévennes ridge. D 907 meanders up the Gardon valley from St-Jean, following the river closely. Just before l'Estréchure, turn left onto D 152 towards Col de l'Asclier. Beyond Milliérines, the landscape becomes wild; the road overlooks the valleys of several tributaries of St-Jean-Gardon, then runs round the Hierle ravine.

Col de l'Asclier★★

The road runs beneath a bridge, part of the Margeride track (*draille*) used by flocks of sheep on their way to high pastures. From the pass there is a magnificent panoramic view to the west.

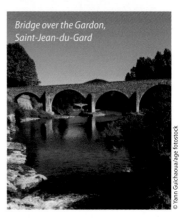

Bridge over the Gardon, Saint-Jean-du-Gard

© Yann Guichaoua/age fotostock

Col de la Triballe

From the pass there is an extensive view of the Cévennes range; the village of St-Martial can be seen in the valley below. The picturesque D 420 leads down into the Hérault valley, with a few hamlets hanging onto the slopes on both sides.

Cross the river Hérault in Peyregrosse then turn left onto D 986 to Pont-d'Hérault.

Anduze

Anduze, a centre of Protestantism, is the last town on the plain and the first in the Cévennes mountains. It nestles between two folds in the rock at a narrow entrance that gives into the Cévennes proper.

SIGHTS
Tour de l'Horloge
Dating from 1320, the clock tower is all that remains of the town's fortifications.

Temple Protestant
The temple was built in 1823 on the site of former barracks; it is one of the largest temples in France.

The Old Town
The narrow tortuous streets of the Old Town, like the rue Bouquerie and the rue Droite are a delight to explore.

▶ **Population:** 3 437.

⛓ **Michelin Map:** 526: Q7.

🔲 **Info:** Plan de Brie - BP 6 - 30140 Anduze. ☏04 66 61 98 17. www.cevennesgrandsud.cool.

◐ **Location:** 17km/11mi SW of Alès, and 13km/8mi from St-Jean-du-Gard.

👥 **Kids:** Take them to the music museum.

🕐 **Timing:** Allow half a day or more.

😊 **Don't miss:** The old town, and the multi-coloured bamboo jungle at Prafrance.

👥 Musée de la Musique
Rte d'Alès. 🕐*Open Jul–Aug 3–6.30pm.* ☏*04 66 61 86 60. www.musee-musique.com.*

An excellent opportunity to brush up on musical instruments through the ages.

EXCURSIONS
👥 Bambouseraie de Prafrance★★

17km/10.5mi SW. Leave Alès on N 110, turn right on D 910A then right on D 129.
🚹🕐*Open late-Feb–late-Mar and Oct 9.30am–6pm; late-Mar–Sept 9.30am–7pm; 1st 2 weeks in Nov 9.30am–5pm.* 👌€10.50.
📞*04 66 61 70 47.*
www.bambouseraie.com.

This 10ha bamboo plantation was founded in 1855 by Cévennes native Eugène Mazel. Mazel became fascinated with bamboo while studying silkworm breeding in Asia, where bamboo is used for making everything from baskets, umbrella handles, ladders, irrigation pipes, scaffolding and building houses to making musical instruments. Mazel imported bamboo cuttings, and in this soil enriched by alluvial deposits of the Gardon, the bamboo grew into a spectacular 20m jungle. The plantation also contains Californian sequoias, palm trees, a Virginian tulip tree, and a Laotian bamboo village with trees from Japan, China and America.

Château de Tornac

4km/2.5mi from Anduze via D 901 towards Nîmes then D 982 in the direction of St-Hippolyte-du-Fort.
The castle was built in the 12C around a watch tower. It was damaged by fire during the Revolution.

🚗 DRIVING TOUR

DES CAMISARDS

26km/16mi from Anduze to St-Jean-du-Gard by the Gardon de Mialet. Allow half a day.

Musée du Désert★

🕐*Open daily Mar–Nov 9.30am–noon, 2–6pm (Jul–Aug 9.30am–6.30pm).*
🕐*Closed Dec–Feb.* 👌€5. 📞*04 66 85 02 72. www.museedudesert.com.*

Le Mas Soubeyran overlooks the rugged countryside around River Gardon, where a few huddled houses stand out on a plateau surrounded by mountains.

▶ Continue along the D 50.

Grotte de Trabuc★★

👋*Jul–Aug guided tours 10.15am, 11am, 11.45am, 12.30pm, 1.15pm, 2pm; Apr–Jun and Sep 10am–5.30pm; Feb–Mar and Oct–mid-Nov 2–4.30pm.*
🕐*Closed mid-Nov–Jan.* 👌€10.30 (child 5–12, €6.20. 📞04 66 85 03 28.
www.grotte-de-trabuc.com/en.
Trabuc cave, the largest in the Cévennes, was inhabited in the Neolithic period and later used by the Romans. During the Wars of Religion, Camisards hid in its labyrinthine galleries. The cave is named after a band of brigands known as the Trabucaires, who used it as their den.

Cave highlights include the Gong chamber, which resonates like a gong, the *gours*, or underground lakes formed by weirs of calcite, the 'red cascades', petrified calcite torrents coloured with oxides, and the aragonite crystallisations, tinted black by manganese. Most impressive is the underground landscape formed by the **'Hundred thousand soldiers'★★**, extraordinary concretions formed in *gours* resembling the Great Wall of China.

Le Gardon de Mialet

On the return to Mas Soubeyran, you run along the Gardon de Mialet (many opportunities for swimming) by a narrow and sinuous route and through a landscape that it typically Cévenols. The scenery is superb, and after 6.5km/4mi you reach the impressive **pont des Abarines**.

Saint-Hippolyte-du-Fort

Sheltered by the southern foothills of the Cévennes, Saint-Hippolyte-du-Fort opens out onto the plains of Languedoc, perfumed with the heady scent of thyme and rosemary. From the past, the city has retained a couple of towers and a few narrow streets lined with houses that possess noble façades. But the most important reason to go there is to discover the mysteries of silk-worm breeding, which has made a significant contribution to the prosperity and well-being of the people of the region.

▸ **Population:** 3 997.

Michelin Map: 526: P8.

Info: Pl. du 8-Mai-1945 - Les Casernes. &04 66 77 91 65. www.cevennes-garrigue-tourisme.com.

Location: 49km/31mi N of Montpellier, and 38km/24mi SW of Alès.

Timing: Allow at least half a day to explore the town and surrounding area.

Don't miss: The silk museum (Musée de la Soie), and the fascinating medieval streets of Sauve.

VISIT
Musée de la Soie
Pl. du 8-Mai-1945. Open Jul–Aug 10.30am–12.30pm, 2–6pm; rest of year daily except Mon. Closed Jan–mid-Feb, 25 Dec. €5.50. &04 30 67 26 94. www.museedelasoie-cevennes.com.
Housed in a former barracks, the museum traces through old documents and tools, the traditional silk manufacturing techniques, many of which are still used today. For those intrigued by this activity, the museum demonstrates the peculiar life cycles of the silkworm.

EXCURSIONS
Sauve
8km/5mi to the E along the D 999.
Built in an amphitheatre along the Vidourle, Sauve is the capital of Salavès, the lords of which bore the title 'Satraps'. This seemingly random maze of narrow streets, often crossed by arches and vaulted passageways, is a place of great charm and intrigue.

Conservatoire de la Fourche – *Les Casernes, r. des Boisseliers.* Open Tue–Sat 2–6pm. €4. &04 66 80 54 66. www.lafourchedesauve.fr. Sauve has an industry that is quite original; it makes hay forks. The museum is a place of living memory where craftsmen still produce hayforks by traditional methods. They are sold to individuals and professionals who use them in daily agriculture.

Mer de rochers – *20min there and back.* At the top of the cliff, from where there is a beautiful view of the village rooftops below, the scented garrigue and a chaos of rocks ripples to the horizon, and from this wild land rises an ancient dungeon, the remains of the castle of Roquevaire, surrounded by cypress trees.

Corconne
22km/14mi S by the D 999.
Corconne is an agreeable medieval village set at the foot of a steep cliff, part of the limestone massif of Coutach. Above the village, out of sight, is a strange natural arch, that is worth a visit.

Durfort
11km/7mi NE, along the D 999 and the D 982 (direction Anduze).
At the edge of the Sor valley, Durfort has always been a centre of coppersmithing. Coppersmiths continue this industry today, working with the last tilt-hammer (15C) still in operation to produce copper objects.

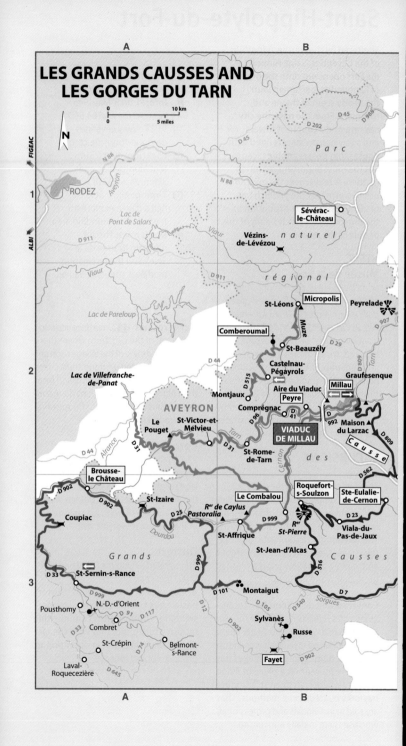

LES GRANDS CAUSSES AND LES GORGES DU TARN

0   10 km
0   5 miles

N

FIGEAC
ALBI

RODEZ

Lac de Pont de Salars

Lac de Pareloup

Lac de Villefranche-de-Panat

AVEYRON

Le Pouget

St-Victor-et-Melvieu

Brousse-le Château

Coupiac

St-Izaire

St-Sernin-s-Rance

N.-D.-d'Orient

Pousthomy

Combret

St-Crépin

Belmont-s-Rance

Laval-Roquecezière

Grands

Dourdou

Pastoralia

R^{er} de Caylus

St-Affrique

Montaigut

Sylvanès

Russe

Fayet

Le Combalou

St-Jean-d'Alcas

Roquefort-s-Soulzon

R^{er} St-Pierre

Ste-Eulalie-de-Cernon

Viala-du-Pas-de-Jaux

Causses

Sorgues

Parc

naturel

régional

Sévérac-le-Château

Vézins-de-Lévézou

St-Léons

Micropolis

Peyrelade

Comberoumal

St-Beauzély

Castelnau-Pégayrols

Aire du Viaduc

Graufesenque

Millau

Montjaux

Peyre

Comprégnac

VIADUC DE MILLAU

Maison du Larzac

Causse

St-Rome-de-Tarn

des

Muze

Tarn

Cernon

Aveyron

Viaur

Viaur

Alrance

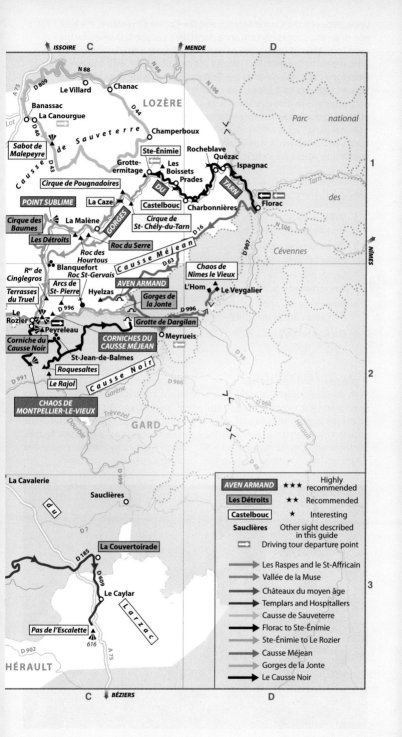

ISSOIRE C   MENDE   D

A 75   D 809   Le Villard   Chanac
Banassac   N 88
La Canourgue   LOZÈRE
Lot   D 46   N 106
                D 44   Champerboux   Parc   national
Sabot de   Sauveterre
Malepeyre   de   Ste-Énimie   Rocheblave
D 43   Causse   Grotte-   Quézac
                ermitage   Les   Ispagnac
Cirque de Pougnadoires   Boissets   TARN
                    Prades   des
POINT SUBLIME   La Caze   Castelbouc   Charbonnières   Florac
Cirque des   La Malène   GORGES   Cirque de   Tarn
Baumes   St-Chély-du-Tarn
Les Détroits   Roc du Serre   D 16   N 106
            Causse Méjean   D 63   Cévennes   NÎMES
Roc des
Hourtous   Chaos de
Rer de   Blanquefort   Nimes le Vieux
Cinglegros   Roc St-Gervais   L'Hom   Le Veygalier
Arcs de   AVEN ARMAND
Terrasses   St-Pierre   Hyelzas   Gorges de
du Truel   la Jonte   D 996
Le   D 996   D 18
Rozier   Grotte de Dargilan
Peyreleau   Meyrueis
Corniche du   CORNICHES DU
Causse Noir   CAUSSE MÉJEAN
D 991   Roquesaltes   St-Jean-de-Balmes   D 986
Le Rajol   Causse Noir
            Garène
CHAOS DE   Trévezel   GARD
MONTPELLIER-LE-VIEUX
                Double   D 986   Hérault
            D 999
La Cavalerie   2
du   Sauclières   D 7

D 185   La Couvertoirade
D 609
        Le Caylar
Larzac
Pas de l'Escalette
616
D 902   A 75
HÉRAULT   3
C   BÉZIERS   D

AVEN ARMAND	★★★	Highly recommended
Les Détroits	★★	Recommended
Castelbouc	★	Interesting
Sauclières		Other sight described in this guide
⇨		Driving tour departure point

⟶ Les Raspes and le St-Affricain
⟶ Vallée de la Muse
⟶ Châteaux du moyen âge
⟶ Templars and Hospitallers
⟶ Causse de Sauveterre
⟶ Florac to Ste-Énimie
⟶ Ste-Énimie to Le Rozier
⟶ Causse Méjean
⟶ Gorges de la Jonte
⟶ Le Causse Noir

LES GRANDS CAUSSES *and Les Gorges du Tarn*

Lying between the Causse Méjean and the Causse Sauveterre, the beautiful and dramatic Gorges du Tarn are essentially a canyon fashioned by the river Tarn. Most of the gorges lie within the Lozère department, but a little bit creeps into Aveyron. The *causses* are part of a huge, wild and beautiful limestone plateau, known as the Grands Causses, lying at an altitude of between 800m and 1,250m. The curious delight with the causses is that they defy attempts to pinpoint them with accuracy. This is a vast, amorphous plateau sprawling across three departments, and embraced within their own national park. This is wilderness in the true sense of the word, a place that leaves you bewildered, and in which to enjoy many happy days of random wandering where serendipity is the best guide.

Highlights

1   **Millau** is a bustling and engaging place to visit (p173)

2   The **Millau viaduct**: a masterpiece of engineering (p175)

3   Simply stunning, **La Couvertoirade** (p181)

4   Drive the largest of the *causses*, the **Causse du Larzac** (p183)

5   The **Gorges du Tarn** are sublime (p187)

A place of hidden riches

With its bewitching light, rocky chaos, limpid waters, verdant gorges and limestone steppes, the Grands Causses have long fascinated the touring visitor. But those who come to study nature, will find riches beyond compare among the 1 500 species of plants, including many orchids, abundant wildlife, especially the griffon vulture, which was reintroduced here in 1981. The historical geography of the region is exemplified in the stunning legacy of historic buildings dating from Neolithic dolmens more than 7 000 years old to the frankly breathtaking viaduct above Millau.

The Middle Ages, a time of uncertainty throughout Europe, saw the development of an agri-pastoral economy under the care of the Knights Templar, whose fortified villages, like La Couvertoirade, still rise above the Larzac causse.

In spite of containing no fewer than 94 towns and villages, with a population of more than 66 000, this brilliant landscape still contrives to retain all the essential qualities of a natural terrain, barely touched by man's presence and influences. Nature is supreme!

Peyreleau, Causse Noir

© Pierre Jacques/hemis.fr

Millau★

This bustling valley town at the confluence of the Tarn and Dourbie makes a great base for excursions to the Causses and the Tarn gorges. The nearby slopes of Borie Blanque and Brunas and Andan peaks are popular for paragliding and hang-gliding.

A BIT OF HISTORY

A glove-making town – In this ewe's milk cheese-making part of the Causses, a leather industry naturally developed, and Millau became known for lambskin gloves. Today, Millau annually produces some 250 000 pairs of gloves exported around the world, and has also expanded into *haute couture*, shoe-making, diverse leather goods and furnishings.

The Graufesenque potteries – During the 1C this town, called Condatomagus – 'the market where the rivers meet', was a Roman centre for earthenware production, with its fine local clay, plentiful water supply and wood from the forests. Condatomagus produced *terra sigillata* ware, bright-red glazed pottery decorated with floral, geometric or historiated patterns of Hellenistic influence. Over 500 potters created millions of pieces for export throughout Europe, the Middle East and even India. Visit the Graufesenque archaeological site and see the Musée de Millau's large collection of earthenware.

●☆ WALKING TOUR

TOWN
Place du Maréchal-Foch

This most attractive part of the old town has a covered square embellished with 12C–16C arcades.

Église Notre-Dame-de l'Espinasse

This church once possessed a thorn from the Crown of Thorns, hence its name. An important pilgrimage centre in the Middle Ages, the Romanesque building was partly destroyed in 1582 and rebuilt in 17C. The frescoes decorating the chan-

▶ **Population:** 23 123.
Ϛ **Michelin Map:** 338: K-6.
🛈 **Info:** Office du tourisme Millau Grands Causses, 1 pl. du Beffroi, 12100 Millau. ℘05 65 60 02 42. www.millau-viaduc-tourisme.fr.
◉ **Location:** 116km/72.5mi N of Montpellier. A lookout on the N 9 over the causse du Larzac offers a spectacular **view★** of Millau and its 15C mill and 12C arched bridge.
🅿 **Parking:** There is ample covered parking in place Emma-Calvé.
◉ **Don't Miss:** The paleontology section of the musée de Millau; the viaduct viewpoint; the musée de la Peau et du Gant.
👥 **Kids:** The city has many 'Station Kid' activities.

cel (1939) are by Jean Bernard and the stained-glass windows by Claude Baillon.

◉ Follow rue des Jacobins.

Continue through **passage du Pozous**, a 13C fortified gateway. Rue du Voultre leads to boulevard de l'Ayrolle.

◉ Turn right onto this boulevard.

Musée de Millau★

Pl du Mar-Foch. ◷Open Jul–Aug daily 10am–12.30pm, 2.30–7pm; Sept–Jun daily except Sun and public holidays 10am–noon, 2–6pm. €5.50 (no charge 1st Saturday in the month). ℘05 65 59 01 08. www.museedemillau.fr.
The museum is housed in the 18C Hôtel de Pégayrolles. Its **paleontology** section includes fossils from secondary marine sediments and the 4m-long 180-million-year-old skeleton of a plesiosaurus marine reptile from Tournemire. There is a remarkable collection of Gallo-Roman **earthenware★**,

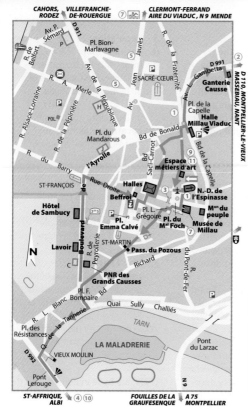

found at Graufesenque, including moulds and potter's chisels and accounts books. The **Maison de la Peau et du Gant★** includes exhibits on glove-making and a magnificent collection of evening gloves.

La Maison du peuple

Today the city theatre, but in the early 20C this was a popular gathering place, and a place of entertainment. In 1935, it was the site of a strike by the town's glovemakers.

▷ Return to the place du Mar-Foch and turn left into the rue des Jacobins.

The street goes under the **passage du Pouzous**, a 13C fortified gateway. Rue du Voultre leads to boulevard de l'Ayrolle and place Frédéric Bompaire.

▷ Turn right from the square onto boulevard de l'Ayrolle.

Boulevard de l'Ayrolle

You come successively to the curious **lavoir de l'Ayrolle** (18C) hemispherical in shape and topped by a nice roof, and then the 17C **Hôtel de Sambucy** *(visit the gardens during Jul–Aug, book at tourist office).*

▷ Follow the boulevard as far as rue Droite and there turn right.

Beffroi (Belfry)

⏱*Open Jul–Aug 10am–noon, 2–6pm; May–Jun and Sept 2.30–6pm.* ⌖€3.50. ☎05 65 59 01 08.
Standing in rue Droite, this Gothic tower is all that remains of the old town hall. The 12C square tower used as a prison in the 17C is topped by an octagonal 17C one. Good view from **place Emma-Calvé**.

▷ Return to rue Droite, and go into the street opposite towards Les Halles.

Millau Viaduct★★★

It is impossible not to be excited when first you see the Millau viaduct, spanning the Tarn gorge (☛*see region map p170*).

This immense span of architectural ingenuity, designed by the British architect, Norman Foster, in collaboration with the celebrated French engineer, Michel Virlogeux, carries the A75 autoroute through the clouds on its way from Clermont Ferrand to Béziers.

The structure, built at a cost of 394 million euros, and consuming two million working hours, is so impressive that there is a specially constructed viewing point just so that you can come and get a good look at it. But to fully appreciate the viaduct you need to find your way out of Millau and along the road to Peyre – one of France's 'Most Beautiful Villages' – which will take you directly under the viaduct, and on to the village. The bridge is awesome; the village quite simply beautiful.

The 2.5km/1.5mi structure stands on seven huge but slender concrete pillars, and with a total height 343m, it is the tallest bridge in the world. More than 150 steel stays hold it all in place, and the effect of late afternoon sunlight catching this metal network is quite magical, the whole edifice shimmering in a most captivating way.

Nominally, the life-span of the bridge is 120 years. How will it age? Will it survive as well as the Pont du Gard near Nîmes? Will it become a regional icon, a symbol of Anglo-French technical achievement? Or simply a high-speed link that takes people away from the town of Millau? Only time will tell. Unlike the Millau viaduct, however, the Pont du Gard never had to cope with thousands of high-speeding vehicles carrying goods and holiday-makers south to the summer sun and sea of Languedoc.

Millau viaduct from Peyre

At the end of the 19C, **Les Halles** housed a covered market. The former hôtel de Galy today houses the tourist office which shows evidence of its medieval construction.

◖ Take rue Sarret, to the right, and then rue de la Capelle.

Espace Métiers d'art

10 r. de la Capelle. ⦿*Open Jun–Sep Mon 3–7.30pm, Tue–Fri 10am–1pm, 3–7.30pm, Sat 10am–1pm; Sep–Dec and Mar–May afternoons only.* ℘*05 65 62 39 73.* *www.espacemetiersdartmillau.com.* The Association Millau'Art et Savoir-Faire pulls together some 30 craftspeople – wood turners, potters, book binders, etc., many with workshops open to the public.

◖ Go back to the place decr. la Capelle, then along the boulevard Gambetta to find a manufacturer of gantier Causse, the only one left in Millau *(www.causse-gantier.fr).*

EXCURSIONS
Fouilles de la Graufesenque

1km/0.6mi S. Leave Millau towards Montpellier and Albi, then turn left after the bridge over the Tarn. ♿⦿*Open Mar–Apr and Oct–Dec Tue–Sun 19am–noon, 2–5pm; May–Jun and Sept 10am–noon, 2–6pm; Jul–Aug 10am–12.30pm, 2.30–7pm.* ⦿*Closed Jan–Feb and public holidays.* ⊗€*4 (no charge 1st Sunday in the month Oct–Apr).* ℘*05 65 60 11 37.* *www.graufesenque.com.* This archaeological site contains the foundations of a Gallo-Roman potters' village with central street, canal, workshops, slaves' houses and kilns which fired 30 000 vases at a time.

🚗 DRIVING TOUR

LES RASPES AND LE ST-AFFRICAIN
⦿*See map on p170. Allow about 4h.*

◖ Leave Millau to the SW on the D 41 (direction Comprégnac). The route passes beneath the viaduct.

Peyre★

This is one of the Most Beautiful Villages in France, and a charming place of narrow streets and with a grandstand view of the Millau viaduct, both of which are valid reasons for visiting. An 11C church has an interesting façade.

◖ Continue on the D 41. Take a left into the village of Comprégnac, parking the car under the shady chestnut trees.

Comprégnac

Home to the **Maison de la Truffe** (℘*05 65 61 16 19, www.truffefrance.com)*, this is a perfect place to become familiar with truffles.

◖ Continue on the D 41, and take a left on the D 96 which continues to St-Rome-de-Tarn. Go over the river to join the D 31. The "Raspes" cut deep into the valley.

St-Victor-et-Melvieu

This commune is the home to the interesting **Centre de l'art mural et d'interprétation de la fresque** which holds exhibitions illustrating the art of painting murals. It includes some exquisite **frescoes★** by Nicolaï Greschy (1912–1985).

◖ After St-Victor, turn right on the D 150 then take a left on the D 73.

The verdant area around **Le Pouget** is the site of one of the most important hydroelectric centres in France.

◖ Leave to the west of the village. When you reach Truel, climb the plateau then take a right on the D 25.

Lac de Villefranche-de-Panat

One of the great, beautiful lakes in southern Aveyron. There are opportunities for swimming, canoeing and windsurfing here.

▶ Return to Truel and cross the Tarn river to rejoin the D 527 towards Les Costes-Gozon. Continue through the village and take a right and then another right towards Crassous. Rejoin the D 993 after Tiergues.

St-Affrique
A small town that developed around the tomb of the bishop Saint Affrique.

▶ Return to Millau on the D 999 and D 992.

ADDRESSES

🛏 STAY

⊖ **Hotel de la Capelle** – *7 pl. de la Capelle.* ☎*05 65 60 14 72. www.hotel-millau-capelle.com. 45 rooms.* This hotel has two distinct advantages: reasonable prices and an air of tranquillity.

⊖⊖ **Ferme-auberge de Quiers** – *In Quiers, 12520 Compeyre, 12km/7.4mi N of Millau by N 9 and D 907.* ☎*05 65 59 85 10. www.quiers.net. 5 rooms. Meals* ⊖⊖. This old restored farmhouse offers comfortable rooms with charm of yesteryear, several with exposed beams and stonework.

⊖⊖ **Hôtel Le Cévenol** – *115 r. du Rajol.* ☎*05 65 60 74 44. www.cevenol-hotel.fr.* ♿🅿. *42 rooms.* Just 300m from the centre of town; comfortable with fine view of the causses.

⊖⊖ **Château de Creissels** – *2 km/1.25mi S of Millau, rte de St-Affrique.* ☎*05 65 60 16 59. www.chateau-de-creissels.com. Closed Jan–Feb.* 🅿. *Meals* ⊖⊖. This 12C château dominates the town of Millau. The main building houses a salon bourgeois and two dining rooms; lovely panoramic terrace and rooms with old furniture.

⊖⊖⊜ **Chambre d'hôte La Saisonneraie** – *Hameau de Luzençon, 12100 St-Georges-de-Luzençon.* ☎*05 65 62 58 86. www.lasaisonneraie.com.* 🅿🍴. *5 rooms.* In a small perched village, with superb views.

🍽 EAT

⊖ **Brasserie L'Estaminet** – *Pl. des Halles. Open Wed–Thu 7am–2pm, Fri 7am–7pm, Sat–Sun 8am–2pm.* Food fresh from the market.

⊖⊖ **Les Arcades** – *2-3 pl. du Mar. Foch.* ☎*05 65 60 87 88.* Salads and grills in the heart of the old town.

⊖⊖ **La Marmite du Pêcheur** –*14–16 bd de la Capelle.* ☎*05 65 61 20 44. Closed Mon, plus Tue–Wed out of season.* Perfect for traditional cuisine; cool in summer.

⊖⊖ **Au Jeu de Paume** – *2 r. St-Antoine.* ☎*05 65 60 25 12. Closed Sun and Sat lunch.* Grilled fish and meat; piano bar Fri evening (Oct–Apr, jazz and blues).

⊖⊖ **La Mangeoire** – *10 bd de la Capelle.* ☎*05 65 60 13 16. www.restaurantlamangeoire.com. Closed Sun pm (Nov–Apr) and Mon (May–Oct).* Ideal for meats grilled on an open fire, and for trying aligot.

⊖⊖ **Capion** – *3 r. Jean-François-Alméras.* ☎*05 65 60 00 91. www.restaurant-capion.com. Closed Tue pm and Wed.* ♿. A great place for traditional cuisine of the region.

⊖⊖ **La Braconne** – *7 Pl. du Mar. Foch.* ☎*05 65 60 30 93. Closed Sun pm and Mon.* This old house in the centre of Millau has a fine 13C vaulted dining room. Grilled dishes cooked in the fireplace at the back and local specialities cooked by the owner.

ACTIVITIES

Walking – The main waymarked footpaths are the GR 62 ('Causse Noir-Lévezou-Rouergue') and several PR, 'Causse Noir' (13 itineraries around Millau for rambling and mountain biking). There are also footpaths around St-Affrique, Camarès and Roquefort.

Children – 👥 Millau organises many activities for children. Information is available from the tourist office.

PNR des Grands Causses – *71 boulevard de l'Ayrolle.* ☎*05 65 61 35 50.* The Parc provides useful addresses for finding accommodation, practising unusual activities and discovering the local cultural heritage.

Castelnau-Pégayrols

Isolated on the rugged southern slopes of the Lévézou plateau, this small village boasts a red sandstone castle and a Romanesque church. For many centuries known as Castelnau du Lévézou, this remarkable place was the capital of the region. Today, the patina of its stone buildings and its narrow alleyways add greatly to the charm of the place.

THE TOWN

Two **churches** – Notre Dame and St-Michel – both with 11C characteristics, are worth visiting. But more so the ancient **castle** of the lords of Lévézou and Arpajon. This 11C building was refurbished in the 18C by the marquis de Pégayrolles, and used as his summer residence (◎*open Jun–Jul daily except Tue 2.30–6.30pm;* ℘*05 65 62 05 05*).

🚗 DRIVING TOUR

VALLÉE DE LA MUSE
40km/25mi. Allow 2h.

Roquefort-sur-Soulzon★

The name of this market town, situated in the heart of the Parc Naturel Regional des Grands Causses, has become synonymous with one of the most widely appreciated of French cheeses, Roquefort.

ROQUEFORT CAVES
Roquefort Société

◎*Open mid-Jul–Aug 9.30am–5.30pm; mid-Mar–Jun and Sep–Oct 9.30am–noon, 1.30–5pm (May–Jun and Sep 5.30pm); rest of year 10am–noon, 1.30–4.30pm.* ◎*Closed 1 Jan and 25 Dec.* ⊜€5. ℘05 65 58 54 38. www.roquefort-societe.com.

▸ **Population:** 343.
⚲ **Michelin Map:** 526: J7.
🄸 **Info:** Mairie, 12620 Castelnau-Pégayrols. ℘05 65 62 02 97. www.castelnau-pegayrols.fr.
▷ **Location:** 20km/12.5mi NW of Millau by the D 911 and then the D 515.

▷ Leave Castlenau SW via the D 515.

Montjaux boasts several fine old houses along the street leading to the Romanesque **church**. From the same era, the **Comberoumal priory★**, of the order of Grandmontains, comprises four buildings around a a small cloister.
Continuing on the D 30, **St-Beauzély** has the remains of a 15C feudal Château, and the interesting Musée Mémoire de la vie rurale which covers local agricultural history in the area.
👥 **Micropolis★** is a fascinating insight into the world of insects (&◎*open mid-Feb–Oct; times vary; check website;* ⊜€13.80, children under 12, €9.50; ℘05 65 58 50 50; www.micropolis-aveyron.com).

▸ **Population:** 637.
⚲ **Michelin Map:** 338: J-K7.
🄸 **Info:** Ave. de Lauras, 12250. ℘05 65 58 56 00. www.roquefort.com.
▷ **Location:** 26km/16mi SW of Millau on the D992 and 62km/39mi NW of Lodève by the A75. Follow the D999 before turning left onto the D23 and enter Roquefort.
◎ **Timing:** Allow one hour.

Roquefort Papillon

◎*Open Jul–Aug 9.30am–6.30pm; Sep–Jun 9.30–11.30am, 1.30–5.30pm; Oct–Mar 9.30–11.30am and 1.30–4.30pm.* ◎*Closed 1 Jan, 25 Dec.* ⊜No charge.

Roquefort cheese

Strict boundaries define the area of production of ewe's milk and the region of caves in which Roquefort cheese is matured. French law decrees that only ewe's milk cheese produced within these boundaries may be labelled 'Roquefort.' As an official label of origin (*appellation d'origine*), 'Roquefort' is one of the oldest in France. Roquefort is known to have been appreciated in Rome by Pliny and by Charlemagne. The cheese's official status was confirmed by decree on 22 October 1979. In the dairies, the milk is first made into a cheese in which the curd has been mixed with a natural mould, *Penicillium roqueforti*, which comes from the caves at Combalou. The cheese is transported to Roquefort for maturation.

Cave of Roquefort Société

© Christian GUY/imageBROKER/age fotostock

FARM VISITS

See how ewes are milked, how and where the cheese is made before being taken to mature in the Roquefort cellars. Five sheep farmers offer farm visits followed by tastings, *(by reservation, Jun–mid-Sep, daily from 4pm).*
Martine Fabrèges, ☏*05 65 62 76 19*;
Alice Ricard, ☏*05 65 99 06 46*;
Anne-Marie Gineste, ☏*05 65 62 53 22*;
Isabelle Anglars, ☏*05 65 47 69 40*;
Annie Bernat, ☏*05 65 99 51 53*.

☏*05 65 58 50 00. www.roquefort-papillon.com.*
Above the town of Roquefort, which lies at the foot of the cliff, is a little limestone plateau known as 'Combalou,' the northeast side of which collapsed when it slipped on its clay substratum. These special conditions gave rise to natural caves between the displaced rocks, in which temperature and humidity are constant and ideal for curing cheese.

Rocher St-Pierre

This rock (alt 650m) against the Combalou cliff offers a **view★** (*viewing table*) as far as the Lévézou mountains to the left, over the Soulzon valley and Tournemire cirque to the right, opposite to the tabular cliffs of the Causse du Larzac, and to the town of Roquefort at the foot of the cliff.

Sentier des Échelles

Allow 2h30; some difficult sections (narrow passages, slippery ladders in rainy weather).
🚶 On the way out of the village, this path leads to the Combalou plateau (alt 791m), from which there is a **panoramic view**.
🚶 There are two more walking trails around Roquefort: Sentier du Menhir *(3.5km/2.2mi)* and Sentier de Trompette *(4km/2.5mi).*

Saint-Sernin-sur-Rance

The village perched on a rocky shoulder above the Rance enjoys an agreeable climate and a privileged position between Toulouse-Albi and Millau-Montpellier. This quiet Aveyron village is a place of narrow streets at the heart of a countryside that produces mushrooms, game, trout and crayfish – it's a superb place to come and relax.

▶ **Population:** 773.
🖢 **Michelin Map:** 526: H8.
🖪 **Info:** Av. d'Albi - 12380 St-Sernin-sur-Rance.
    ℘05 65 99 29 13.
◖ **Location:** 111km/69mi to the NW of Béziers, and 64km/40mi SW of Millau.
◕ **Timing:** At least a full day is need to appreciate this lovely village.
◔ **Don't miss:** The circuit visiting the statues-menhirs.

🚗 DRIVING TOUR

Chateaux du Moyen Âge
113km/70mi. Allow half a day.

◖ Leave St-Sernin to the N on the D 999 then take the direction for Plaisance on the D 33. 3km/2mi after Plaisance, turn right onto the D 60.

Coupiac
👥A big castle flanked by three round towers, one carrying a clock, has occupied the centre of the village since 15C; it was rebuilt in 18C to make it more comfortable (*www.chateaudecoupiac.com*).

◖ Go back to the D 33 and take the D 159 to the N of the village. Head for Brousse-le-Château.

Brousse-le-Château★
At the confluence of the Alrance and the Tarn, Brousse, perched on a hill, is dominated by its church and château fort (*www.brousselechateau.net*). 17C and 18C houses border the Alrance, which is spanned by a Gothic bridge.

◖ Go back to the D 902 and turn left. At Faveyrolles, take the D 60 to the left, towards St-Izaire.

St-Izaire
Birthplace of **Father Hermet** (1856–1939), inventor, among other things, of the statue-menhir known as St-Sernin, St-Izaire concentrates its red sandstone houses along the left bank of the Dourdou.

👥 The town is dominated by its 14C château, a rectangular building with a fortified gate opening onto an inner courtyard (*www.saint-izaire.com*).

◖ Cross the Dourdou and turn right on the D 25 towards St-Affrique. Turn right towards Vabres and follow the D 999 as far as Querbes. There, turn left on the D 101. Go past Montlaur then turn left on a narrow lane for Château de Montaigut.

Château de Montaigut
👥🔊*Guided visits from Easter–Oct daily 10am–noon, 2.30–6.30pm (Jul–Aug 10am–6.30pm); Oct–Easter Mon–Fri 10am–noon, 2.30–6.30pm.* ◈€6 *(child 6–12, €2.50).* ℘05 65 99 81 50. *www.chateau-de-montaigut.com.*
Built on a hill, this 11C medieval fortress dominates the countryside of Rougier, which takes its name from the earth, coloured by iron oxide. The rooms on the ground floor were built over rock-carved tombs from the early Middle Ages (7C–8C). Parts of the castle were used as residences many years later: a pantry, large living room with fireplace, and bedrooms can still be seen.

◖ Go back to Montlaur then to Querbes and turn left onto the D 999 which leads back to St-Sernin.

Ancient Abbaye de
Sylvanès

Here the music is sacred, making the most of the splendid acoustics. This former Cistercian abbey, built in the 12C, is the jewel of a wooded area dotted with hills. Romantics will avow that the first music here was that of the Dourdou, which fed a 19C spa. Times have changed, and the abbey is now the focal point for cultural events, including spiritual music.

- **Michelin Map:** 526: J8.
- **Info:** Bd de Verdun - 12400 St-Affrique. ℘05 65 98 12 40. www.ot-dusaintaffricain.com.
- **Location:** 82km/50mi N of Béziers, and 55km/34mi S of Millau.

SIGHTS

Open Jan–mid-Mar and Nov–mid-Dec Mon–Fri 9.30am–12.30pm, 2–6pm; mid-Mar–Jun and Sept–Oct daily 9.30am–12.30pm. 2–6pm; Jul–Aug daily 9.30am–1pm, 2–7pm. Closed mid-Dec–early Jan and during concerts. €2.50 (guided visits Jul–Aug, €5). ℘05 65 98 20 20. www.sylvanes.com.

The pirate Pons de Léras, repented and redeemed himself by founding the abbey in 1138. The sandstone church was built less than 20 years later.

At the back of the church, an impressive modern organ with 4 600 pipes was added in 1997.

Abbey buildings

The church is extended southwards by the abbey buildings: a gallery and cloisters open out into three sections, including the chapter house and the old sacristy. The great hall of the monks, the scriptorium, is vaulted on intersecting arches, and divided into two aisles by bare columns.

La **Couvertoirade** ★★

This tiny fortified town on the limestone Larzac plateau, once belonged to the Knights Templars. By 1880, La Couvertoirade had only 362 inhabitants, but today it is popular with weavers and artisans working in enamel and pottery. Not surprisingly, it ranks as one of the Most Beautiful Villages in France. It has many lovely, robustly built houses typical of the region.

- **Population:** 181.
- **Michelin Map:** 338: L7.
- **Info:** Point info tourisme de La Couvertoirade. ℘05 65 58 55 59. http://lacouvertoirade.com.
- **Location:** 81km/50.6mi NW of Montpelier.
- **Don't Miss:** The view of the village from the ramparts.

WALKING TOUR

Park near the north gate (charge), outside the ramparts. The village is open all year to the public.

Ramparts

Open Jul–Aug 10am–7pm; Apr–Jun and Sep 10am–noon, 2–6pm; Mar and Oct–mid-Nov 10am–noon, 2–5pm. Guided tours possible by request,

€3. Closed mid-Nov–early Mar. ℘05 65 58 55 59. www.lacouvertoirade.com.

Go through the north gateway and climb the steps at the foot of a Renaissance house. Following the watch-path round to the left to the round tower for a view over the town and its main street, rue Droite.

La Couvertoirade

© Eric Teissedre/Photononstop

The 'Cardabelle'

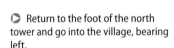

Many doors in La Couvertoirade and other nearby villages are adorned with a dried plant resembling a sunflower surrounded by ragged spiny leaves – the *Carlina acanthifolia* thistle known locally as the **cardabelle**. It opens and closes according to the humidity, making it the local equivalent of seaweed hung outside to forecast the weather.

▶ Return to the foot of the north tower and go into the village, bearing left.

Fortified church

This fortified 14C church, an integral part of the town's defences, has two disc-shaped steles showing different representations of the cross and a graveyard with unusual disc-shaped gravestones.

Château

This fortress was built by the Templars in the 12C and 13C; the two upper floors have since disappeared.

▶ Keep left until you reach a large square, once a village pond, where you walk round a block of houses to the right to reach rue Droite.

Rue Droite

This main street has very attractive houses with outside stone steps leading to a balcony and door into the living area. Sheep were kept on the ground floor below. Just past the corner of the town wall is a fine example of a *lavogne*, or village sheep pond, common in the *causses*.

▶ Walk along the outside of the ramparts, round to the right, to get back to the car.

EXCURSION
♟♟ Musée d'Automates de Sauclières

13km/8mi to the NE along the D 7, near the junction with the D 999.
♿☉*Open mid-Feb–Mar Mon–Fri 2–5pm; Apr–Jun Sun–Fri 2–6pm; Jul–Aug Tue–Sun 10am–6.30pm, except Sat am; Sept Mon–Fri 10am–noon, 2–5.30pm, Sat–Sun 2–6pm; Oct Mon–Fri 10am–noon, 2–5pm, Sun 2–5pm; Nov–Dec Mon–Sun 2–5pm.* ☉*Closed Jan.* ☞€4.80 (child 5–12, €3.30). ℘05 65 62 11 81. www.santonsdecreche.fr.*
More than automatons, two rooms here are devoted to detailed reconstruction of villages and traditional skills and trades.

Causse du Larzac★

The Causse du Larzac, dotted with villages and Templar estates, is famous for Roquefort cheese.

A BIT OF HISTORY

The Causse du Larzac, with its arid limestone plateaux and green valleys, is the largest of the *causses*. Like other causses, Larzac is full of limestone rock 'chimneys' like **Mas Raynal**, explored in 1889 by E A Martel, L Armand, G Gaupillat and E Foulquier.

In the 12C, the Order of the Knights Templar built a local headquarters at Ste-Eulalie-de-Cernon. After the Order was dissolved in 1312, the Hospitallers of St John of Jerusalem (or Malta) took over the Templars' estates, including fortress towns on the Causse du Larzac. In the turbulent 15C the Hospitallers erected the many walls, towers and fortified gates which give the Causse du Larzac its rugged appearance.

🚗 DRIVING TOUR

TEMPLARS AND HOSPITALLERS

166km/103mi round tour from Millau (See MILLAU). Allow one day. Take the N 9 towards Béziers.

The road crosses the Tarn département and climbs up the northern flank of the Causse du Larzac, offering superb panoramas of Millau, the Causse Noir and the Dourbie gorge.

Maison du Larzac

🚃🕙*Open May–Sept 10am–7pm.* 🎫*No charge.* 🖉*06 51 52 06 44.*
To the right of N 9 is an enormous sheepfold roofed with limestone slabs (*lauzes*) called La Jasse. Here the outdoor **Écomusée du Larzac** provides an excellent introduction to the Causse du Larzac, with a traditional farm, an ultra-modern sheepfold and exhibitions on local architecture, archaeology and history.

- **Info:** Office de Tourisme Larzac, Place du Claux, 12230 Nant. 🖉05 65 62 23 64. www.tourisme-larzac.com.
- **Location:** This is the closest causse to Montpellier.
- **Don't Miss:** Roquefort cheese-making caves.
- **Kids:** Ste-Eulalie-de-Cernon's Reptilarium. 🖉05 65 61 32 08. www.reptilarium-larzac.com.

Carry on to La Cavalerie. The road runs alongside Larzac Military Camp.

La Cavalerie

This large fortified village with ancient ramparts evokes the age of chivalry.

From N 9, take D 999 on the right towards St-Affrique. After 3.4km/2mi, take the road to Lapanouse-de-Cernon on the left.

Ste-Eulalie-de-Cernon★

In the valley of the Cernon, Ste-Eulalie was a seat of the Templars' commandery and this medieval fortress has kept most of its ramparts, towers and gates.

Follow D 561 S; right onto D 23.

The road goes through another Templar village, **Le Viala-du-Pas-de-Jaux**.

Roquefort-sur-Soulzon★

See ROQUEFORT-SUR-SOULZON.

Drive S from Roquefort along D 93 towards Fondamente then turn right at the signpost 'St-Jean-d'Alcas'.

St-Jean-d'Alcas

The fortified Romanesque church is enclosed within the ramparts of this picturesque village. Some restored houses feature round doorways and mullioned windows.

Take the D 93, then the D 500.

St-Paul-des-Fonts
Pretty little village containing the **Espace botanique-Hippolyte Coste**, a small museum and garden.

Rejoin the D 93, to Fondamente, turn left on the D 7. Keep forward on the D 185 towards La Couvertoirade.

La Couvertoirade ★★
See LA COUVERTOIRADE.

Follow the D 55 southwards and head for Le Caylar.

Le Caylar
The name of this village crowned by jagged rock formations means 'rock'. From afar these eroded rocks look like impressive ramparts and fortified tow-ers. The small Romanesque chapel of **Notre-Dame-de-Roc-Castel** contains a 12C stone altar. The old town's **clock tower** is all that remains of the ramparts. Some medieval houses retain their 14C and 15C doors and windows.

Leave Le Caylar S on the road past the cemetery and turn left onto a slip road under the A 75. Take D 155E to St-Félix-de-l'Héras, then turn left onto D 155. Where the road crosses the motorway, continue on foot.

Pas de l'Escalette★
This rocky cleft between towering cliffs offers good **views** of the Lergue water-fall. Steps cut into the rockface lead down from the Larzac plateau.

Return to A 75 and Millau.

Chaos de
Montpellier-le-Vieux ★★★

The chaos of Montpellier-le-Vieux is an extraordinary collection of eroded dolomite formations on the Causse Noir. Shepherds thought this gigantic rock jumble resembled a vast ruined city, and locals thought this chaos of rocks was a haunt of the devil himself. Stray sheep or goats that entered vanished into the night, devoured by wolves. In 1883 Montpellier-le-Vieux was discovered by J. and L. de Malafosse and De Barbeyrac-Saint-Maurice, who were amazed at the intricate maze of alleyways, arches and ledges.

VISIT
Open Apr–Oct 9.30am–5.30pm (Jul–Aug 9am–7pm) – 1st train departs 10am; €6.80 (child 5–15, €4.70).
05 65 60 66 30.
www.montpellierlevieux.com.

The **Petit Train Vert** goes to the most picturesque rock formations (*round trip 50min*).
Montpellier-le-Vieux's captivating rock formations have names like Skit-tle, Crocodile, Mycenae Gate, Sphinx, and Bear's Head, after their shapes. **Douminal** offers fabulous views of 'Rocher de la Croix,' the Cirque du Lac, Tarn gorge cliffs, the Dourbie valley, the Cirque des Rouquettes and the Chaos de Roquesaltes.
Enjoy five pedestrian waymarked strolls, from 1 hour to 3 hour in the biggest rocky chaos of Europe. Even so, Mont-pellier-le-Vieux is too vast to be seen in one visit.

Porte de Mycènes
Martel thought Montpellier-le-Vieux's Mycenae Gate resembled the Lion Gate of ancient Greece for its sheer size and grandiose natural arch (12m).
This path crosses a culvert before leading to the **'Baume Obscure'** cave where Martel discovered the bones of cave-bears. Look out for the **'Nez de Cyrano'** Cyrano de Bergerac's huge

Chaos de Montpellier-le-Vieux

© jamesdavidphoto/iStockphoto.com

rocky nose. From here walk up towards the viewpoint.

Belvédère

A fine view of the cirque des Rouquettes which skirts around the enclosed valley of the Dourbie to the south, and the cirque de la Millière to the north.

The trail returns to the starting point, crossing, at mid-height, the cirque de la Millière.

On the right, about 200m from the viewpoint, the valley of the Aven opens out to a depth of 53m. From there, the trail returns directly to the parking area.

Sévérac-le-Château ★

This once fortified town is built on the slopes of an isolated hill in the middle of a depression fed by the rivers and streams of Aveyron. Today, all that remains of the medieval city are the remains of its imposing castle.

▶ **Population:** 2 474.
& **Michelin Map:** 525: K6.
🛈 **Info:** 5 r. des Douves - 12150 Sévérac-le-Château. ✆05 65 47 67 31. www. severac-le-chateau.com.
◖ **Location:** 38km/24mi N of Millau.
🕓 **Timing:** Allow 2 hours, or maybe stay for lunch.

The Sévérac barony, one of the oldest and most powerful in France, included famous personages like **Amaury de Séverac** (1365–1427), a Marshall of France who undertook daring feats of arms, and the composer **Déodat de Séverac** (1873–1921), born in St-Félix-Lauragais, and profoundly influenced in his vocal and choral music by his native Languedoc. His compisitions for solo piano have won critical acclaim.

Opposite the tourist office, narrow streets and archways leading to the château contain **picturesque old houses** (15C–16C) with corbelled turrets and upper storeys overhanging the street. A 17C entrance gate leads into the main courtyard of the **château** (🕓open Jul–Aug 9.30am–7pm; Apr–Jun and Sep 10am–12.30pm 2–6pm; ✆€7. ✆05 65 47 67 31; www.severac-le-chateau.com).

Causse de
Sauveterre

Bordered to the north by the river Lot, this is the most northerly and least arid of the Grands Causses. Its western section has vast stretches of woodland and fairly steep hills.

🚗 DRIVING TOUR

Round trip of 66km/41mi. Allow 5h.

La Canourgue

Narrow canals carry water from the River Urugne through this ancient city overlooked by an imposing clock tower. The former collegiate church built in Provençal style between the 12C and the 14C is surrounded by old corbelled houses straddling canals.

▶ Leave La Canourgue along D998 towards Ste-Énimie and, after 2km/1.2mi, turn right onto D 46; 1.8km/1.1mi further on, leave the car on the left near the Sabot de Malepeyre.

Sabot de Malepeyre★

This enormous clog-shaped (*sabot*) rock, 30m tall, also known as the *pont naturel* (natural bridge) *de Malepeyre* was formed by the erosive action of the water which once flowed on the surface of the *causse*.

▶ Continue and turn left onto D 43 which joins up with D 32; turn left again, drive on to D 998 and turn right. 6km/3.7mi further on, turn left towards Roussac and Sauveterre.

Champerboux

Picturesque hamlet with typical causses houses.

▶ Follow D 44 left.

The road to Chanac is lined with drystone shepherds' huts.

> **Location:** N of Gorges du Tarn; W of Sévérac.
> **Info:** Quartier de la Vignogue, 48230 Chanac. ℘04 66 48 29 28. www.chanac.fr.

Chanac

The old keep is proudly camped at the top of the village (*from the tourist office, follow the signpost to 'La Tour'*). Note the clock tower in place du Plö (*market on Thursdays*).

▶ Cross the River Lot and turn left onto N 88.

Le Villard

This charming village overlooking the Lot valley was once guarded by a fortress built in the 14C to protect the inhabitants from roaming bands of robbers.

▶ The road follows the River Lot southwards. Cross over to reach Banassac.

Banassac

Housed in the town hall, the **Musée archéologique** (&🕐*open daily except Sat–Sun and public holidays 8am–noon, 2–6pm; ℘04 66 32 82 10; www.banassac.fr*) displays sigillated pottery, sought after all over Europe between the 1C and 3C.

ADDRESSES

🏠 STAY

🛏 **Chambre d'hôte La Vialette** – *La Vialette, 48500 La Canourgue, 9km/5.5mi SW of La Canourgue. ℘04 66 32 83 00. www.gite-sauveterre.com.* ⚞. *3 gites, and 3 rooms.* Within the walls of a restored 14C farm.

🍴 EAT

Ferme-Auberge Pradeilles – *Le Gazy, 48230 Chanac, 6km/4mi SW of Chanac. ℘04 66 48 21 91. R*Farmhouse accommodation, with dining room serving regional dishes.

Gorges du Tarn ★★★

Lozère and Aveyron

The Tarn gorges are one of the most spectacular sights in the Causses region. Stretching over more than 50km/30mi, the gorges offer a seemingly endless succession of admirable landscapes and sites.

The course of the Tarn – The Tarn rises in the uplands of Mont Lozère, and gushes turbulently down the Cévennes slopes. On its way, it picks up many tributaries, notably the Tarnon near Florac.

The Tarn then reaches the Causses region, its course now determined by a series of rifts which it has deepened into canyons. In this limestone region, it is fed solely by 40 resurgent springs from the Causse Méjean or Causse de Sauveterre, of which only three form small rivers over a distance of a few hundred yards. Most of them flow into the Tarn as waterfalls.

🚗 DRIVING TOURS

TARN GORGES ROAD
The scenic road D 907bis runs along the floor of the gorges, on the right bank of the Tarn. The journey is never monotonous owing to the constantly changing appearance of the gorges, tinted with different hues depending on the time of day.

FLORAC TO STE-ÉNIMIE
30km/18mi. About 1h30.
All along this road, there are one or two houses still roofed with the heavy schist slabs known as *lauzes*; the roof ridge is made of slabs laid out like the sails of a windmill, which is evidence of the proximity of the Cévennes.

Florac
🕪*See FLORAC.*
N 106 heads north along the Tarn valley bordered to the east by the Cévennes

▷ **Location:** North of Millau. Drive along the scenic road; take boat trips along the most spectacular stretch of the valley (🕪*see Boat Trips);* or stride out along the many footpaths.

⊚ **Don't Miss:** Glorious views of the gorges, perhaps the finest is from Point Sublime.

👪 **Kids:** The gorges are a wonderland for kids, with walking trails, rocky outcrops, lone castles and cliffside villages.

and to the west by the cliffs of the Causse Méjean which tower above the river-bed by 500m.

▷ Within sight of the village of Biesset, on the opposite bank of the Tarn, leave the road to Mende via Montmirat Pass to the right and take D 907bis to the left, which runs along the north bank of the river.

Level with Ispagnac, the Tarn makes a sharp meander; this is where the canyon really begins, as a gigantic defile separating the Causse Méjean and the Causse de Sauveterre.

Ispagnac
At the mouth of the Tarn canyon, the little dip in which Ispagnac lies, sheltered from the north and northwest winds and basking in a mild climate which has always been renowned, is planted with orchards and vineyards.

▷ Continue 1km/0.6mi after Ispagnac then bear left.

Quézac
At Quézac a Gothic **bridge** spans the Tarn enabling pilgrims to reach the sanctuary founded by Pope Urban V in Quézac.
A narrow street, lined with old houses, leads to **Quézac Church**, built on the same site where a statue of the Virgin

Mary was discovered in 1050. A major pilgrimage takes place in September.

▶ Return to D 907bis.

Between Molines and Blajoux stand two castles. First, on the north bank, is the **Château de Rocheblave** (16C) – with its distinctive machicolations – overlooked by the ruins of a 12C manor and by a curious limestone needle. Farther down, on the south bank, stands the **Château de Charbonnières** (16C), situated downstream of Montbrun village.

Castelbouc★
On the south bank of the Tarn. The strange site of Castelbouc ('Goat's Castle') can be seen from the road. The name is said to date from the Crusades. A lord, who stayed at home with the womenfolk, died of his complacency. The story goes that when his soul left his body, an enormous billy-goat was seen in the sky above the castle, which after that became known as Castelbouc.

▶ Shortly after, to the left of the road, Prades Castle comes into view.

Château de Prades
Perched on a rocky spur overhanging the Tarn, this castle was built in the early 13C to protect Ste-Énimie abbey and to defend access to the gorges. At the outset, it belonged to the bishops of Mende then, from 1280 to the Revolution, to the priors of Ste-Énimie abbey.

Sainte-Énemie
See SAINTE-ÉNEMIE.

STE-ÉNIMIE TO LE ROZIER
60km/37mi. Allow 2h30.

▶ Leave Ste-Énimie S on D 907bis.

Cirque de St-Chély-du-Tarn★
The pretty village of St-Chély stands on the south bank of the Tarn at the threshold of the huge desolate cirque of St-Chély with its superb cliffs, at the foot of the Causse Méjean.

D 986 on the opposite bank of the Tarn also affords fine **views★★** of the cirques of St-Chély and Pougnadoires.

Cirque de Pougnadoires★
The houses in Pougnadoires village are embedded in the rock. The village is built against the colossal cliffs of the Pougnadoires cirque, pocked with caves. The reddish hue of the rocks indicates the presence of dolomite.

Château de la Caze★
This 15C château stands in a romantic setting on the banks of the Tarn.

La Malène
Located at the junction of the roads which wind through the Causse de Sauveterre and Causse Méjean, La Malène has always been a thoroughfare. Tourists should visit the 12C Romanesque **church**, the little street lined with historical houses beneath Barre rock, and the 16C castle which is now a hotel.

▶ Cross the bridge over the Tarn out of La Malène and take D 43.

Just off the road to the right stand a cave chapel and a statue of the Virgin Mary from where there is a fine view of the village and its surroundings. The climb up the south bank of the Tarn is spectacular – 10 hairpin bends offer a splendid view of **La Malène** tucked in its hollow.

▶ At Croix-Blanche, take D 16 to the right; 5km/3mi farther on, turn right again. After passing through the village of Rieisse, take the road signposted 'Roc des Hourtous-Roc du Serre' near a café.

Roc des Hourtous★★
Follow the signs along the surfaced track off to the left. Car park. This cliff overlooks La Momie cave, just upstream from the Détroits gully, which is the narrowest section of the Tarn canyon. From here there is a superb **view★★** of the Tarn gorges, from the hamlet of L'Angle to the Cirque des Baumes and the Point Sublime.

Gorges du Tarn at St-Chély-du-Tarn

© Pierre Jacques/hemis.fr

▶ Go back to the fork in the road; leave the car and take the track on the right to the Roc du Serre.

Roc du Serre★★

🚶 This is the only place that gives this marvellous **view★★** of the narrow river gorge as it squeezes between the Causse de Sauveterre and Causse Méjean, with, farther off, Mont Lozère, the Aigoual range, the village of La Malène and the hairpin bends of D 16 as it wends its way up the causse.

Take D 16 on the right across the causse and down to Les Vignes via an impressive cliff-face road that runs past the ruins of the **Château de Blanquefort**.

On leaving **La Malène**, the road runs through narrow straits known as the **Détroits★★** (*see Boat Trips p190*). A **viewpoint**, on the left, offers a good view over this, the narrowest part of the gorges.

Farther along, the road passes round the foot of the **Cirque des Baumes★★** (*see Boat Trips*).

Pas de Soucy

At this point, the Tarn disappears beneath a chaotic heap of enormous boulders – the result of two rock slides, the more recent being due to an earthquake in 580.

🚶 Steps lead up to the **viewpoint** on **Roque Sourde** will give an aerial view of the Pas de Soucy.

▶ At Les Vignes turn right onto D 995, a cliff road with tight hairpin bends. After 5km/3mi, take D 46 to the right which runs across the Causse de Sauveterre and, at St-Georges-de-Lévéjac, turn right once more.

Point Sublime★★★

From the Point Sublime, there is a splendid view over the Tarn gorges, from the Détroits to the Pas de Soucy and the Roche Aiguille.

▶ Return to Les Vignes and the Tarn gorges road.

Soon, flanking the Causse Méjean, the last remaining ruins of **Château de Blanquefort** can be seen clinging tenaciously to a large rock.

Farther along, the huge Cinglegros rock looms into sight, jutting up starkly detached from the Causse Méjean. On the right bank, cliffs at the edge of the Causse de Sauveterre slope away from the Tarn as the cirque of St-Marcellin. Finally, having crossed a bridge over the river adorned with a monument in honour of Édouard-Alfred Martel, the road comes to **Le Rozier**, on the confluence of the Jonte and Tarn. Dwarfed by the cliffs of the Causse Sauveterre, Causse Noir and Causse Méjean, the village is the threshold for the Tarn gorges.

Château de Peyrelade

Open May–Jun Sat–Sun and public holidays 10.30am–5.30pm; Jul–Aug daily 10am–6pm; 1–mid-Sept daily except Tue 10.30am–5.30pm. Closed Tue in mid-end Jun and Sept. €3.50 (child 8–12, €1.50). 05 65 59 74 28. www.seigneurs-du-rouergue.fr.

Visible from the road, this 12C castle was one of the most important fotresses of Rouergue in the Middle Ages. The castle was dismantled on the orders of Richelieu in 1633; even so, the remains still dominate the valley.

BOAT TRIPS
La Malène–Cirque des Baumes

It is advisable to make this trip in the morning, since this section of the canyon is at its best in the morning light. Apr–Oct guided tours daily by a local boatman. €88 per boat of 4 people or €22 for an individual. Bateliers des Gorges du Tarn, 48210 La Malène. 04 66 48 51 10. www.gorgesdutarn.com.

Les Détroits★★

This is the most spectacular, and the narrowest, section of the Tarn gorges.

Cirque des Baumes★★

Downriver from Les Détroits, the gorge widens, flowing into the splendid Cirque des Baumes (*baume* means cave).

Canoeing through Les Détroits

© Pierre Jacques/hemis.fr

WALKS
1 Corniche du Tarn

Round tour from Le Rozier – 21km/13mi by car, then 3h30 on foot.
From Le Rozier, take the road along the Tarn gorges (D 907) as far as Les Vignes. Turn right towards Florac. The steep road climbs in a series of hairpin bends above the gorges. Turn towards La Bourgarie and park the car there.

At the end of the hamlet, follow the red waymarked path. It passes the Bout du Monde ('End of the World') spring. Soon after a right fork leads to the Pas de l'Arc.

▷ Turn back to the fork and then continue to Baousso del Biel.

Baousso del Biel

This opening is the largest natural arch in the region. The path reaches the point where the arch merges with the plateau. Several hundred yards after this bridge, follow the path up to the left to reach the abandoned farm of Volcégure.

▷ From here, a forest footpath (GR 6A) leads back to La Bourgarie.

2 Tarn valley footpath

From La Malène to St-Chély-du-Tarn – 3h one way.
In La Malène, cross the bridge and follow the yellow and green waymarked footpath, which leads to another path running along the river bank towards Hauterives (crowded in summer).

The path first runs through a wooded area where weeping-willows lean over the river. On the opposite bank stand the Causse de Sauveterre limestone cliffs. The path then climbs steps hewn out of the rock, affording a totally different landscape: the luxuriant vegetation growing close to the river has given way to Mediterranean-type scrubland with stunted oaks and sparse wild grasses. Follow the path across a scree to the ghost hamlet of Hauterives (abandoned ruins) then through a forest of pines and oaks.

Sainte-Énimie ★

Ste-Énimie lies in terraced rows below the steep cliffs bordering a loop of the Tarn, where the canyon is at its narrowest. The village is named after a Merovingian princess who chose to live in a grotto in order to dedicate her life to God, and founded a convent.

THE TOWN
A leisurely stroll through the pretty little streets of Ste-Énimie is a good way to discover the village's charm.

Former monastery
Start from the place du Plot. Follow the arrows to the chapter house. Go through a vaulted room, and up a staircase that goes to the crypt.
You can still see the remains of the chapter house, and the fortifications that surrounded the monastery.

Place au Beurre and halle au Blé
At the heart of the ancient village, this square has a lovely old house, while the corn exchange retains its identity and its links with the sale of wheat.

▶ **Population:** 553.
Michelin Map: 526: M5.
Info: 48210 Ste-Énimie ℘04 66 48 53 44. www.gorgesdutarn.net.
Location: 27km/17mi W of Florac, and the same from Mende.
Timing: Use the village as a base to explore.

Le Vieux Logis
Open mid-Jun–mid-Sep daily except Tue and Sat 10am–12.30pm, 3.30–6.30pm. ℘04 66 48 53 44.
This small museum houses various utensils and gives an idea of living conditions in the area in past times.

Église
Originally dating from the 12C, the church has undergone many changes.

Source de Burle
This is the resurgence of all the rain water falling on the causse de Sauveterre, which, according to legend, cures leprosy.

Causse Méjean ★

The Causse Méjean has a harsh climate with freezing winters, scorching summers, and temperature extremes between day and night.

NATURE
The plateau of dolomite limestone outcrops is scattered with megaliths, indicating the habitation by Stone Age people. The Causse Méjean is sheep (*brebis*) country and has a low population density. The griffon vulture was re-introduced in 1970, and Przewalski horses (the last surviving wild horse sub-species) have recently been seen in the region.

Michelin Map: 330: H-9 to I-9.
Info: Office du tourisme du Rozier, Route de Meyrueis, 48150. ℘05 65 62 60 89. www.officedetourisme-gorgesdutarn.com.
Location: 30km/18.75mi NE of Millau via the D 907.
Don't Miss: The Przewalski horses at Villaret; the chaos de Nîmes-le-Vieux and a walk on the corniches.
Kids: The Caussenarde farm at Hyelzas.

Aven Armand

© Pierre Jacques/hemis.fr

🚗 DRIVING TOUR

Round trip 87km/54mi from Florac –
Allow 3h.

▷ Leave Florac W along D 16 and turn left onto D 63.

The D 63 passes through Le Villaret where a stud farm breeds small wild Mongolian Przewalski horses. See them galloping across nearby fields.

Aven Armand★★★
&*See Excursion, opposite.*

👥 Hyelzas
🕐*Open Mar–Oct at various times;*
check website. 🕐*Closed public holidays*
and Nov–Easter. ↔€6.20 (child 6–17,
€3.10). ✆04 66 45 65 25.
www.ferme-caussenarde.com.
At **Hyelzas** you can tour a traditional Causses farmstead with models of Meyrueis' clock tower, the Millau viaduct, Causses farmsteads and Lozère houses.

▷ Return to the D 986 intersection and turn right.

Meyrueis
&*See MEYRUEIS.*

▷ Follow D 996 towards Florac.

Note the contrast between the Causse Méjean and the forested Aigoual massif.

▷ Turn left at Col de Perjuret.

Chaos de Nîmes-le-Vieux★
From the pass, head towards Veygalier
or l'Hom or Gally; park the car. This
walk is not good in rainy and foggy
weather or when winter winds drop the
temperature to –15°C.
The Chaos de Nîmes-le-Vieux rises like a ruined city from the bare expanse of the Causse Méjean. During the Wars of Religion, royal armies pursuing Protestants were shocked at their surroundings because they thought they'd reached their intended destination, Nîmes.

🚶 From **Veygalier** – *Apr–Sep unaccompanied tours from Hom or Gally.*
This typical Veygalier house has an exhibit on local geology. From here a trail leads off through 'streets' of stone overlooked by rock formations 10–50m high. From high above Veygalier, enjoy views over the cirque, where stone houses blend in with their dolomitic surroundings.

🚶 **From l'Hom or Gally** – *1h30 on foot from Gally to Veygalier.*

This Parc National des Cévennes discovery trail is a window onto the Causses natural environment.

▶ Drive back to Florac along D 907.

EXCURSION
Aven Armand★★★
Hidden beneath the Causse Méjean, the Aven Armand is one of the wonders of the underground world, opened to the public in 1927.

Przewalski horse, Parc du Villaret, Causse Mejean

© Eric Baccega/age fotostock

Discovery of the Aven Armand
The famous speleologist E.A. Martel began exploring the *causses* in 1883, accompanied by **Louis Armand**, a locksmith from Le Rozier. On 18 September 1897 Armand returned from an outing to the Causse Méjean greatly excited. The next day an expedition investigated the enormous crevice, known by local farmers as *l'aven* ('the swallow-hole'). Armand was enraptured at this wonderland of rock formations.

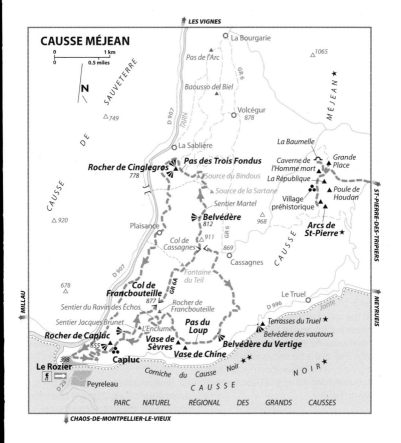

Cave

The tour explores the vast subterranean gallery. Spectacular concretions form a luxuriant jungle of fantastically shaped trees up to 15–25m in height. Glistening with calcite crystals, they have trunks resembling palm trees or cypresses, and large jagged 'leaves' measuring three feet across.

Stalagmites explode into a riot of arabesques, needles, palm branches and elegant pyramids. The variety of concretions is amazing: gigantic candles, monstrous figures with club-shaped heads and curly cabbages and delicately engraved fruit.

WALKS

1 Corniches Causse Méjean ★★★

🚶 *Walking tour from Le Rozier.*
Allow 7h. This well-maintained footpath has spectacular clifftop passages requiring great care; the path can be slippery and is crowded in July and August. Wear stout walking shoes and carry a day's worth of food and water.

▶ Behind the church in Le Rozier, the footpath leads off from the junction of two roads (GR 6A waymarked in red and white).

Half an hour's climb brings you to the pretty little hamlet of **Capluc**, now deserted.

2 Rocher de Capluc

Not recommended for anyone suffering from vertigo.

Bear left towards Capluc rock at the far end of a promontory on the southwest edge of the Causse Méjean.
At the top of a flight of stone steps is a house leaning against the rock face. The terrace around the rock leads to a dizzying climb to the summit, with exhilarating views of Peyreleau and the Jonte and Tarn rivers and villages of Liaucous and Mostuéjouls.

▶ Return to Capluc.

3 Climb to the Col de Francbouteille

Beyond Capluc are two ways of reaching the Francbouteille Pass: The 'Ravin des Echos' along a section of the GR 6A footpath, winds gently uphill, with fine views of the causse. The steep, vertiginous Jacques-Brunet path climbs through juniper, boxwood and pine then threads between little chimneys to a crest offering magnificent views of the Tarn and Jonte canyons.

After a stretch through cool undergrowth with views of the Tarn valley, the path reaches the pass.

Col de Francbouteille

At this 'pass of the two canyons' the Francbouteille rock looms like the prow of a colossal ship.

▶ Follow the arrows to the GR 6A footpath.

Soon, Teil spring comes into view, much appreciated by walkers.

▶ At the Col de Cassagnes, leave the Martel footpath leading to Cinglegros rock (♿ see below) to the left, and bear right towards the isolated village of Cassagnes.

The footpath crosses the causse. Leave a pine plantation and follow the footpath over the Jonte gorge.

4 Belvédère du Vertige

An hour's walk leads to an impressive view over the Jonte canyon. Later on the footpath runs in front of a cave once used as a sheep pen, then between two natural bridges. The steep descent is called **Pas du Loup** ('Wolf's step'). Immediately after, the **Vase de Chine** and **Vase de Sèvres monoliths** come into sight and then distant Peyreleau and Le Rozier, Capluc rock and Causse Noir cliffs.

▶ Return to the footpath which drops downhill amid jagged dolomitic rocks. Leave the footpath to the Col de Francbouteille to the right, and return to Capluc and Le Rozier along the Ravin des Echos and Brèche Magnifique paths.

5 Rocher de Cinglegros

One day walking tour from Le Rozier.
This walk is for the fit and nimble who do not suffer from vertigo.

Follow the route of the Corniches du Causse Méjean as far as the Col de Cassagnes, then turn left to Cinglegros rock. This well laid out path offers exhilarating views of cliffs overhanging the Tarn, the Cinglegros gap and the Cinglegros rock itself.

Return to base by a footpath leading down to the hamlet of Plaisance, then to Le Rozier on the path to La Sablière.

6 Arcs de St-Pierre★

1h30 on foot there and back.
There are two ways to get to the Arcs de St-Pierre:

Either via D 63 which branches off D 986 at Hures-la-Parade; after 3km/2mi, take the little road on the right to St-Pierre-des-Tripiers; 1km/0.6mi past this village, take the small unsurfaced road, again to the right, opposite the junction for La Viale.

Or up the steep, narrow hairpin road branching off D 996 from Le Truel towards St-Pierre-des-Tripiers, in the Jonte Valley. Level with the junction for La Viale, take the small unsurfaced road to the left.

The 'Arcs de St-Pierre' is a mass of eroded rock formations resembling ruins.
Take the footpath downhill (*waymarked in red*) to the **Grande Place**. In this rocky amphitheatre stands a 10m high monolith.
The footpath climbs up to the cave of **La Baumelle**. After returning to the Grande Place, follow the waymarked path leading from it to the **Caverne de l'Homme mort** ('Dead Man's Cave'); 50 skeletons similar to that of Cro-Magnon man were discovered here; most of them had had their skulls operated on with flint.

Past the huge boulders **Poule de Houdan** ('Houdan's hen') and **La République**, the path leads to the site of a **prehistoric village** and finally arrives at the **Arcs de St-Pierre**, three natural arches, some of the finest in the Causses.

ADDRESSES

STAY

Camping Le Pont du Tarn – *Route du Pont de Montvert, 48400 Florac.* 04 66 45 18 26. www.camping-florac.com. *Closed Oct–Mar. 153 places.* On the banks of the Tarn, this camping site has places that are both sheltered and spacious. On summer afternoons you can benefit from the swimming pool, with separate pool for children, or take to the little beach created on the banks of the river. Also available for mobile homes.

Hôtel Doussière – *48150 Le Rozier.* 05 65 62 60 25. www.hotel-doussiere. com. *Closed mid-Nov to Easter.* **P** *20 rooms.* In the village, the hotel comprises two buildings on either side of the Jonte. Some rooms have been renovated, and these have better soundproofing. The breakfast room has a lovely view.

Hôtel Mont Servy – *48210 Mas St-Chély.* 04 66 48 52 14. www.hotel-montservy.com. *Closed Jan–Mar.* **P** *7 rooms. Restaurant.* On the causse Méjean, this hotel-restaurant is in two parts: the hotel, which occupies a newer building, and the restaurant, which has a comprehensive menu of local and regional dishes. The rooms are all well equipped and comfortable.

EAT

Auberge du Chanet – *Hameau de Nivoliers, 48150 Hures-la-Parade.* 04 66 45 65 12. *Closed 20 Nov–25 Mar.* This old sheep farm at the heart of the Causse is an oasis of peace and quiet. Being on the GR 60, it is convenient for a number of walking routes. Traditional cuisine is served in the vaulted dining room or on the sunny terrace. The auberge also offers several accommodation options, from rooms to dormitories.

Meyrueis

Clear mountain air and varied attractions make Meyrueis a popular destination. Ancient plane trees decorate place Sully, generating a relaxing ambiance. Meyrueis was the birthplace of Guilhem Ademar (1190), a troubadour of some renown.

THE TOWN

While strolling along quai Sully, look out for the elegant Renaissance windows of Maison Belon, and the **Tour de l'Horloge** a clock tower left from the town's fortification.

🚗 DRIVING TOURS

GORGES DE LA JONTE★★
Drive down the D 996 from Meyrueis to Le Rozier, rather than up; it's more impressive.
The Jonte gorge can also be visited on foot along the clifftop footpaths over the Causse Méjean (see Causse MÉJEAN) and the Causse Noir (see opposite).

Downstream from Meyrueis the road along the Jonte gorge follows the river's north bank. Some 5km/3mi from Meyrueis, the mouths of two Causse Méjean caves open into the cliff, the **Grotte de la Vigne** and the **Grotte de la Chèvre.** Beyond these caves the gorge becomes narrower and in summer the Jonte disappears. Outside Les Douzes, the river enters a second gorge so deep that you can scarcely see its huge poplars.

Arcs de St-Pierre★
4.5km/3mi, then 1h30 on foot there and back. Leave from Le Truel. See Castelnau-Pégayrols.

👥 La Maison des Vautours
Open Apr and Oct daily except Mon 10am–6pm; May–Jun and Sept daily except Mon 9.30am–7pm; Jul–Aug daily 9.30am–7pm. €6.70 (child 5–12, €3). ☎05 65 62 69 69. www.vautours-lozere.com.

- ▶ **Population:** 963.
- **Michelin Map:** 330: I-9.
- **Info:** Tour de l'Horloge, 48150 Meyrueis. ☎04 66 45 60 33. www.meyrueis-office-tourisme.com.
- **Location:** 43km/28.8mi E of Millau and 58km/36.25mi N of Vigan.
- **Don't Miss:** Mont Aigoual, Jonte Gorge, and the chaos de Montpellier-le-Vieux.
- **Kids:** Dargilan cave.

Vultures were reintroduced into the area in 1970, and this exhibition explains their way of life and feeding habits. You can watch them at close range with a camera and giant screen.

Le Rozier
See GORGES DU TARN, Driving Tour.

Peyreleau
At the confluence of the Jonte and the Tarn and built on the steep slopes of a hill, Peyreleau is an interesting place. A modern church and an old crenelated square keep tower above the village.
From D 29 which climbs onto the Causse Noir, there are views of the 15C **Château de Triadou** where a treasure stolen by its owner from the Protestant army in the 17C was eventually found by peasants during the 1789 Revolution.

Walk the corniche du causse Noir★★
6h. Leave the car at Les Rouquets (E of Peyreleau) and take the road for la Jonte. Follow red waymarks; in places you need to climb metal ladders.

The trail runs along the Jonte, then climbs to the right through beech and pine trees to the Hermitage St-Michel. There is a fine **view★★** from the rocky promontory of Pointe Sublime. Later, the trail climbs through woodland, and the waymarking switches to red and yellow, passing a rock known as the Mushroom. Press on to reach a TV relay station from where there is a fine **view★★** over Payreleau at the confluence of the Jonte and the Tarn. Stay on the path as far as a clearing, and there turn right. Now the path descends along the ravine of the Costalade, continuing through pine forest to a path alongside a vineyard on the outskirts of Rouquette.

▷ Reach the Causse Noir via D 29 S of Peyreleau. After 7km/4.3mi, turn right onto D 110.

LE CAUSSE NOIR★
75km/47mi from Peyreleau – Allow about 4h. ᓬSee map on p171.
It is hard to believe today, but thick pine forests once covered this plateau, which is how it got its name. It is less extensive than the Grands Causses, but its land-scapes are stunning.

▷ Join the Causse Noir by the D 29 to the S of Peyreleau.

As you climb onto the Causse Noir, you can see the château de Triadou, which belonged to the Albignac family until the Revolution.

▷ After 7km/4mi turn right onto the D 110.

Chaos de Montpellier-le Vieux ★★★
ᓬ*See Chaos de MONTPELLIER-LE-VIEUX.*

▷ Come back along the D 110 and turn right onto the D 29.

St-Jean-de-Balmes
At the heart of the plateau, stands a square clock tower of St Benedict's priory, built in 11C.

▷ After La Roujarie, turn right onto the D 124 leading to St-André-de-Vézine. In St-André-de-Vézines, turn right to Roquesaltes.

Chaos de Roquesaltes et du Rajola
🚶 *2h on foot. Medium difficulty.*
Leave the car at the intersection of the road with an unsurfaced path and walk along this path, signposted 'Roquesaltes', tothe right. The path runs down through forest pines and junipers.

▷ When you reach Roquesaltes farm, take GR 62 towards Montméjean.

Roquesaltes, meaning 'tall rocks', looks for all the world like a natural fortress overlooking the hamlet of Roquesaltes. From these rocky ramparts, the view extends over Montpellier-le-Vieux.

▷ From the television mast, turn left onto a track leading to the surfaced road which you had previously followed from St-André; turn left to return.

Grotte de Dargilan★★
In 1880 a shepherd called Sahuquet chased a fox into a huge dark under-ground chamber, which he thought looked like the antechamber to Hell. He fled, and so it was not until 1888 that Dargilan cave was explored, by E A Martel and six companions. Even-tually Dargilan became the property of the Société des Gorges du Tarn which fitted it with iron steps, ramps and railings to accommodate visitors. In 1910 electric lighting was installed in all the galleries.

Cave
🕐*Open Easter–Oct; check website for tour times.* ∞*€10 (child 6–18, €6.50).* 𝄞*04 66 45 60 20.*
http://grotte-dargilan.com.
You first enter the **Grande Salle du Chaos**, a gallery that looks like a cha-otic underground heap of rocks. The smaller Salle de la Mosquée contains many beautiful stalagmites. Other cave wonders include the 'corridor of petri-fied cascades' – **magnificent calcite drapery★★** 100m long and 40m high, a labyrinth, underground lakes and stalag-mitic frozen falls.The 'Mosque' formation of stalagmites with glints of mother-of-pearl is flanked by the 'Minaret', a lovely column. The 'clocher', a slender pyramid, is quite unexpected and beautiful.

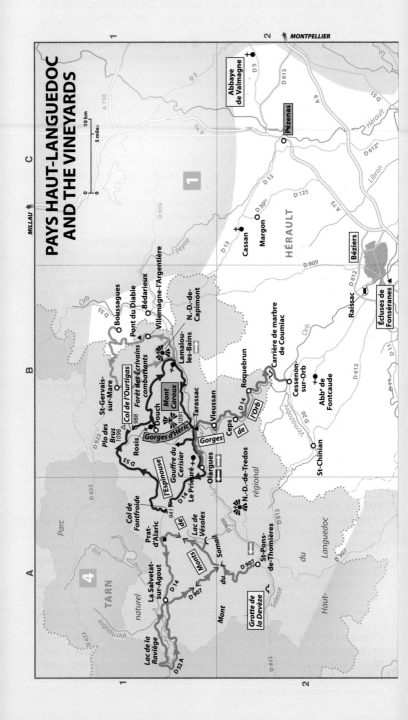

PAYS HAUT-LANGUEDOC
AND THE VINEYARDS

MILLAU

MONTPELLIER

Abbaye de Valmagne

Pézenas

Béziers

HÉRAULT

Cassan

Margon

Raissac

Écluses de Fonsérannes

Boussagues

Pont du Diable

Bédarieux

Villemagne-l'Argentière

N.-D.-de-Capimont

Lamalou-les-Bains

Mont Caroux 1091

Forêt des Écrivains combattants

St-Gervais-sur-Mare

Col de l'Ourtigas 988

Plo des Brus 1098

Douch

Rosis

Gorges d'Héric

l'Espinouse

Gouffre du Cerisier

D 53

Col de Fontfroide 941

Prat-d'Alaric

Lac de Vésoles

Monts

de

Tarassac

Vieussan

Gorges

Ceps

de

l'Orb

Roquebrun

Carrière de marbre de Coumiac

Cessenon-sur-Orb

Abb¹ de Fontcaude

St-Chinian

Olargues

Le Prieuré

N.-D.-de-Tredos

régional

N.-D.-de-Trèdos

Somail

Mont du

St-Pons-de-Thomières

Grotte de la Devèze

La Salvetat-sur-Agout

Lac de la Raviège

Parc

naturel

TARN

Languedoc

du

Haut-

10 km

5 miles

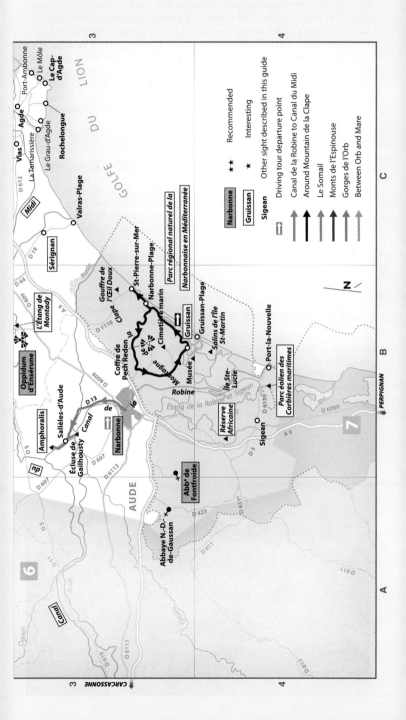

GOLFE DU LION

Port-Ambonne
Le Môle
Le Cap-d'Agde
Agde
Rochelongue
Le Grau-d'Agde
Vias
La Tamarissière
D 612
Midi
D 19
Sérignan
D 64
D 609
Valras-Plage
L'Étang de Montady
Oppidum d'Ensérune
A 9
D 1118
Gouffre de l'Œil Doux
St-Pierre-sur-Mer
Narbonne-Plage
Clape
Coffre de Pech Redon
la
Cimetière marin
Parc régional naturel de la Narbonnaise en Méditerranée
Sallèles-d'Aude
Amphoralis
D 5
Canal
de
la
D 6009
Montagne
Gruissan
Gruissan-Plage
Musée
Salins de l'Île St-Martin
D 13
Écluse de Gailhousty
Narbonne
D 607
D 6113
D 607
Robine
Étang de la Robine et Sigean
 Île Ste-Lucie
Réserve Africaine
Parc éolien des Corbières maritimes
Port-la-Nouvelle
Sigean
D 6139
A 9
D 3
D 6009
Abbᵉ de Fonttroide
D 423
Abbaye N.-D.-de-Gaussan
D 611
D 6113
np
Canal
AUDE
D 5
D 611
D 6113
D 610
Ognon
Orbiel
Aude
D 11

→ PERPIGNAN

↑ CARCASSONNE

N↗

★★   Recommended
★   Interesting

★   Other sight described in this guide

⇧   Driving tour departure point

Narbonne	Canal de la Robine to Canal du Midi
	Around Mountain de la Clape
Gruissan	Le Somail
	Monts de l'Espinouse
Sigean	Gorges de l'Orb
	Between Orb and Mare

199

PAYS HAUT-LANGUEDOC *and the Vineyards*

Today renowned for its fine wines, Haut-Languedoc is blessed with stunning cities, towns and villages, all with pedigrees that reach back to Gallo-Roman times. The secret here is to take an almost aimless tour through the rugged landscape, the *garrigue*, where you pass numerous private and co-operative vineyards. Here, the sampling of wine is taken seriously; as is olive oil, which is also produced in this region in large quantities. Away from the brouhaha of the towns and cities, the countryside is a wonderland of heady scents, sounds and sights, where a host of charming villages lie lost in delightful rambling scenery. Of course, it is impossible to ignore the influence of the Canal du Midi: one man's vision of a highway heaven, even if he had to sacrifice his daughter's dowry to realise it.

Highlights

1 Take the sun at the coastal resort of **Cap d'Agde** (p206)

2 Follow in Molière's footsteps in **Pézenas** (p208)

3 Walk or cycle beside the **Canal du Midi,** or take a boat trip (p214)

4 Visit bustling **Narbonne** (p216)

5 Be sure to stay in the car at the **Réserve Africaine de Sigean** (p224)

Well Oiled

Without doubt, wine is one of the major supports of the regional economy, but so is the production of olives and olive oils. The olive producer has enjoyed renown here since antiquity, and olive oil has played an important role in the life of the Mediterranean populations, who think of the olive tree as sacred. Many of the olive producers of Languedoc were wiped out by a severe frost in 1956, after which they switched to producing wine. But in recent times, olives have come back in vogue, and the 25 November, the Feast of Sainte Catherine Labouré, is officially the first day on which olives can be harvested.

Languedoc Vineyards

The wines of the Languedoc-Roussillon AOC are drawn from a massive area of over 50 000ha, stretching from Narbonne to Nîmes, and embracing 156 communes, of which five are in Aude, fourteen in Gard, and all the rest in Hérault. The annual production exceeds 70 000 gallons of red or rosé, and more than 150 000 gallons of white. You could have quite a party with all that at your disposal!

Hérault vineyards

© clodio/iStockphoto.com

Béziers★

Perched high on a spur overlooking the river Orb and topped by a cathedral, Béziers is the wine capital of Languedoc. It is also the birthplace of Pierre Paul Riquet, the illustrious inventor of the Canal du Midi, and, if you like, the conservatory of the Occitan culture and history, among which lurk the insidious deeds of the crusade against the Cathars.

- ▶ **Population:** 76 382.
- 🕒 **Michelin Map:** 339: E8.
- **Info:** Place du Forum, 34500 Béziers. ✆04 99 41 36 36. www.beziers-tourisme.fr.
- ▶ **Location:** 76km/47.5mi SE of Montpellier.
- **Parking:** Underground car parks in the centre.
- **Timing:** Take at least a day to explore the city.
- **Don't Miss:** Museum du Biterrois; ceramic collection in the château de Raissac.

A BIT OF HISTORY

Béziers was a thriving city when the Romans colonised it during 1C. It was renamed Julia Baeterrae and fell within the Naronensis province.

Modern Béziers occupies the same pre-Roman site of its origins, on a plateau on the east bank of the Orb. The old Roman forum, surrounded by temples and a market, probably stood in front of the site of the present town hall. Between rue St-Jacques and place du Cirque, the old houses, with their neat urban gardens and garages, are laid out in an elliptical pattern, reflecting the presence of Béziers' buried Roman amphitheatre. During the 3C Barbarian threat, the amphitheatre's stones were used to build a wall around the city.

During the Albigensian Crusade, Béziers was besieged in 1209. The resident Roman Catholics fought alongside Cathars to defend their town. One of the commanders of the crusade was the Papal Legate Arnaud-Amaury. When asked by a Crusader how to tell Catholics from Cathars once they had taken the city, the abbot callously replied, 'Kill them all, God will know His own'. All were butchered in the ensuing massacre, even those hiding in the churches. Béziers was pillaged and torched and not a creature there remained living.

Béziers miraculously rose from these ashes, but was a sleepy backward community until the 19C, when the development of its vineyards revived its old wealth and vigour. Béziers was the home town of **Pierre-Paul Riquet**, designer of the Canal du Midi, and of **Jean Moulin**, hero of the World War II Resistance movement commemorated in Béziers' 'Plateau des Poètes', an English style park laid out by landscape artists, the Bulher brothers.

Cathédrale St-Nazaire

© Jean-Marc Barrere/hemis.fr

♻ WALKING TOUR

Leave the car in the Jean-Jaurès car park. This walk starts from the statue of Pierre-Paul Riquet (♿ see Canal du MIDI) in the centre of Pierre-Paul Riquet avenue. Walk NW towards the theatre.

Allées Paul-Riquet

This road avenue shaded by plane trees bustles with life. David d'Angers' statue of Riquet stands at the centre of the avenue, and the mid-19C theatre, also by d'Angers, has a façade decorated with allegorical sculptures.

▶ At the end of the avenue, turn left onto boulevard de la Répulique, then right onto rue Casimir-Péret, and left again onto rue Vannières.

Basilique St-Aphrodise

The church dedicated to the town's patron saint contains a handsome 4C–5C **sarcophagus** carved with the scene of a lion hunt. Opposite the pulpit is a 16C polychrome wood Crucifix.

▶ Turn back along rue Casimir-Péret then, just before reaching boulevard de la Répulique, take rue Trencavel (right).

Église de la Madeleine

Peaceful now, this Romanesque church remodelled during the Gothic period and again in the 18C was one of the sites of the 1209 massacre (♿ see A Bit of History).

▶ From place de la Madeleine, follow rue Paul-Riquet; cross place Semard to the right and take rue Tourventouse.

A vaulted passageway leads to rue du Capus and the **Hôtel Fayet**, an annexe of the Fine Arts Museum.

▶ Turn right onto rue du Gén.-Pailhès then left onto rue du Gén.-Crouzat leading to place des Bons-Amis (note the charming small fountain), then to place de la Révolution.

Ancienne cathédrale St-Nazaire★

On a terrace above the river Orb, the cathedral symbolised the power of Béziers bishops between 760 and 1789. The Romanesque building was badly damaged in 1209, and repairs on it continued from 1215 until the 15C. The west front, flanked by late 14C fortified towers, contains a magnificent rose window. The Jardin de l'Évêché has a pretty view of the church of St-Jude and the river Orb spanned by the 13C Pont Vieux (the newer Pont Neuf dates from the 19C). The terrace near the cathedral affords a view of the Orb flowing through vineyards, the Canal du Midi and the hill fort of Ensérune. Beyond are Mont Caroux, the Pic de Nore and Canigou.

▶ From place de la Révolution, follow rue de Bonsi: the **Hôtel Fabrégat** houses one of two Fine Arts Museums in Béziers. Take rue Massot to your right then continue along rue des Dr-Bourguet. From place St-Cyr, follow rue St-Jacques.

You are now in the district known as *'Quartier des arènes romaines'*, a reminder that the town was once a Roman colony in the Naronensis province.

Musée des Beaux-Arts

Hôtel Fabrégat, place de la Révolution. ⏰*Open Oct–May Tue–Fri 10am–5pm, Sat–Sun 10am–6pm; Jun–Sept Tue to Sun 10am–6pm.* ⌨€3 *(children under 12, free) (combined ticket with Musée du Biterrois).* ✆04 67 28 38 78.

The museum of fine art occupies two old private mansions near the cathedral. The **Hôtel Fabrégat** contains works by Martin Schaffner, Dominiquin, Guido Reni, Pillement, Languedoc painter J Gamelin, Géricault, Devéria, Delacroix, Corot, Dauigny, Othon Friesz, Soutine, Chirico, Kisling, Dufy and Utrillo, among others. Another fine arts museum in the **Hôtel Fayet** houses 19C paintings, a bequest by J G Goulinat (1883–1972) and the contents of the workshop of Béziers sculptor **J A Injalert** (1845–1933).

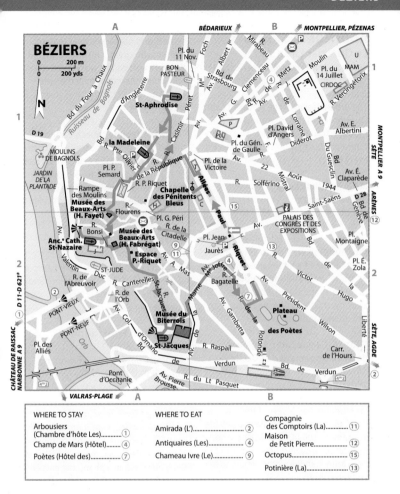

BÉZIERS

WHERE TO STAY		WHERE TO EAT		
Arbousiers (Chambre d'hôte Les)	①	Amirada (L')	②	Compagnie des Comptoirs (La) ⑪
Champ de Mars (Hôtel)	④	Antiquaires (Les)	④	Maison de Petit Pierre ⑫
Poètes (Hôtel des)	⑦	Chameau Ivre (Le)	⑨	Octopus ⑮
				Potinière (La) ⑬

Walk past the Musée du Biterrois and follow avenue de la Marne to place Garialdi then turn right onto avenue du Mar.-Joffre.

Musée du Biterrois

Same hours as the the Musée des Beaux-Arts above). ℘04 67 36 71 01. Contained in the 1702 St-Jacques bar-racks designed by Charles d'Aviler, this museum features local archaeology, ethnology and natural history. Here are dioramas on regional fauna; displays of Greek, Iberian and Roman amphorae discovered on the seabed nearby at Cap d'Agde; galleries on geology and volcanic activity in the Languedoc region, and Bronze and Iron Age life. Gallo-Roman treasures excavated in the city include sigillated pottery from La Graufesenque (*see MILLAU),* the mile-stones which once lined the Via Domitia, and the 'Trésor de Béziers'– three large chased silver platters found in 1983 in a vineyard on the city's outskirts.

Plateau des Poètes

Busts of poets line the path in this hilly landscaped park which runs on from allées Paul-Rique. Designed by the Bühler brothers in the 19C, it features a Caucasian elm, Californian sequoia, magnolias and the Cedar of Lebanon. The Fontaine du Titan (fountain) was designed by Injalert.

Return to place Jean-Jaurès along allées Paul-Riquet.

ADDITIONAL SIGHTS
Le Quartier Latin
Access from the theatre on av. Georges-Clemenceau, then right into av. Jean-Moulin.

The urban design of the so-called Latin Quarter is organised around a former military training ground, a vast rectangular area that now hosts a market every Friday.

MAM (Médiathèque André-Malraux)
1 pl. du 14-Juillet. ℘04 99 51 05 50. www.mediatheque-beziers-agglo.org.
Designed by Jean-Michel Wilmotte, this building has clean lines and a sleek façade of white marble laminate. Its three level auditorium plays host to concerts and shows, and also houses a library, children's play area, music centre, cinema and theatre.

CIRDÒC (Centre Inter-Régional de Développement de l'Occitan)
1 bis boulevard Du Guesclin.
℘04 67 11 85 10. www.locirdoc.fr.
This centre acts as a national library for students and lovers of the 'Langue d'Oc', preserving and making available as many as 100 000 books and prints. Its location in Béziers demonstrates the city's long-standing commitment to the Occitan culture.

EXCURSIONS
Écluses de Fonséranes
0.8km/0.5mi to the W, towards Narbonne. See CARCASSONNE.

Château de Raissac
3.2km/2mi NW towards Murviels-lès-Béziers by Lignan-sur-Orb (D 19) Rte de Lignan. Open: visits to the Ceramics museum, château and park, on request; visit to the cellars of the château with wine tasting daily except Sun. ℘04 67 49 17 60. www.raissac.com.
Contemporary artist Christine Viennet displays her work alongside an important collection of European ceramics from the 19C. The great manufacturers of France are especially well represented, and homage is paid to Bernard Palissy who greatly inspires Christine. Possible visit to the workroom. Shop, and wine cellars complete the visit.

Sérignan★
11km/7mi S on D 19 towards Valras.
The old **collegiate church**, dating from the 12C–14C, graces the southwest bank of the Orb. Its exterior evidences traces of fortifications such as loopholes, machicolations and remnants of watch turrets. Inside, admire the nave's ceiling and elegant heptagonal apse.

Valras-Plage
15km/9.5mi S on D 19.
This fishing port and yachting harbour at the mouth of the Orb has a fine sandy beach. The Théâtre de la Mer hosts various summer shows.

Abbaye de Fontcaude
18km/11mi NW via D 14.
Open daily except Sun morning: Jun–Sep 10am–noon, 2.30–7pm (Jul–Aug Mon–Fri 10am–7pm); Oct–May 10am–noon, 2.30–5.30pm. Closed Jan (except Sun afternoon). ℘04 67 38 23 85. www.abbaye-de-fontcaude.com.
This Romanesque Premonstratensian abbey was destroyed during the Wars of Religion. The transept and the east end are all that remains of the **abbey church**. The large scriptorium, where monks once copied and illuminated manuscripts, is now a **museum** displaying fragments of the **capitals** from the cloisters.

St-Chinian
24km/15mi NW of by the D 612.
This large town, one of the main centres of the Languedoc vineyards, gives its name to an important wine AOC.
To learn more, go to the Maison des Vins on the main square.

ADDRESSES

⌂ STAY
Hotel Champ de Mars – *17 r. de Metz. ℘04 67 28 35 53. 10 rooms.* Quiet family hotel in a quiet street (except market

day, Friday) in the heart of Béziers. The rooms are medium sized and are fully equipped.

🛏️ **Hôtel des Poètes** – *80 Allées Paul-Riquet.* ✆*04 67 76 38 66. www.hotel despoetes.net.* 🅿️. *14 rooms.* Ideally situated opposite the park des Poètes, a small hotel with simple rooms, just a short walk from the railway station.

🛏️ **Chambre d'hôte les Arbousiers** – *i mp. de la Pharmacie, 34370 Maureilhan. 9km/6mi NW of Béziers towards Castres on D 112.* ✆*04 67 90 52 49. 3 rooms.* This large hotel with Mediterranean-style rooms offers a friendly ambience. A menu featuring home-made cold cuts, home-grown vegetables, and the proprietor's wine.

🍽️ EAT

🍽️ **Cannelle** – *11 Pl. de la Mairie.* ✆*04 67 28 06 01. Closed Sun.* This *salon de thé* also has a lunchtime menu or a choice of salads. Contemporary decor.

🍽️ **Le Chameau Ivre** – *15 pl Jean Jaurès.* ✆*04 67 80 20 20. Closed Sun, Mon.* Nice wooden decor in this tapas and wine bar. Exceptional list of over 1 000 wines to be enjoyed with charcuterie and cheese in the shade of plane trees and palms.

🍽️ **L'Amirada** – *Av de la Méditerranée, 34420 Villeneuve-les-Béziers, 7km/4.5mi S of Béziers.* ✆*04 67 93 83 97. Closed Mon evening, and Tue.* On the way to the beach, this modern building houses a fine restaurant serving regional and traditional cuisine in a relaxed atmosphere.

🍽️ **La Potinière** – *15 r. Alfred-de-Musset.* ✆*04 67 11 95 25. Closed Sun evening.* Popular with the locals, this restaurant has a cosy ambience and appealing sophisticated menu.

🍽️ **La Maison de Campagne** – *22 av. Pierre-Verdier.* ✆*04 67 30 91 85. Closed Sun, Mon and Tue–Thu evenings.* ♿. This modern tapas bar has a look of the hacienda about it, with a large patio-terrace and a main house that is beautiful, rustic and chic!

🍽️ **Les Antiquaires** – *4 r. Bagatelle, bas des Allées Paul-Riquet.* ✆*04 67 49 31 10. Closed lunchtime and Mon. Reservations required.* Popular restaurant decorated with ancient porcelain, black and white photographs and musical instruments. Seasonal market produce.

🍽️ **La Compagnie des Comptoirs** – *15 pl. Jean Jaurès.* ✆ *04 99 58 39 29. Closed Sun. Reservations required.* A well-stocked wine list of local and regional wines accompanies an inventive cuisine marrying flavours from the south and east that will delight your taste buds. Shaded terrace dining also.

🍽️ **Octopus** – *12 r. Boïeldieu.* ✆*04 67 49 90 00. www.restaurant-octopus. com. Closed Sun and Mon.* Well prepared daily menus of local produce, served in a dining room or outside on the terrace.

SHOPPING

Main market hall – *Tue–Sun 6am–1pm.*
Other food markets – *8am–12.30pm: Tue pl. Émile-Zola; Wed quartier de l'Iranget; Fri morning pl. David-d'Angers; Mon, Wed and Sat morning pl. du 11-Novembre; Tue, Thu and Sat morning la Devèze.*
Clothing market – *Friday pl. du 14-Juillet.*
Les Caves de Béziers – *3 rte de Pézenas.* ✆*04 67 31 27 23. 9am–12.30pm, 3.30–7.30pm. Closed Sun and public holidays.* This co-operative sells the wines of the region, including the Vins de Pays d'Oc. Also available is regional produce: olive oil, eaux de vie, cheese...
Antolin Délices – *21 r. Martin-Luther-King.* ✆*04 67 62 03 10. 8am–noon, 2–6pm. Closed weekends and public holidays.* Open since 1916, this ice cream factory was located in the city centre, but moved to this building in 1979. Here you can buy ice cream direct from the people who make it.

ACTIVITIES

Boat trips on the canal du Midi – *Les Bateaux du Soleil.* ✆*04 67 94 08 79. www. bateaux-du-soleil.com.* Boat trips on the canal (2h, from Béziers) ; cruise (6h, from Cap d'Agde), to the lock at Ronde d'Agde and the étang de Thau.

EVENTS

Feria – *Arènes de Béziers, SAS du Plateau de Valras, 34536 Béziers.* ✆*04 67 76 13 45. www.arenes-de-beziers.com* – mid-August.

Fête des primeurs – ✆*04 67 76 20 20.* Taking place at the end of October, this festival includes dancing and the blessing of the new wine.

Le **Cap d'Agde**

Originally, the site of Cap d'Agde was little more than a promontory formed by a lava flow from Mont St-Loup. Created in 1970, today's Cap d'Agde is one of Languedoc-Roussillon's most popular coastal resorts and a favourite haunt of kite-flying enthusiasts, an important port and marina, a spa centre and a naturist resort.

BEACHES

The resort's beaches – Footpaths known as 'ramblas' access 14km/8.7mi of golden sandy beaches offering pedalos, wind-surfing, volleyball and children's clubs. Plage **Richelieu** is the largest and Plage du **Môle** the most popular. The sands of Grande Conque are black and Plage de la **Roquille** is beached with seashells. **Nearby beaches** – Le Grau-d'Agde is *5km/3mi W beyond the harbour* and Plage de la **Tamarissière** is on the other side of the Grau-d'Agde canal.

SIGHTS
👥 Île des Loisirs

This leisure island offers mini golf, amusement park, discotheques, casino, cinema, bars and restaurants.

👥 Aquarium

11 r. des Deux-Frères. ♿🕐*Open Jan–Mar and Oct–Dec 2–6pm; Apr–May 2–7pm; Jun and Sept 10am–7pm; Jul–Aug 10am–9pm.* ⊛€8 (children €6). ☎04 67 26 14 21. www.aquarium-agde.com.
Squids, sharks, sea breams and colourful corals occupy some 30 pools.

👥 Aqualand

🕐*Open Jul–early Sep 10am–6pm (Jul–Aug 7pm).* ⊛€28 (child 5–10, €20.50) – online discounts. ☎04 67 26 85 94. www.aqualand.fr.
This 4ha aquatic leisure park features wave pools, giant water chutes, shops and restaurants.

▶ **Population:** 25 695.
🚗 **Michelin Map:** 339: G9.
ℹ **Info:** Rd-Pt du Bon-Accueil, 34305 Le Cap-d'Agde. ☎04 67 01 04 04. www.capdagde.com.
▶ **Location:** 27km/17mi W of Béziers. This town of pastel walls, tiled roofs, shady winding streets and plazzas has eight marinas.
👥 **Kids:** The Aquarium, Aqualand and Île des Loisirs. Cap d'Agde has been nominated a 'Station Kid' resort for its activities and facilities.

Musée de l'Éphèbe

Mas de la Clape. ♿🕐*Open Mon–Fri 10am–noon, 2–6pm, Sat–Sun 9am–noon, 2–5pm (Jul–Aug daily 10am–6pm).* 🕐*Closed 1 Jan, 1 May, 25 Dec.* ⊛€5 (child 11–18, €2). ☎04 67 94 69 60. www.museecapdagde.com.
This underwater archaeology museum contains 25 years of excavated treasures from the Mediterranean and coastal lagoons – including Ancient Greek and Roman boats and amphorae, the magnificent **Éphèbe d'Agde**★★, and a statue of a young Greek man, unearthed in 1964.

EXCURSIONS
Agde

5km/3mi N along D 32E.
Many buildings in Agde are made from the dark grey lava from nearby Mont St-Loup, an extinct volcano. The town enjoys with neighbouring Sète the tradition of *joutes nautiques*, or jousting in boats.
The fortified **Ancienne cathédrale St-Étienne**★ was rebuilt in the 12C, probably to replace a 9C Carolingian building. Note the small round window in the vault through which food and ammunition were passed in times of siege.
The **Musée agathois** *(5 rue de la Fraternité;* 🕐*open mid-Jun–Oct 9.30am–*

Agde by River Hérault

© Jean du Boisberranger/hemis.fr

12.30pm, 2–5pm; ◔*closed Tue, except Jun–Oct;* ✆*04 67 94 82 51) focuses on local folk art and traditions. It occupies a Renaissance mansion converted to a hospital in the 17C.*

In addition to reconstructions of the interiors of local houses, model boats, memorabilia of local seafarers, liturgical exhibits and collected amphorae from the ancient Greek port, the museum includes artefacts, paintings, glazed earthenware and local costumes and exhibits on traditional seafaring, fishing, viticulture, crafts and other aspects of daily life in Agde.

Vias

4km/2.5mi W of Agde along the D 612.
An ancient fortified village, Vias is a place of pilgrimage for visitors who come to pray to a wooden statue brought from Syria by sailors. The church is built in the Gothic style from the black lava.

ADDRESSES

🛏 STAY

⊖ **Camping Neptune** – *34300 Agde, 2km/1mi S of Agde near the Hérault.* ✆*04 67 94 23 94. www.campingleneptune.com. Open Apr–mid-Sep. Reservation recommended. 160 sites.* This landscaped campsite has a swimming pool surrounded by a pleasant beach, games for young and old.

⊖ **Camping Californie-Plage** – *34450 Vias, 3km/2mi SW of Vias.* ✆*04 67 21 64 69.*

Apr–Oct. Shady spot by the sea, with swimming pool. Chalets, bungalows and studios for hire.

⊖⊖ **Hotel les Grenadines** – *6 imp. Marie-Céleste, 34300 Agde.* ✆*04 67 26 27 40. www.hotelgrenadines.com.* 🅿 *20 rooms.* This hotel in a quiet residential area has tidy rooms with whitewashed walls, swimming pool and simple meals.

♈/ EAT

⊖ **Restaurant-bar Casa Pepe** – *29 r. Jean-Roger, 34300 Agde.* ✆*04 67 21 17 67. Daily 8am–midnight (except Wed Sep–Jun). Closed Nov.* This small popular bar and seafood restaurant has a clientele of regulars, fishermen, rugby players and jousters.

⊖ **Mamita Café** – *41 quai Jean-Miquel, 34300 Agde.* ✆*04 67 26 92 84.* The Latino-salsa music, terrace and friendly welcome makes this a great venue for a few tapas.

ON THE TOWN

La Guinguette – *Rte de Mareillan, 34300 Agde.* ✆*04 67 21 24 11. Jun–Sep daily 8am–midnight. Closed Oct–Mar.* This delightful open-air café-bar near the Canal du Midi bewitches with its magical spell of accordion tangos and waltzes.

ACTIVITIES

Canal du Midi boat trips – ✆*04 67 94 08 79. www.bateaux-du-soleil.com.* ⮑*See CANAL DU MIDI.*

Jousting – From Jun to Sep, Agde, like Sète, has water tournaments involving jousting from boats that provide great entertainment.

Pézenas★★

This little town, once called 'Piscenae', is built in a fertile plain covered in vineyards. Pézenas prides itself on its past, reflected in its fascinating little streets and its mansions unchanged since the 17C. A fortified town at the time of the Romans, Pézenas was even then an important trading centre for woollen cloth. After it became part of the royal estate in 1261, its trade fairs took place three times a year.

A BIT OF HISTORY
The 'Versailles' of the Languedoc

For the first time, in 1456, the States General of Languedoc met at Pézenas. The town later became the residence of the governors of Languedoc: the Montmorencys, then the Contis. Armand de Bouron, Prince de Conti, transformed Pézenas into the 'Versailles', or royal court, of the Languedoc and surrounded himself with a court of aristocrats, artists and writers. Each session of the States General was celebrated with lavish entertainments.

🐾 WALKING TOUR

OLD PÉZENAS★★
👥 Scénovision Molière

Pl. des États-du-Languedoc. ⏱*Open Jul–Aug 9am–7pm, up to 10pm on Wed and Fri; Sep–Jun 9am–noon, 2–6pm (10am Sun).* 🎫*€7 (children, €6). Duration 55min.* 📞*04 67 98 35 39. www.scenovisionmoliere.com.*

Centuries may have passed, but the enthusiasm for Molière (1622–1673), a playwright and actor considered to be one of the greatest masters of comedy in Western literature, has not waned, and his memory lives on the this permanent commemoration in the 17C Hotel Peyrat. This interactive exhibition traces Molière's life in five episodes, each one acted out in a different room and with a different setting. Equipped with 3D glasses, you take a stroll through the life of this remarkable character, from

▸ **Population:** 8 606.
🚗 **Michelin Map:** 339: F8.
🏛 **Info:** Pl. des Etats-de-Languedoc, 34120 Pézenas, 📞04 67 98 36 40. www.pezenas-tourisme. fr. Guided tour of the town; Discovery tours Jul–Aug daily except Sun. Enquire at tourist office, or at www. vpah.culture.fr.
⊙ **Location:** 50km/30mi SW of Montpellier. Place du 14-Juillet is the town's main square.
🅿 **Parking:** Try the large parking area near Promenade du Pré-St-Jean if you're headed downtown; for sights south of Cours Jean-Jaurès, use the car park at Place Boy-Lapointe.
⊙ **Timing:** The walking tour of Old Pézenas could take a good part of a day, including visiting the museum and meandering through the shops.

the infancy of the young Jean-Baptiste Poquelin (his real name) to his triumph at the court of Louis XIV, followed by an all-too-rapid decline passing his years wandering around France and with the decline of his illustrious theatre. Thanks to the magic of technology, Molière, accompanied by his loyal friends, like the famous barber Gély, is now back in Pézenas.

▶ Go to the place du 14-Juillet and head into the old town down the rue François-Oustrin.

Old mansions, or *hôtels*, with elegant balconies and ornate doorways, and workshops, now occupied by craftsmen and artists, follow one after the other along streets with evocative names: rue de la Foire, rue Triperie-Vieille, rue Fromagerie-Vieille (Fair, Old Tripe Shop, Old Cheese Shop).

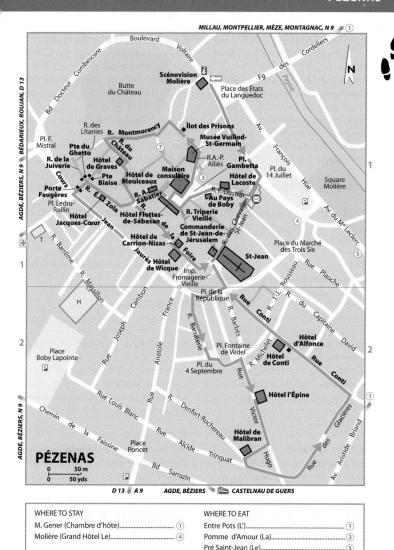

PÉZENAS

```
0    50 m
0    50 yds
```

MILLAU, MONTPELLIER, MÈZE, MONTAGNAC, N 9

WHERE TO STAY	
M. Gener (Chambre d'hôte)	①
Molière (Grand Hôtel Le)	④

WHERE TO EAT	
Entre Pots (L')	①
Pomme d'Amour (La)	③
Pré Saint-Jean (Le)	⑤
5 Gallery (Le)	⑦

 Leave from place du 14-Juillet.

Hôtel de Lacoste★

This early-16C mansion has a very fine staircase and galleries with Gothic arches.

Place Gambetta

This square, once known as 'Place-au-led' ('village square'), has retained its medieval structure. On the left is Gély's old barbershop (which now houses the tourist information office) where Molière liked to go. On the right, stands the **Consular House**; its 18C façade with pediment and wrought-iron work conceals the main building, which dates from 1552. The States General of Languedoc often met here; a particularly memorable session was held in 1632, at which the rebellion of Henry II of Montmorency against the king was hatched.

At the far end of the square, there is **rue Triperie-Vieille**, once lined with market

209

stalls. Farther down, at No. 11, in a court-yard at the end of a vaulted passageway, is a fine early 17C stairwell.

At the corner of Place Gambetta and Rue Alfred Saatier stands the **Hôtel Flottes de Sébasan** with a wide 16C façade and a Renaissance (1511) corner niche which houses a 19C statue of St Roch. A plaque records that Queen Anne of Austria slept in the mansion in 1660.

▷ Take rue A.-P.-Alliès on the right.

The Hôtel de Saint-Germain (*No. 3*) is home to the **Musée Vulliod-St-Germain**.

▷ Take rue Béranger on the left (17C house) which leads onto rue de Montmorency.

Rue de Montmorency
On the right stand the watchtowers of the **Ilôt des prisons**. On the way back up the street, note on the left a 17C faïence **Pietà**, and on the right the gateway from the curtain walls of the old castle demolished on Cardinal Richelieu's orders, after the rebellion of Henry II of Montmorency.

Rue du Château
The beautiful ogee doorway of the **Hôtel de Graves** dates from the 16C.

Rue Alfred-Sabatier
At No. 12 the **Maison des Pauvres** (almshouse) possesses a fine staircase and 18C wrought-iron work.

Rue Émile-Zola
At No. 7 the **Hôtel Jacques Cœur** features a façade adorned with culs-de-lampe in the shape of little figures. At the end of this street the **Porte du Ghetto** opens onto r**ue de la Juiverie**, two names which indicate the past role of this district.

On the left, **Porte Faugères**, which leads onto cours Jean-Jaurès, was once part of the old 14C ramparts.

▷ Take the cours Jean-Jaurès on the left.

Cours Jean-Jaurès (Le Quay)
Cours Jean-Jaurès was constructed by Henry II of Montmorency. At the time it was called Le Quay, and it supplanted rue de la Foire as the town's main centre of activity. Aristocratic mansions were built facing south, the back of the house opening onto rue de la Foire. These mansions can be entered through vaulted passageways leading into court-yards with attractive open staircases. The most interesting buildings are at No. 18, the **Hôtel de Landes de Saint-Palais** and, on the other side of the road, No. 33, the **Hôtel de Latudes**.

▷ Retrace your steps to rue du Château and turn right onto Rue de la Foire.

Rue de la Foire
Once known as rue Droite, this street was the setting for fairs and processions. At No. 16, there is a carved lintel representing some charming child musicians. Note the elegant Renaissance façade of the **Hôtel de Wicque** surmounting an art gallery. Opposite stands the **Hôtel de Carrion-Nizas** with a 17C doorway.

Collégiale St-Jean
This church, designed by Avignon architect Jean-Baptiste Franque, was built in the 18C on the site of an old Templars' church which collapsed in 1733.

Commanderie de St-Jean-de-Jérusalem
The commandery features two well-preserved early 17C façades with their mullioned windows. A corner turret is supported by a masonry buttress.

▷ Follow rue Kléer to place de la République to the right of the collegiate church.

Le Faubourg
This is where this tour leaves the old town centre to carry on into the faubourg that grew up in the 17C and 18C around rue Conti.

Staircase, Hôtel de Lacoste

© Yann Guichaoua /age fotostock

▶ From the square, take rue Barraterie (5th on the right at the end of the square) and turn left onto rue du Commandant-Bassas.

On the right, a porch leads through to the narrow rue du Jeu-de-Paume. This is believed to be the site of the theatre where Molière performed. No. 3 has a fine diamond-fret door.

▶ Turn right onto rue Victor-Hugo.

At No. 11 is the fine façade of the **Hôtel l'Epine** (18C).

Hôtel de Maliran★
This mansion's magnificent 18C façade is embellished with fine windows surmounted by masks representing smiling women, whereas the balconies are supported by garlands of leaves. The door leads straight to an interior 17C staircase supported by two tiers of superimposed columns.

▶ At the end of rue Alcide-Trinquat, walk down a flight of steps, cross rue Victor-Hugo and follow rue des Glacières opposite. Turn left onto rue Conti.

Rue Conti
Many private mansions were built along this street, which, in the 17C, was also full of inns and shops. Carry on past the **Hostellerie du Griffon d'Or** (No. 36).

Molière and Pézenas

During one of the celebrations, Molière, attracted by the town's reputation, came to Pézenas with his Illustrious Theatre in 1650. In 1653, having been permitted to put on a performance for Conti himself, he was given the title of 'Actor to His Supreme Highness the Prince of Conti'. A statue of Molière, by Injalert (1845–1933) stands in a small garden situated on *place du 14-Juillet.*

Hôtel d'Alfonce★
No. 32 rue Conti. ⏱&*Open Jun–Sep but call for hours; rest of the year by request.* ℘*04 67 98 10 38.*
This fine 17C building, one of the best preserved in Pézenas, was used by Molière from November 1655 to February 1656. In the entrance courtyard is a pretty interior terrace adorned with balustrades. On the right, there is a fine 15C spiral staircase.
At No. 30, the **Hôtel de Conti** features a façade, renovated in the 18C, with Louis XV balconies and wrought-iron window sills.

▶ Return to St John's collegiate church via place de la République and turn right onto rue des Chevaliers-St-Jean, which leads back to place du 14-Juillet.

ADDITIONAL SIGHT
Musée Boby-Lapointe
www.bobylapointe.fr.

👥 Boby Lapointe (1922-1972), born in Pézenas, was a singer especially noted for his humorous texts, alliterations, 'spoonerisms' and play on words. He never achieved the fame of Molière, but distinguished himself by his amusing verbal acrobatics. His fame grew when the actor Bourvil sang Lapointe's song *Aragon et Castille* in the 1954 film *Poisson d'avril*.

EXCURSIONS
Château-abbaye de Cassan
11km/7mi. Leave Pézenas heading NW on the D 13. Continue for 2km/1mi beyond Roujan. 🚶⏰*Open mid-Apr–Jun and Sept 2–7pm; Jul–Aug 11am–7pm; Oct Sat–Sun 2–7pm.* 🎫€10. 📞04 67 24 52 45. www.chateau-cassan.com.

Founded in 1080, probably on a Gallo-Roman site, this Augustinian priory became a Romanesque church and basilica in 1115. Over the centuries, the canons extended their power and influence, and rebuilt the priory in the 18C, adding a sumptuous abbey-palace. In time, this Royal Priory became one of the largest castles in Languedoc, and has been classified as an Historic Monument. In 2002, the site was acquired by the group SERCIB, and has been put to social and cultural use since then. Since 2008, Cassan is a member of the association of 'Sites d'exception en Languedoc' with headquarters in the Tourist Office of Pézenas.

Margon
13km/8mi to the NW of Pézenas by the D 13 as far as Roujan, then to the left.

At the heart of this medieval village stand three round towers that formed part of a magnificent castle. The inner courtyard, terraces and garden are open to the public.

Abbaye de Valmagne★
14km/9mi NE along N 9, N 113 to Montagnac then left on D 5. 🚶⏰*Open mid-Jun–Sep 10am–7pm; Easter–mid-Jun Mon–Fri 2–6pm, Sat–Sun and public holidays 10am–6pm; Oct–Mar Mon–Sat 2–6pm, Sun and public holidays 10am–6pm.* 🗣️*Guided tours in season at 10.30am, 11.30am, 2.45pm, 3.45pm, 4.45pm, 5.15pm.* ⏰*Closed 1 Jan, 25 Dec.* 🎫€7.90. 📞04 67 78 47 32. www.valmagne.com.

The great rose-coloured abbey of Valmagne, set in splendid isolation amid a clump of pine trees, rises serenely above the surrounding sea of Languedoc vineyards.

This Cistercian abbey was begun in the mid-13C and completed in the 14C. The abbey church, with its architecture and soaring nave, is an example of a classic Gothic style, as far removed from the traditions of Languedoc as it is from those of the Cistercians.

The **cloisters**, rebuilt in the 14C, are charming with their golden-coloured stonework. The 12C **chapter-house** contains a delightful **fountain★★**.

ADDRESSES

🛏️ STAY

🍴 **Chambre d'hôte M. Gener** – *34 av. Pierre-Sirven, 34530 Montagnac.* 📞*04 67 24 03 21. 4 rooms.* The rooms of this constabulary building dating from 1750 have been set up in the old stables. In the peace and quiet of a large shady courtyard, some of them have retained their loosebox separations. Breakfast is served on a terrace upstairs.

🍴 **Le Molière** – *pl. du 14-juillet.* 📞*04 67 98 14 00. www.hotel-le-moliere.com.* 🅿️ *21 rooms.* Sculptures ornament the façade of this ravishing hotel located in the centre of town. Comfortable, air-conditioned rooms renovated in the southern style. Frescoes evoking the works of Molière decorate the patio-salon.

🍴 **Côte Mas** – *Route de Villeveyrac, 34530 Montagnac.* 📞*04 67 24 36 10. www.cote-mas.fr.* 🅿️.*2 suites.* This home of the award-winning Côte Mas restaurant 🍴, this establishment now offers two luxury suites at the very heart of the domaine's vineyards. Live jazz from local musicians every Thursday during the summer months.

♥ EAT

🍴 **La Pomme d'Amour** – *2 bis r. Alert-Paul-Allies. ℘04 67 98 08 40. Closed Jan, Feb, Mon evening and Tue. Reservation recommended Jul and Aug.* This 18C house near the Office de Tourisme shelters a small, intimate dining room with beams overhead. In summer the street becomes a pedestrian zone and the terrace in the shade of neighbouring houses comes into its own. Sunny southern fare.

🍴🍴 **Le Pré Saint-Jean** – *18 av. du Mar.-Leclerc. ℘04 67 98 15 31. Closed Thu eve, Sun eve and Mon.* Choose from modern regional cuisine and a good selection of local wines.

🍴🍴 **Le 5 Gallery** – *5 r. Canabasserie. ℘04 67 39 54 41. Closed Sun (except Jul–Aug).* Located at the foot of castle hill, this beautiful old house serves salads and quiches, but also has a menu 'Terroir chic' featuring *foie gras* and Iberian hams, as well as Languedoc wines.

🍴🍴🍴 **L'Entre Pots** – *8 av. Louis-Montagne. ℘04 67 90 00 00. Closed Sun, Mon lunch and Wed lunch.* Fresh regional produce, served in a beautiful and intimate interior; pleasing enclosed terrace.

Oppidum d'Ensérune★★

The Ensérune hill fort above the Béziers plain has a Mediterranean location, extraordinary pine wood and a fascinating archaeological story: in 1915, traces of an Iberian-Greek settlement and a crematorium dating from the 4C and 3C were uncovered.

- ♿ **Michelin Map:** 339: D9.
- 🚩 **Info:** Office du tourisme de Nissan-lez-Enserune, Sq. René-Dez. ℘04 67 37 14 12. www.office-tourisme-nissan.com.
- ▶ **Location:** 15km/9.3mi SW of Béziers via D11.
- 👁 **Don't Miss:** The silos, cistern and funerary objects in the Museum.

OPPIDUM

Excavated food stores show that Ensé-rune began as a 6C BCE settlement of mud huts clustered around a hillfort. The Romans arrived in 118 and installed a sewage system, laid paving stones, plastered and painted walls and after 1C *Pax*

Oppidum d'Ensérune, Étang de Montady in the background

© Bertrand Rieger/hemis.fr

Romana people abandoned the hillfort to settle on the plains.

The **Site archéologique d'Ensérune★** (◐*Apr and Sept 10am–12.30pm, 2–6pm; May–Aug 10am–7pm; Oct–Mar 9.30am–12.30pm, 2–5.30pm;* ◐*closed Mon from Sept–Apr, 1 Jan, 1 May, 1 and 11 Nov, 25 Dec;* ☞€5.50; ℘04 67 37 01 23; www.enserune.fr) built on the ancient city's site contains artefacts of daily life from the 6C to the 1C BCE *dolia* (jars) buried beneath houses, ceramics, vases, amphorae, and pottery of Phocaean, Iberian, Greek, Etruscan, Roman and local origins. Funerary objects (5C–3C BCE) include Greek vases and urns used for cremation or offerings. The Mouret room displays an egg found inside a grave, symbolising the renewal of life. The hillfort encompasses a panorama of the Cévennes to Canigou and across the coastal plain. The **view★** to the north takes in the **old Montady Lake★**, drained in 1247.

ADDRESSES

☞ STAY

⌂ **Chambre d'hôte Le Plô** – *7 av. de la Cave, 34440 Nissan-lez-Enserune, 1km/0.6mi E of Ensérune by the D 609.* ℘04 67 37 38 21. ⊠ 🅿. *4 rooms.* At the centre of the village, an imposing mansion, the rooms of which are characterised by Zen décor.

⌂⌂ **Chambre d'hôte Villa les Cigalines** – *R. de Terre-Rousse, 34440 Nissan-lez-Ensérune.* ℘04 67 37 16 20 or 06 86 44 77 62. ⊠. *4 rooms.* The house is located a short way outside the village, but it's still easy to find. Its four bedrooms are tidy and air-conditioned, while the shaded terrace is an agreeable place to take breakfast and barbecues.

⌂⌂ **Hôtel Résidence** – *34440 Nissan-lez-Enserune.* ℘04 67 37 00 63. www.hotel-residence.com. *18 rooms. Restaurant*⌂⌂. A pleasant mansion in the heart of a small village. The rooms are decorated with antique furniture, and there is more space in the annex, which was a 19C wine house. In fine weather, meals are served on the shaded terrace by the pool.

Canal du Midi★

Today's tourists enjoying the calm and beauty of the Canal du Midi have little idea of the phenomenal natural obstacles to building this canal which links the Atlantic to the Mediterranean.

A BIT OF HISTORY

Even the Romans envisioned a canal linking the Atlantic to the Mediterranean, yet by the time of François I, Henri IV and Richelieu, nothing had been achieved. Finally **Pierre-Paul Riquet**, Baron of Bonrepos (1604–80) began the project at his own expense, spending 5 million livres, burdening himself with debts and sacrificing his daughters' dowries to do it. He died exhausted in 1680, six months before

- ⛭ **Michelin Map:** 343: AK1 and 339 AF9.
- ▤ **Info:** www.canalmidi.com.
- ▶ **Location:** Between Naurouze and Béziers.
- ⟲ **Don't Miss:** The cité de Carcassonne; the treasure of the church of Quarante; the three Malpas tunnels and Fonséranes locks.
- ♟ **Kids:** The Aiguille locks; the oppidum of Ensérune; a family cruise on the canal.

the Canal du Midi opened. **Riquet's** descendants regained their rights to a share of the canal profits, and in 1897 sold the canal to the State.

THE PRACTICAL CANAL
WHEN TO CRUISE ALONG THE CANAL

– March to November is the best time. During July and August boats for hire are difficult to find, lock traffic is intense, and prices are higher. May and June brighten the canal banks with irises and various water plants. September and October bring settled weather, mild temperatures and the countryside wears a beautiful russet mantle. Locks operate between June and August from 9am–12.30pm and 1.30–7.30pm.

Hiring a boat – No licence is needed; instruction is usually provided by the boat-hire company just before departure. Maximum speed allowed: 6kph/3.7mph. Boats can be hired for a week or a weekend, for a one-way journey or for a return trip. For summer cruising, book well in advance. Bikes are very useful to have on board for shore excursions (some boat-hire companies also hire bikes). For addresses of boat-hire companies, consult the *Planning Your Trip* section at the beginning of the guide.

Béziers Croisières (*Port Neuf 34545 Béziers; ℘04 67 49 08 23*) offer cruises between Béziers and Poilhès; timetable, prices and bookings by phone.

Croisières du Midi (Luc Lines) (*35 quai des Tonneliers, BP 2, 11200 Homps; ℘04 68 91 33 00*) offer 2h trips aboard traditional *gabares*, starting from Homps, from April to late October.

Boat trips – Several companies organise 2 to 6h trips along the Canal du Midi, with or without lunch.

A great read: *Impossible Engineering: Technology and Territoriality on the Canal du Midi*, Chandra Mukerji (Princetown University Press, 2009).

Heritage and future projects

Riquet's 240km/150mi-long canal begins at Toulouse at the Port de l'Embouchure and runs into the Thau lagoon, through 91 locks. Today only pleasure-craft cruise this scenic waterway, and several companies rent houseboats or offer river cruises.

Canal architecture

Along the canal's banks are buildings erected to house engineers, workers and lock-keepers; buildings for technical and administrative tasks, as well as inns and mills. Canal du Midi lock-keeper's houses are rectangular, with one/two rooms on the ground floor. The façade's plaque indicates the distance to the nearest lock.

Ports

Ports usually have a stone pier and an inn, and in the past there were stables for the draught-horses, a wash-house, chapel and sometimes an ice house, as at Somail. Ports like Castelnaudary and Port St-Sauveur in Toulouse have dry docks for repairing boats.

Vegetation

The canal is lined with great trees which provide shade and beauty, but also limit the evaporation of canal water. Most are fast-growing species like plane trees, poplars and maritime pines. At points like Naurouze, landscaping is extensive.

🚗 DRIVING TOURS

HARNESSED WATER

114km/70mi from Saissac to the Seuil de Naurouze. Allow 5h.
🚗*See LA MONTAGNE NOIR SOUTH.*

This itinerary follows the water-supply system of the Canal du Midi.

SEUIL DE NAUROUZE TO CARCASSONNE

50km/31mi along N 113. Allow 1h.
🚗*See CARCASSONNE.*

From the watershed ridge, N 113 runs along the north bank of the canal all the way to Carcassonne.

Narbonne★★

Narbonne, which has been in its time the ancient capital of Gallia Narbonensis, the residence of the Visigoth monarchy and an archiepiscopal seat, is now a lively Mediterranean city playing an important role as a wine-producing centre and a road and rail junction.

A BIT OF HISTORY

A sea port – Narbonne may well have served as a harbour and market for a 7C BCE Gallic settlement on the Montlaurès hill to the north of the modern city. The town of 'Colonia Naro Martius', established in 118 BCE by decree of the Roman Senate, became a strategic crossroads along the Via Domitia as well as a flourishing port. It exported oil, linen, wood, hemp, the cheeses and meat from the Cévennes so much appreciated by the Romans, and later on sigillated earthenware. Most of the river shipping business, however, was centred on the Italian, Iberian and then Gallic wine trade. During this period the city expanded dramatically and was embellished with magnificent buildings.

A capital city – In 27 BCE, Narbonne gave its name to the Roman province created by Augustus. After the sack of Rome in 410 by the Visigoths, Narbonne became their capital. Later, it fell to the Saracens; in 759 Pépin the Short recaptured it and Charlemagne created the duchy of Gothie with Narbonne as the capital.

From the 14C, the change in course of the Aude, the havoc wrought by the Hundred Years War and plague, and the departure of the Jews caused Narbonne to decline.

🐾 WALKING TOURS

PALAIS DES ARCHEVÊQUES★

The façade of the Archishops' Palace overlooks the lively **place de l'Hôtel-de-Ville**, in the heart of the city, where a section of the Roman Via Domitia was

▶ **Population:** 54 369.

Michelin Map: 344: J3.

Info: 31 r. Jean Jaurès, 11100 Narbonne. ℘04 68 65 15 60. www. narbonne-tourism.co.uk.

Location: 30 km/19mi SW of Béziers by the N 9, and 60 km/37.5mi E of Carcassonne by the A 61.

Parking: There are plenty of parking areas along the canal, near the Quai Valière; do not be tempted to drive into the centre.

Don't Miss: The Archaeological Museum, with its Roman paintings.

Timing: Allow a full day.

discovered. It has three square towers: framing the Passage de l'Ancre, the Tour de la Madeleine (the oldest) and Tour St-Martial; and farther to the left the Donjon Gilles-Aycelin. Between the last two, Viollet-le-Duc built the present Hôtel de Ville (town hall) in a neo-Gothic style. The Archishops' Palace is an example of religious, military and civil architecture bearing the imprint of centuries, from the 12C to the 19C Hôtel de Ville.

Donjon Gilles-Aycelin★

Open Jun–Sep 10am–6pm; Oct–May daily except Tue 9am–noon, 2–6pm. Closed 1 Jan, 25 Dec. ℘04 68 90 30 65. Entrance on the left inside the town hall.

This fortified tower with its rusticated walls stands on the remains of the Gallo-Roman rampart which once protected the heart of the old town. It represented the archbishops' power as opposed to that of the viscounts, who occupied a building on the other side of place de l'Hôtel-de-Ville. From the sentinel path on the platform (162 steps), the **panorama★** stretches over Narbonne and the cathedral, the surrounding plain and away across La Clape summit, the Corbières and the coastal lagoons as far as the Pyrenees on the horizon.

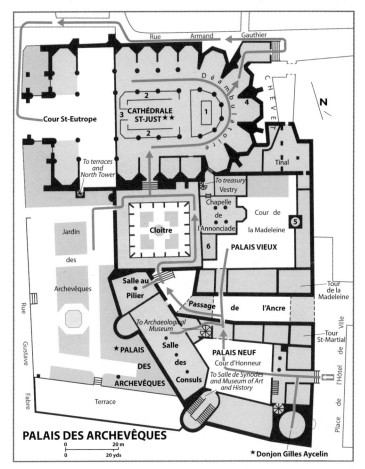

PALAIS DES ARCHEVÊQUES

⊙ Walk through the town hall to the main courtyard of the Palais Neuf.

Palais Neuf (New Palace)

The New Palace complex surrounds the Cour d'Honneur and comprises the façade over the courtyard of the town hall, the Gilles-Aycelin keep, the St-Martial tower, the synods building and the north and south wings.

Archaeological Museum★★

Palais Neuf. ⊙*Open Jun–Sep 10am–6pm; Oct–May daily except Tue 9am–noon, 2–6pm.* ⊙*Closed 1 Jan, 25 Dec.* ⊛€6 *(Museum Pass €9 includes all museums, and is valid for 15 days).* ☎*04 68 90 30 54.*

Narbonne undoubtedly possesses one of the finest collections of **Roman paintings★★** in France. For the most part the items came from the archaeological site of Clos de la Lombardia, north of the ancient city, where they once adorned the homes of the wealthy.

Museum of Art and History★

⊙*As for the Archaeological Museum.*
This museum occupies the old episcopal apartments where Louis XIII stayed during the siege of Perpignan in 1642. Many rooms are hung with portraits of Narbonne's consuls during the 16C, while the King's Chamber is decorated with a beautiful coffered ceiling representing the nine muses.

217

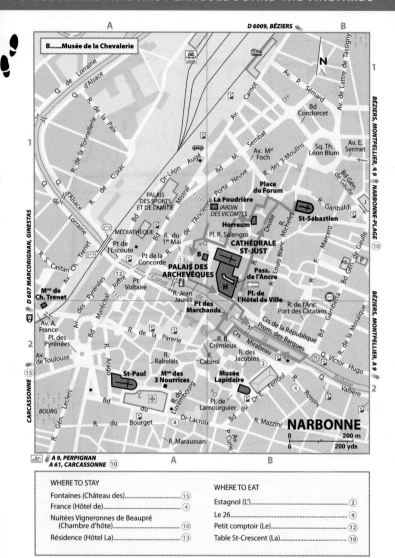

WHERE TO STAY	
Fontaines (Château des)	⑮
France (Hôtel de)	④
Nuitées Vigneronnes de Beaupré (Chambre d'hôte)	⑩
Résidence (Hôtel La)	⑬

WHERE TO EAT	
Estagnol (L')	②
Le 26	④
Petit comptoir (Le)	⑫
Table St-Crescent (La)	⑩

Salle des Consuls

Enter via the Cour d'honneur. Located on the ground floor of the synods building, the room is supported on part of the old Roman fortified city wall.

▶ Leave the Palais Neuf via the door on the north side of the courtyard and enter the Palais Vieux via the door opposite, on the other side of passage de l'Ancre.

Palais Vieux (Old Palace)

The Old Palace consists of two main buildings flanking the Madeleine tower. To the east, a square staircase tower divides a Romanesque façade pierced by arcades. Other monuments stand around Madeleine courtyard: the square Carolingian bell-tower of the church of St-Théodard, the apse of the Annonciade Chapel overlooked to the north by the imposing cathedral chevet, and the 14C **Tinal** (the canons' old storeroom), which has recently been restored.

Palais des Archevêques

© J. A. Moreno/age fotostock

▶ Come out onto passage de l'Ancre and walk to the right.

Passage de l'Ancre
This almost fortified street with its impressive walls separates the old and new palaces and leads from place de l'Hôtel-de-Ville (between the St-Martial and Madeleine towers) to the cloisters.

▶ Enter the Salle au Pilier via a door to the left of the stairs leading to the cathedral cloisters.

Salle au Pilier
◷Open Jul–Sep 10am–6pm; Oct–Jun 9am–noon, 2–6pm. ◷Closed 1 Jan, last 3 weeks in Jan, 1 May, 1 and 11 Nov, 25 Dec. ✆04 68 90 30 65.
This 14C room houses the Palais shop, and owes its name to the enormous pillar that supports the vault.

Cathédrale St-Just-et-St-Pasteur★★
It is possible to enter the cathedral via passage de l'Ancre and through the cloisters.
The first stone was laid on 3 April 1272 and by 1332, the radiating chancel had been completed in the same style as the great cathedrals of northern France. Building the nave and the transept would have involved reaching the ancient rampart which still served in troubled medieval times, so this was postponed. Today, the edifice consists of the chancel flanked by cloisters on the south side.
Cloisters – The cloisters (14C) are at the foot of the south side of the cathedral. The west gallery gives access to the archbishops' gardens. From the 18C **Jardin des Archevêques**, there is a fine view of

The Via Domitia
The Via Domitia is the oldest of the Roman roads built in Gaul. It was named after the Consul of the Roman province of Gallia Narbonensis, Domitius Ahenoarus, who had it built in 118–117 BCE at the time the province was founded.

Following an ancient route once used by the Ligurians and Iberians, the Via Domitia ran from Beaucaire (Gard) to Le Perthus (Pyrénées–Orientales), forming a communications route between Rome and Spain. Beyond the Rhône, the Via Domitia led into the Via Aurelia. Spanned by ridges and punctuated along its length by milestones marking every Roman mile (1 481.5m) and staging posts, the Via Domitia linked Beaucaire (Ugernum), Nîmes (Nemausus), Béziers (Julia Baeterrae), Narbonne (Naro Martius) and Perpignan (Ruscino).

Originally intended for military use, to enable Roman legions to reach the furthest outposts of the empire, Roman roads also aided the transportation of commercial goods and, of course, the spread of new ideas.

Covered market in Narbonne

©fanou11/Fotolia.com

the flying buttresses, the south tower of the cathedral and the synods building. Inside, the strikingly well-proportioned chancel was the only part to be completed. The height of its vaulting (41m) is exceeded only by that in the cathedrals of Amiens (42m) and Beauvais (48m). The chancel houses numerous works of art (&see diagram). Located opposite the high altar is the **organ case** flanked by fine 18C **choir stalls**. The Lady Chapel dedicated to Ste-Marie-de-Bethléem has regained its large Gothic **altarpiece★**, discovered in 1981 under a coat of stucco.

Treasury – ☜Museum/Monuments Pass €9. &04 68 90 30 65. The treasury includes illuminated manuscripts and, together with other church plate, a fine gilt chalice (1561). The most remarkable exhibit is a late-15C Flemish tapestry depicting the **Creation★★**, woven in silk and gold thread.

▷ Leave the cathedral via a door located in the second radiating chapel from the left.

Exterior – Note in particular the chevet with its High Gothic lancets, the great arches surmounted by merlons with arrow slits overlooking the terraces of the amulatory, the flying buttresses, the turrets and the powerful defensive buttresses, and the lofty towers.

OLD NARBONNE

Start from place de l'Hôtel-de-Ville and follow pedestrianised rue Droite.

Place du Forum

Remnants of a 1C temple on the site of the Antique forum and Capitol.

▷ Turn right onto Rue Girard then left onto Rue Michelet.

Église St-Sébastien

This 15C church with 17C extensions, was built, according to legend, on the site of the saint's birthplace.

▷ Return to Place Bistan and, from the SW corner, follow Rue Rouget-de-l'Isle.

The itinerary takes you past the **Horreum**, a Roman warehouse.

▷ Turn right onto Rue du Lieut.-Col.-Deymes and right again onto Rue Armand-Gauthier which leads to place Salengro.

La Poudrière

Situated behind the Jardin des Vicomtes, this 18C powder magazine houses temporary exhibitions.

▷ Return to Place Salengro; right on Rue Chenneier and left on Rue du Lion-d'Or to the embankment; turn left.

Banks of the Robine

The Robine canal links the Sallèles-d'Aude junction canal to **Port-la-Nouvelle**.

▷ When you reach the end of Promenade des Barques, take Pont de la Lierté across the Robine canal. Note the fine metal-framed covered market. Follow the south bank to Pont des Marchands.

Pont des Marchands★

This picturesque bridge, a pedestrianised street lined with colourful shops overlooking the canal, follows the old Roman road (Via Domitia).

▷ Return to Place de l'Hôtel-de-Ville.

ADDITIONAL SIGHTS
MUSÉE LAPIDAIRE★

🕓*As for the Archaeological Museum.* This is in the deconsecrated 13C church of Notre-Dame-de-la-Mourguié.

Basilique St-Paul

🕓*Open daily except Sun afternoon.* This basilica was built on the site of a 4C–5C necropolis near the tomb of the city's first archbishop.

Maison natale de Charles Trenet

13 av. Charles-Trenet. 🕓*Open Jun–Sep 10am–6pm; Oct–May daily except Tue 9am–noon, 2–6pm.* 🕓*Closed 1 Jan, 1 May, 1 and 11 Nov, 25 Dec.* ✆€6. *(Museum Pass €9 includes all museums, and is valid for 15 days).* ✆*04 68 65 15 60.* Birthplace of Charles Trenet, writer of fantasy songs and poetry, and much influenced by jazz.

🚗 DRIVING TOUR

From canal de la Robine to Canal du Midi

🕓*See region map. Allow 4h.*

The creation of the Canal du Midi ignored Narbonne, but its people, not to be outdone, realised that an old canal, the Robine, could be connected to the Midi, bringing them within the canal's sphere of prosperity. This was done in 1787.

▷ Leave Narbonne to the N on the D 13 as far as Cuxac-d'Aude, then turn left onto the D 1626 towards Sallèles.

Canal de jonction

Above and below Sallèles, this canal has many beautiful bays lined with pine.

▷ Take a narrow lane on the left before arriving in Sallèles in order to reach the locks of Gailhousty.

Écluse de Gailhousty

The lock allows the canal to cross the Aude; at this point there is remarkable stonework pediment in bas relief.

▷ 11km/6.5mi to Sallèdes-d'Aude.

Sallèles-d'Aude

This agreeable village has a wine producing pedigree extending back 2 000 years to Gallo-Roman times.

▷ From Sallèdes-d'Aude, take D 1626 NE and follow the signs to 'Musée des Potiers'.

Amphoralis-Musée des Potiers gallo-romains★

🕓*Open Jul–Sep 10am–noon, 3–7pm; Apr–Jun Tue–Fri 2–6pm, Sat–Sun 10am–noon, 2–6pm.* 🕓*Closed 1 Jan, 1 May, 25 Dec.* ✆€5.50. ✆*04 68 46 89 48. www.amphoralis.fr.* The central section of the modern museum building houses an exhibition on the craft of making amphorae, which was both varied and prolific.

ADDRESSES

🛏 STAY

🍽 **Hôtel de France** – *6 r. Rossini.* ✆*04 30 37 01 47. www.hotelnarbonne.com. 15 rooms.* A hotel in a late-19C building located on a quiet street downtown. The rooms are rather plain; those on the back promise a good night's sleep.

🛏 **Camping la Nautique** – *4km/2.5mi S of Narbonne. ☎04 68 90 48 19. www. campinglanautique.com. Reservations advised. 390 places.* A large site with direct access to the Pages lagoon.

🛏🛏 **Chambre d'hôte Nuitées Vigneronnes de Beaupré** – *Rte d'Armissan. ☎04 68 65 85 57. www. domaine-de-beaupre.fr. 4 rooms.* Wine buffs will delight in this small B&B close to the centre of Narbonne.

🛏🛏 **Hôtel Méditerranée** – *11210 Port-la-Nouvelle. ☎04 68 48 03 08. www. hotelmediterranee.com. 29 rooms.* Well placed along the promenade.

🛏🛏 **Hotel la Résidence** – *6 r. du 1er-Mai. ☎04 68 32 19 41. www.hotel residence.fr. Closed 20 Jan–15 Feb. 26 rooms* A fine hotel in a renovated 19C building.

🛏🛏🛏🛏 **Château des Fontaines** – *2 av. de la Distillerie, 11200 Canet (14km/8.7mi W via the D 6113 in the direction of Lézignan-Corbières, then the D 11 from Villedaigne). ☎04 68 49 72 48. www. chateaudesfontaines.com. Easter–Sept. 5 rooms.* A prestigious 19C house where luxury and serenity reigns.

⦿ EAT

🍽🍽 **L'Estagnol** – *5 bis Cours Mirabeau. ☎04 68 65 09 27. Closed 16–24 Nov, Sun and Mon eve.* This lively brasserie situated near Les Halles, popular with the locals, specialises in traditional cuisine.

🍽🍽 **Le 26** – *8 bd Dr Lacroix. ☎04 68 4146 69. Closed Sun eve and Mon.* The chef loves to cook things slowly, filling the restaurant with the appetising aromas of cooking.

🍽🍽🍽 **Le Petit Comptoir** - *4 bd du Mar.-Joffre. ☎04 68 42 30 35. Closed 15 Jun–Jul, Sun–Mon. (May–Sep).* Bistro-style restaurant where one can try local specialities.

🍽🍽🍽🍽 **La Table St Crescent** – *Rte de Perpignan, au Palais du vin. ☎04 68 41 37 37. www.la-table-saint-crescent.com. Closed Sat lunch, Sun eve and Mon.* Located at the edge of the town in a former oratory transformed into a temple of wine; inventive cuisine and superb wines.

SHOPPING

Les Cuisiniers Cavistes – *1–5 pl. Lamourguier. ☎04 68 32 96 45. www. cuisiniers-cavistes.com. Open 8am–7.30pm. Closed Sun afternoon and Mon.* This location invites you to discover the wines of the region while offering local produce in jars ready to take away. Cookery workshops.

Gruissan★

Gruissan once served as a point of defence for the port of Narbonne. The new resort adjoins the old village on the shores of the Grazel lagoon, and coastal houses are set on high stilts. Gruissan makes an ideal centre for exploring Languedoc beauty spots like the montagne de la Clape.

▸ **Population:** 4 815.
▯ **Info:** Bd. du Pech-Meynaud. ☎04 68 49 09 00. www. gruissan-mediterranee.com.
◖ **Location:** 20km/12.5mi SE of Narbonne on the D32
⊛ **Don't Miss:** The ruins of the Barbarossa Tower.

SIGHTS
Old Village
The old village was home to fishermen and salt-pan workers, and their houses form concentric circles around the ruins of the **Barbarossa Tower**.

Resort
The demands of tourism have thrown up hundreds of pastel-coloured apartments stacked like freight containers on a ship, plus all the trappings of a marina and popular beach-side holiday resort.

Gruissan-Plage

This resort has chalets built upon piles to protect them from floods.

EXCURSIONS
Cimetière marin

4km/2.5mi, then 30min on foot. Leave Gruissan on the D 32 towards Narbonne; at the crossroads take the road for N.-D.-des-Auzils into the massif de la Clape. Keep left, and then leave the car in the parking area.

🚶 Along a stony path, among broom, pine, oak and cypress, moving headstones remind us of sailors lost at sea.

Salins de l'Île St-Martin

Rte. de l'Ayrolle 3km/1.8mi S.
🐾 *Guided visits on demand; Écomusée* 🕐 *open 10am–noon, 3–6pm.* 🕐 *Closed Nov–Feb.* 📞 *04 68 49 59 97.*
Sea water invades this salt marsh along 35km/22mi of channels, and salt is harvested in September.

Le Parc Naturel★

(RN9) Domaine de Montplaisir, 11100 Narbonne. 26.4km/16.4mi W on the D 32 and D105.
Maison du Parc naturel régional de la Narbonnaise – *www.parc-naturel-narbonnaise.fr.* The Regional Natural Park of Narbonne in the Mediterranean extends from the Massif de Clape in the north to the Leucate plateau in the south, and embraces the massif de Fontfroide. Here, the extraordinary diversity of landscapes and natural environment is conducive to the development of flora and fauna of great richness. At the heart of the park, a vast lagoon complex is a major halt for migrating and wintering birds.

🚗 DRIVING TOUR

AROUND MONTAGNE DE LA CLAPE
⏱ *See region map. Allow about 2hrs.*

The limestone massif of la Clape rises to 214m, dominating the coastal lagoons around Guissan.

▷ Leave Gruissan following the D 332 towards Narbonne-Plage.

Cité de la vigne et du vin

Domaine INRA de Pech Rouge 5km/3mi from Gruissan. 🕐 *Open Jul–Aug 10am–8pm; Apr–Jun and Sept 9am–noon, 2–6pm; rest of the year, 2–6pm.* 🕐 *Closed Jan.* 📞 *04 68 75 22 62.*
Located at the heart of the Languedoc vineyards, this 'museum' is presented on several levels, from general to more technical, and visits are organised around different themes from viticulture to winemaking.

Narbonne-Plage

This resort stretching along the coast is typical of the traditional Languedoc seaside resorts. There is sailing and water-skiing here.

▷ From Narbonne-Plage, continue N to St-Pierre-sur-Mer.

St-Pierre-sur-Mer

Family seaside resort. The chasm of l'Oeil-Doux to the north is a curious natural phenomenon. It is 100m wide and contains a salt water lake 70m deep into which the sea surges.

▷ Turn round and, at the exit of Narbonne-Plage, turn right onto the D 168 (direction Narbonne).

La montagne de la Clape

The winding and hilly road traverses a rocky terrain where pine forests compete with vineyards nestled in small valleys. From the high point of the 'mountain' there is an excellent **view★** of Narbonne.

▷ After 14km/9mi, turn left onto a road returning you to Gruissan.

Réserve Africaine de Sigean★

This **safari park** (nearly 300ha) owes much of its unique character to the wild landscape of coastal Languedoc, with its *garrigues* dotted with lagoons, and to the fact that for each species large areas have been set aside, which resemble their original native environment as closely as possible.

PARK TOUR
Visit by Car
Please observe the safety instructions displayed at the entrance. ♿🕐*Open all year from 9am; closing hours vary.* 👓€*32 (child 4–14, €23).* 📞*04 68 48 20 20. www.reserveafricainesigean.fr.* The route for visitors in cars goes through four areas, reserved for free ranging animals: **African bush** (ostriches, giraffes, impalas), **Tibetan bear park**, **lion park** and **African savannah** (white rhinoceros, zebras, ostriches, etc).

Visit on Foot
3h. Start from the central car parks, inside the safari park.
🚶 Walking round the safari park, visitors will come across the fauna of various continents – Tibetan bear, dromedaries, antelope, zebra, cheetah, alligator

- ▷ **Location:** 18 km/11m S of Narbonne and 54 km/34m N of Perpignan by the N9. After Sigean follow signs.
- ⊘ **Don't Miss:** Tibetan bears.
- 🕐 **Timing:** Allow half a day.
- 👪 **Kids:** A fascinating visit for children.

– and, near the lagoon of L'Oeil de Ca, bird life such as pink flamingo, crane, white stork, sacred ibis, macaw, swans and pelican.

ADDRESSES

🏠 STAY

🍽 **Chambre d'hôte la Milhauque –** *11440 Peyriac-de-Mer. 2km/1.25mi NW of Peyriac-sur-Mer.* 📞*04 68 41 69 76. www.la-milhauque.gites11.com.* A sheepfold, tastefully restored, offers three rooms in a superb setting out in the *garrigue* and amid vineyards. *Bourride d'anguille* is a speciality dish.

🍽🍽 **Domaine de la Pierre Chaude –** *Les Campets, 11490 Portel-des-Corbières. 6km/3.7mi W of Réserve Africaine, towards Duran by D 611 A.* 📞*04 94 54 47 48. www.lapierrechaude.com. Closed Jan–Mar. 4 rms, 2 self-catering options.* This former *chai* (18C), nestled in a hamlet amid vines and garrique, was renovated by a student of the architect Gaudí. Ravishing guestrooms and Andalusian-style patio shaded by fig trees.

Abbaye de Fontfroide★★★

Fontfroide's spectacular **Cistercian abbey** enjoys a tranquil setting amidst cypress trees, and sunset lights up its flame-coloured ochre and pink Corbières sandstones.

ABBEY
The welcome centre contains the ticket office, bookstore, winery and restaurant.

- 🛈 **Info:** 📞*04 68 45 11 08. www.fontfroide.com.*
- ▷ **Location:** 14km/8.75mi SW of Narbonne.
- ⊘ **Don't Miss:** The cloister and exquisite early 20C windows.

🕐*Open Nov–Mar 10am–12.30pm, 1.30–5pm; Apr–Jun and Sept–Oct 10am–6pm; Jul–Aug 9.30am–7pm.*

Cloister, Abbaye de Fontfroide

© J. Langley/age fotostock

⊛€11 (child 6–18, €7): guided visits +€2.
&04 68 45 11 08.
www.fontfroide.com.

In 1093, a Benedictine abbey was founded on land belonging to Aymeric I, Viscount of Narbonne, and the 12C and 13C saw great prosperity. Pope Pierre de Castelnau's legate, whose assassination sparked off the Aligensian Crusade, stayed here after his trip to Maguelone. Jacques

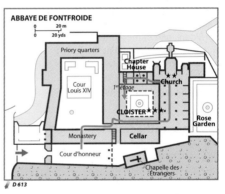

ABBAYE DE FONTFROIDE

Priory quarters

Cour Louis XIV

Chapter House

Church ★★

1er étage

CLOISTER ★★★

Rose Garden

Monastery

Cellar

Cour d'honneur

Chapelle des Etrangers

D 613

Fournier, who reigned under the name of Benedict XII, was abbot here from 1311 to 1317.

Most abbey buildings were erected in the 12C and 13C. The tour begins in the 17C Cour d'honneur, moves through the 13C guard-room and on to the medieval buildings. The cloisters are an example of architectural elegance. The oldest gallery (mid-13C) adjoins the church. Building began on the **Abbey church** in the mid-12C and south chapels were added in the 14C–15C.

The Chapter house is roofed with nine Romanesque vaults supported on decorative ribs that spring from slender marble colonnettes.

The Monks' dormitory above the storeroom is roofed with 12C fine ribbed barrel-vaulting. The **Rose garden** contains about 3 000 rose bushes (11 varieties). Follow footpaths around the abbey to appreciate the charms of its setting.

EXCURSION
Abbaye N.-D.-de-Gaussan

8km/5mi W of Fontfroide along the D 423.

The original buildings of this former abbey-farm were built 12C–14C, and the abbey remained in occupation until the Revolution. In the 19C, major restoration work was carried out, and a Benedictine monastic community has occupied the abbey since 1993. Mass is sung in Gregorian chant at 10am.

Saint-Pons-de-Thomières

This pretty mountain town in the upper Jaur valley, near the river's source, grew up around a Benedictine abbey founded in 936 by Count Raymond Pons of Toulouse. The town is a good base for exploring the region.

▶ **Population:** 2 180.

🛈 **Info:** 2 Place du Foirail, 34220 Saint-Pons-de-Thomières. ℘04 67 97 06 65. http://ot-pays-saint-ponais.fr.

▶ **Location:** 51km/32mi NW of Béziers via the N112; 19km/12mi SW of Olargues.

🕐 **Timing:** Allow one hour.

SIGHTS
Maison du Parc

🛈 34220 Saint-Pons-de-Thomières. ℘04 67 97 38 22. www.parc-haut-languedoc.fr.
St-Pons is now the administrative centre for the Haut Languedoc Regional Nature Park; founded in 1973 to preserve the natural wealth of the region, the park comprises the Caroux-Espinouse massif, the Sidore, part of the Montagne Noire and the Lacaune mountains. It injected new life into these breathtakingly beautiful, but isolated regions, which are too remote for any industrial development to be viable.

Ancienne cathédrale

The old cathedral dates from the 12C, with modifications in the 15C, 16C and 18C. The north side retains some fortified features: two of the original four crenellated corner towers and a row of arrow slits above the windows. The richly sculpted doorway presents something of a puzzle in the shape of seven niches and four unidentified figures above the archivolt.

Musée de Préhistoire régionale★

♿🕐Open Jun–Sept Wed–Fri 10am–noon, 3–6pm, Sat–Sun 3–6pm (Jul–Aug Tue–Sun 10am–noon, 3–6pm). ⚌€3.50. ℘04 67 97 22 61. The museum contains objects discovered on archaeological digs in caves in the region (particularly that at Camprafaud).

Source of the river Jaur

Access via the right river bank. The crenellated tower of the Comte de Pons, which formed part of the fortifications of the former bishopric, can be seen from the ridge over the Jaur. The river Jaur springs up at the foot of a rock then flows on.

EXCURSIONS
Chapelle Notre-dame-de-Tredos

17km/10.5mi. Leave St-Pons on the D 908, to the E (direction Bédarieux). At St-Étienne-d'Albagnan, turn right on the D 176E. The road climbs to Sahuc, which

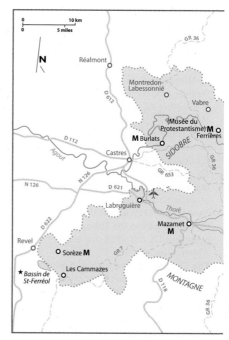

dominates the Esparasol ravine. At a col, 1.5km/1mi before Sahuc, climb to the chapel, on the right.

Notre-Dame-de-Tredos, among the trees, is a place of pilgrimage.

Fine **view** of the mountains of Espinouse to the northwest and over Minervois to the southwest.

Grotte de la Devèze★

5km/3mi W along D 612, beneath Courniou station.

Guided tours 1–mid-Jun and mid-end Sept Wed, Sat–Sun and public holidays 2.30pm and 4pm; mid-end Jun daily 2.30pm and 4pm; Jul–Aug daily 11.30am–6pm; 1–mid-Sept daily at 11.30am, 1pm, 3pm, 4pm. Closed Jan. €8.50 (child 6–12, €5). 04 67 97 03 24. http://grottedeladeveze.fr.

This cave was discovered by chance in 1886 when a tunnel was being drilled through Devèze mountain to carry the Bédarieux-Castres railway line. The tour begins on the middle level, a place of beautiful mineral shapes and colours. A waymarked trail (*yellow markings*) starting near the entrance

Canal du Midi at Le Somail
© P. Michel/age fotostock

to the cave leads (*1h15*) to seven drystone shepherd huts.

🚗 DRIVING TOUR

LE SOMAIL

76km/47mi round tour. Allow 2h.

The Somail is the most fertile part of the Espinouse uplands. It is an area of rolling hills covered with chestnut or beech

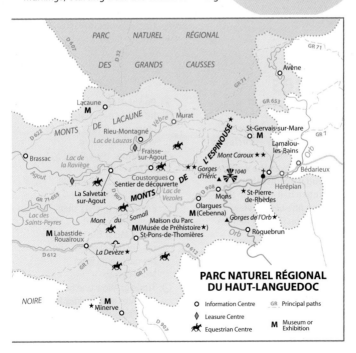

PARC NATUREL RÉGIONAL DU HAUT-LANGUEDOC

O Information Centre
◆ Leisure Centre
🐎 Equestrian Centre
GR Principal paths
M Museum or Exhibition

227

groves and carpeted with heather that takes on russet tones in the autumn.

▶ Leave St-Pons via D 907, the Salvetat-sur-Agout road.

The road winds picturesquely uphill, providing some fine views of St-Pons and the Jaur valley before reaching the Col de Cabaretou.

▶ Beyond the pass, turn right onto D 169 that crosses the Somail plateau. A narrow road to the right signposted Saut de Vésoles leads to the shores of a lake set in the middle of woodland (parking area).

Lac de Vésoles

15min on foot there and back.

🚶 The Bureau, which flows through rugged countryside, used to form an impressive waterfall with a 200m drop over gigantic granite boulders before joining the Jaur.

▶ Return to D 169 and head back to Fraisse-sur-Agout. The road crosses superb heather-clad moorland and the Col de la Bane.

Prat-d'Alaric

🕐 *Jul–Aug: guided tour (2hr) Wed only from 10.30am. Departs from tourist office of Monts de l'Espinouse in Fraisse-sur-Agout.* ℘04 67 97 53 81.

This typical Espinouse farmstead has been renovated by the Haut-Languedoc regional park authority and is now used as a visitor centre (*maison du pays*). The peaceful village of **Fraisse-sur-Agout** is famous for its angling.

▶ From the village, either head for the Col de Fontfroide and the tour through the Espinouse uplands or continue to La Salvetat.

La Salvetat-sur-Agout

This is a summer holiday resort perched on a rocky promontory high above the confluence of the Vère and Agout.

▶ From La Salvetat, return to St-Pons via D 907.

ACTIVITIES

👥 **Les Randonnées des Signoles** – *34330 La Salvetat-sur-Agout.* ℘04 67 97 63 61. *www.signoles.com.* Walks with a donkey that allow you to explore Haut-Languedoc and its lakes.

Olargues
and Monts de l'Espinouse

This village with its steep streets occupies a promontory encircled by the river Jaur. The village skyline is dominated by a tower, the vestige of an 11C feudal fortress that was converted into a bell-tower in the 15C. There is a fine overall view from the ridge, on the way in from St-Pons-de-Thomières.

🐾 WALKING TOUR

OLD TOWN

Start from place de la Mairie. Enter the old town through the Porte Neuve (*to the left at the bottom of the square*).

▶ **Population:** 663.
ℹ **Info:** Ave. de la Gare, 34390 Olargues. ℘04 67 23 02 21. www.olargues.org.
▶ **Location:** 19km/12mi NE of St Pons de Thomières by the D908 and 68km/42.5mi, NW of Béziers by the N12 then the D908.
👁 **Don't Miss:** The view from the Col de l'Ourtigas and the panorama from Mont Caroux.
🕐 **Timing:** Allow one hour for Olargues and one day for the Monts de l'Espinouse.

From the terrace beside the bell-tower, there is a pleasant **view** of the Jaur and the 13C humpback bridge which spans it, the Espinouse mountains, and Mont Caroux to the northeast.

From rue de la Place, take the covered stairway of the Commanderie on the right; it leads to another street just below the bell-tower. The **Musée d'Olargues** is located halfway along (🕐*open daily except Mon 3–6pm;* 📞*04 67 97 71 26*), and contains displays on traditional crafts and agricultural practices, most of which have now disappeared in the wake of modern technology.

On the way out of Olargues to the west is the **Cebenna** 🏃🏻🧗 (♿🕐*open Sept–early Jul Tue, Wed and Fri 9am–noon, 2–6pm; mid-Jul–Aug Tue–Fri 9am–12.30pm, 4–6pm, Sat 10am–12.30pm;* 🕐*closed 21 Dec–3 Jan and public holidays;* 📞*04 67 97 88 00; www.cebenna.org*), a multimedia centre offering a reference library, lectures and activities.

🚗 DRIVING TOURS

MONTS DE L'ESPINOUSE★
80km/50mi round tour. Allow 6h including the walk to the Caroux viewing table. See region map.

▶ Take D 908 out of Olargues and head W towards St-Pons then turn right onto D 14 to Fraisse-sur-Agout and La Salvetat. It is possible to do this tour taking Lamalou-les-Bains as a starting point.

The pass road leading to the Col de Fontfroide along the western slopes of the Espinouse mountains starts in a Mediterranean setting of vines, olive trees, holm-oaks and chestnut trees. At higher altitudes, the Mediterranean vegetation gives way to moorland.

From the Col du Poirier, the view extends over the mountains in the Somail to the left beyond the Coustorgues gully. There is an even wider view to the south towards the Jaur valley *(viewpoint)*.

Col de Fontfroide
The Col de Fontfroide is a mountain pass set in an impressively wild spot. It marks the watershed between the Mediterranean and Atlantic sides of the range.

▶ Turn right onto D 53 to Camon.

The road runs along the banks of the Agout, through the village of Camon which gets quite lively in summer, and continues through rugged, lonely, mountainous scenery.

Forêt domaniale de l'Espinouse★
From the road near the Espinouse summit, the roof of the Espinouse farm or **Rec d'Agout** is visible farther down the hill to the right.

The road then reaches the foot of the bare dome-shaped crest of Espinouse and runs on down through rugged countryside with ravines to each side, before crossing the **Pas de la Lauze**, a slender ridge linking the Espinouse and Caroux ranges.

Col de l'Ourtigas★
An observation platform provides an interesting **view★** of the rugged Espinouse range gashed by ravines. To the left is the Montagne d'Aret and to the right the two outcrops forming the Fourcat d'Héric.

🚶 *To the right is a path leading to the Plo des Brus (45min on foot there and back).*

▶ Continue to the road junction with D 180E branching off to Douch on the right.

On the side of the road is the **Église de Rosis**, a church with a stone bell-tower.

Douch
This village is typical of the Caroux region. The narrow streets are flanked by stone houses roofed with stone slabs *(lauzes)*.

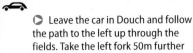

▷ Leave the car in Douch and follow the path to the left up through the fields. Take the left fork 50m further on.

Table d'orientation du Mont Caroux★★

2h on foot there and back.

🚶 The path climbs through clumps of broom, then a beech forest. To the left, at the top of the hill, is the highest point on Mont Caroux itself. The path then runs across a vast plateau to a viewing table, with the Plo de la Maurelle to the right. The rugged Caroux peak towers above the Or and Jaur valleys. The **panorama★★** is magnificent.

▷ Return to D 180.

Forêt des Écrivains Combattants

By car via chemin Paul-Prévost.

🚶 *On foot via a flight of steps 200m further on opposite an old inn.*

After the catastrophic floods in 1930, the slopes of the Caroux range had to be reafforested. The Association des Écrivains Combattants, the Touring Club de France and the villages of Combes and Rosis replanted the forest dedicated to writers who had laid down their lives for France.

▷ The picturesque D 180 leads to Lamalou-les-Bains.

Lamalou-les-Bains

♿See LAMALOU-LES-BAINS.

▷ Drive W out of Lamalou-les-Bains along D 908 to Colomières-sur-Or; leave the car on the left, just beyond the bridge, and follow the path along the gorge.

Gorges de Colomières

30min on foot there and back.

🚶 *The footpath is fitted in places with metal ladders and handrails to allow walkers to get past difficult passages. The more adventurous will follow a 13km/8mi loop (about 5h30) waymarked with blue triangles.*

The path follows the stream which cascades down from one pool to the next. The section upstream from the gorge is renowned for the rock climbing opportunities it offers. The short itinerary stops by a small dam.

▷ In Mons-la-Trivalle, travel NE along D 14E; leave the car at the entrance to the gorge. A footpath runs along the gorge to the hamlet of Héric.

Gorges d'Héric★★

🚶 *3h on foot there and back.*

Follow the stream to the **Gouffre du Cerisier**. Farther on is a majestic amphitheatre, the **Cirque de Farrières**. The path leads past Mont Caroux before arriving in **Héric**, a hamlet of stone slated-roofed houses. The gorge attracts swimmers, picnickers and rock climbers.

▷ Turn right off D 908 onto D 14E20 passing beneath the railway line.

Prieuré de St-Julien

This 12C priory is surrounded by vineyards, wooded hills and cypresses.

▷ Return to D 908 and Olargues.

GORGES DE L'ORB

28.8km/17.9mi, from Olargues to Cessenon-sur-Orb. ♿See region map. Allow 2h.

▷ Leave Olargues to the E on the D 908. Cross the Orb by the Tarassac suspension bridge.

Moulin de Tarassac

From the suspension bridge there is a fine view overlooking a beautiful mill transformed into a leisure centre by the Regional Natural Park of Haut-Languedoc. The landscape is typically Meditarranean with olive, fig and oak trees interspersed with vines and fields.

Roquebrun

This village with its cobbled streets is dominated by the ruins of its medieval tower. Sheltered from the north winds, it enjoys an equable climate conducive to growing mimosas in abundance.

◗ Climb towards the Carolingian tower.

Laid out above the village, the **Mediterranean garden** brings together some 400 Mediterranean and exotic species including the prickly pear, strawberry trees, jujube trees, junipers and Japanese medlar (◖*open mid-Feb–Jun and Sept–late Nov daily except Sat morning 9am–noon, 1.30–5.30pm; Jul–Aug daily 9am–7pm; ⊛€5.50; ℘04 67 89 55 29; www.jardin-mediterraneen.fr*).

◗ Leave by the D 19 (direction Murviel-lès-Béziers), then turn right on the D 136, towards Cessenon-sur-Orb.

Carrière de marbre de Coumiac

This quarry, producing red marble, was used until 1965. Marble from here was chosen as decoration in the American White House.
Follow the road that winds through the vineyards of St Chinian AOC as far as Cessenon-sur-Orb. From there, you can return to Olargues or go to Béziers (20km/12.5mi to the SE).

Lamalou-les-Bains

Lamalou springs were discovered in the 13C and their soothing powers were quickly appreciated. This spa treats people with poliomyelitis and other mobility problems. Mounet-Sully, Alphonse Daudet, André Gide have all taken the waters here. Lamalou-les-Bains makes a base for excursions around the Caroux region.

St-Pierre-de-Rhèdes★

This 12C rural parish church has an elegant apse decorated with Lombard arcades.

EXCURSION
Bedarieux
9km/5.5mi E along the D 908.
This small town has a spectacular viaduct, built in 1853, and the longest bridge on this stretch of railway.

🚗 DRIVING TOUR

BETWEEN ORB AND MARE
40km/25mi. See region map. Allow 2h.

🛈 **Info:** 1 Ave. Capus. ℘04 67 95 70 91. www.ot-lamaloulesbains.fr.
◗ **Location:** 38km/23.75mi N of Béziers on D909.
⊛ **Don't Miss:** The parish church.

◗ Leave Lamalou to the E on the D 908 head towards Hérépian on the D 13.

The **Sanctuaire de Notre-Dame de-Capimont★** is a pilgrimage chapel and offers a fine view of the Orb valley. **Villemagne** was the seat of a Benedictine abbey in the 7C to the late 18C. The village is named after nearby silver mines, and at least one 12C house survives. The **Pont du Diable**, is a well-worn bridge probably dating from the 12C–13C. Continue on the D 922, and before St-Étienne-Estréchoux, turn right to **Boussagues**, a village dominated by the ruins of its citadel, 14C castle, Romanesque church and bailiff's house.
Go back along the D 922 as far as **St-Gervais-sur-Mare**, a peaceful village that has known periods of prosperity thanks to the presence of coal… and chestnut trees.

◗ Take the D 22 back to Lamalou.

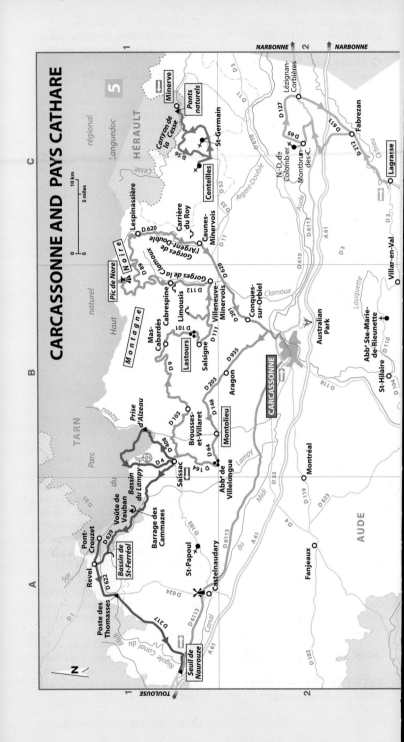

CARCASSONNE AND PAYS CATHARE

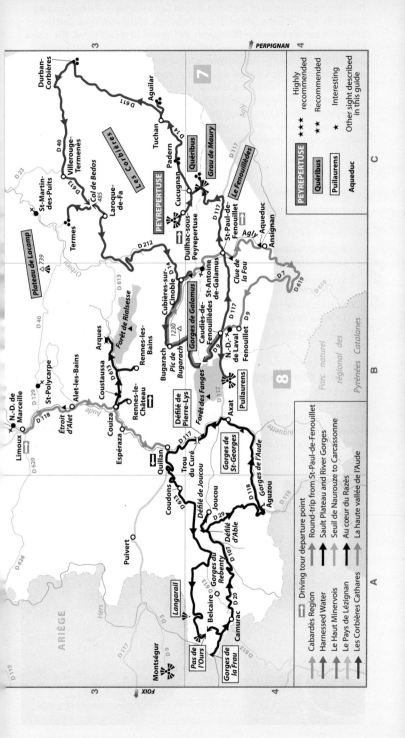

PERPIGNAN

Highly recommended
Recommended
Interesting
Other sight described in this guide

PEYREPERTUSE
Quéribus
Puilaurens
Aqueduc

Durban-Corbières

D 40

Villerouge-Termenès

Col de Bedos 485

St-Martin-des-Puits

Les Corbières

Aguilar

Tuchan

Padern

Quéribus

Grau de Maury

D 611

PEYREPERTUSE

Cucugnan

Laroque-de-Fa

Termes

St-Paul-de-Fenouillet

Le Fenouillèdes

Plateau de Lacamp

739

Orbieu

D 40

D 23

St-Polycarpe

Arques

Forêt de Rialsesse

Rennes-les-Bains

D 212

Dulhac-sous-Peyrepertuse

St-Antoine de-Galamus

Aqueduc

Assignan

Ansignan

Agly

D 117

Cubières-sur-Cinoble

Pic de Bugarach 1230

Gorges de Galamus

Caudiès-de-Fenouillèdes

Clue de la Fou

D 7

D 619

D 619

N.-D. de Marceille

Limoux

D 620

St-Polycarpe

Alet-les-Bains

Étroit d'Alet

Aude

D 118

D 129

Coustaussa

Couiza

Rennes-le-Château

Espéraza

D 613

Bugarach

Défilé de Pierre-Lys

Forêt des Fanges

N.-D.-de Laval

D 9

D 117

D 9

Puilaurens

Parc naturel régional des Pyrénées Catalanes

Quillan

Trou du Curé

Défilé de Joucou

Coudons

Puivert

D 626

D 117

D 613

Joucou

D 29

Axat

Aiguette

Gorges de St-Georges

Gorges de l'Aude

Aguzou

D 118

D 118

ARIÈGE

FOIX

Hers

D 117

D 119

D 5

Montségur

D 9

Langarail

Belcaire

Gorges du Rébenty

D 613

D 20

Camurac

Pas de l'Ours

Gorges de la Frau

D 619

D 107

Défilé d'Able

Cabardès Region
Harnessed Water
Le Haut Minervois
Le Pays de Lézignan
Les Corbières Cathares

Driving tour departure point
Round-trip from St-Paul-de-Fenouillet
Sault Plateau and River Gorges
Seuil de Naurouze to Carcassonne
Au cœur du Razès
La haute vallée de l'Aude

7

8

CARCASSONNE *and Pays Cathare*

The abiding impression of the lands around Carcassonne is of never-ending vineyards, for this is the fabled land of Corbières, Minervois, Fitou and the delightful bubbly known as Blanquette de Limoux. In recent times, the region has become the historical focus of attention of the persecuted sect known as the Cathars; indeed, 'Le Pay Cathare' is these days a seal of authenticity, and numerous 'Routes de Cathare' are actively promoted by the tourist boards. But underlying the history is a landscape that is divine. Ruined castles still turn their walls to the winds as they have done down the centuries, and white-foamed rivers bully a way through rocky gorges. And everywhere, the hillside is dotted with villages and hamlets where life is programmed to *andante moderato*: slipping by with a time-honoured ease.

Highlights

The First 'Champagne'

Blanquette de Limoux, a sparkling white wine, was 'invented' more than a century before champagne. The first reference to blanquette – the Occitan word for white – appears in papers written by Benedictine monks in 1531 at the abbey of St-Hilaire. They write of the production and distribution of St-Hilaire's blanquette in cork-stoppered flasks. Local folklore asserts that Dom Pérignon invented sparkling white wine while serving in the abbey, before leaving for the Champagne region and there popularising the drink.

Home Cooking

The extreme western part of Aude is consumed by the Pays du Lauragais, which centres on the town of Castelnaudary, arguably – and they really do argue – the cassoulet kingdom of the world. Like all French classics, cassoulet has a legion of 'genuine' recipes. This stick-in-the-ribs concoction is the very antithesis of junk food; it's mother's cooking, an icon of the simple life, a dish of white haricot beans, Toulouse sausage, duck and belly pork. Bon appetit!

Castelnaudary cassoulet and Corbières wine

© Kevin O'Hara/age fotostock

Carcassonne★★★

A visit to fortified Carcassonne, a UNESCO World Heritage site, is a return to the Middle Ages. On Bastille Day (14 July), a dramatic fireworks display seemingly make the citadel go up in flames. The romantic old town contrasts sharply with the commercial Ville Basse (lower town), a *bastide* town, where Carcassonne shows off its role as the centre of the Aude *département's* wine-growing industry.

▶ **Population:** 48 287.
◔ **Michelin Map:** 344: F3.
▯ **Info:** 28 rue de Verdun, 11000 Carcassonne. ℘04 68 10 24 30. www.tourisme-carcassonne.fr.
20min guided tour of the ramparts by miniature railway – May–Sep, departs Pte Narbonnaise.
▶ **Location:** 96km/60mi SE of Toulouse, 60km/37.5mi W of Narbonne.
✿ **Don't Miss:** The 'Cité'.

A BIT OF HISTORY

Carcassonne commands the main communication route between the Mediterranean and Toulouse. For 400 years, Carcassonne remained the capital of a county, then of a viscountcy under the suzerainty of the counts of Toulouse. After the annexation of Roussillon under the Treaty of the Pyrenees, Carcassonne's military importance dwindled to almost nil, as some 200km/125mi separated it from the new border, guarded by Perpignan. Carcassonne was abandoned and left to decay until the Romantic movement brought the Middle Ages back into fashion.

Prosper Mérimée, appointed general inspector of Historical Monuments, celebrated the ruins in his travel memoir, *Notes d'un voyage dans le Midi de la France*, 1835. Local archaeologist Jean-Pierre Cros-Mayrevieille was passionately committed to the restoration of his native town. After visiting Carcassonne, **Viollet-le-Duc** returned to Paris with an enthusiastic report that the Commission of Historical Monuments agreed to undertake the restoration of the Cité in 1844.

☙ WALKING TOURS

LA CITÉ★★★

The 'Cité' of Carcassonne on the Aude's east bank is the largest fortress in Europe. It consists of a fortified nucleus, the Château Comtal, and a double curtain wall: the outer ramparts, with 14 towers, separated from the inner ramparts (24 towers) by the outer bailey, or lists *(lices)*. A resident population of fewer than 150 and school and post office saves Carcassonne cité from becoming a ghost town. ✿*It is especially agreeable to wander the streets in the evening, once most of the tourists have left.*

▶ Leave the car in one of the car parks outside the walls in front of the gateway to the east, Porte Narbonnaise.

Tour of the ramparts aboard a **tourist train** (♿◔*open May–Sept leaving from the Porte Narbonnaise with explanation of the defence system 10am-noon, 2–6pm; ℘04 68 24 45 70)* or a **horse-drawn carriage** *(◔open Apr–Nov: discovery of the ramparts in a caleche, with historical commentary; ⇔€8,children 2–10, €5; Route de la Cavayère, Montlegun, Carcassonne; ℘04 68 71 54 57; www.carcassonne-caleches.com).*

Porte Narbonnaise

On either side of the gateway to the original fortified town are two massive Narbonne towers, and between them, a 13C statue of the Virgin Mary. Inside, the 13C rooms restored by Viollet-le-Duc house **temporary exhibitions** of modern art.

CATHARE

Ramparts of Carcassonne

© L. Montico/hemis.fr

Rue Cros-Mayrevieille
This street leads directly to the castle, although you might prefer to get there by wandering the narrow winding streets of the medieval town, with its many crafts and souvenir shops.

Château Comtal
🕐*Open Jan–Mar and Oct–Dec daily 9.30am–5pm; Apr–Sept daily 10am–6.30pm.* 🕐*Closed 1 Jan, 1 May, 1 and 11 Nov, 25 Dec.* ⬿€8.50. 𝄐04 68 11 70 70.
www.remparts-carcassonne.fr.
The castle was originally the palace of the viscounts, and built in the 12C by Bernard Aton Trencavel. It became a citadel after Carcassonne was made part of the royal estate in 1226. Since the reign of St Louis IX, it has been defended by a large semicircular barbican and formidable moat.
The tour begins on the first floor, now an archaeological museum (**Musée lapidaire**). This museum exhibits archaeological remains from the fortified town and local region, including a 12C marble lavabo from the abbey of Lagrasse, late 15C stone **calvary**★ from Villanière and the recumbent figure of a knight killed in battle. A collection of prints shows the fortified town as it was before Viollet-le-Duc's restoration.
Cour d'honneur – The buildings surrounding the large main courtyard have been restored.

The building to the south has an interesting façade reflecting its three periods of construction: Romanesque, Gothic and Renaissance.
Cour du Midi – The tallest of the fortress' watchtowers, the Tour de Guet, affords a view of up to 30km/19mi away.

▷ Leave the castle and follow rue de la Porte d'Aude on the left.

Porte d'Aude
A fortified path, the Montée d'Aude, weaves from the church of St-Gimer up to this heavily defended gateway.
The **Tour de l'Inquisition** was the seat of the Inquisitor's court, and its central pillar with chains and cell bear witness to the tortures inflicted upon heretics. The Bishop's **Tour carrée de l'Évêque** was appointed much more comfortably.

▷ Return towards the Porte d'Aude and continue along the Lices Basses.

The itinerary takes you past the **Tour de la Justice**. The Trencavels, protectors of the Cathars, sought refuge here with the count of Toulouse during the Albigensian Crusade. This circular tower has windows whose tilting wooden shutters enabled those inside to see (and drop things on) attackers.

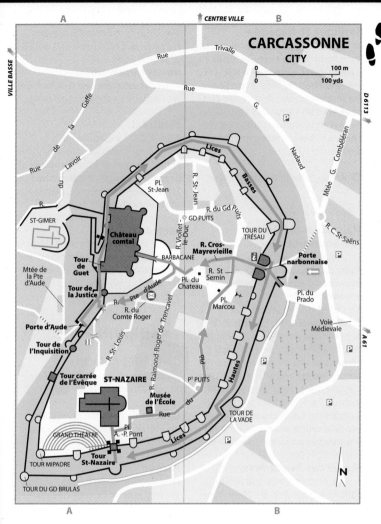

CARCASSONNE
CITY

▶ Walk beneath the drawbridge by the Porte Narbonnaise and continue SE.

'Lices basses' and 'Lices hautes'

These wide gaps between the inner and outer ramparts, edged with moats, were used for weapons practice and jousting. The 'lices basses' are the part contained between the two main walls, between the Porte d'Aude and the Porte Narbonnaise at the northern end of the city. The 'lices hautes' run south from Porte Narbonaise to the Tour St-Nazaire.

Beyond Porte Narbonnaise, note the three-storey Tour de la Vade on the outer curtain wall to the left. This fortified tower kept watch over all of the eastern ramparts.
Carry on to the Tour du Grand Brulas, on the corner opposite the Tour Mipadre.

Tour St-Nazaire

This tower's postern was only accessible by ladders. A well and an oven are still in evidence on the first floor. At the top of the tower is a viewing table.

▶ Enter the Cité through the Porte St-Nazaire.

Basilique St-Nazaire★

All that remains of the original church is the Romanesque nave. The basilica's **stained-glass windows★★** (13C–14C) are considered the most impressive in the south of France. Remarkable **statues★★** adorn the pillars around the chancel walls, and one of the most eye-catching bishops' tombs is that of Pierre de Roquefort (14C).

▶ Return to the Porte Narbonnaise via rue du Plô.

LOWER TOWN
Maison des Mémoires Joë-Bousquet

53 rue de Verdun. ⚐🕐*Open daily except Sun, Mon and public holidays 9am–noon, 2–6pm.* ✆*No charge.* 𝄞*04 68 72 50 83.*

Paralysed during World War II, Joë Bousquet lived in this house from 1918 to 1950 and never left his closed-shutter first floor bedroom. Here he wrote his poetry and letters and received the famous writers and artists of his time – André Gide, Paul Valéry, Aragon, Michaux, Paul Éluard and Max Ernst. He founded the Carcassonne Group with two local writers and published articles in the literary magazine *Cahiers du Sud.*

Musée des Beaux-Arts

1 rue de Verdun. Entrance: sq Gambetta. 🕐*Open mid-Jun–mid-Sep 10am–6pm; mid-Sep–mid-Jun Tue–Sat 10am–noon, 2–6pm.* 🕐*Closed public holidays.* 𝄞*04 68 77 73 70.*

On display are 17C and 18C paintings of French, Flemish and Dutch masters, and faïence from Moustiers, Marseille and elsewhere. Works of Carcassonne painter Jacques Gamelin (1738–1803) add local interest. Note Chardin's *Les Apprêts d'un déjeuner.* Works by Courbet and other artists from the French Academy represent 19C painting.

EXCURSIONS
Australian Park

Chemin des Bartavelles. 👥🕐*Open Apr–Oct daily during school holidays 10.30am–7pm; outside school holidays*

Mon–Fri 2–6pm, Sat and Sun, guided visits only. ✆*€10.50 (child 4–11, €7.50).* 𝄞*04 68 25 86 83.* *www.leparcaustralien.fr.*

A French take on the beasts of Australia, with wallabies, kangaroos and emus.

Montréal

16km/10mi W of Carcassonne.

This village overlooks the vineyards of the Carcassès and the vast plains of Razè and Lauragais; it's dominated by 14C St Vincent's collegiale, built in the southern Gothic style.

Fanjeaux

9km/5.5mi further, along the D 119.

A sacred place since Roman times – the name comes from Fanum Jovis, the Temple of Jupiter – the village is closely linked with the Cathar story.

🚗DRIVING TOURS

CABARDÈS REGION★

Round trip from Carcassonne 165km/ 103mi – Allow 1 day. ⚐*See region map.*

▶ Leave Carcassonne along N 113 towards Castelnaudary. After Pezens, turn right onto D 629.

Aragon

Proudly standing on its rocky outcrop, this little jewel of Cabardès is a place of narrow streets, charm and heritage, with a 16C castle that now serves as a B&B.

▶ Take the D 203 NW towards Fraisse-Cabardès then the D 148 to the left (direction Montolieu).

Montolieu★

This village in the Cabardès region is devoted to the world of books, with 20 or so bookshops, craft workshops (bookbinder's, copyist's, engraver's) and a **Musée des Arts et Métiers du livre** (⚐🕐*open Apr–mid-Nov Mon–Fri 10am–noon, 2–6pm, Sat 2–6pm, Sun 3–6pm; mid-Nov–Mar Mon–Sat 2–5pm, Sun 3–5pm;* 🕐*Closed 1 Jan, 25 Dec;* ✆*€3;* 𝄞*04 68 24 80 04; www.montolieu-livre.*

fr) dedicated to book design and production.

▷ A small road (D 64) S of the village leads to Villelongue Abbey.

Ancienne Abbaye de Villelongue

🕐*Open Apr–Oct daily except Fri–Sat 10am–noon, 2–6.30pm (Jul–Aug daily 10am–noon, 2–7pm). *€6.
🕐*Closed Nov–Mar.* ℘*04 68 24 90 38. www.abbaye-de-villelongue.com.*
This old abbey church was built to a Cistercian design and was rebuilt in the late 13C and early 14C. It's interesting for its refectory with ribbed vaulting, the south gallery of the cloisters and its chapter-house.

▷ D 164 on the right leads to Saissac.

Saissac

This village high over the Vernassonne ravine is shadowed by the ruins of a 14C castle. The largest tower in the old curtain wall affords a beautiful panorama of the site.

▷ Drive E along D 103.

Brousses-et-Villaret

An 18C **paper mill** manufactures paper the traditional way, and its **Gutenberg Museum** (℘*04 68 26 67 43)* relates the history of printing techniques.

▷ Continue on D 103 to D 118 and turn right. Beyond Cuxac-Cabardès, turn right onto D 73, follow D 9.

Mas-Cabardès

The ruins of a fortified castle tower over this village and its narrow streets. Near the **church** belfry topped by a 15C octagonal tower of Romanesque appearance, look for a 16C stone cross carved with a shuttle, emblem of the Orbiel valley weavers.

▷ Drive S along D 101.

Châteaux de Lastours★

Departure from the village centre, at the 'Accueil Village'.
🕐*Open Jul–Aug 9am–8pm; Apr–Jun and Sept 9am–6pm; Oct 10am–5pm; Nov–Mar days and times vary.* 🕐*Closed Jan and 25 Dec.* *€7. ℘04 68 77 56 02. www.chateauxdelastours.fr.*
The ruins of four castles stand out in this rugged rocky landscape between the Orbiel and Grésillou valleys. The **Cabaret**, Tour Régine, Fleur d'Espine and Quertinheux castles comprised the Cabaret fortress in the 12C. Cathar refugees sought protection at Cabaret, which resisted every attack. For an exquisite **view** of the Châteaux de Lastours ruins, drive up to the viewpoint on the opposite side of Grésillou valley.

▷ Follow D 701 to Salsigne.

Salsigne

Mining has given a livelihood to this area long before Roman and Saracen invaders extracted iron, copper, lead and silver here. After gold was discovered in 1892, mining concessions grew up at Salsigne, Lastours and Villanière. 92t of gold, 240t of silver and 30 000t of copper has been extracted since 1924.

▷ From Salsigne, follow the signs to the Grotte de Limousis.

Grotte de Limousis

Guided tours daily: Jul–Aug 10.15am–6pm; Apr–Jun and Sept 10.30am, 11.30am and hourly 2.30–5.30pm; Mar and Oct–mid-Nov 2.30pm, 3.30pm, 4.30pm. 🕐*Closed rest of year.* *€10.30 (child 5–12, €6.20). ℘04 68 77 50 26. www.grotte-de-limousis.com.*
Discovered in 1811, this cave is set in an arid, bare limestone countryside of vines and olive trees. The cave's chambers extend for 663m with curiously shaped concretions alternating with mirrors of limpid water. An enormous **chandelier★** of white aragonite crystals is the main feature of the cave.

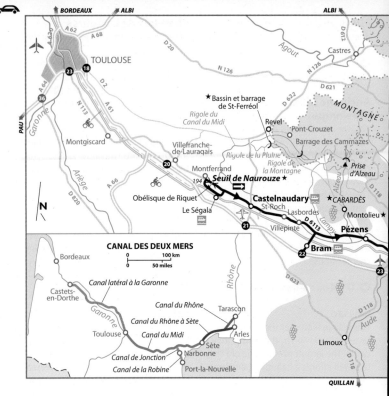

Return on D 511 to D 111 and there, follow the signs to Villeneuve-Minervois. Go through the village, which earns a living mainly from wine-growing, and take D 112 towards Cabrespine.

Gorges de la Clamoux

These gorges show the striking contrast between the two slopes of Montagne Noire. The road traverses the floor of the valley and its orchards and vineyards as far as Cabrespine.

Take the road on the left which climbs to the Gouffre de Cabrespine.

Gouffre de Cabrespine

Guided tours: Jul–Aug 10am–6.30pm; Apr–Jun and Sep–Oct 10.30am–5.30pm; Nov–mid-Dec and Feb–Mar 2–5pm. Closed rest of year. €10.30 (child 5–12, €6.20). 04 68 26 14 22. www.gouffre-de-cabrespine.com.

The upper part of this gigantic chasm is a huge network of subterranean galleries drained by the River Clamoux. The 'Salle des Éboulis' (chamber of fallen earth) is 250m high.

Follow the balconied walkway through stalactites and stalagmites, dazzling curtains of aragonite crystals, the 'Salles Rouges' (red galleries) and the 'Salle aux Cristaux' (crystal gallery).

Return to D 112. The road reaches Cabrespine, overlooked by Roc de l'Aigle, then winds up bends between chestnut groves. At Pradelles-Cabardès, take D 87 to the right towards the Pic de Nore.

Pic de Nore★

Montagne Noire's highest point, the Pic de Nore (*1 211m*), towers over the undulating heath-covered countryside. The **panorama★** stretches from the Lacaune, Espinouse and Corbières

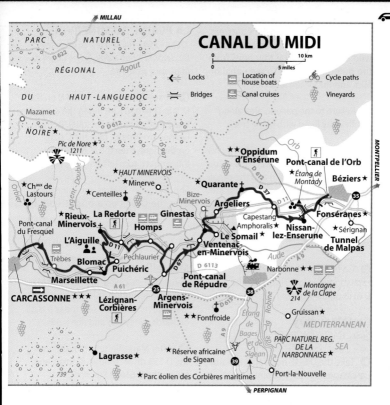

CANAL DU MIDI

| Locks | Location of house boats | Cycle paths |
| Bridges | Canal cruises | Vineyards |

mountains, to Canigou, the Carlit massif and Midi de Bigorre.

▶ Return to Pradelles-Cabardès and turn left onto D 89 then right onto D 620 towards Caunes-Minervois.

Lespinassière
Built on an isolated peak inside a mountain cirque, Lespinassière has a castle with a 15C square tower.

Gorges de l'Argent-Double
The river Argent-Double, which springs up near Col de la Salette, flows through a deep and sinuous gorge.

Caunes-Minervois
The village is known for its grey and white-veined red marble quarried nearby. This marble was used to decorate the Grand Trianon in Versailles, the Palais Garnier in Paris and the St-Sernin Basilica in Toulouse.

Fine mansions dominate the town hall square: Hôtel Sicard (14C) and Hôtel d'Alibert (16C). The former Benedictine abbey church has retained its 11C Romanesque east end.

▶ Drive SW along D 620. Beyond Villegly, turn right onto D 35.

Conques-sur-Orbiel
This pretty village has traces of its earlier fortifications, including the 16C south gateway and the church belfry-porch.

SEUIL DE NAUROUZE TO CARCASSONNE
50km/31mi along N 113. Allow 1h.
See map, above.
From the watershed ridge, N 113 runs along the north bank of the canal all the way to Carcassonne.

Seuil de Naurouze★
Walk the shady path round the octagonal reservoir built 1669–1673 amidst an

arboretum of Aleppo pines, nettle trees, sycamores, North-African cedars and wild cherry trees. The tour goes from the pumping station to the Canal du Midi and the Ocean lock (1671).

▷ Return to the parking area along an alleyway lined with plane trees.

The Riquet obelisk, raised in 1825 by his descendants, stands between the col de Naurouze (on the D 113) and the canal. It is surrounded by a ring of cedars, and, according to legend, when the cracks in the stones close up, the society will sink into debauchery and the end of the world will arrive.

▷ Go back along the D 217 to Labastide-d'Anjou. Then take the D 6113 on the right.

Castelnaudary
See CASTELNAUDARY.

▷ Take the D 6113 heading E towards Carcassonne. After Villepinte, turn right onto the D 4.

Bram
Birthplace of writer and journalist Jean Cau (1925–93), Bram is a typical example of urban planning in Languedoc, known as *circulades*, with villages built in concentric circles around the church.
Bram was the scene of one of the worst atrocities of the Albigensian crusade, when Simon de Montfort besieged the town in 1210. The siege lasted just three days, but de Montfort took revenge by cutting off the top lip of all his prisoners and blinding all but one. For the last he gouged out only one eye, so that he could lead the others out of the town to the château of Lastours.

▷ Turn round and go back along the D 4 and then turn right onto the D 6113.

Pézens
Pézens has contrived to retain some vestiges of its ramparts and fortified gate.

▷ Continue to Carcassonne.

LA PLAINE DU MINERVOIS
120km/75mi; allow a few extra miles for detours – half a day. See Canal du Midi map, p240–41.

▷ Leave Carcassonne to the N on the D 118. The road runs along the canal, and passes over the Fresquel. At the Bezons crossroads, take the D 620 on the right, then the D 201. After Villedubert, turn left onto the D 101.

Shortly before **Trèbes**, the canal passes over the Orbiel on a bridge built by Vauban in 1686.

▷ Leaving Trèbes, turn right on D 157.

Marseillette
Here is the so-called 'dry pond' of Marseillette, although this plain was formerly covered by the sea; today it is all orchards, vineyards and rice fields.

▷ After Marseillette turn right on the D 157, drive through Blomac, and follow the D 610 to Puichéric.

Puichéric is a place of narrow streets, ancient mansions, a church and castle burned down by the Black Prince in 1355. The crosses the canal at the ▲▲ l'Aiguille lock, which is surrounded by folk-art-inspired sculptures. **Rieux-Minervois★** is a large wine-producing village at the heart of the Minervois vineyards. Likewise is **La Redorte**, which was established in a loop in the canal. Continue on the D 11, and then take a left onto the D 610 to **Homps**, another village that was destroyed during the Albigensian crusade, and again during the Wars of Religion.

▷ Leave Homps by the D 65, and after 1.5km/1mi turn right on the D 124. The route now runs alongside the canal towpath towards Argens-Minervois.

Argens-Minervois
The village clings to a hill on which stands the castle rebuilt in the 14C after its capture by Montfort.

Port du Somail, Saint-Nazaire-d'Aude

© Jean-Pierre Degas/ hemis.fr

▷ Drive to Lézignan-Corbières to the S by the D 611.

Pont-canal de Répudre

This is the first canal-bridge built in France by Riquet in 1676. The castle overlooking **Venténac-en-Minervois** offers a fine view of the canal and surrounding plain.

▷ Drive N along D 26.

Ginestas

This village set among vineyards has a **church** with a 17C gilded wood altarpiece and a 15C naïve polychrome statue of St Anne.

▷ Drive E for 2km/1.2mi to Le Somail.

Le Somail★

This peaceful hamlet has preserved its humpback bridge and inn dating from 1773. The **Musée de la Chapellerie** contains hats and head-dresses from around the world, dating from 1885.

▷ From Le Somail, drive N to join D 5.

The road to Béziers follows the canal part of the way. Alternatively, make a detour by taking the D 607 towards **Argeliers**. This medieval village has a grand fortified church. **Quarante★** is a hilltop village to the north, surrounded by vineyards. The beautiful Église Ste-Marie was consecrated here in 1053.

▷ In Capestang, take D 37 S to Nissan-lez-Ensérune.

Nissan-lez-Enserune is home to the 14C gothic Église St-Saturnin.

From there, the Oppidum d'Ensérune is signposted.

Oppidum d'Ensérune★★

Ġ See Oppidum d'ENSÉRUNE.

▷ Continue to Colomiers, turn E onto D 162E then left onto N 9 and follow signposts to Écluses de Fonséranes.

Écluses de Fonséranes★

A sequence of eight locks makes up a 312m-long 'staircase' enabling river craft to negotiate a drop of 25m. Today, locks have been replaced by a single lock, lying parallel to the original system.

Pont-canal de l'Orb

Access via the towpath downstream from the locks.

⚐ Since 1857, a canal-bridge carrying the Canal du Midi over the Or provides an alternative to the somewhat daunting stretch of river.

Béziers★

Ġ See BÉZIERS.

ADDRESSES

🛏 STAY

Camping Le Martinet Rouge – *11390 Brousses-et-Villaret.* 𝒫*04 68 26 51 98. www.camping-martinet.fr. Open Mar–Nov. ♿ ⛺. 63 places.* In a fabulous setting in the Montagne Noire.

Chambre d'hôte l'Olivette – *R. Pierre-Duhem, 11160 Cabrespine.* 𝒫*04 68 26 19 25. www.olivette-cabrespine.com. 🅿 ⛺. 3 rooms.* Charming simplicity; located not far from the gouffrede Cabrespine. Table d'Hôte by arrangement.

Hôtel Espace Cité – *132 r. Trivalle.* 𝒫*04 68 25 24 24. www.hotelespacecite.fr. 48 rooms.* Modern hotel at the foot of the citadel, with bright and functional rooms, warm welcome, and breakfast buffet.

Auberge du Château – *Château de Cavanac, 11570 Cavanac.* 𝒫*04 68 79 61 04. www.chateau-de-cavanac.fr. 🅿 ♿. 24 rooms.* Beautiful rooms with view over vineyard; fine restaurant.

Chambre d'hôte La Maison sur la Colline – *Lieu-dit Ste-Croix.* 𝒫*04 68 47 57 94. Closed end Dec–mid Feb. 🅿 ⛺ 5 rooms. Restaurant.* This restored farm has a view of the Cité from its garden. Rooms are spacious and colourful.

Hôtel la Bergerie – *Allée Pech-Marie, 11600 Aragon.* 𝒫*04 68 26 10 65. ♿ 8 rooms. Restaurant.* In a lovely village; rooms have views over vineyard.

Hôtel Montmorency – *2 r. Camille-St-Saëns.* 𝒫*04 68 11 96 70. www.lemontmorency.com. 🅿. 20 rooms.* Close to La Cité. Very smart rooms, well furnished, but simple.

Hôtel Best Western Le Donjon – *2 r. du Comte-Roger.* 𝒫*04 68 11 23 00. www.hotel-donjon.fr. ♿. 62 rooms.* This hotel combining old stonework and renovated decor occupies part of a 15C orphanage at the heart of the Cité.

🍽 EAT

Le Bar à Vins – *6 r. du Plo.* 𝒫*04 68 47 38 38. ♿.* In the heart of the medieval Cité, this wine bar's shady garden has a view of the St-Nazaire basilica. Tapas and fast food.

Auberge de Dame Carcas – *3 pl. du Château.* 𝒫*04 68 71 23 23. www.damecarcas.com. Closed lunch and Wed.* This popular establishment in the medieval Cité has a generous menu.

La Tête de l'Art – *37 bis r. Trivalle.* 𝒫*04 68 47 36 36. ♿ ⛺.* This restaurant specialises in pork dishes.

La Marquière – *13 r. St-Jean* 𝒫*04 68 71 52 00. Closed Wed and Thu.* Roughcast building near northern ramparts. Serves traditional cuisine.

Comte Roger – *14 r. St-Louis.* 𝒫*04 68 11 93 40. www.comteroger.com. Closed Sun and Mon.* A sheltered spot.

Castelnaudary

The town famous for its thick *cassoulet* stew makes an excellent stop-over for anyone cruising the Canal du Midi. The Grand Bassin offers plenty of mooring space. The restored 17C Moulin de Cugarel testifies to Castelnaudary's once important flour-milling activity.

▶ **Population:** 12 043.
🜨 **Michelin Map:** 344: C3.
🛈 **Info:** Pl. de Verdun, 11400 Castelnaudary. 𝒫04 68 23 05 73. www.castelnaudary-tourisme.fr.
◑ **Location:** 63km/39mi SE of Toulouse, and 39km/24mi W of Carcassonne.
🕐 **Timing:** Allow half a day, and stay for lunch.
👁 **Don't Miss:** The Grand Bassin.

 WALKING TOUR

THE TOWN

The **bell tower** of Église St-Michel is impressive, as are the Gothic and Renaissance **gates** in the north façade.

Go into rue du Collège, then right into rue Goufferand. Cross rue de Dunkerque to reach the **Grand Bassin**. The basin forms part of the Canal du Midi as a reservoir for the locks at St-Roch.

Go a short way up ave. des Pyrénées and turn right into rue de la Haute-Baffe, then rue des Batailleries. Turn left towards the **Musée archéologique du Présidial** (🕐 open Jul–Sept daily except Tue 2.30–6.30pm; ✆€2; ✆04 38 23 00 42; www.musees-mediterranee.org), which traces the early history of the country from Gallo-Roman to modern times. One room is dedicated to regional products and ceramics.

Go back into the rue des Batailleries to visit the **chapel**, which has a fine display of gilded woodwork. Return along rue de l'Hôpital.

VISIT
Moulin de Cugarel
N of the town along the rue des Moulins.
At the start of the 20C, a dozen mills were still operating on the heights above Castelnaudary. The 17C Cugarel mill commands a fine **view** of the Lauragais plain. It was restored in 1962.

WALKS
🚶 A forest road stretches from the Prise d'eau d'Alzeau to the Bassin du Lampy (15km/9.3mi). The GR 7 long-distance footpath traverses woodland, skirting the Rigole de la Montagne from the Bassin du Lampy to the Cammazes dam (11km/6.8mi).

The GR 653 long-distance footpath, the 'Pierre-Paul Riquet' variation of GR 7, starts from the Bassin de St-Ferréol, links with the Rigole de la Plaine in Revel, skirtings it as far as the Poste des Thommasses (9km/5.6mi) before running on to the Seuil de Naurouze (another 24km/15mi).

EXCURSION
Abbaye de St-Papoul
5km/3mi NE on the D 103.
♿🕐 *Open Easter–Oct daily.*
✆€3.50. ✆04 68 94 97 75.
http://saintpapoul.free.fr.
Founded in 768 by Pepin the Short, the abbey became a cathedral in 1317 before becoming a simple parish church.

La Montagne Noire South★

The Montagne Noire, or Black Mountain, forms the south-western tip of the Massif Central and is separated from the Agout massif (Sidobre and the Lacaune and Espinouse ranges) by the furrow formed by the Thoré.

GEOGRAPHICAL NOTES
The mountain's densely forested northern slope rises sharply over the Thoré and culminates in the Pic de Nore. Its more Mediterranean southern slope drops gently down to the Lauragais and Minervois plains. The rainy northern slopes shelter oak, beech, fir, spruce forests, and the rugged southern slopes are scattered with *garrigue*, gorse, sweet chestnut trees, vines and olive trees.

- ⚪ **Michelin Map:** 344: E-2 to F-2.
- ⚪ **Info:** Office de Tourisme Intercommunal "Aux sources du Canal du Midi Lauragais Revel et Sorézois" 20 rue Jean Moulin, 31250 Revel. ✆05 62 71 23 33. www.revel-lauragais.com.
- ⚪ **Location:** La Montagne Noire comprises the extreme SW of the central Massif.
- ⚪ **Don't Miss:** Saint-Ferréol basin and the Abbey-école of Sorrèze.
- ⚪ **Kids:** Sylvea à Revel; Explorarôme à Montégut-Lauragais.

St-Ferréol reservoir

© Jean-Paul Azam/hemi.fr

The Montagne Noire's greatest wealth lies in its abundant reserves of water and its beautiful countryside. Only a meagre income can be made by raising stock or growing crops here, but the Salsigne gold mines still operate and marble is mined at Caunes-Minervois.

🚗 DRIVING TOURS

CABARDÈS REGION★
Round tour from Carcassonne –
See CARCASSONNE.

HARNESSED WATER★
From the Prise d'Alzeau to the Seuil de Naurouze. 114km/71mi. Allow 5h.
See regional map p232.

This itinerary follows the water-supply system of the Canal du Midi first devised in the 17C by Pierre-Paul Riquet and improved upon over the centuries.

▷ From Saissac, follow D 408 towards Lacombe then a forest road on the right.

Prise d'Alzeau
A monument commemorating Pierre-Paul Riquet, designer and builder of the Canal du Midi, retraces the various stages of canal construction.

▷ Turn back and continue to Lacombe. Turn left towards Lampy along forest roads.

Forêt domaniale de la Montagne noire
This 3 650ha forest of beech and fir trees includes the Ramondes and Hautaniboul forests. The road crosses the Alzeau in a lovely woodland setting at La Galaube.

Bassin du Lampy
This reservoir on the Lampy was built between 1776 to 1780 to supply the Canal du Midi. It flows into the Montagne Noire channel where a pleasant footpath runs for 23km/14.5mi to the village of Les Cammazes. Magnificent beech groves and shady paths make the Bassin du Lampy a popular place for a stroll.

▷ Follow D 4 towards Saissac then turn right onto D 629. Just before Les Cammazes, turn right onto a road leading to the dam.

Barrage des Cammazes
The reservoir retained by this dam feeds the Canal du Midi, supplies 116 towns and villages with drinking water and irrigates the Lauragais plain. Footpaths lead down to the edge of the Sor.

▷ Return to D 629 and turn right. Continue along the Rigole de la Montagne.

Voûte de Vauban

Outside Cammazes, the Rigole de la Montagne runs through the Voûte de Vauban, a 122m-long tunnel.

Bassin and barrage de St-Ferréol★

The reservoir on the Atlantic side of the Montagne Noire stretches for 67ha between wooded hillsides. The magnificent lake is ideal for sailing and swimming, and its shores pleasant for strolling. The **dam's construction** between 1667 and 1672 employed 1 000 men, women and children. The English-style **park** has winding paths through forest of cedar, maritime pines and sequoias. **Canal du Midi Museum and Gardens★** – ☏05 61 80 57 57. http://museecanal-dumidi31.blogspot.co.uk. In the house once lived in by Riquet himself, this museum retraces the incredible history of the canal. The gardens are a delightful bonus.

Revel

On the edge of the Montagne Noire and the Lauragais region, Revel's economy is based on cabinet-making, marquetry, bronze work, gold-plating and lacquer work. This bastide has a geometric street layout around a main square surrounded by covered arcades or *garlandes*. The 14C **covered market** features its timber roof and belfry, renovated in the 19C. **Sylvea** (*13 r Jean-Moulin*) is a **museum** providing an overview of the wood trade, and the skills of cartwrights, clog-makers, coopers and violin-makers.

▷ Follow D 85 E to Pont-Crouzet.

Pont-Crouzet

The Rigole de la Plaine starts here. This canal collects water from the Sor and takes it to the Poste des Thommasses.

▷ Return to Revel and follow D 622 S then D 624 towards Castelnaudary.

Poste des Thommasses

This catches the water of the Laudot from St-Ferréol and that of the Sor, diverted from Pont-Crouzet via the Rigole de la Plaine. This water is then sent onto the Seuil de Naurouze.

▷ Turn right onto D 217.

Seuil de Naurouze★
&*See CARCASSONNE.*

Minerve★

Minerve occupies a picturesque **site★★** on a promontory with views of rugged gorges.

A BIT OF HISTORY

In the Middle Ages a proud fortress that stood atop this spur witnessed one of the most dramatic events in the Albigensian Crusade. In 1210, Simon de Montfort, at the head of 7 000 men, laid seige to Minerve's proud fortress. After five weeks of siege, the townspeople, having run out of water, were forced to capitulate. They were given the choice of converting or being slaughtered. The 180 'Parfaits' who refused to surrender are commemorated by J L Séverac on place de la Mairie.

▸ **Population:** 133.
&* **Michelin Map:** 339: B8.
🛈 **Info:** 9 R. des Martyrs. ☏04 68 91 81 43. www.minervois-tourisme.fr.
▷ **Location:** 32km/20mi NW of Narbonne via the D 607.
👁 **Don't Miss:** The two natural bridges sculpted by the Cesse; the château de Minerve's octagonal tower.
👫 **Kids:** Le musée Hurepel.

▰ WALKING TOUR
Allow 1h30. Take D 147 SW of the village. The Grand Pont is the setting of many summer cultural events.

Minerve

©Unclesam/Fotolia.com

Ponts naturels★

The road affords views of natural bridges formed at the beginning of the Quaternary Era when the Cesse abandoned two meanders it once formed before flowing into the Briant, to attack the limestone cliff. As it forced its way through the many cracks in the wall, gradually enlarging them as it passed, two tunnels were formed. The first, the 250m long **Grand Pont**, ends in an opening 30m high. Upstream, the Cesse flows through the **Petit Pont**, about 15m high. Climb up to the narrow rue des Martyrs, lined with craft workshops like Maison des Templiers.

Église St-Étienne

This small Romanesque church has an 11C oven-vaulted apse and 12C nave.

▷ Walk on towards the tower standing N of the village.

This 13C octagonal tower known as '**La Candela**' and sections of the curtain wall overlooking the Briant valley are all that remains of the fortress dismantled in 1636 on order of Louis XIII.

▷ Go back down rue des Martyrs and turn left into a narrow alley leading to the ramparts. Parts of Minerve's 12C double curtain wall, including the pointed archway of the southern postern, still remain. Follow the path to the left along the lower edge of the village.

Musée d'Archéologie et de Paléontologie de Minerve

⏰Open Mar–mid-Nov 10am–1pm, 2–6pm. ⏰Closed rest of year. ⌦€3. ☎04 68 91 22 92.
This museum covers prehistory and archaeology up to the Roman and Visigoth invasions, and features a mould of Upper Paleolithic human footprints discovered in the **Grotte d'Aldène** (see The Haut Minervois below) dating from the Aurignacian period 15 000 years ago.

Musée Hurepel

⏰Open Jul–Aug 10am–1pm, 2–7pm; Apr–Jun and Sep–Oct 10am–12.30pm, 2–6pm. ⌦€3. ☎04 68 91 12 26.
Learn about the main episodes in the Albigensian Crusade through these dioramas.

Puits St-Rustique

This well supplied water to the townspeople during the siege of 1210. Simon de Montfort destroyed it with a powerful catapult from across the river, forcing Minerve to capitulate.

Vallée du Briant

A narrow path skirts the village along the steep narrow Briant valley, to emerge under the ruined 'Candela'.

🚗 DRIVING TOUR

LE HAUT MINERVOIS★
35km/22mi round tour. Take D 10 E1 W towards Fauzan.

Canyon de la Cesse
In the early Quaternary Era, the Cesse hollowed out a canyon, enlarged existing caves and made new ones. Upstream of Minerve, the valley narrows and the river flows for 20km/12mi underground, emerging to ground level in heavy winter storms.

▷ Turn left onto the road to Cesseras. Go through Cesseras and turn right onto D 168 to Siran. After 2km/1mi, turn right again.

Chapelle de St-Germain
This Romanesque chapel has an apse with interesting decorations.

Return to D 168 and carry on to Siran.

🚶 Stop the car beyond the bridge over a track and take the footpath up to the top of the hill to discover an interesting **dolmen** of the covered-alleyway type, called **Mourel des Fades** ('fairies' dolmen').

Chapelle de Centeilles★
N of Siran.
Surrounded by cypress trees, holm-oaks and vines, this 13C chapel looks onto a panorama of vineyards, La Livinière and its basilica and the distant Pyrenees. Around the chapel are drystone huts known as capitelles.

▷ Return to Siran and take a small road on the left which skirts the St-Martin peak and rejoins D 182 to the N, overlooking the Cesse gorge. Turn right towards Minerve. Just after Fauzan, take a small road to the left.

After 1.5km/1mi enjoy a view of the Cesse gorge and the **caves** in the cliff face. In one of these caves – **Aldène** – Paleolithic human footprints were discovered (♨ *see Musée de Minerve opposite*). A small path leads to the **Grotte de Fauzan** where traces of prehistoric footprints were found.

▷ Return to Minerve along the Cesse canyon.

Lagrasse

On the shores of the river Orbieu, the town owes its existence to its majestic abbey. An outpost of the Carolingian civilisation near Frankish Catalonia, the abbey's fortifications were added in the 14C and its embellishments added in the 18C. See the 11C humpback bridge and covered market.

▷ **Population:** 569.
ℹ **Info:** 16 r. Paul-Vergnes, 11220 Lagrasse. ☎04 68 43 11 56. www.lagrasse.com.
▷ **Location:** 42km/26.25mi SW of Narbonne. The D 212 from Fabrézan offers a sweeping view of the fortified town.
◉ **Don't Miss:** A walk along the Orbieu river.

👣 WALKING TOUR

MEDIEVAL CITY
Enter the walled town via Porte du Consulat and follow the street of the same name before turning left onto Rue Paul-Vergnes. The old medieval city developed around the monastery. Stroll the narrow streets lined with medieval houses where craftsmen have set up workshops.

Lagrasse and Abbaye Sainte-Marie-d'Orbieu
© btrenkel/IStockphoto.com

Église Saint-Michel
This Gothic church is flanked by nine side chapels. Note the keystones decorated with the guilds' symbols.

▶ Retrace your steps and turn left onto rue de l'Église; cross place de la Bouquerie; follow rue des Mazels.

Place de la Halle
The 14C covered market has 10 stone pillars supporting a timber framework. Medieval façades, some half-timbered, surround the square (note the 14C **Maison Maynard**). See the 16C Maison Sibra in Rue Foy, then follow Rue des Deux-Ponts to **Pont Vieux**, for access to the abbey.

Abbaye Sainte-Marie-d'Orbieu
🕐*Open mid-Jan–Mar and Nov–mid-Dec 10am–5pm; Apr–mid-Jun and mid-Sept–Oct 10am–6pm; mid-Jun–mid-Sept 10am–7pm.* ✆€4.
📞*04 68 43 15 99.*
www.abbayedelagrasse.com.
The **abbot's chapel**★ contains rare late-14C ceramic paving and traces of mural paintings. The Palais Vieux includes the oldest parts of the abbey. A lapidary museum displays fragments from the original cloisters. The lower level contains cellars, store rooms and bakery. The **Cloisters** were built in 1760 on the site of the visible remains of the 1280

cloisters. The 13C abbey church was built on the foundations of a Carolingian church. The 40m bell-tower built in 1537 affords an attractive view from the top.

EXCURSIONS
St-Martin-des-Puits
8km/5mi S of Lagrasse on the D 23 then the D 212.
The church has a choir of the pre-Romanesque period, along with 12C murals.

Plateau de Lacamp★★
27km/17mi SW on D 23 and D 212.
Between Caunette-sur-Lauquet and Lairière, the Louviéro Pass on D 40 gives access to the 'forest track' of the western Corbières. The Plateau de Lacamp, with an average altitude of 700m, forms a breakwater towards the Orbieu. The track runs along the southern edge of the causse for about 3km/2mi, with sweeping **views** of the Orbieu valley, the Bugarach and Canigou peaks, St-Barthélemy, the threshold of the Lauragais and the Montagne Noire.

Villar-en-Val
17km/10.5mi W Lagrasse by the D 3 then, to the left, the D 603 towards Serviès-en-Val and the D 10.
The birthplace of poet Joseph Delteil (1894-1978). A Poetry Trail has been made through the forest and garrigue to the clearing where he spent his early years with his grandfather.

🚗DRIVING TOUR

LE PAYS DE LÉZIGNAN★
See region map. Allow about 2h.

▶ Leave Lagrasse on the D 212 to the N (direction Lézignan).

Fabrezan
Dominating the Orbieu valley, the village with its winding streets houses a small museum in the town hall dedicated to scientist and poet Charles Cros (1842–1888), who invented the paléophone, precursor of Edison's phonograph.

◐ Turn left twice, on the D 212, then the D 111. Before Moux, turn right. At Conilhac, turn left onto the D 165.

The road climbs a hill then opens out onto the **vineyards** of Montbrun-des-Corbières which it dominates.

◐ The D 127 and D 611 lead to Lézignan. Return to Lagrasse on the D 611, then the D 212.

ADDRESSES

🏠 STAY

◐◐ **Le Clos des Souquets** – *47 av. de Lagrasse, 11200 Fabrezan.* ✆*04 68 90 48 04. www.le-clos-des-souquets.com.* 🅿 *9 rooms.* This small auberge offers traditional cuisine, along with a choice of hotel or B&B. A find.

◐◐◐ **Hôtel La Fargo** – *11220 St-Pierre-des-Champs.* ✆*04 68 43 12 78. www. lafargo.fr.* 🅿 *6 rooms. Restaurant* ◐◐. This former Catalan forge in a magnificent wooded park along the riverbank, is renovated with Colonial style furnishings.

◐◐◐◐ **Chambre d'hôte La Bastide de Donos** – *11200 Thézan-des-Corbières.* ✆*04 68 43 32 11. www.chateaudonos.com. 4 rooms and 2 suites.* Offers superb view of the chateau and the old washing place. On site wine tasting. Access to private lake.

🍴 EAT

◐◐ **La Balade Gourmande** – *B d Léon-Castel, D 6113, 11200 Lézignan-Corbières.* ✆*04 68 27 22 18. Closed weekends. Reservations recommended.* ♿🅿. Two dining rooms decorated in southern colours. The perfect place to try cassoulet.

◐◐ **Le Tournedos** – *Pl. de Lattrede-Tassigny, 11200 Lézignan-Corbières.* ✆*04 68 27 11 51. Closed Sun pm and Mon.* Grills and tournedos are the chef's specialties, served in a bright and airy dining room. 19 bedrooms also available.

◐◐ **Les Calicots** – *17 r. du Commerce, 11200 Fabrezan.* ✆*04 68 49 18 54. Closed Tue.* Tucked in an alley in this charming medieval village, this former haberdashery provides a pleasant setting for a meal, opening out onto a patio. Regional cuisine made with local produce.

Les Corbières★★

Corbières is best known for its ruined castles and its wine, and a massif landscape showered with luminous Mediterranean light. The spiny sweet-smelling *garrigue* covers much of the countryside.

A BIT OF HISTORY

Vines have overgrown the area east of the Orbieu and around Limoux, the region producing sparkling white *blanquette*. The **Corbières** has been awarded the *Appellation d'Origine Contrôlée* for its fruity, full-bodied wines (mainly red, some white and rosé) with bouquets evocative of local flora.
The region's widely differing soil types produce a variety of grapes – Carignan, Cinsaut and Grenache, making any *dégustation* tour a real voyage of discovery. The red wines of neighbour-

🛈 **Info:** Office Intercommunal de Tourisme des Corbières Sauvages, 2 Route de Duilhac, 11350 Cucugnan. ✆04 68 45 69 40. www. corbières-sauvages.com.

◐ **Location:** Bounded on the S by the D 117 between Perpignan and Quillan, on the W by the D118 between Quillan and Carcassonne, to the N by the A61 between Carcassonne and Narbonne, and to the E by the A9 linking Perpignan.

◐ **Don't Miss:** The chateaux de Peyrepertuse, Quéribus and Puilaurens.

👥 **Kids:** Cathar castles and Cucugnan's 'Pocket'. Theatre de poche.

ing **Fitou**, also an *Appellation d'Origine Contrôlée*, are dark and robust with a hint of spiciness.

Many local villages have their own wine cooperatives (*cave coopérative*) and encourage customers to taste their wares, but private producers often require reservations, which makes having a wine guide listing telephone numbers quite useful.

DRIVING TOURS

LES CORBIÈRES CATHARES★★

ROUND-TRIP FROM DUILHAC-SOUS-PEYREPERTUSE

117km/73mi. Allow an overnight stopover.

Magnificent castles and castle ruins, including the 'Five Sons of Carcassonne,' dot the Corbières landscape. These vertiginous feudal fortresses sheltered Cathars fleeing from the Inquisition.

Duilhac-sous-Peyrepertuse

Leaving the upper town to the north, note the village fountain fed by a bursting spring.

Château de Peyrepertuse★★★
See Château de PEYREPERTUSE.

▷ Return to Duilhac; drive to Cucugnan (*See Château de Queribus*).

Château de Padern

20min on foot round-trip. Be careful; the ruins are dangerous in places. To reach the castle, follow the yellow-marked 'Sentier Cathare.'

The Château de Padern, owned by the abbots of Lagrasse until 1579, was completely rebuilt in the 17C. You can see the remains of a round tower, leading to the upper part of the keep (now in ruins) and fine views of the village and the river Verdouble.

▷ At end of D 14, turn left onto D 611.

Tuchan

This town is a production centre for Fitou wines (AOC). The picturesque D 39 winds through the Tuchan valley.

▷ East of Tuchan, a surfaced path going through vineyards branches off D 39 to the left and leads to Aguilar Castle.

Château d'Aguilar

10min on foot from the parking area. Enter the enclosure from the SW.

On the orders of the king of France the Château d'Aguilar fortress was reinforced in the 13C, with a hexagonal curtain wall flanked by six reinforced round towers. The wall and a Romanesque chapel remain intact.

▷ Return to Tuchan and turn right onto D 611 to Durban.

Durban-Corbières

The castle overlooking the village includes a crenellated rectangular two-storey building with 13C twin bays and 16C mullioned windows, as well as remains of curtain walls and towers.

▷ Drive W out of Durban along D 40.

Villerouge-Termenès

At the heart of the medieval village stands the (12C–14C) **castle** flanked by four towers which was owned by the bishops of Narbonne and in 1321 witnessed the burning at the stake of the last Cathar Parfait, Guilhem Bélibaste. Audio-visual exhibits describe Bélibaste's life and works and the daily life of medieval Villerouge and its inhabitants. Enjoy views of the village and its surroundings from the sentry walk.

Every summer Villerouge re-enacts medieval banquets and various activities evocative of life in medieval Languedoc.

▷ Follow D 613 SW of Villerouge to Col de Bedos then turn right onto D 40.

Col de Bedos

Bedos Pass is located on D 40, a **ridge road★** winding through wooded ravines. From the dip formed by the lower gorge of the Sou, see the ruins of the Château de Termes.

Château de Termes

Open Mar and Nov Sat–Sun and public holidays 10am–5pm; Apr–Jun and Sept–Oct daily 10am–6pm; Jul–Aug daily 10am–7.30pm.
Closed Jan–Feb. €4. 04 68 70 09 20. www.chateau-termes.com.
Leave the car at the foot of the hill, beyond the bridge.
30min on foot round-trip; follow a steep track up then climb a succession of tiers that mark the curtain walls.

The castle held by Cathar Raymond de Termes succumbed to Simon de Montfort after a four month siege (August to November 1210) during the first stage of the Albigensian Crusade.

The site on the promontory defended by the natural trench of the Sou valley (Terminet gorge) is more interesting than the fortress ruins, offering good views of the **Terminet gorge** from near the northwest postern (*dangerous slopes*) and top of the rock.

Return to Col de Bedos and turn right onto D 613.

Laroque-de-Fa

The village watered by the Sou occupies a picturesque site on a fortified spur.

Beyond Mouthoumet, as you reach Orbieu bridge, turn left onto D 212 and drive past the ruins of Auriac Castle. In Soulatgé, turn right onto D 14 to Cubières. Turn left onto D 45 just before Bugarach.

Gorges de Galamus★★

See Le FENOUILLÉDES, Driving Tour.

Follow the D14. Just before Bugarach, turn left onto the D 4.

Pic de Bugarach

The rugged Bugarach summit is visible from the virtually deserted valleys surrounding it. The ascent to the Col du

Corbières vineyards in autumn

© B. Merle/Photononstop

Linas, winding through the upper Agly valley, is particularly impressive.

Turn left onto D 46 before St-Louis, it leads to D 9 heading for Caudiès-de-Fenouillèdes.

Forêt domaniale des Fanges

This forest massif covers 1 184ha acres and shelters exceptional Aude firs. The **Col de St-Louis** (*alt 687m*) is a good departure point for ramblers (rocky, often very uneven ground).

Drive on to Caudiès and turn right onto D 117 to Lapradelle. From Lapradelle, take the small road (D 22) and then the uphill road to the right 800m beyond Puilaurens.

Château de Puilaurens★

Open Feb–Mar Sat–Sun; Apr and Oct–mid-Nov 10am–5pm; May 10am–6pm; Jun and Sept 10am–7pm; Jul–Aug 9am–8pm. Closed mid-Nov–Jan.
€5. 04 68 20 65 26. www.payscathare.org/histoire-6.
Leave the car and continue on foot; 30min round-trip. Closed in bad weather.
The castle high above the upper Aude valley, with its crenellated curtain wall, four towers and projecting battlements, is impregnable from the north and remains more or less intact.

Rejoin D 117 and turn right to Maury then left onto D 19.

Grau de Maury★★

From this little pass, the southern gateway to the Corbières, is a fine panorama of mountain chains and the jagged ridge overlooking the dip formed by the Fenouillèdes to the south.

▷ A steep narrow road to the right leads up from the Grau de Maury to the ruined fortress of Quéribus.

Château de Quéribus★★
See Château de QUÉRIBUS.

▷ Head back to Cucugnan and turn left onto D 14 to return to Duilhac.

LE HAUT VALLÉE DE L'AUDE
120km/75mi round-trip from Limoux.
See LIMOUX: Driving Tour.

Château de
Quéribus★★

Perched on a narrow, rocky peak at 729m, and beaten by the winds, Quéribus was the last refuge of the Cathars, a real eagle's nest overlooking Corbières and Fenouillèdes on the edge of the Pyrénées-Orientales.

VISIT
♟ Château★

⚐ 30min. Stout walking shoes recommended. Audioguides available ∞€4. ⏰Open daily: Jan and Mar 10am–5pm; Feb and Nov–Dec 10am–5.30pm; Apr 10am–6pm; May–Jun and Sept 9.30am–7pm; Jul–Aug 9am–8pm; Oct 10am–6.30pm. ∞€6.50 (child 6–15, €3.50) ticket combined with the Théâtre de poche Achille-Mir de Cucugnan. ℘04 68 45 03 69. www.queribuscucugnan.fr.
Three successive enclosures protect the main tower, placed at the very summit of the rock. Polygonal in shape, it has two floors: a lower hall, and a high, vaulted Gothic rooms. The simplicity of

CATHAR SITES

Centre d'Études Cathares – *Maison des Mémoires, 53 r. de Verdun, BP 197, 11004 Carcassonne Cedex. ℘04 68 47 24 66. www. cathares.org.* Research and information centre on Cathar history; open to the public.

Carte intersites – This card gives reductions on visits to 16 Cathar sites: the châteaux of Lastours, Arques, Quéribus, Puilaurens, Termes, Villerouge-Termenès, Saissac, Peyrepertuse, Usson, the Château comtal de Carcassonne, the abbeys of Caunes-Minervois, Saint-Papoul, Saint-Hilaire, Lagrasse, Fontfroide and the Musée du Quercorb in Puivert. Available at all the sites.

'Pays Cathare' – This is a trademark acquired by the Conseil Général de l'Aude. The logo guarantees the authenticity and the 'extra' quality of the certified food products, hotels and restaurants.

- ♿ **Michelin Map:** 344: G5.
- 🛈 **Info:** Office Intercommunal de Tourisme des Corbières Sauvages, 2 Route de Duilhac, 11350 Cucugnan. ℘04 68 45 69 40. www. corbieres-sauvages.com.
- ▷ **Location:** 40km/25mi NW of Perpignan, and 50km/31mi E of Quillan.
- 👥 **Kids:** Take them to see *Le Sermon du curé de Cucugnan.*
- 🕐 **Timing:** Allow a minimum of 30min, but it can take longer.

its design has given rise to speculation that it has some astronomical or solar symbolism, similar to Montségur. But speculation is all it is for nothing remains of the pre-Crusade castle. What you see today was built in the late-13C, and remodelled in the 16C to accommodate advances in artillery. Even so, it is a moving experience to climb to the top for the panoramic **views★★**.

Château de Quéribus

© Bertrand Rieger/hemis.fr

EXCURSION
Cucugnan
This pretty village is well known from the tale of *Le Sermon du curé de Cucugnan* adapted into French by Alphonse Daudet in the second half of the 19C. The **Achille-Mir theatre** on place du Platane hosts a virtual theatre performance on this theme. (&⊙*open check chateau website for details; €6.50 (child 6–15, €3.50) (ticket combined with the château de Quéribus); 04 68 45 03 69).*

ADDRESSES

🏠STAY AND ⑨/EAT

🍽 **Auberge du Vigneron** – *2 R. Achille-Mir, 11350 Cucugnan. 04 68 45 03 00. Closed 13 Nov–28 Feb, Mon noon in Jul–Aug; Sun eve and Mon.* This village house offers guests the delights of simple cooking, Corbières wine and cosy little rooms. The restaurant occupies an old wine shop, opening onto a fine summer terrace with mountain views.

Château de **Peyrepertuse★★★**

The craggy outline of the ruined fortress of Peyrepertuse only properly comes into view when seen from the outskirts of Rouffiac, to the north. The largest of the 'Five sons of Carcassonne', it sits on a crest in the Corbières, standing boldly atop its rocky base.
The château is one of the finest examples of a medieval fortress in the Corbières.

A BIT OF HISTORY
In the 11C–12C, the castle was associated with the counts of Barcelona and Narbonne, and during the Albigensian Crusade it was handed peacefully over to the French, never actually having been held under siege. Even at the height of the Cathar persecution, Peyrepertuse seems to have survived largely

ℹ **Info:** Office Intercommunal de Tourisme des Corbières Sauvages, 2 Route de Duilhac, 11350 Cucugnan. 04 68 45 69 40. www.corbieres-sauvages.com.
▶ **Location:** Get here from Duilhac: 3.5km/2mi up a steep, narrow road. Visitors should have a good head for heights and take great care while exploring the castle, particularly if there is a strong wind. During the summer, bring water, sunhats and suncream.
👁 **Don't Miss:** The view over the surrounding valley from east of the castle.

unscathed. Today, it is a moving and atmospheric theatre of French history.

VISIT

From the car park, follow a path along the north face, leading up to the castle entrance. Sturdy footwear advised. There is very little shade within the castle. Be sure to take adequate protection as well as water.

Open Jan 10am–4.30pm; Feb 10am–5pm; Apr 9.30am–7pm; May–Jun and Sept 9am–7pm; Jul–Aug 9am–8pm; Mar and Oct 10am–6pm; Nov–Dec 10am–4.30pm. No visits during stormy weather. €6.50. 06 71 58 63 36. www.chateau-peyrepertuse.com.

The layout of the chateau is complex, and barely discernible from below. From the main entrance you go left or right, turning into walled alleyways, castle rooms, ramparts or clambering up and down steps to explore the numerous rooms. It is quite a haul on a warm day to the highest point of the château.

The château, which was first mentioned in the 9C and probably occupied from Gallo-Roman times, occupies a tapered promontory, which the lower walls parallel to create a strong curtain wall, although it is not complete on the north side. The views from the curtain wall are especially impressive.

The name 'Peyrepetuse' derives from the Occitan language and simply means Pierced Rock. The castle, which is on two distinct levels, was built on a strategic location along the French/Spanish border by the king of Aragon (lower) in the 11C and by Louis IX (Saint Louis) later on. The two castles are linked together by a huge staircase of more than 60 steps carved from the rock, and winding from the curtain wall to the citadel. However, the castle lost its strategic importance when the border of the two countries was moved to the south in 1659.

From the approach road it is difficult to identify clearly just where the castle is, not least because from a distance its walls fuse so well with the rocks around it. But on closer inspection, the castle is most impressive, and far larger than might be imagined.

This is one of the so-called 'Five Sons of Carcassonne', along with Queribus, Termes, Aguilar and Puilaurens: five castles strategically placed to defend the new French border against the Spanish. This border, since relocated, corresponds roughly with the present border between the Aude and Pyrénées-Orientales departments.

Château de Peyrepertuse

© Bertrand Rieger/hemis.fr

Le Fenouillèdes ★★

The Fenouillèdes region between the southern Corbières and Conflent evokes the aromatic plant known as fennel, and surprises you with its wild beauty; a delight to explore by car. The region links the furrow hollowed out between the Col Campérié and the more populated Estagel area (including the Maury vineyards and 'Côtes du Roussillon') and a rugged mountain range that becomes quite arid between Sournia and Prades.

🛈 **Info:** Office du tourisme de St-Paul-de-Fenouillet, 26 bd de l'Agly. ℘04 68 59 07 57. www.st-paul66.com.

▶ **Location:** Estagel, 24km/ 15mi W of Perpignan on the D117, is the gateway to Fenouillèdes.

👁 **Don't Miss:** Roman aqueduct bridge of Ansignan.

🚗 DRIVING TOUR

ROUND TRIP FROM ST-PAUL-DE-FENOUILLET
60km/37mi. About 4h.

St-Paul-de-Fenouillet
This town is on the east bank of the Agly near its confluence with the Boulzane.

Clue de la Fou
Strong winds blow through this valley gouged out by the Agly. Cross the river and follow D 619 as it bends around the Fenouillèdes furrow and its vineyards. See the ruined Quéribus castle on its rocky pinnacle and Canigou peak in the distance. The road skirts the still-used Roman aqueduct at **Ansignan** before reaching Sournia via Pézilla-de-Conflent.

▶ Turn right onto D 7 towards St-Prats-de-Sournia.

The road offers a fine view of the Corbières and the Mediterranean Sea through the Agly valley.

▶ Beyond Le Vivier, turn left onto D 9 towards Caudiès.

Notre-Dame-de-Laval
Previously a **hermitage**, this Gothic church on an olive-lined esplanade contains a 15C statue of Mary and Joseph. The road climbs to **Fenouillet** with delightful views of the hermitage of Notre-Dame-de-Laval and the Bugarach summit, before reaching **Caudiès-de-Fenouillèdes**, the gateway to the Fenouillèdes.

▶ Continue N along D 9 to Col de St-Louis then turn right onto D 46 and right again onto D 45.

Pic de Bugarach
↩ *See Les CORBIÈRES, Driving Tour.*

▶ Turn right onto D 14.

Cubières
A rest area near the old mill has picnic tables on the shady banks of the Agly.

▶ Turn right onto D 10 which runs alongside the Cubières stream then the river Agly.

Gorges de Galamus
© Jason Langley/age fotostock

Gorges de Galamus★★

The spectacular rock-carved road and the hermitage clinging to the hillside create a fantasy world bathed in Catalan sunlight. The narrow gorge offers glimpses of the mountain stream below.

Ermitage St-Antoine-de-Galamus

Leave the car in the car park at the hermitage before the tunnel. 🚶 *30min on foot round-trip.*

The path runs down from the hermitage terrace (**view** of Canigou). The hermitage building conceals the chapel in the dim depths of a natural cave.

▶ The D 7 follows a sinuous course through vineyards enroute to St-Paul-de-Fenouillet.

ADDRESSES

🏠 STAY

◌◌◌ **Domaine de Coussères** – *66220 Prugnanes – 5km/3mi NW of St-Paul-de-*

Fenouillet by D 117 and D 20. ☎*04 68 59 23 55. www.cousseres.fr. Closed 15 Oct–1 Apr. 5 rooms.* Perched on a small hill amid the vines, this superb *bastide* dominates a majestic landscape of mountains and *garrigues*. Large, tastefully decorated rooms, and a warm welcome in the dining room.

🍽 EAT

◌◌ **Le Relais des Corbières** – *10 Ave. Jean-Moulin, 66220 St-Paul-de-Fenouillet.* ☎*04 68 59 23 89. www.lerelaisdescorbieres. com. Closed 2–28 Jan, Sun eve and Mon except Jul–Aug and public holidays.* Enjoy a warm welcome and simple honest fare in a dining room with rustic decor or terrace.

ACTIVITIES

Train touristique du Pays cathare et du Fenouillèdes – ☎*04 68 59 99 02. www. tpcf.fr.* The train runs daily during July and August, but at other times according to demand, providing a 60km/37.5mi journey from Rivesaltes to Axat.

Quillan

Plateau and river gorges

This town is a major tourist centre for the upper Aude valley and one of the best points of departure for forays into the forests of the Pyrenean foothills. Until the Second World War, hat-making was big business in the area; these days local industry other than tourism, which plays a major part in the area's economy, includes the production of laminates (Formica), luxury and garden furniture, trousers and shoes.

- ▶ **Population:** 3 372.
- 🧭 **Michelin Map:** 344: E5.
- 🅸 **Info:** Square André-Tricoire, 11500 Quillan. ☎04 68 20 07 78. www.pyrenees audoises.com.
- ▶ **Location:** 28 km/17.5m S of Limoux by the D118 and 76km/47.5m W of Perpignan by the N9 then the D117.
- 👁 **Don't Miss:** The Belvédère du Pas de l'Ours.

VISIT

On the esplanade in front of the station there is a quaint little monument to Abbot Armand (🧭 *see Défilé de Pierre-Lys below*). On the east bank of the Aude stand the ruins, sadly being left to fall into disrepair, of a 13C fortress with a square

ground plan – most unusual in this region.

EXCURSION
Puivert

The **Musée du Quercorb** on local history, traditions and livelihoods displays casts of medieval musical instruments which once ornamented the castle (*open mid-Jul–Aug 10am–7pm; Apr–mid Jul and Sep Wed–Sun 10am–1pm, 2–6pm; €4.10, child 6–15, €1.70; ℘04 68 20 80 98; www.museequercorb.com).*

All that remains of **Puivert Castle** dating from before the siege of 1210, are sections of wall to the west. Of the partly destroyed 14C castle, a keep and a tower-gate decorated with the Bruyères lion are still standing.

Visit the keep, chapel and 'Minstrels' room evoking Puivert court life during the age of the troubadours (*open Easter–mid-Nov daily 9am–7pm; mid-Dec–Easter daily 10am–5pm; closed mid-Nov–mid-Dec; €5; ℘04 68 20 81 52; www.chateau-de-puivert.com).*

🚗 DRIVING TOUR

SAULT PLATEAU AND RIVER GORGES★★
144km/90mi round tour. Allow one day.

This trip includes a large stretch of the **Route du Sapin de l'Aude**, a drive through woodland where there are conifers over 50m tall.

▶ Leave Quillan W along D 117 and turn left onto D 613 which runs across the Sault plateau. Beyond Espèze, watch out for a crossroads marked with a cross and turn right onto D 29 towards Bélesta. Take the left turn past the forest lodge, drive along the forest road to a left bend and park the car by the Langarail drinking troughs.

Langarail pastures★
🚶 *45min on foot there and back.*
As its name suggests, this is a rural site. Follow the stony track until the bumpy stretch from which there is a **view** to the north, beyond the Bélesta forest as far as the foothills of the chain towards the Lauragais.

▶ Get back onto the forest road and continue W.

Quillan

Pas de l'Ours★
The road runs along a rocky cliff above the Gorges de la Frau.

▶ At Col de la Gargante, take the steep road to the left which is signposted 'Belvédère 600m'.

Belvédère du Pas de l'Ours★★
15min on foot there and back.
🚶 From the look-out point, there is a magnificent view of the **Gorges de la Frau★**; 700m lower down are the Montségur outcrop and the Tabe mountain; beyond these, and much higher up, the white patches of the Trimouns quarry can be seen.

▶ Beyond Col de la Gargante, follow the road to Comus and turn right.

Gorges de la Frau★
1h30 on foot there and back.
🚶 Park the car at the entrance to a wide forest track climbing a tributary valley. The path runs along the base of yellow-tinged limestone cliffs. After a 45min walk, turn back at the point where the valley makes a sharp bend.

▶ Return to Comus and take the road to the right towards Camurac.

Camurac ski area
Alt 1 400m–1 800m.
Camurac is a family resort equipped with 16 Alpine ski runs suitable for all levels of proficiency, a country-skiing loop and a marked track for snowshoeing.

The road climbs up to Col des Sept Frères. Turn left onto D 613 then right onto D 20 to Niort de Sault; turn left.

Drive down the **Rebenty gorge**, passing beneath the impressive overhangs of the **Défilé d'Able** and through the **Défilé de Joucou**, where the road follows a series of tunnels and overhangs, to reach **Joucou**, a sheltered village gathered around an old abbey.

Turn back. After driving through a couple of tunnels, turn left onto D 29 which runs through Rodome, Aunat and Bessède-de-Sault before joining D 118. Turn left towards Axat.

This pretty stretch of road runs along the edge of the Sault plateau.

Grottes de l'Aguzou

The cave is open to visitors all year round, by reservation. Make your reservation several days in advance in summer (Jul–Aug) , and from 2 to 3 weeks in advance during the rest of the year.; departure at 9am. 1 day (9am–5pm): €60. Take light walking boots or shoes and a cold meal. 04 68 20 45 38. www.grotte-aguzou.com.

This complex network of caves was discovered in 1965. On the tour, visitors can see a large number of crystals and some wonderful examples of aragonite.

Gorges de St-Georges★

This river gorge, cutting straight down through bare rock, is the narrowest in the upper Aude valley.

In the **Aude gorge**, a reach of some 10km/6mi, the river surges along between high cliffs thickly covered with plant life.

Drive on to Axat, a white-water sports resort, left onto D 177 to Quillan.

Défilé de Pierre-Lys★

This is an impressive stretch of road between the ravine's sheer cliff walls, to which the odd bush clings tenaciously. The final tunnel is known as the **Trou du Curé** ('priest's hole') in memory of Abbot Félix Armand (1742–1823), parish priest of St-Martin-Lys, who had the passage cut through the rock with pickaxes.

Rennes-le-Château

Rennes-le-Château stands on a plateau over the Aude valley. Rumour still abounds about the fortune of the enigmatic Father Béranger Saunière, parish priest from 1885 to his death in 1917. How from 1891 onwards was he able to fund the complete restoration of his ruined church, build a sumptuous mansion (the Villa Bétania), a bizarre, semi-fortified library-tower (the Tour Magdala) and a tropical greenhouse, and lead a life fit for a prince? The abbot must have discovered some hidden treasure – of the Knights Templar, the Cathars, or treasure brought back from the Holy City by the Visigoths, perhaps?

- **Michelin Map:** 344: E5.
- **Info:** 11190 Rennes-le-Château. 04 68 31 38 85. www.rennes-le-chateau.fr.
- **Location:** 16km/10mi N of Quillan.
- **Parking:** The village is closed to traffic during Jul–Aug, but 3 car parks are available at the bottom of the village.
- **Timing:** Allow at least 1 hr.

SIGHTS
Église Ste-Marie-Madeleine

The church is decorated with 19C neo-Gothic murals and polychrome statues. At the entrance to the church is a font supported by the Devil.

Domaine de l'abbé Saunière

The **Espace Bérenger Saunière** in the presbytery includes a local history **museum** displaying the Visigothic pillar said to have contained Father Saunière's treasure.

In the **Domaine de l'abbé Saunière**, is the priest's garden, private chapel, Villa Bétania and the curious crenelated Magdala tower (🕐 *open daily: mid-Mar–Apr 10am–1pm, 2–4.30pm; May 10am–6.30pm; Jun–Aug 10am–7pm; Sept 10am–5.15pm; Oct–late Nov 10.30am–1pm, 2–4.30pm; ⊚€5; ℘04 04 68 74 72 68; www.rennes-le-chateau.fr*).

▷ Return to Couiza and follow D 118 towards Quillan.

🚗 DRIVING TOUR

AU COEUR DU RAZÈS
ℰ *See region map.*

First a Roman then a Visigoth city, in the 12C, Rennes (Rhedae) became the seat of the powerful but short-lived county of Razès, which for a time drew much envy before being united in the county of Carcassonne in 835. The county had feudal jurisdiction in Occitania, and was founded in 781 after the creation of the kingdom of Aquitania.

▷ 3.5km/2mi from Rennes-le-Château.

Couiza
Couiza, in the foothills of the Pyrenees on the Aude river and at the foot of the hill leading to Rennes-le-Château, is an industrious place, mainly manufacturing shows and hats. The old **castle** of the Dukes of Joyeuse is mid 16C, flanked by round towers and quite well preserved; today it houses a hotel with a Renaissance courtyard.

▷ Take the D 613 towards Villerouge-Termenès.

The road passes Coustaussa and the ruins of its castle (inaccessible and dangerous). Constructed in the 12C by Rai-

mond-Roger Trencavel, it was attacked by Simon de Montfort in 1210 and 1211 as a stronghold of Cathars. Members of the breakaway religious sect were still present in the village in the 14C.

▷ 8.5km/5mi from Couiza by the D 613 then the D 14 on the right.

Rennes-les-Bains
Crossed by a stream this small community is a source of treatment for rheumatological problems.

▷ Return to the D 613. 9km/5.5mi from Rennes-les-Bains. From Arques, 500m along D 613.

Donjon d'Arques
🕐*Open Mar and Oct–mid-Nov Sat–Sun and public holidays 10am–1pm, 2–5pm; Apr–Sept 10am–1pm, 2–6pm (Jul–Aug) 10am–1.30pm, 2–7pm). ⊚€6 (child 6–15, €3). ℘04 68 69 84 77. www.chateau-arques.fr.*
👥 Used as living quarters since the late 13C, this keep of beautiful gold-coloured sandstone has three rooms open to the public. **Maison Déodat Roché** presents an audio-visual exhibition on the Cathar doctrine compiled by the eponymous Déodat Roché (1877–1978), a specialist in Catharism, and, some might say, something of a Cathar himself.

▷ Slightly farther on to the left, a forest track leads through the Rialsesse forest.

Forêt de Rialsesse
The forest is well established, mainly in Austrian pine, and today is popular with walkers and cyclists alike.

ADDRESSES

🛏 STAY

⊚⊚ **Au Coeur de Rennes** – *R. de l'Église, 11190 Rennes-les-Bains. ℘04 68 69 59 68. www.aucoeurderennes.com. 5 rooms.* Comfortable rooms, sometimes decorated a little quirkily, but a friendly atmosphere, and a gourmet break.

Magdala tower, domaine de l'abbe Saunière, Rennes-le-Château

© Jean-Paul Garcin/Photononstop/Tips Images

Conspiracies of Rennes-le-Château

As you move south from Carcassonne into the beautiful but complex folds of the mountains that were the Cathar stronghold, so you delve deeper into a world of mystery. Until recent times, the tiny and largely obscure village of Rennes-le-Château was virtually unknown. But then rumours started to surface, originating in the mid-1950s, concerning a local 19C priest. Father Bérenger Saunière arrived in the village in 1885, and acquired large sums of money during his tenure by selling masses and receiving donations. This was not uncommon, but the source of the wealth became a topic of conversation, and stories circulating within the village ranged from the priest having found hidden treasure to espionage for the Germans during World War I. During the 1950s, these rumours, in true entrepreneurial fashion, were given wide local circulation by a local man who opened a restaurant in Saunière's former estate (L'Hotel de la Tour), and hoped to use the stories to attract business.

From then on Rennes-le-Château became the centre of conspiracy theories claiming that Saunière had discovered hidden treasure and/or secrets about the history of the Church that could threaten the foundations of Roman Catholicism. Suddenly, the area became the focus of increasingly outlandish claims involving the Knights Templar, the Priory of Sion, the Rex Deus, the Holy Grail, the treasures of the Temple of Solomon, the Ark of the Covenant, ley lines and sacred geometry alignments. Saunière's story, true or false, found its way into contemporary novels, notably *Sepulchre*, by Kate Mosse, who had previously penned a novel set in the times of the Cathars, *Labyrinth*.

This is all grist to the mill of speculation. Is there treasure here? Or is it wishful thinking?

Limoux

Limoux is the production centre of sparkling **blanquette**, made from the Mauzac, Chenin and Chardonnay grapes using the *méthode champenoise*. The town's skyline features the Gothic spire of St Martin's Church and its lively narrow streets are still partly enclosed within a 14C fortified wall.

SIGHTS
Musée du Piano
Pl. de 22 Septembre. ⏱*Open May–Sept.* ⬡*€4.* ✆*04 68 31 85 03.*
An interesting exhibit of French pianos from late 18C to today, presenting the evolution of the instrument.

Musée Petiet
Prom. du Tivoli. ⏱*Open Jun and Sept Tue–Fri 9am–noon, 2–6pm, Sat 10am–noon, 2–5pm; Jul–Aug Tue–Sun 9am–noon, 2–6.30pm; rest of year Wed–Fri 9am–noon, 2–6pm, Sat 10am–noon, 2–5pm.* ⏱*Closed 1 Jan, 1 May and 25 Dec.* ⬡*€3.50.* ✆*04 68 31 85 03.*
This museum in the former workshop of the Petiet family, displays local paintings such as *The Ironers* by Marie Petiet (1854–93), battle scenes from the 1870 Franco-Prussian War by Étienne Dujardin-Beaumetz, and works by Henri Lebasque (*Reading*) and Achille Laugé (*Notre-Dame de Paris*).

EXCURSIONS
Jardin aux Plantes parfumées
Leave Limoux on the road for Carcassonne then turn right under the railway line as far as the commerical centre. Turn right at the first roundabout and follow signs for ' R. Dewoitine ' - domaine de Flassian.
⏱*Open May–Jun and Sept Wed–Fri, Sun and public holidays 1–6pm; Jul–Aug Wed–Sun and public holidays 1–6pm, and Mon mid-May–mid-Aug.* ⬡*€8.* ✆*04 68 31 49 94.*
www.labouichere.com.
A garden of a thousand-and-one scents: a perfumed rose garden, dry garden, medieval garden with plants for the

▶ **Population:** 10 816.
ℹ **Info:** 7 av. du Pont-de-France, 11300 Limoux. ✆04 68 31 11 82. www.tourisme-limoux-in-aude.fr.
◗ **Location:** 26km/16mi S of Carcassonne and 28km/17.5mi N of Quillan via D 118.
👁 **Don't Miss:** A tasting of blanquette de Limoux, and Limoux's carnival (January to April) with streets full of costumed dancers and musicians.
👪 **Kids:** The Arques dungeon, and nautical activities. Musée des Dinosaurs.

Cathar centuries. Simply an enchanting place spread over 2ha, with more than 2 500 plants… and donkeys?

Notre-Dame-de-Marceille
2km/1mi N of Limoux on the D 104.
This 14C pilgrimage church is built in the Gothic style.

St-Hilaire
12km/7.5mi N of Limoux on the D 104. It was the Benedictine monks of St-Hilaire who are traditionally credited

Vineyards of Limoux
© clodio/iStockphoto.com

with the discovery of the techniques for making the *blanquette de Limoux*.

Abbaye Ste-Marie-de-Rieunette

19km/12mi to the NW. After St-Hilaire turn right onto the D 110 and continue for 6km/4mi after Ladern-sur-Laquet. In 1994, Ste-Marie-de-Rieunette came back to life thanks to a community of five Cistercian nuns for the Boulaur abbey in Gers.

St-Polycarpe

8km/5mi SE along D 129.
The **fortified church** here was part of a Benedictine abbey which was dissolved in 1771. On display are the 14C head reliquary (bare head) of St Polycarp, St Benedict and of the Holy Thorn, as well as 8C fabrics. The walls and vault feature the restored remains of 14C frescoes.

🚗 DRIVING TOUR

LA HAUTE VALLÉE DE L'AUDE

120km/75mi round tour from Limoux – Allow one day. ⏱See region map.

▷ Leave Limoux south along D 118.

Castles along this route had quite efficient defences during the Albigensian Crusade. The Aude valley cuts across a fold in the Corbières mountain massif, before narrowing into the **Étroit d'Alet** gorge.

Alet-les-Bains

Surrounded by 12C ramparts Alet's **old town** has many interesting house on **place de la République**. Picturesque narrow streets branch off from the square to the city gates: Porte Calvière and Porte Cadène. Not far from D 118 are the **ruins** of the 11C abbey church, raised to the status of cathedral from 1318.

▷ Turn left off D 118 onto D 70 then right onto a minor road towards Arques.

Couiza

⏱*See RENNES-LE-CHÂTEAU, Driving Tour.*

▷ Leaving Couiza, turn left on the D 12.

Espéraza

This small town on the banks of the Aude was an important hat-making centre, whose past is commemorated in the **Musée de la Chapellerie** (&⏱*open Jan–Jun and Sept–Dec 10.30am–12.30, 1.30–5.30pm; Jul–Aug 10am–7pm; ⏱Closed 25 Dec; ≈€2; ℘04 68 74 00 75; www.museedelachapellerie.fr).* Organised like a factory, the museum shows the stages of making of a felt hat and displays various headdress. The **Musée des Dinosaures** 🚶🚶 reconstructs a local 19C dinosaur dig and displays bone fragments, semi-fossilised eggs and the skeleton of an enormous sauropod (&⏱*open daily 10.30am–12.30pm, 1.30–5.30pm; ⏱closed 1 Jan, 25 Dec; ≈€8.70, children €6.20; ℘04 68 74 26 88; www.dinosauria.org).*

Quillan ⏱*See QUILLAN.*

ADDRESSES

🛏 STAY

🛏 **Camping Val d'Aleth** – *Chemin de la Paoulette, 11580 Alet-les-Bains. ℘04 68 69 90 40. www.valdaleth.com.* & *Reservations advised, 37 places.* Close to the village centre, pleasantly shaded along the river.

🍴 EAT

Good to know – If you're feeling hungry, then you will be spoiled for choice in the place de la République where there are many places to buy tapas, gargantuan salads and grills including the **Café Gourmand**.

SHOPPING

Blanquette de Limoux – For details of the producers who accept visitors contact the tourist office or the Union of Limoux AOC (*20 av. du Pont-de-France; ℘04 68 31 12 83).*

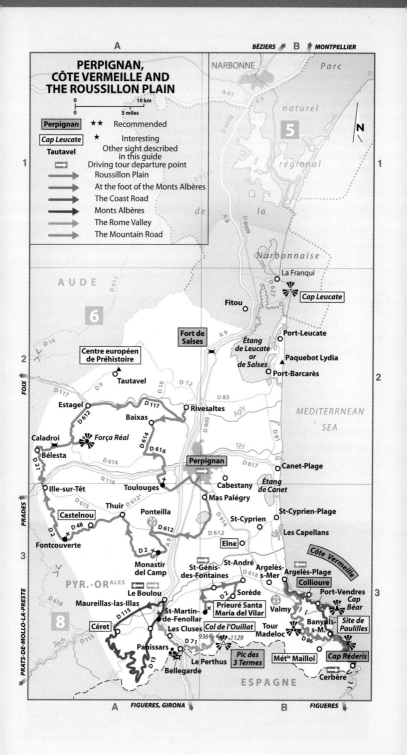

PERPIGNAN, CÔTE VERMEILLE AND THE ROUSSILLON PLAIN

| | 10 km |
| 0 | 5 miles |

Perpignan
★★ Recommended
Cap Leucate
★ Interesting
Tautavel
Other sight described in this guide
Driving tour departure point
Roussillon Plain
At the foot of the Monts Albères
The Coast Road
Monts Albères
The Rome Valley
The Mountain Road

BÉZIERS B MONTPELLIER

NARBONNE

Parc

naturel

régional

de la

Narbonnaise

La Franqui
Cap Leucate
Fitou
Port-Leucate
Fort de Salses
Étang de Leucate or de Salses
Paquebot Lydia
Centre européen de Préhistoire
Tautavel
Port-Barcarès

AUDE

Estagel
Baixas
Rivesaltes
MEDITERRNEAN SEA
Caladroi
Força Réal
Bélesta
Ille-sur-Têt
Toulouges
Perpignan
Canet-Plage
Cabestany
Étang de Canet
Mas Palégry
Thuir
Ponteilla
St-Cyprien
St-Cyprien-Plage
Castelnou
Les Capellans
Fontcouverte
Elne
Côte Vermeille
Monastir del Camp
St-Génis-des-Fontaines
St-André
Argelès-s-Mer
Argelès-Plage
Collioure
Port-Vendres
Cap Béar
PYR.-OR^ALES
Le Boulou
Sorède
Valmy
Maureillas-las-Illas
Prieuré Santa Maria del Vilar
Banyuls-s-M.
Site de Paulilles
Céret
St-Martin-de-Fenollar
Col de l'Ouillat
Tour Madeloc
Cap Réderis
Panissars
Les Cluses
Le Perthus
Pic des 3 Termes
Mét^le Maillol
Bellegarde
Cerbère

ESPAGNE

FIGUERES, GIRONA
FIGUERES

The Vermilion Coast, the undiscovered Spanish facet of France, has been the source of inspiration for many of the world's leading artists, and led to its own style of painting. Bathed in a magical light, here the waves dash against rocky shores, craggy mountains do battle against the sea, and steeply sloping vineyards cling to the hillsides. The area has been settled since prehistoric times, as the remains of Tautavel Man testify, but the principal town of Perpignan seems to have been founded only in the 10C. France this is, of course, but above all else it is Catalonia, as evidenced by the mix of languages used across the Franco-Spanish border. Here, in this frontierland, the buildings speak of past times, of the counts of Roussillon, the kings of Majorca, the Catalans and Aragonese, and then the French. Inevitably, over centuries of cultural co-habitation, a unique identity has formed.

Highlights

1 Enjoy a town walk in ancient **Perpignan** (p268)
2 Check out the half-buried **Fort de Salses** (p273)
3 Spend some time in the artists' paradise that is **Collioure** (p277)
4 Chill out in the sheltered village of **Banyuls-sur-Mer** (p280)
5 Make the intimate acquaintance of the local **wines** (p281)

Tautavel Man

Tautavel man is the name of an extinct hominid that lived about 300 000–450 000 years ago. The being is named after fossils found in an ancient karst cave on the site known as *Caune de l'Arago*, very close to the village of Tautavel. Although excavations had been going on for some years, the skull of this early ancestor of man was found there only in 1971. It has a flat and receding forehead and a well-developed arch of the eyebrows; the face is big and has rectangular eye sockets.

Littorally Speaking

This lovely stretch of coastline – the littoral, in French – has numerous enchanting border villages, where the influence of Spain is plain to see. Castle ruins pepper the landscape, and peaceful, hidden villages are found at every turn. This is the best of both worlds: a launch pad from which to explore the Mediterranean, yet only a few minutes from the Spanish Costa Brava. This, the Côte Vermeille, is the last stretch of French coast before Spain, and extends from Argelès-sur-Mer, a superb halt for families, to the border village of Cerbère in the secluded valley of Cervera.

Beach of Collioure and Église Notre-Dame-des-Anges

© I.Astar/age fotostock

Perpignan★★

Perpignan, once the capital city of the counts of Roussillon and the kings of Majorca, is an outlying post of Catalan civilisation north of the Pyrenees, and a lively commercial city, with shaded walks lined with pavement cafés. The economy is largely based on tourism, wine and olive oil, and the production of cork, wool and leather.

A BIT OF HISTORY

During the 13C, the city profited from the great upsurge in trade between the south of France, and the Levant stimulated by the crusades. In 1276, Perpignan became the capital of Roussillon as part of the kingdom of Majorca.

The second Catalan city – After the kingdom of Majorca had ceased to be in 1344, Roussillon and Cerdagne were integrated into the princedom of Catalonia which, in the 14C and 15C, constituted a kind of autonomous federation in the heart of the State of Aragón. Catalan 'Corts' sat at Barcelona, but delegated a 'Deputation' to Perpignan. Between the two slopes of the Pyrenees, a commercial, cultural and linguistic community came into being.

French or Spanish? – In 1463, Louis XI helped King John II of Aragón to defeat the Catalans and took possession of Perpignan and Roussillon. However, hostilities with France broke out once more and French armies besieged the city. The people of Perpignan put up fierce resistance and surrendered only when ordered to do so by the king of Aragón, who gave the city the title of 'Fidelissima' (most faithful).

In 1493, Charles VIII gave the province of Roussillon back to the Spanish. Later, however, Cardinal Richelieu seized the opportunity offered by a Catalan rebellion against Spain, forming an alliance with rebels and, in 1641, Louis XIII became count of Barcelona.

The final siege of Perpignan – As a Spanish garrison was holding Perpignan, the city was laid to siege. Louis XIII arrived with the elite of the French army

▶ **Population:** 123 089.

🛈 **Info:** Place François Arago, 66000 Perpignan. ℘04 68 66 30 30. www.perpignan tourisme.com.

◗ **Location:** The A 9 (exit 42) and the N 9 both lead to Perpignan; access to the centre by Boulevard Edmond Michelet (west), Avenue des Baléares (south) or Pont Arago (north, over the Têt River).

🅿 **Parking:** Park near the Promenade des Platanes.

⊘ **Don't Miss:** Le Castillet, symbol of Perpignan.

🕓 **Timing:** Take the town walk first, to get the lay of the land; save time for the Palace of the Kings of Majorca. A visit to Rousillon Plain will require a day.

👪 **Kids:** Palais des Rois de Majorque.

and Perpignan finally surrendered on 9 September 1642.

The Treaty of the Pyrenees ratified the final reunification of Roussillon with the French crown.

Castillet with the Catalan flag

©Bertrand Rieger/Hemis/Photoshot

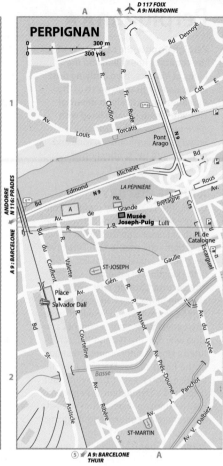

PERPIGNAN

WHERE TO STAY

Alexander (Hôtel)	①
Domaine du Mas Boluix (Chambre d'hôte)	③
Domaine du Moulin (Chambre d'hôte)	⑤
Kyriad (Hôtel)	⑨
Mas des Arcades (Hôtel Le)	⑪
New Christina (Hôtel)	⑬

WHERE TO EAT

Antiquaires (Les)	①
Chap' (Le)	⑤
Galinette (La)	⑦
Nature et Gastronomie	⑳
Passerelle (La)	⑨

 WALKING TOUR

HISTORIC PERPIGNAN

Le Castillet★

This monument, an emblem of Perpignan dominates place de la Victoire. Its two towers are crowned with exceptionally tall crenellations and machicolations.

Promenade des Platanes

This wide avenue is lined with plane trees and adorned with fountains. Palm trees grow along the side avenues.

La Miranda

This is a small public park behind the church of St-Jacques. It is given over to the plant life of the *garrigue* and shrubs which are either native or have been introduced to the region.

Église St-Jacques

At the west end of the nave, a vast chapel added in the 18C was reserved for the brotherhood of La Sanch ('of the precious Blood'). From 1416, this penitents' brotherhood performed a solemn procession on Maundy Thursday (now Good Friday), carrying its *misteris* to the singing of hymns.

▷ Turn right down R. de L'Anguille.

Campo Santo

韡🕐*Open daily except Mon.* 🕐*Closed 1 Jan, 25 Dec.* ✆*04 68 66 30 30.* *www.perpignantourisme.com.*

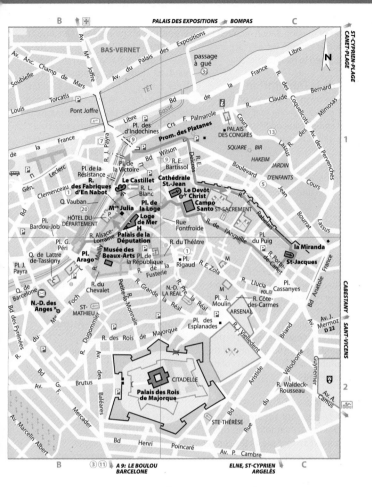

Situated south of the cathedral (☉ see below), the Campo Santo is a vast square graveyard which exhibits great architectural unity with its pointed funeral alcoves and marble recesses, set into walls adorned with pebbles and courses of brick. It is one of the few medieval graveyards remaining in France.

Cathédrale St-Jean★

The church was begun in 1324 by Sancho, second king of Majorca, and was consecrated in 1509. The oblong façade of the basilica is constructed from pebbles alternating with bricks. It is flanked on the right by a square tower with an 18C wrought-iron campanile housing a 15C bell.

Place de la Loge

This square and the pedestrianised rue de la Loge, paved in pink marble, form the lively centre of town life. Here, in summer, the *sardana* is danced several times a week.

Loge de Mer★

This fine Gothic building, dating from 1397 and refurbished and extended in the 16C, once housed a commercial tribunal in charge of ruling on claims relating to maritime trade.

Hôtel de Ville★

In the arcaded courtyard stands a bronze by Maillol: *The Mediterranean*. On the façade of the building, three bronze arms, which are said to symbolise the 'hands' or estates of the population required to elect the five consuls, were in fact originally designed to hold torches.

Palais de la Députation
During the reign of the kings of Aragón this 15C palace was the seat of the permanent commission or *députation* representing the Catalan 'Corts'.

▶ Follow the rue d'Alsace-Lorraine. On the right, the rue Mailly gives access to the musée des Beaux-Arts.

Musée d'Art Hyacinthe-Rigaud
Hôtel de Lazerme. ⏱*Closed for renovation.* ☎*04 68 35 43 40.*
Hyacinthe-Rigaud (1659–1743) was a French baroque painter of Catalan origin whose career was largely based in Paris. He is renowned for his portrait paintings of Louis XIV, the royalty and nobility of Europe, and members of their courts, and was considered one of the most notable French portraitists of the Classical period.

Place Arago
This lively, pleasant square, adorned with palm trees, magnolias and cafés, attracts crowds of people. In the centre stands the statue of the famous physician, astronomer and politician **François Arago** (1786–1853).

▶ Return to the Palais de la Députation.

Opposite the Palais de la Députation, take a little detour down the small rue des Fabriques d'En Nabot, The **Maison Julia**★ at No. 2 is one of the few well-preserved *hôtels* of Perpignan, possessing a patio with 14C Gothic arcades.

▶ Return to Le Castillet.

ADDITIONAL SIGHTS
♣♣ Palais des Rois de Majorque★
⏱↝*Open Jun–Sep 10am–6pm; Oct–May 9am–5pm.* ⏱*Closed 1 Jan, 1 May, 1 Nov, 25 Dec.* ☎*04 68 34 64 93.*

When the kings of Majorca came to the throne in 1276, they built their palace on the hill of Puig del Rey. A vaulted slope leads across the red-brick ramparts to a pleasant Mediterranean garden. Pass beneath a tower to the west, the **tour de l'Homage**, to get to the square-shaped main courtyard. This is open on the east and west sides with two storeys of arcades.
On the first floor of the south wing, the **great hall of Majorca** has a chimney-piece with three fireplaces. Beyond it, the Queen's suite has a superb ceiling painted with the Catalan colours (green and red). The most splendid part of the building is the **chapel-keep** of Ste-Croix rising above the east wing. It comprises two sanctuaries built one above the other in the 14C by Jaime II of Majorca.

Chapelle N.-D.-des-Anges
32 r. du Mar.-Foch.
This old Gothic chapter house (13C) of the monastery was turned into a military hospital in the 19C; it stages temporary exhibitions.

Musée Numismatique Joseph-Puig★
42 Ave. de Grande-Bretagne.
⏱*Open Tue–Sat by appointment only.* ☎*04 68 62 37 64.*
Part of the Villa 'Les Tilleuls' (1907) has been converted into a museum, at the donor's request, to display the numismatic collection bequeathed by Joseph Puig to his native city of Perpignan.

EXCURSIONS
Cabestany
5km/3mi on D 22 to the SE.
Inside the church of **Notre-Dame-des-Anges**, on the wall of the chapel on the right is a famous Romanesque **tympanum**★ by the 12C travelling sculptor, the master of Cabestany.

Tautavel
27.7km/17.2mi NW, D 117 and D59.
This little village of just under 900 inhabitants, on the banks of the Verdouble, is an important centre of prehistory

following the discovery here of objects of vital significance in the study of the origins of human life. Tautavel is in a wine growing area in the Catalan, the Corbières, between the sea and the mountains, at the bottom of the foothills of the high Pyrenees. In spite of its pre-historic notoriety, the village is equally renowned, in rather different circles, for the quality of its wine which uses grenache, syrah and carignane grapes. The remains of the village's castle are nearby, and while Tautavel is close to the mountain areas occupied by the Cathars, the village and surrounding area seem to have escaped the attention of the Crusading army.

Centre Européen de Préhistoire★★
Avenue Léon Jean Grégory. Open mid-Jul–Aug 10am–7pm; rest of year 10am–12.30pm, 2–6pm. Closed 1 Jan, 25–26 and 31 Dec. €8. 04 68 29 07 76. http://450000ans.com.
Devoted to the evolution of man and his environment (based on the signifi-cant discoveries made in the Caune de l'Arago and surrounding area).

🚗 DRIVING TOUR

ROUSSILLON PLAIN
128km/80mi. Allow one day.

▷ Leave Perpignan S, turn left onto N 114 then take a little road on the right towards Villeneuve-de-la-Raho.

Situated among vineyards, **Mas Palégry** is the setting for an **Aviation museum**. (*visit by arrangement; 06 18 92 64 14; http://pyreneescatalanes.free.fr*).

▷ Follow D 612 towards Thuir, and then turn right to Ponteilla.

The **Jardin Exotique de Ponteilla** (*open Jun–Aug Sun–Fri 10.30am–7pm, Sat 2–7pm; May and Sep Wed 2–6.30pm; closed rest of year; €7.50; 04 68 53 22 44; http://jardinexotiquede-ponteilla.fr*) has a signposted botanical trail.

Turn back, cross D 612 and drive on to Trouillas, turn right onto D 37 to Vil-lemolaque and continue along D 40 towards Passa, where the **Prieuré du Monastir del Camp** is an imposing building with an elegant fortified front (*guided tours daily except Thu; 04 68 38 80 71*).

Drive along D 2 to Fourques, then turn right to D 615 to **Thuir**, known mainly for its wine cellars.

Continue along the D 48. The road climbs the slopes of the Aspre. Sud-denly the medieval, fortified village of **Castelnou★** comes into sight with Mont Canigou rising in the background, making a wonderful **view★**. Continue to the **Église de Fontcouverte**, an iso-lated church shaded by oak trees. This is a beautiful, solitary site.

Take the D 2 north to **Ille-sur-Têt** (*see Ille-sur-Têt*). The D 21 leads to **Bélesta**, a remarkable village built on a rocky nose rising from the vineyards. The village has long been known to archaeologists for its wealth of prehistoric remains. The **Chateau-musée** (*open mid-Jun–mid-Sep 2–7pm; rest of year daily except Tue and Sat 2–5.30pm; 04 68 84 55 55*) gives an insight into the prehistoric finds.

Drive in the direction of the col de la Bataille (D 38). **Castle Caladroi** soon appears in the middle of a park planted with exotic species. From the col you reach the **ermitage de Força Réal**, which offers a superb **panorama★★**.

Go back to the col, and from there reach **Estagel**, and continue on the D 117 to **Rivesaltes**, one of the wine capitals of Roussillon.

Head SW on the D 614 to **Baixas**, an agreeable medieval village dominated by the silhouette of its **church★**.

Continue on the D 614, then turn left at the D 616. At **Baho**, take the road south, passing over **la Têt** and the D 116.

Turn right, then left to reach **Toulouges** (church).

▶ Return to Perpignan on the D 900.

ADDRESSES

🏠 STAY

⊝⊝⊜ **Chambre d'hôte Domaine du Mas Boluix** – *Chemin du Pou de les Colobres. 5km/3mi S of Perpignan towards Argelès.* ☎04 68 08 17 70. &.ᴛᴀ. *7 rooms.* Removed from the bustle of Perpignan, this nicely restored 18C *mas* is a peaceful place in the middle of Cabestany grapevines. Each guest room is named after a local artist.

⊝⊝⊜ **Hôtel Alexander** – *15 Bd. Clemenceau.* ☎04 68 35 41 41. www.hotel-alexander.fr. *24 rooms. Restaurant* ⊝⊝. This little downtown hotel has balconied, air-conditioned guestrooms on three levels (with elevator). Enthusiastic welcome.

⊝⊝⊜ **Hôtel New Christina** – *51 cours Lassus.* ☎04 68 35 12 21. *25 rooms. Restaurant* ⊝⊝. A small modern hotel, close to city centre, with a swimming pool on the roof.

⊝⊝⊜ **Hôtel Kyriad** – *8 bd. Wilson.* ☎04 68 59 25 94. www.kyriad.com. *38 rooms.* Functional room furnishings; intergral courtyard with fountain.

⊝⊝⊜ **Le Mas des Arcades** – *840 av. d'Espagne 2km/1mi on the D 9.* ☎04 68 85 11 11. www.hotel-mas-arcades.fr. *62 rooms. Restaurant* ⊝⊝. Tidy rooms, half with balconies; fine restaurant.

🍴 EAT

⊝⊝ **Les Antiquaires** – *Pl. Desprès.* ☎04 68 34 06 58. *Closed Sun eve and Mon.* This family restaurant is decorated with antique china; the chef serves a traditional cuisine.

⊝⊝ **La Galinette** – *23 R. Jean-Payra.* ☎04 68 35 00 90. *Closed Sun and Mon.* Contemporary furnishings, beautifully set tables and southern-style dishes created with market-fresh ingredients.

⊝⊝ **La Passerelle** – *1 cours Palmarole.* ☎04 68 51 30 65. *Closed Mon lunch, and Sun.* A cosy restaurant where seafood stars and reminds you that the sea is not far away.

⊝⊝ **Casa Bonet** – *2 R. du Chevalet.* ☎04 68 34 19 45. This *casa* in the pedestrian area of town houses a restaurant offering a buffet, tapas and different brochettes.

⊝⊝⊜ **Le Chap** – *Park Hôtel. 18 bd Jean-Bourrat.* ☎04 68 35 14 14. *Closed lunch time (Mon, Fri, Sat) and Sun.* Lovely décor; excellent choice of regional wines.

TAKING A BREAK

Espi – *43 bis quai Vauban.* ☎04 68 35 19 91. *Winter: daily 7.30am–7.30pm; summer: 7.30am–12.30am.* Immense store where each type of product (sweets, pastries, etc) features specialities original to the house.

ACTIVITIES AND EVENTS

Centre Équestre de Loisirs du Barcarès – *Chemin de l'Hourtou, 66420 Le Barcarès.* ☎04 68 80 98 26. *Daily 10am–noon, 2–8.30pm.* Tours on horseback, by the hour or the day, round Salses lake by the sea. 2–5 day excursions around the Cathar castles or along the Roussillon wine route.

Jazzèbre – Open air concerts, and in bars. End of Sept. www.jazzebre.com.

SHOPPING

Markets – Fruit and vegetable markets are held daily except Mon on the pl. de la République and every morning on place Cassanyes. Flea market Av. du Palais-des-Expositions on Sun morning. Organic market on pl. Rigaud Wed and Sat mornings.

Shopping streets – Clothes shops can be found in the pedestrianised city centre (Rue Mailly). The avenue du Gén.-de-Gaulle, in a lively part of town, is full of shops. The rue de l'Adjudant-Pilote-Paratilla, also called la rue des Olives by locals, is known for its two grocery shops and delicatessen.

Au Paradis des Desserts – *13 Ave. du Gén.-de-Gaulle.* ☎04 68 34 89 69. *Tue–Sun 8am–12.10pm, 4–7.30pm. Closed public holiday afternoons and 3 wks in Aug.* Here a talented patissier devotes himself to the creation of a wide range of truly individualised taste sensations.

IN THE EVENING

A number of bars in the old part of the city have live music in the evenings, such as O'Shannons Irish pub, le Corto Maltese and le Tio Pepe or le Mediator.

Fort de **Salses**★★

Rising above the surrounding vineyards, this half-buried fortress is surprisingly big. The colour of the brickwork, bronzed by the sun, blends harmoniously with the golden sheen of the stonework, mainly of pink sandstone. Built in the 15C, on a site with a source of spring water, the fort is a unique example of the medieval military architecture of Spain, adapted by Vauban in 1691 to the needs of the military of the time. The Treaty of the Pyrenees of 1659 redrew the border with Spain, and Salses then lost its strategic importance.

A BIT OF HISTORY

Hannibal's passage – In 218 BCE, Hannibal made plans to cross Gaul and invade Italy. Rome immediately sent emissaries, to ask the Gauls to resist the Carthaginians' advance. The Gauls declined and Hannibal was allowed through as 'a guest'. When the Romans, who remembered the episode with bitterness, occupied Gaul, they built a camp at Salses.

After Roussillon had been restored to Spain in 1493, Ferdinand of Aragón had this fortress built. Designed to house a garrison of 1 500 men, it could also withstand attack by newly evolving artillery. French troops reconquered Roussillon in mid-17C.

Info: ℘04 68 38 60 13. www.salses.monuments-nationaux.fr.

Location: 16km/10mi N of Perpignan by the N 9 (direction Sigean).

VISIT

Jan–Mar and Oct–Dec 10am–12.15pm, 2–5pm; Apr–Sept 10am–6.30pm. Closed 1 Jan, 1 May, 1 and 11 Nov, 25 Dec. €7.50.

The fortress illustrates the significant transition from that of medieval castle to a modern fortress. With walls from 6–10m thick, the construction has three wholly independent parts running from east to west. The various levels are connected by a labyrinth of passages with a zigzagging complex network of internal underground defences. The fortress today houses rotating exhibitions of contemporary art.

EXCURSION
Le vignoble de Fitou
To the N on the D 900.

Here, separated from the sea by the lake of Leucate, lie the vineyards of Corbières Maritime, whose centre is at Fitou, which gave its name to a robust AOC .

Fort des Salses

© R. Manin/age fotostock

Le-Barcarès

The urban planners of this resort developed this site to satisfy tourists, providing for easy access to swimming and other outdoor activities and building self-catering accommodation, family camps and conventional hotel facilities. Residential areas have been grouped together, saving the seafront from overbearing blocks of buildings that would stifle the horizon.

- ▶ **Population:** 4 089.
- ⏱ **Michelin Map:** 344: J6.
- ⓘ **Info:** Pl. de la République, 66420 Port-Barcarès. ☏ 04 68 86 16 56.
- ▶ **Location:** 25km/15.5mi N of Perpignan and 50km/31m SW of Narbonne by the A9.
- 🅿 **Parking:** Along the beaches or near the Tourist Office.
- 👪 **Kids:** Aquamagic.
- 🕐 **Timing:** Allow 30 minutes for sightseeing.

VISIT
Paquebot Lydia

This ship, which was deliberately run aground in 1967, is the main attraction of the new Roussillon shoreline (disco and casino). Just by the *Lydia*, along an esplanade by the sea, the **Allée des Arts** (*signposted*) hosts a small display of contemporary sculpture including the 'Soleillonautes', totem poles sculpted from the trunks of trees from Gabon.

👪 Aquamagic

In Port-Leucate. 🕐*Open mid-Jul–Aug 10am–7pm; mid-Jun–mid-Jul 10am–6pm.* ⊛*€23 (child 5–10, €17) – online discounts.* ☏*04 68 40 99 98. www.aqualand.fr.*
This seaside leisure park (water chutes, swimming pool) is particularly suitable for young children.

The new harbour complex of **Port-Leucate** and **Port-Barcarès** constitutes the largest marina on the French Mediterranean coast.

🐾WALK

Cap Leucate★

🚶 *2h via a footpath running along the cliffs. Start from the Sémaphore du cap, at Leucate-Plage (10km/6mi N of Port-Barcarès along D 627).*
From the look-out point by the signal station on the cape, there is a **view★** from Languedoc to the Albères mountains.

Port-Barcarès

© FOURGEOT/iStockphoto.com

Canet-Plage

This seaside resort named after the nearby Étang de Canet has a busy yacht marina, sports facilities and casino, and lots of activities for kids.

SIGHTS
Beaches
Plage Sardinal is ideal for camping. Shady family-friendly beaches and minigolf, volleyball and sailing schools.

⚏ Aquarium
Boulevard de la Jetée, at the harbour.
♿🕐*Open Jul–Aug 9.30am–8.30pm; Sep–Jun: 10am–noon, 2–6pm.* ∞€6.50 *(child, €5.50).* ☎*04 68 80 49 64.*
Children will enjoy the colourful display of local and tropical species.

Étang de Canet
W of Canet-Plage along D 81 towards St-Cyprien. Accessible by car (parking area), on foot or by bus.
Canet lagoon is a protected natural environment with **300 bird species**. Fishermen's huts cluster around the lagoon's banks and a footpath weaves through the lagoon's flora and fauna.

EXCURSIONS
St-Cyprien
9km/5.6mi S.
This small elegant residential town with palm tree-lined streets has preserved its historic Catalan village.

Collections de St-Cyprien
4 rue Émile-Zola, near the town hall.
🕐*Open Jul–Aug 10am–noon, 3–7pm; Sep–Jun daily except Tue 10am–noon, 2–6pm.* 🕐*Closed 1 Jan, 1 May, 11 Nov, 24–25 and 31 Dec.* ∞€6.50. ☎*04 68 21 06 96. www.collectionsdesaintcyprien.com.*
This museum contains works of local painter **François Desnoyers** (1894–1972), as well as his collection of works by Gleizes, Picasso, Pierre Ambroggiani etc.

St-Cyprien-Plage
The seaside resort has a residential district, harbour and 3km/1.8mi of sandy beaches. Its lively marina is the second-largest in Mediterranean France.

▶ Population: 12 681.
⚙ Michelin Map: 344: J6.
ℹ Info: Pl. de la Méditerranée, 66140 Canet-en-Roussillon. ☎04 68 86 72 00. www.ot-canet.fr.

ADDRESSES

🏠 STAY

⊖🍽 **Hôtel La Lagune** – *66750 St-Cyprien, 9km/6mi S of Canet on D 81A.* ☎*04 68 21 24 24. www.hotel-lalagune.com.* 🅿 *49 rooms.* Two swimming pools and beach makes this hotel between land and sea a pleasure. Rooms are functional.

⊖🍽 **Chambre d'hôte La Vieille Demeure** – *4 r. de Llobet, 66440 Torreilles.* ☎*04 68 28 45 71. www.la-vieille-demeure. com.* 🍴. *5 rooms.* This house located in the heart of the village has lots of character: Andalusian-style patio, orchard of citrus fruits, and elegant rooms.

🍷 EAT

⊖🍽 **Le Don Quichotte** – *22 av. de Catalogne.* ☎*04 68 80 35 17. Closed Tue noon, Wed noon in Jul–Aug, Mon–Tue (except eves in Jul–Aug).* The vibrant dining room serves up classical cuisine.

ACTIVITIES

Getting to the beach – *Tram operates in Jul–Aug from Canet.* ☎*04 68 61 01 13.*

Club nautique Canet-Perpignan – *Zone technique, Le Port.* ☎*04 68 73 33 95. Daily 9am–noon, 2–6pm.* Sailing club.

Aqualand – ⚏ *Av. des Champs de Neptune, Les Capellans 66750 St-Cyprien, south of Les Capellans.* ☎*04 68 21 49 49. Mid-Jun–mid-Sep.* Aquapark.

Club Omnipêche Plaisance – *Quai Rimbaud, 66750 St-Cyprien.* ☎*06 09 54 78 12. Jun–Sep.* Fishing trips and fishing lessons.

Aéro Service Littoral – *Rte de Ste-Marie, 66440 Torreilles.* ☎*04 68 28 13 73. www. ulm66.fr. Daily 8am–12.30pm, 2–7pm.* ULM and motorised hang-gliding courses.

Elne★

Set among apricot and peach orchards by the coast, Elne was named after the Empress Helen, Constantine's mother, and Iberians knew it as 'Illiberis'. At the end of the Roman Empire, it was the true capital of the Roussillon area and is a major stopping point on the road to Spain. The superb cathedral cloisters testify to Elne's former splendour.

- ▶ **Population:** 8 552.
- **Michelin Map:** 344: I7.
- **Info:** Office du tourisme d'Elne, Pl. Sant-Jordi. ℰ04 68 22 05 07. www.elne-tourisme.com.
- **Location:** 14km/8.75mi S of Perpignan on the N114.
- **Don't Miss:** Adam and Eve column in the Cathédrale Ste-Eulalie-et-Ste-Julie.
- **Kids:** Cathedral; Tropique du Papillon.

SIGHTS
Cathédrale Ste-Eulalie-et-Ste-Julie

Building of the cathedral began in the 11C. The ribbed vaulting of the six chapels in the south aisle, built from the 14C to the mid-15C, reflects the three stages in the evolution of Gothic architecture. **Cloisters★★** – *Open mid-Jan–Apr and Oct–Dec 10am–12.30pm, 2–5pm; May–Sept 10am–12.30pm, 2–6.30pm. Closed 1 Jan, 1 May, 25 Dec. €4.50–€8 (depending on sites visited). ℰ04 68 22 70 90.* The south cloisters were built in the 12C; the other three date from the 13C and 14C. The superb **capitals** on the twin columns are decorated with imaginary animals, biblical and evangelical figures, and plants, but the most remarkable work is Capital 12, depicting Adam and Eve, in the Romanesque south gallery.

Cathédrale Ste-Eulalie-et-Ste-Julie
© Isaac Medina Alcázar/iStockphoto.com

Musée d'Archéologie – *Entrance up the staircase at the end of the east cloisters.* The archaeological museum in the old chapel of St-Laurent exhibits 15C to 17C earthenware, Attic ceramics (4C BCE) and sigillated ceramic ware from Illiberis (Elne under Roman rule) and reconstructions of Véraza culture huts of wood and reeds.
Musée d'Histoire – *Entrance via the west cloisters.* The history museum contains archives, literature and town seals, along with statues of the Virgin Mary, the Vierge des Tres Portalets (13C) and the Vierge du Portail de Perpignan (14C).

Musée Terrus

Open same hours and charges as cloisters. Closed 1 Jan, 1 May, 25 Dec. ℰ04 68 22 88 88.
This museum named after Étienne Terrus (1857–1922) displays works by him and other artists whose company he kept, such as Luce, Maillol and G de Monfreid.

Le Tropique du Papillon

Entrance via avenue Paul-Reig, at the intersection with the Argelès-Perpignan road (N 114). Open Apr–Sept 10am–12.30pm, 2.30–6pm (Jul–Aug 10am–7pm). Closed a number of days in May. €8 (child 3–12, €6). ℰ04 68 37 83 77. www.tropique-du-papillon.com.
Night and day, butterflies and moths flutter freely around this tropical hothouse; there is a nursery and an educational area.

Argelès-Plage

Argelès-Plage, with its beautiful sandy beaches, is the camping capital of Europe, with tens of thousands of holidaymakers descending on 60 parks contained within a 5km/3mi radius. Argelès-Plage is the 'Kid Station' resort par excellence with 5km/3mi of supervised golden sand beaches (June to September) and a 2km/1.2mi-long seafront promenade with umbrella pine trees and aloe, mimosa, olive and oleander.

Argelès-sur-Mer
2.5km/1.5mi W along D 618.
In the heart of the old town, the **Casa de les Albères** *(4 Pl des Castellans ◷ open Jun–Sept Tue–Sat 10am–1pm, 2–6pm; rest of year Tue–Fri 10am–noon, 2–5pm, Sat 10am–1pm; ☎04 68 81 42 74)* is a Catalan museum of folk art and traditions such as wine making, manufacturing barrels, espadrilles (rope-soled sandals) and wooden toys.

👫 Château de Valmy
♿◷*Open Mon–Sat 9.30am–12.30pm, 2.30–6pm/7pm. ☎04 68 81 25 70. www.chateau-valmy.com.*
In the grounds of the Château de Valmy are a discovery trail and falconry featuring **eagles**, kites, vultures and other birds of prey. Wine tastings, too.

- **Info:** Pl. de l'Europe, 66700. ☎04 68 81 15 85. www.argeles-sur-mer.com.
- **Location:** 28km/17.5mi S of Perpignan. A bus service operates from Jun–Sep from Argelès-sur-Mer (the town) to the beach.

ADDRESSES

🛏 STAY
Camping Pujol – ☎04 68 81 00 25. *Open Jun-Sep. Reservations required. 249 pitches.* This shady camp site with jacuzzi, health club, evening dances and children's entertainment has pitches on the site of a sailing base.

🍴 EAT
L'Amadeus – *Av. des Platanes.* ☎04 68 81 12 38. *Closed Tue, Wed and Thu in Feb–Mar and Mon except Jul–Aug.* This restaurant has a light and airy dining room, a terrace and patio. Well-cooked regional cuisine.

Collioure★★

This colourful little fortress town on the Côte Vermeille attracts huge crowds of tourists. Its lovely setting amidst the Albères foothills has been immortalised on canvas by painters like Derain, Braque, Othon, Friesz, Matisse, Picasso and Foujita. Its many attractions include a fortified church, royal castle, seaside promenade, brightly coloured Catalan boats, old streets with flower-bedecked balconies, outdoor cafés and inviting boutiques.

- **Population:** 3 096.
- **Michelin Map:** 344: J7.
- **Info:** Collioure Tourism Office, Pl du 18 Juin. ☎04 68 82 15 47. www.collioure.com.
- **Location:** 31km/19.3mi S of Perpignan via the N114 then D114.
- **Don't Miss:** Boramar beach; anchovy tastings; the Old Port; Museum of Modern Art.
- **Kids:** A diving orientation with Centre International de Plongee (CIP).

A BIT OF HISTORY

When Catalan naval forces ruled the Mediterranean as far as the Levant, medieval Collioure was the trading port for Roussillon. In 1463 Louis XI's invading troops marked the beginning of a turbulent period in which the castle was built on the rocky spur separating the port into two coves. After the Peace Treaty of the Pyrenees, the enclosed town was razed to the ground in 1670 and the lower town became the main town.

WALKING TOUR

Walk to the old port or 'Port d'Amont' via quai de l'Amirauté on the banks of the 'Ravin du Douy.'

Chemin du Fauvisme

A marked route through the streets of Collioure passes 20 stages celebrating city views painted by Henri Matisse and André Derain. (*Guided tours available In Jul–Aug; contact the tourist office for details, or l'Espace Fauve ℘04 68 98 07 16*).

Église Notre-Dame-des-Anges

Built between 1684 and 1691 this church's distinctive bell-tower was once the lighthouse for the old port.

Inside are nine ornately carved and gilded **altarpieces★** Including the 1698 high altar work of Catalan artist Joseph Sunyer. An immense three-storey triptych completely hides the apse. The sacristy houses a beautiful Louis XIII vestment cupboard, 15C paintings, a 16C reliquary and 17C Madonna.

Ancien îlot St-Vincent

The former island is connected to the church by two beaches. Behind the little chapel, a panorama takes in the Côte Vermeille and a sea wall leads to the lighthouse.

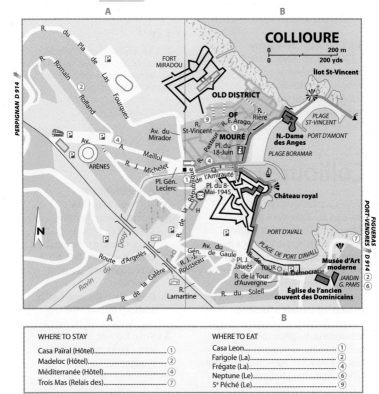

WHERE TO STAY	
Casa Païral (Hôtel)	①
Madeloc (Hôtel)	②
Méditerranée (Hôtel)	④
Trois Mas (Relais des)	⑦

WHERE TO EAT	
Casa Leon	①
Farigole (La)	②
Frégate (La)	④
Neptune (Le)	⑥
5e Péché (Le)	⑨

Old district of Mouré

Enjoy pleasant strolls through the steep flower-filled back streets of this old district near the church.

▶ Cross the Douy, at the end of the marina.

Château Royal

🕐 *Open 9am–5pm (Jul–Aug 10am–7pm).* 🕐 *Closed 1 Jan, 1 May, 15–16 Aug, 25 Dec.* ☎*04 68 82 06 43. www.ledepartement66.fr.*
This imposing castle built on a Roman site juts into the sea between the Port d'Amont and the Port d'Avall. It was the summer residence of Majorcan kings from 1276 to 1344 until it was taken over by the kings of Aragón. Tour the underground passages and main courtyard, parade ground, 16C prison, 13C chapel, Queen's bedchamber and upper rooms and ramparts. The 17C barracks house exhibitions on grape vines, cork, Sorède whips, *espadrilles* (rope-soled sandals) and Catalan boats.

▶ Continue to the Port d'Avall beach called the 'Faubourg'

Église de l'ancien couvent des Dominicains

This old church now houses the local wine co-operative.

Musée d'Art moderne

🕐 *Open Jun–Sep 10am–noon, 2–6pm; Oct–May daily except Tue 10am–noon, 2–6pm.* 🕐 *Closed 1 Jan, 1 May, 1 Nov and 25 Dec.* ☎*04 68 82 10 19.*
The artistic success of Collioure is well deserved, and it is down to one man, Jean Peské (1870–1949), who was the inspiration and driving force. Collections are housed in the villa Pams at the foot of a terraced garden abundant in olive trees. The collection, enriched by regular donations, is regular put on display in exhibitions.

ADDRESSES

🛌 STAY

🛏️ **Casa Païral** – *Imp. des Palmiers.* ☎*04 68 82 05 81. www.hotel-casa-pairal. com.* 🅿️. *27 rooms.* A noble old house within a beautiful Mediterranean garden. The rooms have lots of personality.

🛏️ **Hôtel Méditerranée** – *Av. Aristide-Maillol.* ☎*04 68 82 08 60. www. mediterranee-hotel.com. 23 rooms.* Retro building; rooms with balconies. Garden; solarium.

🛏️ **Hôtel Madeloc** – *R. Romain-Rolland.* ☎*04 68 82 07 56. www.madeloc. com.* 🅿️. *27 rooms.* Rooms furnished in rattan; some with terraces. Garden.

🛏️ **Relais des Trois Mas** – *Rte Port-Vendres.* ☎*04 68 82 05 07. www. relaisdestroismas.com.* 🅿️. *23 rooms.* Lovely rooms; garden, pool, jacuzzi.

🍴 EAT

🍴 **La Frégate** – *24 quai Camille-Pelletan.* ☎*04 68 82 06 05. www.fregate-collioure.com.* Coastal cuisine, of course; some rooms.

🍴 **La Farigole and Hotel l'Arapède** – *Rte de Port-Vendres.* ☎*04 68 98 09 59.* 🅿️ *www.arapede.com.* Decorated with aerial photos of Collioure; terrace, regional cuisine.

🍴 **Neptune** – *Rte de Port-Vendres. Closed Mon in Jul and Wed Oct–Jun.* ☎*04 68 82 02 27.* Seafood dishes, and regional specialties; unhindered view of the Old Port from the terraces.

🍴 **Le 5e Péché** – *18 r. de la Fraternité.* ☎*04 68 98 09 76. Closed Mon–Tue (except Jul–Aug).* Strictly for gourmands who appreciate this mix of Japanese and Catalan cuisine.

🍴 **Casa Leon** – *2 r. Rière - 66190 Collioure.* ☎*04 68 82 10 74.* Popular with Colliourencs, this little restaurant offers excellent seafood. You'll appreciate the grilled tuna or the fried prawns, and everything is incomparably fresh.

ACTIVITIES

CIP – *15 r. de la Tour d'Auvergne, 66190 Collioure.* ☎*04 68 82 07 16. www.cip-collioure.com. Children must be over 8 years old to partake.* This diving centre in the heart of the village offers diving and snorkelling excursions and courses of different levels.

Banyuls-sur-Mer

Set on a promontory, Banyuls is France's most southerly seaside resort, known for its lovely bay, yacht harbour, vineyards and sea-water therapy centre. Sheltered from the *tramontane*'s harsh north-westerly gusts, tropical flora like carob, eucalyptus and palms thrive along this Mediterranean coast all the way to the Riviera.

THE RESORT

The main beach is sheltered by a cove and two islands, Île Petite and Île Grosse. The Côte Vermeille's coastal waters are deep, clear and teeming with fish.

♟♟ Aquarium du Lab. Arago

www.obs-banyuls.fr.
This **Aquarium** displays Mediterranean fauna in a recreated environment.

Écrin bleu: Underwater Trail

Part of the Banyuls-Cerbère Marine Nature Reserve. ◐*Open Jul–Aug noon–6pm. Equipment rental from noon to 5pm. Meeting point on the Peyrefite beach and information area on the yachting harbour.* ⊗*No charge.* ☎*04 68 88 56 87.*
Observe red mullets, bass, rainbow wrasse, and on a lucky day, dolphins, loggerhead turtles and spotted sea

▶ **Population:** 4 749.
▯ **Info:** Av. de la République, 66650 Banyuls-sur-Mer. ☎04 68 88 31 58. www.banyuls-sur-mer.com.
▶ **Location:** 38km/23.75mi S of Perpignan on the N 114.
◉ **Don't Miss:** The view from Cap Réderis.

horses. This 250m supervised underwater trail has five observation stations (at depths up to 5m) marked by buoys. Underwater information plaques guide you along.

Réserve Marine Naturelle de Banyuls-Cerbère

Created in 1974 to protect marine species endangered by intensive fishing, tourism activities and waste water pollution this conservation area covers 650ha and 6.5km/4mi of rocky Languedoc-Roussillon coastline.

EXCURSION
Métairie Maillol★

5km/3mi SW. ◐*Open May–Sep 10am–noon, 3–6pm; Oct–Apr 10am–noon, 2–5pm.* ◐*Closed public holidays.* ⊗€5. ☎*04 68 88 57 11.*
Aristide Maillol (1861–1944) was born in Banyuls. At 20 he 'went up' to Paris to learn painting and became interested in pottery and tapestry. After the age of 40

Seafront, Banyuls-sur-Mer, the hills with vineyards in the background

© Tree4Two/iStockphoto.com

he gained renown for his sculptures of nude figures, remarkable for their grace and power. Maillol enjoyed his little country retreat, which now as the Musée Maillol, displays many of his sculptures, terracotta, paintings and drawings.

Banyuls wine

The famous **Banyuls wine** complements the best of tables, served as an apéritif, with dessert, or foie gras and strongly flavoured cheeses and game. Several cellars (**caves**) welcome the public, including two on the vertiginous Route des Crêtes. At the **Grande Cave** (*www.banyuls.com*) see a video on the history of Banyuls and enjoy a guided tour of the oak barrel storage rooms, wines maturing in the sun and cellars containing antique casks.

The **Cellier des Templiers-cave du Mas Reig** (&⊙—*open Apr–early Nov daily 10am–7.30pm; rest of year 10am–1pm, 2.30–6.30pm;* ⊙*closed 1 Jan, 25 Dec;* ✆*04 68 98 36 70*) dates from the days of the (13C) Knights Templar, whose feudal castle and sub-commandery (Mas Reig) are next door.

Côte Vermeille ★★

The resorts along this rocky stretch of coast, tucked into little bays, were once small maritime fortresses. The 'vermilion' coast is named after the local landscape, whose colour is enhanced by the clear light of this region. Explore the Côte Vermeille via the Route des crêtes (N 114) mountain road, and Route du littoral, the coast road, via Collioure and Port-Vendres (heavy summer traffic).

& **Michelin Map:** 344: J7– K8.

🛈 **Info:** Office du Tourisme de Collioure, Pl du 18 Juin. ✆04 68 82 15 47. www.collioure.com.

▶ **Location:** 30km/18.75mi SW of Perpignan by D 914. Argelès Plage is the gateway to the Vermeille Coast.

☺ **Don't Miss:** The picturesque port of Collioure and the Spanish ambience of Cerbère.

👪 **Kids:** Swimming off the beaches along the coast!

☎ DRIVING TOURS

THE MOUNTAIN ROAD

37km/23mi from Argelès-Plage to Cerbère. About 2h30.

Argelès-Plage

&*See ARGELÈS-PLAGE.*

Beyond Argelès and the stretch of beach to the north, the coast becomes much more dramatic as the (D 114) climbs into the Albères foothills and cuts across rocky headlands lapped by the Mediterranean.

▶ At the roundabout just before Collioure, take D 86 left. The road heads uphill, through the Collioure vineyards. Turn left again at the first intersection, onto a downhill road.

Notre-Dame-de-Consolation

This hermitage is well known throughout Roussillon. Its chapel contains votive offerings from sailors.

▶ Turn back to D 86 and turn left. (☺*Note: this stretch of mountain road has no safety barriers or other protection.*)

Cork-oaks appear between patches of exposed black rock schist.

▶ Follow the signs for the 'Circuit du vignoble' wine route through the vineyards towards Banyuls.

This spectacular road leads to a viewing table and ruins of an 1885 barracks.

▶ Take the steep, narrow track to the right leading up to Tour Madeloc. (⊘ *Note: extreme caution required: gradient of 1:4, with tight hairpin bends and no space for passing.*)

The road passes two more fortified constructions before reaching a small level plateau.

Tour Madeloc

Alt 652m. 15min on foot round-trip.
This old round signal tower was part of a network of lookout posts during the reign of the kings of Aragón and Mallorca. Tour de la Massane surveyed the Roussillon plain and Tour Madeloc kept watch out to sea. Enjoy a splendid **panorama★★** of the Albères mountains, the Vermeille and Roussillon coasts. The track back down to D 86 gives breathtaking **views★** of the sea and Banyuls.

▶ Turn right onto D 86.

The road leads to Banyuls, passing the Mas Reig underground wine cellar situated in the oldest vineyard in the Banyuls area, as well as the modern cellar in which wines from the Cave des Templiers are aged.

Banyuls-sur-Mer
Ġ*See BANYULS-SUR-MER.*

Cap Réderis★★
Where the road edges the cliff, you'll have a magnificent **panorama** of the Languedoc and Catalonia coasts as far south as the Cabo de Creus. Farther along you'll see the bay of Banyuls, spectacular at high tide.

Cerbère
This charming seaside resort is the last French town before Spain and the Costa Brava. Set in a little cove with a pebble beach, it has white houses, outdoor cafés and narrow pedestrian streets.

THE COAST ROAD
33km/21mi from Cerbère to Argelès-Plage – about 2h.
Beyond Cerbère, the road winds through vineyards overlooking a vast seascape.

Cap Réderis★★ Ġ*See above.*

Cap Réderis

©Franck Guiziou/Hemis/Photoshot

Site de Paulilles★
Opened in 2008 this is a free ecological recreational park which was once the site of a dynamite factory. The coast itself is protected, as it cultivates a rare breed of seagrass. Visitors enjoy diving, bike riding and hiking here.

Banyuls-sur-Mer
See BANYULS-SUR-MER.
Leaving Banyuls, the road passes a seaside spa for heliotherapy. Before Port-Vendres is an excellent view of the port.

▶ Turn right towards Cap Béar then, after the Hôtel des Tamarins, cross the railway line and drive to the S of the bay.

Cap Béar
From the lighthouse on the headland, you can see down the coast from Cap Leucate to Cabo de Creus.

Port-Vendres (Port of Venus)
This town developed as a naval port and became a major port for trade.

Collioure★★ *See COLLIOURE.*
The road leaves the foothills of the Albères before reaching Argelès.

ADDRESSES

STAY AND ¶/EAT

Hôtel les Elmes – *Plage des Elmes.* ℘*04 68 88 03 12. www.hotel-des-elmes.com. 31 rooms. Restaurant* . Welcoming hotel on the beach.

Al Fanal and El Llagut – *18 av. du Fontaulé.* ℘*04 68 88 00 81.* Catalan cuisine centred on seafood. Rooms also available.

Ferme-auberge Les Clos de Paulilles – *66660 Port-Vendres, 3km/2mi N of Banyuls on D 114.* ℘*04 68 98 07 58.* Terrace restaurant serving country cooking.

Le Boulou

This spa resort at the foot of the Albères mountains makes an ideal base for exploring the Roussillon. On the fringe of an exotic cork-oak wood, Le Boulou has two cork-making factories.

VISIT
The town's medieval past is reflected in remnants of its 14C curtain wall and early 15C chapel of St-Antoine.

Église Notre-Dame d'El Voló
Of the original 12C Romanesque church, the white-marble **portal** by the Master of Cabestany has survived.

🚗 DRIVING TOURS

MONTS ALBÈRES
49km/30mi round tour. Half a day.
The Albères mountain range is the last outcrop of crystalline rocks on the eastern flank of the Pyrenees. Its highest

▶ **Population:** 5 626.
Michelin Map: 344: I7.
Info: 1 r. du Château, 66162 Le Boulou. ℘04 68 87 50 95. www.ot-leboulou.fr. Guided tours *(1h30)* leave at 3pm on Thu from the tourist office.
▶ **Location:** 27km/17mi S of Perpignan by D 900.
Don't Miss: Céret Museum of Modern Art, the panorama from Fort de Bellegarde and Pic des Trois Termes.

peak, Pic Neulos, towers 1 256m above sea level.

▶ Leave Le Boulou W on D 115.

Céret★ *See CÉRET.*

▶ Leave Céret heading SW on D 13F towards Fontfrède.

This road climbs through chestnut groves, offering many pretty views. Turn right off the Las Illas road at the Col de la Brousse into a very winding road to the **Col de Fontfrède** (June 1940–June 1944).

▶ Return to the Col de la Brousse and turn right towards Las Illas.

The road winds through dense vegetation, terraced gardens and scattered farmhouses. The Case Nove mas (farmhouse) and the Mas Liansou are traditional Albères dwellings. After Las Illas, the road follows the river, clinging to the rock face and affording excellent views of the river gorge.

Maureillas-las-Illas

In this holiday village amidst cork-oak groves and orchards, cork-cutters have created a cork museum, **Musée du Liège** (✿open Jul–Aug 10am–noon, 2.30–6.30pm; Sep–Nov and Feb–Jun daily except Tue 2–5pm; ✿closed 1 Jan, 1 May, 1 Nov, 25–26 Dec; ✿€3.50; ☎04 68 83 15 41). Learn about cork and see astonishing cork sculptures and magnificent oak casks showcasing local handicrafts.

Chapelle St-Martin-de-Fenollar

This modest 9C chapel founded by Benedictines from Arles-sur-Tech contains interesting 12C **mural paintings★**.

▶ D 9 leads back to Le Boulou.

THE ROME VALLEY

53km/33mi from Le Boulou to Pic des Trois Termes – allow half a day.

Panissars, Fort de Bellegarde in the background

© Rtsubin/iStockphoto.com

From Boulou guided tours of the Rome valley are organised by the **Association pour le patrimoine de la vallée de la Rome** *(Information and reservations: Le Boulou tourist office.* ☎04 68 87 50 95).

The **Vallée de la Rome** is an essential communication route between France and Spain, traversed for two millennia since the Via Domitia's construction in c.120 BCE. Leave the 'Catalane' motorway to discover awesome megalithic, Gallo-Roman and medieval sites in a superb landscape.

▶ Leave Le Boulou on D 900, S towards Le Perthus, until you reach Chapelle St-Martin-de-Fenollar (✿see left). Go back to D 900.

Les Cluses

These hamlets on either side of the gorge between the Via Domitia and the Rome valley contain 3C–4C Roman remains: the **Château des Maures** or 'Castell d els Moros' and **Fort de la Cluse Haute**. Next to the fort, the **church of St-Nazaire** is a pre-Romanesque construction with three naves and traces of frescoes attributed to the Master of Fenollar.

Le Perthus

Since prehistory, Le Perthus has seen the comings and goings of nomadic hordes, armies, refugees and tourists. The hamlet became a town in the late 19C.

▶ From the centre of Le Perthus, turn left towards the Fort de Bellegarde.

Fort de Bellegarde

✿*Open mid-Jun–mid-Sept 10.30am–6.30pm.* *Guided tours Mon, Fri–Sun 2.30pm and 4pm; Tue–Thu 2.30pm.* ☎04 68 54 27 53. www.le-perthus.com.

This fortress overlooking Le Perthus was rebuilt by Saint Hilaire, and then by Vauban between 1679 and 1688. The terrace offers a **panorama★★** of the Canigou and Fontfrède peaks, the Rome valley, Le Perthus, the Panissars site and in Spain, the Rio Llobregat valley.

Panissars

During the Roman occupation, the Panissars Pass was the main Pyrenees route. In 1984, foundations of a huge Roman monument were discovered and thought to be the remains of the Trophy of Pompey.

▶ Turn back and, N of Le Perthus, turn right onto D 71 to the Col de l'Ouillat.

This road passes by groves of chestnut trees and the magnificent oaks of St-Martin-de-l'Albères, with views of the Canigou and the southern Albères slopes and St-Christophe summit.
From a right-hand bend catch a view of Trois Termes Peak.

Col de l'Ouillat★

A cool stopping place with a viewing terrace on the edge of the Laroque-des-Albères forest. The road winds through beeches and pines to the rocky outcrop of Trois Termes.

Pic des Trois Termes★★

Enjoy a **panorama** of the Albères mountains, Roussillon plain and coastal lagoons, the Confluent and Vallespir valleys, and the Spanish Costa Brava.

▶ Turn back.

The unsurfaced road between the Pic des Trois Termes and Sorède is accessible only by four-wheel-drive.

AT THE FOOT OF MONTS ALBÈRES

32km/20mi. Allow 3h.

▶ Tour begins from Saint-Génis-des-Fontaines 10km/6mi E of Le Boulou. Drive W of Argelès-Plage along D 2 to Sorède.

Saint-Génis-des-Fontaines

Open Jul–Aug 9.30am–12.30pm, 3–7pm; Apr–Jun and Sept 9.30am–12.30pm, 3–7pm; rest of year 9.30am–noon, 2–5pm. Closed 1 Jan, 25 Dec. www.saint-genis-des-fontaines.fr.

The decorations in the parish church and cloisters, namely the white-marble sculpted lintel from 1020, show the importance of this former Benedictine abbey.

▶ Continue E along D 618.

Saint-André

Leave the car in the shaded square to the right of the village high street. Reach the church by walking through an archway.
This 12C church's exterior has pre-Romanesque fishbone features, a marble lintel and foiled altar table.
Wind up your visit at the **Maison transfrontalière d'art roman** (*open mid-Jun–mid-Sep daily except Mon 10am–noon, 2.30–7pm; Apr–mid-Jun and mid-Sep–Oct daily except Sun and Mon 10am–noon, 3–6pm; closed Nov–Mar; €2; 04 68 89 04 85; www.saint-andre66.fr*).

Sorède

This village is a centre for the breeding and study of tortoises.
Vallée des tortues – This 2ha park (*open Apr–mid-May 10am–6pm; mid-May–mid-Aug 9am–8pm; mid-Aug–Sept 10am–6pm; Oct 11am–4.30pm. €12 (child 3–10, €8). 04 68 95 50 50. www.lavalleedestortues.com*) houses some 25 species of land and international water tortoises.

▶ Return to Sorède and continue left along D 2 to Laroque-des-Albères, then follow D 11 to Villelongue-dels-Monts. In the village, take Cami del Vilar to the priory 2km/1.2mi away.

Prieuré Santa Maria del Vilar★

Open Apr–Oct 3–6pm (Jul–Aug 6.30pm); Nov–Mar 2.30–5.30pm. €4. 04 68 89 64 61. www.prieureduvilar.free.fr.
The 11C priory is shaded by olive trees, holm oaks and cypresses.

▶ Return to Villelongue-dels-Monts, turn left onto D 61A then right onto D 618 to Génis-des-Fontaines.

There is about the long valley north of Canigou a certain mellow softness, like the downy skin on the peaches and apricots that grow here in abundance. The whole setting is relaxed, gentle, pleasing. The local economy is founded these days on tourism, and much of this is geared towards exploring the mountains, which provide dazzling walking potential at all standards as well as plentiful opportunity for those who enjoy messing about in snow. The absence of heavy industry makes this the most attractive of places, set against a stupendous backdrop of high mountains. The old province of Roussillon is an historical and cultural region, comprising what is now the southern French department of Pyrénées-Orientales lying between the eastern extremities of the mountains and the Mediterranean coastal lowlands.

Highlights

1 The annual **Pablo Casals Music Festival** (p293)

2 Spend a relaxing morning and lunch in **Villefranche-de-Conflent** (p294)

3 Visit **Prades** on market day for a colourful experience (p296)

4 Take a relaxing stroll around **Vernet-les-Bains** (p296)

5 Spend time in **Andorra** (p308)

Pablo Casals

Prades was chosen by the world-renowned cellist Pablo Casals (1876–1973) as his exiled home, one that while not in his homeland of Spain nevertheless remained in his beloved Catalonia. He is generally regarded as the pre-eminent cellist of the first half of the 20C, and one of the greatest cellists of all time. He made many recordings throughout his career, of solo, chamber, and orchestral music, also as conductor. Not surprisingly, many of the surrounding villages and their fine buildings are ambraced in an annual Pablo Casals Festival from mid July to mid August, which the maestro founded in 1950. The main venue is the Abbaye Saint Michel-de-Cuxa (&see *ABBAYE SAINT MICHEL-DE-CUXA*).

Andorra

Set his among the eastern Pyrenees, the principality of Andorra, is no mere tax-free shopping haven. This tiny Catalan-speaking nation is also a wild, scenic land of lofty plateaux and precipitous valleys.

Abbaye Saint-Michel-de-Cuxa

© eyemagic/Zoonar GmbH RM/age fotostock

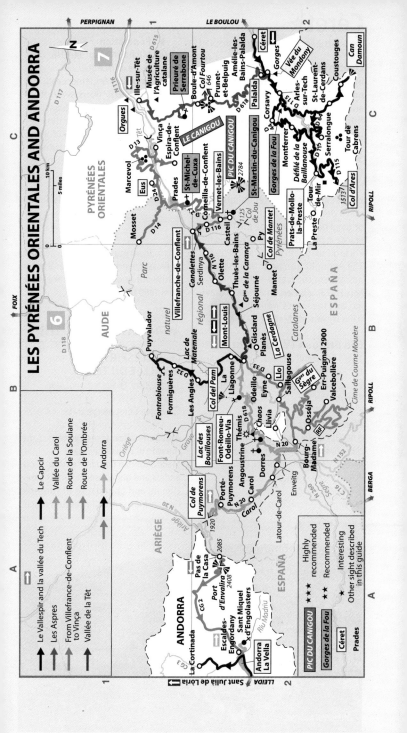

LES PYRÉNÉES ORIENTALES AND ANDORRA

Le Vallespir and la vallée du Tech

Les Aspres

From Villefranche-de-Conflent to Vinça

Vallée de la Têt

Le Capcir

Vallée du Carol

Route de la Soulane

Route de l'Ombrée

Andorra

★★★ Highly recommended

★★ Recommended

★ Interesting

Other sight described in this guide

PIC DU CANIGOU

Gorges de la Fou

Céret

Prades

PYRÉNÉES ORIENTALES

PERPIGNAN

LE BOULOU

FOIX

ANDORRA

ESPAÑA

Parc naturel régional

287

Céret★

Amélie-les-Bains and around

Céret in the Vallespir region is the lively hub of Catalan tradition in the northern Pyrenees, with bullfights and *sardana* dancing. This major fruit-growing area is becoming a popular arts and crafts centre.

SIGHTS
Old Céret

Majestic plane trees shade strollers between place de la République and place de la Liberté. Remnants of the original ramparts include the Porte de France in place de la République and the Porte d'Espagne in place Pablo-Picasso. The wrought iron and stainless steel monument to Picasso – *Sardane de la Paix* (1973) is based on a Picasso drawing, and the town's World War I Memorial is by Aristide Maillol.

Old Bridge★ (Vieux pont)

The 14C 'Devil's Leap' bridge spans the Tech in a single arch. Enjoy lovely views of the Canigou massif and the Albères range.

Musée d'Art Moderne★★

8 bd Mar. Joffre. ♿⟳*Open Jul–Sept daily 10am–7pm; rest of the year daily except Mon 10am–5.30pm.* ⟳*Closed 1 Jan, 1 May, 1 Nov, 25 Dec.* ⊜€8. ℘*04 68 87 27 76.* *www.musee-ceret.com.*

▶ **Population:** 7 885.
♿ **Michelin Map:** 344: H8
  ♿*see also Le BOULOU.*
🛈 **Info:** 1 av G-Clemenceau.
  ℘04 68 87 00 53. www.ot-ceret.fr. Amélie-les-Bains Tourism Office, 22 av de Vallespir. ℘04 68 39 01 98. www.amelie-les-bains.com.
🅿 **Location:** 33km/20.65mi SW of Perpignan.
👁 **Don't Miss:** La Féria and Folklore Festival in July.

This modern museum features ceramics by Picasso, works from the Céret period (1909–50) and contemporary works from 1960 to 1970.

🚗 DRIVING TOUR

LE VALLESPIR AND la VALLéE DU TECH★

130km/81mi. ♿*See regional map.*

🅿 Leave Céret on the D115.

Amélie-les-Bains is a town named after the wife of Louis-Philippe. Mediterranean flora like mimosas, oleanders and palm trees reflect the mild climate and abundance of sunshine. Queen Marie-Amélie made France's

Medieval town of Palalda

© T. Grun/age fotostock

southernmost spa fashionable in the 19C.

From here it is possible to make a cool and pleasant walk around the **Gorges and vallée du Mondony** (🚶30min round-trip on foot).

▶ 6km/3.5mi on D 115 to Mas Pagris.

The road to Montalba climbs the rocky spur of Fort-les-Bains and skirts the clifftops overlooking the **Vallée du Mondony★** gorge. It then crosses a series of stepped terraces.

▶ 3km/2mi on the D 618.

The medieval town of **Palalda★** is a fine Catalan village. The **Palalda Museum** (🕐 open May–Sep daily except Sun 10am–noon, 2–6.30pm, Mon, Sat and public holidays 2–6.30pm; mid-Feb–Apr and Oct–mid-Dec daily except Sun 10am–noon, 2–5.30pm, Mon, Sat and public holidays 2.30–5.30pm; ⬤€3.50; ℘04 68 39 34 90) is divided into two sections: **Museum of Folk Arts and Traditions** – antique tools and a reconstruction of an early 20C kitchen, wherein local dishes like cargolade (grilled snails with aïoli – garlic mayonnaise) were enjoyed. **Roussillon Postal Museum** – This reconstruction of a late 19C post office presents the history of the local postal service and the Roussillon lighthouse system.

Go back to Amélie and follow the D 115 to **Arles-sur-Tech**, a place dealing with traditional Catalan fabrics, originally built around an abbey, c.900.

Stay on the D 115 as you leave Arles for the **Gorges de la Fou★★**; a walk here is something you won't forget!

Continue on the D 115 for 3km/2mi, then turn left on the D 3, and after 10km/6mi reach **St-Laurent-de-Cerdans**, the most populous town of the southern part of Vallespir (small **museum**).

Only 4km/2.5mi further on, **Coustouges** is a small mountain village occupying the site of a Roman guard. **Can Damoun★** is a panoramic site above the valleys.

Turn round and drive to La Forge-del-Mitg, and left onto the D 64, then head for **Serralongue**, where there is a Romanesque **church** and medieval **museum**.

Turn round again and take the D 64, and then the D 115 towards Le Tech. The **Défilé de la Baillanouse** is renowned for a huge landslide in 1940 that completely blocked the road to a depth of 40m. In the climb to the **Col d'Ares**, on the frontier with Spain, you pass **Prats-de-Mollo★** (⬤see PRATS-DE-MOLLO) the **Tour de Mir**, one of the highest signal towers in Roussillon.

Go back to Le Tech, and turn left onto the D 44, passing through **Montferrer** (chateau ruins).

ADDRESSES

🛏 STAY

🍽 **Ensoleillade La Rive** – R. J. Coste. ℘04 68 39 06 20. 🅿. 14 rooms. Simple family hospitality by the Tech river.

🍽🍽 **Le Rousillon** – Av. Beau-Soleil. ℘04 68 39 34 39. 🅿. 30 rooms. Restaurant 🍽🍽. Situated on the way into town; bright and spacious rooms.

🍴 EAT AND DRINK

🍽🍽 **Carré d'As** – Q4 av. du Dr Bouix. ℘04 68 39 20 00. Closed Mon–Tue except public holidays. Local specialities in the restaurant and pasta and pizzas in the brasserie.

La Rosquilla Fondante Séguéla (Pâtisserie Pérez-Aubert) – 12 r. des Thermes. ℘04 68 39 00 16. In 1810 pastry cook Robert Séguéla created the rousquille, a lemon-flavoured iced biscuit, here.

Bar le Chateau – Rte d'Arles-sur-Tech. ℘04 68 39 31 71. Thu and Sat 9pm–1am, Sun 3–7pm. Closed Oct–May. Charming nightspot where dancers show off traditional tangos and waltzes.

SHOPPING

Fruit and vegetable market – Pl. de la République. Daily 7am–noon.

Les Caves du Roussillon – 10 r. des Thermes. ℘04 68 39 00 29. Open daily 9am–12.30pm, 4–7.30pm. Tastings of local vintages, plus more than 300 Roussillon wines.

Prats-de-Mollo-la-Preste★

Prats-de-Mollo lies in the broad upper Tech valley overlooked by the close-cropped slopes of the Costabonne massif and Mont Canigou. It combines the character of a walled fortress town designed by Vauban with the charm of a lively Catalan mountain town.
A picturesque Fête de l'Ours (Bear festival) takes place in February.

▶ **Population:** 1 099.
Michelin Map: 344: F-8.
Info: Pl. du Foiral, 66230 Prats-de-Mollo-la-Preste. 𝒫04 68 39 70 83. www.pratsdemollo lapreste.com.
Location: 63km/39.5m SW of Perpignan by the A9 then the D115.
Timing: Allow 2 hours for the town.
Kids: Fort Lagarde.

WALKING TOUR

Enter the town through Porte de France and follow the shopping street of the same name.

Opposite place d'Armes, climb the steps up rue de la Croix-de-Mission, overlooked by a Cross and Instruments of the Passion.

Église

A Romanesque church, of which only the crenellated belltower remains, predated the present building which has a Gothic structure, despite dating from the 17C.

▶ Follow the south side of the church and take a fortified rampart walk round the chevet. Leave the precinct and walk uphill for about 100m towards Fort Lagarde. Turn round for a good view of the roof and upper sections of the church.

Fort Lagarde

Open Jul–Aug 10.30am–1pm, 2–6.30pm; Apr–Jun and Sept–Oct daily except Mon 2–5.30pm. €3.50 (children under 12, no charge). 𝒫04 68 39 70 83.
The fortress was built in 1692 on a rocky spur overlooking the town, and at the centre of the site there are now the remains of the old castle.

▶ Take the steps up the side of the curtain wall to get to the fort.

▶ Return to the church and take the street to the right.

In sight of the **almshouse**, go down the steps on the left and follow the street as it runs along below the almshouse gardens.

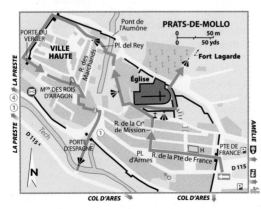

WHERE TO STAY

Bellevue (Hôtel)............ ①

Val du Tech (Hôtel Le)................... ④

WHERE TO EAT

Ribes................................. ①

◖ Cross the torrent over the fortified bridge, just downstream of the old humpback bridge of La Guilhème, to get to the upper town.

Ville haute (Ville d'Amoun)★

Place del Rey, where an old house once belonging to the military engineers stands, used to be the site of one of the residences of the counts of Besalù, who, in the 12C, reigned over one of the pieces of land that formed part of the patchwork of Catalan territory.

Where rue des Marchands leads off to the left, take a carved stairway up to the right.

◖ Continue along the curtain wall. Leave the town through a modern gateway, and return to it through the next one round (a gatehouse), the 'Porte du Verger'.

The street leads to a crossroads, overlooked by a house in the shape of a ship's prow; some people think this was once a palace of the kings of Aragón, and others think that it once housed the trade union of the weavers' guild. An alleyway leads downhill to the exit from the upper town. Go through Porte d'Espagne onto the footbridge over the Tech, from where there is a good view of the south side of the town.

EXCURSION
La Preste

8km/5mi NW from Prats-de-Mollo along D 115A.
This spa town has five springs (temperature 44°C) recommended for the cure of infections of the colon.
Napoléon III had this road up to the spa built. He had intended to follow a course of hydrotherapy at the spa, but the war of 1870 intervened, and he was forced to abandon the idea.

ADDRESSES

STAY

◖◖ **Hotel Bellevue** – *Pl. du Forail. ℘04 68 39 72 48. www.hotel-le-bellevue.fr.*

Prats-de-Mollo-la-Preste

©Claudio Giovanni Colombo/iStockphoto

Closed Tue and Wed from 30 Oct–30 Mar. 17 rooms. Restaurant◖◖. Spa guests and tourists alike are attentively looked after in this guesthouse whose owner cooks the Catalan dishes served in the restaurant. Fresh, well-kept rooms with wood furniture. Terrace and small garden.

◖◖ **Hôtel Le Val du Tech** – *La Preste, 66230 Prats-de-Mollo-La-Preste. ℘04 68 39 71 12. www.hotel-levaldutech.com. 25 rooms.* This hotel–restaurant clings to the hillside a short distance from the thermal baths. Walkers will enjoy the rustic dining room, and the delicious traditional dishes. The rooms look out over the valley.

♈ EAT

◖◖ **Ribes** – *La Preste, 66230 Prats-de-Mollo-La-Preste. ℘04 68 39 71 04. www.hotel-ribes.com.* Secluded in the middle of meadows, with a relaxing and beautiful view of the Pyrenees and the valley of the Tech, this lovely restaurant has a convivial family atmosphere, and generous regional dishes at the table. This place exudes authenticity, and the rooms are clean and well equipped.

ACTIVITIES

Guided tours of the fort *(mid-Jul–mid-Aug daily except Sat show at 3pm; ℘04 68 39 70 83)* with a military theme: costumed horsemen give demonstrations of 18C French military training.

Prieuré de
Serrabone★★

The steep, winding road up to Serrabone in the rather bleak part of Roussillon known as Les Aspres, does not at any stage give so much as a glimpse of the splendid Romanesque priory which lies at the end of it.

▶ **Location:** 41km/25.5mi W of Perpigan by the N116. After Ille-sur-Têt, turn left on the D618.

◉ **Don't Miss:** The pink marble tribune in the church.

◷ **Timing:** Allow 45 minutes.

VISIT

Entrance to the church is through the south gallery. ◷*Open 10am–6pm.* ◷*Closed 1 Jan, 1 May, 1 Nov, 25 Dec.* ⊙*€4.* ✆*04 68 84 09 30.* *www.ledepartement66.fr.*

The exterior of the priory has an impressive, if somewhat forbidding, appearance with its rugged architectural style and dark schist stonework. The priory was founded in 1082, on the site of a pre-existing that church was enlarged and reconsecrated in 1151. Once a prosperous and flourishing priory, it saw the first signs of decline towards the end of the 13C.

South gallery★ – *12C.* Overlooking the ravine, the gallery was used as a covered walkway by Augustinian canons. It is imbued with serenity and harmony, and decorated with capitals reflecting oriental themes, typical of the romantic sculptors of Roussillon.

Church – The nave dates from the 11C; the chancel, transept and the north side aisle are 12C. The church contains a pink-marble **tribune★★** with impressively rich ornamentation.

The most remarkable feature is the delicate ornamentation of three archivolts – an ornamental moulding or band following the curve of the underside of an arch.

ADDRESSES

SHOPPING

Relais de Serrabone – *66130 Boule-d'Amont.* ✆*04 68 84 26 24. At the foot of the road which leads to the priory. Jul–Aug, daily 11am–7pm; Apr–Jun and Sep–Oct, daily exc Tue.* Run by local producers, this shop presents a mouthwatering selection of honeys, aromatic herbs, charcuterie, preserved ducks and other tasty treats.

Ille-sur-Têt

This little town in the Roussillon plain between the Têt and the Boulès is an important fruit and vegetable market.

SIGHTS
Hospici d'Illa

◷*Open Feb–May and Oct–Nov daily except Wed, Sat–Sun and public holidays 2–6pm; Jun and Sept daily except Wed 10am–noon, 2–6pm; Jul–Aug daily 10am–1pm, 2–6pm.* ⊙*€4.* ◷*Closed Dec–Jan and mornings of Sat–Sun Jun–Sept.* ✆*04 68 84 83 96.* The former Hospice St-Jacques (16C and

ℹ **Info:** Place Henri Demay, 66130 Ille-sur-Têt. ✆04 68 84 02 62 www.ille-sur-tet.com.

▶ **Location:** On the N116, 26km/16.25mi W of Perpignan and 21km/13mi E of Prades.

◉ **Don't Miss:** The Hospici d'Illa sculptures and fairy landscapes of Orgues d'Ille.

18C) houses Romanesque and Baroque paintings, sculpture and gold and silver plate, and runs cooking workshops.

🚶 Les Orgues d'Ille-sur-Têt★
North of Ille-sur-Têt; 15min on foot.
🕐*Open dates and times vary; call for details;* 👜€5. 📞*04 68 84 13 13. www.ille-sur-tet.com.*
Earth pillars known as the 'Organ Pipes'. Towards Montalba, look for deep ochre formations to the left of the road.

🚗DRIVING TOUR

LES ASPRES★
56km/35mi from Ille-sur-Têt to Amélie-les-Bains. Allow 3h.

In this rugged sparsely inhabited region, the beautiful Mediterranean landscape is covered by olive groves and cork oaks.

▷ Leave Ille-sur-Têt S on D 2, then turn right onto D 16 to Bouleternère.

D 618 (*turn left in Bouleternère*) leaves the orchards in the Têt valley for the garrigues (scrubland) along the Boulès gorge.

▷ After 7.5km/4.5mi turn right to Serrabone. TSee Prieuré de SERRABONE.

Boule d'Amont
A winding and narrow road leads to this small village, and then up to the Col Fourtou, for a view of the highest Corbières summits.

Prunet-et-Belpuig
The **Chapelle de la Trinité** has a door with scrolled hinges. Brooding **castle ruins** on a rocky spur overlook Mont Canigou, the Albères, the Roussillon and Languedoc coasts and the Corbières.

▷ Continue on the D 618 to Palada (👣see CÉRET, Driving Tour).

Abbaye
Saint-Michel-de-Cuxa★★

The success of this Romanesque abbey is evidenced by its rich ornamentation and an impressive number of relics that it sheltered in the Middle Ages – 90, plus the graves of two martyrs – at which time it was the largest pilgrimage church in Catalonia. Despite the effects of history, the floral decorations are the most beautiful in Roussillon.

VISIT
One of the finest gems of the Pyrénées, the abbey's sturdy, crenellated bell tower is visible from afar. You may notice that half of the cloisters are missing: they are to be found in the Cloisters Museum in New York.
The 10C pre-Romanesque church is the biggest in France, and a superb aesthetic and acoustical venue for the summer

- ♿ **Michelin Map:** 344 F7.
- 🔖 **Info:** 📞04 68 96 15 35.
- ▷ **Location:** The abbey is located 45km/28mi W of Perpignan along the D 116, then from Prades on the D 127 (direction Taurinya).
- 🕐 **Timing:** 1hr is sufficient.
- 🅿 **Parking:** Nearby car park.
- 👁 **Don't Miss:** The oriental influences displayed in the capitals of the cloister.

cello concerts. The six-voice Gregorian vespers service held (rather sporadically) at 7pm in the monastery next door is hauntingly simple and medieval in tone and texture. The abbey is the main venue for the annual **Pablo Casals Music Festival**, founded in 1950. Some concerts are held in St Pierre in Prades (*Festival Pablo Casals, 33 rue de l'Hospice, 66502 Prades;* 📞*04 68 96 33 07; http://prades-festival-casals.com*). Pablo Casals himself participated up to the age of 90.

Villefranche-de-Conflent★

Villefranche-de-Conflent, founded in 1090 by Guillaume Raymond, Count of Cerdagne, occupies a remarkable site on the confluence of the Cady and the Têt, closely surrounded by rock cliffs. Villefranche was a fortified town from the start. Its fortifications were improved over the centuries and finally completed in the 17C by Vauban.

THE FORTIFIED TOWN★

The fortified town of Villefranche and Cova Bastera were inscribed in 2008 among the World Heritage Sites as representative of the finest examples of the work of Sébastien Le Prestre de Vauban (1633-1707), a military engineer of King Louis XIV. The town is also ranked among the Most Beautiful Villages of France.

Park the car outside the ramparts, in the car park by the confluence of the Têt and the Cady.

Go through the fortified wall at the Porte de France, built in Louis XVI's reign, to the left of the old gateway used by the counts.

Info: Pl d l'Eglise, 66500 Villefranche-de-Conflent. &04 68 96 22 96. www.villefranchedeconflent.fr.

Location: 42km/25mi E of Font-Romeu by the N116 and 8km/5mi SW of Prades.

Don't Miss: Guided tour of the town, or a trip on the **Train Jaune** linking Villfranche-de-Conflent and Latour-de-Carol .

Timing: Allow two hours, and stay for lunch.

Ramparts★

Open Jul–Aug 10am–8pm; Jun and Sep 10am–7pm; Mar–May 10.30am–12.30pm, 2–6pm. Rest of year 10.30am–noon, 2–5pm (Dec 2–5pm). Closed Jan and 25 Dec. €4.50. &04 68 05 87 05.

The tour of the ramparts takes in two storeys of galleries, one above the other: the lower watch-path, dating from the construction of the fortress in the 11C, and the upper gallery, dating from the 17C.

Villefranche-de-Conflent

© Franck Guiziou/hemis.fr

Église St-Jacques

The church, which dates from the 12C and 13C, comprises two parallel naves. Enter through the doorway with four columns; the capitals are by the St-Michel-de-Cuxa School.

Porte d'Espagne

This gateway, like the Porte de France, was refurbished as a monumental entrance in 1791.

Rue St-Jean

After returning to the Porte de France, walk through the village along rue St-Jean with its 13C and 14C houses, many of which still feature their original porches with rounded or pointed arches.

Fort Liberia★

Access via the staircase of a 'Thousand steps', via a footpath or by means of a 4-wheel-drive vehicle.
Open May–Jun 10am–7pm; Jul–Aug 9am–8pm; rest of year 10am–6pm.
€7 (child 5–11, €3.80). 04 68 96 34 01. www.fort-liberia.com.

Overlooked as it is by Mont Belloc, the town was rather too exposed to attack from any enemy encamped above it. Therefore, from 1679 when he was in charge of the project to fortify the town, Vauban planned to protect it by building a fort.

This fort, equipped with a cistern and powder magazines, clearly illustrates some of Vauban's strategic defensive designs. The 'Stairway of a Thousand Steps' (there are in fact 734) was built from pink Conflent marble to link the fort to the town by the little fortified St-Pierre bridge over the Têt.

From the fort, there are **wonderful views★★** of the valleys below and Mont Canigou. *We recommend taking the 'Stairway of a Thousand Steps' back down into the village.*

CAVES
Grottes des Canalettes

The site comprises three cave systems close to the village of Villefranche. Les Canalettes was originally opened in 1954 by the Castillo family. In 2003, it

merged with Les Grandes Canalettes opened in 1984 by the Delonca family. Later, the Cova Bastera owned by Bernard Castillo joined the other two caves, but this system (*see below*) is no longer open to the public. This creates a unit out of these three different and a complementary cave system that is unique in Europe.

€10 (child €6) for each cave system, or €15/€7 for the two. 04 68 05 20 20. www.grottescanalettes.com.

Les Canalettes

Guided visits only (1h) Jul–Aug Sun–Fri at 11am, noon, 1pm, 2pm, 3pm, 4pm.

The concretions in this cave take on an amazing variety of shapes: petrified calcite torrents and eccentrics. Some of the finest include the Table, a natural hollow (*gour*) that gradually filled up with calcite, and some dazzling white draperies.

Les Grandes Canalettes

Open Apr–Jun 10am–5pm; Jul–Aug 10am–5.30pm; Sept–Oct 10am–4pm; 1st 2 wks in Nov 11am–4pm; mid-Nov to Christmas Sat–Sun only 11am–4pm.
Closed rest of year.

This cave forms part of the same network as the Canalettes cave, and was discovered after Les Canalettes.

Cova Bastera

Not open to the public

This cave, situated on the Andorra road opposite the ramparts, is at the far end of the network. It controlled the road from Vernet-les-Bains, and reveals Vauban's underground fortification system and the various phases of occupation of the site, portrayed in life-size tableaux.

🚗 DRIVING TOUR

FROM VILLEFRANCE-DE-CONFLENT TO VINÇA
68km/42.2mi. Allow about 6h.
See region map.

▷ Leave Villefranche-de-Conflent to the S on the D 116.

Corneilla-de-Conflent

The beautiful Romanesque **church** belonged to a former Priory of Canons Regular of St. Augustine. Flanked by a square tower built of granite, the short façade is pierced by a gate of six marble columns of the 12C.

▷ The road climbs the valley of the Cady, domain of shepherds, and fruit growers.

Vernet-les-Bains★

Maison du Patrimoine, 2 rue de la Chapelle ℘04 68 05 55 35; www.vernet-les-bains.fr.
At the foot of the wooded foothills of Canigou, the village is both refreshing and peaceful, and a spa resort of some importance. The weekly market here is small but comprehensive.

▷ In Vernet, take the narrow route du Canigou, and drive 2.5km/1.5mi.

Casteil

Parc animalier de Casteil ⛄⛄ (◷*open: check website for variable dates and times. ⬤⬤€13 (child 3–12, €10); ℘04 68 05 67 54; www.parcanimaliercasteil.com)* has a number of trails for you to follow in search of bears, wolves, lions and more peaceful herbivores.

▷ Go back to Vernet, and take the D 27 towards Taurinya.

Abbaye St-Michel-de-Cuxa★★
See ABBAYE ST-MICHEL-DE-CUXA.

Prades

The main town hereabouts, Prades is a lively, brightly coloured market town set among orchards, and renowned both for its bustling Tuesday street market and its buildings and pavements, many of which are constructed from the soft-hued, variegated pink Conflent marble quarried locally. In 1939, Prades was chosen by the world-renowned cellist Pablo Casals (1876–1973) as his exiled home,

and the **Musée Pablo-Casals** enables you to discover much about the man and his music.

▷ Follow the D 619 NW for 12km/7.5mi, then take the D 14.

Mosset

Mosset is a delightful little place of narrow streets, the remains of a chateau, and a **perfumed garden** (℘04 68 05 38 32; www.mosset.fr) wherein the aromas of mountain flowers – lavender, valerian, rosemary, chamomile, cat mint – assault the senses and brings a new dimension to the silence of the mountains.

▷ Continue on the D 14, and go as far as Catlar on the D 619. There, turn left onto the D 24.

Eus★

This pyramidal pile – not unlike a child's sand castle or a precarious tower of playing cards – originally built for defensive reasons, has repelled both French and Spanish attempts at possession by force. Eus is an unmissable location, perched on a hillside just a short way to the east of Prades.

▷ Follow the D 35, leaving to the right the pont de Marquixanes.

Prieuré de Marcevol

Below a tiny village, home to shepherds and winemakers, is a 12C priory founded by the canons of the Holy Sepulchre.

▷ Turn right onto the D 116, then left onto the D 25, and finally the D 55.

Espira-de-Conflent

The furniture inside the Romanesque church of Espira (1165) illustrates the heyday of Baroque sculpture between 1650 and 1730.

Vinça

Another fortified village, this with a church displaying fine Baroque features and rich decoration.

Abbaye de
Saint-Martin-du-Canigou★★

This abbey perched in its eagle's eyrie 1 055m above sea level is one of the prime sights to be seen in the area around Vernet-les-Bains. Guifred, Count of Cerdagne, great-grandson of Wilfred le Velu, founder of the Catalonian dynasty, chose Mont Canigou, a solitary place venerated by his people, to found a Benedictine monastery in 1001.

VISIT

Guided visits only (1hr, in French only, but with written translations) Jun–Sep 10am, 11am, noon, 2pm, 3pm, 4pm, 5pm (Sun and public holidays 10am, 12.30pm, 2pm, 3pm, 4pm, 5pm); Oct–May 10am, 11am, 2pm, 3pm, 4pm (Sun and public holidays 10am, 12.30pm, 2pm, 3pm, 4pm). Closed Jan. €6. 04 68 05 50 03. http://stmartinducanigou.org.

Cloisters – At the beginning of the 20C, all that remained of the cloisters were three galleries with somewhat crude semicircular arcades. Restoration work included rebuilding a south gallery overlooking the ravine, using the marble capitals from an upper storey which was no longer extant.

Churches – The lower church (10C), dedicated to 'Notre-Dame-sous-Terre' in accordance with an old Christian tradition, forms the crypt of the upper church (11C). The latter, consisting of three successive naves with parallel barrel vaults, conveys an impression of great age with its rugged, simply carved capitals.

Walk to the **viewpoint** (*after reaching the abbey, take a stairway to the left which climbs into the woods. Just past the water outlet turn right; 30min on foot there and back*) to appreciate the originality of St-Martin's site. From here, there is an impressive view of the abbey. Its **site★★** dominating the Casteil and Vernet valleys is most striking.

🛈 **Info:** 66820 Casteil. 04 68 05 50 03. http://stmartinducanigou.org.

📍 **Location:** 14km/8.75mi S of Prades by N 116. The abbey can be reached from Vernet-les-Bains. Alternatively, park in Casteil and continue on foot (1h).

👁 **Don't Miss:** The view of the abbey from the woods above.

🕐 **Timing:** Allow one hour.

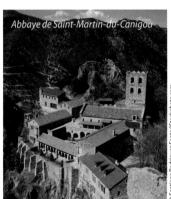
Abbaye de Saint-Martin-du-Canigou

© Santiago Rodriguez Fonto/iStockphoto.com

EXCURSION
Col de Mantet★

20km/12.5mi to the SW – about 1hr.
The cliff road is very steep and narrow upstream of Py.

After leaving Vernet to the west, from Sahorre on, the road (D 27) climbs the Rotja valley, first amid apple trees then along a gorge sunk into the granite rock. Above Py, a pretty village 1 023m above sea level, the road scales steep slopes with granite outcrops bristling here and there. After 3.5km/2mi, in a wide bend in the road, a **look-out point★** gives a good view of the village with its red roofs and Mont Canigou.

The Mantet Pass opens up at an altitude of 1 761m, near the evergreen forest of La Ville. On the opposite slope, the strikingly austere site of **Mantet**, an almost deserted village can be seen huddled in a dip.

Le Canigou★★★

Towering above the Roussillon orchards, Pic du Canigou is revered by Catalonians from France and Spain, who still light the first of their Midsummer Eve bonfires on its summit. The best season for **climbing** is autumn, with mild temperatures and perfect visibility. Patches of snow cover northern slopes in spring and early summer. Mid-summer brings heat and crowds.

A BIT OF HISTORY

A geographer's mistake recorded Canigou as the highest peak in the Pyrenees for quite some time. Ever since the first ascent, reputedly by King Peter of Aragon in 1285, Catalonian sportsmen have vied to conquer this peak: by bicycle in 1901, on skis and on board a Gladiator 10 CC automobile in 1903, and by horseback in 1907. Vernet-les-Bains and Prats-de-Mollo are linked only by forest roads.

⚡ WALKS

1 FROM VERNET-LES-BAINS VIA MARIAILLES

12km/7.5mi – 45min by car and 10hr on foot for the return trip. Experienced walkers only. From Vernet-les-Bains (See VERNET-LES-BAINS) take D 116

Michelin Map: 344: F7.

Location: 69km/43mi W of Perpignan by N 116/D 27.

to the Col de Jou via Casteil and park the car at the pass. Follow the GR 10 footpath via Mariailles, to the refuge at the summit. Continue to Canigou along the Haute Randonnée Pyrénéenne.

Pic du Canigou★★★

Alt 2 784m.

On the Canigou summit are a cross and remains of a stone hut used in the 18C and 19C for scientific observations. Listen for the tinkling of bells from grazing animals in the Cady valley below. The viewing table offers a **panorama** of the Roussillon plain, Mediterranean coast and Costa Brava in Catalonia. Sometimes you can see Canigou all the way from Marseille's church of Notre-Dame-de-la-Garde, 253km/157mi as the crow flies.

2 FROM VERNET-LES-BAINS VIA THE CHALET-HÔTEL DES CORTALETS

23km/14.5mi – about 1h30 by car and 3h30 on foot there and back.

The track starting from Fillols is closed on the way up from 1pm to 6pm

Pic du Canigou

© Jean-Paul Garcin/Photononstop/Tips Images

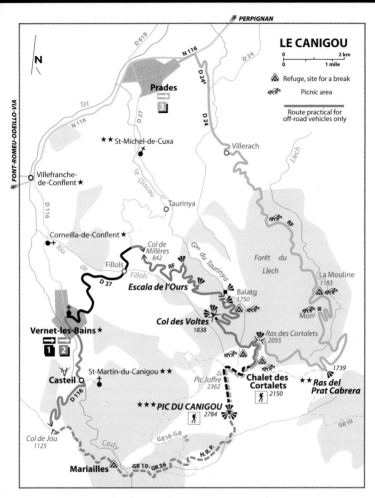

LE CANIGOU

0 ——— 2 km
0 ——— 1 mile

🔺 Refuge, site for a break

Picnic area

Route practical for
off-road vehicles only

PERPIGNAN

D 619
N 116
D 24ª
Prades
3
D 27
★★ St-Michel-de-Cuxa
Villerach
Tét
le Llisou
Villefranche-
de-Conflent ★
D 116
Taurinya
FONT-ROMEU-ODEILLO-VIA
N 116
D 24
Llech
Corneilla-de-Conflent ★
Riu
Col de
Millères
842
Fillols
RF
D 27
Fillols
Escala de l'Ours
RF
Forêt du
Llech
La Mouline
1183
Gᵉ du Taurinya
Balatg
1750
Monᵗ
Col des Voltes
1838
Ras des Cortalets
2055
Vernet-les-Bains ★
1
2
1739
Casteil
D 116
St-Martin-du-Canigou ★★
Pic Joffre
2362
Chalet des
Cortalets
2150
★★ Ras del
Prat Cabrera
★★★ PIC DU CANIGOU
2784
GR 10
Col de Jou
1125
Cady
GR10-GR 36
H.R.P.
GR10-GR 36
Mariailles

and on the way down from 8am to
3pm. The old Cortalets road built for
the Club Alpin in 1899 is a picturesque
but rough mountain road, accessible
only in July and August, in dry weather,
in a four-wheel drive or Jeep. Jeep and
Land-Rovers excursions are organised
from **Vernet-les-Bains**: consult the
Tourist Office (☎04 68 05 55 35) or from
Corneilla-de-Conflent.
Beware of the road's poor condition,
and a very narrow 21 percent gradient
(protected by a parapet) and 31
harrowing hairpin bends.
Start your tour from Vernet-les-Bains
(⚠ See VERNET-LES-BAINS) and take
D 27 in the direction of Prades. After
Fillols, turn right.

After leaving Vernet-les-Bains, beyond
Col de Millères, alt 842m, the road corkscrews along the rocky crest between
the Fillols and Taurinya valleys, with
views of Prades and St-Michel-de-Cuxa.
You'll wind through larch trees and
rocky outcrops to a stunning view of
the Cerdagne and Fenouillèdes regions.

Escala de l'Ours

This vertiginous cliff road is the trip's
most spectacular. It cuts a narrow tunnel through the rock itself, over the
Taurinya gorges far below, with viewpoints along the way. Arolla pines thin
out beyond the Baltag forest hut, and
the countryside becomes a pastoral with
open meadows.

Catalan Midsummer Celebrations

Every summer on the feast of St John, or Midsummer Day, Canigou celebrates the bond between French and Spanish Catalans. On 24 June a flame is lit in the Castillet at Perpignan and carried to the Canigou summit where Catalans from Spain gather to receive it. The same evening, the flame is used to light fires all over Catalonia and other parts of Perpignan before it is returned to the Castillet.

Contact **Perpignan Tourist Office for details**: ✆ *04 68 66 30 30.*

Col des Voltes

From the pass is a view of the northern slopes of Canigou and the Cady basin.

▶ At the Ras dels Cortalets (picnic area), turn right.

Chalet des Cortalets

Hotel-chalet at the mouth of the cirque formed by the Canigou, Joffre and Barbet peaks.

🚶 West of the hotel-chalet, follow the path waymarked by red and white flashes along the lakeshore, then up the eastern face of Joffre peak. Leave the path as it descends to Vernet and continue the ascent on the left, below the ridge. A zigzag path between the rocks leads to the summit (3hr30min there and back).

Pic du Canigou★★★
♿*See* 1 *above.*

3 FROM PRADES VIA THE CHALET-HÔTEL DES CORTALETS

20km/12.5mi – allow 2h by car and 3h30 on foot there and back. ♿ *Accessible only in dry summer weather, the road is very rough along the Llech gorge; a 10km/6mi stretch cuts into the rock face. Excursions by Jeep or four-wheel drive are organised from Prades. This tour leaves Prades on N 116, towards Perpignan, then turn right onto D 24B.*

After leaving Prades, beyond Villerach, the D 24 traverses the Conflent orchards and overlooks the Llech gorge 200–300m below, before pushing up to the La Mouline forest hut *(alt 1 183m; picnic area).*

Ras del Prat Cabrera★★

This delightful rest stop *(1 739m)* overlooking the La Lentilla valley offers a panorama of the Roussillon plain, Albères mountains and the Mediterranean. The road opens out in the upper cirque of the Llech valley with stupendous **views★★★** of the Corbières southern border and the Galamus gorge.

▶ Follow the 'Balcon du Canigou' road W to the Chalet des Cortalets (Tsee C above) and then continue on foot to the **Pic du Canigou★★★** (♿*see* 1 *above).*

Canigou from Vernet-les-Bains

© curtoicurto/iStockphoto.com

Mont-Louis★

Mont-Louis was originally a fortified town founded in 1679 by Vauban to defend the new borders laid down in the **Treaty of the Pyrenees**. Mont-Louis became an excellent border stronghold. A statue in the church square of this austere fortress town pays tribute to General Dagobert, who drove the Spaniards out of the Cerdagne in 1793, during the invasion of Roussillon.

▶ **Population:** 193.
Michelin Map: 344: D7.
Info: 6 boulevard Vauban, 66210. ℘04 68 04 21 97. www.mont-louis.net.
Location: 36km/22.5mi SW of Prades, and 9km/5.6mi E of Font-Romeu-Odeillo-Via.
Don't Miss: The Forçats artesian wells.

VISIT
The fortified town
Guided tours (1h): Jul–Aug daily at 10.30am, 11.30am, 2pm, 3pm, 4pm and 5pm on Mon and Thu; rest of year 11.30am and 2pm: Apr–Jun and Sept Mon–Sat, Oct–Mar Mon–Fri. Closed Christmas period. €5.50 (child 7–10, €2, 11–18, €2.50). ℘04 68 04 21 97.
This consists of a citadel and a lower town, built entirely within the ramparts. The citadel has a square layout, with cut-off corners extended by bastions. Three demilunes protect the curtain walls.

As the town, named after Louis XIV, the reigning monarch during its construction, was never besieged, the ramparts, the main gatehouse (Porte de France), the bastions and the watchtowers have remained intact.

Note the **Puits des Forçats**, an 18C well designed to supply the garrison with water in the event of a siege.

Solar Furnace
guided tours every 30min in summer, and hourly during the rest of the year; check website for details. Closed 1 Jan, 25 Dec. €6.50 (child 7–17, €5). ℘04 68 04 14 89. www.four-solaire.fr.
The solar furnace was installed in 1953. The concentrating panel refurbished in 1980, consists of 860 parabolic mirrors and the heliostat of 546 flat mirrors. The structure focuses the sun's rays into its centre where temperatures reach up to 3 000°C–3 500°C. Since July 1993 it has been used for commercial rather than research purposes.

EXCURSIONS
Planès
6.5km/4mi S on the road to Cabanasse and St-Pierre-dels-Forçats.
Leave the car in front of the Mairie-École in Planès and take the path on the right to the church.

A small cemetery around the church offers a beautiful **view★** of the Carlit massif. The tiny **church** has a curious ground plan in the shape of a sort of five-pointed star, the 'rays' of which are formed by alternately pointed or blunted semicircular chapels. The central dome rests on three semi-domes. The origins of this monument have given rise to intense speculation over the years, as its structure was extremely rare in the medieval western world. Local tradition attributes it to the Saracens, hence the church was known locally as *la mesquita* or mosque. It is probably a Romanesque building inspired by the symbol of the Holy Trinity.

Lac des Bouillouses★
14km/9mi NW of Mont-Louis on the D 118; 300m after a bridge over the Têt, turn left onto the D 60.
A dam has transformed the lake into an impressive reservoir. The walk to Pic Carlit starts at the lake (3h).

🚗 DRIVING TOURS

VALLÉE DE LA TÊT
See region map. Allow about 4h.

Train Jaune

The 'Canary' (℘08 92 35 35 35), painted in Catalonia's yellow and red, has been running between Villfranche-de-Conflent and Latour-de-Carol (62km/38.5mi) since 1910. The Mont-Louis to Olette crosses the Giscard bridge and Séjourné viaduct.

▷ Leave Mont-Louis on the D 116 (direction Prades).

The road runs across a cliff between Mont-Louis and Olette. During the descent, at every turn, high peaks appear on the bank of the Têt.

Pont Gisclard

This railway bridge is named after the engineer who built it, but who was accidentally killed during testing. The road becomes more tortuous as it descends to pass Fontpédrouse.

Viaduc Séjourné

An elegant and robust viaduct, named after its builder, Paul Séjourné (1851–1939).

▷ Follow the road to Thuès-Entre-Valls.

Gorges de la Carança

🚶 *Leave Thuès-Entre-Valls by a path running along the Carança or use the car parks. Start of the walking route is above the parking, after the railway bridge.* ⊘ *Good walking shoes recommended; no pets allowed.*
A small loop of about 1h30 runs along the gorges, past a waterfall and a bridge. The road climbs steeply on the other side to a junction where you turn right (signposted *'Parc auto par chambre d'eau'*). After a fairly narrow ridge, the path descends to the parking.
A larger loop (3h) is available to strong walkers. This, too, starts along the river to the first bridge, but instead of crossing the bridge, go forward along an ascending path. The main difficulty is the return on the other side of the river.

Thuès-les-Bains

A modest location that has established itself as a spa resort.

The road passes through **Olette**, where many of the houses back against the cliff face. Quite soon the ruins of **château de la Bastide** come into view.

LE CAPCIR

⌚*See region map. Allow half a day.*

▷ Leave Mont-Louis and head N on the D 118.

Rising gently, the road offers a view of the citadel rising above the wood, before the massif of Cambras d'Azé. The mountains of Capcir are covered in a thick cloak of pine dotted with lakes. At any time of year, this is a paradise for walkers, and in winter for cross-country skiing.

La Llagonne

The name of this village means 'The Lagoon', and, indeed, before the construction of the Bouillouses dam, the land was often marshy, especially after the resurgence of water in springtime.

▷ At the col de la Quillane which marks the entry into the Capcir mountains, turn left onto the D 32F.

Les Angles

12 av. de l'Aude, 66210 Les Angles.
🕐*Open Jul–Aug 9am–12.30pm, 2–7pm; rest of year 9am–12.30pm, 2–6pm.* ℘*04 68 04 32 76. www.lesangles.com.*
Overlooking the Capcir plateau, this important station was established in 1964 around an old village.

Parc animalier des Angles

🕐*Open Jul–Aug 9am–6pm; rest of the year 9am–5pm.* ⊘*€14 (child 4–14, €12).* ℘*04 68 04 17 20. www.faune-pyreneenne.fr.*
At the S entrance to the village, branch left on the path to Pla del Mir to visit wild animals living in the Pyrenean landscape.
Areas of **Alpine and Nordic skiing** extend over 40km/25mi of tracks. The

station is equipped for **extreme sports** like ice diving or ice surfing.

Formiguères

This small resort has 18 ski runs, and cross-country trails.

▶ Turn left on the D 32B and follow the signs for 'Grotte de Fontrabiouse'.

👥 Grotte de Fontrabiouse

Guided visits: Jul–Aug 10.15am–6pm; May–Jun and Sept 10.30am–5.30pm; Oct–mid-Nov 2.30pm, 3.30pm, 4.30pm; early Dec–Apr 10.30am, 11.30am, 2.30pm, 3.30pm, 4.30pm. ⏱ *Closed early–end Nov, 24–25*

and 31 Dec, 1 Jan.* ✎€10.50 (child 5–12, €6.50).* ✆*04 68 30 95 55. www.grotte-de-fontrabiouse.com.*
This cave was discovered in 1962, when quarrying for onyx used in the Palais de Chaillot in Paris and the Palace of the Majorcan kings in Perpignan.

Puyvalador

The name of this station means 'Mountain Sentinel', and rightly so. It has 16 ski runs, facing the Puyvalador lake, much loved by windsurfers.

▶ Continue beyond the D 118 to reach Quillan (🧭*See QUILLON via Axat.*)

Font-Romeu-Odeillo-Via★

Font-Romeu is a health resort on the sunny side of the French Cerdagne, higher than any other mountain village. It is protected from northerly winds and offers a superb valley panorama. Its impressive sports facilities (swimming pool, ice rink and stables) attract international athletes for altitude training.

FONT-ROMEU/PYRÉNÉES 2000 SKI AREAS

Accessible by road or by gondola from the centre of Font-Romeu (2.5km/1.5mi via the route des pistes leading off from the calvary).
Forty downhill slopes accommodate skiers of all levels. The Pyrénées 2000 resort specialises in ski techniques for people with physical disabilities. Font-Romeu's **Centre Européen d'Entraînement Canin en Altitude** offers dog-sledding instruction year-round.

LA FONTAINE DU PÈLERIN

This hermitage bears witness to the famous Catalan pilgrimage that gave Font-Romeu its name (*Fontaine du Pèlerin* or 'Pilgrim's fountain').

ℹ **Info:** Office du tourisme de Font-Romeu, 82 av Emmanuel-Brousse-66120. ✆04 68 30 68 30. www.font-romeu.fr.
▶ **Location:** 89km/55mi W of Perpignan and 9km/6mi W of Mont-Louis via the D618.
🙂 **Don't Miss:** The panorama from the Calvary.

The **hermitage★** is known for its statue of the Blessed Virgin Mary called the 'Vierge de l'Invention'. The **chapel★** dates from the 17C and 18C. Its magnificent **altarpiece★★** by Joseph Sunyer dates from 1707. The staircase to the left of the high altar leads to the **camaril★★★**, the Virgin Mary's small 'reception room', Sunyer's masterpiece *(For guided tours contact the tourist office).* Some 300m from the hermitage on the road to Mont-Louis, turn right onto a path lined with stations of the cross. The calvary affords a **panorama★★** over Cerdagne.

EXCURSIONS
Col del Pam★

🚶 *15min round-trip.* The observation platform over the Têt valley affords a

view of the Carlit range, Bouillouses plateau, Capcir and Canigou summit.

Llivia
9km/5.6mi S along D 33E.
This is Spanish enclave on French territory (☞*See La CERDAGNE*) with picturesque lanes and the remains of a medieval castle and old towers.

Musee municipal
🕐*Closed for renovations. Contact for opening dates* 📞*04 68 30 10 22.*
This local museum houses the famous **Pharmacie de Llivia★**, with ceramic jars and 17C and 18C objects commonly found in apothecary shops.

La **Cerdagne★**

The half-French, half-Spanish Cerdagne region in the eastern Pyrenees lies in the upper valley of the Sègre, between St-Martin gorge (alt 1 000m) and La Perche Pass (alt 1 579m). This peaceful sunlit valley framed by majestic mountains is a rural idyll of fields, pastures and streams lined with alders and willows. To the north the granite massif of Le Carlit towers at 2 921m and to the south lies the Puigmal range (alt 2 910m) with its forests and ravines.

SKI AREAS
Espace Cambre d'Aze à Eyne 🎿
Alt 1 600m–2 400m.
The resorts of Eyne and St-Pierre-del-Forçats comprise 27 Alpine ski runs for all levels of skiers.

Err-Puigmal 2900 🎿🏂
Alt 1 850m–2 520m.
18 Alpine runs and 10km/6mi of cross-country trails on Mont Puigmal.

Porté-Puymorens 🎿
Alt 1 615m–2 500m.
In March the Grand Prix Porté-Puymorens is held at this ski resort with 16 downhill slopes, 25km/15mi of cross-country trails, snowboarding and ski-biking.

- ♿ **Michelin Map:** 344: C7/D8.
- 🛈 **Info:** Porté-Puymorens. 📞04 68 04 82 41. www. porte-puymorens.net.
- ◉ **Location:** SW of Perpignan, 1hr from Spanish border.
- ⊘ **Don't Miss:** The panorama from col Puymorens and col de l'Ombrée.
- 👪 **Kids:** The solar furnace at Odeillo and the Cerdagne Museum at Ste-Léocadie.

🚗 DRIVING TOUR

VALLÉE DU CAROL★★
27km/16.5mi from Col de Puymorens. Allow 1h.

After leaving gentle slopes of the Ariège's upper valley, the road descends deeper into the valley.

Col de Puymorens★
Alt 1 920m.
The pass lies on the Atlantic-Mediterranean watershed between the Ariège and the Sègre. The road crosses a bridge and leads down into the **Carol valley**, with views of **Porté-Puymorens** (☞*see The Puymorens Tunnel panel, p380)* and the glacial threshold beneath the Tour Cerdane's ruins. Beyond Porté, the road traverses a narrow ravine, the Défilé de la Faou, before squeezing between sheer valley walls on the way to Enveitg. Before Bourg-Madame, look for the Grand Hôtel de Fort-Romeu on the left,

Col du Puymorens

© J.-D. Sudres/hemis.fr

with the Spanish enclave of Llivia in the foreground. To the right, on the Spanish side, see Puigcerdà on the hilltop.

Bourg-Madame

In 1815 the duke of Angoulême named this village on the River Rahur to honour his wife Madame Royale.

ROUTE DE LA SOULANE★
36km/22.5mi. Allow 2h.

▷ Start at Bourg-Madame (see above); leave north on N 20.

Ur

Note the church's Lombardy banding surmounted by a cogged frieze, and the altarpiece by Sunyer.

▷ At Ur, turn right onto D 618 and at Villeneuve-des-Escaldes take D 10 to the left.

Dorres

The **church's** north side altar Our Lady of Sorrows typifies the Catalans' penchant for dressing up their statues. The south chapel has an impressive Black Madonna *(contact the town hall ℘04 68 04 60 69)*. The path from the hôtel Marty in Dorres leads to a **sulphur spring** used for open-air thermalism *(○open 8.30am–8pm, Jul and Aug 8am–9pm; ℘04 68 04 66 87; 30min round-trip on foot)*.

▷ Go back to D 618.

Angoustrine

The Romanesque **church** offers guided tours *(○mid-Jul–Aug daily except Sat–Sun 10am–noon; ℘04 68 30 22 89)*.

Chaos de Targasonne

This gigantic heap of contorted granite boulders dates from the Quaternary Era. A short distance *(2km/1.2mi)* away, view the border mountains from Canigou to Puigmal and the jagged Sierra del Cadi.

Thémis

Many experiments on solar energy have been conducted in the region, as evidenced by this prototype solar tower plant closed in 1986. It remains an imposing building with 100m high tower dominating the Catalan landscape.

Odeillo

Near the village stands the huge **solar furnace** inaugurated in 1969 *(&○open: call for details; ○closed 1 Jan, mid-Nov–mid-Dec and 31 Dec; €7 (child 7–17, €3.50; ℘04 68 30 77 86; www.foursolaire-fontromeu.fr)*.
This valley's sunny slopes are reflected in the enormous parabolic surface covered with over 9 000 mirrors, whose temperatures can exceed 3 500°C.

Font-Romeu-Odeillo-Via★

See FONT-ROMEU-ODEILLO-VIA.
The road runs through the pine forest above the picturesque village of **Bolquère** to the Mont-Louis plateau and Aude valley and Conflent region.

Mont-Louis★

See MONT-LOUIS.

ROUTE DE L'OMBRÉE

112km/70mi. Allow half a day.
From Mont-Louis, D 116 climbs steadily to the La Perche Pass (*alt 1 579m*) linking the valleys of the Têt (Conflent) and the Sègre (Cerdagne).
To the south rises the Cambras d'Azé. Driving through the high moorland enroute to Eyne, you'll enjoy an ever-broadening **panorama★** of the Cerdagne: the ragged outline of the Sierra del Cadi, Puigcerdà, the mountains on the border with Andorra and the Carlit massif.

▶ Turn left onto D 29.

Eyne

At the entrance to this attractive terraced village is an annex of the **Musée de Cerdagne** ▲ (*see Ste-Léocadie*), the casa de la Vall d'Eina all about water, and a botanical garden of endemic plants.

▶ Follow D 33 S towards Llo.

Llo★

This steeply sloped village has an interesting watchtower and Romanesque church.

Gorges du Sègre★

Leave from the church in Llo.
The Sègre flows down from the Puigmal massif, creating torrents and a beautiful needle-shaped rock.
At **Saillagouse**, look for the famous Cerdagne charcuterie.

▶ Continue along D 116 towards Puigcerdà.

▲ Ste-Léocadie

Cal Mateau farm houses the **Musée de Cerdagne** (*open Jan–Apr and Oct–Dec Mon, Wed–Fri 2–5pm; May Mon, Wed–Fri 11am–1pm, 3–5.30pm; Jun and Sept daily except Tue 11am–1pm, 3–5.30pm; Jul–Aug daily except Tue 11am–1pm, 3–7pm; closed 1–11 Nov, 25 Dec, 1 Jan; €4.50 (child 7–18, €2.50); 04 68 04 08 05; www.pyrenees-cerdagne.com*). This fine 17C–18C building houses exhibitions on shepherds, horse-breeding and traditional flask-making (*annex in Eyne, see left*).

▶ Turn left onto D 89 leading to the Puigmal ski resort; at the edge of the forest, take the surfaced forest road to the right just after a hairpin bend.

Table d'Orientation de Ste-Léocadie

Alt 1 681m.
The viewing table here offers a **panorama★** of the Cerdagne, the Carol valley and Fontfrède summit.

▶ Go back to D 89 and turn right. The mountain road leads up the Err valley. Go back to D 116, turn left and a little further on left again (D 30).

Route forestières d'Osséja★

Just above Osséja, leave the Valcebollère road to follow the route forestière to the edge of one of the Pyrenees largest forests. Take the right fork to boundary post 504 (Courne Mourère summit, 2 205m above sea level). Enjoy **views★** of the Cerdagne, the mountains on the Andorra border and Catalonia sierras.

▶ Descend to Osséja by a branching forest road, and then turn right onto the D 30.

Valcebollère

Lost at the end of a road in a cul-de-sac, Valcebollère is the southernmost village of Catalonia. Nicely restored, it is dominated by ancient ruins clinging to an austere mountain of shale. Athletes enjoy the locality which is a good starting point for walking and skiing.

▶ Go back to the D 116 and turn left.

Hix

🐚 *Off season, guided tours by request at the Bourg-Madame tourist office.* ℘*04 68 04 55 35.*

Hix was the residence of the counts of Cerdagne and the commercial capital of the region until the 12C. The little Romanesque **church** contains an early 16C altarpiece dedicated to St Martin, a 13C seated Madonna and Romanesque Christ.

ADDRESSES

🍴 **STAY AND** ⍟ **EAT**

😊😊 **Hôtel Planes (La Vieille Maison Cerdane)** – *6 pl. de Cerdagne, 66800 Saillagouse.* ℘*04 68 04 72 08. http:// chezplanes.com. 19 rooms.* Old coaching inn with refurbished rooms. Restaurant 😊😊 offers 'mountain' cuisine in a rustic décor – Catalan dishes, omelettes and salads.

😊😊 **Planotel** – *6 pl. de Cerdagne, 66800 Saillagouse.* ℘*04 68 04 72 08. http://chezplanes.com. 20 rooms.* Built in the 1970s, this hotel is ideal for a relaxing and calm break. All the rooms have been refurbished, and all but two have balconies. Swimming pool with sliding roof. Generous country cuisine.

😊😊 **Auberge Catalane** – *10, av. du Puymorens, 66760 Latour-de-Carol.* ℘*04 68 04 41 63. www.aubergecatalane.fr. Closed Sun evening and Mon. 10 rooms. Restaurant* 😊😊. At 1 200m, a cosy inn with charming, renovated rooms. Rustic dining room with a Catalan ambiance and cuisine.

😊😊 **Hotel Marty** – *3 carrer Major, 66760 Dorres.* ℘*04 68 30 07 52.* 🅿 *21 rooms.* This popular family-run guest house has a large dining room serving hearty regional meals; a terrace, and some rooms with verandas.

😊😊 **Clair Soleil** – *29 av. François-Arago, rte d'Odeillo.* ℘*04 68 30 13 65.* 🅿 *29 rooms. Restaurant* 😊😊. This family guest house faces the Odeillo solar furnace. Modest rooms with balcony or terrace. Regional cuisine served in a small dining room.

😊😊 **La Brasserie de la Vieille Maison Cerdagne** – *6 pl. de Cerdagne, 66800 Saillagouse.* ℘*04 68 04 72 08. http://*

chezplanes.com. ♿. *19 rooms.* At the Hôtel Planes, an old coaching stop in Saillagouse village, enjoy a range of family cuisine, and accommodation 😊😊.

😊😊😊 **Auberge les Écureuils** – *Carrer de la Coma, 66340 Valcebollère.* ℘*04 68 04 52 03. www.aubergeecureuils. com. 16 rooms.* This old barn has been converted into a cosy country inn. Nicely decorated rooms. Garden at the edge of the stream. Organised walks, skis and snowshoes available. Restaurant 😊😊😊 of character, classical menu and Catalan dishes. Small crêperie.

SHOPPING

Charcuterie Bonzom – *Rte d'Estavar, 66800 Saillagouse.* ℘*04 68 04 71 53. www.charcuterie-catalane-bonzom.com. Open 8am–12.30pm, 3–7.30pm. Closed Mon and Wed.* Here, at the heart of one of the centres for the renowned Catalan sausage, is a shop where you will have no trouble filling your bags with sausages or dried hams, with over 1 500 to choose from!

ACTIVITIES

SPA RESORTS

Les Bains de Llo – *Rte des Gorges de Llo, 66800 Llo.* ℘*04 68 04 74 55. www. bains-de-llo.com. Open 10am–7.30pm.* Bathe in sulphurous springs at 35°C–37°C. Snack bar with freshly squeezed fruit juice, pancakes and waffles.

Bains chauds de Dorres – *66760 Dorres.* ℘*04 68 04 66 87. www.bains-de-dorres.com. Open 8.30am–8pm.* Down the concrete road, below the hôtel Marty at Dorres, you reach (30min on foot, there and back) a sulphur source (41°C) where Cerdan and summer visitors come to enjoy the outdoor spa.

FLYING

École de parapente Vol'Aime – *92 r. Creu-de-Fé, 66120 Targassonne.* ℘*04 68 30 10 10. www.volaime.com. 8am–5pm for paragliding. Closed Nov–Mar.* Discovery courses, lessons, or just flights.

EVENTS

Grand Prix Porté-Puymorens – *March.* Alpine skiing competition.

Andorra★

This small independent state has a total area of 468sq km/180sq mi (about one and a third times the area of the Isle of Wight). Andorra lies at the heart of the Pyrenees and has remained curiously apart from its neighbours, France and Spain. Visitors are attracted by its rugged scenery and picturesque villages.

▶ **Population:** 85 000.
📍 **Michelin Map:** 343 G9.
ℹ **Info:** Pl. de la Rotonda, Andorra la Vella. ℘(+376) 89 11 72 from UK. www.visitandorra.com.
▶ **Location:** From France, there is only one road, the N 22 which passes through the border post Pas de la Casa.
🕐 **Timing:** At least a day.
👁 **Don't Miss:** The panorama from the port d'Envalira.

A BIT OF HISTORY

'Charlemagne the great, my father, delivered me from the Arabs' begins the Andorran national anthem, which then continues, 'I alone remain the only daughter of Charlemagne. Christian and free for 11 centuries, Christian and free I shall carry on between my two valiant guardians, my two protecting princes.'

From co-principality to independent sovereignty

Until 1993, Andorra was a co-principality under a regime of dual allegiance, a legacy from the medieval feudal system. Under such a contract, two neighbouring lords would define the limits of their respective rights and authority over a territory that they held in common fief. Andorra was unusual, however, in that its two lords came to be of different nationality, but left the status of the territory as it was under feudal law, with the result that neither of them could claim possession of the land. This dual allegiance to two co-princes was established in 1278 by the Bishop of Urgell and Roger Bernard III, Count of Foix. However, while the bishops of Urgell remained co-princes, the counts of Foix passed their lordship on to France (when Henri IV, Count of Foix and Béarn, became king in 1589) and thus eventually to the President of the French Republic. On 14 March 1993 the Andorrans voted in a referendum to adopt a new democratic constitution making the principality a fully independent state. The official language of the country is Catalan. The principality has signed a treaty of cooperation with France and Spain, the first countries to officially recognise its independence. It has also become a member of the United Nations.

A taste for liberty

Andorrans pride themselves above all on seeking and fiercely defending their liberty and independence. A long-standing system of representative government and 11 centuries of peace have given them little incentive to alter the country's administration. The country is governed by a General Council, which holds its sessions at the 'Casa de la Vall' (©see p310) and ensures the proportional representation of the various elements of the Andorran population and the seven parishes. Andorrans do not pay any direct taxes, nor do they have to do military service. They also have free postal services within their country. Most of the land is communally owned, so there are very few private landowners.

Work and play

Until recently this essentially patriarchal society traditionally made a living from stock rearing and crop cultivation. In between the high summer pastures and the hamlets you can still see the old cortals, groups of barns or farmhouses, which are gradually becoming more accessible as the tracks leading up to them are made suitable for vehicles. The mountain slopes exposed to the sun are cultivated in terraces. Tobacco, the main crop in the Sant Julià de Lòria Valley, is

grown up to an altitude of 1 600m. The first roads suitable for vehicles linking it with the outside world were not opened until 1913, on the Spanish side, and 1931, on the French. The population of Andorra numbered 82 000 in 2009, most of whom speak Catalan; it has increased slightly since then, and is now around 85 000.

ANDORRE LA VELLA

Andorra's capital, 1 409m above the Gran Valira valley, is a bustling commercial town, but hidden away from the busy main axis you'll find traditional quiet old streets. This is the highest capital city in Europe, and also, at 3 hours driving time, the furthest from

Pas de la Casa

©bysinka/Fotolia.com

the nearest airports at Toulouse, Girona, Perpignan and Barcelona.

Casa de la Vall
The Casa houses Andorra's Parliament building and its Law Courts in a massive 16C stone building.

🚗 DRIVING TOURS

VALIRA D'ORIENT VALLEY★
From Pas de la Casa to Andorre la Vella. 30km/18.6mi – Allow half to a full day.
♿ See map p309.

Pas de la Casa
A simple border crossing, this village, the highest in the Principality, became an important ski centre. The town consists mainly of large hotel complexes and duty-free shops: there is throughout the year an intense animation, accompanied, especially in the summer, with impressive congestion!
Undulating and winding, the road winds through the mountains before reaching the port of Envalira. The climb offers beautiful views of the pond and the Circus Font-Negro.

Port d'Envalira★★
😊The port d'Envalira can be obstructed by snow but is usually re-opened within 24 hours. Even so, you can avoid this pass by a tunnel. The highest pass in

the Pyrenees, marking the watershed between the Mediterranean (Valira) and the Atlantic (Ariège) has a good road. Its **panorama** includes the Andorra mountains (2 942m) stretching away to Coma Pedrosa. The road descends to Pas de la Casa, offering spectacular views of the **Font-Nègre** cirque and lake.

Saint Joan de Caselles
This romanesque church dominates the surroundings at one of the highest points in the area.

Canillo
This village church has the tallest belltower in Andorra (27m). Nearby is Andorra's national shrine, the **chapel of Our Lady of Meritxell**.

Encamp
In addition to two churches of note, the village contains the **Casa Cristo★**, which has retained its original furniture and is now a museum; the **Musée national de l'Automobile** 👥 is also of interest, it invites you to explore the history of the automobile.

Escaldes-Engordany
Here you will find the **Musée des Maquettes**, displaying models that illustrate the architecture of the region. And nearby, the **Musée du Parfum**, which explores the many facets of perfume.

Port d'Envalira

©Claudio Giovanni Colombo/Bigstockphoto.com

Andorre la Vella
See p309.

VALIRA DEL NORD VALLEY★
Allow half to a full day. See map p309.

Sant Julià de Lòria
This village houses the **Musée du Tabac★**, displayed in a former tobacco factory.

Gorges de Sant Antoni
From a bridge across the Valira del Nord you can see the old humpback bridge used by muleteers. The Coma Pedrosa peaks loom in the distance beyond the Arinsal valley.

Before La Massana, turn left towards Sispony.

La Massana
The Casa Rull de Sispony was one of the finest and richest houses in the parish of Massana.

Ordino
This village's picturesque streets are worth exploring. Old Catalan forges produced attractive wrought-iron works like the balcony of 'Don Guillem's' house, the gates of the church and (1676) **Casa Areny-Plandolit** (*open daily except Mon 9.30am–1.30pm, 3–6.30pm (Sun 10am–1.30pm); 6€; closed 14 Mar, 1 May, 8 Sep, 25–26 Dec; 00 376 83 69 08).*

Musée de la Microminiature
In a small space, in keeping with its subject, the museum houses the miniatures by Ukranian artist Nikolai Siadristy.

Musée iconographique et du Christianisme
The museum contains about 80 religious icons from 17C–19C, mainly from Russia.

La Cortinada
Village highlights are its pleasant setting, a splendid house with galleries and dovecot, and the Romanesque frescoes and Baroque altarpieces in the **church of Sant Marti**.

ESTANY D'ENGOLASTERS
9km/5.5mi, then 30min round-trip on foot. See map p309.

Leave Escaldes E of Andorra, on the road to France, and at the outskirts of the village turn right, doubling back slightly, to follow the Engolasters mountain road.

The outstanding landmark on the Engolasters plateau is the lovely Romanesque bell-tower of **Sant Miguel**. Enjoy a walk to the dam, and lake reflections of the dark forest lining its shores.

ADDRESSES

STAY

Hôtel Coray – *Caballers 38, Encamp. 00 376 831 513. 85 rooms.* Good location in the hills above the town; large and bright dining room.

Hôtel Coma Bella – *Sant Julià de Lòria. 7km/4mi au SW of Andorra la Vella. 00 376 742 030. www.hotelcomabella. com. 30 rooms.* This hotel in the peaceful La Rabassa forest features rooms decorated with contemporary Andorran furnishings.

Hôtel Guillem – *C/ dels Arinsols 10, Encamp. 00 376 733 900. www. hotelguillem.net. 42 rooms. Restaurant.* This hotel is peaceful, and offers every comfort.

Hôtel Coma – *Ctra Gral d'Ordino, Ordino. 00 376 736 100. www.hotelcoma. com. 48 rooms. Restaurant.* Conveniently located, this welcoming hotel offers comfortable rooms with private terraces.

Hôtel Univers – *R. René-Baulard, Encamp. 00 376 731 105. www. hoteluniversandorra.com. 31 rooms. Restaurant.* Located on the banks of the East Valira and close to the futuristic city hall, friendly hotel with comfortable rooms.

Hôtel de la Espel – *Pl. Creu Blanca 1, Escaldes-Engordany. 00 376 820 855. www.hotelespel.com. 84 rooms. Restaurant.* Rooms with wooden floors and functional furnishings.

Andorran Influences

Until the 1950s, Andorra's population, almost entirely Andorran-born, barely exceeded 6 000. These days only about 25 percent of the population – almost two-thirds of whom live in Andorra la Vella and around – are Andorran nationals. The remainder are largely Spanish, French and Portuguese.

The official language is Catalan (Català), a Romance language closely related to Provençal, but with roots in Castilian and French. Local spin has it that everyone in Andorra speaks Catalan, Spanish and French, but there are plenty of people who can't understand more than a few words of French; hardly anyone speaks English.

Andorran cuisine is mainly Catalan, with significant French and, perhaps surprisingly, Italian influences. Sauces are typically served with meat and fish. Pasta is also common. Local dishes include *cunillo* (rabbit cooked in tomato sauce), *xai* (roast lamb), *trinxat* (bacon, potatoes and cabbage) and *escudella* (a stew of chicken, sausage and meatballs).

Given the fondness of the Catalans for music, it is no surprise that Andorra has a Chamber Orchestra, and that it also stages a famous international singing contest. In 2004, Andorra participated in the Eurovision Song Contest for the first time. This attracted media attention from Catalonia, since it was the first song to be sung in Catalan.

But the single most important event in Andorran cultural life is the Escaldes-Engordany international jazz festival, which has featured such international stars such as Miles Davis, Fats Domino and B.B. King.

Typical dances, such as the marratxa and the contrapàs, are especially popular at feasts, at which exuberant Andorran people tend to celebrate enthusiastically and loudly.

♥/EAT

Borda Estevet – *Rte de La Comella 2, Andorra la Vella.* ℘*00 376 86 40 26.* This old stone-walled house welcomes its clients with rustic decor, local Pyrenean cooking and a wow of a dessert trolley.

Can Benet – *Antic carrer Major 9, Andorra la Vella.* ℘*00 376 828 922. www.restaurant-canbenet.com.* Small ground floor bar; main dining room is upstairs.

La Borda Pairal 1630 – *R. Dr-Vilanova 7, Andorra la Vella.* ℘*00 376 869 999. Closed Sun evening and Mon.* Old Andorran stone farm, retaining its rustic décor.

Taberna Angel Belmonte – *R. Ciutat-de-Consuegra 3, Andorra la Vella.* ℘*00 376 822 460. www.tabernaangel belmonte.com.* A pleasant tavern-style restaurant serving seafood.

El Rusc – *La Massana.* ℘*00 376 838 200. Closed Sun evening and Mon.* 🅿. Beautiful local house with an attractive rustic dining room. Traditional dishes, Basque specialties and good cellar.

SHOPPING

Shoppers love Andorra for its many luxury products at duty-free prices. Usual store hours are 9am–1pm and 4–8pm (9pm during holiday periods).

ACTIVITIES

Andorra has to ski centres with 180 pistes over 285km/178mi, 110 ski lifts, and almost 1 400 snow cannons.

Caldea – This gigantic futuristic water sports complex fed by the 68°C spa waters of Escaldes-Engordany was designed by French architect Jean-Michel Ruols (℘*00 376 80 09 99*).

Walking – Andorra has numerous pathways through the mountains, with refuges, climbing walls and via ferrata.

Chapelle de Piétat, Saint-Savin, Hautes-Pyrénées
© Jean-Paul Azam/hemis.fr

DISCOVERING MIDI TOULOUSAIN

TOULOUSE AND AROUND

Nicknamed the 'Pink City' for its preponderance of red-brick buildings, Toulouse, is the fourth-largest conurbation in France and capital of the country's largest region (Midi-Pyrénées). It stands squarely in the Midi, between the Atlantic Ocean and the Mediterranean and within easy reach of the ski slopes of the Pyrenees. The Garonne river runs through the middle of it and its banks provide pleasant promenades, picnic spots and vantage points. Although Toulouse has plenty of history to offer, this is very much a contemporary city. Thanks to the Airbus assembly plant beside Blagnac airport, it is the leading aerospace city in Europe with a thriving research sector. The presence of the third-largest student population in France – almost 90 000 – coupled with a benign climate creates a vibrant, outdoor atmosphere. It's a cosmopolitan place with clear influences derived from Spain, but it proudly retains and cultivates its Occitan identity – street names and announcements on the metro, for instance, are bilingual.

Highlights

1 Admire the great brick pilgrimage church of **St Sernin** (p320)
2 Get your bearings over a coffee in the lively **place du Capitole** (p324)
3 Explore the art collections of the **Fondation Bemberg** (p326)
4 Go for a leisurely boat ride on the **Garonne** river (p336)
5 Get out of orbit in the fascinating **Cité de l'Espace** (p333)

Orientation

Old Toulouse is bordered on three sides by broad and busy avenues: the boulevards Lascrosses, Arcole, Strasbourg and Lazare Canot and the Allées Feuga, Guesde and Verdier. To the west it is limited by the Garonne river. The central square and the best spot to get your bearings is the Place du Capitole. Almost all sights worth seeing are within walking distance of here, without a slope in sight.

A short way to the north is the city's main church, St Sernin, its tiered spire acting as a landmark. To the south of Capitole are a cluster of medieval streets briefly interrupted by the bustling Rue de Metz and Place Esquirol.

Across Pont Neuf and Pont St Pierre from the centre there is another group of sights in the St Cyprien quarter, most notably the Hotel Dieu, distinguished from afar by its large green dome.

Place du Capitole

© Christophe Boisvieux/hemis.fr

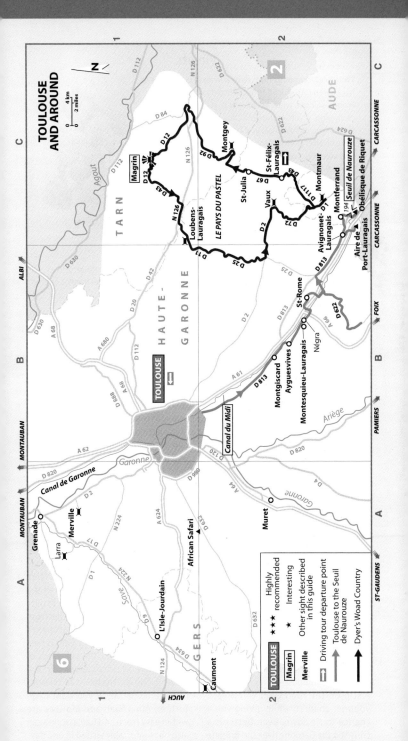

TOULOUSE AND AROUND

N

0   4 km
0   2 miles

2

CARCASSONNE

AUDE

MONTAUBAN

MONTAUBAN

ALBI

TARN

HAUTE-GARONNE

Magrin

Montgey

St-Félix-Lauragais

Montmaur

Montferrand

LE PAYS DU PASTEL

St-Julia

Vaux

Avignonet-Lauragais

Loubens-Lauragais

Seuil de Naurouze

Obélisque de Riquet

CARCASSONNE

Aire de
Port-Lauragais

FOIX

St-Rome

TOULOUSE

Négra

Montgiscard

Ayguesvives

Montesquieu-Lauragais

Canal du Midi

PAMIERS

Ariège

Garonne

Canal de Garonne

Grenade

Larra

Merville

African Safari

Muret

Garonne

L'Isle-Jourdain

GERS

Caumont

AUCH

ST-GAUDENS

6

★★★   Highly
          recommended

★   Interesting

        Other sight described
        in this guide

TOULOUSE   Driving tour departure point

Magrin

Merville   Toulouse to the Seuil
                de Naurouze

                Dyer's Wood Country

317

Violets

The violet, originally from Parma in Italy, is thought to have been introduced to Toulouse during the 19C by French soldiers who had fought in Napoleon's Italian campaign. It was enthusiastically received by the people of Toulouse, and became the most sought-after item at florists', perfume-makers' and confectioners' (the famous sugared violets). At the beginning of the century, some 600 000 bouquets a year were being sent to the capital, Northern Europe and even Canada. Sadly, disease and mildew soon got the better of this delicate winter plant with its tiny purple flowers. However, from 1985, scientists began research into ways of saving the plant. Ten years later, they succeeded in cultivating it under glass. Nowadays, the greenhouses of Lalande, north of Toulouse, are once again fragrant with the scent of this pretty flower and Toulouse has had its emblem restored.

R. Corbe/MICHELIN

Every year, the *fête de la violette*, a festival in honour of this lovely bloom, is held in late February–early March.

Other sights require a car or bus ride to reach: chiefly the Cité de l'Espace (in the western suburbs) and the Airbus assembly complex and the new Aeroscopia musuem (at Blagnac to the east).

Toulouse for Children

Kids might not be thrilled by too many churches, streets and museums but there are several possible ways to keep them entertained in the city.

Chief attraction is the **Cité de l'Espace** (*see p333*) which will satisfy their curiosity about all things to do with the universe and extraterrestrials while also supplying plenty of physical sensations. Allow the best part of a day to get the most out of it and, as with any theme park, plan your visit ahead around the shows you want to see.

The latest addition to the attractions of Toulouse is **Aeroscopia** (*see p333*), a modern museum that features a collection of iconic aircraft at its centre adjacent to Toulouse-Blagnac airport.

A trip on the road train will please younger children while giving you a chance to sit down. Even better is a cruise on the Garonne river and Brienne canal. If you prefer to get around by bicycle, the Canal du Midi has pleasant, shady tow paths converted into cycletracks on both sides. With a car there are more possibilities out of town. The labyrinthe de Merville is a maze involving clue-solving and punching in codes to open gates which keeps brains and bodies occupied at the same time. Take a picnic and take your time.

Getting Out of the City

Toulouse is the capital of its own *département*, Haute Garonne, which stretches south as far as the Pyrenees. Being the hub of a road, rail and canal network, the city makes a good base from which to explore the hinterland. This takes in the rich farmland of the Lauragais, once important for its production of blue dye made from the woad plant; the upper reaches of the Canal du Midi (the tow path is best followed by bicycle); the vineyards of Fronton (one of France's less well known wine regions) and the towns and villages of eastern Gascony. If you want to go further, Albi, Auch and Moissac are within easy reach and Carcassonne can also be comfortably visited in one day.

Toulouse★★★

Bathed in Mediterranean light, Toulouse can take on a variety of hues depending on the time of day, ranging from scorching red to dusky pink or even violet. Once the capital of all the regions united by the Occitanian dialects *(langues d'oc)*, Toulouse is now a famous centre of the French aeronautical construction industry, which has attracted numerous high-tech industries, as well as a lively university town.

▶ **Population:** 466 219.

ℹ **Info:** Donjon du Capitole, 38001-31080 Toulouse. ☎08 92 18 01 80. www. toulouse-tourisme.com.

▶ **Location:** 245km/153mi SE of Bordeaux by A 62; 95km/59mi NW of Carcassonne by A 61.

ℙ **Parking:** Street parking in the centre of the city is limited but there is a multi-storey car park beneath the place du Capitole.

◉ **Don't Miss:** The Old Town, Basilique St-Sernin.

A BIT OF HISTORY

From Celtic to 'Capitoul' rule – The ancient settlement of the Volcae, a branch of Celtic invaders, was probably situated in Vieille-Toulouse *(9km/5mi S)*, but moved site and expanded into a large city which Rome made the intellectual centre of Gallia Narbonensis. In the 3C, it was converted to Christianity and became the third most important city in Gaul. Visigothic capital in the 5C, it then passed into the hands of the Franks. After Charlemagne, Toulouse was ruled by counts, but it was far enough removed from the seat of Frankish power to keep a large degree of autonomy. From the 9C to the 13C, under the dynasty of the counts Raimond, the court of Toulouse was one of the most gracious and magnificent in Europe. The city was administered by consuls or *capitouls*, whom the count would systematically consult concerning the defence of the city or any negotiation with neighbouring feudal lords. The administration of the *capitouls* meant that the merchants of Toulouse had the possibility of becoming members of the aristocracy (to mark their rise in station, the new-fledged noblemen would adorn their mansion with a turret). By the time the city passed under the rule of the French crown in 1271, only

PUBLIC TRANSPORT

Toulouse is served by 84 bus routes, two metro lines and two tram lines. Complementary to the bus, tram and metro, there are 9 on-demand lines, serving the areas on the periphery of Toulouse (*www.tisseo.fr/en/getting-around*).

A **night service** operates from 9.30pm to 3am on Friday and Saturday and from 9.30pm to midnight from Sunday to Thursday. **Metro, tram and bus** network tickets start at €1.60 for a single trip and up to €13.40 for 10 trips. Network maps are available at www.tisseo.fr/en/network-maps.

PASS TOURISME

With the **Pass Tourisme**, you gain free entry to museums in the city centre, a guided visit from the Tourist Office, and free travel on the local public transport network: metro, tram, bus and airport shuttle bus. You will also benefit from reduced rates at most tourist sites and in a number of shops. With the **Pass Tourisme Premium**, you can also take advantage of a free river cruise along the Garonne or the Canal du Midi with Bateaux Toulousains, as well as a trip on the Tourist Train. Cards are personalised and are valid for 1, 2 or 3 days: Pass Tourisme: €15, €22, €29; Pass Premium: €20, €27, €35.

12 *capitouls* remained. A Parliament, established in 1420 and reinstated in 1443, supervised law and finance.

The oldest academy in France – After the turmoil of the Albigensian conflict, Toulouse once more became a centre of artistic and literary creativity. In 1324, seven eminent citizens desiring to preserve the *langue d'Oc* founded the 'Compagnie du Gai-Savoir', one of the oldest literary societies in Europe. Every year on 3 May, the best poets were awarded the prize of a golden flower. Ronsard and Victor Hugo were honoured in this way, as was poet, playwright and revolutionary journalist Philippe-Nazaire-François Fabre (1755–94), author of the Republican calendar and the ballad *'Il pleut, il pleut, bergère'*, who immortalised his prize by changing his pen-name to **Fabre d'Églantine** (wild rose). In 1694, Louis XIV raised the society to the status of **Académie des Jeux floraux**.

The dyer's woad boom – In the 15C, the trade in **dyer's woad** (*see sidebar p338*) launched the merchants of Toulouse onto the scene of international commerce, with London and Antwerp among the main outlets. Clever speculation enabled families like the Bernuys and the Assézats to lead the life of princes. Sumptuous palatial mansions were built during this period, symbolising the tremendous wealth and power of these 'dyer's woad tycoons'. The thriving city of Toulouse, which had been largely medieval in appearance, underwent harmonious changes influenced by Italian architectural style, in particular that of the Florentine revival. However, with the introduction of indigo into Europe and the outbreak of the Wars of Religion, the boom collapsed after 1560 and recession set in.

No head is too great – **Henri de Montmorency**, governor of Languedoc, 'first Christian baron' and member of the most illustrious family of France, was renowned for his courage, good looks and generosity and soon became well loved in his adopted province. In 1632, he was persuaded by Gaston d'Orléans, brother of Louis XIII, to take up arms in the rebellion of the nobility against Cardinal Richelieu, a decision that was to cost him dearly. Both Orléans and Montmorency were defeated at Castelnaudary, where Montmorency fought valiantly, sustaining more than a dozen wounds, before being taken prisoner. He was condemned to death by the Parliament at Toulouse.

Nobody could believe that such a popular and high ranking figure would be executed, but the king, who had come in person to Toulouse with Cardinal Richelieu, turned a deaf ear to the pleas of the family, the court and the people, claiming that as king he could not afford to show favour to any particular individual. He did, however, concede that the condemned man could be beheaded inside the Capitole, instead of the market place. So, on a specially constructed scaffold in the interior courtyard, the 37-year-old duke met his death with all the dignity befitting a noble lord. When his head was shown to the crowd in front of the Capitole, there were howls of vengeance levelled at the cardinal.

Born in Toulouse – Toulouse is the birthplace of several famous French figures, including Jean-Pierre Rives, champion of the Toulouse rugby team, and Claude Nougaro (1929–2004), a late 20C troubadour. Those familiar with the little round tins of Lajaunie sweets (in aniseed and other flavours) will be interested to know that Lajaunie, a chemist, was also a native of Toulouse.

BASILIQUE ST-SERNIN★★★

This is the most famous and most magnificent of the great Romanesque pilgrimage churches in the south of France, and one which can also boast the largest collection of holy relics. The site was home, in the late 4C, to a basilica containing the body of St Sernin (or Saturninus). This Apostle from the Languedoc, the first bishop of Toulouse, was martyred in 250 by being tied to the legs of a bull he had refused to sacrifice to pagan gods, which dragged him down a flight of stone steps.

With the donation of numerous relics by Charlemagne, the church became a focus for pilgrims from all over Europe,

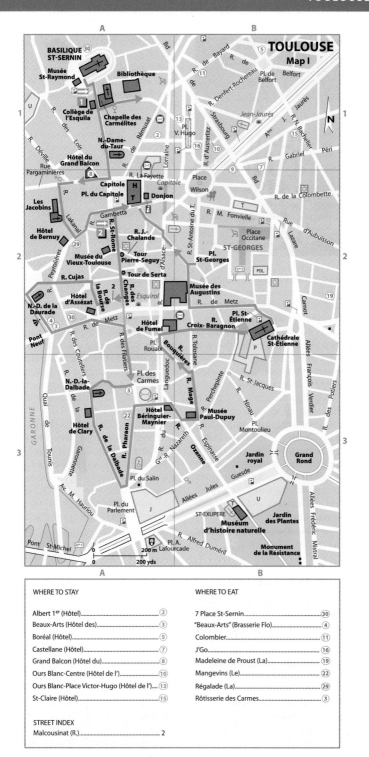

TOULOUSE
Map I

Bell-tower, Basilique Saint-Sernin

© Philippe Blanchot/hemis.fr

and also a stopping place for pilgrims on their way to Santiago de Compostela. The present building was constructed to meet these growing needs. It was begun in c.1080 and completed in the mid-14C. General restoration was undertaken in 1860 by Viollet-le-Duc.

Exterior – St-Sernin is constructed from red brick and white stone. In the apse, begun in the late 11C, stone is much in evidence, whereas the nave is built almost all of brick, which in turn is the only material used in the belfry. The 11C **apse** is the oldest part of the building. It forms a magnificent ensemble of five chapels and four transept chapels combining with the tiered roofs of the chancel and transept, and the elegant bell-tower rising out of the whole.

The five-tier octagonal **bell-tower** stands majestically above the tran-

sept crossing. The three lower tiers are embellished with early 12C Romanesque round arches. The two upper storeys were added 150 years later; the openings, shaped like mitres, are surmounted by little decorative pediments. The spire was added in the 15C.

Interior – St-Sernin is the epitome of a major pilgrimage church. It was designed to accommodate large congregations, with room for a choir of canons and consists of a nave flanked by double side aisles, a broad transept and a chancel with an ambulatory from which five radiating chapels open off.

Chancel – Beneath the dome of the transept crossing, there is a fine table of Pyrenean marble from the old Romanesque altar signed by Bernard Gilduin and consecrated in 1096 by Pope Urban II.

Transept – The vast transept is laid out as three aisles with east-facing chapels. The capitals of the tribune gallery and the Romanesque mural paintings are worthy of attention. In the north transept, two groups of Romanesque mural paintings have been uncovered (the Resurrection and the Lamb of God presented by angels).

One of the south transept chapels is dedicated to the Virgin Mary (note the 14C statue of 'Notre-Dame-la-Belle'); on the chapel's oven-vault are frescoes one above the other mingling the theme of the Virgin seated 'in Majesty' (13C) with the Coronation of the Virgin.

The **Ambulatory and crypt** displays numerous altarpieces and reliquaries, leading to it being known as the Corps Saints, or Holy Relics, since the 17C. On the wall curving round the outside of the crypt are seven impressive late 11C **low-relief sculptures★★** in St-Béat marble from the studio of Bernard Gilduin: Christ in Majesty, with the symbols of the Evangelists, surrounded by angels and Apostles.

A 'Red-Brick' City

Brick, the only construction material available in any sufficient quantity in the alluvial plain of the Garonne, has long predominated in the buildings of Toulouse, lending the city its unique style and beauty. As brick is so light and mortar adheres to it easily, the master masons of Toulouse were able to construct extravagantly wide vaults spanning a single nave.

WALKING TOURS

① **OLD TOWN★★★**
From St-Sernin follow rue du Taur, one of the favourite haunts of students, lined

with many bookshops selling new and second-hand books.

Musée St-Raymond★★
Place St-Sernin. ♿🕐*Open daily 10am–6pm.* 👓€4. 📞*05 61 22 31 44. www.saintraymond.toulouse.fr.*
This museum, housed in one of the buildings of the old Collège St-Raymond (13C), rebuilt in 1523 and restored by Viollet-le-Duc, was recently refurbished and now displays its collections of archaeology and antique art.

Collège de l'Esquila
This opens off No. 69 rue du Taur through a doorway decorated with bosses, a Renaissance work by Toulouse sculptor N. Bachelier.

▶ Turn left onto rue du Périgord.

Chapelle des Carmélites
♿🕐*Open daily except Mon 10am–12.30pm, 2–6pm.* 🕐*Closed 1 Jan, 1 May, 25 Dec.* 📞*05 34 44 92 05.*
The decoration of this chapel – woodwork and paintings commemorating the Carmelite order (by the Toulouse painter Despax) – is a fine example of 18C art.

▶ Return to rue du Taur.

Bibliothèque d'étude et du patrimoine
Civic pride and the importance of learning are celebrated in this 1930s library by Montariol. The reading room is brilliantly lit by large windows decorated with a laurel leaf motif and by a cupola composed of gold, blue and white roundels of stained glass.

Église Notre-Dame-du-Taur
This church, known as St-Sernin-du-Taur until the 16C, replaced the sanctuary erected where the martyr saint was buried.

▶ On reaching place du Capitole, turn right onto rue Romiguières.

Hôtel du Grand Balcon
In the 1920s this hotel, then a pension, provided a place to rest for pioneers of French aviation working for Aerospatiale. The middle floors were reserved for pilots – Saint-Exupéry occupied room No. 32 and Mermoz No. 20 – while the top floor accommodated mechanics.

Les Jacobins★★
St Dominic, alarmed by the spread of the Albigensian heresy, founded the Order of Preachers (Dominican Order) and the first Dominican monastery was founded in Toulouse in 1216. The red-brick church is a masterpiece of the southern French Gothic, marking a milestone in the evolution of this style.

Convent des Jacobins★★
Rue Lakanal. Exterior described above. ♿🕐*Open daily except Mon 10am–6pm.* 👓€4. 📞*05 61 22 23 82. www.jacobins.toulouse.fr.*
The awesome **main body★★** of the church, which has two naves, is the result of successive enlargements. It reflects the Dominican Order's prestige, its prosperity and its two aims: serving God and preaching his word.
On the floor of the church, the ground plan of the original rectangular sanctuary (1234), which was covered by a timber-frame roof, is indicated by five black-marble slabs (the bases of the old pillars) and by a line of black tiles (the old walls). The church's roof vault, which reaches a height of 28m up to the keystones, is supported on seven columns. The **column★★** at the far east end supports the entire fan vaulting of the apse; its 22 ribs, alternately wide and narrow, resemble the branches of a palm tree. Up as far as the sills of the clerestory windows, the walls are decorated with painted imitation brickwork in ochre and pink. Other stripes of contrasting colours are used to emphasise the upward thrust of the engaged colonnettes and the graceful sweep of the ribs on the roof vault.
The stained-glass windows were inserted from 1923: *'grisaille'* (monotonal) windows round the apse, and

brighter-coloured windows in the nave. The façade's rose windows are 14C. Since the ceremony for the seventh centenary of the death of St Thomas Aquinas in 1974, the relics of the 'saintly doctor' have been on display beneath a high altar of grey marble, from Prouille.

Cloisters – The north door opens into cloisters adorned with twin colonnettes, typical of Languedoc Gothic (other examples may be found in St-Hilaire in the Corbières and Arles-sur-Tech).

Chapelle St-Antonin – This delicate Gothic chapel, on the left of the chapter-house, was built from 1337 to 1341 as a funeral chapel by friar Dominique Grima, who became bishop of Pamiers (keystone of the arch above the head of Christ of the Apocalypse). The bones were transferred from tombs in the nave into an ossuary beneath the altar.

Chapter house (c.1300) – Two very slim facetted columns support the roof vault. The graceful apsidal chapel once more boasts colourful mural decoration.

Grand Réfectoire (*open during temporary exhibitions of modern art*) – The great refectory (north-east corner of the cloisters) is a vast room (built 1303), with a timber-frame roof supported on six transverse arches separating the bays.

Hôtel de Bernuy (Lycée Pierre-de-Fermat)

Open: Visits organised by the tourist office. Closed school holidays, 1 Jan, 25 Dec. 05 62 15 42 15.

This mansion was built in two stages in the early 16C. The beautiful main doorway (*1 rue Gambetta*) blends curves and counter-curves, in typically Gothic style, with medallions. An octagonal corbelled **staircase turret★**, one of the tallest in old Toulouse, is lit through windows that neatly follow the angle where two walls meet.

▷ Rue Gambetta leads to place du Capitole.

Place du Capitole

Along the east side of this vast square, the main meeting point for local residents, stretches the majestic façade of the Capitole building. At the centre of the square, inlaid into the paving, is an enormous bronze Occitan cross, surrounded by the signs of the zodiac, by Raymond Moretti.

Capitole★

Open Easter–end Oct 9am–7pm; rest of year 9am–5pm (first weekend of month and public holiday, 9am–7pm). Closed 1 Jan. No charge. 05 61 22 29 22.

This is the city hall of Toulouse, named after the 'capitouls', or consuls, who used to run the city. The courtyard was the scene of the execution of the duke of Montmorency in 1632 (*see A Bit of History*), about which there is a commemorative plaque set into the flagstones.

The staircase, hall and various rooms, most notably the **Salle des Illustres** dedicated to the most glorious representatives of Toulouse, were decorated with appropriate grandiosity at the time of the Third Republic, by specially commissioned, officially approved painters. Cross the courtyard and walk diagonally through the gardens to get to the keep (*donjon*), a remnant of the 16C Capitole, restored by Viollet-le-Duc. It now houses the tourist office.

2 SOUTH FROM THE PLACE DU CAPITOLE

▷ Leave place du Capitole heading south along rue Saint-Rome.

Rue St-Rome

Pedestrian street.

This busy shopping street is part of the old *cardo maximus* (Roman road through town from north to south). At the beginning of the street (No. 39) stands the interesting house of Catherine de' Medici's physician (Augier Ferrier). Pierre Séguy's fine Gothic turret is tucked inside the courtyard of No. 4 **rue Jules-Chalande**. At No. 3 rue St-Rome is an elegant early 17C town house, the Hôtel de Gomère.

Musée du Vieux Toulouse

Open mid-Apr–Nov Mon–Sat 2–6pm. €2.50. *05 62 27 11 50.* *http://toulousainsdetoulouse.fr*

The beautiful Hôtel Dumay was built in red brick embellished with stone at the end of the 16C by Antoine Dumay, chief physician to queen Marguerite de Valois. The museum it now houses brings together collections on the history of Toulouse: paintings and sculptures, portraits of local dignitaries, plans for buildings, and archaeological finds excavated in the city and surrounding area. Regional folk arts include costumes, ceramics and everyday objects.

Rue des Changes

The square known as 'Quatre Coins des Changes' is overlooked by the Sarta turret. Nos. 20, 19 and 17 boast some interesting decorative features (timbering, window frames etc), whereas No. 16, the 16C Hôtel d'Astorg et St-Germain, has a façade with a gallery just beneath the eaves – a local feature known as *mirandes* – and a courtyard with timber galleries and diagonally opposed spiral staircases with wooden handrails.

▷ Turn right before reaching the place Esquirol crossroads.

Rue Malcousinat

At No. 11, the 16C Hôtel de Cheverny, the attractive main building, which is Gothic-Renaissance, is flanked by an austere 15C keep.

▷ Turn right onto rue de la Bourse.

Rue de la Bourse

Note at No. 15 the Hôtel de Nupces (18C). No. 20, the late-15C Hôtel Delfau, is the house of Pierre Del Fau, who hoped to become a *capitoul,* but who never fulfilled his ambition.

The 24m-high turret, pierced with five large windows, is quite remarkable.

▷ Turn left onto rue Cujas.

Basilique Notre-Dame-de-la-Daurade

The present church, which dates from the 18C, occupies the site of a pagan temple that was converted into a church in the 5C, and a Benedictine monastery. Take the **quai de la Daurade** upstream, past the fine arts academy (École des Beaux-Arts). There is a good view across the river of the Hôtel-Dieu.

(*For sights going the other way along the riverbank, see p326).*

Pont Neuf

Despite the name, this is the city's oldest bridge, completed in 1632. It effectively connects Gascony on the left bank of the river with Languedoc on the right.

▷ Rue de Metz (left); bear left again.

Hotel d'Assézat★★

This, the finest private mansion in Toulouse, was built in 1555–57 according to the plans of Nicolas Bachelier, the greatest Renaissance architect of Toulouse, for the Capitoul d'Assézat, who had made a fortune from trading in dyer's woad.

The façades of the buildings to the left of and opposite the entrance are the earliest example of the use of the Classical style in Toulouse, characterised by the three decorative orders – Doric, Ionic, Corinthian – used one above the other, creating a marvellously elegant effect. To add a bit of variety to these façades, the architect introduced rectangular windows beneath relieving arches on the ground and first floors. On the second floor, the lines are reversed, with round-arched windows beneath straight horizontal entablatures.

The sophistication of this design is matched by the elaborate decoration on the two doorways, one with twisted columns and the other adorned with scrolls and garlands. Sculpture underwent a revival in Toulouse at the time of the Renaissance, when stone began to be used again, in conjunction with brick. On the inside of the façade facing the street, there is an elegant portico with four arcades, surmounted by a gallery.

Hôtel d'Assézat

© Jean-Marc Barrère/hemis.fr

The fourth side was never completed, as Assézat, having converted to the Protestant faith, was driven into exile, a ruined man. The wall is adorned only by a covered gallery resting on graceful consoles.

Fondation Bemberg★★

Pl. d'Assézat. & ⏱Open daily except Mon 10am–12.30pm, 1.30–6pm (Thu 8.30pm). ⏱Closed 1 Jan, 25 Dec. ⬡€8. ℘05 61 12 06 89. www.fondation-bemberg.fr.

The Hôtel d'Assézat now houses the donation of private art collector Georges Bemberg. This impressive collection comprises painting, sculpture and objets d'art from the Renaissance to the 20C. Old Masters (16C–18C) are displayed as they would be in a private home. There are paintings by the 18C Venetian School (vedute by Canaletto and Guardi), 15C Flemish works such as *Virgin and Child* from the studio of Rogier Van der Weyden and 17C Dutch painting, with *Musicians* by Pieter de Hooch. Displayed with the paintings are 16C objets d'art such as a nautilus and a grisaille Limoges enamel plaque depicting Saturn.

The **Renaissance portrait gallery** includes paintings (*Charles IX* by François Clouet, *Portrait of a Young Woman with a Ring* by Ambrosius Benson and *Portrait of Antoine de Bourbon* by Franz Pourbus) and 16C sculpture groups. The small room adjoining this contains

bronzes from Italy, such as a superb figure of Mars attributed to Giovanni Bologna, alongside Limoges enamels, leather-bound books and paintings by Veronese, Tintoretto and Bassano.

An open gallery overlooking the courtyard leads to the staircase up to the second floor, which is devoted to **Modern Masters** (19C–20C). The collection's highlight is the series of paintings by Bonnard, executed in a vibrant palette (*Woman with a Red Cape, Le Cannet, Still Life with Lemons*). The collection features other works by almost all the great names of the Modern French School from Impressionism and Pointillism to Fauvism. Artists featured include Louis Valtat, Paul Gauguin, Matisse, H-E Cross, Eugène Boudin, Claude Monet and Raoul Dufy.

▷ Take rue des Marchands (right), then rue des Filatiers (right), then rue des Polinaires (right) and rue H.-de-Gorsse, in which there are some attractive 16C houses. Turn left onto rue de la Dalbade.

Église Notre-Dame-la-Dalbade

This church was built in the 16C, on the site of an earlier building. In 1926 the bell-tower fell in, damaging the church, which was subsequently restored, with particular attention paid to its beautiful brickwork.

Rue de la Dalbade

This street is lined with the elegant mansions of former local dignitaries. Nos. 7, 11, 18 and 20 have fine 18C façades. Note No. 22, the Hôtel Molinier, which boasts an extravagantly ornate, sculpted doorway (16C) of quite profane inspiration. The **Hôtel de Clary**, at No. 25, has a beautiful Renaissance courtyard.

Rue Pharaon

This really pretty street has a number of interesting features: the Hôtel du Capitoul Marvejol at No. 47 (charming courtyard); 18C façades at No. 29; turret dating from 1478 at No. 21.

⬭ Walk along rue Pharaon to place des Carmes then turn right onto rue Ozenne.

Hôtel Béringuier-Maynier (Hôtel du Vieux-Raisin)

The main building at the back of the courtyard marks the first manifestation of the Italian Renaissance in Toulouse, in the style of the châteaux of the Loire Valley (stone as well as brick work).

⬭ Behind the mansion, take rue Ozenne.

Rue Ozenne

At No. 9 the Hôtel Dahus and Tournoër turret make a handsome 15C architectural group.

⬭ Take rue de la Pleau to the left.

Musée Paul-Dupuy★

13 r. de la Pleau. 🕐*Open daily except Mon 10am–6pm.* 🕐*Closed 1 Jan, 1 May, 25 Dec.* ✺€4. ✆*05 31 22 95 40.* This museum, in the Hôtel Pierre-Besson, is devoted to the applied arts from the Middle Ages to the present: metal and wood work, clock-making, weights and measures, coins, musical instruments, enamel work, gold plate, costumes and weapons.

Rue Mage

This is one of the best-preserved streets in Toulouse, with period houses at Nos.

20 and 16 (Louis XIV) and No. 11 (Louis XIII); the Hôtel d'Espie (No. 3) is an example of French Rococo (Louis XV or Regency style).

Rue Bouquière

Note the splendid architecture of the Hôtel de Puivert (18C).

Hôtel de Fumel (Palais Consulaire)

This mansion houses the Chamber of Commerce. It features a fine 18C façade, at right angles, overlooking the garden. From the corner of rue Tolosane, the façade and tower of the cathedral can be seen, whereas to the left the tower of Les Augustins rises from among trees. No. 24 **rue Croix-Baragnon** is home to the city's Cultural Centre. No. 15, 'the oldest house in Toulouse', dating from the 13C, is distinguished by its gemel windows.

Place St-Étienne

In the square stands Toulouse's oldest fountain, 'Le Griffoul' (16C).

Cathédrale St-Étienne★

Compared to St-Sernin, the cathedral appears curiously unharmonious in style. It was built over several centuries, from the 11C to the 17C, and combines the Gothic styles of both southern and northern France.

⬭ Enter through the west doorway.

The vast single nave, as wide as it is high, is the first manifestation of the southern French Gothic style and gives a good idea of the progress made in architectural techniques: St-Étienne's single vault spans 19m, and St-Sernin's Romanesque vault a mere 9m.
Leave by the south door and walk round the church to appreciate the robust solidity of the buttresses supporting the chancel, evidence that they were intended to support greater things...

⬭ Turn left onto rue de Metz then right onto rue des Arts and left again onto rue de la Pomme, which leads back to place du Capitole.

Musée des Augustins★★

Rue de Metz. &🕐*Open daily except Tue 10am–6pm (Wed 9pm).* 🕐*Closed 1 Jan, 1 May, 25 Dec.* ⊚€5. ✆*05 61 22 21 82. www.augustins.org.*

This museum is housed in a former Augustinian monastery designed in the southern French Gothic style (14C and 15C); specifically the chapter-house and the great and small cloisters.

Religious painting (14C–18C) – The paintings are from the 15C, 16C and 17C (Perugino, Rubens, Murillo, Guercino, Simon Vouet, Nicolas Tournier, Murillo), and the sculptures from the 16C–17C.

Romanesque sculptures★★★ (12C) – In the western wing, built on plans by Viollet-le-Duc and punctuated by great arches, the admirable historiated or foliated capitals were mostly taken from the cloisters of St-Sernin Basilica, the monastery of Notre-Dame de la Daurade and buildings from the chapter-house of St-Étienne Cathedral.

French painting (17C–19C) – Upstairs, the *salon rouge*, which is evocative of 19C museums in its presentation (there are many paintings on the walls, some of them quite high up), is largely devoted to 19C French painting.

The *salon brun* is devoted to works created in Toulouse in the 17C–18C. The *salon vert* displays 17C–18C French paintings: Philippe de Champaigne (*Réception d'Henri d'Orléans*), Largillière, Oudry.

After visiting the museum, return to the **cloisters**, where different gardens have been recreated as they would have existed in medieval monasteries and abbeys.

Galeries Lafayette

4-8 rue Lapeyrouse.
There is a panoramic view of rooftops and church spires from the terrace on the top floor of this department store.

ALONG THE RIVERBANK

This walk starts from the quai de la Daurade in front of the church of the same name (&see p323).

River/Canal Cruises

A good way to get an introduction to Toulouse is to take a cruise on a modern passenger barge departing from the quai de la Daurade. Off-season you can turn up and walk on board, but in summer you'll need to reserve in advance.

The most popular route, which takes one and a quarter hours, travels up the Canal de la Brienne into the Port de l'Embouchure, where the Canal du Midi sets off for the Mediterranean and the Canal de la Garonne for Bordeaux.
Toulouse Croisières: ✆05 61 25 72 57. *www. toulouse-croisieres.com.*
Péniche Baladine: ✆05 61 80 22 26. *www.bateaux-toulousains.com.*

▷ Walk downstream along quai Lucien Lombard to Place St Pierre.

Pont St-Pierre

The handsome steel bridge of Pont St Pierre was originally built in 1852 but entirely rebuilt in 1987. Across the river is the green dome of the Hôpital de la Grave, a prominent landmark.

▷ Continue along the river bank on quai St Pierre.

Ecluse St Pierre and canal de Brienne

The last manually operated lock in the city lets boats into the short but picturesque Canal de Brienne. Set back from the lock is the oldest church in southwest France. the Eglise St-Pierre-des Cuisines.

▷ Continue down quai St Pierre.

Espace EDF Bazacle

Standing beside a weir across the Garonne, this working hydroelectric power station combines splendid river views, art exhibitions and insights into eight centuries of industrial history. The site was occupied by water mills from 1189 until 1890 when turbines were installed to power the city's street lighting. Hands-on exhibits explain how electricity is generated. The basement is below water level and a window allows visitors to observe fish as they navigate a special 'ladder' in order to migrate downstream towards the ocean (May–July).

▶ Retrace your steps to place St Pierre and turn left up Rue Valade.

The University Cloister
In the university campus, to the left stands an 18C cloister, part of the former monastery of St-Pierre de Chartreux.

AROUND JARDIN DES PLANTES
Muséum d'Histoire Naturelle★★
Located in the Jardin des Plantes (botanical gardens). ◐*Open daily except Mon 10am–6pm.* ◐*Closed 1 Jan, 1 May, 25 Dec.* ✆€7. ℘05 67 7384 84. *www.museum.toulouse.fr.*
The natural history museum has extensive collections, most notably of ornithological, prehistoric and ethnographical exhibits.

Jardins
Take this opportunity to discover the **Jardin des Plantes**, the **Jardin Royal** and the **Grand Rond**, well laid out gardens that make a very pleasant place for a stroll. At the southern end of allée Fréderic-Mistral, in the botanical gardens, stands the **Musée Départemental de la Résistance et de la Déportation** (&◐*open daily except weekends 9.30am–noon, 2–6pm;* ◐*closed public holidays;* ✆*no charge;* ℘05 61 14 80 40). An arrangement of lenses ensures that sunlight enters the crypt only on 19 August, the anniversary of the liberation of Toulouse.

Musée Georges-Labit★
Along the Canal du Midi, near rue du Japon. &◐*Open daily except Mon 10am–6pm.* ◐*Closed 1 Jan, 1 May, 25 Dec.* ✆€4. ℘05 31 22 99 80.
This museum is located in the Moorish villa in which Georges Labit (1862–99), an enthusiastic collector of anything to do with the Orient, assembled the artefacts brought back from his travels.

SAINT-CYPRIEN QUARTER
Les Abattoirs (Musée d'Art Moderne et Contemporain)★
76 allées Charles-de-Fitte (west bank of the Garonne). &◐*Open daily except Mon and Tue noon–8pm.* ✆€7. ℘05 34 51 10 60. *www.lesabattoirs.org.*
The brick buildings of the former slaughter houses have been turned into a museum of modern and contemporary art illustrating various post-war trends.

Le Château d'eau
Just across the Pont Neuf from the city centre is this brick-built 1823 water tower which supplied the 90 public fountains of the city until 1870. In 1974 it was transformed into a gallery dedicated to exhibitions on photography.

Hôtel-Dieu
Before becoming a hospital at the beginning of the 15C, the Hotel-Dieu was charitable institution accommodating and feeding the poor, the sick and pilgrims en route to Santiago de Compostela. Notable in it are two rooms: the immense, wood-pannelled Salle des Pèlerins and the salle des Colonnes, which takes its name from the pillars supporting the roof.
The hospital's Viguerie wing houses two museums to do with medicine.

Musée d'Histoire de la médecine de Toulouse
◐*Open Thu–Fri and some Sundays and public holidays 11am–5pm.* ✆*No charge.* ℘05 61 77 84 25. *www.musee-medecine.com.*
The city's museum of the history of medicine consists of four rooms including the ancient pharmacy complete with pots, mortars and scales. Other items on display illustrate the evolution of medical techniques taught in Toulouse's medical schools. On the walls are portraits of benefactors and celebrated doctors.

Musée des Instruments de médecine
◐*Thu–Fri 1–5pm, first Sun of month 10am–6pm.* ✆*No charge.* ℘05 61 77 82 72. *www.chu-toulouse.fr.*

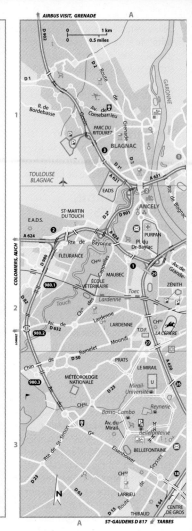

TOULOUSE
Map II

WHERE TO STAY

Athénée (Hôtel) .... ⑤

Brienne (Hôtel de) .... ⑦

Manoir St-Clair
(Chambre d'hôte) .... ⑧

Mermoz (Hôtel) .... ⑨

WHERE TO EAT

Bellevue (Le) .... ③

Table des Merville (La) .... ⑩

Galerie municipale
du Château d'eau .... D

A collection of medical objects dating from the last half of the 19C to the present day, relating to divers specialities including surgery and obstetrics.

EXCURSIONS
Canal de Garonne
The northern extension of the Canal du Midi stretches 193km/120mi from the Port de l'Embouchure in Toulouse to Castets-en-Dorthe. A cycling and walking route follows it for the first 20km/12mi from Toulouse.

Grenade
30km/18.6mi northwest of Toulouse on the D 902.
This bastide founded in 1290 is visited for its 14C covered market hall, the oldest such building in France, and its 14–15C Languedoc Gothic church with its 47m brick bell tower inspired by that of the Jacobins in Toulouse.

Château de Merville
20km/12.4mi northwest of Toulouse by the D 902 in the direction of Grenade; 6km/3.7mi after Seilh, turn left on the D 87A. The chateau is on the right as you

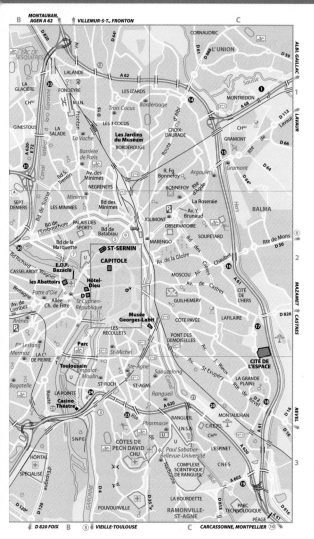

enter the village. ⏱Open mid-end Apr daily; May–Jun and Sept–Oct Sat–Sun and public holidays; Jul–Aug daily. House open 2–6pm. ⚲€8 (child 4–18, €6). ℘05 61 85 67 46. www.chateau-merville.com.

Europe's largest boxwood maze opens to visitors from spring to autumn in the grounds of this brick-built country house which was erected between 1750 and 1759 by the marquis de Chalvet-Rochemonteix, grand seneschal of Toulouse.

6km/4mi of paths between tall mature box hedges shaded by ancient oak trees provide the basic structure for the maze which changes its configuration annually. Two themed routes, each taking approximately an hour and a half, lead from start to finish. The way is blocked, however, by locked gates and arches of cascading water which can only be passed by solving clues and punching the relevant code into a keypad.

The house, with its elegant rooms decorated in period style, can be visited before or after exploring the maze, or in between the two routes.

Aerospace Industry★★

A Bit of History

'La Ligne' – During the inter-war period, Toulouse became the departure point for France's first ever scheduled airline, thanks to the efforts of industrialists such as P Latécoère, administrators such as D Daurat, and pilots such as Mermoz, Saint-Exupéry and Guillaumet.

25 Dec 1918: First trial flight from Toulouse to Barcelona.

1 Sep 1919: First airmail service between France and Morocco.

1 Jun 1925: Aircraft reach Dakar. Pioneers pilot routes to and in S. America.

12 May 1930: First commercial South Atlantic crossing.

Post-war – After the World War II and the maiden flight of the Leduc 010, prototype of high-speed aircraft on 21 April 1949, four important projects helped to boost the French aeronautical industry. Two military aircraft (Transall, Breguet Atlantic) and two civil aircraft (Caravelle, Concorde) enabled French engineers and research consultants to hone their talents as aircraft designers and to develop teamwork with their British and German counterparts.

1 May 1959: Caravelle's maiden flight on the Paris-Athens-Istanbul route.

2 Mar 1969: First test flight of 'Concorde 001,' the first supersonic airliner, piloted by André Turcat.

1 Jan 1970: Founding of Aérospatiale, amalgamation of Nord-Aviation, Sud-Aviation and Sereb.

Airbus – A product of European ambition (initially Anglo-French, then Franco-German from 1969, and Franco-Spanish after 1987), Airbus Industrie has in 20 years become the world's second most important civil aviation manufacturer

Airbus Visit

Village Aéroconstellation, r. Franz Joseph Strauss (Blagnac, in the western suburbs of the city). 🕐➤Tours daily except Sun and public holidays. Reservation essential. Identity card or passport required. ✆From €15.50. 📞05 34 39 42 00. www.taxiway.fr. Visits to the Airbus site are by guided tour. There are three stages, each taking about 1h30. 1. The Panoramic Tour is by bus and gives an overview of the installations. 2. J.L. Lagardère Plant: from a belvedere built into the plant, enjoy the view over the interior and exterior general testing stations, and over the whole site. 3. Telemetry room: presentation of the A380 programme and its certification campaign (first flights and test campaigns).

Cité de l'Espace

© Didier Zylberyng/hemis.fr

Aeroscopia

With its unique collection, Aeroscopia is the home of a rich local aviation heritage and a place of memory, creating a link between the past, the present and the future of aviation (*www.musee-aeroscopia.fr*).

🏛️ Cité de l'Espace★

Parc de la Plaine, along the eastern side of the ringroad. Early Jul–Aug 9.30am–7pm; rest of year 9.30am–5pm (weekends and school holidays 9.30am–6pm). 🚗16–22€ (children 5–15 years, 12–14.50€); 🚶guided visit possible (1hr) 4€. 📞0 820 377 223. www.cite-espace.com. Visible from quite a distance thanks to a 53m/170ft high replica Ariane 5 rocket, Toulouse's 'space city' is great fun for older kids and adults, and is also educational. Attractions include a Mir space station, IMAX cinema, planetarium and moon walk simulator.

Château de Larra

25km/15.5mi northwest of Toulouse. From Merville take the D87a. cross the D17 and turn right on the D87. A road to the left leads to Larra.

This grand house on a square plan was built in the 18C by the architect of the façade of the capitol, Guillaume Cammas. All the rooms are decorated with white or coloured stucco. The salon looks out on to a fleur-de-lys of clipped box hedges and four fountains.

African Safari

41 r. des Landes, Plaisance-du-Touch, (14km/8.6mi southwest of Toulouse). 🕐Open daily Apr–Sep 9.30am–7.30pm; Oct–Mar 10am–6pm. 🚗€16.50 (child 2–10, €12.50). 📞05 61 86 45 03. www.zoo-africansafari.com.

The visit begins with a car tour through enclosures inhabited by lions, camels, zebras, gnus and rhinoceroses. The rest of the zoo is explored on foot. Animals to see, each to its enclosure, include big cats, wolves, monkeys, kangaroos, parrots and sea lions.

Muret

16km/9.9mi south of Toulouse by motorway.

A decisive battle in the Albigensian crusade was fought here on 12 September 1213 when Simon de Montfort routed the army of count Raymond of Toulouse. The aviation pioneer Clément Ader was born in Muret in 1841. In 1890 he achieved a flight of 50m, 13 years before the Wright brothers. A small museum celebrates his life and achievements.

🚗DRIVING TOUR

TOULOUSE TO THE SEUIL DE NAUROUZE

For the route of this tour from Toulouse to the Seuil de Naurouze, refer to the region map – Allow around 2h.

▶ Leave Toulouse on the N 113 heading southeast.

This route crosses the ferile Lauragais plain. Chateaux and churches in Toulousain Gothic style with belfry walls testify to an age when woad production made this a prosperous region.

Montgiscard

Bastide founded by Alphonse de Poitiers, brother of Saint Louis, in the 13C. The 14C gothic church has a belfry wall pierced by six mitre-arched openings and flanked by two turrets. It was built by Nicolas Bachelier, architect of the hôtel d'Assézat in Toulouse. Behind the church there is a curious house decorated with an ironwork canopy.

▶ From Montgiscard take the N 113 in the direction of Ayguesvives.

Écluse d'Ayguesvives

This picturesque lock in the centre of a hamlet faces an 1831 mill.

N 113 crosses the canal.
In Avignonet-Lauragais, take D 80 towards Baraigne.

Aire de Port Lauragais

This rest area on the A 61 motorway between Villefranche-de-Lauragais and Castelnaudary is on the Canal du Midi. A harbourmaster's office welcomes passing boats.

Return to Avignonet; continue east on N 113, then turn off to Montferrand.

Montferrand

This hilltop village was the site of a Cathar fortress that fell in 1211. All that remains is the gate. Note the 16C belfry-wall of the deconsecrated church.

Go back to N 113 and cross via D 218.

Obelisque de Riquet

Leave the car in the parking area near the monument.
The obelisk, built in 1825 by Riquet's descendants, stands in an enclosure formed by the 'stones of Naurouze', between the Naurouze Pass (N 113) and the canal.

Seuil de Naurouze

See CARCASSONE.

ADDRESSES

STAY

Hotel Albert 1er – *8 r. Rivals. 05 61 21 17 91. www.hotel-albert1.com. 47 rooms.* Ideally placed from which to explore the city on foot.

Hôtel St-Claire – *29 pl. Nicolas-Bachelier. 05 34 40 58 88. www.stclaire hotel.fr. 16 rooms.* Five minutes from place Wilson, a small hotel with elegant rooms, inspired by Feng Shui. Discounts at certain periods.

Hôtel de l'Ours Blanc-Place Victor Hugo – *25 pl. Victor-Hugo. 05 61 23 14 55. www.hotel-oursblanc.com. 38 rooms.* Opposite the market, but well soundproofed and air-conditioned; simple and very comfortable.

Hôtel Castellane – *17 r. Castellane. 05 61 62 18 82. www.castellanehotel.com. 53 rooms.* This small hotel close to the Capitole is slightly set back from the main thoroughfare. The rooms are housed in three different buildings; some well suited to families.

Chambre d'hôte Manoir St-Clair – *20 ch. de Sironis, 31130 Balma. 05 61 24 36 98. www.manoirsaintclair.com. 3 rooms.* An authentic 17C manor with brick walls circulating a grand park with trees and flowers. The pretty rooms are decorated with inspiration from the region.

Hôtel Athénée – *13 bis r. Matabiau. 05 61 63 10 63. www.hotel-toulouse-athenee.com. 35 rooms.* Just 500m from St Sernin; a lovely relaxing place.

Hôtel de Brienne – *20 bd du Mar.-Leclerc. 05 61 23 60 60. www.hoteldebrienne.com. 77 rooms.* A place most suitable for business people, but equally appropriate for those on holiday.

Hôtel de l'Ours Blanc-Centre – *14 pl. Victor-Hugo. 05 61 21 25 97. www.hotel-oursblanc.com. 44 rooms.* Close to the centre of the city; sound-proofed and air-conditioned rooms.

Hôtel des Beaux-Arts – *1 pl. du Pont-Neuf. 05 34 45 42 42. www.hoteldesbeauxarts.com. 19 rooms.* An 18C house refurbished with taste to create cosy and comfortable rooms. Most have a view over the Garonne river and No. 42 has its own small terrace.

Hôtel Mermoz – *50 r. Matabiau 05 61 63 04 04. http://privilegetoulouse.com. 52 rooms.* The inner flower garden of this hotel near the city centre provides a haven of calm. Spacious rooms furnished in 1930s style.

Hôtel du Grand Balcon – *8 r. Romiguières. 05 34 25 44 09. www.grandbalconhotel.com. 47 rooms.* Very close to the place du Capitole is this legendary hotel which once lodged the pioneer aviators Saint-Exupéry and Mermoz. The rooms and suites are decorated in different styles. The lounges, bars and restaurant all have a touch of elegance about them.

EAT

J'Go – *16 pl. Victor-Hugo. 05 61 23 02 03. www.lejgo.com. Closed 1 Jan, 24 and 31 Dec.* Both cuisine and decor pay homage to the region. A diner appreciated by the locals.

🍽🛏 **7 Place St-Sernin** – *7 pl. St-Sernin - 📞05 62 30 05 30. www.7placesaintsernin. com. Closed Sat lunch and Sun.* The outdoor tables of this well-known restaurant enjoy a view of the Basilica St-Sernin. Exquisite food.

🍽🛏 **Le Bellevue** – *1 av. des Pyrénées, 31120 Lacroix-Falgarde. 📞05 61 76 94 97. www.restaurant-lebellevue.com. Closed Tue, Wed.* This former dance hall was in its prime in the 1940s. Now a restaurant, it is enjoying a revival of fortunes.

🍽🛏 **Colombier** – *14 r. Bayard. 📞05 61 62 40 05. www.restaurant-lecolombier.com. Closed Mon lunch, Sat lunch and Sun. Reservation recommended.* Opened in 1874, this is an essential stopping point for culinary pilgrims in search of authentic cassoulet. Delightful dining room with pink bricks and wall paintings. Friendly and efficient service.

🍽🛏 **La Madeleine de Proust** – *11 r. Riquet. 📞05 61 63 80 88. www.made leinedeproust.com. Closed Sat lunch, Sun eve and Mon.* Childhood memories inspire the original, carefully designed decor of this restaurant featuring yellow walls, waxed tables, antique toys, an old school desk, a time-worn cupboard. The cuisine gives the starring role to vegetables that have fallen out of common use.

🍽🛏 **Le Mangevins** – *46 r. Pharaon. 📞05 61 52 79 16. Closed weekends.* In this local tavern where salted foie gras and beef are sold by weight, the bawdy, fun atmosphere is enhanced by ribald songs. There is no menu, but a set meal for hearty appetites.

🍽🛏 **Rôtisserie des Carmes** – *138 r. Polinaires. 📞05 61 53 34 88. www. cartesurtables.com. Closed Sat, Sun and public holidays.* Next to the market, the chef serves whatever is available that day.

🍽🛏 **La Table des Merville** – *3 pl. Richard. 31320 Castanet-Tolosan. 📞05 62 71 24 25. www.table-des-merville. com. Closed Sun & 24 Dec–4 Jan.* The appetising cuisine of this welcoming restaurant reflects the availability of ingredients in the market. Modern art is displayed on the walls.

🍽🛏🛏🛏 **Brasserie Flo 'Beaux Arts'** – *1 quai Daurade. 📞05 61 21 12 12. www.brasserielesbeauxarts.com. Daily.* The atmosphere of a 1930s brasserie is recreated here with bistro-style chairs, wall seats, retro lighting, wood panelling and mirrors. The cuisine, in keeping with the decor, features seafood, sauerkraut and a few regional specialities.

TAKING A BREAK

Maison Octave – *21 rue Bellegarde. 📞05 61 12 38 38. Open daily. www.octave.eu.* Famous ice cream parlour serving an overwhelming choice of sherbets, ice cream, *vacherins*.

ON THE TOWN

Au Père Louis – *45 r. des Tourneurs. 📞05 61 21 33 45. Mon–Sat 8.30am– 2.30pm, 6–11.30pm. Closed Aug.* First opened in 1889 and now a registered historical building, this wine bar is a local institution. Wine is sipped around fat-bellied barrels; an appetizing choice of open-faced sandwiches is available in the evening.

Cinémathèque de Toulouse – *69 r. du Taur, BP 824 . 📞05 62 30 30 10. www. lacinemathequedetoulouse.com.* This cinematic citadel, founded in 1950 by Raymond Borde, was overseen by Daniel Toscan du Plantier between 1996 and 2003. Numerous theme cycles and film festivals. Exhibition hall, library and bar.

SHOPPING

Markets – The Sunday morning country market held round the Eglise St-Aubin is where farmers sell their fruit, vegetables and poultry, live or butchered. Wednesday and Friday from November to March, geese, ducks and foie gras are sold at place du Salin. Saturday mornings an organic farmers' market is held at place du Capitole. Sunday mornings L'Inquet, a renowned flea market, takes place at Place Arnaud Bernard. Used-book sellers gather around place St-Étienne Saturdays and place Arnaud-Bernard Thursdays (many are present at L'Inquet as well).

Shopping streets – The main shopping streets are rue d'Alsace-Lorraine, rue Croix-Baragnon, rue St-Antoine-du-T., rue Boulbonne, rue des Arts and the pedestrian sections of rue St-Rome, rue des Filatiers, rue Baronie and rue de la Pomme. There is also a shopping mall, St-Georges, in the centre of the city.

La Maison de la Violette – *Bd de Bonrepas, Canal du Midi. 📞05 61 99 01 30. www.lamaisondelaviolette.fr. Mon–Sat*

9.30am–12.30pm, 2–7pm. Closed Mon in Nov, and from Jan–Mar. The celebrated Toulouse violet is the star of this shop and café on a pastel barge. The owner's enthusiasm for this noble flower is contagious.

Olivier Confiseur-Chocolatier – *20 r. Lafayette. ℘05 61 23 21 87. www. chocolatsolivier.com. Mon 2–7pm, Tue–Sat 9.30am–7pm. Sun 10am–1pm (exc summer).* Olivier, a master chocolate maker, produces irresistible specialities, including the famous sugared violets, capitouls (almonds covered in dark chocolate), *Clémence Isaure* (Armagnac-soaked grapes covered in dark chocolate), *brindilles* (nougatine covered in chocolate praline) and *Péché du Diable*, The Devil's Sin, (dark chocolate ganache with orange peel and ginger). Heaven help us!

ACTIVITIES

Touch and Go – *Blagnac airport. Mon–Sat by appointment only. ℘06 08 67 72 84.* A guided tour taking visitors behind the scenes of a modern airport to see all the processes needed in order for a plane to take off.

Toulouse Croisières – *Quai de la Daurade. ℘05 61 25 72 57. www.toulouse-croisieres. com. Cruises all year, Jul–Aug: also night cruises.* Embark upon the pleasure steamer Le Capitole for a cruise along the Garonne. You'll discover the Pont Neuf, the Saint-Michel lock, the untamed banks of the Île du Grand Ramier.

Péniche Baladine – *℘05 61 80 22 26 or 06 74 64 52 36. www.bateaux-toulousains. com. Departs quai de la Daurade. Oct–May: Wed, Sat, Sun and public holidays; Jun-Sep and school holidays: open every day.* Canal du Midi cruises *(1h15)* depart at 10.50am and 4pm, Garonne cruises *(1hr15mins)* depart at 2.30pm, 5.30pm and 7pm. Details of night cruises on request.

EVENTS

Fête de la violette – *Feb. ℘05 62 16 31 31.* The ideal opportunity to learn all about the flower that is the city's emblem.

Printemps du rire – *Late Mar–early Apr. ℘05 62 21 23 24. www.printempsdurire. com.* Spring comedy festival.

Le Printemps de Septembre – *Late Sept, noon–7pm Mon–Fri, 11am–7pm Sat–Sun. ℘01 43 38 00 11. www.printempsde septembre.com.* Festival of photography and visual arts.

Festival Occitania – *Oct. ℘05 61 11 24 87, www.ieotolosa.free.fr.* Regional culture celebrated through various media (cinema, poetry, song etc…).

Jazz sur son 31 – *Oct (2nd and 3rd) weeks. ℘05 34 45 05 92, www.jazz31.com.* Large jazz festival established 18 years ago.

Saint-Félix-Lauragais
and Dyer's Woad Country

Saint-Félix in a pretty site★ overlooking the Lauragais plain, passed into history (or legend, as some see it) when the Cathars held a council here to set up their church.

A BIT OF HISTORY

Saint-Félix prides itself on being the birthplace of this composer (1873–1921) of melodies evoking the beauty of nature and the countryside. Debussy said of De Séverac's music that 'it smelt good'. A pupil of Vincent d'Indy and

- ▶ **Population:** 1 337.
- **Michelin Map:** 343: J-4.
- **Info:** Pl. Guillaume-de-Nogaret, 31540 St-Félix-Lauragais. ℘05 62 18 96 99. www.revel-lauragais.com.
- **Location:** 10km/6mi W of Revel, not far from Toulouse and Canal du Midi.
- **Don't Miss:** The Château-Musée du Pastel at Magrin.
- **Timing:** Allow half a day for the driving tour.

Magnard at the Schola Cantorum in Paris, Déodat de Séverac was also profoundly influenced by Debussy's work.

SIGHTS

Castle

There is a pleasant walkway round this castle, built in the 13C and later extended and remodelled, which affords fine views to the east over the Montagne Noire with Revel at its foot. To the north, the belfry of St-Julia and, high up, the castle of Montgey can be seen.

Church

This collegiate church dates from the 14C and was rebuilt at the beginning of the 17C. To the right of the church stands the façade of the chapter house.

Walk

Not far from the church, a vaulted passageway leads to an area where there is a view to the west over peaceful countryside with hills and cypresses.

🚗 DRIVING TOUR

TOULOUSE TO THE SEUIL DE NAUROUZE

52km/32mi tour. Allow around 2h.
♿ *See TOULOUSE.*

DYER'S WOAD COUNTRY

80km/50mi. About 2h.
♿ *See region map.*

Today the plain is given over to the cultivation of wheat, barley and rape seed, and stock raising (cattle, sheep and poultry). An offshoot of poultry rearing has been the installation of factories for food processing.

▶ From St-Félix-Lauragais head N on D 67.

St-Julia

An old fortified 'free' town, with some ramparts and a church with an unusual belfry-wall.

▶ Drive north to the intersection with D 1, turn left towards Montégut-Lauragais, then immediately left towards Puéchoursi; after the village turn right.

Belfry-wall of St-Julia

©Franck Guiziou/Hemis/Photoshot

Montgey

High on a hill, this village has a big **castle** (🕐 *park and terraces always open, chateau visits 10am–6pm by appointment only;* 📞*05 63 75 75 81)*, an old medieval fortress that was captured by Simon de Montfort in 1211, then renovated in the 15C and 17C. From the terrace, there is a view over the Lauragais hills.

▶ Drive W to Aguts along D 45 then N along D 92 to Puylaurens and turn left onto D 12 to Magrin.

Château de Magrin-musée du Pastel★

🕐☕*Guided tours: Jul–Sep 3–5.30pm (and mornings in Aug); rest of year Sun and public holidays, 3–5.30pm.* 🕐*Closed mid-Dec–mid-Jan.* ☜€8. 📞*05 63 70 63 82. www.pastel-chateau-musee.com.*
Perched on top of a hill, the Château de Magrin (12C–16C) offers a splendid **panorama★** of the Montagne Noire and the Pyrenees.
The dyer's woad museum contains a woad mill and drying rack and presents the various stages involved in making blue dye from dyer's woad, including the history of the *Isatis tinctoria* plant.

▶ Leave the château heading southwest to join the D 130 in Algans. At the junction with the N 126, turn right towards Toulouse, then left on the D 20D.

Loubens-Lauragais

This charming village, bright with flowers in season, is tucked up against a

Woad

Known as the source of a deep blue hue since ancient times, woad (*Isatis tinctoria*, pastel in French), was introduced into the Languedoc in the 13C, from either Spain or the orient. The so-called 'Blue Triangle' formed by Albi, Toulouse and Carcassonne was found to have just the right soil and climate for it – mild winters, wet springs and sunny summers – and production increased rapidly in response to export demand from the 14C to the 16C.

At the height of the Renaissance, Languedoc woad was highly praised by the dyers of Europe and fortunes were made, not by growers, but by the merchants of Toulouse, a financial capital that stood in a strategic position between the woad plantations and the Atlantic ports, especially Bordeaux. These 'princes de pastel' built themselves country chateaux and city mansions on the proceeds, the Hotel d'Assézat being the finest surviving example.

Woad is a yellow-flowering crucifer of the cabbage family. Between June and September its leaves are picked, washed, dried and crushed in a mill. The resulting paste is formed into balls called cocagnes, derived from the Occitan word for cake. From them comes the phrase 'Pays de Cocagne', the French version of 'the land of milk and honey'.

The peak of woad production only lasted about 60 years. Decline from the 1560s on was rapid, largely due to the Wars of Religion, financial instability and the arrival of indigo from India, which was preferred by dyers. The woad industry lingered on – Napoleon used woad to dye the uniforms of his soldiers – until the synthetic blue pigments were invented in the 19C.

Recently there has been a revival of interest in woad as a dye by artisanal textile weavers and as a pigment for applications in the fine arts. It has also found new uses in herbalism and in the elaboration of natural cosmetics.

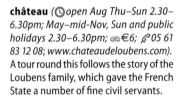

château (🕐 *open Aug Thu–Sun 2.30–6.30pm; May–mid-Nov, Sun and public holidays 2.30–6.30pm;* 🎫€6; 𝄞*05 61 83 12 08; www.chateaudeloubens.com).* A tour round this follows the story of the Loubens family, which gave the French State a number of fine civil servants.

▷ Drive S along D 11 to Caraman, then follow D 25 towards Villefranche-de-Lauragais; 8km/5mi farther on, turn left on D 2.

Vaux

This hilltop village has a Gothic church, which has retained its turreted belfry-wall (1551). The **château** is a Renaissance work (1550–60), as illustrated by the many mullion windows.

▷ Leave Vaux S on D 72 to Mourvilles-hautes then turn left onto the D 79.

Château de Montmaur

Outside only open to the public.

This castle was taken time and again by Simon de Montfort, in 1211 and 1212; pillaged by Protestants in 1577; and rebuilt in the 16C–17C. The main building is square, flanked by four round towers.

▷ Return to St-Félix-Lauragais.

ADDRESSES

EVENT

Fête historique de la cocagne – Easter Sun and Mon. Concerts, circus shows, jugglers, costumed parades, traditional craft fair.

Festival Déodat de Séverac – Jun–Jul. Chamber music, opera, Occitan and Catalan music. For information on both events. 𝄞*05 62 18 96 99 (St Felix Lauragais tourist office).*

l'Isle-Jourdain
and Le Gimontois

Isle Jourdain was a stopover on the road to Santiago de Compostela. Bertrand de l'Isle, founder of Saint-Bertrand-de-Comminges, was born here (*See St-Bertrand-de-Comminges*). Its lake has water sports facilities.

TOWN CENTRE

The main attraction in place de l'Hôtel-de-Ville are the stained-glass windows and façade sculptures on the turn-of-the-century house of Claude Auge. The 18C Collegiate Church has arresting neo-Classical architecture and painted frescoes.

Musée d'Art Campanaire★

Open Tue–Sat and 1st Sun of the month 10am–noon, 2–6pm. Closed 1 May, 25 Dec, 1st two weeks of Jan. €4.50. 05 62 07 30 01.

This bell museum has over 1 000 bells from around the world.

The 'foundry' exhibit explains how bells are made. There are several carillons, some which visitors may play, bells from Europe, America, the South Pacific, Asia and Africa, and **subrejougs** (harness bells from Vallée de la Save) with remarkable polychrome decorations.

EXCURSION
Château de Caumont

10km/6mi southwest of L'Isle-Jourdain. Leave L'Isle-Jourdain heading southwest on the D 634 and after 7km/4mi turn right on the D 243. After la Save turn right on the D 39. Cazaux-Savès.

Guided tours: mid-Apr–Jun Sun and public holidays 3–7pm; Jul–Aug daily 3–6.30pm; Sept–Oct Sat–Sun 3–6.30pm. €8 (children €3.50). 05 62 07 94 20. www.caumont.org.

Built in the 16C by Pierre de Nogaret de La Valette over the ruins of an ancient castle, this 'Loire chateau in Gascony' stands in a remarkable setting overlooking the vallée de la Save.

Pierre's grandson, Pierre, Jean-Louis de Nogaret de La Valette, was born here in

1554. He began his career as a favourite of Henri III and went on to reach the highest positions: duc d'Épernon, governor of Provence, colonel-general of the infantry and admiral.

Flanked by four square towers, the château is composed of three wings arranged in the form of a horse shoe. The north wing, with its balcony over the courtyard, is the oldest part of the building.

Inside, note the Red Room, with its splendid Pyrenean marble fireplace and the beautiful coffered ceiling in the White Room. The visit also takes in the magnificent staircase, the chapel and the king's bedroom which was used on a visit by the future Henry IV.

Château de Caumont

© De Agostini/C. Sappa/age fotostock

ALBIGEOIS *and the Black Mountain*

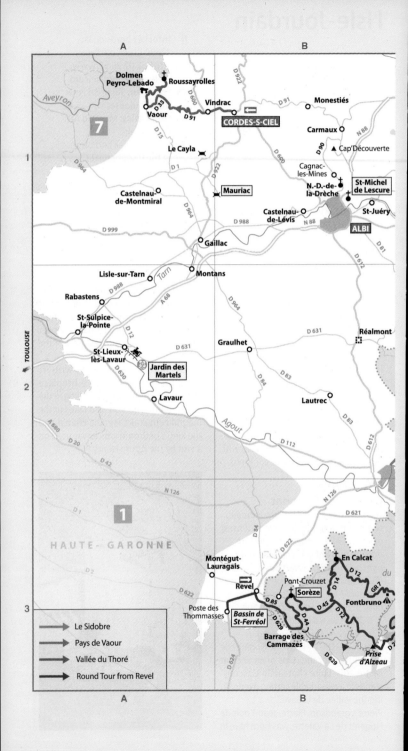

Dolmen Peyro-Lebado
Roussayrolles
D 922
D 91
Monestiés
D 600
Vindrac
Vaour
D 33
D 91
Carmaux
N 88
D 90
▲ Cap'Découverte
D 15
CORDES-S-CIEL
D 600
D 964
Le Cayla
D 1
Cagnac-les-Mines
D 322
Mauriac
N.-D.-de-la-Drèche
St-Michel de Lescure
Castelnau-de-Montmiral
D 964
D 988
Castelnau-de-Lévis
N 88
St-Juéry
D 999
ALBI
D 81
Gaillac
D 612
Lisle-sur-Tarn
Tarn
Montans
D 988
A 68
D 964
Rabastens
D 631
Réalmont
St-Sulpice-la-Pointe
D 12
D 631
Graulhet
TOULOUSE
D 630
St-Lieux-lès-Lavaur
Jardin des Martels
D 631
D 83
D 84
Lautrec
D 83
Lavaur
Agout
D 612
A 680
D 20
D 112
D 42
N 126
N 126
D 621
D 1
1
HAUTE- GARONNE
D 2
D 84
Montégut-Lauragais
D 622
En Calcat
du
D 622
D 12
Revel
Pont-Crouzet
D 14
GR 7
Sorèze
D 85
Fontbruno
Poste des Thommasses
D 45
D 12
Bassin de St-Ferréol
D 629
D 44
Barrage des Cammazes
D 629
Prise d'Alzeau
D 024

7

Aveyron

1

2

3

A   B

→	Le Sidobre
→	Pays de Vaour
→	Vallée du Thoré
→	Round Tour from Revel

A   B

340

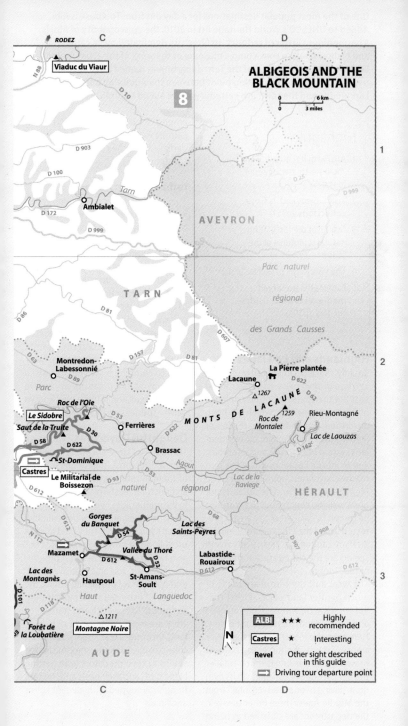

ALBIGEOIS AND THE BLACK MOUNTAIN

RODEZ

Viaduc du Viaur

8

Ambialet

AVEYRON

Parc naturel

régional

des Grands Causses

TARN

Montredon-Labessonnié

Parc

Roc de l'Oie

Le Sidobre

Saut de la Truite

St-Dominique

Castres

Le Militarial de Boissezon

Ferrières

Brassac

La Pierre plantée

Lacaune

△1267

MONTS DE LACAUNE

Roc de Montalet △1259

Rieu-Montagné

Lac de Laouzas

Agout

naturel

régional

Lac de la Raviège

HÉRAULT

Gorges du Banquet

Lac des Saints-Peyres

Mazamet

Vallée du Thoré

Lac des Montagnès

Hautpoul

St-Amans-Soult

Labastide-Rouairoux

Haut

Languedoc

Forêt de la Loubatière

△1211

Montagne Noire

AUDE

N

		Highly recommended
ALBI	★★★	Highly recommended
Castres	★	Interesting
Revel		Other sight described in this guide
		Driving tour departure point

341

One of the most popular destinations for a day out from Toulouse is Albi. Added to UNESCO's World Heritage list in 2010, the episcopal city of Albi is a harmonious cluster of redbrick architecture dominated by its cathedral and bishop's palace containing a museum of the work of the artist Toulouse-Lautrec. Albi is the capital of the Tarn department, named after its principal river, which sits at the meeting point between the Aquitaine basin, the Languedoc and the southern extremity of the Massif Central.

Highlights

1 **Albi** with its cathedral and Toulouse-Lautrec museum (p343)

2 Visit Castres and its **Goya collections** (p351)

3 Marvel at the fascinating natural sculptures of the **Sidobre** (p353)

4 The **vineyards** of Gaillac (p362)

5 Explore the preserved **medieval town** of Cordes-sur-Ciel (p364)

Highlands and Lowlands

Broadly, the department can be divided into two distinct parts. To the south and east are the sparsely popular uplands of the Montagne Noir, which has been described as a massive water tower feeding the Canal du Midi by an ingenious system of channels and reservoirs; and Monts de Lacaune, where the Tarn reaches its highest point, the Puech de Montgrand 1 267m. The uplands are great walking country but they can also be toured by car. Part of this area is protected under the Parc Naturel Régional du Haut-Languedoc. Particularly worth seeing are the curious rock formations of the Sidobre.

The west and the centre are made of much gentler landscapes, either rolling farmland or, approaching Toulouse and the Garonne, agricultural plains. Here are to be found most of the major sights. Albi is, of course, the biggest draw. Cordes-sur-Ciel is much smaller but almost equally appealing in its own right, having been preserved intact from the Middle Ages. Three other towns in the department are classified as being among the most beautiful in France: Lautrec – known for its production of garlic – Monesties and Castelnau-de-Montmiral.

Industrial Heritage

The Tarn is a mainly rural region with a low population density and an economy based on the service sector, especially tourism. In the past, however, it had important industries and while some continue into the present others have ceased and their installations turned into tourist attractions. Such is the case of Carmaux, where installations from coal-mining and glassmaking have been put to new uses to attract visitors.

The department's second city, Castres, on the banks of the Agout river, manages to combine a thriving industrial economy with a pleasant city centre noted for culture. It has a well known gallery specialising in Spanish art.

Delightful Dovecotes

The Tarn has France's highest concentration of dovecotes (pigeonniers), 1 700 of them in total, many of them mini-architectural masterpieces.

In the middle ages, with the rural population rising, pigeons provided a highly-prized source of food. They bred quickly, providing not only eggs and meat but also fertiliser for the fields. A pigeonnier, however, was an expensive luxury that only the wealthy could afford, the degree of ostentation demonstrating the proprietor's wealth and status.

They are most common in rich, lowland farming areas. Many stand on stilts crowned with mushroom shaped stones to keep predators from getting at the birds and their nests and they are frequently topped with elegant spires and finials.

Albi★★★

The beautiful Renaissance mansions of Albi 'la rouge' on the banks of the Tarn are showpieces of the city's mid-15C–mid-16C economic boom in the textile and dyeing industries.

A BIT OF HISTORY

The 'Albigensian Crusade' – The 12C–13C crusade against the followers of Catharism became known as the Albigensian Crusade, perhaps because Albi offered them refuge. The crusade, launched by Pope Innocent III, brought Occitania into the sphere of the French monarch, but it was to take an Inquisition, torture, murder and the 1244 massacre at Montségur to end the so-called heresy.

Henri de Toulouse-Lautrec – The famous artist born in Albi in 1864 was the son of Comte Alphonse de Toulouse-Lautrec Montfa and Adèle Tapié de Celeyran. Childhood accidents left Toulouse-Lautrec crippled for life. In 1882 he moved to Montmartre and lost himself in the seamy life of Paris bars

▶ **Population**: 51 567.
▫ **Info**: Palais de la Berbie, pl. Ste-Cécile, 81000 Albi. ✆05 63 36 36 00. www.albi-tourisme.fr.
◗ **Location**: 76km/47.5mi NE of Toulouse. View this charming town from the 11C **Pont Vieux**, or on a stroll through its narrow winding streets. **Restored mills** now contain local tourist board offices, a museum honouring Lapérouse, a hotel and private residences. The terrace in Botany Bay square affords **views** of the Tarn, the Pont Vieux and the towering cathedral.
⊛ **Don't Miss:** Cathédrale Ste-Cécile; Palais de la Berbie; Musée Toulouse-Lautrec.

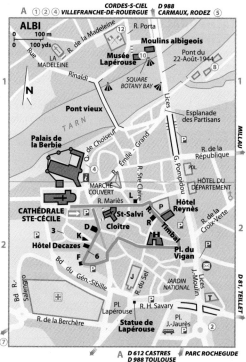

Albi the Red

As in Toulouse, moreso in Albi: brick has always been the building material of preference, giving the city a sheen of pink or varied hues of red, especially at sunrise or sunset. The primary reason for using it was because it was readily available and therefore cheap. The banks of the River Tarn yielded clay in abundance which was easily shaped by hand – you can still see the finger marks left by artisans. In addition, brick is a quick and versatile to build with; it lends safety – the more brick and the less wood, the less susceptible would be a building to the risk of fire; and brick can bear the weight of tall and heavy buildings such as towers.

As a result, brick is everywhere starting with the catheral and bishop's palace, both buildings intended to impress and intimidate.

The golden age of brick construction came after the upheavals of the Albigensian crusade, when Albi was growing wealthy on the proceeds of woad (*see SAINT-FELIX-LAURAGAIS*). Brick was put to glorious effect in the city's hotel particulars built by wealthy citizens who could afford to lift their brick homes above the ordinary by the addition of stone features and artistic decoration.

and brothels, and portrayed them in his paintings. From 1891 his talent as a lithographer won him fame. By 1899, his alcoholism and debauchery landed him in a sanatorium in Neuilly.

Toulouse-Lautrec left Paris in 1901, died in the family château at Malromé on 9 September of that year, and was buried in Verdelais.

CATHÉDRALE STE-CÉCILE★★★

The cathedral's massive proportions are best appreciated from the Pont du 22-Août bridge or from the cathedral square.

&⊙*Open May–Oct daily 9am–6.30pm; Nov–Apr 9am–1.15pm, 2–6.30pm.*

⚭*Chancel: €5 with audioguide; Treasury €2; combined ticket €6.* ℘*05 63 38 47 40. http://cathedrale-albi.com.*

The Catholic Church reclaimed its authority after the Albigensian Crusade. Roman Catholic bishops became as powerful as lords. **Bernard de Combret**, bishop from 1254 to 1271, began constructing a bishops' palace in 1265, and **Bernard de Castanet** (1276–1308) began building the cathedral of Ste-Cécile, which took 200 years. Successive bishops added finishing touches.

The sheer red-brick walls were replaced in 1849 by false machicolations, a rampart walk and bell turrets.

Doorway and canopy porch★ – The main entrance through a 15C doorway

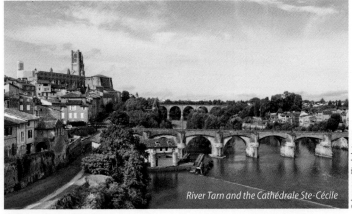

River Tarn and the Cathédrale Ste-Cécile

© dvoevnore/iStockphoto.com

winds up a grand staircase to a carved stone canopy forming the porch. This work of art was added under Louis I of Amboise (1520).

Bell-tower – The original tower was a square, keep-like structure about as high as the nave. Between 1485 and 1492, Louis I added three storeys.

Rood screen★★★ – After the church was consecrated around 1480, Louis I of Amboise built the chancel, closed off by a carved stone rood screen. The resulting interlaced motifs, pinnacles and arches typify Late Flamboyant Gothic decoration. The carved stone screen around the outside of the choir consists of ornate ogee arcading with Flamboyant tracery and the Chi-Rho Christogram. Against each of the pillars between the arches is a polychrome statue of an Old Testament figure, fine examples of the naturalism of Gothic sculpture in France.

Chancel

Statues of Charlemagne and the Emperor Constantine gaze down from the entrance doorways, and other statues depict New Testament figures. The 15C stained-glass windows around the apse were restored in the 19C. The chapel of the Sainte-Croix is worth a view. The monumental **organ** built by Christophe Moucherel in 1734–6 was restored in 1981.

Below the organ stands the new **high altar★**, a creation in black marble by Jean-Paul Froidevaux.

Treasury

As long ago as the 13C this chapel was designated to house the cathedral's archives and precious objects, including a 14C polychrome reliquary of St Ursula, a 13C crosier from the Limoges region, a 14C episcopal ring and Sienese polyptych.

The Last Judgement – This magnificent three-tiered mural, executed in the late 15C, was stripped of its image of Christ in 1693, when the chapel of St-Clair was added to the cathedral.

Cathedral vault – Louis II of Amboise commissioned Bolognese artists to embellish the nave of the cathedral with dazzling paintings inspired by the Italian Renaissance, the Quattrocento (15C).

PALAIS DE LA BERBIE★

The name of Bernard de Combret's bishops' palace 'Berbie' derives from bisbia or 'bishopric' in local dialect. Bernard de Castenet transformed the original building with a massive keep and curtain wall. The Edict of Nantes in 1598 removed the need for this fortress, and since 1922 it has housed the Musée Toulouse-Lautrec.

Musée Toulouse-Lautrec★★

Palais de la Berbie, Place Ste Cécile.
Open Jan 10am–noon, 2–5pm; Feb–Mar and Nov–Dec 10am–noon, 2–5.30pm; Apr–May 10am–noon, 2–6pm; 1st 3 wks of June and Oct 10am–noon, 2–6pm; last wk of Jun–Sept 9am–6pm. Closed Tue Oct–Mar, 1 Jan, 1 May, 1 Nov, 25 Dec.. €8; Free admission to the terraces and gardens of the Palais de la Berbie, all year.
05 63 49 48 70.
www.museetoulouselautrec.net.

A grand 17C staircase leads to archaeological exhibits on the first floor; note the tiny, 15 000-year-old *Vénus de Courbet* discovered at Penne in the Tarn *département.*

The 13C chapel of Notre-Dame has ribbed vaulting and colourful decor by the Marseille artist Antoine Lombard.

Musée Toulouse-Lautrec

©Alexandre Ménard/iStockphoto.com

This was indeed Paris

The **Musée Toulouse Lautrec** contains one of Toulouse-Lautrec's most famous works: *Au Salon de La Rue des Moulins*, with the pastel study and finished painting of 1894 on opposite walls. The work shows the artist's supreme skill as a draughtsman and his sensitivity as an observer of the harsh realities of life. Other works portray the world of Parisian music halls and theatres that Toulouse-Lautrec knew so well. Here are portraits of Valentin 'le Désossé' ('boneless') who danced with La Goulue at the Moulin de la Galette; the singer-songwriter Aristide Briant, who sang in slang at the cabaret Le Mirliton; the café-concert artist Caudieux; Jane Avril, nicknamed 'Le Mélinite,' and the singer Yvette Guilbert, once passionately pursued by the artist.

The comprehensive **Toulouse-Lautrec collection** was bequeathed to Albi by the artist's mother, the Comtesse Alphonse de Toulouse-Lautrec in 1922 and was augmented by other family members. Javal's portrait of the artist captures the dignity in Toulouse-Lautrec's gaze. Early works such as *Artilleur sellant son cheval* – a soldier saddling his horse, painted when the artist was only 16 show his early interest in animals and people. Other works evoke Toulouse-Lautrec's life in Montmartre.

⌷ WALKING TOURS

OLD ALBI★★
1h.

▷ From place Ste-Cécile, take rue Ste-Cécile and then rue St-Clair (2nd on the right).

A covered passage on the left offers glimpses of the Saint-Salvi cloisters, a later stop on this walk.

Hôtel Séré de Rivières
This 15C–18C mansion belonged to a family of dyer's woad merchants ennobled in the 18C. A notable member was General **Raymond Séré de Rivières** (1815–95), designer of France's border defence system after the eastern provinces fell to Prussia (1870–71).

Maison du vieil Alby
This restored medieval house, between pretty Croix-Blanche and Puech-Berenguier streets, hosts local craft exhibitions and has literature on Albi. Beneath the eaves of this building is a solelhièr, or woad drying room.

Rue Toulouse-Lautrec
At No. 8, the **Hôtel Decazes** on the site of the 14C fortifications features a handsome courtyard with a balustraded staircase and galleries. The Maison Lapérouse, named after a seaman (1741–88) (☉*see Musée Lapérouse*), houses a **nautical museum** and the Hôtel du Bosc, where Toulouse-Lautrec was born.

▷ Turn left onto rue de Verdusse then right onto rue Saunal.

Note a wealthy 16C woad merchant's mansion and the fine 17C town hall on the corner of rue des Pénitents and rue de l'Hôtel-de-Ville. Rue de l'Hôtel-de-Ville leads to the restored **place du Vigan** with its 81 fountains and the Jardin National.

▷ Follow rue Timbal.

Hôtel de Reynès★
Headquarters of the local chamber of commerce. This wealthy merchant family's Renaissance stone and brick mansion has a courtyard featuring busts of François I and Eleanor of Austria, and window mullions adorned with mermaids.

Pharmacie des Pénitents★ (or Maison Enjalbert)
This 16C house features timbering and crisscross-pattern brickwork typical of the Albi region. The façade's decoration is typically Renaissance.

◯ Take rue Mariès towards the cathedral.

Note No. 6 on the right, an attractive 15C timber-and-brick building.

Collégiale St-Salvi

St Salvi was a lawyer before becoming Bishop of Albi in the 6C. He brought Christianity to the region and is buried on the site of this church, which has seen a turbulent history. The church's layout and foundations date from the Carolingian period. The 11C saw the building of a church and Romanesque cloisters. Work was interrupted by the Albigensian Crusade and was resumed in the 13C, in the Gothic style.

Interior – *Enter by the north door.* All that remains of the Romanesque doorway is the archivolt, the arch mouldings and two capitals. The first four bays are Romanesque and retain their 12C capitals. Two apsidal chapels in the chancel also remain from the original construction. The chancel and the remaining bays of the nave are in the Flamboyant Gothic style. The **cloisters** were rebuilt by Vidal de Malvesi in the 13C. All that remains is the east gallery, with Romanesque historiated capitals and Gothic ones decorated with plant motifs.

BERGES DU TARN★★

Follow the Azure circuit starting from the tourist office.

The banks of the Tarn offer splendid **views★★** of the town and the old fortifications and a peaceful stroll away from the town's bustle.

Les Moulins albigeois

On the right bank of the Tarn stand these ancient brick-built mills which have been beautifully restored to accommodate a hotel, the departmental tourism authority and the Musée Lapérouse.

Musée Lapérouse

Botany-Bay Square, entrance in rue Porta. ◯*Open Jul–Aug 9am–noon, 2–6pm (weekends 10am–noon, 2–7pm); Mar–Jun and Sep–Oct daily except Mon 9am–noon, 2–6pm; Nov–Feb*

daily except Mon 10am–noon, 2–5pm. ◯*Closed 1 Jan, 1 May, 1 Nov, 25 Dec.* ✆€3.50. ✆05 63 46 01 87. *www.laperouse-france.fr.*

The navigational instruments, maps, charts and model ships in these handsome vaulted rooms recall the expeditions of Admiral Jean-François de Galaup de Lapérouse, born in the Manoir du Go outside Albi in 1741. In 1785, Lapérouse embarked upon a scientific expedition with two frigates, the *Boussole* and the *Astrolabe*, but he perished when the latter was shipwrecked off Vanikoro Island, north of the New Hebrides. An international team carried out investigations of the wreck of the *Astrolabe* in 1986. A memorial to the seaman graces the square named in his honour.

EXCURSIONS

Église St-Michel de Lescure★

5km/3mi NE towards Carmaux-Rodez, then right at the signpost to Lescure.

The old priory church in Lescure cemetery was built in the 11C by Benedictine monks from Gaillac Abbey. Its 12C Romanesque doorway is most interesting. Four capitals display narrative scenes, like those of the St-Sernin basilica in Toulouse and the church of St-Pierre in Moissac.

Notre-Dame-de-la-Drèche

5km/3mi N on the road to Carmaux-Rodez, then left towards Cagnac-les-Mines. This strikingly large 19C shrine built is consecrated to the 'Vierge d'Or de Clermont', a mid-10C gold statue of the Virgin Mary in Majesty from the Auvergne. The interior of this octagonal rotunda contains murals designed by Bernard Bénézet and executed by Father Léon Valette. The **musée-sacristie** contains a remarkable gold brocade altar hanging made by nuns of the Order of St Clare in Mazamet.

Castelnau-de-Lévis

7km/4.5mi W. Leave Albi on the road to Cordes-sur-Ciel, then take D 1 left. The remains of this 13C fortress offer pleasing views of Albi, its towering cathedral and surrounding Tarn valley.

St-Juéry

6km/3.7mi E towards Millau, follow signs for 'Site du Saut du Tarn'.

Musée culturel du Saut du Tarn (🕐*open Apr–mid-Nov daily except Sat 2–6pm – 2–7pm in Jul–Aug; ⚐ guided visits in Jul–Aug 2.30pm; ⚐€5; 🕐closed 1 May, 1 Nov; ✆05 63 45 91 01; www. musee-saut-du-tarn.com),* is located in a former hydroelectric power station, and **Amblalet** *(20km/12.4mi E)* on a peninsula formed by a meandering river.

Amblalet

20km /12mi E of Albi via D 100 to Saint-Juéry and then scenic D 172 which follows the course of the river Tarn.

Amblalet enjoys an impressive natural site on a presqu'île formed by an exaggerated meander of the Tarn river. A promontory in the middle of the loop is crowned by an old priory while the village clings to the rocky isthmus. The route to the priory passes in front of the chapel of Notre-Dame-de-l'Auder, a Romanesque chapel with a finely sculpted portal founded in the 11C. It houses the wooden polychrome statue of a virgin (17C) named after the Occitan word for the evergreen tree, Phillyrea media, which stands in the priory's grounds. It is said to have been grown from a twig brought back from the Holy Land by a returning crusader.

Réalmont

18 km/11mi S on the N112.

Its name deriving from regius mons ('hill of the king'), this bastide was founded in 1272 by order of king Philippe le Hardi at the foot of the Puech du Caylou. With its large arcaded square, picturesque streets of medieval houses and central well (19C) it has kept much of its historical atmosphere. Note the sundial on the wall of the church which bears the inscription 'la vie passe comme cette ombre' (life passes like this shadow). Inside the church is a remarkable altarpiece. The fontaine de la Féjaire, fed by the heads of three lions, dates from the 17C.

Musée de la Mine, Cagnac-les-Mines

10km/6mi north on D90 in Carmaux.
🕐*Open mid-Feb–Apr and Nov–23 Dec daily except Mon 10am–noon, 2–5pm; May–Jun and Sept–Oct daily 10am–noon, 2–6pm; Jul–Aug daily 10am–12.30pm, 1.30–7pm.* 🕐*Closed 24 Dec–2 Jan, 1 May, 1 Nov.* ⚐*€7 (child 5–18, €4).* ⚐*✆05 63 53 91 70.* http://musee-mine.tarn.fr.

The town of **Carmaux** sits at the centre of a coal field. This museum explains the difficult and dangerous life of the miner. One room is dedicated to a strike of 1914 and the role of Jean Jaurès.

Viaduc de Viaur★

37km/23mi via the N88 N towards Rodez. After the Tanus turn off follow the signs along little roads to 'Viaduc de Viaur'.
This great iron railway bridge built in 1902 over the thickly wooded Viaur valley is the work of engineer Paul Bodin. It is 410m long and carries the Albi to Rodez railway in a single arch 116m above the river. There are good views of it from the terrace outside the hotel of the same name.

ADDRESSES

🛏STAY

⚐ **Chambre d'hôte à la Ferme "Naussens"** – *81150 Castanet.* ✆*05 63 55 22 56. 5 rooms. Closed Nov–mid Apr.* A convivial farmer's welcome and Mediterranean-accented cuisine.

⚐ **Chambre d'hôte au Bouquet de Roose** – *Jussens, 81150 Castelnau-de-Levis (5km/3mi from Albi by D 1).* ✆*05 63 45 59 75. 3 rooms. Closed 15 Dec–15 Jan.* Within sight of the city centre, but essentially out in the countryside, offering peace and quiet.

⚐⚐ **Hotel Cantepau** – *9 r. Cantepau.* ✆*05 63 60 75 80. www.hotel-cantepau-albi.com.* 🅿. *33 rooms.* Wicker furniture, subdued hues and fans give this hotel a colonial feel.

⚐⚐⚐ **Grand Hôtel d'Orléans** – *pl. Stalingrad.* ✆*05 63 54 16 56. www.hotel-orleans-albi.com. 56 rooms.* Simple and unfussy hotel; swimming pool; traditional dishes.

⊜⊜🖥 **Hôtel Mercure** – *41 bis r. Porta.*
℘*05 63 47 66 66. www.mercure.com.* 🅿
56 rooms. This modern hotel in an 18C
red-brick mill on the banks of the Tarn has
lovely views of the river and cathedral.

♈/EAT

⊜🖥 **La Fourchette Adroite**– *7 pl. de
l' Archevêché.* ℘*05 63 49 77 81.* A modern
decor within ancient walls. Creative
cuisine.

⊜🖥 **L'Épicurien** – *42 pl. Jean-Jaurès.*
℘*05 63 53 10 70. www.restaurant
lepicurien.com. Closed Sun and Mon.* ♿.
The address to know in Albi. Minimalist
yet comfortable and bright Bistro and
gourmet menus.

⊜🖥 **Le Jardin des Quatre Saisons** –
19 bd de Strasbourg. ℘*05 63 60 77 76.
www.le-jardin-des-quatre-saisons.
com. Closed Sun eve and Mon.* A reliable
favourite with a good selection of wines
and traditional cuisine.

⊜🖥 **Le Robinson** – *142 r. Édouard-Branly.*
℘*05 63 46 15 69. Closed Nov–Feb, Mon
and Tue.* Dating from the 1920s, this old-
fashioned dance hall has an exuberant
charm.

⊜🖥 **La Table du Sommelier** – *20 r. Porta.*
℘*05 63 46 20 10. www.latabledusommelier.
com. Closed Sun and Mon.* This wine-
focused bistro serves refined cuisine with
fresh ingredients in a rustic dining room
with a mezzanine.

Lautrec

**This medieval village perched on a
hill that was once a fortified position
is today renowned for its production
of 'Ail rose de Lautrec', a variety of
pink-flushed garlic.**

▶ **Population:** 1 822.
🚗 **Michelin Map:** 338: E8.
🅸 **Info:** Rue du Mercadial.
℘05 63 97 94 41.
www.lautrectourisme.com.
◐ **Location:** 15km/9.3mi
northwest of Castres.
🅐 **Don't Miss:** Colline de la
Salette.

👣WALKING TOUR

Lautrec's overhanging half-timbered
houses are built around a rocky outcrop,
the colline de la Salette, rising out of the
middle of the village. From the calvary
on the top there is a view which takes
in the Monts de Lacaune and the
Montagne Noir.
Some sections of the 13C fortifications
that protected the village have been
preserved, notably the porte de la
Caussade. The rue du Mercadial leads
through the ramparts. Immediately on
the left is former Benedictine convent
which houses the tourist information
office. Beyond the attractive place des
Halles (15C–17C) is the collégiale Saint-
Rémy which has a marble altarpiece over
the high altar. Two interesting visits in
Lautrec are to a working windmill and
clogmaker's workshop.
Musée archéologique – ⏱*Contact
tourist office for details of opening hours.*
An exhibition of objects found during
excavations as well as documents to do
with local history

Purple garlic from Lautrec

Coveted by gourmets for its
flavour and storage-life, the purple
garlic cultivated in and around
Lautrec has an annual production
exceeding 4 000 tonnes. On the
first Friday in August, locals hold
a competition of garlic sculpting,
followed by a tasting. Locals share
an enormous pot of *cassoulet*
accompanied by *confit de canard*.
Lautrec cuisine features garlic
crushed into sauces, rubbed onto
croutons, added to soups and
stews, and in old days, a handful
of raw garlic cloves and a chunk
of bread was the favourite packed
lunch of local labourers.

Castres★

This busy city on the banks of the Agout makes an excellent base for excursions to the Sidobre region, the Lacaune mountains and Montagne Noire. Castres has a remarkable museum devoted to Spanish painting, particularly the works of Goya. The Castres area is the French wool-carding centre, and with textile and spinning mills, dyeing and dressing workshops, its wool industry is second only to that of Roubaix-Tourcoing.

- ▶ **Population:** 43 273.
- **Michelin Map:** 338: F-9.
- **Info:** Office du tourisme de Castres, 2 place de la République, 81100 Castres. ℘05 63 62 63 62. www.tourisme-castres.fr.
- ▶ **Location:** 40km/25mi S of Albi.
- **Don't Miss:** Le musée Goya
- **Kids:** Le planétarium-observatoire de Montredon-Labessonnié.

A BIT OF HISTORY

A self-governed city – Castres grew up on the west bank of the Agout, around a Benedictine monastery founded c.810. At the end of the 9C veneration of the relics of St Vincent, one of the preachers who took the Gospel to Spain, made Castres a stopping place on the pilgrim route to Santiago de Compostela. In the 10C, the town came under the rule of the viscounts of Albi and Lautrec. In the 11C, the viscount of Albi granted Castres the right to self-government by a college of 'consuls' or capitouls.

The town managed to keep out of trouble during the Cathar heresy by submitting to Simon de Montfort.

The Reformation – From 1563, the Reformation attracted numerous followers. Once the city's capitouls had renounced Roman Catholicism, Castres became one of the strongholds of Calvinism in Languedoc. It was caught up in the Wars of Religion, which the Peace Treaty of Alès, Henri IV's ascent to the throne and the promulgation of the Edict of Nantes eventually brought to an end. In the 17C, the city hosted one of the four chambers set up by the Edict of Nantes to regulate differences between Protestants and Roman Catholics. This was a prosperous period during which local magistrates and merchants built luxurious town houses and the bishopric a magnificent episcopal palace.

However, the confrontations between Protestants and Roman Catholics persisted after the revocation of the Edict of Nantes until the French Revolution, forcing numerous Huguenots to flee into exile.

Jean Jaurès – The famous Socialist leader was born in Castres on 3 September 1859 and spent part of his childhood in Saïx, a little village on the banks of the Agout, southwest of Castres. He was a student at the lycée that now bears his name, and went on to train as a teacher at the École Normale Supérieure in Paris, after which he taught philosophy at the lycée in Albi and at the University of Toulouse. Attracted by politics, he was elected Republican Member of Parliament for the Tarn in 1885, then Socialist Member for Carmaux, where he took up the miners' cause in 1893.

At the next elections, however, Jaurès was defeated, largely because of his support for Dreyfus, victim of what was eventually proved to be a military conspiracy which led to his being falsely convicted of selling sensitive information to the Germans, an affair which provoked bitter controversy throughout France. Jaurès nonetheless became head of the United Socialist Party (SFIO) not long after its foundation in 1905. As war approached, he put his influential voice to the service of promoting peace and devoted himself to the cause of international brotherhood.

He was assassinated at the Café du Croissant in Paris on 31 July 1914. War was declared two days later. In 1924, his remains were transferred to the Panthéon, Paris.

🐾 WALKING TOUR

OLD CASTRES
1h30

▶ Start from the theatre.

Opposite are the superb **formal gardens** (Jardin de l'Évêché) designed by Le Nôtre in 1676. The town hall **Hôtel de Ville** occupies the **former bishops' palace** designed by Mansart and built in 1669. The massive Romanesque **Tour St-Benoît** is all that remains of the former abbey of St-Benoît.

Musée Goya★

🕐 *Open Jul–Aug 10am–6pm; Apr–Jun and Sept daily except Mon 9am–noon, 2–6pm; Oct–Mar Tue–Sat 9am–noon, 2–5pm, Sun 10am–noon, 2–5pm.*
🕐 *Closed 1 Jan, 1 May, 14 Jul, 1 Nov, 25 Dec.* ⊜€5 *(children under 18, free); no charge 1st Sunday in the month.*
📞 *05 63 71 59 30. www.ville-castres.fr.*
This museum in the Hôtel de Ville (🔵*see above*) contains works by **Goya★★**, as well as 14C Spanish Primitives, and 17C works by Murillo, Valdès Leal and Ribera. Admire Goya's etchings *Los Desastres de la Guerra* (The Disasters of War) inspired by the Spanish War of Independence (1808–14). *Los Caprichos* (Caprices) expresses the isolation and contemplation provoked by the artist's deafness in 1792.

Self-portrait with glasses (1800) by Francisco de Goya

J.-C. Ouradou/Musée Goya, Castres

Cathédrale St-Benoît

This cathedral dedicated to St Benoît de Nursie and designed by the architect Caillau in 1677 was built on the site of a 9C Benedictine abbey. Eustache Lagon took charge of construction of this enormous Baroque edifice in 1710.

Quai des Jacobins

The Pont Neuf and quay afford attractive **views★** of bright coloured medieval houses lining the banks of the Agout. Homes of weavers and dyers in the Middle Ages, they are built over vast stone cellars opening directly onto the water.

Quai des Jacobins

© clodio/iStockphoto.com

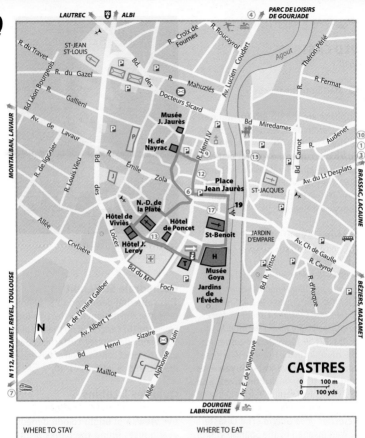

CASTRES

0   100 m
0   100 yds

Place Jean-Jaurès

The early 19C houses around this square feature Classical sandstone façades. Admire Gaston Pech's statue of Jean Jaurès and the fountain inspired by that on place de la Concorde in Paris.

▶ Cross place Jean-Jaurès; right onto rue Henri-IV; left onto rue du Consulat.

Centre national and Musée Jean-Jaurès

♿⏱*Open Jul–Aug daily 10am–noon, 2–6pm; rest of year daily except Mon*

10am–noon, 2–6pm (Oct–Mar 5pm). ⏱*Closed Sun from Nov–Mar, 1 Jan, 1 May, 1 Nov, 25 Dec.* ⌨€3. ☎05 63 72 01 01. www.ville-castres.fr.

This museum devoted to the life and work of the great Socialist, as well as society in the late 19C and early 20C, also has an information centre on the history of socialism.

Hôtel de Nayrac★

12 rue Frédéric-Thomas.
Beautiful 1620 brick and stone mansion typical of Toulouse civil architecture.

▶ Take rue Émile-Zola and rue Victor-Hugo.

Église Notre-Dame-de-la-Platé

This Baroque-style church was rebuilt between 1743 and 1755. Note the high altar's Assumption of the Virgin in Carrara marble, by Isidora and Antonio Baratta (Bernini School), and the fine 18C organ.

▶ Retrace your steps and turn left onto rue de l'Hôtel-de-Ville.

At No. 31, admire the doorway with its round arch on fluted columns surmounted by a carved pediment depicting pistol, sabre and cannon.

▶ Turn left onto rue de la Platé leading to rue Chambre-de-l'Édit.

Hotel de Viviès

No. 35. This 16C building has a square corner tower.

▶ Admire Hôtel Jean-Leroy (no 31, 16C) and Hôtel de Poncet (rue Gabriel-Guy, 17C). Rue Chambre-de-l'Édit goes back to the theatre.

🚗 DRIVING TOUR

LE SIDOBRE★

53km/33mi round tour. Allow 3h.

The Sidobre massif is littered with granite rock formations sculpted into curious forms by erosion.

▶ Leave Castres on D 622 to Brassac. Turn right at the hamlet of La Fontasse.

Chaos de St-Dominique

This river of rocks in a wooded setting covers the River Lézert for 4km/2.5mi *(slippery in wet weather).*

Grotte de St-Dominique

15min on foot round-trip.

Le Sidobre rocks
© &#169 Jean-Yves Benedeyt/iStockphoto.com

🚶 The cave overlooks a glade and once gave refuge to a disciple of St Dominic during the Revolution.

▶ Return to D 622 and head back towards Brassac. After 5km/3mi, just past a café, turn left. In Loustalou stop at the café-tabac 'Au Rocher Tremblant'.

Rocher de Sept-Faux

This extraordinary rocking-stone consists of two blocks poised on top of one another, weighing 900 tonne, which can be rocked by simply pressing on a wooden lever.

▶ Return to the Brassac road and turn left towards Lacrouzette.

Lac du Merle

This fine lake surrounded by forests is fed by the waters of the Lignon.

Chaos de la Resse (or 'River of Rocks')

A chaotic heap of rocks covers the River Lignon, whose roar is quite impressive.

Peyro Clabado

The Peyro Clabado rock is a 780 tonne granite boulder balanced on a tiny pedestal of rocks.

Lacrouzette

Most of the town's inhabitants earn their living from quarrying granite.

▶ From Lacrouzette, take D 58 to Thérondel. Stop at the village of Ricard and take the footpath to the Trois Fromages and Roc de l'Oie.

Trois Fromages; Roc de l'Oie

45min on foot round-trip. Follow the red and white flashes marking the GR footpath through the woods.

The **Trois Fromages** ('three cheeses') rock is a single boulder fractured by erosion into three rounded fragments. Further on, the **Roc de l'Oie** resembles a goose – hence its name.

▶ Return to D 58 and follow signs to Lacrouzette and Burlats. About 2km/1mi beyond Lacrouzette, after the turnoff to Campselves, take the little road left.

Saut de la Truite

Stop near the River Lignon.
Take a footpath to the right of the torrent. 10min on foot round-trip as far as the foot of the waterfall.

At this gushing waterfall the fresh green landscape becomes more arid.

Burlats

The remains of this Benedictine abbey founded in the 10C retain their Romanesque doorways, capitals and mouldings and mullioned windows. The **Pavillon d'Adélaïde was the** 12C home to Adélaïde de Toulouse and her court, whose troubadours sang of courtly love.

▶ Return to Castres via Les Salvages and D 89.

EXCURSIONS
Montredon-Labessonnié

21km/13mi NE along D 89 then left 5km/3mi beyond Roquecourbe.

The **Planétarium-Observatoire (Planet Tarn)** stages shows for children, on the solar system, constellations and their associated legends. ◔**Planétarium**: *Jul–Aug Mon–Fri 3pm; ℘05 63 75 63 12 www.planetarn.com).* **Ateliers fusées à eau:** *Jul–Aug Mon–Fri 4.30pm.* **Seasonal soirées d'observation** *Jul–Aug 9pm by appointment.* ◔*Closed 25 Dec–1 Jan. ℘05 63 75 63 12.*

Brassac

24 km/15mi E of Castres by the D 622.

On the edge of the Sidobre and of the monts de Lacaune, Brassac is a pleasant summer resort surrounded by wooded hills for which it is classed as a Station Verte (a base for countryside holidays). It still has a textile industry. Its old bridge, the **Pont Gothique**, has withstood the currents of the Agout river since the 12C. It has enormous iron hooks attached to which dyers would hang wooden poles to dry their fabrics. There is a good view of the town from the bridge, a harmonious ensemble with the towers of the château seeming to rise out of the river.

Ferrières

31km/19mi E by D 622 to Brassac, then D 53 towards Vabre.

This village on the northeastern edge of the Sidobre is something of a cultural hub for the Parc naturel régional du Haut-Languedoc. Its history is intimately connected with the Reformation because the local seigneur, Guillaume de Guilhot, who had the chateau rebuilt in the 16C, was the leader of the local Reformation party.

Musée du Protestantisme

&♿◔*Open Jul–Sep daily 10am–noon, 3–7pm (Tue and Sun 2.30–6.30pm); rest of year Mon–Fri 2–5pm, Sun 3–6pm.* ◔*Closed mid-Dec–mid-Mar. ⊛€4 (children over 10, €1). ℘05 63 74 05 49. http://mprl.fr/en.*

Installed in the house of a musical instrument maker (16C), this museum contains an important collection of documents related to the history of Protestantism and the events that brought conflict to the region.

The Edict of Nantes, the Edict of Castres, the revocation of the Edict of Nantes, the period 'in the Desert' (when Protestantism went underground) and the emigration of persecuted protestants are evoked in engravings, documents and objects. Also on display are 'dark lanterns' designed to not be visible from far away. A special place is reserved for engravings illustrating the fate of Jean

Calas, a Protestant merchant of Toulouse who was executed in 1762.

Le Militarial de Boissezon

15km/9.4mi SE on the D 612 then the D 93 - La Bastide du Fort. ⏱*Open mid-Jun–mid-Sep Wed–Mon 10am–noon, 2–6pm; rest of the year Sun and public holidays 2–6pm.* ⏱*Closed mid-Dec–mid-Feb.* ⊜*4€ (children 2€).* *℘05 63 50 86 30. www.lemilitarial.com.* This small museum brings together a large collection of objects related to warfare: arms (including pistols, revolvers, rifles, bazookas and machine guns), uniforms, photographs, books, identity cards and so on from the World War I onwards. It illustrates the evolution of fighting techniques and equipment.

ADDRESSES

🛏 STAY

⊜ **Auberge de Crémaussel** – *81210 Lacrouzette. ℘05 63 50 61 33. www.gitedecremaussel.com. Closed 1st week Sep, 25 Dec–Jan. 5 rooms.* This rural auberge has bright rooms facing onto the countryside. Regional cuisine.

⊜ **Camping le Plô** – *81260 Le Bez. ℘05 63 74 00 82. www.leplo.com. Open from mid-May–mid Sep. Reservations advised. 60 pitches.* Isolated in Montagne Noire at the edge of a forest. Everything is simple, but spick and span.

⊜ **Chambre d'hôte le Pasteillé** – *La Ferme, 81290 Viviers-les-Montagnes. ℘05 63 72 15 64. 4 rooms.* An ancient farm in large private grounds; one room for people of reduced mobility; peaceful and welcoming.

⊜⊜ **Hôtel la Renaissance** – *17 r. Victor-Hugo. ℘05 63 59 30 42. www.hotel-renaissance.fr. 20 rooms.* 17C house in a pedestrianed area of the old town; the rooms are original and decorated in various styles.

⊜⊜ **Hôtel le Miredames** – *1 pl. Roger-Salengro. ℘05 63 71 38 18. www.hotel-miredames.com.* ♿. This address has a certain notority in Castres for it was once a "resto philo". Regular philosophical and political discussions, debates and

conferences took place within these walls. The **restaurant** is known for its delicious traditional dishes ⊜⊜.

⊜⊜⊜ **Hôtel le Castel de Burlats** – *8 pl. du 8-Mai-1945, 81100 Burlats. ℘05 63 35 05 98. www.lecasteldeburlats.fr. Closed 13 Feb–1 Mar.* 🅿. *10 rooms.* This fine 14C and 16C palace in a formal French style garden has comfortable spacious rooms overlooking the hill, and a charming Renaissance style salon.

⅋/EAT

⊜ **Brasserie de l'Europe** – *1 pl. Jean-Jaurès. ℘05 63 59 01 44. Closed Sun.* The most popular brasserie in Castres, close to Agout; good choice of meat dishes, pizzas and salads.

⊜ **Café de Paris** – *8 pl. de l'Hôtel-de-Ville, 81260 Brassac. ℘05 63 74 00 31. Closed Fri eve except Jul and Aug.* A lovely and simple place without pretensions, close to the 12C bridge; simple regional and traditional cuisine.

⊜ **La Mandragore** – *1 r. Malpas. ℘05 63 59 51 27. Closed Sun–Mon.* This little restaurant in Old Castres offers reasonable, family-style traditional cuisine amidst a contemporary decor.

⊜⊜ **Le Pescadou** – *18-20 r. des 3-Rois. ℘05 63 72 32 22.* Specialising in seafood dishes, including bouillabaisse; simple decor, and terrace in summer.

⊜⊜ **Le Victoria** – *24 pl. 8-Mai-1945. ℘05 63 59 14 68. Closed Sat lunch–Sun.* Three underground dining rooms with cosy decor and attractive stone archways. Take a look at the pretty cave à vins behind a window pane. Traditional cuisine.

TAKING A BREAK

Signovert – *5 r. Émile-Zola. ℘05 63 59 21 77. Closed Mon 8.15am–12.15pm, 2.15–7.15pm.* This pastry shop and chocolatier founded in 1928 sells a local nougat, *le Granit du Sidobre.*

ACTIVITIES

Le Coche d'eau – *R. Milhau-Ducommun. Daily May–Sept. ℘05 63 62 41 76. Leaves from the city centre. Closed Nov–Apr.* For a cruise on the Agout, hop aboard the *Miredames*, a wooden boat inspired by the old 'water coaches' once pulled by horses.

Lacaune

This spa and summer resort is a popular base for exploring the surrounding hills of Monts de Lacaune by foot, bicycle or car.

VISIT

The chief point of interest in the town itself are the Musée-Filature, a museum in an old textile factory, and, in place du Griffoul, a fountain known as the Font dels Pissaïres, which consists of a group of four young men in blackened steel who appear to urinate fresh water into two 14C stone basins below.

Statues-menhirs

The Monts de Lacaune are renowned for their unusual prehistoric monuments, 'statues-menhirs'. These erect monoliths made of granite or sandstone differ from standing stones elsewhere in that they are carved in stylised bas relief as human figures – both men and women. Their purpose is unknown. Experts believe they date from the Chalcolithic, around 3500–2300 BCE, making them the earliest examples of statuary occurring in Europe. Some of them have been removed to the Musée Fenaille in Rodez (see RODEZ, p480), but 30 others stand in situ, the best known being **La Pierre Plantée**, just outside Lacaune.

A room in the museum at Murat-sur-Vèbre (east of Lacaune) is dedicated to them.

▶ **Population:** 2 620.
Michelin Map: 338: I8.
Info: 05 63 37 04 98. www.lacaune.com.
Location: 46km/28.5mi northeast of Castres.

Mazamet

Situated at the foot of the Montagne Noire, Mazamet still thrives on the wool industry that brought prosperity to the area in the 18C. Specialising in the 'pulled wool' technique, the town is also renowned for tawing the pelts once the wool has been removed. Today, sheepskins are mainly imported from Australia, South Africa and Argentina, wool is exported to Italy and skins to Spain, Belgium, Italy and the USA.

A BIT OF HISTORY

Hilltop village – In the 5C, the Visigoths built Hautpoul clinging to a hilltop to protect it from would-be attackers. Nonetheless, Simon de Montfort managed to storm the stronghold in 1212 and the Wars of Religion finished off what he left standing. In the valley below, the textile industry expanded, thanks to the supply of pure water from the Arnette ideal for washing wool. With the advent of the industrial age the inhabitants of Hautpoul were thus persuaded to abandon their hilltop site to found Mazamet.

Centre of the wool industry – With woad, madder and saffron produced in the neighbouring plains, the Montagne Noire specialising in sheep rearing, and the Arnette and Thoré providing water, Mazamet became a major wool industry centre. In 1851, the company of Houlès Père et Fils et Cormouls imported sheepskins from Buenos Aires, opening up an industry for 'pulled wool'.

Learn about this along two marked trails 'Mazamet au fil de la laine' from the tourist office or public park.

▶ **Population:** 10 587.
Michelin Map: 338: G-10.
Info: 3 rue des Casernes, 81200 Mazamet. 05 63 61 27 07. www.tourisme-mazamet.com.
Location: 60km/37.5mi south of Albi.
Kids: La Maison du Bois et du Jouet.

VISIT
Maison Fuzier
R. de Casernes, 81200 Mazamet.
⊙*Open Feb–Mar and Nov–Dec Wed–Sat 10am–noon, 2–5pm; Apr–Jun and Sept–Oct Tue–Sat 10am–noon, 2–5pm; Jul–Aug Mon–Sat 10am–noon, 2–6pm; Sun 2.30–6.30pm.* ⊙*Closed Jan, 1 May, 24–25 and 31 Dec.* ⊛€3. *℘05 63 61 56 56. www.maison-memoires.com.*
The Maison Fuzier houses the tourist office and **Maison des Mémoires de Mazamet**, with an exhibition on Cathar history and types about local burial procedure dating back to earliest times.

EXCURSIONS
Hautpoul
4km/2.5mi S along D 54 then the first road on the right.
This hamlet directly above the **Gorges de l'Arnette** was the birthplace of Mazamet and offers an attractive **view★** of Mazamet and the Thoré Valley.
👥 Adults and children will appreciate the **Maison du Bois et du Jouet**, a craft centre (⊙*open Jul–Aug 2–7pm; Oct–May Tue–Sun 2–6pm; Jun and Sept daily 2–6pm;* ⊙*closed 1 Jan, 25 Dec;* ⊛€6 (child 4–14, €4); *℘05 63 61 42 70; www.hautpoul.org).*

Lac des Montagnès
6km/3.7mi S along D 118.
Set against a backdrop of hills and woodland, this beautiful reservoir is popular with anglers, swimmers and walkers.

Labastide-Rouairoux
23km/14mi E on the D 612.
The traditional industry of this village is the manufacture of woollen yarn. A 24-stop 'Art and Textiles' walking tour (ask for details in the tourist information office) leads around the various sights and viewpoints.
Musée du Textile – (*℘05 63 98 08 60; call for opening times).* All the stages of textile manufacture – spinning, dyeing, weaving, tissage, printing and finishing – are explained in this 19C factory, with demonstrations on the relevant machines.

🚗DRIVING TOUR

VALLÉE DU THORÉ
41 km/25.5mi. Allow around 2h.

▷ Leave Mazamet heading east on the D 612 in the direction of St-Pons.

Saint-Amans-Soult
In 1851 the town of Saint-Amans-la-Bastide decided to change its name in honour of its famous son, Marshal Jean-de-Dieu Soult (1769–1851), who played an important role in military and political affairs during the Napoleonic wars and after. As commander of the French army in Spain during the Peninsular War he was the chief adversary of Wellington. Later, he became prime minister of France three times. His tomb is to be seen on the right side of the church.

▷ Turn left off D612 on to D 53. Some way after St-Amans-Valtoret, look out for a sign saying 'Gorges du Banquet, belvédère à 150 m'. Park here.

Gorges du Banquet
🚶*15min on foot.* From the balcony there are superb views over the deep gorge carved through granitic rocks by the river Arn.

▷ The tour can be extended by a detour from Le Vintrou on the D 161.

Lac des Saints-Peyres
This picturesque reservoir stretching for around 10km/6mi down the Arn valley is surrounded by forests. It is popular with windsurfers.

▷ From Le Vintrou return to Mazamet on D 54.

ADDRESSES

🛏 STAY AND 🍴EAT

⊖ **Hotel Mets et Plaisirs** – *7 ave. A.-Rouvière.* *℘05 63 61 56 93. www.metset plaisirs.com.* **11 rooms.** This old family mansion opposite the post office serves traditional country fare. Simple rooms.

La Montagne Noire North

Named the 'Black Mountain' for its dark, brooding appearance from a distance, this range of sedimentary and metamorphic hills is the southwestern extension of the Massif Central. It has two distinct faces to it. While the south-facing slopes are distinctly Mediterranean, dry, sparsely vegetated and suited to vineyards and olive groves, the north-facing slopes are damp and cool, with beech, oak, pine and spruce woods as the dominant ground cover. *See also LA MONTAIGNE NOIRE SOUTH.*

DRIVING TOURS

ROUND TOUR FROM REVEL

Leave Revel SE along D 629 then turn left onto D 44 running through the picturesque Sor gorge.

Durfort

At the edge of the Sor valley, Durfort has always been a centre of coppersmithing. Coppersmiths continue this industry today, working with the last tilt-hammer (15C) still in operation to produce copper objects. The **copper museum** (*open Jun–Sept Fri–Sun 3–7pm; 05 63 74 22 77*) is in an old coppersmith house.

Continue to Pont-Crouzet and turn right onto D 85 to Sorèze.

Sorèze★

Sorèze is one of the centres for the Parc Naturel Régional du Haut Languedoc. This village developed in the 8C around the abbey, now in ruins except for its majestic 13C octagonal **bell-tower**. The abbey's famous **college★** founded in the 17C by Benedictine monks became a royal military school during the reign of Louis XVI but was eventually bought back by the Dominicans in 1854. The college closed down in 1991.

As you leave Sorèze, turn right onto D 45 then bear right again onto D 12.

Arfons

Arfons is a peaceful mountain village with slate-roofed houses. On the corner of a house in the main street is a 14C stone statue of the Virgin Mary. Surrounded by forests, Arfons is the point of departure for a number of walks (*GR 7 waymarked footpath*).

From Arfons, drive SE to Lacombe through the Montagne Noire Forest, then rejoin D 203 heading N across La Loubatière forest.

Forêt de la Loubatière

D 203 makes a pleasant drive, winding through a beech, oak and fir forest.

Fontbruno

The war memorial to the Montagne Noire resistance forces stands here above a crypt. There is an attractive view of the plain.

Just past the monument, turn left into the forest of Hautaniboul.

The forest road comes to the **Pas du Sant**, at the intersection of three roads.

Take D 14 to the left, and after Massaguel turn left again onto D 85 to St-Ferréol.

En Calcat

Two Benedictine abbeys were established here by Father Romain Banquet on his personal estate. The **Monastère de St-Benoît**, for men only, was consecrated in 1896 and is still an active community. Monks here create and pro-

duce pottery, stained glass and zithers. Close by, the **Abbaye Ste-Scholastique** founded in 1890, shelters a contemplative order of nuns who operate weaving and binding workshops.

Continue on to **Dourgne**, a village which makes its living quarrying slate and stone.

▶ Take D 12 to the left to return to Sorèze via Mont Alric.

Mont Alric viewing table
Alt 788m. The view to the west stretches as far as the Revel plain, whereas the Pyrenees can be seen in the south. In the foreground, to the east, is Mont Alric (alt 813m).

▶ Take D 45 right to Sorèze then D 85 back to Revel.

LES EAUX CAPTIVES★
75km/46.5mi tour.
See LA MONTAGNE NOIR SOUTH.

EXCURSION
Explorarôme
Montégut-Lauragais: 7km/4mi W of Revel on the D 1. Open for guided visits only on spring and summer holidays. ℘05 62 18 53 00.
A plunge into the world of scents and perfumes via a laboratory, garden and exhibition hall. Of interest to children and adults alike.

Lavaur

Lavaur, located on the west bank of the Agout, at a crossroads linking Toulouse, Castres and Montauban, still has the charming old districts typical of a small fortified town in Languedoc. Lavaur was defended by the castle of Plo, the only remains of which are a few walls holding up the Esplanade du Plo, in the southern part of the town.

A BIT OF HISTORY
During the Albigensian Crusade, the town was besieged by the troops of Simon de Montfort and surrendered on 3 May 1211, after two months of resistance organised by Guiraude, a lady of the town, and 80 knights who had espoused the Cathar cause. They were hanged, other heretics were burnt at the stake, and Lady Guiraude was thrown into a well which was then filled with stones.

SIGHTS
CATHÉDRALE ST-ALAIN★
The original Romanesque building destroyed in 1211, was rebuilt in 1254.

▶ **Population:** 11 166.
Info: Tour des Rondes. ℘05 63 58 02 00. www.tourisme-lavaur.fr.
▶ **Location:** On the W bank of the Agout, between Lauragais and Albigeois.
Don't Miss: The Jack-o'-the-clock of Saint-Alain Cathedral.
Kids: The steam train at Saint-Lieux-les-Lavaur.

At the top of a Romanesque tower the famous 1523 painted **Jack-o'-the-clock** strikes the hour and half-hour.
The cathedral's southern French Gothic style interior has an imposing single nave (13C–14C) and seven-sided apse (late 15C–early 16C).
The Romanesque door that leads to the first chapel on the right is part of the original building. In the chancel, the 11C white-marble altar-table (Moissac School) comes from Ste-Foy, the oldest church in Lavaur. The west side of the nave leads to the porch underneath an octagonal belfry.

Jardin de l'Évêché

This garden, on the site of the former bishops' palace, has ancient cedars and carefully tended flowerbeds, making it a pleasant place for a quiet walk.

Église Saint-François

Until the Revolution this church built in 1328 was the chapel of the Couvent des Cordeliers, founded in Lavaur in 1220 by Sicard VI de Lautrec, Baron of Ambres. On the right of the entrance is a beautiful building of wood and brick.

EXCURSIONS

♟♟ Giroussens
Jardins des Martels★

9km/5.6mi NW along D 87 and D 631.
♿⏰*Open Apr and Sept daily 1–6pm; May–Aug 10am–6pm; 1st 2 wks in Oct Wed, Sat–Sun 1.30–6pm; last 2 wks in Oct daily 1.30–6pm.* ⌕€8 *(child 4–10, €4.20, 11–17, €5.20).* ⏰*Closed Dec–Mar.* ✆*05 63 41 61 42. www.jardinsdesmartels.com.*
These English-style gardens feature water lily pools, flower beds, woodland and a mini-farm for children.

St-Lieux-lès-Lavaur

10km/6mi NW on D 87 and D 631 to the left.
The Tarn tourist **steam train** ♟♟ (⏰*Apr–Oct: times vary;* ⌕€7, *child 4–10,* €5.50; ✆*05 61 47 44 52; www.cftt.org*) running as far as Giroussens leaves from this charming site in the Agout valley.

Saint-Sulpice-la-Pointe

11 km/7mi NW on D 630.
Souterrain du Castela – ♿*Open all year.* ⌕€5 *(child 6–12,* €3). ✆*05 63 41 89 50. www.ville-saint-sulpice-81.fr.* A ruined chateau dominates this bastide town. Beneath the ruis is a subterranean gallery 142m long of galleries used as a refuge and by forgers.
A new attraction in Saint-Sulpice is a pigeonnier which has been converted to a small museum on two levels to explain the life and uses of homing pigeons.

Graulhet

21km/13mi NW by D 87 and D 631.
Graulhet once prospered from the trade in Languedoc woad. When that industry declined it dedicated itself to tanning and established a reputation as a leading centre for the preparation of hides for the manufacture of shoes, gloves and clothing. Its monuments include the 13C Pont Vieux (rebuilt in the 17C) and the Panessac quarter which has some half-timbered houses.

Maison des métiers du cuir

R. St-Jean. ♿⏰*Open May–Sep Mon–Fri 9am–noon, 2–5.30pm, Sat by appointment;* ⌕€5 *(children under 12 years,* €2.50). ✆*05 63 42 16 04. www.ville-graulhet.fr.*
Graulhet's most important industry is explained in this former factory, now the Centre for Leatherworking Skills.

Jardins des Martels

Jardins des Martels

Gaillac

For many years Gaillac's wealth came from riverboat traffic and trade on the Tarn. The old town has charming squares with fountains and narrow streets lined with old timber and brick houses.

SIGHTS
Abbatiale Saint-Michel
In the 7C, Benedictine monks founded an abbey here dedicated to St Michael. The abbey church, built between the 11C and 14C, contains a 14C polychrome statue of the Madonna and Child. Abbey buildings now house the **Maison des Vins de Gaillac** and the **Musée de l'Abbaye**, about journeymen (*compagnons*), work in local vineyards, and objects of local historical interest.

Tour Pierre-de-Brens
This brick tower dating from the 14C and 15C has gargoyles, mullioned windows and a remarkable projecting gallery.

Parc de Foucaud
The terraced gardens above the Tarn were laid out by André Le Nôtre, the famous 17C French designer of the Versailles gardens. The château contains the **Musée des Beaux-Arts** (*open 10am–noon, 2–6pm: Apr–Oct daily except Tue; Nov–Mar Fri–Sun; €2.50; 05 63 57 18 25; www.ville-gaillac.fr)* showing works by local painters and sculptors.

Musée d'Histoire naturelle Philadelphe-Thomas
Pl. Philadelphe-Thomas. Open 10am–noon, 2–6pm: Apr–Oct daily except Tue; Nov–Mar Fri–Sun; €2.50. 05 63 57 36 31. www.ville-gaillac.fr. The eponymous Dr Thomas donated the contents of this natural history museum to the town of Gaillac in 1912. It has impressive collections of minerals and fossils as well as specimens of birds, insects and reptiles.

▶ **Population:** 14 626.

Info: Abbaye St-Michel, 81600 Gaillac. ℘0 805 400 828. www.ville-gaillac.fr.

Location: Gaillac is a transportation crossroads linking Montauban and Albi by river, rail and road.

Don't Miss: A local wine tasting and the Château de Mauriac's 'herbarium'.

Kids: The Musée'art du Chocolat at Lisle-sur-Tarn.

EXCURSIONS
Montans
4km/2.5mi S on D 87.
First settled at least as early as the Iron Age, Montans became one of the most important pottery producing centres of Roman Gaul. Fragments of imported amphorae hint at the export of wine from Gaillac via the Tarn and Garonne rivers.

Archéosite de Montans – *Open Apr–Oct Mon–Fri 9am–noon, 2–6pm, Sat–Sun and public holidays 2–6pm; Nov–Mar Mon–Fri 9am–noon, 1–5pm. Closed 1 May and Christmas. €4 (children under 6 years free). 05 63 57 59 16. http://archeosite.ted.fr.* Through archaeological finds and reproductions, and information panels, this museum explains the daily life of Montans' Gallo-Roman potters who produced beautiful and functional pieces in terra sigillata (sealed clay).
One highlight of the Archéosite is the Rue Antique, a realistic recreation of a 1C street during the reign of Tiberius with its tavern, baker's and pottery.
Also remarkable is the hoard of treasure of 40 aurei (gold coins) contained in an inkwell which was unearthed in 1992.

Castelnau-de-Montmiral
13km/8mi NW on D 964.
This picturesque village high above the Vère valley and Grésigne forest is an old bastide founded in the 13C by Raymond VII, Count of Toulouse. **Place**

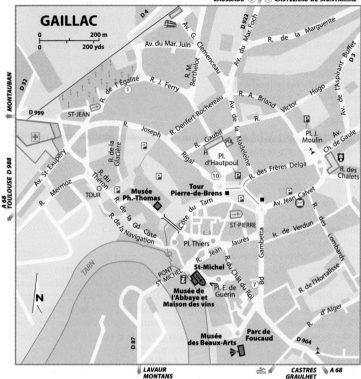

WHERE TO STAY	
Château de Salettes (Hôtel)	③
Verrerie (Hôtel La)	①

WHERE TO EAT	
Falaise (La)	④
Sarments (Les)	⑦
Table du Sommelier (La)	⑩

The Gaillac vineyards

The south bank of the Tarn grows red grapes: Gamay, Braucol, Syrah and Duras. Vineyards on the north bank grow red varieties (Duras, Braucol, Syrah, Cabernet and Merlot) and also Mauzac, Loin de l'œil and Sauvignon varieties for white wines. Gaillac wines are AOC (*Appellation d'Origine Contrôlée*) and these vineyards rank among the foremost wine producers in the southwest of France.

des Arcades is flanked by arcades topped with corbelled half-timbered houses, some dating from the 17C. In the 15C **parish church**, note the polychrome stone statue of Christ Bound (15C), Baroque altarpiece and 13C **gem-encrusted cross-reliquary★** of the counts of Armagnac known as the Montmiral Cross.

Château de Mauriac★

11km/7mi N on D 922. Turn right just before Cahuzac. ℘05 63 41 71 18. www.bistes.com.

This castle dating from the 14C has a beautiful façade and rooms displaying paintings by Bernard Bistes, the castle's owner.

The French-style ceiling of the 'Polish Room' is decorated with 360 panels depicting a fresh-looking **herbarium★**.

Lisle-sur-Tarn

9km/5.5mi SW via N 88.

This town has a vast **square** with covered arcades and fountain, vestiges of its *bastide* days (1248), and 16C to 18C brick and timber houses. **Notre-Dame de la Jonquière** church has a Romanesque portal and Toulouse style bell-tower.

The **Musée Raymond-Lafage** (☉*open daily except Tue 10am–noon, 3–6pm;* ℘*05 63 40 45 45; http://museeraymondlafage. wifeo.com*) presents work by Raymond-Lafage, the 17C Lisle draughtsman; Gallo-Roman and medieval artefacts; works of sacred art; and portraits by Victor Maziès.

Musée'art du Chocolat – *Open Tue–Sun 10am–12.30pm, 2–7pm (Jan–Mar closes at 6pm).* ⬳*3.50€ (children under 12 years 2.50€).* ℘*05 63 33 69 79.* The pieces on display in this museum combining art and chocolate are dreampt up and created by Michel Thomaso-Défos, master chocolatier, and Casimir Ferrer, painter and sculptor. Their subjects are widely varied and include Albi cathedral, the obelisk in the place du Concorde. A film shows the stages by which cacao is transformed into the finished product.

Rabastens

17 km/10.5mi SW om the D 988.

Rabastens is a wine town forming part of the Gaillac appellation and also a stop on the pilgrimage route to Santiago de Compostela. As a pro-Cathar town during the times of the Albigensian crusade it was obliged to pull down its fortifications but there are still plenty of old buildings to be seen. There are good views of the old town from the bridge. Especially worth visiting is the Eglise Notre-Dame du Bourg which was founded by monks from Moissac in the lower town in the 12C. It has eight beautiful Romanesque capitals set into its portal. Inside, the ceiling is magnificently painted.

The collection of the Musée du Pays Rabastinois, housed in the beautiful Hotel de la Fite (late 17C) includes a superb 4C mosaic from a Gallo-Roman villa.

ADDRESSES

🛏 STAY

⬯⬯ **Hôtel Verrerie** – *R. de l'Égalité.* ℘*05 63 57 32 77. www.hotel-tarn-la-verrerie.com. Closed 23–30 Dec, 17 Feb–2 Mar.* 🅿. *14 rooms.* This 19C glass-making factory has contemporary rooms; the dining room opens onto a terrace.

⬯⬯⬯⬯ **Château de Salettes** – *3km/1.86mi S of Cahuzac-sur-Vère via the D 922.* ℘*05 63 33 60 60. www.chateau desalettes.com. Closed 2–16 Jan, 28 Feb–13 Mar. 18 rooms. Restaurant* ⬯⬯⬯⬯. At the heart of vineyards the original 13–16C château has been entirely rebuilt. Beautiful contemporary decor with spacious rooms; there is a terrace and outdoor pool. Try the proprietor's wine.

🍽 EAT

⬯⬯ **La Table du Sommelier** – *34 Pl. du Griffoul.* ℘*05 63 81 20 10. www.latable dusommelier.com. Closed Sun and Mon.* Warm, rustic decor attracting regulars with appetizer plates and interesting wines.

⬯⬯⬯ **Les Sarments** – *27 r. Cabrol derrière abbaye St-Michel.* ℘*05 63 57 62 61. www.restaurantslessarments.com. Closed 1–7 Mar Tue eve, Oct– Feb Wed lunch, Mar–Sep Sun eve and Mon.* Discover Gaillac wine-producing methods in this Maison des vins which neighbours a Medieval wine warehouse. Traditional cuisine.

WINE SHOPPING

Domaine du Moulin – *Chemin de Bastié.* ℘*05 63 57 20 52.* These vineyards have found favour with French celebrities. Tastings.

Maison des Vins de Gaillac – Caveau St-Michel – *Abbaye St-Michel.* ℘*05 63 57 15 40. www.vins-gaillac.com. Closed Christmas.* This wine centre on the River Tarn sells products from 82 different vineyards and 3 cooperatives producing Gaillac wine. Tastings.

Cordes-sur-Ciel ★★★

Cordes-sur-Ciel occupies a remarkable **site★★** on the Puech de Mordagne rocky outcrop, overlooking the Cérou valley. On a bright day the sunlight enhances the soft pink and grey hues of the old façades. The village may owe its name to the textile and leather industry which prospered here in the 13C and 14C.

▶ **Population:** 989.
⌚ **Michelin Map:** 338: D-6.
ℹ **Info:** Office du tourisme de Cordes, Maison Gaugiran 38-42 Grand Rue Raimond VII, 81170 Cordes sur Cie. ☏05 63 56 00 52. www.cordessurciel.fr.
◑ **Location:** NW of the Tarn, 27km/16.8mi from Albi.
◉ **Don't Miss:** A promenade through the Upper Town.
👥 **Kids:** Jardin des Paradis; Musée de l'Art du Sucre.

A BIT OF HISTORY

Fortified town – In 1222, during the Albigensian Crusade, the Count of Toulouse, Raymond VII, decided to build the fortified town of Cordes in response to destruction of the stronghold of St-Marcel by Simon de Montfort's troops. The charter of customs and privileges enjoyed by the inhabitants of Cordes included, among other things, exemption from taxes and tolls. The town-cum-fortress rapidly became a favourite haunt of heretics, and the Inquisition found rich pickings during its work here. The end of the campaign against the Cathars ushered in a period of prosperity. In the 14C, the leather and cloth trades flourished; craftsmen wove linen and hemp cultivated on the surrounding plains, whereas the dyers on the banks of the Cérou used the **pastel** (blue dyer's woad) and saffron which grew so abundantly in the region. The beautiful houses built during this period bear witness to the wealth of the inhabitants.

Decline and revival – The quarrels among the bishops of Albi, which affected the entire region, the resistance of Cordes to the Huguenots during the Wars of Religion and two plague epidemics put an end to this golden age in the 15C. After a brief burst of life at the end of the 19C, due to the introduction of mechanical embroidery looms, Cordes, which had originally been designed to be isolated, finally fell into decline, cut off as it was from the main communication routes. Fortunately,

Cordes-sur-Ciel

©Fred Challis/iStockphoto.com

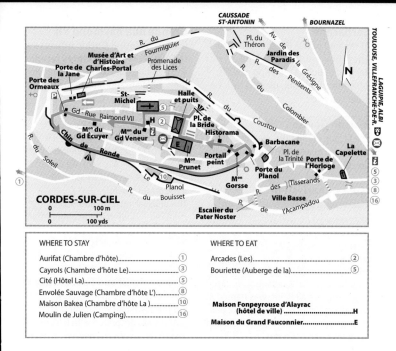

CAUSSADE ST-ANTONIN · BOURNAZEL · TOULOUSE, VILLEFRANCHE-DE-R., LAGUIPIE, ALBI

CORDES-SUR-CIEL

WHERE TO STAY

Aurifat (Chambre d'hôte) ... ①
Cayrols (Chambre d'hôte Le) ... ③
Cité (Hôtel La) ... ⑤
Envolée Sauvage (Chambre d'hôte L') ... ⑧
Maison Bakea (Chambre d'hôte La) ... ⑩
Moulin de Julien (Camping) ... ⑯

WHERE TO EAT

Arcades (Les) ... ②
Bouriette (Auberge de la) ... ⑤

Maison Fonpeyrouse d'Alayrac (hôtel de ville) ... H
Maison du Grand Fauconnier ... E

the threatened demolition of its Gothic houses spurred the population into action and a number of measures to classify some of its buildings as historic monuments were taken in 1923. But those most susceptible to the charm of Cordes were the artists and craftsmen who rallied to the cause and helped to put the town back on the map. Restoration is still being carried out, preserving the original character of Cordes. In 1970 the town also became a venue for musical entertainment.

The winding, steeply sloping, stone streets are home to an ironmonger, an enameller and a sculptor of figurines, not to mention weavers, engravers, sculptors and painters, who practise their crafts in the beautiful old houses whose original appearance has been so successfully conserved.

✦ WALKING TOURS

UPPER TOWN★★
Traffic is banned in the upper town in summer. Park for a fee as near as you

can to either the Porte de la Jane or the tourist information office in Place Jeanne Ramel-Cals, at the bottom of Grande Rue de l'Horloge (the square you arrive at when coming from Albi).

Porte de la Jane and Porte des Ormeaux
Laid out in a diamond-shape, Cordes had two curtain walls built around it in 1222. The **Porte de la Jane**, a remnant of the second curtain wall, doubled the Porte des Ormeaux. Assailants who fought their way past the Porte de la Jane were surprised to be confronted by the massive towers of this second fortified gateway, the **Porte des Ormeaux.**

Chemin de ronde
The southern wards (Planol haut) and those of rue du Planol offer attractive views of the surrounding countryside.

Porte du Planol (or Vainqueur)
A 13C gateway guarding the eastern approach to the town.

Barbacane

At the end of the 13C the town developed beyond its walls and it was decided to build a third ring of walls, of which this barbican, pierced by loopholes, survives.

Maison Gorsse

The façade of this house features some beautiful Renaissance mullioned windows.

Musée Charles-Portal

Maison du Grand Fauconier. ⓒ*Open mid-Mar–May Fri–Sun and public holidays 2.30–6pm; Jun–Aug daily except Tue 2.30–6.30pm; Sept–Oct Fri–Sun and public holidays 3–6pm.* ⊕€2.50. ℘06 09 61 00 45.

This local history museum, located inside the Portail Peint, was named in honour of Charles Portal, keeper of public records for the Tarn *département* and great historian of Cordes.

On the ground floor are some antique grain measures, a rather unusual sarcophagus from the Merovingian necropolis (6C) in Vindrac *(5km/3mi W of Cordes)*, the beautiful studded door from the Maison du Grand Fauconier and the falcons (faucons) to which this house owes its name.

A room on the first floor is devoted to the architecture of Cordes. The second floor houses interesting collections of local prehistoric exhibits and some opulent Gallo-Roman furniture which belonged to the temple at Loubers. Another room contains the *libre ferrat* or iron book, so-called because its binding incorporated an iron chain. This record book contains the town's regulations from the end of the 13C to the 17C. New consuls were sworn in on the Gospel extracts inside it. The third floor displays objects found during excavation of the Vindrac necropolis: jewellery, buckles, a set of antefixes and earthenware from Gallo-Roman times.

Portail peint

The Painted Gate is probably named after the painted Madonna which once adorned it.

Grande Rue Raymond VII

Cordes' beautiful **Gothic houses★★** (13C–14C) have richly **sculpted façades** and the largest and best-preserved line the cobbled Grand-Rue (or rue Droite).

Musée de l'Art du sucre

33 Grande Rue Raymond VII. ⓒ*Open mid-Feb–Mar and Nov–Dec 10.30am–12.30pm, 1.30–6pm; Apr–Oct 10am–7pm (Jul–Aug 9am–8pm).* ⊕€5 (child 6–14, €4). ℘05 63 56 02 40. www.artdusucre.fr.

This unusual museum housed in a rose-coloured Prunet mansion contains art made entirely of sugar, paintings and miscellaneous exhibits (stamp album, Provençal market, musical instruments).

Maison du Grand Fauconnier★

This beautiful old mansion now housing the town hall was named after its roof corbels decorated with falcons. Its remarkably elegant façade was restored in the 19C.

Musée d'Art moderne et contemporain – *Housed in the Maison du Grand Fauconnier.* ⓒ*Open mid-Mar–mid-Nov daily except Tue 10.30am–12.30pm, 2–6pm.* ⊕€4 (children under 14, free). ℘05 63 56 14 79. www.mamc.cordessurciel.fr. A 15C spiral staircase leads to the **Salle Yves-Brayer** containing the painter's drawings, lithographs, etchings and watercolours. The **Salle de la Broderie cordaise** offers embroidery demonstrations on a tambour frame. The mechanical embroidery frames, from St-Gall in Switzerland, brought Cordes prosperity in the late 19C and early 20C.

The **Salle de la Fresque**, so-called because of its 14C wall paintings, is now the **Espace André-Verdet**. It displays the donated collection of the eponymous poet who often visited Cordes. Works here include modern and contemporary paintings, stained glass and ceramics by Picasso, Léger, Prévert, Klee, Miró, Arman, Magnelli and others.

Covered market and well

This market place once rang to the sound of cloth merchants and today is the city's hub. Its roof is supported by 24 octagonal wooden pillars. Nearby is a **well**, 114m deep.

The shaded **Place de la Bride** offers sweeping views of the Cérou Valley to the northeast, against the slender silhouette of the Bournazel belfry to the north.

▲▲ Église St-Michel

This church has its original 13C chancel and transept and a splendid 14C rose window. Enjoy the panorama from atop the watchtower.

Maison Fonpeyrouse d'Alayrac

This late 13C mansion which now houses the tourist office has an interesting inner courtyard. Two timber galleries give access to the upper storeys.

Maison du Grand Veneur★

This mansion named after the Master of the Royal Hunt, has a distinctive three-storey façade depicting hunting scenes.

Maison du Grand Écuyer

The elegant façade of this mansion is built of beautiful Salles sandstone and adorned with imaginative figures sculpted in the round.

LOWER TOWN
Porte de l'Horloge

From the Place Jeanne Ramel-Cals the Grand Rue de l'Horloge climbs directly towards this handsome clocktower-cum-gate built in the 14–16C. The Escalier du Pater Noster up to the gateway from the place de Lacampadou is a staircase with as many steps as the Lord's Prayer has words.

La Capelette

Grand-Rue. To see inside, refer to the sign on the the door.
The interior of this old chapel, built in 1511, was decorated by Yves Brayer.

▲▲ Jardin des Paradis

Pl. du Théron. Open daily Apr–Oct 10am–6pm. 05 63 56 29 77. www.jardindesparadis.eu.

This exquisite garden in the lower part of the town combines contemporary, oriental and medieval influences. It is intended to be a 'living' garden, in the sense of attracting wildfe by the application of natural gardening methods. A series of cultural and educational events in the garden, and activities for children, brings it alive in the human sense too. The various enclosures include ponds, paths, hedges, interesting species of plants, garden features, games and shady places to sit – choice among them the Persian Pavilion. There is also a small museum with exhibitions about nature. Vegetables from the kitchen garden are available for sale by arrangement.

EXCURSIONS
Monestiés★

8km/5mi west on D 91 in the direction of Cordes-sur-Ciel.

Chapelle St-Jacques★★

Open Jul–Aug 10am–noon, 2–6.30pm; rest of the year call for opening times. Closed 1 Jan and 25 Dec. €3. 05 63 76 19 17. www.tourisme-monesties.fr.
The **Mise au tombeau★★** has remarkable elegance, and presents, on three levels, the final episodes of the Passion.
The **Centre contemporain Bajén-Vega** (*open mid-Apr–mid-Jun and mid-Sept–Oct 10am–noon, 2–5.30pm; mid-Jun–mid-Sept 10am–12.30pm, 2–6pm; closed 1 Jan and 25 Dec; €3; 05 63 76 19 17; www.tourisme-monesties.fr*) houses paintings by Spanish political refugees Martine Vega and Francisco Bajén.

Le Cayla

11km/7mi SW on D 922 (signposted).
Musée Maurice-et-Eugénie-de-Guérin commemorates the short-lived romantic writer **Maurice de Guérin** (1810–39) and his sister **Eugénie** (1805–48). Born into a noble family in the Chateau du Cayla, they were contemporaries of Lamartine, George Sand and Victor Hugo.

🚗 DRIVING TOUR

PAYS DE VAOUR
27 km/16mi. Allow 1.5h.

▶ Leave Cordes on D 600 through Cabannes.

Vindrac
This village has several half-timbered brick houses and a small church with a sundial and octagonal belfry.

▶ Turn left on D 91. After 9 km/6mi turn left on D 33 towards Vaour (2.5 km/1.5mi).

Vaour
Vaour was one of the first headquarters to be founded (mid-12C) by the enigmatic military order of the Knights Templar. A small, twisting road leads from the edge of the hamlet to what is left of the **Commanderie des Templiers**: the remains of a porch, a tower and a building divided into three rooms with vaulted ceilings, also incorporating a bread oven and a fireplace.

▶ Take D15 in the direction of de Saint-Antonin-Noble-Val.

Dolmen Peyro-Lebado
The largest dolmen in the Tarn stands at a route intersection. It is orientated on an axis between the rising and setting sun and dates from 4 000 years ago.

▶ Turn right at the dolmen towards Cordes, then left for Roussayrolles.

Église de Roussayrolles
Built in the 13C, this small Gothic church contains frescoes (1952) by Nicolaï Greschny, master iconographer and refugee from the Russian Revolution, influenced by the oriental tradition of sacred art.

▶ To return to Cordes take the little road to Marnaves and turn right on to D600.

ADDRESSES

🛏 STAY

🛏 **Camping Moulin de Julien** – ℘05 63 56 11 10. www.campingmoulindejulien.com. Open May–Sep. Reservation recommended. 130 sites. Pitch your tent at the foot of the medieval city. This campsite has a pool, a children's play area and chalets for hire.

🛏 **Chambre d'hôte le Cayrols** – Livers Cazelles. ℘05 63 56 22 46. www.lecayrols.com. Closed end Nov–end Feb. 5 rooms. This old farm, tastefully restored houses simple rooms; many leisure activities suitable for children, including swimming pool, toboggan, minigolf...

🛏 **La Maison Bakea** – 26 le Planol. ℘05 63 56 22 24. www.maisonbakea.fr. Closed 15 Oct–30 Mar. 5 rooms. This 13C house in the medieval town has a delightful courtyard, and charming, well-furnished rooms.

🛏🛏 **Chambre d'hôte Aurifat** – ℘05 63 56 07 03. Closed mid-Dec–mid-Feb. 4 rooms. The restored 13C watch tower in an enchanting spot has charming rooms, swimming pool and terraced garden.

🛏🛏 **Hôtel la Cité** – 19 Grand Rue Raymond VII. ℘05 63 56 03 53. 8 rooms. Restaurant🍽🍽. Built into the ramparts of the city; rooms are decorated in the original styles.

🛏🛏🛏 **Chambre d'hôte L'Envolée Sauvage** – La Borie, Livers Cazelles Village. ℘05 63 56 88 52. www.lenvolee-sauvage.com. 4 rppms. Closed 5 Jan–28 Feb. The rooms of the 18C farm are decorated with good taste; cuisine is based on domestic and market produce.

🍽 EAT

🍽 **Les Arcades** – 3 pl. de la Halle. ℘05 63 56 93 96. Closed Christmas to Feb. Eating here won't break the bank; simple rustic dishes inspired by regional produce.

🍽🍽 **Auberge de la Bouriette** – Campes – 4km/2.5mi NE of Cordes-sur-Ciel on D 922 then D 98. ℘05 63 56 07 32. www.domainelabouriette.com. Closed end Nov–Feb. This working farm offers five B&B rooms and has a dining room with a view in the old barn.

With only 150 000 inhabitants and a population density (30 per sq km) less than a third of the national average, the department of the Ariège is a predominantly rural region. Its largest town, Pamiers, is home to just 17 000 people and the capital Foix, 10 000. Everything is dictated by the presence of the Pyrenees which form a solid wall across the south of the *departement* reaching over 3 000m and pierced by only one road, the N20 from Ax to Andorra. Away from this north–south axis along the Ariège valley and the east–west main road through St-Girons in the west and Lavalenet in the east the *departement* is a compendium of small settlements, Romanesque churches and ruined castles dominated by the natural features of the landscape: fast-flowing rivers, waterfalls and forests. Half of the department is covered by the Parque Natural Régional Pyrénées Ariégoises.

Counts and Princes

In the Middle Ages, the territory of what is now the Ariège formed part of the county of Foix; a powerful, autonomous dominion that stretched along the central French Pyrenees to the Béarn around Pau.

The most famous count of Foix was Gaston III (1331–1391). Because of his physical beauty and long blond hair he adopted the name of Gaston Fébus in allusion to Phoebus, an epithet of the God Apollo. A proto-Renaissance man, Gaston Fébus attracted artists and troubadours to his court and wrote a classic book on his favourite pastime hunting, the *Livre de la Chasse* (Book of the Hunt). The title of count of Foix passed to the French crown in the 17C and subsequently to the president who, because of this, now holds the honorary title of co-prince (along with a Spanish bishop) of the independent Pyrenean enclave of Andorra.

The Cathars' Last Stand

Although the so-called 'Pays Cathare' is further to the east, the Ariège could lay claim to the name as it was here that the Cathar church was definitively defeated by its persecutors. The last Cathars took refuge in the remote and easily defended fortresses of the Ariège where they thought they would be safe. For the Catholic Church and the Inquisition, however, no pocket of heresy could be allowed to survive. The Cathar's symbolic last act of resistance was at the castle of Montségur, where over 200 people who refused to renounce their faith were burnt at the stake.

Highlights

1 Climb the tower of the **Château de Foix** (p372)

2 See the site of the Cathars' last stand at **Montségur** (p374)

3 Find out about prehistoric cave painting in the **Grotte de Niaux** (p378)

4 Stroll around pretty old town of **Saint-Lizier** (p385)

5 Marvel at the extraordinary **Mas-d'Azil** cave (p388)

Underworlds

France's largest concentration of caves is here in the Ariège. The massive drive-through tunnel of Mas d'Azil, 50m high at its opening, cannot fail to impress by its sheer scale. The Grotte de Lombrives, meanwhile, is believed to be the largest cave in Europe. Labouiche is certainly the continent's longest navigable underground river open to the public. As well as being natural wonders in their own right, many caves contain remains of prehistoric occupation. Niaux, in particular, has superb paintings on its walls of bison, horse and ibex. The Parc de la Prehistoire at nearby Tarascon-sur-Ariège explains as much as is known about the life and work of prehistoric cave painters.

There are more underground wall paintings in the church at Vals, this time 12C frescoes.

L'ARIÈGE

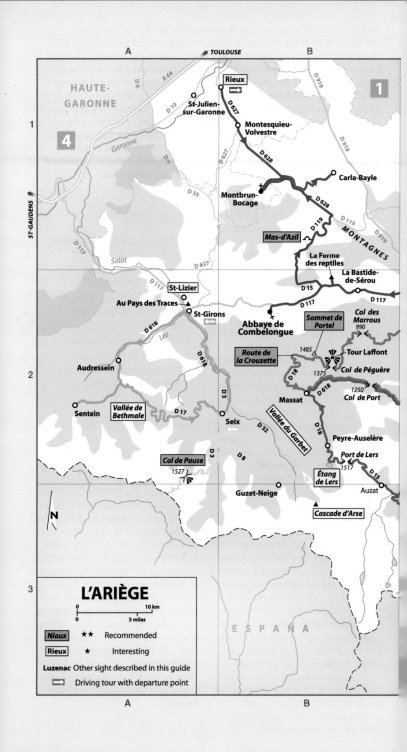

TOULOUSE

HAUTE-GARONNE

ST-GAUDENS

Rieux ➡

St-Julien-sur-Garonne

Garonne

Montesquieu-Volvestre

Carla-Bayle

Montbrun-Bocage

MONTAGNES

Mas-d'Azil

Salat

La Ferme des reptiles

La Bastide-de-Sérou

St-Lizier

Au Pays des Traces

Lez

St-Girons ➡

Abbaye de Combelongue

Sommet de Portel

Col des Marrous
990

1485

Route de la Crouzette

Tour Laffont

Col de Péguère

1375

Col de Port
1250

Audressein

D 618

Massat

D 618

Peyre-Auselère

Vallée de Bethmale

Seix

Vallée du Garbet

Port de Lers
1517

Sentein

Étang de Lers

D 15

Col de Pause
1527

Auzat

Guzet-Neige

Cascade d'Arse

ESPAÑA

N

L'ARIÈGE

0 _____ 10 km
0 _____ 5 miles

Niaux ★★ Recommended

Rieux ★ Interesting

Luzenac Other sight described in this guide

➡ Driving tour with departure point

370

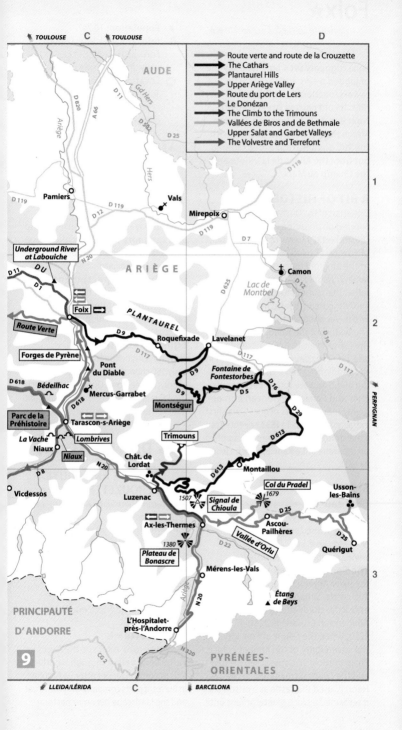

Route verte and route de la Crouzette
The Cathars
Plantaurel Hills
Upper Ariège Valley
Route du port de Lers
Le Donézan
The Climb to the Trimouns
Vallées de Biros and de Bethmale
Upper Salat and Garbet Valleys
The Volvestre and Terrefont

TOULOUSE C TOULOUSE D

AUDE

Pamiers
Vals
Mirepoix
Camon
Lac de Montbel

ARIÈGE

Underground River at Labouiche

Route Verte

Foix

PLANTAUREL
Roquefixade Lavelanet

Forges de Pyrène

Pont du Diable

Fontaine de Fontestorbes

Bédeilhac

Mercus-Garrabet
Montségur

Parc de la Préhistoire
Tarascon-s-Ariège

La Vache
Niaux Lombrives
Niaux

Trimouns

Chât. de Lordat

Vicdessos

Luzenac

Montaillou

Col du Pradel

Usson-les-Bains

1507 Signal de Chioula

Ax-les-Thermes

1380 Ascou-Pailhères

Vallée d'Orlu

Quérigut

Plateau de Bonascre

Mérens-les-Vals

Étang de Beys

PRINCIPAUTÉ D'ANDORRE

L'Hospitalet-près-l'Andorre

PYRÉNÉES-ORIENTALES

LLEIDA/LÉRIDA C BARCELONA D

Foix★

Route Verte & Crouzette★★,
Cathars, Plantaurel Hills

Foix, ruggedly set★ against a skyline of jagged peaks and three castle towers, overlooks the Plantaurel hills. Its old narrow streets radiate from Rue de Labistour and Rue des Marchands, starkly contrasting with the 19C administrative area fanning out from the Allées de la Villote and the Champ de Mars.

▶ **Population:** 10 247.
🛈 **Info:** 29 R. Delcassé, 09000 Foix. ✆05 61 65 12 12. www.foix-tourisme.com.
◐ **Location:** 88km/55mi S of Toulouse. The old town's centre and fountain is at the corner of rue de Labistour and des Marchands.
👫 **Kids:** The Reptile Farm, and Labouiche river; Les Forges de Pyrène.

A BIT OF HISTORY

Once part of the Duchy of Aquitaine, the Foix region became a county in the 11C. Under the 1229 Treaty of Paris, the count of Foix was forced to become a vassal to the king of France. In 1290 the Foix family inherited Béarn and settled there rather than submit to royal authority. In 1607 King Henri IV inherited the county and it was annexed to the crown.

The waters of the Ariège contain gold dust. Between the Middle Ages and late 19C, *orpailleurs* panned for gold in the sandy river beds. Nuggets weighing 15g/5oz were found between Varilhes and Pamiers. Pyrenean iron ore, highly reputed for its richness, was first extracted long ago. In 1833, seventy-four 'Catalan' iron foundries were still supplied by the mine at Le Rancié, which closed in 1931.

SIGHTS
Château

ⓘ*Open: dates vary; check website for details.* ⓘ*Closed public holidays from Nov–Mar.* ⊜€5.60. ✆05 61 05 10 10. www.sites-touristiques-ariege.fr.
The Pont de Vernajoul bridge over the River Arget has a great view of this 10C castle. Simon de Montfort did not attack this sturdy stronghold during the Albigensian Crusade in 1211–17, but in 1272, when the Count of Foix ignored the sovereignty of the King of France, Philip the Bold's troops sacked the town and the count surrendered. In the 16C, Henri IV used the castle as a prison and it remained a place of internment until

1864. Today it houses a museum and offers a **panorama★** of Foix, the Ariège Valley, and the Pain de Sucre ('sugar loaf') in Montgaillard.
The **Musée Départemental de l'Ariège** houses collections of military and hunting weapons that recall the castle's original function.

Église St-Volusien

This fine Gothic church has a 14C nave, an early 15C chancel and a Renaissance altar of polychrome stone. Opposite the church (*no 1 Rue de la Préfecture*) see the elegant mansion decorated with caryatids.

🚗 DRIVING TOURS

ROUTE VERTE AND ROUTE DE LA CROUZETTE★★
Round-trip 93km/58mi. Allow 5h.
🚶*See region map.*
⚠*The road is usually blocked by snow from mid-December to mid-June between the Col des Marrous and the Col de la Crouzette. It may also be blocked at the Col des Caougnous.*

◐ Head W from Foix along D 17.

Route Verte★★
The 'green road' climbs up the **Arget** (or Barguillère) **valley** through woodland and becomes steeper after La Mouline. In Burret, it parts company with the Arget and the landscape becomes pastoral.

Col des Marrous

Alt 990m.

From the pass, extensive views to the south overlook the Arget valley and Arize forest.

The road climbs through a beech forest into fine views of the Plantaurel area and La Bastide-de-Sérou. Beyond the Col de Jouels, the road clings to the upper slopes of the wooded Caplong cirque, with panoramic views of countryside. In the background is the truncated pyramid of Mont Valier (*alt 2 838m*).

Col de Péguère (*alt 1 375m*) offers an uninterrupted panorama.

Tour Laffon

🚶 *15min on foot round-trip. Follow the path to the right behind the hut.*

Magnificent **vista★** of the central and Ariège Pyrenees, from Pic de Fontfrède (1 617m) to Pic de Cagire (1 912m) beyond the Col de Portet d'Aspet.

Route de la Crouzette★★

This hilltop road skirts the bracken-covered crests of the Arize range and overlooks the forested cirques to the north and gently hollowed out Massat valley to the south.

Sommet de Portel★★

🚶 *15min on foot round-trip.*

Alt 1 485m. Leave the car in a wide bend on the road, at a mountain pass 3.5km/2mi beyond the Col de Péguère.

Climb the grassy bank to the northwest, to the foundations of an old beacon. Enjoy the **panorama** of the peaks in the upper Couserans region. From this summit, the old track drops down to the Coulat spring in just a few minutes, ideal for a picnic or a stroll. Beyond the Col de la Crouzette, during the steep descent to Massat via Biert and then D 618 to the left, is a view of the upper Couserans region and peaks below the Col de Pause, Aulus and the Garbet Valley.

Massat

This small local capital boasts a gabled church flanked by an elegant 15C octagonal tower 58m high. On the top, the muzzles of decorative cannon project through diamond-shaped apertures.

▷ Continue along D 618.

East of Massat the upper Arac basin widens with attractive views of the Massat countryside. Farther on, the majestic Mont Valier range looms into sight and the road climbs to the Col des Caougnous. Before this pass, the gap formed by the Col de Port offers views of the jagged summit of Pic des Trois Seigneurs. The road winds through hamlets with impressive views of Mont Valier before entering a moorland of ferns and broom.

Col de Port

Alt 1 250m.

This pass marks a natural boundary between the 'green' Pyrenees on the Atlantic watershed and the 'sunny' Pyrenees towards the Mediterranean. The road traverses the Saurat valley's fertile land exposed to sunshine, and beyond Saurat is the Montorgueil tower and two enormous rocks named Soudour and Calamès.

Grotte de Bédeilhac

♿*See TARASCON-SUR-ARIÈGE.*

Tarascon-sur-Ariège

♿*See TARASCON-SUR-ARIÈGE.*

▷ Leave Tarascon N on the road to Mercus-Garrabet, along the east bank of the Ariège.

Beyond the Pic de Soudour (alt 1 070m) look out for the Romanesque church of **Mercus-Garrabet** on a rocky outcrop in the middle of its graveyard.

Pont du Diable

Keep following the road along the east bank of the Ariège. Leave the car just beyond the level crossing.

This fortified bridge spanning the Ariège once struck terror into the hearts of local people. It was rebuilt over a dozen times as, legend has it, all the work done each day collapsed during the night – hence the bridge's name (*diable* meaning 'devil'). Observe the system of fortification on the side of the west bank (door and lower chamber). Beyond the turn-off to Lavelanet, the **Pain de Sucre** ('sugar loaf') looms into view with the village of **Montgaillard** below.

▷ Drive into the village and follow signs for 'Les Forges de Pyrène'.

Les Forges de Pyrène★

&♿○*Open mid-Feb–Apr daily 10am–noon, 1.30–6pm; May–Jun and Sept–Oct Mon–Fri 10am–6pm, Sat–Sun 10am–6.30pm; Jul–Aug daily 10am–7pm; mid-end Dec 10am–noon, 1.30–6pm. ○Closed 7–25 Mar, 2–17 Dec, 24–25 and 31 Dec. ⊗€8.80 (child 5–18, €6) ℘05 34 09 30 60. www.forges-de-pyrene.com.*
👥 This open-air museum covering 5ha celebrates 120 traditional crafts and trades, from the dairywoman with her dog team to the wax maker's candles. Workshops show smithies, bakers, sculptors and their like demonstrating their skills.

THE CATHARS

55 km/34mi – Allow at least half a day. See region map.
The Cathars are most often associated with the Pays Cathare of the Corbières southeast of Caracassonne (&*see CARCASSONNE*), but they were equally present in the country around Foix, in the pays d'Olmes, pays de Sault and the Plantaurel. Here, to some extent, they were lost in the Pyrenean foothills away from the major routes of communication, and they were able to establish themselves in citadels safe from the bloodthirsty persecutors. They made what is always described as their last stand at Montségur, which has become the symbol of Cathar resistance.
More substance is added to the story of the Cathars by a renowned book (&*see p376*) looking in detail at the village of Montaillou and the work of the Inquisition which continued after the crusades had finished.

▷ Leave Foix heading south on D 117 towards Montgaillard, then fork left on D 9 through Soula to reach Roquefixade. The road is windy.

Roquefixade

The peaceful village de Roquefixade, a bastide founded at the end of the 13C, is organised around a square with a fountain-cum-drinking trough in the middle.
🚶 From the square a footpath (allow 3/4h) climbs to the top of the huge rock above the village on which sit the ruins of the château. Built in the 11C, this fortress served as a refuge for Cathars during the Albigensian crusade and could communicate with Montségur by beacon. It became a royal fortress in 1278 and was finally demolished in 1632 on the orders of Louis XIII.

▷ Continue on D 9 until the D 117. Turn left towards Lavelanet.

Lavelanet
Musée du Textile

Rue Jean Canal. ○*Open mid-Apr–Oct Tue–Sun 2–6pm (Jul–Aug daily 2–7pm). ⊗€5 (children €3). ℘05 61 03 89 19. www.museedutextileariege.fr.*
Housed in a former mill, this museum has an impressive collection of machines used in the local textile industry from the 17C to the 19C.

▷ Return to the west entry of Lavelanet and fork left on D 109. This joins the D 9 that leads to Montségur.

Montségur★★

○*Open daily: Feb and Nov–Dec 11am–4pm; Mar and Oct 10am–5pm; Apr–Jun and Sept 10am–6pm; Jul–Aug 9am–7pm.* 🗣*Guided visits available.* ⚠ *Can be closed in bad weather conditions. ⊗€5.50/€6.50 according to season). ℘05 61 01 10 27/06 94. www.montsegur.fr.*
⚠ *It's worth bringing good walking shoes. Allow at least an hour for the steep ascent to the château on foot and the return to the car park. The path to the chateau begins outside the village on the D9 to Lavalanet and Foix.*

Montségur castle

© gladiatoria/iStockphoto.com

It would be hard to imagine a better site for a castle than that of Montségur which is built on a rock, the 'Pog', at an altitude of 1 207m. But this is not just another spectacular fortress. What draws visitors here is the story of its downfall and its consequences.

By 1243, the Albigensian crusades were over and the Inquisition was at work rounding up the remaining heretics. The last Cathars were reduced to a few remote enclaves, of which the castle of Montségur was the main one. It was inhabited by a community of Cathar faithful protected by a garrison of soldiers. While Catharism was still practised, the Inquisition had unfinished business. Siege was laid to Montségur by Hugh d'Arcis, seneschal of Carcassonne, and for some time success was not assured.

Then the east tower was damaged by a projectile from trebuchet and subsequently overrun by intrepid Basque volunteers after they had scaled the impossible slopes.

On 2 March 1244 the castle capitulated but on favourable terms. The soldiers, most of whom were not Cathars, would be allowed to depart in return for a light penance. Everyone else was given 15 days grace before they faced their fate, a delay which has never been satisfactorily explained. On 16 March over 200 unrepentant Cathars were marched down the mountainside in chains and burnt alive on pyres. Catharism lingered on for a few years but it never recovered from after the fall of Montségur.

The fortress as seen today, a stretched pentagon following the contours of the platform on top of the rock is not quite the same as the one that existed in 1244 – but is still impressive. The views over the valley and over the surrounding hills and towards the Pyrenees are superb. The village of Montségur is in the Lasset valley below the château. An **archaeological museum** (🕒 *opening times vary;* 📞*05 61 01 10 27*) in the town hall (*mairie*) contains information on Cathar philosophy and displays objects from the excavations.

▶ Continue on D9 towards Bélesta passing Fougax-et-Barrineuf.

Intermittent fountain of Fontestorbes

Fontestorbes spring, which emerges from a rock cave in the Hers valley, is the resurgence of water that has soaked into the chalky soil of part of Sault plateau.

▶ From Bélesta take the right turning on D16 to traverse the beautiful forest of Bélesta. The D16 becomes the D29. The route climbs to the plateau de Sault (🚶see QUILLAN, Driving Tour) in curves to meet D613.

Turn right towards Ax-les-Thermes. In the village of Camurac, D20 on the right leads to the GR107 along the Gorges de la Frau. Continue on D613.

Montaillou

This hitherto unheard of village acquired sudden notoriety in 1975 with the publication of a book – *Montaillou, Cathars and Catholics in a French Village 1294 –1324* by Emmanuel Le Roy Ladurie. Based on the records of the Inquisition led by bishop of Pamiers, Jacques Fournier, the book describes the daily life of the inhabitants of a 14C Ariegeois commuity in detail and the continuing repression of heresy long after the famous battles of the crusade against the Cathars had been fought.

◗ Continue in the direction of Ax-les-Thermes.

Signal du Chioula★

👣*See AX-LES-THERMES.*

◗ Turn right on to the small D 2 towards Lordat.

Château de Lordat

Parking (free) in the upper part of the village. 🕐*Open Jun–mid-Jul 10.30am–12.30pm, 2–6pm; mid-Jul–Aug 10am–12.30pm, 1.30–6.30pm; Sept 10.30am–12.30pm, 2–5pm; Oct 2–5pm.* 👓€4.50 *(child 8–16, €2.50).* 📞*05 61 01 34 22.*

This château overlooking the valley of the Ariège served as a refuge for Cathars after the siege de Montségur. It was demolished by Richelieu and little of it remains. Nevertheless, it provides a tremendous **viewpoint★** over the Pyrenees.

◗ Turn right on N 20 at Luzenac towards Tarascon-sur-Ariège and Foix.

🔎 For more Cathar châteaux to explore 👣see *LES CORBIÈRES.*

PLANTAUREL HILLS

58km/36mi from Foix. Allow half a day.

◗ Leave Foix N along the west bank of the River Ariège to Vernajoul and turn left onto D 1.

These Pyrenees foothills extend from east to west along the northern edge of the range. The Touyre, Douctouyre, Ariège and Arize rivers have dug through the hills, forming transverse valleys.

👥 Underground river of Labouiche★

🚤*Guided tours by boat for 12 people: Jul–Aug 9.30am–5pm; Apr–Jun and Sept 10–11am, 2–4.30pm; Oct–Nov Tue–Fri 2–4pm, Sat–Sun, school and public holidays 2–4.30pm.* 👓€10.80 *(children €8.80).* 📞*05 61 65 04 11. www.labouiche.com.*

The **subterranean gallery** hollowed out by the Labouiche underground river was first explored in 1905. The boat trip runs 70m below ground level through high and low-vaulted galleries, with two changes of craft. Enjoy stalactites and stalagmites and the vision of a beautiful underground waterfall.

◗ Continue along D 1, turn left onto D 11 and left again onto D 117.

La Bastide-de-Sérou

The church in the old part of town contains a 15C carved-wood crucifix from the Rhine region and a late 15C Pietà.

◗ Continue along D 117 then turn right onto D 49 to Brouzenac.

👥 La Ferme des reptiles

♿🕐*Open mid-Jun–mid-Sept daily 10am–7pm; rest of year Sat–Sun and holidays 2–6pm.* 🕐*Closed Jan.* 👓€9 *(child 3–11, €6).* 📞*05 61 65 82 13. www.lafermedesreptiles.fr.*

Hands-on guided tour of this zoo showcases reptiles from common grass snakes to powerful pythons, and iguanas and tortoises.

◗ Return to D 117 and turn right then right again onto D 15.

Beyond Durban, the road follows the shaded Arize valley towards Mas-d'Azil. Along the way, note the small chapels clinging to the slopes.

Grotte du Mas-d'Azil★★
See GROTTE du MAS-d'AZIL.

▷ Continue alongside the River Arize, which flows through a narrow gorge, to Sabarat; left on D 628 to Daumazan-sur-Arize. In the village, left on D 19.

Montbrun-Bocage
See RIEUX.

ADDRESSES

🛏 STAY

🍽🍽 **Hôtel du Lac** – *Rte Nationale 20. 𝄞05 61 65 17 17. www.hoteldulac-foix.fr.* 🅿. *25 rooms.* Peaceful hotel beside a lakes. An air conditioned bungalow can be rented. Wi-Fi access.

🍽🍽 **Hôtel Eychenne** – *11 rue Peyrevidal. 𝄞05 61 65 00 04. 16 rooms.*

Centrally located and easily identified by its twooden corner tower .

🍽🍽 **Chambre d'hôte Château de Benac** – *09000 Benac. 𝄞05 61 02 65 20. www.chambres-hotes-gite-ariege.com.* 🅿 🍽. *5 rooms.* A beautiful bed and breakfast in a 17C house surrounded by forests and fields. Meals are mainly vegetarian although fowl and fish are also sometimes served.

🍽 EAT

🍽 **Au Grilladou** – *7 R. La Faurie. 𝄞05 61 64 00 74. Closed Sat lunch and Sun from Sep–late Jun.* This little restaurant offers pizzas, salads and grilled dishes at very reasonable prices. Simple décor, efficient service and warm welcome.

ACTIVITIES

Sentir Cathare – *www.lesentiercathare. com.* A 250km/155mi long-distance footpath leaqds from Foix to the Mediterranean in 12 stages, visiting Cathar sites along the way. it intersects with another footpath, the Chemin des Bonshommes *(The Path of Good Men, GR107)* which crosses the mountains into Spain.

Tarascon-sur-Ariège

Upper Ariège valley★ and Route du Port de Lers

Tarascon lies in an accessible, sheltered site in the centre of the Ariège valley floor. The surrounding chalk cliffs carved out by the river's passage, and the tributary River Vicdessos add to the charm of the site. The town is a major centre in the Pyrenees for speleological experts (mainly engaged in studies of the Neolithic period). It is also of interest to amateur enthusiasts, seeking to unravel the mysteries in the many caves that pepper the slopes at this confluence of river valleys, called Sabarthès in the Middle Ages.

▷ **Population:** 3 407.
🛈 **Info:** Ave Paul-Joucia, 09400 Tarascon-sur-Ariège. 𝄞05 61 05 94 94. www. montagnesdetarasconet-duvicdessos.com.
▷ **Location:** 15km/9.5mi S of Foix on the N20.

VISIT
Old Tarascon (Vieille Ville)
There's not much left of the old town of Tarascon but it's worth an hour's stroll even if it is necessary to apply a little imagination to fill in the gaps where historic buildings have disappeared. The natural point of entry is the rue du Barri which sets off from near the bridge

over the Ariège. This street was outside the town's walls and became a gathering place for the poor. At a crossroads marked by a fountain the porte de Leule leads into the rue Naugé where many of the houses have arched doorways. The stepped rue de la Tour climbs up to Tarascon's distinctive free-standing clocktower, the tour du Castella, erected in 1775 on the site of the vanished castle keep. Going back down into the town is the Château Lamotte, a 13C fortress which is best seen from the square behind it, rather than the street.

PREHISTORICAL EXCURSIONS

With its 12 decorated caves and its splendid park devoted to prehistoric art, the Ariège *département* can rightly claim to be one of the main centres of Prehistory in France.

♣♣ Parc de la Préhistoire★★

1km/0.6mi N. Drive along N 20 towards Foix then follow the signposts (parking area). ◷*Open Jul–Aug 10am–8pm; Apr–Jun 10am–6pm (Sat–Sun and public holidays 10am–7pm); Sept–Oct daily except Mon, 10am–6pm (Sat–Sun and public holidays, 10am–7pm).* ◷*Closed Nov–Mar.* ▨€10.80 *(child 5–12, €6.90; 13–18, €8.30).* ✆05 61 05 10 10. www.sites-touristiques-ariege.fr.

This museum of prehistoric art, located in a beautiful mountain setting at Lacombe on the road to Banat is devoted to cave wall paintings. A resolutely contemporary building beside a lake houses the **Grand Atelier**, where visitors wearing infrared helmets go round an initiatory exhibition in semi-darkness. In the entrance corridor, drops of water falling on steel cylinders evoke the passage of time, while the history of art since its origins unfolds on screens on the walls. A reconstruction of the Dune des Pas gallery from the Clastres network at Niaux (⊙*some sections not open to the public*) shows the poignant imprint of children's feet in the ground made thousands of years ago. From the same part of the subterranean network, the skilfully executed sketches of a wea-

sel and a horse have been reproduced on a neighbouring wall. The next part of the visit is a short film on methods of excavation and dating used by archaeologists with an overview of cave wall art from all over the world. It illustrates the path taken by prehistoric artists as they searched for the right place to adorn with their images of animals. The exhibition also covers themes such as painted symbols, carved weapons and jewellery, other carvings and techniques used by artists of the Magdalenian period. At the end of the exhibition there is a life-size reproduction of the Salon Noir at Niaux, its walls decorated with paintings of horses, ibex and bison and carved symbols.

Grotte de Niaux★★

5km/3mi S. Turn right off N 20 onto D 8. Take a road uphill just after leaving the village of Niaux. ▰*Guided tours only, see website for details.* ◷*Closed 1 Jan, 25 Dec.* ▨€12 *(child 5–12, €7; 13–18, €8).* ✆05 61 05 10 10. www.sites-touristiques-ariege.fr. ☞ *The path to follow for the visit is long and over rough ground, wear sturdy shoes or boots in rainy weather; reservations strongly recommended.* ✆05 61 05 88 37 or 05 61 05 10 10.

This cave in the Vicdessos valley is famous for its remarkably well-preserved prehistoric wall drawings.

On entering the cave's vast entrance porch, 678m above sea level, the extent of the glacial erosion that occurred many thousands of years ago in the massif of the Cap de la Lesse, where the cave is situated, becomes immediately clear. **The Cave★★** consists of vast, high chambers and long passageways leading, 775m from the entrance, to a kind of natural rotunda known as the **'Salon Noir'** ('Black Chamber'). This is where the best pictures are. They show bison, horses and other animals observed with an extraordinary sense of realism.

Grotte de la Vache

8km/5mi S. Carry on along D 8 and turn right towards Alliat. ◷*For reasons of security the cave system is currently*

closed; check website for the latest information. 📞*05 61 05 95 06. www.grotte-de-la-vache.org.*
This cave was occupied at the end of the Magdalenian period and consists of two galleries, one of which is called Monique, explored up until 1967.

Grotte de Bédeilhac
6km/3.7mi NW along D 618.
🚶 *Guided visits only: May–Sept; check website for variable dates and times.* 🎟*€10 (child 5–11, €5).* 📞*05 61 05 95 06. www.grotte-de-bedeilhac.org.*
This cave has a huge entrance (36m wide by 25m high), large enough to allow a plane to take off and land during a film that was once shot here.

Grotte de Lombrives★
3km/1.9mi S. 🔒*No longer open to the public. www.grotte-lombrives.fr.*
These vast caves, south of Tarascon and just north of Ussat-les-Bains, have certainly been used as a shelter for many centuries. While the first people to enter the cave may have been seeking protection from wild animals or bad weather, later the cave become a hideout for bandits, or a place of refuge for those fleeing religious persecution.

🚗 DRIVING TOURS

UPPER ARIÈGE VALLEY★
From Tarascon-sur-Ariège towards the Col de Puymorens – 54km/33.6mi – Allow half a day.

The Ariège rises on the Andorra border, in the Font-Nègre cirque, and flows into the Garonne just south of Toulouse, having covered 170km/106m. In its upper reaches, the river flows along a glacial channel which widens out and changes direction at Ax. The traces of the old glacier are much in evidence around Tarascon. The Ariège then flows through the Labarre ravine, cutting across the limestone Plantaurel range to reach the Pamiers plain, laid down by the river's own alluvial deposits, where it finally leaves the Pyrenees.

▷ Leave Tarascon along N 20 towards Ax-les-Thermes.

Grotte de Lombrives★
♿*See opposite.*

Luzenac
♿*See Ax-les-Thermes.*
The route continues along the left bank of the Ariège river as far as Ax-les-Thermes. Notice the beautiful Romanesque tower of the church at Unac on the other bank.

Ax-les-Thermes
♿*See AX-LES-THERMES.*

▷ Continue along N 20 towards Puymorens and Andorra.

The road runs alongside some of the bridges – remarkable engineering feats – of the trans-Pyrenean railway line, one of the highest in Europe. It connects Toulouse with Latour-de-Carol near the border in Spain. It is the only railway line through the central Pyrenees.

Mérens-les-Vals
The village was rebuilt along the roadside after the fire that destroyed Mérens-d'en-Haut in 1811 in an arson attack by the 'Miquelets' (Spanish mercenaries feared since the 16C), during the Franco-Spanish Napoleonic War. Beyond Mérens and the Mérens gorge, the road runs upstream along the upper valley of the Ariège in between magnificent forests. On the left is the peak called 'Dent d'Orlu'.

Centrale de Mérens
Alt 1 100m.
This automated power plant is the middle stage of the hydroelectric project of the same name, made possible by the raising of the level of Lake Lanoux. This reservoir, fed by redirecting the tributary waters of the River Segre (and so also the River Ebro) in Spain into the Garonne Valley, is the object of an agreement between the French and Spanish governments, to compensate Spain for the loss of water.

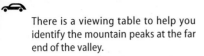

There is a viewing table to help you identify the mountain peaks at the far end of the valley.

L'Hospitalet-Prés-l'Andorra
Alt 1 436m.
This is the first village in the Ariège valley. As the road climbs towards it, the landscape becomes bleaker and more rugged; keep careful watch for the troops of wild horses that frequently follow this route.

Beyond L'Hospitalet, one can either continue up to the **Col de Puymorens★** *(alt 1 920m)* (&see LA CERDAGNE, p304) and drive through the Cerdagne region into Spanish Catalonia or follow N 22 towards Pas de la Casa and **Andorra** (&see ANDORRA).

ROUTE DU PORT DE LERS
87km/54mi round trip. Allow 3h.

▷ Leave Tarascon-sur-Ariège towards Ax-les-Thermes and turn immediately right onto D 8 towards Alliat.

The Port de Lers road reveals the marked contrast between the wooded, coppiced landscape of the Atlantic watershed and the harsher, more rugged countryside towards the Mediterranean.

Grotte de Niaux★★
See p378.

The Puymorens Tunnel

Since 20 October 1994, a tunnel has enabled traffic to avoid the trip across the Puymorens Pass itself, which tends to be a difficult journey in the winter. The building of the Puymorens tunnel, almost 5km/3mi in length, was welcomed by local residents, although it was less well received by ecologists. The tunnel is a physical realisation of the economic and cultural connections between the Ariège region and Catalonia. &See p304.

Niaux
On the edge of the village, the **musée pyrénéen de Niaux** (Ⓛopen for guided visits by appointment only; Jul–Aug 9am–8pm; Sept–Jun 10am–noon, 2–6pm; ℘05 61 05 88 36 www.musee-pyreneen-de-niaux.com) is devoted to traditional popular crafts of the region. High on a rocky promontory, stand the ruins of the 14C Château de Miglos.

The route continues to Junac, where the monument to the dead of World War I was sculpted by Bourdelle. At Laramade the valley opens out to the left as it is joined by the Siguer valley. The Port de Siguer (alt 2 396m) is a pass that was frequently involved in the exchanges between France, Andorra and Spain.

The road follows the deep, rugged **vallée du Vicdessos** where the extended pasturelands play host to flocks of sheep and herds of cattle, with little sign of human habitation. To the right the villages of Orus and Illier perch on the steep mountainside.

Vicdessos
This mountain village is built on a site carved out by glacial action below the hanging Suc valley.

▷ Take D 18 to the right up to Port de Lers.

Port de Lers
Alt 1 517m.
As you climb, look back for a good view of the Goulier valley. The road runs alongside a rushing stream, past several waterfalls.

Étang de Lers★
This superb, solitary lake at the foot of the Pic de Montbéas is set in mountain scenery carved out long ago by glacier action.

L'Etang de Lers-Trois Seigneurs ski area
Alt 1 275m–1 600m.
Some 35km/21mi of cross-country trails go around the lake, at the foot of the Pic de Montbéas.

Drystone Huts

The countryside around Auzat and Vicdessos is dotted with numerous drystone shepherd's huts – known as *orris* – with corbelled roof vaults covered with tufts of a particular species of local grass which keeps the water out. They were used during the summer grazing season. Two footpaths have recently been marked out to enable visitors to explore the area and its huts, some of which date from the 13C. The first path leaves from Pradières and for much of its length follows the GR 10 long-distance footpath, going past the huts at La Caudière and Journosque and running above Lake Izourt and the Arties valley. The second leaves from the Carla huts, which have just been restored, and leads past several more huts and the lakes of Roumazet and Soucarrane.
Further details are available from the local tourist office (*rue des Pyrénées, Auzat; ℘05 61 64 87 53*).

The road carries on round the Cirque de Lers, where horses, sheep and herds of cattle share the pastures.

Peyre Auselère

This is the first hamlet in the sparsely inhabited Courtignou valley. Leave the car in the village to see the waterfalls of the Courtignou.
After Mouréou the landscape becomes less austere, then the road runs across narrow valleys cut through schist.

Massat
♨ *See FOIX.*

Col de Port
♨ *See FOIX.*

▶ D 618 leads back to Tarascon-sur-Ariège.

ADDRESSES

🖌 STAY

◯ **Chambre d'hôte Domaine Fournié** – *Lieu-dit "Fournié" , 09400 Tararscon-sur-Ariège. ℘05 61 01 73 23. www.domaine-fournie.com. Closed at Christmas.* 🅿 ▢ *5 rooms.* Rooms in this 17C house are named after famous films. Indoor swimming pool.

◯◯ **Le Manoir d'Agnes** – *2, rue Saint Roch, 09400 Tarascon-sur-Ariège. ℘05 61 02 32 81. www.manoiragnes.com. 15 rooms.* Bright and modern rooms that combine charm and tradition; excellent in-house restaurant – *see Saveurs du Manoir, opposite.*

🍾/EAT

◯◯ **La Petite Auberge de Niaux** – *09400 Niaux. ℘05 61 05 79 79. www.aubergedeniaux.com. Closed Sun eve, Mon.* Occupying a stone house, this likeable restaurant has a smart dining room with exposed beams, wooden chairs and coloured tablecloths.

◯◯ **Saveurs du Manoir** – *Hôtel Le Manoir d'Agnès, RN20, 2, rue Saint Roch, 09400 Tarascon-sur-Ariège. ℘05 61 02 32 81. www.manoiragnes.com. Closed Sun eve, Mon except certain public holidays, and Sat lunch.* The cuisine in this hotel restaurant changes with the seasons and uses high quality products from local producers wherever possible; a touch of fine dining in this bistrot setting. *15 rooms in the hotel* ◯◯.

SHOPPING

Hypocras – *1 R. Croix-de-Quié, 09400 Tarascon-sur-Ariège. ℘05 61 05 60 38. www.hypocras.com. Open Tue–Sat 3–7pm.* Shop selling a medieval aperitif.

Ax-les-Thermes
and the Donézan

The valley spa and winter sports town of Ax, at the confluence of the Oriège and Lauze rivers, really bustles, summer or winter.

▶ **Population**: 1 351.
◐ **Location**: 128km/80mi S of Toulouse.
👪 **Kids**: Maison des Loups.
◉ **Don't Miss**: Réserve Nationale d'Orlu.

THE SPA
Eighty mineral springs, at temperatures ranging from 18°C–78°C, supply three pump rooms: the Couloubret, the Modèle and the Teich. The main afflictions treated here are rheumatism, respiratory disorders and some skin problems. The focal point of the resort is the Promenade du Couloubret.

WALKING TOUR

OLD TOWN
45min.
Although modern Ax-les-Thermes is dominated by its facilities for health, leisure and pleasure, there are signs of its much tougher past. The old town was once delineated by a set of defensive walls with eight towers but these have long since vanished.
Start from the **casino** (1903) and first visit the adjacent **Eglise Saint Vincent**, built in stages from the 12C to the 19C in a composite of styles.
From here, cross the road to the spacious place du Breilh, where the old town starts. A cloud of water vapour indicates the town's most popular sight, the **Bassin des Ladres**, a pool of thermally heated water. This is said to have been placed here by 13C Saint Louis (King Louis IX) for the benefit of soldiers returning from the Crusades infected with leprosy. It has since been put to different uses including washing wool and washing pig carcasses.
On the square is the **Hôpital Saint Louis** which was founded in 1260 and was expanded in 1846.
Next to it is the **Thermes de Breilh**, today closed. In the maze of small streets south and east of the Place du Breilh – espeically rues Coustou, Constant Alibert, Moulinas and Boucarie –

there are various fountains and medieval half-timbered houses.

🏃 WALKS
Réserve Nationale d'Orlu
8.5km/5mi to the starting point of the footpath. Leave Ax on the road to Andorra and turn off towards Orlu just before the bridge over the Oriège; stay on the north bank of the river.
This walk (3h round-trip) is suitable for all walking enthusiasts.
The road skirts the **Orlu valley★** and reservoir shore, with Orgeix manor house reflected in the waters of the dam. Take the road on the left before the old Orlu ironworks. Leave the car in Pont de Caralp carpark and walk along the track closed to motorised vehicles.
The path climbs the west bank of the Oriège to the En Gaudu shelter. Look for marmots and izards in early morning and late afternoon. Farther up (2h round-trip), the path crosses a stream and from Pas de Balussière continues along the east bank of the Oriège.
Farther up still, the **Étang de Beys** comes into view.

Signal du Chioula★
45min on foot round-trip.
Leave Ax on D 613 N, following the Ariège valley in a series of hairpin bends.
At the Chioula Pass, a wide footpath leads to the beacon (alt 1,507m/4,898ft; 45min round-trip), and a view of the peaks framing the upper Ariège valley.

EXCURSIONS
👪 Maison des Loups
8.5km/5.3mi. Leave Ax on the road to Andorra and turn towards Orlu just before the bridge on the Oriège; drive to the end of the valley as far as Les Forges. ◷Open Jul–Aug daily

Ax-les-Thermes

©Hemis/Photoshot

10am–7pm; Apr–Jun daily except Mon
and Wed 10am–5.30pm; Sept–Oct Thu–
Sun 11am–5pm. ☉Closed Nov–Easter.
⇒€8.90 (child 3–12, €7.30).
☎05 61 64 02 66.
www.maisondesloups.com.
Observation platforms scattered across a
magnificent woodland site, with mountain streams rushing through it, offer an
opportunity to see different species of
wolves roaming around in vast enclosures and being fed. Kids will enjoy the
donkeys, goats, lambs and piglets.

Plateau de Bonascre★

*8km/5mi. Leave Ax on N 20 to
Tarascon and turn off left onto D 820.*
The road climbs steeply in hairpin
bends, with views of the three river
valleys which converge on Ax. On the
Bonascre plateau at the top is the ski
resort of **Ax-Bonascre-le-Saquet**,
and a gondola leading to the **Plateau
du Saquet** (alt 2 030m).
Continue in car or on foot past the 'Sup-
Aero' holiday home and turn left on the
track to Campels which goes along the
side of the mountain for 1.5km/0.9mi.
From here you have a superb **view★★**
over the valley and the heights of
the Ariège towards the frontier with
Andorra. Down below, the main road
and the railway intertwine.

SKI AREAS
Ax-Bonascre-le-Saquet
Alt 1 400m–2 400m.

The ski area has 75km/44mi of forested
Alpine ski runs for all levels of skiers, and
grass skiing in summer!
The **gondola** goes to the Saquet plateau (☉open at varying times throughout the year; check locally for current
information; ☎05 61 64 60 60; www.
vallees-ax.com).

Ascou-Pailhères
Alt 1 500m–2 030m.
This family resort offers 15 Alpine ski
runs for all levels.

Mijanès-Donézan
Alt 1 530m–2 000m.
The 'Québec of Ariège' on the Donézan
plateau offers 10 downhill slopes and
25km/15.6mi of cross-country trails. This
family resort caters to children with play
groups and sledding.

Le Chioula
Alt 1 240m–1 650m.
There are 65km/40.6mi of cross-country trails and 6km/3.6mi of free trails
for those learning cross-country techniques. Lodging adjacent to the trails.

Plateau de Beille
*16 km/10mi west on N 20. Continue to
Cabannes then turn left on D 522.*
At an altitude of between 1 800m–
2 000m this is considered the premier
site for cross-country ski-ing in the Pyrenees. The 12 pistes have a total length
of 70 km/43 miles.

The Izard

About 40 years ago, the izard, a variety of wild goat found in the Pyrenees, had been all but killed off by hunters' bullets. Nowadays it is a protected species. There are over 1 000 in the Orlu valley, which has been designated a nature reserve since 1981. The izard is found between 1 600m–2 500m above sea level, but it does venture below 900m. It is gradually taking over those areas which have been abandoned by man. The izard's coat changes colour depending on the season: it is red-gold in the summer and dark brown with patches of white in the winter, when it also becomes much thicker to combat the cold. The animals are not that timid and can be observed quite easily, especially during spring or autumn. The summer heat and winter cold force them to take refuge in the undergrowth. Izards are perfectly suited to their environment and can climb up and down even quite steep slopes with impressive agility.

🚗 DRIVING TOURS

LE DONÉZAN

For a map of this 42km/26mi tour see region map. Allow 3h.

Note that this route cannot be driven in winter because access to the col de Pailhères and Pradel may be blocked by snow.

The Donézan offers beautiful countryside at mid-altitude (around 1 200m) consisting of forests, lakes and hamlets. It is a popular region for hiking in summer and has some skiing in winter.

▶ Leave Ax-les-Thermes heading east on D 613 towards Chioula and Quérigut. The road is steep and winding. Turn right on D 25, towards Ascou and Quérigut. In the hamlet of Lavail turn left on D 22.

Col du Pradel★

The distinctive **Dent d'Orlu** (alt 2 222m) can be seen to the southeast. The road corkscrews up the pass (alt 1 680m) around tight hairpin bends with views of the mountains.

▶ Return to D 25 and turn left. The ski resort of Ascou-Pailhères is on the right. Cross the col de Pailhères .

Mijanès and the Étang du Laurenti

Mijanès is a pleasing cluster of mountain houses. Leaving the village, take the track towards Bruyante (*5.5km/3.5mi*) which brings you to the refuge du Laurenti. From here there is an easy walk to the beautiful mountain lake of Laurenti (*3h30*).

▶ Return to D 25 and follow D 16 to Quérigut through La Pla.

Château de Donézan

All that is left of this medieval château at the top of the village of Quérigut is a ruined tower.

▶ Return to Le Pla. Turn right on D 16 towards Rouze.

Ponts Vauban

30min. Rouze has two bridges built by the 17C engineer Vauban. To see them, follow the marked footpath which begins in the place de la Mairie.

▶ Leave Rouze on D 16 towards Usson-les-Bains and the château d'Usson.

Château d'Usson

15mn from the parking at the bottom of the chateau. Open Jul–Aug 10am–1pm, 3–7pm; Sept Fri–Mon 2–6pm; rest of the year by appointment. €4 (child 5–12, €2.10). 04 68 20 41 37. www.donezan.com.

This imposing castle was built between the 11C and 12C. Its stables house a visitor's centre for the Donezan with displays on the geography, wildlife and human life of the region.

THE CLIMB TO TRIMOUNS ★★
For a map of this 39km/24mi tour, see region map. Allow around 3h.

▶ Leave Ax-les-Thermes heading NW on N 20 towards Tarascon.

Luzenac
This village has been famed since the late 19C for its French chalk quarried at the **Carrière de Trimouns★**. Find tourist infromation at 6 rue de la Mairie.

▶ Cross the bridge and take D 2 towards Caussou.

Unac
Note the pretty Romanesque church with its tall belfry.

▶ Continue on D 2, the route des Corniches. Turn left towards Lordat to visit its chateau (*see Foix, Driving Tour*). Return to the crossroads on the route des Corniches. Go straight on for Trimouns.

Carrière de Trimouns★
Guided tours only (1h). Open mid-May–early Jul and early Sept–mid-Oct Mon–Fri at 4pm; Jul–mid-Sept at 10am, 11am, 2pm, 3pm and 4pm. €8.20 (6–20 years, €5.50). Visits depend on the weather – telephone one hour in advance. ☎05 61 64 60 60. www.vallees-ax.com.
French chalk (talc) is mined in this quarry at an altitude of 1 800m in the massif du Saint-Barthélemy. The talc is brought down to a factory in the valley where it is dried, ground and conditioned.

▶ Return down to Lordat and head for Luzenac via Vernaux.

Vernaux
Below the village, the road runs past an isolated Romanesque church.

▶ On reaching Luzenac, turn left for Ax-les-Thermes on N 20.

Saint-Girons
Le Couserans, Upper Salat and Garbet valleys★

Situated at the confluence of three rivers, St-Girons soon became an important market town and the main administrative centre of the Couserans region, known locally as '18 valleys' country. This region, just north of the 'axial zone' or backbone of the Pyrenees, was closely linked with the neighbouring district of Le Comminges in medieval times.

EXCURSIONS
Saint-Lizier★
2km/1.2mi N of Saint-Girons.
Above the functional modern town of St-Girons, on the main road down in the valley, is the far more attractive Gallo-Roman citadel of St-Lizier on the hill. It is

▶ **Population:** 6 750.
▶ **Michelin Map:** 343: E-7.
▶ **Info:** Pl. Alphonse-Sentein, 09200 St-Girons. ☎05 61 96 26 60. www.ville-st-girons.fr.
▶ **Location:** 28km/17.5mi S of Junction 20 of the A64 Toulouse to Bayonne Autoroute.
▶ **Don't Miss:** Le Col de Pause; La Cascade d'Arse.
▶ **Timing:** Allow one and a half days to see the whole area.

only small but a delightful place to stroll around. The cathedral is something of an architectural jumble built over five centuries and distinguished by its 14C

Saint-Lizier

octagonal belfry. Inside are 12C frescoes of the apostles which have a Byzantine air to them. The two-storey 12C cloister has sculpted Romanesque capitals. Other notable buildings are the Hotel Dieu which contains an 18C pharmacy and the massive bishop's palace built in the 17C.

Au Pays des Traces

Ferme du Miguet. ⏰*Open Jul–Aug Mon–Sat 10am–7pm, Sun 1.30–7pm; French school holidays 1.30–6.30pm.* ⊜*€11 (child 3–12, €9). Sports shoes recommended.* ✆*05 61 66 47 98. www.paysdestraces.fr.*
Children will have fun in this theme park which teaches principles of ichnology – the tracks, traces and trails of animals.

🚗 DRIVING TOURS

VALLÉES DE BIROS AND DE BETHMALE
Round trip from St-Girons. 78km/48mi. Allow about 4h.

▶ Leave St-Girons SW along D 618 towards Luchon.

The picturesque road follows the River Lez through a wide sunny valley dotted with attractive villages.

Audressein
This is a pleasant little village at the junction of the River Bouigane and River Lez.

▶ The route follows the Lez Valley upstream.

Castillon-en-Couserans
This little village on the east bank of the Lez is built at the foot of a wooded hill. The 12C **Chapelle-St-Pierre**, in Parc du Calvaire, was fortified in the 16C.

Les Bordes-sur-Lez
At the entrance to the village, next to a roadside cross, there is a scenic view of the oldest bridge in the Couserans area and the Romanesque church in Ourjout, marking the beginning of the Biros valley.

Vallée de Biros
Climbing up the valley of the River Lez, the road passes a number of tributary valleys on the south side, at the far end of which are glimpses of the mountains along the border.

Sentein
This village makes a good base camp for mountain climbing.
🚶 Walking enthusiasts and nature lovers could continue to the end of the valley, the road ending at Eylie.

▶ Turn around and go back down the valley to Les Bordes. Turn right on D 17.

Vallée de Bethmale★
The valley is wide open, its hilly slopes dappled with barns and tightly clustered villages.
The village of Bethmale used to be known for the imposing bearing of its population and their distinctive dress – the traditional men's jackets, for example, were made of raw wool with multicoloured facings – a fact which continues to intrigue ethnologists and experts in folklore, for similar garments are a part of ceremonial peasant costume in the Balkans.

Ayet
The church, built on a raised site, contains examples of 18C 'primitive' woodwork.

▶ About 5km/3mi farther on, park by the roadside near a sharp bend to the left and walk into Bethmale forest.

Lac de Bethmale

🚶 *15min on foot round trip.*

The lake sits in an attractive setting surrounded by beech trees.

The road climbs through a cirque of pastureland to Col de la Core, which looks back down over Bethmale valley.

The road goes back down past orchards and barns to the junction of the River Salat and River Garbet near Oust, the geographic centre of the Upper Salat region.

Seix

The village is overlooked by a 16C château.

Vic

The **church** here has a wall-belfry and Romanesque triple apse.

▶ To return to St-Girons, turn left onto D 3 towards the Gorges de Ribaouto. Alternatively, continue your journey through the Upper Salat and Garbet valleys.

UPPER SALAT AND GARBET VALLEYS★

Round tour from Seix 78km/48mi – allow 1 day. From Seix, drive south along D 3 which follows the Salat upstream as far as Salau, close to the Spanish border. For 10km/6mi beyond Seix, the road runs alongside the river; at the entrance to Couflens, branch off towards Col de Pause and Port d'Aula. The surface of this steep, narrow road is poor and badly rutted over the final 3km/1.8mi (generally obstructed by snow from October to May).

The little road climbs above the impressive, forested Vallée d'Angouls. Off to the south, through the gap carved out by the Salat, the summits of the valley's last cirque can be seen above Salau; the highest is Mont Rouch (alt 2 858m). The route continues beyond the strikingly situated village of Faup, perched on a rocky ledge, to the pass.

Col de Pause★★

Alt 1 527m. The road above the pass, on the right-hand slope beneath Pic

de Fonta, offers a different **view** of Mont Valier on the far side of the vallée d'Estours breach. The chasms gashing the east face of the summit and the ridges of its northern foothills are clearly visible.

▶ Beyond Col de Pause, the steep and narrow road to Port d'Aula is in very poor condition. Return to Pont de la Taule and turn right on D 8.

The road follows **vallée d'Ustou**, climbs for a few miles, and then drops down in a series of sharp bends to Aulus-les-Bains. There are views during the descent.

Guzet

This winter resort, its chalets dotted among fir trees, stands in the picturesque Upper Ustou valley.

Aulus-les-Bains

The sulphur, calcium and magnesium-containing mineral waters which rumble through Aulus are used to treat metabolic disorders. Aulus is a convenient starting point for excursions into the three upper valleys of the Garbet (the Fouillet, the Arse and the Upper Garbet), all of which abound in waterfalls and small lakes.

▶ Continue SE up Vallée du Garbet. After 1km/0.6mi, park.

Cascade d'Arse★

🚶 *Take the GR 10 path, on the right (5km/3mi on foot).*

After crossing the river and winding south, GR 10 leads to the foot of these falls which plunge 110m in three stages.

▶ Return to Aulus and take D 32 N down the Garbet valley.

Vallée du Garbet★

This valley in the Upper Couserans was once known as *Terra Santa* (The Holy Land) on account of the large number of chapels and wayside shrines.

▶ At the far end of the valley, the road goes through Oust then Seix.

Grotte du
Mas-d'Azil★★

This cave is one of the most interesting natural sights in the Ariège. It is also a famous prehistoric milestone in the scientific world as it is here that the Azilian culture was studied and defined.

A BIT OF HISTORY

In 1887, as a result of methodical excavations, Édouard Piette discovered a new layer of evidence of human habitation dating from between the end of the Magdalenian (30 000 BCE) period and the beginning of the Neolithic – this was the Azilian period (9 500 BCE). Research continued under Abbé Breuil and Joseph Mandement, and others such as Boule and Cartailhac. The items excavated are exhibited in the cave and the town of Mas-d'Azil.

THE CAVE

🕐 *Open at a wide range of variable hours; check website for details.* ◉ €9 *(child 5–12, €4.50; 13–18, €5.50), ticket combined with the museum.*
05 61 05 10 10.
www.sites-touristiques-ariege.fr.

The cave, hollowed out by the Arize underneath the Plantaurel mountain range, is 420m long with an average width of 50m. Upstream, the entrance forms a magnificent archway (65m high), whereas downstream, a flattened opening (8m or so) pierces a sheer rock 140m high.

Approaching the town of Mas-d'Azil from the south, the D 119, and a footpath alongside it, go through this natural passageway following the course of the torrent whose waters are gradually eroding the limestone walls, then under a majestic vault, shored up in the centre by a huge pillar of rock.

- 🕐 **Michelin Map:** 343: G-6.
- ℹ **Info:** 17 av. de la Gare, 09290 Le Mas-d'Azil. *05 61 69 99 90. www.tourisme-arize-leze.com.*
- ▶ **Location:** North of Ariège, Mas-d'Azil is also a village 23km/14mi northwest of Saint-Girons and 34km/21mi northwest of Foix.
- 👁 **Don't Miss:** The 'fawn with birds' carving at the Musée de la Préhistoire.
- 👪 **Kids:** A large green space in front of the southern entrance to the cave (across the road from the car park) makes a good place for a picnic and for kids to run around.

THE TOUR

To see more, take the guided tour which visits parts of the cave on the right bank of the river which are not visible form the road or footpath.

The tour includes the **Salle du Temple**, a Protestant place of refuge, the intermediate floor of which was destroyed under Richelieu after the fruitless siege of 1625. Display cases contain exhibits dating from the Magdalenian (scrapers, chisels, needles, a moulding of the famous neighing horse head) and Azilian periods (harpoons made from antlers – the reindeer moved northwards as the climate became warmer – arrowheads, coloured pebbles and miniaturised tools).

The Salle Mandement contains the remains of animals (mainly mammoth and bear), coated in rubble and doubtless reduced to a heap of bones by subterranean flooding (the Arize, which was 10 times the volume that it is today, made the water level reach the roof).

The **Musée de la Préhistoire** (*05 61 05 10 10*) in the village in front of the church contains the famous Magdalenian carving of a fawn with birds (*Faon aux oiseaux*).

Mirepoix

In the 13C, many Cathars settled in the town of Mirepoix, including the seigneur, Pierre Roger de Mirepoix who played an important role in the defence of Montségur during the 1243 siege. In the same century Mirepoix was devastated by a flood from the waters of Lake Puivert. The town was rebuilt in a safer place, at the confluence of the River Hers and River Countirou.

▶ **Population:** 3 309.
◔ **Michelin Map:** 343: J-6.
🏠 **Info:** Pl. du Mar.-Leclerc, 09500 Mirepoix. ✆05 61 68 83 76. www.tourisme-mirepoix.com.
◉ **Location:** 22km/13.75mi E of Pamiers.

TOWN

All roads lead into the focal point of the place Principale, with its lovely arcades sheltering cafés and shops, and half-timbered houses supported on pillars.

Place Principale★★

The main square of public gardens, old-world shops and cafés is surrounded by late 13C–15C houses. Note the **Maison des Consuls** with carved heads.

Cathedral St-Maurice

The cathedral, surmounted by an elegant Gothic spire, was built between 1343 and 1865. The early 16C nave is the widest (31.6m) of any built for a French Gothic church. It is flanked with chapels set between the interior buttresses, following Gothic tradition in the south of France.

EXCURSIONS

Camon

8km/5mi SE, on D 625, then D 7.
Camon with its imposing **abbey** is set against the Ariège hills. Visit the fortifications, then enter the village through the Porte de l'Horloge to see the conventual buildings renovated by Philippe de Lévis, Bishop of Mirepoix, in the 16C. There are the remains of the old cloisters and the oratory decorated with 14C paintings.

Vals

12 km/7.5mi W of Mirepoix. Take D 119 going towards Pamiers and turn right at Pujols on to D 40.
This village has an extraordinary subterranean church. Steps climb up a cleft in the rock to a chamber probably carved in the 11C, where the apse has remarkable Romanesque frescoes (12C) on the walls. They show three episodes in the life of Christ and are more drawn than painted with naïve simplicity. Above ground is a 14C tower and a terrace with views.

Pamiers

21km/13mi E along D 922.
Pamiers is situated on the east bank of the River Ariège, on the edge of a fertile plain. Since it became a bishopric in 1295, it has been home to four monastic communities. The **Promenade du Castella** is a walkway which follows the line of the old castle, the foundations of which are still visible between the Porte de Nerviau and the Pont-Neuf. At the top of the hill is a bust of the composer **Gabriel Fauré**, born in Pamiers in 1845. The **Cathédrale St-Antonin**, in place du Mercadel, has a handsome bell-tower in the Toulouse style, resting on a fortified base. All that remains of the original 12C church is the doorway.

The church of **Notre-Dame-du-Camp** features a monumental brick façade with crenellations and towers, and a single 17C nave inside. Pamiers has several interesting **old towers**: the Clocher des Cordeliers (*Rue des Cordeliers*), similar to the tower of this name in Toulouse; the Tour de la Monnaie (*near Rimbaud School*); the square Tour du Carmel (*Place Eugène-Soula*), originally a keep built in 1285; the tower of the Couvent des Augustins (*near the hospital*); and the brick and stone Porte de Nerviau (*near the town hall*).

Rieux-Volvestre★

Although it only has 2 600 citizens, this small town has been a bishopric since 1317 when pope John XXII reorganised the church in southwest France. There is a good view of the cathedral with its octagonal bell tower from across the Pont Lajous over the Arize river. Opposite the cathedral are some half-timbered houses from the 15C and 16C.

EXCURSIONS
👥 Village gaulois de Saint-Jullen

5km/3mi SW via the D 25. ⏱*Open: check website for details of visits.* ⤷*Guided visits (1h) 2–6pm.* ⏱*Closed Dec–Easter.* ☎*05 61 87 16 38. www.village-gaulois.org.*
A recreated Gaulois village complete with wooden palisade and thatched huts. There are demonstrations of traditional skills including basket-making, pottery and weaving.

🚗 DRIVING TOUR

THE VOLVESTRE AND TERREFORT
A 66km/41mi trip from Rieux to Pamiers via Carla-Bayle. Allow 2h.

▶ Take the main road southeast from Rieux, D 627.

Montesquieu-Volvestre
A delightful bastide founded in 1238 on a loop of the on the river Arize. At the centre is a beautiful arcaded square with a market hall (16C). The church was built in the 13C as part of the town's fortifications and and has an unusual belltower with 16 sides.

▶ In Daumazan-sur-Arize, turn right on D 74.

▶ **Population:** 2 640.
🚲 **Michelin Map:** 343: F5.
ℹ **Info:** 9 rue de l'Evêché. ☎05 61 87 63 33. www.tourisme-volvestre.com.
📍 **Location:** SE of Toulouse.
👁 **Don't Miss:** In the 1st week of May Rieux holds the Fête du Papogay in which local archers compete to bring down a mock parrot from the top of a pole.
👥 **Kids:** Village Gaulois de Saint-Julien.

Montbrun-Bocage
The small village **church** contains remarkable 16C **murals★**; in the chancel, note St Christopher, the Tree of Jesse and scenes from the Life of St John the Baptist.

▶ Leave on the D 74 and turn right on D 628 and shortly after turn off on D 14. Follow the signs to Carla-Bayle.

Carla-Bayle
This fortified village on a rocky outcrop changed its name from Carla-le-Comte to Carla-le-Peuple during the Revoulution and then, in 1879, to Carla-Bayle in honour of Protestant philosopher Pierre Bayle who was born here in 1647. He was the author of the influential book, **Historical and Critical Dictionary**, and was in some ways a forerunner of the Englightenment. In recent years the village has been restored and is now a home to artists and craftspeople. There are good views from the ramparts south towards the Pyrenees.

▶ Take D 14 and turn right on D 919 towards Foix. Turn off left on D 27.

St-Martin d'Oydes
This pretty village in a valley has a circular plan with a ring of medieval houses facing the church.

▶ Leave the village heading south on D626. turn left on to D119 and continue to Pamiers Terrefort.

SAINT-GAUDENS *and Around*

It would be hard to find anywhere in Europe with a longer history than this corner of southwest France. Archaeological remains found near the town of Aurignac have given their name to one of the continent's earliest prehistoric cultures which flourished over 30 000 years ago. Almost as old are the enigmatic hand paintings in the Grotte de Gargas. In comparatively recent times, the Roman general Pompey founded one of southern Gaul's most important cities, Lugdunum, in 72 BCE while on his way to campaign in Spain. That this became a prosperous and desirable region to live in late Roman times is indicated by the excavated remains of the villas of Mountmaurin and Valentine. After having been overrun by the Visigoths, the comminges became a part of the Duchy of Aquitaine in the 7C and a county in its own right from the 8C until it was incorporated into the French crown in the late 15C. In the middle ages, the region flourished and the splendid Romanesque-Gothic cathedral of St Bertrand-des-Comminges was built on a hill above Lugdunum.

A Place on the Map

Today, the name Comminges is usually used to refer to the southern part of the department of Haute-Garonne with St-Gaudens as its sub-prefecture. The historical county, however, was broader than this and covered parts of what is now the *départements* of the Gers, Haute-Garonne, Haute-Pyrenées and Ariège. Topographically, the Comminges extends from the undulating hills and valleys of southern Gascony and culminates in the peaks of the Massif de la Maladeta, just over the Spanish border, which includes the highest peak in the Pyrenees Pic d'Aneto, 3 404m).

The Garonne creates a corridor through the north of the Comminges carrying the motorway and railway line linking Toulouse to Bayonne. Two broad valleys thrusting south into the Pyrenees are the only other major routes of communication. At the head of one of these is Bagnères-de-Luchon, an important spa. Mid-way up the other valley is the winter sports resorts of St-Lary-Soulan.

Across the Border

For most of their length the Pyrenees are a formidable barrier inhibiting cross-border connections between Spain and France. But in one place they relent. The main route through the Comminges, the N125, slips effortlessly over the frontier into a into a distinct corner of Spanish Catalonia, the Val d'Aran which geographically has more in common with the French side of the range.

Highlights

1 Visit the excavated Roman villa at **Montmaurin** (p396)
2 Admire the great **St-Bertrand-des-Comminges** cathedral (p398)
3 Puzzle over the enigmatic hand prints in the **Grotte de Gargas** (p401)
4 Take the waters in **Bagneres de Luchon** (p403)
5 Discover the wildlife of the high Pyrenees in the **Reserve Naturelle du Néouvielle** (p408)

The River Garonne

One natural feature gives unity to the Comminges and that is the Garonne, the principal river of southwest France. Rising in the Val d'Aran, it flows across the border at Pont du Roi to become France's fourth largest river after the Loire, Seine and Rhone. From the frontier to its mouth it is 521km/323mi long and drains the Aquitaine basin. It flows north through the marble town of St-Béat before turning sharply east to pass St-Gaudens. After leaving the Comminges it flows towards Toulouse. It receives the Ariège, Tarn and Lot rivers as tributaries before joining the Dordogne to form the Gironde estuary near Bordeaux.

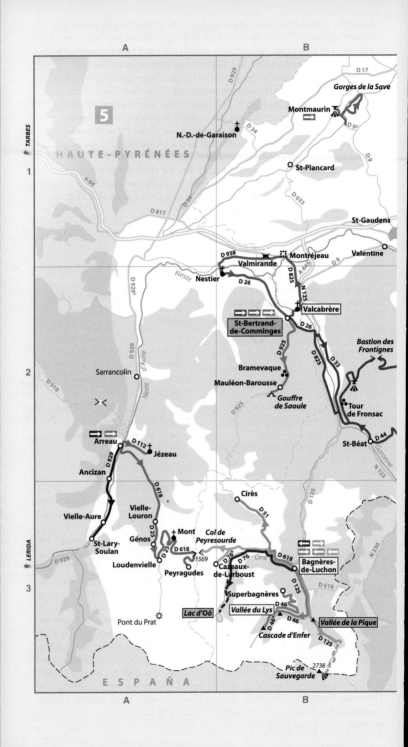

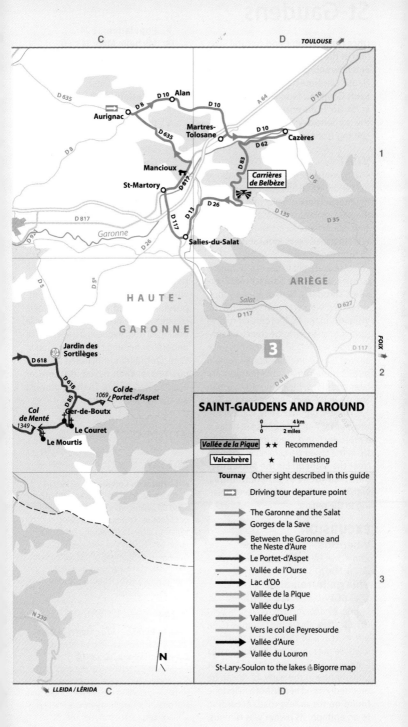

C — D

Alan
D 10
D 8
D 10
Aurignac
D 635
D 635
Martres-
Tolosane
D 10
Cazères
D 62
Mancioux
D 83
Carrières
de Belbèze
St-Martory
D 817
D 26
D 135
D 817
D 13
Garonne
D 117
D 26
Salies-du-Salat
D 35

FOIX

ARIÈGE

HAUTE-

GARONNE

Salat
D 627
D 117
D 117

3

Jardin des
Sortilèges
D 618
D 618
Col de
Portet-d'Aspet
1069
Col
de Menté
Ger-de-Boutx
1349
Le Couret
Le Mourtis

SAINT-GAUDENS AND AROUND

0	4 km
0	2 miles

Vallée de la Pique ★★ Recommended

Valcabrère ★ Interesting

Tournay Other sight described in this guide

Driving tour departure point

The Garonne and the Salat

Gorges de la Save

Between the Garonne and
the Neste d'Aure

Le Portet-d'Aspet

Vallée de l'Ourse

Lac d'Oô

Vallée de la Pique

Vallée du Lys

Vallée d'Oueil

Vers le col de Peyresourde

Vallée d'Aure

Vallée du Louron

St-Lary-Soulon to the lakes Bigorre map

N 230

N

LLEIDA / LÉRIDA C — D

St-Gaudens

Once the economic and cultural hub of the county of Comminges, and now sub-prefectture of Haute-Garonne department, Saint Gaudens, familiarly known as 'St-Go' is the entry point into the modern-day Comminges when coming from Toulouse.

▶ **Population:** 11 241.
◔ **Michelin Map:** 343: C6.
▯ **Info:** 2 rue du Thiers. ℘05 61 94 77 61. www. tourisme-stgaudens.com.
◑ **Location:** 92km/57mi southwest of Toulouse by the A64 motorway.
◉ **Don't Miss:** Collégiale Saint-Pierre-et-Saint-Gaudens.

VISIT

The town is sited on a terrace above the Garonne and has good views of the Pyrenees. There is a viewing table on the balcony beside the Monument des Trois-Maréchaux – a memorial to World War I marshals Foch, Joffre and Gallieni, all from the Pyrenees.

The essential sight to see in St-Gaudens is the **Collégiale Saint-Pierre-et-Saint-Gaudens**. Named after a young shepherd who was martyred by the Visigoths in the 5C for refusing to give up his Christian faith, the church was finished between 1130 and 1150 but since altered. Some original capitals remain but its more remarkable features are later additions, including a 17C organ and three 18C Aubusson tapestries. The 12C cloister, unfortunately, was demolished in 1807 and the one seen today is a reproduction dating from the 1980s. Up in the tower is a carillon of 36 bells. Near the cathedral is the **Musée-de-Saint-Gaudens et du Comminges**, with an eclectic assembly of items relating to the region.

EXCURSION
Valentine
2km/1.5mi SW in the road to Bagnères-de-Luchon (D 5).
Villa gallo-romaine
℘*05 61 89 05 91.* ✿*Guided tours by prior arrangement.*
On a terrace above the Garonne river, out of reach of floods and morning mists, lie the remains of this Roman villa built during the reign of the Emperor Constantine in the early 4C. It can be predisedly dated because of a milestone found on the access road. According to an epitaph, its owner was Nimfius, apparently an important person. Built of river stones, limestone blocks and marble from St-Béat, the villa was only a single storey high but covered a wide area behind its handsome façade. Much of the building can be traced from the ruins which centre on a courtyard in which there is a semicircular Nymphaeum once fed with thermal waters by pipes. The principle rooms of the villa benefited from hypocausts, a system of underfloor heating commonly used in Gaul. Outbuildings included servants quarters, a water tank and a tank for keeping live oysters. To the southwest are the remains of a temple.

ADDRESSES

⌂ STAY

⊖⊖ **Hôtel du Commerce** – *2 avenue de Boulogne, 31800 St-Gaudens. ℘05 62 00 97 00. www.commerce31.com. Closed at Christmas. 48 rooms.* A modern building close to the town centre. The rooms are functional and varied but all have air-conditioning. In the restaurant, the menu combines tradition with modernity. Cassoulet is one of the house specialities.

⏲/EAT

⊖⊖ **La Pyrène** – *60 av. Maréchal Joffre. ℘05 61 89 60 98. www.lapyrene.com. Closed Sun eve and Tue eve.* ▣. This restaurant-pizzeria in the outskirts of St-Gaudens is easy to find. Almost all the dishes – including the starters buffet and the desserts – are homemade. There is a shady terrace for summer use.

Aurignac

To any palaeontologist, Aurignac is familiar as the place that gave its name to a civilisation of early Cro-Magnons who lived long before the great age of cave painters. The town grew up as a fortified base of the Counts of comminges in the hills to the west of the Garonne. Aurignac is built on a hill, with medieval streets on its crest around a castle keep (donjon) and Renaissance houses on the streets below.

SIGHTS

Abri préhistorique – The cave shelter which has made the town famous is just ouside the built-up area on the road to Boulogne-sur-Gesse (D 635). It is reached by a short walk from a car park down the wooded slope and across a stream, although there is not much to see.

Église Saint-Pierre – This 16C church next to the Porte du Clocher (the gateway to the medieval town) has a flamboyant Gothic porch.

Donjon – A flight of steps leads up to the top of this tower from where there is a **panorama★** of the Pyrenees on a clear day from the Pic du Midi de Bigorre to the Ariège.

🚗 DRIVING TOUR

THE GARONNE AND THE SALAT
70km/43mi. Allow around 1h30.

▶ Leave Aurignac going NE on D 8, then continue on D 10 to Alan.

Alan

This bastide founded in 1270 by the seneschal Eustache de Beaumarchés became one of the preferred residencies of the bishops of Comminges. It preserves the remains of its ramparts and a Gothic gateway. The church on the square was rebuilt in the 18C but has its original three-story 14C belfry wall. The **Palais des Évêques** (🕐*open end Jun–Sept Sat–Sun 3–6.30pm; Tour of the*

- **Population:** 1 250.
- **Michelin Map:** 343: D5.
- **Info:** Ave de Boulogne. 𝄪05 61 98 70 06. www.tourisme-aurignac.com.
- **Location:** 21km/13mi northeast of St-Gaudens.
- **Don't Miss:** A climb to the top of the Donjon.

Palace by appointment, for groups only: minimum of 8 people; ⌐€3, children under 12, no charge; 𝄪05 61 98 90 72; www.lepalaisdeseve_quesdecomminges.com) was the winter residence of Jean de Foix Grailly (1466–1501), Bishop of Comminges. It has a Gothic portal with a cow, the **vache d'Alan★**, holding the bishop's coat of arms carved above it.

▶ Continue on D 10.

Martres-Tolosane

Formerly a Gallo-Roman town, today Martres-Tolosane is chiefly distinguished by its Gothic church, église Saint-Vidian, built over an early Christian necropolis. The Musée Angonia is dedicated to the local faïence pottery industry and finds at the nearby Chiragan Roman villa – from which almost 300 busts and statues have been excavated and sent to the Musée Saint-Raymond in Toulouse.

▶ Follow D 10 along the Garonne.

Cazères

Historically, Cazères was an important trading port on the Garonne. In recent years it has become a centre for leisure boating.

▶ Cross the Garonne in the direction of Couladère. At Mauran, take D 83 to the left. There are views of the Petites Pyrénées before Ausseing.

Panorama des carrières de Belbèze★

🐾*15mins on foot. Turn left off the road to Belbèze-en-Comminges, signposted 'Table d'orientation'.*

The view from this high point takes in the Salat basin, the Pyrenees in Ariege, the pic du Midi de Bigorre and the range receding towards the Basque Country. The stone extracted form the quarry was much used in the building of Toulouse.

▷ Take D 26 then D 52 to the left to reach Mazères-sur-Salat. Turn left on D 13.

Salies-du-Salat

The monumental 1930s municipal spa building is testament to the famous waters of Salies which are claimed to be the most mineral rich in Europe.

▷ Take D 117 N.

Saint-Martory

This small town is the starting point of a canal of the same name dug in 1846–1877 to irrigate the higher terraces along the western side of the Garonne valley. It stretchs for 70km/43.7mi as far as the outskirts of Toulouse.

▷ Continue on N 117, now heading NE, for 3km/1.8mi.

Menhirs de Mancioux

These two tall stones erected in prehistoric times stand by the roadside. They are thought to have been used by the Romans as milestones or signposts on the route between Toulouse and Lugundum (Saint-Bertrand-de-Comminges).

▷ Continue on N 117 and turn left on D 635 to return to Aurignac.

Montmaurin

Nestled in the Gascony hills, Montmaurin offers fine views of the Pyrenees and the archaeological attraction of the remains of a Gallo-Roman villa outside the village.

▶ **Population:** 217.
🜏 **Michelin Map:** 343: B-5.
▷ **Location:** Montmaurin is 10km/6.25mi S of Boulogne-sur-Gesse.
👁 **Don't Miss:** The Gallo-Roman Villa.

VISIT
Villa Gallo-Romaine

1km/0.6mi SE.
🕐*Open Jan–Apr and Sept–Dec daily except Mon 9.30am–noon, 2–5pm; May–Aug daily 9.30am–noon, 2–6pm.* 🕐*Closed 1 Jan, 1 May, 1 and 11 Nov and 25 Dec.* ☎*05 61 88 74 73.* ✆€3 *(children under 18, no charge). www.villa-montmaurin.fr.*
The descendants of a certain Nepotius inherited a territory near Montmaurin extending over about 7 000ha. The original *villa rustica* built on this land in the 1C concentrated the agricultural and rural dependencies around the big house, much like large farms do today. In the 4C this residence was replaced by

a marble mansion. This *villa urbana* was adorned with gardens, colonnades and statues of nymphs. Thermal baths and a system of hot air circulating beneath the tiled floors assured comfort, however inclement the weather. The mansion comprised 200 rooms arranged around a row of three separate courtyards graced with peristyles and pergolas. Summer apartments set on tiered terraces completed the complex.

Museum

Ground floor of the town hall (Mairie).
🕐*Open same hours as Villa Gallo-Romaine.* 🕐*Closed 1 Jan, 1 May, 1 and 11 Nov, 25 Dec.* ☎*05 61 88 17 18.*

This museum is devoted to local prehistoric finds and the archaeologists who discovered them, and the local Gallo-Roman civilisation.

EXCURSIONS
Viewing Table
800m N of the village.
The viewing table offers a **panorama★★** extending from the Pyrenees in the Ariège département to Pic du Midi de Bigorre and Pic de Ger. Through the gap carved by the Garonne see the Maladetta massif and glaciated sections of the Luchon heights on the frontier.

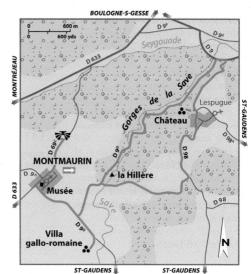

EXCURSIONS
Saint-Plancard
8km/5mi S on D 69c, then D 633 towards Montréjeau.
Built on the site of a Gallo-Roman temple, the chapel of Saint-Jean-des-Vignes dates from the early 11C, but is remarkable for the paintings which survive from the end of that centry. They have faded with time but there is a light (switch opposite the door) in order to see them better. The paintings in the apse show Christ in majesty surrounded by the evangelists (on the left), the Three Kings (centre) and the crucifixion and resurrection (on the right).
In the south apsidiole chapel Christ is shown on his throne in a figure of eight design held by four expressive angels. The paintings on the walls, meanwhile, are dedicated to the work of St-Jean the Baptist. On the right of the entrance is the Fall of Man.

Notre-Dame-de-Garaison
18km/11mi W of Montmaurin by D 17, then D 34 right after Balesta.
In 1515 the Virgin Mary appeared to a young shepherdess, Anglèze de Sagazan, in a remote valley on the plateau of Lannemezan. A shrine, the object of pilgrimage, grew up on the spot. In the mid-19C a school was created. This now has 600 pupils plus a religious community of 20 nuns. The chapel (built in 1702) has naïve paintings showing hooded pilgrims dressed in blue, white, grey and black robes. In the nave, the beautiful 17C furniture ist he work of the toulousain sculptor Pierre Affre.
There are also murals from the 16C. They include a depiction of Garaison around 1550 (high up on north and south walls of the nave), the life of Saint Catherine (first chapel on right) and John the Baptist (2nd chapel on right).

🚗 DRIVING TOUR

GORGES DE LA SAVE
12km/7.5mi. Allow 1h.
See local map above.

▶ Follow the Save valley downstream for 1km/0.6mi, then cross the river.

Château de Lespugue
The ruins crown a rocky spur above Save gorge. Reach them on foot by descending through an oak grove and climbing through the woods on the opposite slope of the valley.

Return to the car and continue down to the river. Just before the bridge, turn left on D 9.

Gorges de la Save

Carving a deep channel through limestone folds of the Lesser Pyrenees, the Save torrent has hollowed out caves beneath the rock. Excavated between 1912 and 1922 by the Comte and Comtesse de Saint-Périer, several of these yielded finds from the Magdalenian (late Palaeolithic) and Azilian (transitional Paleolithic-Neolithic) periods. Notable is the statuette the **Vénus de Lespugue**, whose original is in the Musée des Antiquités Nationales in St-Germain-en-Laye.

La Hillère

On the way out of the gorge, archaeological digs have revealed a sanctuary including temples, baths, fountain and market, built during the 4C on the spot where the River Save resurfaces.

Return to Montmaurin.

ADDRESSES

EAT

Auberge 'La Ferme de Préville' – *Rte d'Auch, 31350 Boulogne/Gesse. 05 61 88 23 12. Closed Sat and Sun.*
Beams and furniture in wood: the decor of this inn is resolutely rustic but renovated. The cooking uses only ingredients sourced from local farmers. Cooking workshops on Monday evenings after the meal (except in July and August).

St-Bertrand-de-Comminges★★

St-Bertrand is one of the most picturesque villages in the foothills of the Pyrenees, perched on an isolated hilltop at the entrance to the upper valley of the River Garonne. It is encircled by ancient ramparts and dominated by an imposing cathedral; the belfry-porch of this sanctuary, crowned by a defensive wooden gallery, is a landmark visible for miles around.

- **Population:** 251.
- **Michelin Map:** 343: B-6.
- **Info:** Les Olivétains – Parvis de la cathédrale. 05 61 95 44 44.
- **Location:** St-Bertrand is 10km/6mi S of Junction 17 of the A64 Toulouse to Bayonne Autoroute.
- **Don't Miss:** The Cloisters and the woodcarvings in the cathedral.
- **Timing:** Allow half a day.

Apart from its remarkable **site★★**, St-Bertrand is noted for the artistic and architectural treasure it contains, and for the charm of its steep, narrow streets crowded with medieval houses and artisans' workshops. In summer, in conjunction with nearby Valcabrère and St-Gaudens, the village holds a music festival. Today St-Bertrand-de-Comminges, formerly a stopping place on the pilgrims' route to Santiago de Compostela, remains one of the most impressive sights on any journey through the Pyrenees.

A BIT OF HISTORY

Memories of Herod – The town that preceded St-Bertrand enjoyed a distinguished Roman past as **Lugdunum Convenarum**, capital of the tribe of Convenae in the 1C BCE; it is thought to have had between 5 000 and 10 000 inhabitants. The Jewish historian Flavius Josephus asserts that it was the place of exile of Herod, the Tetrarch of Galilee, and his wife Herodias, responsible for the decapitation of John the Baptist, four years after the death of Christ.

Ongoing **excavations** have unearthed two Roman bathhouses, the remains of a theatre, a temple probably consecrated to Rome and to Augustus, a 5C Christian basilica and a market place on one side of a large square flanked by porticoes.

Two Bertrands – The Roman colonial capital was eventually sacked by the Barbarians. Subsequently rebuilt on the hill only and enclosed within a wall, it was totally destroyed for a second time by the Burgundians in the 6C. For nearly 500 years after that the town stood empty and fell into decay.

Around 1120 the Bishop of Comminges, Bertrand de L'Îsle-Jourdain, appreciating the site of the old acropolis, had the ruins cleared and built a cathedral. To serve it he appointed a chapter of canons. The effects of the future St Bertrand's actions were felt almost immediately; the faithful flocked to the town that grew up around the church, and pilgrims broke their journey here. The town adopted the name of the man who had brought it back to life.

By the end of the 13C the cathedral founded by St Bertrand was no longer large enough for its congregation. A namesake, Bertrand de Got, who was himself destined to become Clement V, the first Avignon Pope, continued the bishop's work; the enlargement of the church was completed by his successors in 1352.

CATHÉDRALE STE-MARIE★

Allow 2hr. ⏱ *Jun–Sept 9am–7pm (Sun 2–7pm); Feb–Apr and Oct 10am–noon, 2–6pm (Sun 2–6pm); May 9am–6pm (Sun 2–5pm); Nov–Jan 10am–noon, 2–5pm (Sun 2–5pm).* ⊛€4.
☎*05 61 95 44 44. www.cathedrale-saint-bertrand.org.*

The Romanesque part of the cathedral comprises the west front crowned with an 18C belfry, the porch and the three western bays; the rest is Gothic. The tympanum (west door) is carved with an effigy of Bishop St Bertrand and an Adoration of the Magi.

Cloisters★★

The pervading sense of spiritual peace and retreat from the world distilled by the architectural setting is enhanced by the temporal poetry of the splendid mountain landscape visible through the arcades of the south gallery, open to the outside world.

One gallery is Romanesque (12C), the other three are Gothic; the gallery adjoining the church was altered in the 15C and 16C – it houses several sarcophagi. The capitals in the cloisters are exceptional for their carvings showing biblical scenes, foliage and scrolls. Note the celebrated pillar portraying the Evangelists Matthew, Mark, Luke and John, with its capital representing the signs of the zodiac for each of the seasons.

Trésor★

The treasury is located above the northern gallery (*access from inside the church*). The upper level chapel and the former chapter rooms contain 16C Tournai tapestries, episcopal ornaments, a mitre, two liturgical copes (the needlework on these vestments represents the Virgin Mary and the Passion), and the shaft of St Bertrand's crook, fashioned from the tusk of a narwhal whale. The copes, exquisitely embroidered in *broderie anglaise*, were the gift of Bertrand de Got on the occasion of the translation of Bishop St Bertrand's relics (1309).

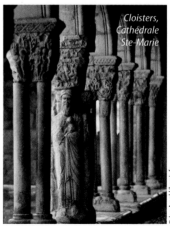

Cloisters, Cathédrale Ste-Marie

© Jon Arnold/hemis.fr

Canons' Chancel★★

The chancel boasts the superb **woodwork★★** commissioned from sculptors in Toulouse by Bishop Jean de Mauléon and inaugurated by him in 1535.

The carvings include the rood screen, the choir screen, the high altar reredos – unfortunately disfigured by painting – a bishop's throne surmounted by a three-tiered pyramidal dome, and 66 **stalls**, 38 of them with tall backs and canopies. Piety, wit, satire – even lechery – are given free reign in the little world created by the craftsmen, the general theme of which is the Redemption.

St Bertrand's Tomb

The tomb is a 15C stone-built tabernacle in the form of a shrine, covered in paintings depicting the miracles of St Bertrand; it supports an altar.

Lady Chapel

The chapel, a 16C addition on the northern side of the church, contains the marble tomb of Hugues de Chatillon, who completed the building in the 14C. The lierne and tierceron vaulting signify the end of the Gothic period.

Nave and narthex

Space for the congregation on the outer side of the rood screen is somewhat limited but this is compensated for in the richness of the furnishings: a 16C **organ★** (recitals are given in season); a 16C pulpit; the former parish altar, which dates from 1621. The altar frontispiece is made of Cordoba leather.

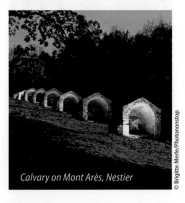

Calvary on Mont Arès, Nestier

© Brigitte Merle/Photononstop

🚗 DRIVING TOURS

BETWEEN THE GARONNE AND THE NESTE D'AURE

32km/20km. Allow 45min.
🕭 See region map.

▷ Leave Saint-Bertrand heading NE on D 26.

Basilique Saint-Just de Valcabrère★

🕐 *Open Jul–Sept daily 9am–7pm; Apr–Jun, 1–15 Oct 10am–noon, 2–6pm; rest of the year Sat–Sun 2–5pm.* 🎫 *€2.50 (children under 10 no charge).* 📞 *05 61 95 49 06.*

The 11C–12C Romanesque **Basilique St-Just** stands isolated in the middle of fields surrounded by cypress trees. Beneath the altar is a curious chamber like a crypt where, it is thought, a sick person would spend the night in order to be impregnated by the healing forces of the sacred objects above him or her.

▷ Take N 125 N towards Valcabrère.

Montréjeau

This former bastide founded in 1272 has several points of interest: the place de Verdun (covered market and public gardens), the place Valentin-Abeille (central fountain, arcades and timber framed house at No. 21) and the boulevard de Lassus (a cliff road with views).

▷ Leave Montréjeau west via D 638.

Château de Valmirande

🕐 *Guided visits mid-Jul–mid-Aug 4pm; 1–13 Jul, 15–31 Aug by appointment with the tourist office on 📞 05 61 95 80 22; rest of the year groups only.* 🎫 *€7 (children under 12, €3).* 📞 *05 62 00 79 55.*

Only the grounds of this château are open to visitors. The gardens are planted with more than 180 species of trees and shrubs.

▷ The D 638 becomes D 938 as it enters the département of Hautes-Pyrénées. Turn left at Saint-Laurent-de-Neste.

Nestier
The **calvary on Mont Arès** consists of 12 stone chapels built in 1854 by the priest of Nestier.

▶ Take D 26 in the direction of Saint-Bertrand-de-Comminges.

👥 Grottes préhistoriques de Grottes de Gargas ★
🕐*Open Jul–Aug 10am–6pm; rest of the year Tue–Sun 10.30am–5.30pm.* ⊛*€10.50 (children €6).* 👁*Visitor numbers are limited. Reservation recommended.* 📞*05 62 98 81 50. www.grottesdegargas.fr.*
Sometime around 26 860 years ago, give or take 460 years, during the time that archaeologists call the Gravettian period, prehistoric people crept into the upper and lower galleries of these Jurassic limestone caverns and made marks on the wall which modern science has been unable to decipher.
Gargas is best known for the negative hand impressions – there are a verified 110 of them – made by men and women of all ages. There are also paintings and engravings, etched with fingers and flints, showing horses, bison, ibex and inscrutable signs.

LE PORTET-D'ASPET
88km/55mi route. Allow around 2h. ♿*See region map.*

▶ Leave St-Bertrand-des-Comminges heading SE on D 26 and turn right on N 125. Cross the Garonne by the pont de Chaum, turn right then after the bend turn left on D 618.

On the right are the ruins of the **tour de Fronsac**, one of the fortresses of the counts of Comminges.

Bastion des Frontignes
The hairpin bend before the village of Antichan offers a fine **view** of the Luchon massif.

▶ Continue on D 618 crossing the pass of **col des Ares** (797 m/2 615ft). After **Juzet-d'Izaut** and the **col de Buret**, turn left on D 5 to reach the village of Sengouagnet.

Le jardin des Sortilèges
🕐*Open: check the website for details of exhibitions and displays.* ⊛*4€ (children under 16 3€).* 📞*06 37 92 44 39. www.jardinsdesortilege.fr.*
These seven gardens reveal the secrets of many common plants that are often ignored. This is the place to discover the multiple virtues of nettles and the culinary uses of what are normally called weeds.

▶ Turn round and turn left onto D 618.

After Henne-Morte, the road steepens on its way through the vallée du Ger, which includes a beautiful wooded gorge as it approaches the col de Portet-d'Aspet.

Col de Portet-d'Aspet
This pass at an altitude of 1 069 m affords great views, particularly of mont Valier (alt 2 838m), which takes the form of a lightly inclined pyramid. A monument at the col commemorates the tragic death of Italian cyclist and Olympic gold medalist 24 year-old Fabio Casartelli who in 1995 became the fourth competitor to die in the Tour de France as he was descending from the col. It was claimed at the time that a helmet would not have saved his life but since then head-protection has become compulsory for professional cyclists.
The road over the pass continues to the east into the Couserans region of the Ariège (♿*see SAINT-GIRONS).*

▶ Turn round. Before Henne-Morte, turn left on D 85, then right on D 44. At the **col de Menté** (alt 1 349m) turn left towards Le Mourtis.

Le Mourtis
This small winter sports resort has chalets and apartments spread out in a forest of lichen-clad fir trees.

The Cave Artists

France's legacy of cave art dates from the Upper Palaeolithic around 26 000–10 000 years ago. Prehistoric artists often worked in inaccessible places by the light of torches. They used three techniques – drawing, engraving and painting – to depict animals, signs and, rarely, human beings. The pigments came from ground minerals and charcoal and were applied with a brush or by blowing through a tube.

▶ Turn round and return to D 44.

The road descends in loops then passes under the packed slate roofs of Boutx and Lez.

Saint-Béat

Despite now being on the busy N125, St Beat has retained considerable charm. The local white and grey marble, renowned since Roman times, was later used to fashion the fountains and statues of Versailles. The exposed workings of the Roman quarry are visible just outside the town on the D44. The Romanesque church dates from the 14C. Its portal has a tympanum showing Christ in majesty. The sacristy contains several polychrome statues.

▶ Return to Saint-Bertrand-des-Comminges by N 125, D 33 and D 26.

VALLÉE DE L'OURSE
12km/7.5mi – Allow 30min.
See region map.

▶ Leave St-Bertrand-des-Comminges going south on D 26 towards Izaourt. After 2 km/1mi turn right in the direction of Mauléon-Barousse.

Still fairly wild, the vallée de l'Ourse (or Barousse) has numerous small villages sown around its slopes.

Bramevaque
Château des Comtes de Comminges
20mins from the car park.
Little remains of this 11C fortress except the restored keep. Good views over the valley.

▶ Continue on D 925.

Mauléon-Barousse
Maison des Sources
Open Thu–Tue 9am–6pm. Closed first weekend of month. Guided visits available. 05 62 39 23 85.
The theme of this visitor's centre is water, its natural cycle and its uses. There is also an arboretum and children's playground.

▶ Go W on D 925 along the Ourse de Ferrère for a short way just past the turning to Ourde.

Gouffre de Saoule
It is possible to walk to the Gouffre from the village.
A viewpoint looks over the natural limestone bridge which spans the cacading Ours de Ferrère river.

ADDRESSES

STAY

Hôtel l'Oppidum – *R. de la Poste. 05 61 88 33 50. http://hoteloppidum.com. Closed 15 Nov–15 Dec, Sun evening and Mon off-season. 15 rooms. Restaurant.* This establishment is very nicely situated at the foot of the Sainte-Marie cathedral. The rather confined rooms are reasonably well fitted-out; many come with new bathrooms. One room also has a terrace.

EAT

Chez Simone – *R. du Musée. 05 61 94 91 05. Closed Toussaint and Christmas school holidays, and evenings off-season.* A couple of streets from the cathedral, Simone offers simple family fare. The rustic dining room features wooden beams, chequered oilcloths and decorative copper vessels, while outside there is a terrace beneath the lime trees.

Bagnères-de-Luchon ★

and local valleys

Bagnères-de-Luchon, or Luchon as it is more commonly known, is a lively spa lying in a beautiful setting half way along the scenic Route des Pyrénées, appreciated for the restorative virtues of the fine climate as well as the waters. It is the busiest and most fashionable cure resort in the region, and also a tourist and winter sports centre with a wide choice of ski runs, climbs and excursions. In the winter, the town serves as a base for skiers attracted by the slopes at Superbagnères, the resort's high-altitude annex, and slopes around other resorts such as Peyragude and Le Mourtis.

▶ **Population:** 2 711.
🖹 **Info:** Allées d'Étigny, 31110 Bagnères-de-L. ℘05 61 79 21 21. www.luchon.com.
◑ **Location:** In the far south of the Haute-Garonne.
☺ **Don't Miss:** Lac d'Oô and Vallée de la Pique.

A BIT OF HISTORY

Baths of Ilixo – In Gallo-Roman times, the Vallée d'One (the land of the Onesii) was already famous for its healing waters. Ilixo, the centre's divine custodian, presided over the magnificent baths which were second only to those in Naples, according to an inscription in Latin on the wall of the bath house. Excavations have revealed traces of enormous pools lined with marble, and systems for circulating warm air and steam. A Roman road linked the baths to Lugdunum Convenarum (St-Bertrand-de-Comminges).

The Great Intendant – In 1759, Baron d'Étigny, who lived at Auch, visited Luchon for the first time. The baron, who was Intendant (Royal Steward) of Gascony, Béarn and Navarre, was so impressed with the spa that he determined to restore it to its former glory. By 1762, a carriage road linked Luchon to Montréjeau in the north. The splendid avenue – which today bears the nobleman's name – was officially inaugurated, and planted with rows of lime trees which had to be guarded by soldiers as the inhabitants were hostile to such innovations. D'Étigny then replaced the original common pool with nine double troughs made of wood, each with a removable cover which had a hole for the bathers' heads.

This was a substantial improvement, though those taking the waters still had to undress in the open air, screened only by a board fence. D'Étigny was also the first person to think of appointing a regular doctor to a thermal spa.

The next step was to advertise the town. D'Étigny persuaded the governor of the province, Maréchal Duc de Richelieu, to take a cure. The duke, enchanted by the Roman ruins, was delighted. He extolled the merits of the spa back at the palace in Versailles and returned for a second cure. From then on, the town's success was assured. Even the premature death of Baron d'Étigny, in 1767, did not halt Luchon's development.

THE SPA

Life in Luchon centres on **allées d'Étigny**, the main avenue leading to the baths. The mansion at no 18, built in the 18C, was where the Duc de Richelieu resided. It now houses the tourist office and local museum.

Cures – Water from some 80 springs is piped from Superbagnères mountain to the spa. Combining the effects of sulphur and radioactivity to treat respiratory disorders, the Luchon cures have long been favoured by famous singers, actors, lawyers and preachers. More recently, there has been increasing success in treating rheumatic complaints and physiotherapy, by combining alluvial mud steeped in colonies of algae and bacteria giving off sulphur, found only in extremely hot water, with sulphurous emanations in a specially fitted-out grotto or **Radio-Vaporarium**,

Spa, Bagnères-de-Luchon

© Jean-Paul Azam/hemis.fr

where the temperature is 38–42°C. The Radio-Vaporarium is located in Luchon's most luxurious spa treatment centre.

Villas of the Spa District

Luchon's spa district has several notable villas particularly on boulevard Edmont Rostand, named after the Belle Epoque playwright (author of *Cyrano de Bergerac*), a frequent visitor to the town.

Musée du Pays de Luchon

Open daily except Tue and public holidays 10am–noon, 3–6pm. €4 (combined ticket with the Musée de l'Aéronautique €6). 05 61 79 29 87.
This local history and folk museum features Iron Age artefacts, statues and votive altars from the Gallo-Roman period, as well as weavers' looms, shepherds' crooks, farming tools and religious items, mementoes of famous Pyrenees climbers, and photographs of the town and its thermal cures.

Musée de l'Aéronautique

R. Albert-Camus. Open Apr–Oct Tue, Thu, Sat 3–6pm. €4 (combined ticket with the Musée du Pays de Luchon €6). 05 61 79 29 87.
Parts of World War II aircraft shot down in the Pyrenees are brought together in this unusual museum.

WALKING

Behind Luchon, the Pyrenees form a barrier of granitic summits all over 3 000m sealing off the vallée d'Oô in the south. There is even a pass, le port de Vénasque, at an altitude of 2 448m.

1 Lac d'Oô★★

Leave Luchon via D 618, the road to Col de Peyresourde. At Castillon, fork left onto the Vallée d'Oô road (D 76), which skirts the base of the huge moraine sheltering the villages of Cazeaux and Garin. 2h30 round trip walk along the footpath marked GR 10. Alt 1 504m.
The lake lies in a magnificent setting with the torrent from Lac d'Espingo cascading down a spectacular 275m. The lake (covering 38ha; maximum depth 67m) fuels the Oô hydroelectric power station.

2 Vallée de la Pique★★

Leave Luchon via D 125. The road follows the Vallée de la Pique upstream. Cross the river and turn left onto the D 125 leading to the University of Toulouse, and its botanical laboratory. Park the car and continue on foot.
Set amid forests, waterfalls and high pastureland typical of the Pyrenees, the Hospice de France, at 1 385m, makes an excellent base for ramblers. Walkers can get a closer view of the Pyrenees' highest point by leaving the Hospice

early morning on the mule track to **Port de Vénasque** (*alt 2 448m*). From the foothills on the Spanish side of the pass (*4h30 round trip*) or from Pic de Sauvegarde, which rises to 2 738m (*6h round trip*), is a panorama of the Maladetta massif.

🚗 DRIVING TOURS

VALLÉE DU LYS★
32km/20mi S from Luchon.
Allow 2h30. 🕐 See region map.

▷ Leave Luchon S along D 125 then turn right onto D 46. Park the car 2km/1.2mi beyond the second Pont de Ravi.

This valley's name *Bat de Lys* comes from *bat*, Gascon for *valley*.

Gouffre Richard
The base of an electricity pylon, offers a good view of a waterfall plummeting down into a rocky cauldron. After the turnoff to Superbagnères on the left, the road veers southwards, revealing a **panorama★** of the highest peaks encompassing the cirque. 🅿Park in the (free) car park of Les Délices du Lys restaurant.

Centrale du Portillon (Portillon Power Station)
The hydroelectric station is powered by water falling from 1 419m, a drop considered sensational when the station opened in 1941.

Cascade d'Enfer (Hell's Waterfall)
This is the last leap of the Enfer stream.

▷ Return to D 46 and take the turnoff to Superbagnères on the left.

Superbagnères
This alpine ski centre can be reached from Bagnères-de-Luchon by cableway. The impressive Grand Hôtel built in 1922 and now owned by Club Méditerranée affords a **view★★** of the Pyrenees and the Maladetta massif glaciers beyond.

VALLÉE D'OUEIL★
15km/9mi NW from Luchon to Cirès – 30min. 🕐 See region map.

▷ Leave Luchon by D 618.

After several sharp bends, turn right on D 51. About 2km/1mi along, a track leads to **Benque-Dessous-et-Dessus**, whose church in the upper village contains 15C murals. The lower **Vallée d'Oueil★** has pretty pastures and clustered villages.

Cirès
The houses in this hamlet have pointed roofs with lofts for storing the hay.

VERS LE COL DE PEYRESOURDE★
20km/12mi from Luchon to Col de Peyresourde. Allow around 45min.

▷ Head west on D 618.

Saint-Aventin
The Romanesque church here has stone carving including a Virgin and child.

▷ Continue on D618. Garin has a small chapel worth a short stop.

Cazeaux-de-Larboust
The church is decorated with 15C sculptures.

Col de Peyresourde
At 1 569m this pass leading into the Louron valley has good views.

ADDRESSES

⌂ **Chambre d'hôte Le Poujastou** – *R. du Sabotier, 31110 Juzet-de-Luchon. ℘05 61 94 32 88. www.lepoujastou.com. Closed Nov. 5 rooms.* This 18C house is the village café; contemporary rooms in ochre hues.

⌂ **La Petite Auberge** – *15 r. Lamartine. ℘05 61 79 02 88. Closed late Oct–26 Dec.* 🅿. *30 rooms.* An historic house mid-way between the spa and the cable car for Superbagnères.

Arreau

This pleasant town of slate-roofed houses was once the capital of the Four Valleys Region. Note the 16C corbelled **Maison du Lys** and the *halles* (covered market) with basket-handled arches forming the ground floor of the town hall. The chapel features a Romanesque doorway with marble columns and storiated capitals. The D 929 follows the River Neste d'Aure upstream along a wide and pleasant valley.

- ▶ **Population:** 854.
- **Michelin Map:** 342: O5.
- **Info:** Château de Nestes, Arreau. ℘05 62 98 63 15. www.vallee-aure.com.
- ▷ **Location:** 32km/20mi south of Lannemezan.
- **Kids:** Workshops at Grottes de Labastide.
- **Don't Miss:** The maison des Lys in Arreau and the painted churches of the Vallée du Louron.

WALKING TOUR

Start from the tourist information office, housed in the Chateau des Nestes, and walk up the road following the rushing waters of the Louron river upstream. Beside the river are the workings of an old sawmill. To the left of the road is the the Chapelle Saint Exupery, a Romanesque chapel with an octagonal 16C belltower which dates from the 1930s but looks as if it should be older.

The ground floor is an arcaded market hall. Offices occupy the first floor and a belfry crowns the building. Across a narrow street is the 16C half-timbered Maison des Lys. The town's most beautiful building, it is named after the fleur-de-lis motifs on its façade.

Up the main street from the town hall is the Romanesque church, the Eglise Notre Dame.

Val d'Aran

The main road through the Comminges crosses the Spanish border into the Val d'Aran, a geographical anomaly. The Garonne river rises in this valley and flows north through the Pyrenees. Until the building of a tunnel in 1948, the valley was more closely connected to France than to the rest of Spain. The Val d'Aran has three languages: Catalan, Spanish and Aranés, related to Occitan.

EXCURSIONS
Sarrancolin
7km/4.5mi N of Arreau by D 929.
Celebrated for its, marble-quarrying and its woollen industry this little village preserves some houses from the 16C and 17C. On the main street stands the **église Saint-Ébons**. This remarkable Romanesque church dating from the 12C is built on the plan of a Greek cross (unique in the region) and has a spire clad in slate rising from a square tower adorned with four corner pinnacles. Inside there is a wrought iron grille from the 15C, statues of gilded wood and the reliquary of St Ébons (13C), an ornate coper and enamel ches.

Espace prehistoire de Labastide
17km/10.5mi N of Arreau by D 292.
Open Jul–Aug daily 10am–6pm; Apr–mid-May and Sept Sun 10am–noon, 2–5pm, Wed–Sat 2–5pm; mid-May–Jun Sun 10am–noon, 2–5pm, Mon–Thu 2–5pm; €6 (children €5). ℘05 62 49 14 03. Guided tours 1h30. www.espace-prehistoire-labastide.fr. Warm clothes recommended.
The son-et-lumière show projected on the limestone wall of the Grotte Blanche explains the scientific importance of the paintings discovered in the Grotte aux Chevaux (which is not open to visitors), and how human beings lived in Magdalenian times. A footpath leads to the Perte de Laspugue – 'Perte' meaning a

place where a river disappears into the ground.

👥 Three workshops introduce children and animals to prehistoric sounds, the art of painting on rock walls and how prehistoric hunters tracked their prey.

🚗 DRIVING TOURS

VALLÉE D'AURE★

A tour of 16km/10mi from Arreau to Saint-Lary-Soulan. Allow 20min.

▷ Leave Arreau heading N on the D 929 main road up the valley which links the two stops on the tour.

Ancizan

A cluster of 16C houses recalls the prosperity of this town. It has two museums. The subject of the Musee de la Valle d'Aure is the traditional life of the valley. The **Musée de la Cidrerie** in a 19C farmhouse celebrates the area's important cider industry, feted each autumn.

Mines de Vielle-Aure

This former magnesium mine has been prepared to receive visitors.

Saint-Lary-Soulan

See SAINT-LARY-SOULAN.

VALLÉE DU LOURON

46km/28mi. Allow 1h.

This tour visits a series of exquisite churches whose vaults and walls were painted by French and Spanish artists in the 16C. To find out when the churches are open check with the tourist information office in Loudenville.

▷ Leave Arreau heading east on D 112.

Jezeau

The church has a beautiful Renaissance altarpiece in sculpted and painted wood.

▷ Return to Arreaux and take D 618 going SE. At the fork before Avajan, take D 25 to the right.

Vielle-Louron

The Eglise Saint-Mercurial is one of the most beautiful painted churches of the vallée du Louron. In the sacristy (16C) demons with sardonic grins submit the damned to torments.

▷ Continue on D 25.

Genós

🚶 *15min on foot.*

Park near the church, on the left and walk around the cemetery to reach the ruin of the 14C château from where there is a view over the lake to the mountains at the head of the valley.

▷ Continue to Loudenville, at the far end of the lake.

Loudenvielle

L'Arixo is a small museum explaining the life of the vallee du Louron. In the Moulin de Saoussas the old mill wheels can be seen in operation.

▷ Continue on D 25 to Estarvielle where there is another painted church. Take D618 to the right, then D 130 left to Mont.

Mont

The Romanesque church here has a painted facade and 16C paintings inside.

▷ Resume D 618 to the left and continue to Luchon over the col de Peyresourde (1 569m).

ADDRESSES

🛏 STAY

🍽🍽 **Chambre d'hôte Domaine Véga** – 65250 St-Arroman. ☎05 62 98 96 77. *www.domaine-vega.fr. Closed Oct–May.* 🅿🚭. *4 rooms.* Beautiful 16C manorhouse standing in its own wooded grounds. The rooms are simple and comfortable, with views over the swimming pool and the surrounding countryside. An outdoor kitchen is available for the use of guests.

Saint-Lary-Soulan

Standing in the middle of the vallée d'Aure, Saint-Lary-Soulan is moderately attractive Pyrenean town of stone houses with slate roofs. It serves both a summer and winter clientele. From spring to autumn, it is a centre for walking and other outdoor activities, and is the principle point of access to the Néouvielle nature reserve.

SIGHTS
Ski Resort
One of the Pyrenees' leading ski resorts, St-Lary-Soulan village is connected to vast domain of slopes on the high western slopes of the valley. The domain is divided into three interconnected parts Pla d'Adet (the usual starting point, at 1 700m connected to the village below by two cable cars), d'Espiaube et du Vallon du Portet. There are 100km/60mi of pistes and the skiing area goes up to 2 515m.

▶ **Population:** 917.
◔ **Michelin Map:** 342: N6.
▯ **Info:** 37 rue Vincent Mir, 65170 St Lary-Soulan. ☎05 62 39 50 81. www.saintlary.com.
◗ **Location:** 43km/27mi south of Lannemezan.
▲▲ **Kids:** Maison de l'ours.

EXCURSION
Maison de l'ours
Access by the Route du Corps-Franc-Pommiès. ◔*Open Jul–Oct daily 9.30am–12.30pm, 2–6.30pm; rest of the year closed Mon.* ∞€6.90 *(children €4.90).* ☎05 62 39 50 83.
▲▲ The desirability of maintaing a population of brown bears in the Pyrenees is fiercely debated. The 'house of the bear' aims to promote understanding of the mountains' most conspicuous and endangered species – its population having been reduced by 90 percent over the last century. Two bears are kept here in captivity.

Reserve Naturelle du Néouvielle★★★

Within the inimitable Pyrenees, there are some corners of the mountains that are particularly special. The uniqueness of the Massif de Néouvielle, a block of granite mountains carved into lakes and crests by glaciers millions of years ago, was first recognised in 1936, but it wasn't until 1968 that the area was given full legal protection as a national nature reserve. The name comes from the Occitan 'nèu vielha', meaning 'old snow'. The highest peak in the reserve is Pic de Néouvielle (3 091m).

◔ **Michelin Map:** 342: M5.
▯ **Info:** 37 rue Vincent Mir, 65170 St Lary Soulan. ☎05 62 39 50 81. www.saintlary.com.
◗ **Location:** Lac d'Ourdon visitor centre is 19km/11.5mi southwest of St-Lary-Soulan on D929.

VISIT
Public access to the reserve is controlled. A single road leads to a visitor's centre beside Lac d'Orédon. The GR10 long distance footpath along the Pyrenees traverses Néouvielle from west to east. There are other signposted footpaths, a mountain refuge and a bivouac area for overnight stays. Camping is forbidden.

Lac d'Aubert and Lac d'Aumar

© Jacques Sierpinski/hemis.fr

WILDLIFE

Néouvielle has 1 250 species of plant, around 20 of them rare. The dominant tree is the mountain pine. At the other extreme of size, two thirds of France's sphagnum mosses are found here.

The most interesting animals, both rare, are the desman, an aquatic mammal with webbed feet and the midwife toad which has the highest range of any European amphibian (up to 2 400m).

Lac d'Aubert

Altitude 2 149m. The access road into the reserve continues to this lake but from July to mid-September it is barred to traffic and a minibus (*navette*) service runs from the visitor's centre at Lac d'Oredon. A better way to get there is on the sentier des Laquettes footpath (allow 1.5hrs).

Lac d'Aumar ★

At the northern end of this peaceful lake, *at an altitude of 2 192m,* the summit of Pic de Néouvielle (alt 3 091m), bordered by a small glacier, comes into view.

Col (ou hourquette) d'Aubert ★★

3h on foot from the lac d'Aubert. Take the marked footpath ('sentier de la hourquette d'Aubert') which goes round the lake to the northeast. The pass (alt 2 498m) joins the basins of the two lakes, Aubert and Aumar, with the desolate valley of Escoubous on the slope above Barèges. There is an impressive **view★★** over the lakes and in the distant south east the glaciated Maladetta massif.

🚗 DRIVING TOURS

ST-LARY-SOULON TO THE LAKES

70 km/43mi from St-Lary-Soulan to lac d'Orédon. Allow around 3h.
see region map.

Check the weather before you set off, especially if you want to do any walking or explore further into the Néouvielle nature reserve. A good time to do this tour is in the early summer. The waterfalls and lakes are at their best when water is most abundant from snowmelt.

▷ Leave St-Lary SW along D 929. The valley narrows to a gorge. Up on the left is the village of Tramezaïgues. From Tramezaïgues take D 19, a road that is only partly surfaced. Beyond Fredançon, the last 4km/2mi of the road are so narrow that traffic is one-way only.

Vallée du Rioumajou★

This is a densely wooded valley with numerous waterfalls. Not far from the Spanish frontier the former Rioumajou hospice (alt 1 560m), now a mountain refuge, stands in a fine amphitheatre.

▷ Return to Tramezaïgues and turn left on D 929.

As the road follows the line of the Vallée de la Neste d'Aure, the silhouette of Pic de Campbieil comes gradually into view. The mountain, one of the highest points in the massif at 3 173m, is recognisable by its twin-peaked crest.

▷ Beyond Fabian turn left on D 118.

The road, climbing alongside the waters of the Neste de la Géla, passes through the scattered hamlets of **Aragnouet**. Below, on the right, the belfry-wall of the 12C **Chapelle des Templiers** (⊙*open mid-Jul–Aug every day except Mon and Tue 3–6pm;* ℘*05 62 39 62 63)* appears.

▷ Leave the route leading to the the 3km/2mi Bielsa tunnel into Aragón in Spain on the left.

Piau-Engaly

At an altitude of 1 850m, the highest ski resort in the French Pyrenees enjoys a superb **site★★** and is a stone's throw from the nature reserves of the Parc National des Pyrénées and the Parque Nacional de Ordesa y Monte Perdido in Spain.

▷ Return to Fabian and turn left on D 929 heading N.

The old road, carved out by the French electricity authority to allow access to the Cap-de-Long site (&*see below*), climbs up through the valley of the Neste de Couplan.

▷ Continue to Lake Cap-de-Long.

Barrage de Cap-de-Long★

The dam has created a volume of 67.5 million m^3/89.7 million cu yd of water and is an important component of the Pragnères hydro-electric power station. It lies at an altitude of 2,160m/7,087ft.

▷ Retrace your steps. The scenic Route des Lacs starts from the Orédon fork and the road stops at the Orédon Lake parking area.

Lac d'Orédon★

Alt 1 849m. The visitor's centre and chalet-hotel makes this spot a good basecamp for excursions further into Néouvielle nature reserve on foot. There are various marked routes to choose from, from the easy to the strenuous.
Leave the car in the car park (charge).

ADDRESSES

STAY

⊖ **Chalet Hôtel du Lac d'Orédon** – *Lac d'Orédon.* ℘*06 23 05 72 60. www. refuge-pyrenees-oredon.com. 80 beds.* Magnificently sited beside a lake in a nature reserve, this simple hotel has a restaurant, bar and panoramic terrace.

TRANSPORT

The **lake road from Lac d'Orégon to Lac d'Aubert** *is closed to traffic during the day in Jul and Aug between 9.30am and 6.30pm. A shuttle service (navette) operates instead. Departures every 30min 9.30am–6pm;* ℘*05 62 39 62 63).*

ACTIVITIES

Domaine skiable de Piau – *65170 Piau-Engaly.* ℘*05 62 39 61 69. www.piau-engaly.com.* Altitude 1 420m–2 600m. One of the most beautiful of Pyrenees ski resorts with 39 pistes (4 green, 17 blue, 11 red, 7 black).

Parcours suspendu du Moudang – *Pont du Moudang.* ℘*06 83 18 13 43. www. parcoursaventuremoudang.overblog.com. Jun–Aug 9.30am–12pm, 1.30–7pm (6.30pm in Jun).* A supervised, overhead obstacle course with rope ladders, monkey bridges, zip-lines and other challenges.

Until the Revolution reorganised France's internal divisions, what is now the department of Haute-Pyrenees was known as Bigorre, a medieval county created in the 9C. As the modern name spells out, mountains dominate this region which ends abruptly to the south in the highest part of the Pyrenees. There are 35 summits over 3 000m and 34 high passes (cols) – several made famous by the gruelling passage over them of the cyclists of the Tour de France. Haute-Pyrenees is home not only to 236 000 people but also 150 000 sheep – giving an indication of the traditional pastoral lifestyle that clings on in the highlands. The population density is low and a third of communes have less than one hundred inhabitants. The Pyrenees thus offer endless space and fresh air, with a range of signposted walks from short to long, easy to strenuous. There are many beautiful places to visit – the mountains have lakes and waterfalls in abundance – but outstanding among them are the Cirque de Gavarnie and the Pont d'Espagne both of which form part of the Pyrenees National Park.

Getting around the Mountains

All the main roads in the Pyrenees travel north to south and it's sometimes necessary to come back down a valley and go up an adjacent one to get to where you want to go. The western mountains of Bigorre are only accessible from the Vallee d'Aure through the Comminges (⟳ *see Saint-Gaudens and Around*). There is, however, a scenic mid-altitude link, the D 918 which crosses a series of spectacular passes (cols).

Foothills and Plains

Down below, in the foothills and on the plains, the scenery is inevitably less spectacular but moving about much easier. The unassuming capital, Tarbes, prides itself on its history of horse breeding but it is overshadowed by the shrine of Lourdes. Its 6 million annual visitors make it one of the most visited towns in France.

Pyrennean Spas

In a way, Lourdes follows an ancient Pyrenean tradition of spas serving healing waters to the needy. The golden age of spa therapy was the 19C but Bagnères-de-Bigorre, Cauterets, Luz-St-Sauveur and Barèges are still much sought out by patients seeking rest cures.

Cycle-mania

Surprisingly perhaps, this mountainous region has a strong association with cycling. The route of the Tour de France – which overshadows all other

Highlights

1 Explore the caves of the **Grottes de Médous** (p418)

2 Take a giddy cable car ride to the summit of the **Pic du Midi de Bigorre** (p420)

3 Join the massed pilgrims at the shrine of **Lourdes** (p420)

4 See the waterfalls above Cauterets at the **Pont d'Espagne** (p431)

5 Marvel at the **Cirque de Gavarnie** (p437)

sport in France during three weeks of July – invariably includes a stage over one or more of the famous passes (cols) of the Pyrenees. The climbs to the Portet d'Aspet, Peyresourde, Aspin, Tourmalet and Aubisque are prodigious tests of stamina and, because they slow the riders down, these stages are popular places to see the Tour go past – on the flat lowlands, the pack flashes in front of you before you have a chance to register what is happening. The rider who does best on the passes is called 'the king of the mountains' and gets to wears a red polkadot jersey.

From spring to autumn, weather permitting, ordinary cyclists can pit themselves against the Tour de France cols and get a 'cycle passport' stamped at the top of each pass as a souvenir.

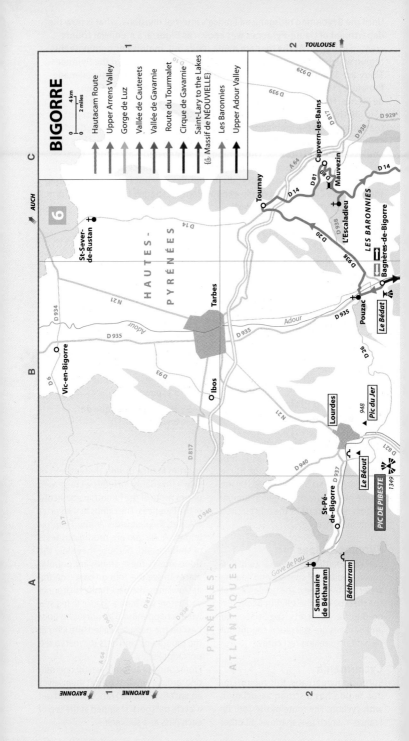

BIGORRE

0 ___ 4 km
0 ___ 2 miles

Hautacam Route
Upper Arrens Valley
Gorge de Luz
Vallée de Cauterets
Vallée de Gavarnie
Route du Tourmalet
Cirque de Gavarnie
Saint-Lary to the Lakes (& Massif de NÉOUVIELLE)
Les Baronnies
Upper Adour Valley

TOULOUSE

AUCH

BAYONNE

BAYONNE

St-Sever-de-Rustan

HAUTES-PYRÉNÉES

Tarbes

Vic-en-Bigorre

Ibos

Adour

Lourdes

Pic du Jer
948

Le Béout

PIC DE PIBESTE
1349

St-Pé-de-Bigorre

Sanctuaire de Bétharram

Bétharram

Gave de Pau

PYRÉNÉES-ATLANTIQUES

Tournay

Capvern-les-Bains

Mauvezin

L'Escaladieu

LES BARONNIES

Bagnères-de-Bigorre

Pouzac

Le Bédat

412

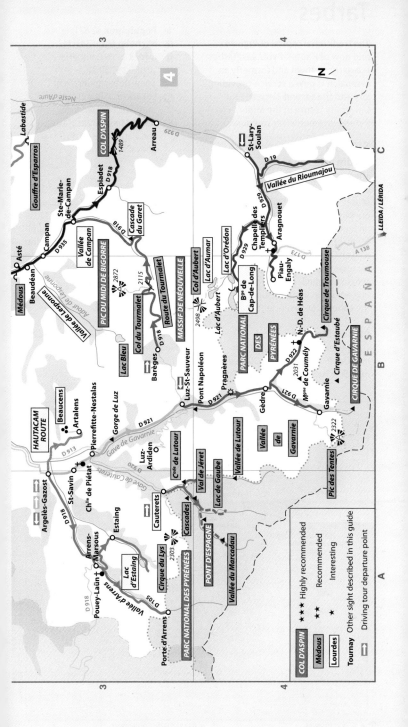

Tarbes

N

3

4

Labastide

Gouffre d'Esparros

Neste d'Aure

COL D'ASPIN

D 918

1489

Arreau

D 929

St-Lary-
Soulan

D 19

Vallée du Rioumajou

Ste-Marie-
de-Campan

Espiadet

Campan

Beaudéan

Médous

Asté

D 935

Vallée
de Campan

Cascade
du Garet

D 918

Aragnouet

D 173

A 138

Chapelle des
Templiers

D 929

Plau-
Engaly

Bge de
Cap-de-Long

Lac d'Orédon

Lac d'Aumar

Lac d'Aubert

Col d'Aubert

Aragnouet

LLEIDA / LÉRIDA

E S P A Ñ A

Adour de Lesponne

Vallée de Lesponne

PIC DU MIDI DE BIGORRE

2872

2115

Route du Tourmalet

MASSIF DE NÉOUVIELLE

Lac d'Aubert

2498

Col du Tourmalet

D 918

Lac Bleu

Barèges

Luz-St-Sauveur

Pont Napoléon

Pragnères

PARC NATIONAL

DES

PYRÉNÉES

N.-D. de Héas

Cirque de Troumouse

Cirque d'Estaubé

Cirque de Gavarnie

CIRQUE DE GAVARNIE

Beaucens

Artalens

HAUTACAM
ROUTE

Pierrefitte-Nestalas

Gorge de Luz

D 921

Gave de Gavarnie

D 913

Luz-
Ardiden

Cⁿᵉ de Lutour

Vallée de Lutour

Vallée
de
Gavarnie

Gèdre

D 921

Mⁿᵉ de Coumély

2031

D 922

Gavarnie

2322

Pic des Tentes

Argelès-Gazost

St-Savin

Chⁿᵉ de Piétat

D 918

Arrens-
Marsous

Estaing

Cauterets

Gave de Cauterets

D 920

Cascades

Val de Jéret

Lac de Gaube

PONT D'ESPAGNE

Vallée du Marcadau

Lac
d'Estaing

Cirque du Lys

2303

PARC NATIONAL DES PYRÉNÉES

Pouey-Laün

D 105

Vallée d'Arrens

Porte d'Arrens

COL D'ASPIN ★★★ Highly recommended

Médous ★★ Recommended

Lourdes ★ Interesting

Tournay Other sight described in this guide

Driving tour departure point

4

3

4

413

Tarbes

The traditional capital of Bigorre and now of Hautes-Pyrénées, Tarbes is a garrison town and formerly an arsenal. it is now a service-providing city and the second-largest university centre in the Midi-Pyrénées region after Toulouse.

SIGHTS

Jardin Massey★

These shaded public gardens, laid out between the fine arts school and the Musée Massey (at their northern end) are within easy reach of the town centre on foot. The only other buildings within them, apart from the museum, are an elegant Orangerie containing a display of cactuses and a refreshment kiosk. Adjacent to the pond stands a reconstructed Romanesque cloister brought here from the abbey of St-Sever-de-Rustan.

Musée Massey

🕒 Open daily except Tue: mid-Apr–mid-Oct 10am–12.30pm, 1.30–7pm; mid-Oct–mid-Apr 10am–noon, 2–5pm.

▶ **Population:** 42 871.
🖉 **Michelin Map:** 343: M3.
🚩 **Info:** 3 cours Gambetta.
   𝒫 05 62 51 30 31.
   www.tarbes-tourisme.fr.
◐ **Location:** 150km/90mi southwest of Toulouse.
☜ **Don't Miss:** Jardin Massey and Haras, Maison du Cheval.

🕒 Closed 1 Jan, 1 May and 25 Dec. ⊛€5 (under 18s no charge). 𝒫 05 62 51 30 31. The city's main museum contains uniforms, equipment and arms tracing the history of the French Hussars cavalry regiment and various local art and archaeological treasures.

Maison natale du Maréchal Foch

2 rue Victoire. 🕒 Open daily except Tue 9.30am–12.15pm, 2–5.15pm. 🕒 Closed 1 Jan, 25 Dec. ⊛No charge. 𝒫 05 62 93 19 02.

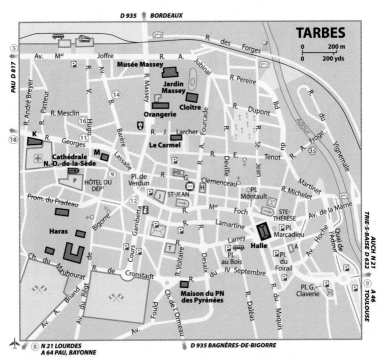

Ferdinand Foch (1851–1929), marshall of France and national hero, was born in this house, now a museum. In April 1918 he was appointed supreme commander of the Allied armies of the Western Front and he was largely responsible for the final counter-offensive which led to the cessation of hostilities and forced the Germans to accept an armistice. He also played a key role in the subsequent peace conference which imposed harsh terms on the vanquished. Pictures, furniture owned by Foch and other objects associated with his life.

Cathédrale N.-D.-de-la-Sède
Pl. Charles-de-Gaulle.
Although Tarbes cathedral is at heart Romanesque, there is little sign of it except in the structure of the apse where stone and brick are used together.

♟♟ Haras, Maison du cheval★
70 av. du Régiment-de-Bigorre. ◷*Open mid Jun–mid Sep Mon–Fri 9am–5.30pm.* ☞*Guided visits Jul–Aug 9am–noon; the rest of the year by appointment.* ♿ ℰ*05 55 73 83 83.*
www.haras-nationaux.fr.
Tarbes like to describe itself as 'the city of the horse', largely because the presence of this national stud farm. It was established in 1806 under the empire of Napoleon I to provide crossbred Anglo-Arabian mounts to the Hussars and other cavalry regiments to make good their losses in the costly Iberian campaign. Nowadays, the stud also raises and keeps cart horses, race horses and horses for amateur recreation.
The various buildings of the stud farm stand in a pleasant park close to the city centre. Visitors are shown the stables, the saddle room, the smithy, the breeding unit and the Maison du Cheval, a shrine-museum to man's association with the horse. Various shows and competitions are staged at the Haras during the course of the year.

Musée de Résistance et de la Déportation
63 rue Georges-Lassalle. ◷*Open Mon–Fri 9am–noon, 2–5pm by appointment.*
◷*Closed public holidays.* ⊜*No charge.* ℰ*05 62 51 11 60.*
www.cheminsdememoire.gouv.fr.
Although only small, this museum tells an important human story, that of the local deportees and resistance fighters who lived or died between 1939–45.

Maison du Parc national des Pyrénées
2 rue du IV-septembre. ◷*Open Mon–Fri 9am–noon, 2–5pm.* ◷*Closed public holidays.* ⊜*No charge.* ℰ*05 62 54 16 40. www.parc-pyrenees.com.*
This Pyrenees national park maintains a network of visitors' centres in the mountains themselves but the head office is a handy place for planning. It provides maps and brochures on the geogrpahy, and the staff can answer questions about where to go and what to see. It also has displays on flora and fauna..

EXCURSIONS
Ibos
7 km/4.5mi. Leave Tarbes on D 817 towards Pau.
With its square tower and massive polygonal apse, the église Saint-Laurent, built in the 14C and 15C, has the distinct air of a castle about it.

Vic-en-Bigorre
17km/10.5mi N on D 935 towards Bordeaux.
This small town on the Echez river has a 19C market hall which comes alive with stalls on Saturday mornings.

Abbaye de Saint-Sever-de-Rustan
22km/14mi. Leave Tarbes on N 21 towards Rabastens. At Escondeaux take D 27 on the right. ☞*Guided visits Jun–Sept daily 2–6pm.* ♿ ⊜€*3.50.* ℰ*05 62 96 65 67.*
www.rabastens-tourisme.com.
This Romanesque-Gothic Benedictine abbey dates from 11C. Although it has lost its cloister to the Jardin Massey in Tarbes it still has some good stone carving and 18C walnut furnishings in the sacristy.

Bagnères-de-Bigorre

This picturesque spa lies in attractive pastureland, north of the vallée de Campan, on the west bank of the River Adour. The waters of the cure centre, which are rich in calcium and sulphur salts, are drawn from 13 bores. These are used in the treatment of respiratory, rheumatic and psychosomatic disorders. Bagnères-de-Bigorre is also a nucleus around which much Pyrenees folklore is centred, and was the home of a well-known 19C literary society, specialising in works inspired by the mountains. A choral society, known as the Chanteurs Montagnards, which travelled to London, Rome, Jerusalem and Moscow in the mid-1800s, still survives.

- **Population:** 8 163.
- **Info:** Office de tourisme Grand Tourmalet Pic du Midi, 3 allée Tournefort, 65200 Bagnères. ℘05 62 95 50 71. www.grand-tourmalet.com.
- **Location:** 22km/14mi S of Tarbes.

SIGHTS
The Spa
Bagnère's spa facilities consist of the **Grands Thermes** and the **Thermes de la Reine** (℮see Addresses). Functioning since Roman times, the waters are rich in magnesium, calcium and sulphates.

They are prescribed for rheumatic complaints, psychosommatic illnesses and breathing difficulties.

Parc thermal de Salut★
45min round trip on foot.
A gateway at the end of avenue Noguès (south of the town plan) marks the entrance to this 100ha park, offering pleasant walks under fine, shady trees. The central avenue crosses the park and skirts the garden leading to the former Établissement thermal de Salut – the old spa centre.

Old Town
Among the attractions of this area (bordered to the east by the busiest part of the town, allées des Coustous)

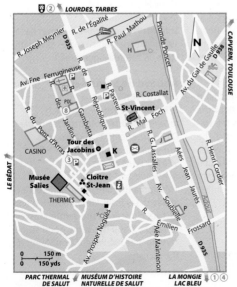

BAGNÈRES-DE-BIGORRE

WHERE TO STAY

Catala (Hôtel) .... ①
Maison Burret (Chambre d'hôte) .... ②
Hostellerie d'Asté .... ④
Petites Vosges (Chambre d'hôte Les) .... ⑧

WHERE TO EAT

Auberge Gourmande (L').........③

Maison à colombages .... K

Pic du Midi de Bigorre from near Bagnères-de-Bigorre

© Jean-Paul Azam/hemis.fr

are **St Vincent's**, a 16C church with a belfry-wall pierced by three rows of arcades, **Tour des Jacobins**, a tower which is all that remains of a 15C monastery destroyed during the Revolution, and the **cloister ruins** on the corner of rue St-Jean and rue des Thermes. The charming **half-timbered house** at the junction of rue du Vieux-Moulin and rue Victor-Hugo dates from the 15C.

Musée des Beaux-arts Salies

🕐*Open May–Jun and Sept–Oct Wed–Fri 10am–noon, 2–6pm, Sat–Sun 3–6pm; Jul–Aug Tue–Fri 10am–noon, 2–6pm, Sat–Sun 3–6pm.* ☜€4. 📞*06 33 79 60 45.*
This museum displays ceramics and paintings by Joos van Cleve, Chasseriau, Jongkind, Picabia and others.

Musée du Marbre

🕐*Open Jul–Aug Wed–Sun 2.30–6pm; Jun and Sept Tue–Sat 2.30–6pm; school holidays Tue–Sat 2.30–5.30pm; rest of year outside school holidays Wed, Fri–Sat 2.30–5.30pm.* ☜€4. 📞*05 62 91 12 05.*
Displays of beautiful marble in colours you'd never dream of, from France, Europe and the Middle East.

🚶 WALKS
Le Bédat★
👣*1h30 round trip on foot.*
At the junction of three by-roads, a path to the left leads to the Fontaine des Fées (Fairy Fountain) and a statue of the Bédat Virgin. Behind the statue, another path follows the crest to the lookout point (alt 881m), encompassing the Baronnies and Lannemezan plateau (*east*) and across the Vallée de Campan to the summits of the Central Pyrenees (*south*).

Lac Bleu★★
Alt 1 944m.
Leave Bagnères S along D 935 and, beyond Baudéan, 1km/0.6mi before Campan, turn right onto D 29.
🚶 *Walk through the Lesponne valley, starting from Bagnères-de-Bigorre. Allow 4h there and back.*
The road runs along the charming **Vallée de Lesponne★**, which offers views of Pic du Midi de Bigorre and Pic de Montaigu, especially attractive in spring and autumn when they are snow-capped. The Chiroulet inns, near the top of the valley, are the starting point of the walk to **Lac Bleu**, a lake-reservoir in a splendidly isolated spot.

🚗 DRIVING TOURS

Les Baronnies★
53 km/33mi. Allow at least half a day.

The Baronnies, its name recalling the feudal divisions of the ancien regime, is a particularly scenic extent of Pyrenean foothills and small valleys between Bagnères-de-Bigorre and Lannemezan.

▷ Leave Bagnères-de-Bigorre going north on D 935 towards Tarbes.

Pouzac
The 16C church contains an impressive 17C sculpted altarpiece by Élie Corau from Bagnères and Jean Ferrère from Asté. Jean Catau painted the late 17C wooden vaulting.

▷ Continue west on D 26.

Tournay
This bastide founded in 1307 has an arboretum of 200 tree species outside it.

▷ Take D 817. In Ozon turn right on D 14. At Gourgue turn left on D 81 towards Capvern-les-Bains.

Capvern-les-Bains
There are good views to be had from the Laca residential quarter of this small spa town.

▷ Leave Capvern-les-Bains going south on D 80. At Mauvezin, follow signs to the chateau.

Chateau de Mauvezin
The counts of Bigorre built this walled keep on a naturally defensive promontory in the 11C. It was rebuilt in the 14C by Gaston Fébus.

▷ Continue on D 938.

Abbaye de l'Escaladieu
The pioneering 12C Cistercian monks of Bigorre built their first house on the remoter higher slopes, but decided to move down to the more hospitable Arros valley to found this abbey. it was largely destroyed during the wars of religion but some parts survive, especially the church and chapter house. It is now subject to a long-term programme of restoration but is often used as a venue for cultural events.

▷ Take D 14.

Gouffre d'Esparros★★
◷☜ *Jun–Sept 10am–noon, 1.30–5.30pm (Jul–Aug: booking advised); school holidays 10am–noon, 1.30–5pm; Feb–Apr and Oct outside school holidays Sat–Sun and public holidays 10am–noon, 1.30–5pm, Wed 1.30–5pm; May Sat–Sun and public holidays 10am–noon, 1.30–5.30pm, Mon–Fri 1.30–5.30pm; Jan Sat–Sun 2–5pm.* ◷*Closed Nov–mid-Dec; Mon and Tue from Oct–Mar, 1 Jan, 25 Dec.* ⊗€8 (child 4–12, €5.50; 13–17, €6.50. ✆05 62 39 11 80. www.gouffre-esparros.fr. *Access is limited and bookings are recommended.* Admire exceptionally fine aragonite formations like snow crystals and the **Salle du Lac gallery**.

▷ Return to Bagneres-de-Bigorre on D 77, D 14 and D 938.

Upper Adour valley
38km/24mi, from Bagnères-de-Bigorre to Arreau. Allow around 1h.

▷ Leave Bagnères-de-Bigorre going south on D 935, along the Adour.

Grotte de Médous★★
☜*Guided tours only (1hr) Jul–Aug 9.30am–noon, 1.30–5.30pm; Apr–Jun and Sept–mid-Oct 10–noon, 2–5pm.* ◷*Closed mid-Oct–Mar.* ⊗€9 (child5–10, €4.50). ✆05 62 91 78 46. www.grottes-medous.com.
In 1948, three speleologists from Bagnères-de-Bigorre, exploring a gallery which did not penetrate very far into the rock, discovered a blow-hole which suggested the existence of a substantial cavern close by. The site, not far from Bagnères, was near a resurgent spring watering the pools in the grounds of Médous Château. The cavers gouged a larger hole in the rock wall, squeezed through an opening not much bigger than a cat flap and found themselves in a series of galleries full of marvellous rock formations.

The 1km/0.6mi route twists through an enchanted land of stalactites, stalagmites and broad petrified flows of calcite (carbonate of lime) which have hardened over the ages into fantastic forms evoking waterfalls, hanging draperies, a magnificent church organ etc; the chambers have subsequently been given suitably fanciful names. After the Gallery of Marvels, the Hindu Temple, the Cervin Halls and the Great Organ Chamber, the visit includes a boat trip along a short subterranean stretch of the River Adour: the caverns have been hollowed out over the millennia by waters siphoned off from the main river through a tunnel near Campan, only emerging into the open-air again in the grounds of Médous Château.

▷ Resume D 935. Cross the Adour towards Asté (D 408)

Asté
A small museum here celebrates a 17C/18C family of sculptors.

▷ Continue south on D 935.

Beaudéan
The birthplace of Dominique Larrey (1766–1842), pioneering military surgeon created baron by Napoleon I, is now a museum. Larrey is credited with many life-saving innovations in battlefield medicine including the use of 'flying ambulances' to rapidly gather up the wounded and take them to field hospitals.

▷ Continue on D 935.

Campan
This small town has a 16C covered market, 18C fountain and 16C church.

▷ In Ste-Marie-de-Campan, turn left on D 918 towards Col d'Aspin.

Espiadet
The marble quarry here supplied its distinctive red- and white-veined green stone for use in the columns of the Grand Trianon in Versailles and Garnier's Parisian Opera House.

Col d'Aspin★★★
This mountain pass (1 489m) offers a panorama of peaks and distant forests. Beyond the pass the narrow road drops steeply in hairpin bends with thrilling views of the Arbizon massif to reach **Arreau** (&see ARREAU).

ADDRESSES

🛏STAY

🏠 **Maison Burret** – *67 Cap-de-la-Vielle, 65200 Montgaillard.* ℘*05 62 91 54 29. www.maisonburret.com. Closed Nov–Jan.* 🅿 🍴. *3 rooms. Restaurant* 😊😊.
A beautiful Bigourdane farmhouse built in 1791 (listed for its value to rural heritage). It has preserved much of its character: sculpted staircase, grand fireplace in the dining room, antique furniture and, outside, a pigeonniers and stables. There is a small museum of country life. A warm welcome and good value.

😊😊 **Les Petites Vosges** – *17 bd Carnot, 65200 Bagnères-de-Bigorre.* ℘*05 62 91 55 30. www.lespetites vosges.com. Closed Nov.* 🍴. *4 rooms.* The mixture of the old and the contemporary give this house an agreeable sense of originality and vitality. Cosy rooms and elegant sitting room. The owner can advise on walks to take in the area.

😊😊 **Hôtel Catala** – *12 rue Larrey, 65710 Beaudéan.* ℘*05 62 91 75 20. www. le-catala-hotel-pyrenees.com. Closed some public holidays and Christmas.* 🅿. *24 rooms. Restaurant* 😊😊. The unasssuming facade belies an original interior: the décor of the bedroom matches the paintings on the doors (of sport, history and so on).

🍴 EAT

😊😊😊 **L'Auberge Gourmande** – *1 bd Lyperon.* ℘*05 62 95 52 01. Closed 15–30 Nov, Tue except Jul–Aug and Mon.* This pretty countryside house harbours an elegant dining room where you will find delicious food of southwest France, masterly prepared and without pretention.

Pic du Midi de Bigorre★★★

Looking due south from lowland Bigorre, there is one peak that stands proud of the rest. Topped by an observatory and a television relay mast the Pic du Midi is an unmistakeable landmark. It looks like a mountain should and, because of its forward position, it appears to be one of the tallest summits. It's not, but it is still a respectable 2 877m. For the visitor, the important thing is that it is easily accessible, making it the best viewpoint in the central Pyrenees.

A two-stage cable car rises up to it from the ski resort of La Mongie. On a clear day there is an unbeatable double panorama of the even higher mountains to the south and the plains of the Adour valley to the north. As well as viewing terraces, there is a museum and restaurant to visit.

- **Michelin Map:** 342: M5.
- **Info:** ☎08 25 00 28 77. www.picdumidi.com.
- **Location:** Above the ski resort of La Mongie.
- **Timing:** Sometimes closed Mon or Tue, call ahead.

Intrepid or foolhardy outdoor activity lovers make full use of the mountain. In winter they can ski down from the summit and in summer they make the desecent by mountain bike – in both cases only after signing a waiver accepting full responsibility for their actions. A more tranquil way to enjoy the Pic du Midi is to spend an evening of star-watching on the top or even spend the night in order to enjoy the sunrise and appreciate the words of the 19C Franco-Irish eccentric explorer of the Pyrenees, Henry Russell who declared 'there are mornings up there which must make the saints long to be on earth'.

Lourdes★

The town of Lourdes, on the banks of the Pau torrent, is famous the world over as a religious pilgrimage centre. Great ceremonies take place from Easter to All Saints' Day, with processions of believers and invalids, buoyed by faith and hope, lending the town a surreal, slightly morbid atmosphere.

PILGRIMAGE

A few figures – Pilgrimages are mainly held at Easter and during Holy Week, attracting over 6 million visitors a year, three-quarters of whom are French and 80 000 sick or disabled. Considered to be the most important place of pilgrimage in the western hemisphere, among French towns, Lourdes is second only to Paris in providing tourist accommodation (350 hotels, 40 000 beds). The town has hundreds of shops, most of them

- **Population:** 14 973.
- **Michelin Map:** 342: L-4.
- **Info:** Place Peyremale, 65100 Lourdes. ☎05 62 42 77 40. www.lourdes-infotourisme.com.
- **Location:** 21km/13mi SW of Tarbes.
- **Don't Miss:** The Lourdes wax museum.
- **Kids:** Musée du Petit Lourdes and aquarium.

selling religious items. Some 700 special trains and 400 planes service Lourdes every year (via the Tarbes-Lourdes Pyrenees International Airport). The TGV Atlantique (high-speed train) has been coming here since 1993. A ring road links D 940 and D 937 (Pau-Lourdes) and N 21 (Tarbes–Argelès-Gazost), diverting traffic from the town centre.

Bernadette Soubirous (1844–79) – The Soubirous family was poor and the parents, millers, brought up their four children with difficulty. Bernadette, the eldest, was born in Lourdes but spent her first few months with a wet-nurse at Bartrès, not far from Lourdes. In early 1858, when she was 14, she was living with her parents in their single room and attending a school for poor children run by the Sisters of Charity. At weekends, preparing for her First Communion, she went to parish Catechism classes.

On Thursday 11 February, a school holiday, Bernadette was gathering wood on the river bank near a local landmark known as Massabielle Rock, accompanied by one of her sisters and a neighbour. It was then, in a grotto hollowed out from the rock, that she saw for the first time the vision of the Immaculate Conception; the beautiful Lady was to appear to her 18 times in total.

Massabielle Grotto – Although Massabielle Rock was not easily accessible at the time, a crowd of believers and unbelievers alike began to form around its cave, and increased daily as news of Bernadette's vision spread. During the ninth apparition Bernadette began to scrabble with her fingers in the earth floor of the cave and suddenly a spring, never before suspected, gushed forth and continued to flow in front of the startled spectators. In 1862 the Church decided that a sanctuary should be built around the grotto. The first procession was organised in 1864 during which a statue dedicated to Our Lady of Lourdes, and lodged within the cave where the apparitions occurred, was officially blessed. In 1866, Bernadette entered the St-Gildard convent belonging to the Sisters of Charity Order. She died in April 1879, was beatified in 1925 and canonised in 1933.

World's largest pilgrimage – The earliest visits, at first at parish and then diocesan level, were expanded in 1873 into a national event organised by the Fathers of the Assumption in Paris. A year later, a second event included arrangements for 14 invalids to be treated at Lourdes. From then on, attention to the sick and the lame became a priority.

Since the celebration of Bernadette's centenary in 1958 and the Vatican II Council, planning of organised pilgrimages has taken a new turn. All the great traditional events, such as the Holy Sacrament Procession and the Torchlight Procession, have been retained but there have been new initiatives concerning meetings, the reception of pilgrims etc. The grotto has been relieved of certain 'accessories' and the Basilique du Rosaire, renowned for its organ and acoustics, now welcomes secular concerts and musical events.

GETTING AROUND

Parking and walking – Because of the crowds and tour buses blocking the streets the best way to get around, particularly around the sanctuaries, is on foot. There is usually space to park along the Avenue du Paradis (beside ther river, near Pont Vieux). Alternatively, there are car parks in the middle of town including in the square where the tourist office is located (*Place Peyremale*).

Tourist train – A small train runs from mid-Apr–Oct; departures from place Mgr-Laurence every 20min between 9–11.30am and 1.30–6pm; the journey takes 45min with the possibility of hopping on and off at your leisure; there is a night train mid-May–mid-Sept 8.30–11pm. Accessible to persons of impaired mobility.

Discounts – The tourist office sells packs for individuals and families to visit the main sites in Lourdes and the Hautes-Pyrenees including the Pic du Midi, the Château de Pau and the Cirque de Gavarnie. Information at the tourist office.

THE VICINITY OF THE GROTTO

The best way to approach the sanctuaries is through the Porte St-Michel, up the broad avenue of Esplanade du Rosaire (used for processions) towards the massive basilica.

Basilique Souterraine de St-Pie X

Buried beneath the avenue (south side) is the colossal **Basilique Souterraine de St-Pie X**, an underground basilica consecrated on 25 March 1958 to solemnise the official centenary of the apparitions. The huge oval hall can hold up to 20 000 pilgrims – more than the normal population of Lourdes. It is one of the largest churches in the world, measuring 201m × 81m at its widest point and covering an area of 12 000 sq m. Pre-stressed concrete supports the low vaulting, with no need for intermediate columns.

Place du Rosaire

A large statue of the crowned Virgin Mary stands in this large square in front of the church. Near it is an information office for pilgrims.

Grotte de Massabielle

Follow the crowds and wheelchairs and you will come to the sacred grotto beneath the mound on which stands

Grotte de Massabielle

S. Sauvignier/MICHELIN

the basilica. There are usually long queues to enter the cave and religious services are sometimes held here. The cave is surprisingly small. A statue of the Virgin carved in Carrare marble by Fabisch in 1864 marks the exact spot of the apparitions.

The spring from which the water flows is visible at the back of the grotto. Pipes feed the water to taps and baths for the benefit of pilgrims. Near the bathhouse, candles are lit in prayer.

The basilica

The great church raised above the grotto is approached by two curving ramps from the Place du Rosaire.

The neo-Byzantine **Basilique du Rosaire**, consecrated and blessed in 1889, occupies the lower level, between the ramps.

On the next level up is the crypt, dug into the rock, the first sanctuary built at Lourdes and reserved in the daytime for silent prayer. Bernadette was present when the **crypt** was consecrated on 19 May 1866.

The neo-Gothic **Basilique de L'Immaculée Conception** (Basilica of the Immaculate Conception), also called the **basilique supérieur**, was inaugurated in 1871 and can accommodate a congregation of 2 000. Mosaics in the side chapels represent the Mysteries of the Rosary.

Espace Ste-Bernadette

Across the river beside the sanctuary is this modern religious complex including a church consecrated in 1988.

Chemin du Calvaire

The Road to Calvary starts beside the grotto and winds up through the trees past 14 Stations of the Cross in bronze statuary. It ends at the Cross of Calvary. Nearby are the grottoes of St Madeleine and Our Lady of Sorrows (Notre-Dame-des-Douleurs), in the natural cavern on the flank of Mont des Espélugues.

Musées des Sanctuaires

The **Musée Sainte Bernadette** (*Bvd. Rémi Sempé;* 🚹 🕐 *open Apr–Oct 9am–*

Basilique du Rosaire

© bbsferrari/iStockphoto.com

noon, 2–7pm. ☜No charge; ☎05 62 42 78 78) contains mementoes of the young saint, together with pictorial material on the site of the 18 alleged apparitions and on the history of the pilgrimages.

Musée des Miraculés – *Accueil Jean-Paul-II, esplanade du Rosaire*. A display presents the 66 'official' miracles attributed to Lourdes.

COMMEMORATIVE SITES
Moulin de Boly:
Maison Natale de Bernadette
12 rue Bernadette-Soubirous.
🕑*Open 9/10am–noon, 2/3–5pm/7pm.*
☜*No charge.* ☎*05 62 42 16 36.*
The old mill where Bernadette was born on 7 January 1844 contains an exhibit on the Soubirous family.

Cachot
15 rue des Petits-Fossés.
&🕑*Open Apr–Oct 9am–noon, 2–7pm; rest of year 10am–noon, 3–5pm.*
☎*05 62 94 51 30.*
At the time of the apparitions, the Soubirous family were living in a state of penury in an unused prison.

Église du Sacré-Cœur
This parish church was built in 1867 and Marie-Bernard (Bernadette) Soubirous was baptised at this font.

Hospice Sainte-Bernadette
2 ave. Alexandre Marqui. Beneath the colonnade, follow the signs marked Visite Chapelle.
Bernadette attended classes at this hospital run by the Sisters of Charity before being admitted as a boarder from 1860–1866. See personal souvenirs of the saint, and her communicant's cape, Catechism, Holy Bible and prayer stool.

Bartrès
3km/1.8mi N.
As a baby Bernadette was entrusted to the wet-nurse Marie Aravant-Lagües in this village. **Maison Lagües** displays mementoes of Bernadette's return visits. &🕑*Open early Apr–mid-Oct: daily except Sun 8.30am–noon, 2–6pm.*
☜*No charge.* ☎*05 62 42 02 03.*

SIGHTS
Château Fort★
25 rue du Fort. Access via the Saracens' Staircase (131 steps) or the castle ramp from rue du Bourg, past the small Basque cemetery. 🕑*Open daily: mid-Oct–mid-Apr daily 10am–6pm (5pm on Mon); mid-Apr–mid-Oct 10am–7pm.*
🕑*Closed 1 Jan, 1 and 11 Nov, 25 Dec.*
☜€7 *(child 6–11,* €3*).* ☎*05 62 42 37 37. www.lourdes-visite.fr.*
The fortress guarding the gateway to the Central Pyrenees, a fine example of medieval military architecture, became

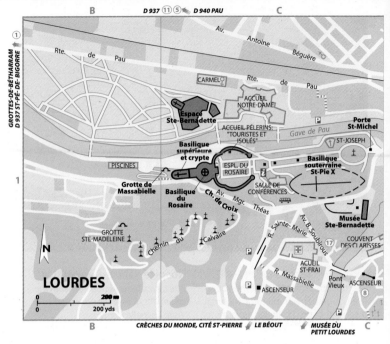

the state prison in the 17C and 18C. The Pointe du Cavalier (Rider's Bluff) panorama covers the valley of the Pau torrent and Pyrenean chain.

The **Pyrenean Folk Museum**★ exhibits local costumes, musical instruments, fine ceramics, a Béarnaise kitchen, *surjougs* (harness bells on wooden frames) and displays on paleontology and prehistory.

Musée de Cire de Lourdes★

87 rue de la Grotte. &. ⊙*Open Apr–mid-Oct 9.30–11.45am, 1.45–6pm (Sun and Wed open at 10am).* ⊙*Closed Nov–Mar.* ⊛*7.50€ (child 6–12, €4).* ℘*05 62 94 33 74.* www.musee-de-cire-lourdes.com. This museum traces the life of Bernadette Soubirous. Its terrace overlooks the château, Pau torrent and sanctuaries.

👥 Musée du Petit Lourdes

68 ave du Peyremale &. ⊙*Open Apr–mid-Oct 9am–noon, 1.30–6.45pm.* ⊛*€6.50 (children €3.50).* ℘*05 62 94 24 36.* This is an open-air reconstruction of Lourdes in the year 1858.

Musée du Gemmail

72 rue de la Grotte. ⊙*Open Easter–Oct 9am–noon, 2–7pm (Sun 2–7pm).* ⊛*No charge.* ℘*05 62 94 13 15.* www.gemmail.com. This museum contains works of art made by 'gemail' a technique involving coloured glass.

Musée de Lourdes

11 rue d'Egalité. &. ⊙*Open Apr–Oct 9am–noon, 1.30–6.30pm; rest of the year Mon–Fri 10am–noon, 2–5pm.* ⊛*€6.50 (children €3.50).* ℘*05 62 94 28 00.* Reconstruction of the town centre around 1858 with artisans' workshops (shoemaker, cabinetmaker and basketmaker) and a pastoral shepherd's hut.

EXCURSIONS
Pic du Jer★

SE of Lourdes.

A **funicular railway** offers a **panorama** of the Central Pyrenees rising to 948m. ⊙*Open Apr–Oct daily 9.30am–6pm (7pm in Jul–Aug).* ⊛*€10.80 return ticket (child 6–11, €8).* ℘*05 62 94 00 41.* www.picdujer.fr.

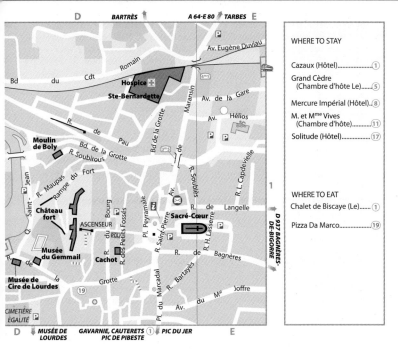

WHERE TO STAY

Cazaux (Hôtel).........................①

Grand Cèdre
  (Chambre d'hôte Le)........⑤

Mercure Impérial (Hôtel)..⑧

M. et Mme Vives
  (Chambre d'hôte)............⑪

Solitude (Hôtel).................⑰

WHERE TO EAT

Chalet de Biscaye (Le)........①

Pizza Da Marco....................⑲

Le Béout★

Alt 791m. S of Lourdes.

🚶 *Take the footpath from the Cité-Secours-St-Pierre rescue centre.*

The **view** of Lourdes, Pic du Jer, Pic de Montaigu, the Argelès valley and Bat-Surguère and Castelloubon valleys is splendid. Continue along the ridge to the far end to admire the Pic du Midi de Bigorre, Lac de Lourdes, Pic Long in the Néouvielle massif, the Marboré Cylinder and Monte Perdido.

St-Pé-de-Bigorre

Leave Lourdes by D 937. Before reaching St-Pé, cross the river then follow the road through Lourdes Forest and rejoin D 937 before St-Pé-de-Bigorre.

This small town's Romanesque abbey on the route to Santiago de Compostela, was the largest and finest religious monument in the Pyrenees until the Wars of Religion and 1661 earthquake.

Grottes et Sanctuaire de Bétharram★

16 km west by D 937.

🕐 *Open 25 Mar–Oct daily 9am–noon, 1.30–5.30pm (Jul–Aug daily 9am–6pm);*
mid-Feb–24 Mar Mon–Thu 2.30–4pm, Fri 2.30pm. ⊜*€14 (child 4–12, €9).* 📞*05 62 41 80 04. www.betharram.com.*

Discovered in 1819, the **grottes** de Bétharram consist of 5 200m of galleries of stalagmites, stalactites and other rock formations on five levels. The tour through the caverns is undertaken on foot, in boat and by a small train.

Bétharram has also been a Marian shrine since the 15C, long before the apparitions at Lourdes. The **sanctuaire** de Bétharram includes a 17C Baroque chapel and the Stations of the Cross depicted in painted bas-reliefs by Alexandre Renoir (1845).

ADDRESSES

🛏️ STAY

⊝ **Hôtel Cazaux** – *2 chemin Rochers.* 📞*05 62 94 22 65. http://fr.federal-hotel. com. Closed Easter–mid Oct. 20 rooms.* This small hotel near the market offers scrupulously kept rooms and a friendly welcome.

⊜⊜ **Chambre d'hôtes A Nousta** – *28 rte de Bartrès, 65100 Loubajac , 6km/4mi*

NW of Lourdes on D 940 towards Pau. &05 62 94 44 17. 🖪. www.anousta.com. Closed 11 Nov–Feb holiday. 5 rooms. Restaurant ⊜🍽. A farm with a stunning backdrop of the Pyrenees. Four rooms with beams and sloping ceilings, and two others with a terrace.

⊜🍽 **Le Grand Cèdre** – 6 r. du Barry, 65270 St-Pé-de-Bigorre. 🗺 🖪. &05 62 41 82 04. www.legrandcedre.fr. 5 rooms. Restaurant⊜🍽. This lovely 17C manor has 4 rooms decorated in art deco, Louis XV, Henri II, Louis-Philippe. Dining room, music room and superb park.

⊜🍽 **Hôtel Mercure Impérial** – 3 av. du Paradis. &05 62 94 06 30. www.mercure. com. Closed 15 Dec–31 Jan. 93 rooms. This 1935 hotel renovated in its original art deco style, is near the cave. Rooms are furnished in soothing mahogany tones. The dining and drawing rooms open onto a garden.

⊜🍽 **Hôtel Solitude** – 3 passage St-Louis. &05 62 42 84 28. www.hotel solitude.com. Closed 12 Apr–4 Nov. 293 rooms. Restaurant ⊜🍽. This imposing modern hotel on the banks of the Gave de Pau has a small rooftop swimming pool. The rotunda dining room has a terrace overlooking the river.

⫝̸ EAT

⊜ **Pizza da Marco** – 47 r. de la Grotte. &05 62 94 03 59. Closed Sun and Mon. A pleasant place for crispy pizza and efficient service.

⊜🍽 **Le Chalet de Biscaye** – 26 rte du Lac. &05 62 94 12 26. www.chalet- de-biscaye.fr. Closed 5–21 Jan, Mon eve, and Tue. A family restaurant with a tasty traditional cuisine. Shady terrace and warm dining room.

Argelès-Gazost

Standing near the confluence of two rivers, the Gave d'Azun and the Gave de Pau, in a valley with a mild climate, Argelès-Gazost became a residential spa town and resort in the 19C. A peaceful and agreeable place to stay, it commands a busy crossroads between a north–south and east–west route, serving a stream of trippers and skiers headed for the higher slopes.

UPPER TOWN

The town stands on the west side of the valley. It centres around a large public park, the Parc Thermal, in which stands a casino.

The oldest buiding in **Argelès-Gazost** is the Tour de Vieuzac, a 14C vestige of the former castle but much restored. There is also a rose garden and a small theatre housed in an old railway shed. Beneath the town runs the Voie Verte des Gaves, an 18km/11mi track between Lourdes and Pierrefitte-Nestalas for cyclists and walkers.

▶ **Population:** 3 300.
◔ **Michelin Map:** 342: L4.
🗊 **Info:** 15 place de la République, Argelés-Gazost. &05 62 97 00 25. www.argeles-gazost.com.
▶ **Location:** 13km/8mi S of Lourdes.

ᯤ Parc animalier des Pyrénées

Situated at the entrance of the town, coming from Lourdes along N 21. ◷Open Apr–Oct 9.30am–6pm (Jul–Aug 9.30am–7pm; 1st 2 wks in Oct 1–6pm). ◷Closed Nov–Mar. ⊜€18 (child 3–11, €13). &05 62 97 91 07. www.parc-animalier-pyrenees.com. During an hour or so spent in this animal park, especially aimed at families with children, you can get to know about the wildlife of the Pyrenees and nine species in particular, including izard, ibex, bear and marmot.

Three exhibition rooms display mounted wildlife from Europe, Africa, America's Far North; from wild boar to antelope and impala.

🚶 WALK
Pic de Pibeste★★★
🚶 *4.5km/2.5mi N via N 21 and D 102 (left) as far as Ouzous. Car park near the church. Allow at least 4h30 round trip on foot. It is essential to have sturdy shoes or boots, warm clothing and a supply of food.*

Despite its relatively modest height (alt 1 349m), the Pibeste Peak offers one of the finest views in the central Pyrenees. The footpath rises gently to the panorama over Ouzous, then climbs in hairpin bends, getting tougher and steeper. From the summit you can see southwards towards Pic du Midi de Bigorre, the Luz and Cauterets mountains, and several distant peaks over 3 000m high.

EXCURSIONS
Beaucens★
👥 Donjon des Aigles★
6.5km/4mi SE. Take D 100 and then D 13 as far as Beaucens.There is a car park at the foot of the castle.
🕐*Open for visits Apr–Sep 10am–noon, 2.30–6.30pm. Flying demonstrations at 3.30pm, 5pm (Aug 3pm, 4.30pm and 6pm).* ⊛*€14 (children €8.50).* ℘*05 62 97 19 59. www.donjon-des-aigles.com.*
The **Beaucens ruins** provide an atmospheric setting for showing off indigenous birds of prey: vultures, eagles, falcons, kites, buzzards, and owls and condors from the Andes, African vultures, and American eagles.

Estaing
👥 Les lamas du Val d'Azun
11km/7mi SW on D 918 to Arras-en-Lavedan, then D 103 through Estaing towards the lake.
🐾*Guided visits only, by arrangement.* ♿ ℘*05 62 97 44 48 or 06 89 48 71 86.*
Lamas are not at all the bad-tempered spitters they are popularly thought to be, say the owners of this farm, which is open to visitors. Rather they are quiet, calm and even huggable. Not only do they serve as pack animals, supply wool and rich fertiliser, but they are also formidable grazers and even guard flocks of sheep.

🚗 DRIVING TOURS

HAUTACAM ROUTE
20km/12mi. Allow 1h. 🕐*See region map.*

▷ Leave Argelès via D 100, which crosses the Azun and climbs, after Ayros, the eastern slope of the Argelès basin.

Artalens
Beyond the village, the road crosses a small valley, where the remains of five old watermills, prominent throughout the Bigorre district in the 19C, flank a stream. After Artalens, the road offers **views★** of the Vignemale beyond vallée de Cauterets, and Balaïtous towering over the mountains surrounding vallée d'Arrens.

UPPER ARRENS VALLEY
24km/15mi. Allow 4h.
🕐*See region map.*
This route explores one of the valleys that make up the Val d'Azun (with the valleys of Ouzom to the west and Estaing to the east.

▷ Leave Argelès going west on D 918.

Monument des Géodésiens (Surveyors' Monument)
Outside Argelès-Gazost is a tower shaped like a geodetic instrument, which was built in 1925 on the hundredth anniversary of the first ascent of the Balaïtous crest, by a team of military surveyors.

▷ Stay on D 918 passing a succession of small villages, on or just off the road.

Arrens-Marsous
Nestled in the valley, this quiet town serves as a base for ramblers at weekends and in summer.
ℹ **Maison du val d'Azun et du Parc national des Pyrénées** – *Pl. du Val-d'Azun.* ℘*05 62 97 49 49. www.valdazun. com.* ♿.
Upstairs in this national park information office there is a permanent exhibi-

tion on the flora, fauna and traditions of the area.

▷ From Arrens take the road towards the barrage du Tech (D105).

Chapelle de Pouey-Laün
A dark blue vault with ribs and stars picked out in gold has earned this church the epithet of 'the golden chapel'.
After Pouey-Laun the road continues up the wild valley of the gave d'Arrens passing the Tech dam.

Porte d'Arrens
Picnic area. This is the point of departure for signposted footpaths heading off into the Balaïtous massif. There is a beautiful view of the col du Souloir, a pass taking the D918 westwards into the Béarn.
🚶 From the porte d'Arrens there is a footpath to the lac de Suyen *(45mins).*

▷ Return to the chapelle de Pouey-Laün and take the road on the right (GR10) to go over a low pass, the col des Bordères. In the village of Estaing, turn right up the glaciated valley of Labat de Bun.

Lac d'Estaing★
Among the 40 or so lakes in the Val d'Azun, this is one of the largest and the most accessible, being served by surfaced road. There is a restaurant and shop at the head of the lake serving the numerous day-trippers who come up here in good weather.
In June the Fête de la Transhumance brings the lakeside alive with more people. Flocks of sheep are driven up here from the valley followed by anyone who wants to walk with them. In the afternoon there are displays of sheepdog handling and sheep shearing.

GORGE DE LUZ
18 km/11mi, from Argelès-Gazost to Luz-St-Sauveur. Allow 1h.
This itinerary skirts the top of the Pierrefitte-Nestalas, with superb excursions into the valley of Cauterets: Pont

d'Espagne, lac de Gaube, Marcadau *(♿See CAUTERETS).*

▷ Leave Argelès going south on D 101 (a minor road on the west side of the valley).

St Savin
Until the Revolution, this village was a centre of religious devotion. Its church belonged to a Benedictine abbey and its abbots were overlords of the St Savin valley. The 11C and 12C building, fortified in the 14C still has its internal watch-path and a lantern belfry crowns the 14C tower. The organ loft (16C) is decorated with masks whose eyes and mouths moved as the organ played.

▷ Continue beyond St-Savin on the same road, although now called D 13.

Chapelle-de-Pietat
A short lane leads to the right. On a small terrace shaded by lime trees stands this delightful chapel, originally Romanesque but rebuilt in the 18C. It offers superb views over the valley below and back towards St Savin. Across the valley are the reddish ruins of Beaucens castle.

▷ Continue on D 13.

Pierrefitte-Nestalas
Incongruously, this small town has an aquarium of tropical marine life which includes a living coral reef.

▷ Pierrefitte-Nestalas merges into Soulom. Take D 921 N up the valley.

Gorge de Luz
Beyond Pierrefitte-Nestalas the road enters the gorge with dark walls of shale and tumbling waterfalls. Before the road as built in the 18C the only direct way to Luz was via a precaripus mule track called the Echelles de Bareges, the Steps of Bareges.
Pont de la Reine marks the end of the enclosed section. Beyond the bridge is the once remote Pays de Toy.

Continue on the main road to reach Luz-St-Sauveur.

ADDRESSES

STAY

⊜ **Chambre d'hôte Mme Vermeil** – *3 r. du Château, 65400 Arcizans-Avant. 5km/3mi S of Argelès on D 101 then D 13. ℘05 62 97 55 96. 3 rooms.* This fine 19C residence typical of the Bigorre region has a splendid view of the valley, and rooms panelled and furnished in pine. The mountaineer owner is happy to advise walkers.

⊜ **Chambre d'hôte Eth Bérye Petit** – *15 rte de Vielle, 65400 Beaucens, 8.5km/5mi SE of Argelès on D 100 and a B-road. ℘05 62 97 90 02. www.beryepetit.com. 3 rooms.* This fine 1790 family mansion has splendid views over the valley.

⊜⊟ **Hôtel Picors** – *Rte d'Aubisque, 65400 Aucun, 10km/6mi W on the rte du col d'Aubisque road. ℘05 62 97 40 90. www.hotel-picors.com. Closed Nov–Easter.* ⊡. *48 rooms.* Impressive façade, fine views of the Pyrenees and the added attractions of sauna, tennis, minigolf and indoor pool.

⊜⊟ **Hôtel les Cimes** – *1 place d'Ourout and 4, rue du Cabaliros, Argelès-Gazost. ℘05 62 97 00 10. www.hotel-lescimes.com.* ⊡. *29 rooms.* On the edge of town, but within walking distance, a charming hotel and restaurant tucked away, and perfect for a restful stay in the valley.

⊻/EAT

⊜⊟ **Lac d'Estaing** – *Au Lac, 65400 Estaing. ℘05 62 97 06 25. Closed 16 Oct–14 May.* Location is everything. The restaurant may be unpretentious but the setting by the lake means there are mountain views all around.

Cauterets★

Set amid high wooded mountains where the Gave de Cauterets meets the Gave de Cambasque, Cauterets is one of the main spas in the Pyrenees. The town is also a bustling summer resort, a popular excursion and mountaineering centre (Vignemale) and a booming winter sports resort.

🐾WALKING TOUR

Start in place du Maréchal-Foch. With the tourist information office in front of you, turn right towards the spa (thermes) along allée du Parc.

The Spa

The thermal district is characterised by its narrow streets and high houses clustered on the right bank of the river, at the foot of Thermes de César, modelled on the thermal baths of Antiquity (triangular pediment and marble columns).

Turn right in front of the spa down rue du Maréchal-Joffre.

- ▶ **Population:** 1 038.
- **Michelin Map:** 342: L5.
- **Info:** Tourism office, 1 Pl du Mar-Foch. ℘05 62 92 50 50. www.cauterets.com.
- **Location:** 16km/10mi south of Argelès-Gazost on D 920.
- **Kids:** Gaube chair lift.
- **Don't Miss:** Pont d'Espagne, Lac de Gaube and the cascades.

Note, opposite the church, the lovely façade adorned with wrought-iron balconies and grey-marble window frames.

Take rue du Général-Castelnau in front of the church, crossing the rue de la Raillère (along which there are more beautiful façades) and the river, the gave de Cauterets. Turn right along the Esplanade des Œufs.

Esplanade des Œufs

Named after the Œufs spring, this is lined with boutiques built from metallic structures left over from the 1889 Paris

World Fair. The Gare des Œufs provides a bus shuttle service to the Griffons spa.

▶ Turn left on avenue du Mamelon-vert.

To extend the walk, go along this street until it turns a sharp corner to see the **Villa Russe**, a house built in 1840 for the princess Galitzine. Beneath the dome is an Orthodox chapel. Turn round and take the first left turning down boulevard Latapie-Fleurin.

Boulevard Latapie-Flurin

This street is bordered by luxury hotels built during Cauterets' heyday. Hôtel Continental and Hôtel d'Angleterre, founded by Alphonse Meillon (one of the gentlemen innkeepers synonymous with the popularity of the Pyrenees at the time), have impressive neo-Classical façades, lavishly decorated with cornices, pillars, caryatids and wrought-iron balconies.

▶ At the end of the boulevard turn right down rue de la Feria which continues as rue du Pont-Neuf. Turn left after the bridge passing the national park information centre.

Old Railway Station

The astonishing wooden construction which formed part of the Norwegian pavilion at the 1889 World Exhibition became the town's **railway station**. After the closure of the line it was turned into a bus station.

▶ From the crossroads outside the national park office, take rue Richelieu to return to the place du Maréchal-Foch.

Musée Cauterets 1900

🕑 *Open during school holidays Mon–Sat 10am–noon, 3–6.30pm; rest of the year call for information.* ✆ *05 62 92 02 02.* ✺ *€6 (child 5–14, €3).*
This museum occupying part of the hôtel d'Angleterre, evokes the Belle Epoque heyday of Cauterets and celebrates the traditional life of the mountains.

EXCURSION
Cirque du Lys★★

Access via the **Lys gondola lift** (🕑 *open Jul–Aug and Dec–Apr 9am–noon, 1.45–5.15pm;* 🕑 *closed rest of year; chair-lift and cable-car for the crêtes du Lys* ✺ *€12 round-trip in summer)* and the **Grand Barbat chair-lift** (🕑 *open same times as the Lys lift).*
As you cross the Cambasque plateau, a superb **panorama** from Crête du Lys (2 303m) overlooks the spectacular Pic du Midi de Bigorre, Vignemale and Balaïtous (*viewing table).* You can take a mountain bike to ride back to Cauterets from the Grand Barbat chair-lift station.
🚶 It takes 1h on foot to get to Ilhéou Lake (or Blue Lake) via the GR10 rambling path.

SKI AREA
Alt 1 450m–1 630m.
The ski fields in Cauterets are divided into two parts. Cirque du Lys is the largest and has a constant snowfall from December through to May. Weather permitting, it is possible to ski down to Cambasque (where the lift makes an intermediate halt). The other, smaller part of the resort is Pont d'Espagne which has four ski-lifts, including the Gaube chair-lift.

🚶 WALKS
Chemin des Cascades ★

🏃 *5h from Cauterets or 4h from the car park at pont de la Raillère, near the thermes des Griffons.*
This beautiful woodland walk visits Cauterets' trio of waterfalls: Cerisey, Pas-de-l'Ours and Boussès. It's especially enjoyable in spring and early summer.

Vallée du Luron and Lac d'Epsom ★★

🏃 *5h from la Fruitière in the Vallée de Lutour.* One of the most beautiful and also one of the easier walks to do in the area. The first hour is along the valley and then the footpath climbs through pine trees to reach the lac d'Epsom.

🚗 DRIVING TOUR

VALLÉE DES CAUTERETS★★
12km/7.5mi there-and-back trip up the valley above Cauterets. Allow around 30mins. See region map.

▶ Leave Cauterets on the GR10.

Cascade de Lutour★★
A footbridge spans the pool below the last four waterfalls of Gave de Lutour.

▶ The road continues up the valley; narrow, steep, heavily wooded, boulder-strewn and cooled by waterfalls.

Cascades de Cerisey, Pas de l'Ours and Boussès★★
These three attractive waterfalls are all very different. Above the Boussès waterfall, the river divides around Sarah Bernhardt's Island *(parking in the glade)*.

Pont d'Espagne★★★
🅿 *Park in the Puntas car park, and take the Puntas* **cable shuttle** *(15min, ⏱open Jun and Sep enquire at tourist office; ⏱closed Oct–early Dec; ✆05 62 92 50 50) as far as Plateau du Clot (activity centre with cross-country ski trails and rambling paths), or go by foot to the bridge.*
This bridge is named after an ancient mule track which once lead to Spain. The magnificent site marks the confluence of the Gave de Gaube and Gave de Marcadau, and several footbridges and viewpoints offer breathtaking scenes of foaming cascades. A path to the Pont d'Espagne from the Puntas parking area meanders through firs and pines, and meadows dotted with mountain flowers stretch across the landscape. Ideal for winter cross-country skiing.

Lac de Gaube★★
🚶 *1h30 round trip by GR 10 rambling path, downstream from Pont d'Espagne.* The **Gaube chair-lift** (⏱open Jul–Aug 9am–6pm; May–Jun and Sep 9.45am–5.30pm; ⏱closed Oct–mid Dec, depending on weather conditions; ✆05 62 92 50 50) from Plateau de Clots can be taken

most of the way, followed by a 15min walk to a bar-café by the lake. At the top of the chair-lift, nature information panels describe forest flora and fauna and the izard, a local species of chamois. Its austere yet beautiful site provides a view of the Vignemale massif and glaciers. A footpath along the river's west bank looks onto Pique Longue du Vignemale, 3 298m, one of the highest peaks in the Pyrenees.

Vallée du Marcadau★★
🚶 *6.5km/4mi; 6hr round trip on foot from the Pont d'Espagne parking area.* Once a favourite route for crossing into Spain, this path has grass-covered shoulders and mountain streams, alternating with glacial thresholds and twisted mountain pines. The Wallon refuge stands at an altitude of 1 866m, and beyond it is a cirque of pastureland scattered with lakes. Marcadau means market place, which this once was.

ADDRESSES

🛏 STAY

🛏 **Chambre d'hôte les Ruisseaux** – *7km/4.2mi N of Cauterets. Rte de Pierrefitte. ✆05 62 92 28 02. www.lesruisseaux.com. 4 rooms.* Bed and breakfast built in the 1920–30s. The rooms are newly furnished and immpeccable.

🛏 **Hôtel du Lion d'Or** – *12 r. Richelieu. ✆05 62 92 52 87. www.hotel-cauterets.fr. Closed 30 Sep–20 Dec. 22 rooms.* A family hotel only 100m from the Lys cable-car, with cosy rooms and wrought iron balconies. The flower adorned patio makes a pleasant place to relax.

🛏🛏 **Chambre d'hôte Grange St-Jean** – *Rte de Lourdes, quartier Calypso. ✆05 62 92 58 58. 3 rooms.* This converted barn B&B with blue and yellow façade has rooms are decorated on a mountain theme and a garden facing a meadow.

🍽 EAT

🍽 **L'Aragon** – *R. de Belfort. ✆05 62 92 54 94. Sun-Thu 7.30am–2am; Fri–Sat 7.30am–3am.* This lively snack bar with cosy wood fire serves salads, soups and omelettes.

Parc National des Pyrénées★★★

The Pyrénées National Park was created in 1967 with the aim of preserving the natural environment. One of six national parks in mainland France, it shares a 15km/10mi common border with the Spanish national park of Ordesa and Mont Perdu (south of Gavarnie). The national park covers 45 700 ha between 1 000m and 3 298m of altitude (the highest point being the summit of Vignemale).

VISIT

The national park proper, the core, is surrounded by a peripheral zone of 206 000ha shared by 86 communes in the *départements* of Hautes-Pyrénées and Pyrénées-Atlantiques. The national park is extended to the east by the Néouvielle nature reserve (&see

⚅ **Michelin Map:** 342: K-5.

🛈 **Info:** 2 rue du IV Septembre, 65000 Tarbes.
𝄞05 62 54 16 40.
www.parc-pyrenees.com.

▶ **Location:** Extends for more than 100km/60mi along the French border region from Vallée d'Aspe in the west to Vallée d'Aure in the east. Seven other 'Maisons du Parc' offer tourist information (&see Addresses).

RESERVE NATIONAL DU NÉOUVIELLE) which is managed by the adminstrators of the park. In order to better protect biodiveristy within its territory, the national park surveys and tracks all flora

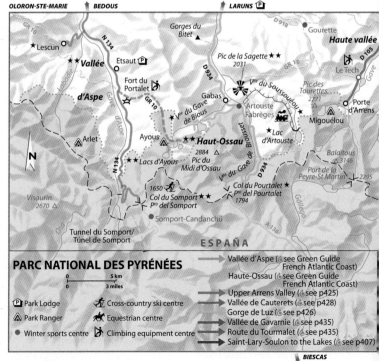

and fauna. The preservation of wildlife in the sensitive central zone does not prohibit human economic activities such as livestock farming or forestry; the park's obective is to reconcile the protection of nature with such economic activities. In the peripheral zone, the park has a policy of encouraging local development in harmony with the protection of the natural environment.

Land without People

No one lives in the central part of the park which is all high mountain except, in the summer months, shepherds and wardens of refuges for climbers. It's this absence of human beings that explains the presence of other animals.

The Six Valleys

The national park covers six vallées of which four are in Hautes-Pyrénées: Arrens, Cauterets, Luz-Gavarnie and Aure. The other two – the **Aspe** and **Ossau** valleys – are in the neighbour-ing department of Pyrenees Atlantiques (see Green Guide Atlantic Coast).

WALKS

There are more than 350km/210mi of marked footpaths in the park. The best known of them is **GR10**, a long distance trail that travels the length of the Pyrenees from one coast to the other crossing through the park on its way. There are plenty of other shorter footpaths of greater or lesser difficulty to choose from.

The park authorities encourage people to explore the path as long as they take sensible precautions for walking in high mountains.

Hunting, picking flowers, lighting campfires and bringing in dogs are all prohibited in the national park. Fishing is allowed, but only with a permit and during the season which runs from March to September.

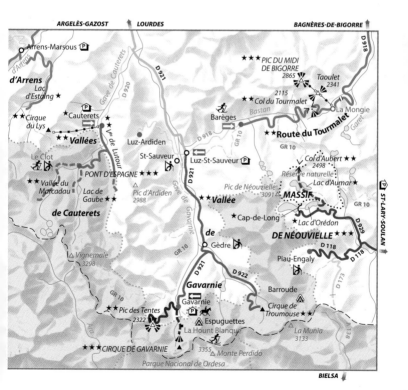

Wildlife of the Pyrénées

An Abundant Flora – The Pyrenees National Park has within its borders 60 endemic species of wildflowers. To each altitude zone, its characteristic vegetation. The lower slopes are classed as damp montane (900m–1 800m) and support luch forests of beech and pine. At the subalpine level (1 800m–2 400m). rhodendrons grow along with birch and mountain ash. The highest slopes are at truly alpine altitudes (2 400m–2 900m), between the upper tree limit and the permanent snowfields. Higher still is the nival zone where only lichen and algae survive.

Animal Life – The park provides shelter for 4 000 izard, a local species of chamois, particularly in the valleys of Ossau and Cauterets, where they can be easily spotted, as well as more than 200 colonies of marmot. Much less conspicuous is the desman (a small, very rare aquatic mammal). With a good pair of binoculars, it is not unusual to see vultures (the griffon vulture, especially, and more rarely the bearded vulture) and golden eagles in flight.

The Fate of the Bear – The national park's largest inhabitant is also its least seen. The European brown bear (*Ursus arctos*) clings precariously to its habitat of rocky slopes and in beech and fir forests which overlook the Aspe and Ossau valleys at an altitude of 1 500m–1 700m. This once carnivorous plantigrade animal now varies its diet according to the season, eating tubers, fruit, insects, acorns but also small mammals and sometimes sheep.

Unfortunately, the extension of the road network as well as forestry work and tourism combined with the bear's slow reproduction cycle (females have a cub every two years), have led to the regression of the species. Other threats to the bear are the hostility of sheep farmers.

On 1 November 2004, the last native Pyrenean bear, Cannelle (a female) was shot by a hunter claiming self-defence. The only hope for the bear is a progamme of reintroduction begun in 1996 which has seen bears from Slovenia released into the wild. There are now thought to be no more than 20 bears in the French Pyrenees but only 4 of them within the protective area of the national park.

The position of the bear remains critical with conservationists insisting that they are a vital part of the ecosystem, but many people in the local community convinced that the mountains are better off without them.

ADDRESSES

VISITOR CENTRES

Vallée d'Aure): *St-Lary-Soulan.* ℘05 62 39 40 91.

Vallée de Luz: *Luz-St-Sauveur* – ℘05 62 92 38 38; and *Gavarnie* – ℘05 62 92 42 48.

Vallée de Cauterets: *Cauterets* – ℘05 62 92 52 56;

Vallée d'Azun: *Arrens-Marsous* – ℘ 05 62 97 43 13;

Vallée d'Ossau: *Laruns.* ℘05 59 05 41 59;
Vallée d'Aspe: *Etsaut.* ℘05 59 34 88 30.

all these offices give out information and can advise on activities and events within the confines of the park.

REFUGES

The national park has several refuge huts for the convenience of walkers and climbers who want to stay overnight. Some are managed by the park authorities, others by the Club Alpin Français. Places in these refuges are in high demand during the summer months and advanced reservation is essential.

CAMPING

Camping is prohibited in the national park, but bivouacking is tolerated (overnight or in case of bad weather, it is permissible to set up a tent, on the condition that you are more than a 1h walk from a road used by motor vehicles). Tourist offices and syndicats d'initiative can provide you with a list of campsites near the park.

Luz-St-Sauveur

Luz-Saint-Sauveur, route centre and capital of a small mountain canton, owes its success to the Empress Eugénie, wife of Napoleon III, who started a fashion for visiting the spas of the Pyrenees in the mid-19C. It is, however, a much more ancient place – as its chateau testifies. Today, it exploits its strategic position, at a three-way crossroads where the routes between Lourdes, Gavarnie, the Col du Tourmalet meet, to offer a range of services to visitors to the mountains. In winter it caters for skiers going up to the winter sports resort of Luz-Ardiden. The Tour de France cycle race frequently passes through Luz-St-Sauveur.

- **Population:** 1 005.
- **Michelin Map:** 342: L5-M5.
- **Info:** Pl 8 Mai, 65120 Luz-St-Sauveur. ℘05 62 92 30 30. www.luz.org.
- **Location:** 18km/11mi southwest of Argelès-Gazost.

SIGHTS
Château Sainte-Marie
🚶 *30min walk. At Esquièze, just before entering Luz on D 921, turn left on D 172 towards Vizos. The narrow footpath departs to the right beside hôtel Montaigu.*
Built in the 10C by the counts of Bigorre, this chateau was occupied by the Knights Hospitaller and then the English before it was retaken 1404. From the ruins there is a superb view over the valley.

Fortified Church
Luz's fortified **church★** was built in the 12C and fortified in the 14C. It has a watch-path, crenellated wall and two square towers. There is a small museum of religious art in the Chapelle Notre-Dame-de-la-Pitié and a museum of ethnography in the Arsenal tower.

Saint-Sauveur
Saint-Sauveur is the spa quarter across the valley from Luz proper. Its single street, a corniche road above the river, is named after two great aristocractic patrons of the town in the 19C, the Duchesse de Berry at one end, and Empress Eugénie on the other. The spa, built in Napoléon III style, is supplied with thermally heated water. A phrase from the book of Isaiah written on an earlier building – 'Vous prendrez joyeusement les eaux de la source du sauveur' ('With joy shall ye draw water out of the wells of salvation') – gave the spa its name.

EXCURSIONS
Thermes de Barèges-Barzun
7km/4.5mi from Luz-Saint-Sauveur on D 918. Rue Ramond. ⏰*Open Jul–Aug daily 9am–12.30pm, 2–6.30pm; rest of the year Mon–Sat.* ℘*05 62 92 68 02. www.cieleo-bareges.com.*
The two halves of the composite name point to different establishments: the Thermes de Barèges treats patients with bone disorders and rheumatism while the Thermes de Barzun concentrates on breathing problems.

Domaine skiable de Luz-Ardiden
15km/9mi from Luz-Saint-Sauveur on D 12.
Luz Ardiden
Luz Ardiden's setting (alt 1 680m–2 450m) still remains unspoilt. The ski area is serviced by 19 lifts. The Aulian and Bédéret slopes offer 32 runs for all levels, totalling 60km/40mi. Skiers can slalom around moguls, and schuss or monoski in Snowboard Space. There is off-piste skiing in the adjacent valley of Bernazaou.

Ski 'Grand Tourmalet'
There are two entry points to this, one of the largest skiing areas in the French Pyrenees: La Mongie or Barèges. Their lifts meet at the Col du Tourmalet making for a choice of 100km/60mi of pistes reaching from 1 400m to 2 500m.

The Pic du Midi (&see PIC DU MIDI DE BIGORRE) also forms part of this mega-ski resort although most skiiers dont get beyond the half-way station of the two-leg cable car.

Domaine skiable de Gavarnie-Gèdre

25km/12mi south of Luz-St-Sauveur on D 921. ◯*Open mid-Dec–mid-Mar. www.gavarnie.com.*
With 11 lifts (from 1 650m–2 400m) and 29 slopes (5 of them black), a snow-boarding park and a children's play area, this is among the smaller Pyrenean ski resorts.

🚗 DRIVING TOURS

VALLÉE DE GAVARNIE★★
20km/12mi itinerary from Luz-St-Sauveur. Allow 3h30.
&*See region map.*

The Vallée de Gavarnie and the Cirque de Gavarnie have been UNESCO World Heritage sites since 1997. The forbid-ding landscape provoked the Baroness Dudevant (George Sand) to write: 'From Luz to Gavarnie is primeval chaos; it is hell itself.' Victor Hugo described the track through the Chaos de Coumély as 'a black and hideous path.' The Prag-nères, Gèdre and Gavarnie basins were gouged by Quaternary Age glaciers. Their melting waters created narrows, the most typical of which is St-Sauveur gorge. Temporary dwellings perch on the ledges; torrents cascade from the tributary valleys.

▷ Leave Luz-Saint-Sauveur via D 921.

Pont Napoléon
☝ *Avoid the 3pm jam of excursion coaches near the Pont Napoléon.*
This arched bridge, ordered by Napo-leon III in 1860, spans the gorge chan-nelled by the Pau Torrent. The road carved from the bed-rock, twists through another gorge and passes through the hamlet of Sia. The bridge is a favourite for bungey jumping.

Centrale de Pragnères
Open for visits except in times of 'Vigipirate' – national security alerts.
The most important hydrolectric power station in Hautes-Pyrénées gathers its water from the high mountains includ-ing the massif de Néouvielle. It oper-ates at full capacity during periods of peak demand in winter. It consists of 40km/25mi of tunnels, four dams including Cap-Long, the biggest in the Pyrenees, a central turbine hall and two pumping stations.

Gèdre
This village at the confluence of the Héas and Gavarnie torrents makes a charm-ing halt enroute to Cirque de Gavarnie, and is base for driving tours to the Trou-mouse and Estaubé cirques.

▷ Follow the toll road to the Cirque de Troumouse (15km/9mi), usually obstructed by snow from Dec–Apr.

Héas
The **chapel** is the site of regular pilgrim-ages. Most of the original building was swept away in an avalanche in 1915 and rebuilt 10 years later, but the north aisle and statues, paintings, the 1643 bell, a stoup and 18C processional Cross still remain.

Cirque de Troumouse★★
This amphitheatre is best viewed from a rocky spur, in the centre of which stands the Vierge de Troumouse (🚶*45min round trip walk).* The amphitheatre can accommodate three million spectators. Carpeted in meadow grass and flowers, it is enclosed by a rampart of mountains 10km/6mi around. The highest peak is Pic de la Munia and below it are twinned rock pinnacles 'the Two Sisters.'

▷ Return to Gèdre and continue along D 921.

The scenery gets wild with the spectacu-lar Cascade d'Arroudet dashing down into the hanging valley of the Aspé Tor-rent. The road crosses the rock-strewn

Chaos de Coumély and begins the final ascent towards Gavarnie. Beyond the Fausse Brèche and Pic des Sarradets the snow-covered ledges of the amphitheatre come into view, with the summits of Le Casque, La Tour and Pic du Marboré. The road follows the hamlet of Bareilles and then, on the Turon de Holle, the monumental statue of Notre-Dame-des-Neiges.

Gavarnie &See below.

ROUTE DU TOURMALET★★
30km /19mi trip on D 918, from Barèges to Ste-Marie-de-Campan. Allow 1h.
&See region map.
The route is extremely windy and exposed on the climb up to the col de Tourmalet from the Barèges side. Check before departing: the pass is often closed because of snow from autumn to spring.
The route begins in the somewhat stark valley of Escoubous. After 4km/2.5mi, you reach the pont de la Gaubie.

After the pont de la Gaubie the rocky pyramid of the pic de Néouvielle appears in the distance. Soon the pic du Midi de Bigorre, topped by an observatory and television mast, can be seen. There are many curves from here to the pass.

Col du Tourmalet ★★
The statue of a cyclist marks this classic mountain pass which is frequently used in the Tour de France. At an altitude of 2 115m this is the highest main road pass in the French Pyrenees.

There are more curves on the way down from the pass to La Mongie.

Pic du Midi de Bigorre ★★★
&See PIC DU MIDI DE BIGORRE.
A cable car departs from the ski resort of La Mongie to the observatory on the top of the Pic du Midi de Bigorre.

The road continues to descend quickly as it reaches the Campan valley and Sainte-Marie-de-Campan.

Cirque de Gavarnie★★★

Part of a trans-fronteral UNESCO World Heritage Site (since 1997) and undoubtedly the unmissable sight of the Pyrenees, the Cirque de Gavarnie inevitably generates superlatives. It is a classic example of a cirque, a depression and headwall carved by a massive glacier. It's almost impossible to imagine the amount of ice that would have been needed to scoop out such a vastly oversized, sheer-walled amphitheatre with 17 summits of over 3,000m rising above it and the longest waterfall in Europe (422m) falling down its face.

SIGHTS
Gavarnie
From the village, you can reach the Cirque de Gavarnie astride a donkey or a horse. Find them near the parking area

- **Michelin Map:** 342: L6-M6.
- **Info:** 65120 Gavarnie-Gèdre. ℘05 62 92 49 10. www.gavarnie.com.
- **Location:** 20km/12mi south of Luz-St-Sauveur.

closest to the main street. ℘*05 62 92 49 10. www.gavarnie.com.*
Since 1864 Gavarnie has provided various mounts for the trek to the Cirque. In summer this small town is packed with day-trippers. Once they've gone and the mules, donkeys and ponies return to their pastures, Gavarnie becomes a base for mountaineers. Gavarnie, the highest village in the Pyrenees, is very crowded in the summer. Park outside the town, and walk into town.
The 14C **church** on the old pilgrims' route to Port de Boucharo contains a polychrome statue of St James of Compostela, two statuettes of Compostela

Cirque de Gavarnie with the Grande Cascade

© Jean-Marc Barrère/hemis.fr

pilgrims, and a Virgin Mary holding a pilgrim's water flask.

🚶 MOUNTAIN WALKS
Cirque de Gavarnie★★★
2h on foot there and back.
At the end of the village, take the unsurfaced path then follow the true left bank of the *gave* (mountain stream). Cross over an old stone bridge and walk up through the woods, with the river now to your right. The last part of the walk climbs through mixed vegetation to the first rocky folds marking the approach of the Cirque itself. Then the Cirque de Gavarnie comes into view. Gazing at its majesty of sheer walls and tiered snow platforms, Victor Hugo exclaimed: 'It is both a mountain and a rampart; it is the most mysterious of structures by the most mysterious of architects; it is Nature's Colosseum – it is Gavarnie!'
The mounted Driving Tours end at the Hôtel du Cirque, but it is possible to continue, on foot (*1h there and back*), to the **Grande Cascade**. This impressive waterfall is fed by melt-water from the frozen lake on Monte Perdido on the Spanish side of the frontier. The cascade drops 422m into the void.

Brèche de Roland
(Roland's Gap)
⟶4h on foot there and back – for experienced mountain walkers only: beware of the névés from September to early July. Follow the marked path heading E from Port de Boucharo.
The path follows the gently rising Haute Route des Pyrénées and fords a waterfall at the foot of the Taillon glacier.

From the pass admire the Grande Cascade of the Cirque de Gavarnie. Cross to the Sarradets refuge. Beyond, the climb to the brèche is long and often made more difficult by the presence of snow. The breach named after the gallant 8C knight Rolland offers a **view** of Monte Perdido and the barren Spanish side.

EXCURSION
Col du Boucharo★★
and Pic de Tentes★★
In the summer months you can drive from Gavarnie up towards the Col bu Bouchara. The final stretch to the col, which is the frontier with Spain, is closed to cars.
Leaving Gavarnie in the direction of Luz (north), turn left just before the bridge. The road skirts the statue of Notre-Dame-des-Neiges at the mouth of the Vallée d'Ossoue, then climbs to enter the Vallée des Espéciéres. When you reach Col de Tentes, leave the car at the saddle and walk to the rounded summit of Pic de Tentes (alt 2 322m), to the NE.
👁It is also worth walking to the Col du Boucharo for a view into Spain.
The Col de Tentes offers a **panorama★★★** of peaks forming the Cirque de Gavarnie, including Le Taillon and Pic du Marboré, gashed by the Grande Cascade glacier.
More distant still rises Le Petit Vignemale and, shouldering the Ossoue glacier, Vignemale itself, so beloved of Henry Russell, who built a cave on the mountain in which he entertained guests.
To the northeast the Néouvielle massif stands in front of Pic du Midi de Bigorre.

The Gers – the modern department based on the ancient province of Gascony – is quintessential rural France. It may have no individual, must-see sights to compete with more famous parts of the country but when its pretty villages, bastide towns, chateaux, ancient abbeys, rolling fields of cereals and sunflowers are taken as whole it makes an enjoyable backroads corner to travel in. The capital city of Auch is easily reached from Toulouse and makes a good base from which to explore the Gers. There is a sense of good living here fostered by good things to eat and drink. In particular, the Gers is renowned for its duck and goose products (foie gras and confit de canard) and for its Armagac brandy – which connoisseurs say can hold its own against Cognac. The region also has four of France's less well-known wine regions: Saint-Mont, Madiran, Côtes de Gascogne and Côtes du Condomois.

Bullfighting

Bullfighting in the Gers comes in two varieties. The *corrida* is a confrontation between man and bull in the Spanish fashion. *Course landaise*, however, is more a demonstration of gymnastic prowess using a cow which is not killed. Instead of a matador there is an *écarteur* who dodges the charging animal and *sauteur*, who jumps over it.

Bastides and Castelnaux

Many towns in the Gers are bastides, new towns founded in the Middle Ages by charter from the king or seigneur. Their purpose was to put wild areas of land into cultivation while at the same time settling and organising the growing population. As a bonus for the landlord, the populace became easier to tax. Most bastides are built to a similar plan with streets of stone or half-timbered houses laid out on a grid. At the centre there is a square with a market hall in the

Highlights

1 Explore the old town of **Auch** (p441)

2 Marciac's annual **jazz festival** (p446)

3 Discover the Gallo-Roman treasure of **Eauze** (p448)

4 Explore the town of **Condom** (p449)

5 Taste **Armagnac** (p451)

middle and arcades around the outside. According to necessity, walls, gateways and other fortifications were added to some bastides. Castelnaux are towns that grew up in the protective shelter of a château.

Other medieval new towns are classified as castelaus, denoting a settlement which grew up under the protection of a local château.

Cathédrale Ste-Marie and River Gers, Auch

© Jean-Marc Barrère/hemis.fr

THE GERS REGION

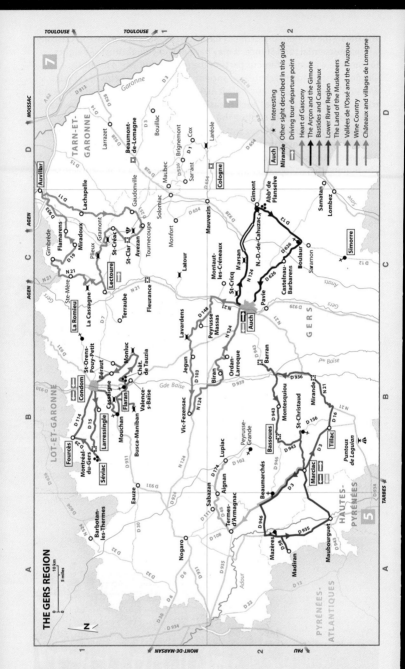

THE GERS REGION

Legend:
- ★ Interesting
- Other sight described in this guide
- Driving tour departure point
- Heart of Gascony
- The Arçon and the Gimone
- Bastides and Castelnaux
- Lower River Region
- The Land of the Musketeers
- Vallées de l'Ossé and the l'Auzoue
- Wine Country
- Châteaux and villages de Lomagne

Auch★

*The Heart of Gascony
and East of Auch*

An important crossroads since Roman times on the busy trade route linking Toulouse to the Atlantic – before traffic was diverted along the River Garonne – Auch was revived in the 18C by the administrator Étigny and embellished during the Second Empire. The bustling street life and busy Saturday markets underline its position as administrative capital of Gascony. The main streets converge on place de la Libération. The Episcopal district stands apart above the River Gers.

OLD TOWN
Escalier monumental
The 232 steps of this monumental staircase link place Salinis, the square next to the cathedral which overlooks the Gers Valley, with the quays below. The statue of d'Artagnan, dating from 1931, is halfway down. Climbing back up the steps, gives you a fine view of the 14C **Tour d'Armagnac** (the 40m-high watchtower of the municipal prison) and the abutments and double-course flying buttresses around the cathedral.

▶ **Population:** 23 247.
◔ **Michelin Map:** 336: F8.
▣ **Info:** 3, place de la République.
  ☎05 62 05 22 89.
  www.auch-tourisme.com.
◖ **Location:** 76km/47.5mi W of Toulouse.
⊛ **Don't Miss:** Cathédrale Ste-Marie.

Cathédrale Ste-Marie★★
◔*Open Jan–Jun Mon–Fri 9.30am– noon, 2.30–5.30pm, Sat–Sun 6pm; Jul–Aug daily 9.30am–7pm; 1st 2 wks in Sept Mon–Thu 9.30am–5.30pm, Fri–Sun 9.30am–6pm; mid-Sept–Dec Mon–Thu 9.30am–noon, 2.30–5.30pm, Fri–Sun 9.30am–noon, 2–6pm.* ⊚*No charge.*
Construction of the cathedral of Ste-Marie began in 1489 and was completed two centuries later. The solid 16C and 17C **façade** presents a balanced relationship between pilasters, columns, cornices, balustrades and niches. The quadripartite vaulting, dating from the mid-17C, lends a stylistic unity to the interior, done in the French Gothic style. Treasures are the early-16C *Christ Entombed in the Chapel of the Holy Sep-*

WHERE TO STAY

Castagné (Chambre d'hôte Le)...............② ⑰
Houresté (Chambre d'hôte Le).............⑦ ⑨
Mme Mengelle (Chambre d'hôte)..................⑨ ⑦
Chalets des Mousquetaires (Camping Les).............⑫
Robinson (Hôtel Le).....................⑮
Château Les Charmettes............⑰

WHERE TO EAT

Papillon (Le).........................③
Table d'Oste (La).........................⑧

Ancien palais archiépiscopal........B
Escalier monumental....................E
Escalier monumental....................E
Ancien palais archiépiscopal........B

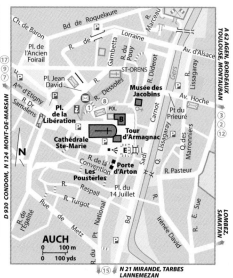

ulchre, and the 16C stone altarpiece of the St Catherine's Chapel.

Stained-glass windows★★ – Eighteen works by the Gascon painter Arnaud de Moles embellish the early 16C ambulatory chapels windows, noted for their rich colours, large panes and expressive figures linking the Old and New Testaments and the pagan world.

Choir Stalls★★★ – Auch woodcarvers took 50 years (c.1500–52) to complete the 113 stalls decorated with over 1 500 exquisitely carved oak figures drawn from the Bible, secular history, myths and legends. The splendid tones of the great organ (1694), constructed by Jean de Joyeuse, ring forth from May to September during **concerts**.

Préfecture (Ancien palais archiépiscopal)

The offices of the préfecture occupy the former **archbishop's palace** (1742–1775), its ornate iron gate framed by Corinthian pilasters, which stands on a square on the north side of the cathedral. A market is held in the halle aux herbes (across the square) on Saturdays.

Place de la Libération

This is the centre of action in the upper town.

Les Pousterles

Pousterles is the medieval term used to designate posterns set in the walls of the fortified upper town. **Porte d'Arton** was the main entrance to the town. Before joining place Salinis, Rue Fabre-d'Églantine skirts the walls of the lycée, founded as a Jesuit college in 1545.

Musée des Jacobins

Displaying Gallo-Roman archaeology and South American colonial art, the Jacobin Museum is housed in the former Couvent des Jacobins (◔open Feb–Mar daily 2–5pm; Apr–Jun daily 10am–noon, 2–6pm; ◔from Jul 2017, the museum will be closed for one year for renovation work; ◎€5; ℘05 62 05 74 79).

EXCURSIONS
Pavie
5km/3mi S via N 21.
Originally a Gallo-Roman villa, Pavie became a *bastide* in 1281. Rue d'Étigny and rue de la Guérite contain beautiful examples of half-timbered houses. The 13C church, restored in the 19C, has kept its 14C square belfry. A Gothic bridge with three arches spans the River Gers.

Montaut-les-Créneaux
10 km/6mi NE on N 21 and D 272.
Built around a château, this castelnau has some beautiful half-timbered houses. The 12C Benedictine church dedicated to St Michael is worth seeing as is the gateway armed with a portcullis.

Lombez
38km/6.6mi SE on D 349 then D 149.
The old town of narrow streets and half-timbered houses is overshadowed by the tower of its fortified cathedral. Octagonal brick southern Gothic toulousain style in five storeys. To the right of the door a

d'Artagnan, the Real Musketeer

The town statue honouring d'Artagnan portrays him as the famous musketeer immortalised by novelist Alexandre Dumas in *The Three Musketeers*. The real-life character, Charles de Batz (born c.1615), borrowed the name d'Artagnan from the Montesquiou family on his mother's side before joining the French Guards (d'Artagnan was more suitable for court use).

As a young soldier, he was already favoured by Cardinal Mazarin (1602–61), Richelieu's successor, and divided his time between battle campaigns, diplomatic missions and bawdy back street life. Louis XIV entrusted him with the arrest of Finance Minister Jules Fouquet, who had grown extremely rich at the State's expense. D'Artagnan, a Captain-Lieutenant in the 1st Company of the King's Musketeers, died a hero's death at the siege of Maastricht in 1673.

plaque commemorates the visit here of the Italian poet Petrarch, coming from Avignon in the summer of 1330. There is a good view of the cathedral from the chapelle Saint Majan reached on foot from the road to the cemetery (park there).

Samatan

2km/1mi NEof Lombez by D 39.

Not only does this town have a lively foie gras market on Monday mornings in winter but it also has a museum dedicated to the Gers' favourite goose product.

Simorre★

18km/6.6mi SW of Lombez by D 632 then D 234.

The church here was built in the 14C and added to in the 16C. it has an octagonal tower. The choir is illuminated by 14 and 15C stained glass windows. The choir stalls have some interesting carvings. In the sacristy there are 14C murals.

🚗 DRIVING TOURS

BASTIDES AND CASTELNAUX

A signposted route connects the bastides and castelnaux of central Gers. ◔*See MARCIAC.*

HEART OF GASCONY

75km/47mi. Allow 1h30.

▷ Leave Auch N on N 21 towards Agen. After 8.5km/5mi, leaving Preignan, turn left on D 272. Passing right of Roquelaure, take D 148 along the ridge. Turn left for Peyrusse-Massas.

👥 Le jardin carnivore, Peyrusse-Massas

☏05 62 65 52 48.
www.natureetpaysages.fr.

With 550 species, this collection of carnivorous plants claims to be one of the largest in the world. The visit begins with a short film, after which an audioguide steers you around the bog garden with its sundews, Venus fly traps, trumpet plants and other ravenous flora. Finally, you go into the nursery where

some of the plants you have seen are on sale. The totem of the garden is the mythical man-eating tree, a spectre which haunted European explorers.

▷ Return to D 148 and on leaving Mérens turn left on D 518, then D 103 to Lavardens. The road runs through an undulating landscape and fine **view★**.

Lavardens

This picturesque village with narrow streets is noted for its imposing castle, attractive church belfry and visible remains of ancient ramparts and towers. The original **castle** (🕐*open mid-end Mar and Nov–Dec Mon–Fri 10.30am–12.30pm, 2–5pm, Sat–Sun until 6pm, except in Mar; Apr–Jun and Sept–Oct10.30am–12.30pm, 2–6pm; Jul–Aug daily 10am–7pm;* 🕐 *closed mid-Jan–mid-Mar:* 👓€ *5–* €*6, entrance fee varies according to the exhibitions;*☏*05 62 58 10 61; www.chateaulavardens.com)* was razed in the 15C. The 17C structure standing today, pierced with mullion and transom windows, has a façade flanked with square towers.

Jégun

This village stands on a rocky spur within the ground-plan of a bastide. Highlights are the old market, fine half-timbered old houses and the 13C collegiate church of Ste-Candide.

Vic-Fézensac

This town holds busy markets and *féria*, traditional festivals with bullfighting.

▷ Head SE via N 124 towards Auch. At St-Jean-Poutge turn right on D 939 towards L'Isle-de-Noé.

After about 4km/2mi, before turning left on D 374, note the unusual **Gallo-Roman pier** with a niche. **Biran** is a small *castelnau* built on a spur; a single road links the fortified gateway to the remains of the keep. The **Notre-Dame-de-Pitié church** shelters a monumental carved stone altarpiece, carved with scenes including the Pietà.

Continue along D 374 and rejoin N 124. After a short way, take the second road on the right.

The pretty little village of **Ordan-Larroque** perched on a rocky outcrop proudly possesses a 200-year-old maple tree. From the place de la mairie, there is a beautiful view over the valley. The **Conservatoire municipal d'archéologie et d'histoire** (by appointment only; 🕿 05 62 67 82 79) contains items from the village's past.

Return to Auch via the N 124.

THE ARÇON AND THE GIMONE
65km/40mi. Allow around 1h30.

Leave Auch heading E via N 124 towards Toulouse.

The 16C **Château de St-Cricq** is now a reception and conference centre.

Continue along N 124 towards Toulouse.

After 7.5km/4.5mi look for the long south façade of the **Château de Marsan** (18C–19C), owned by the Montesquiou family. At the first roundabout at the entrance to Gimont, turn right on D12 towards Saramon. The chapel is on the right.

Chapelle Notre-Dame-de-Cahuzac
This chateau was built of brick and stone in the 16C to mark the apparition of the Virgin Mary to a young shepherd in 1513. Although small, it has a handsome Gothic portal.

Gimont
The main street of this *bastide* founded in 1266 runs through the old covered market place. Local foie gras can be bought at the marchés au gras on Wednesday and Sunday mornings.
Église – An example of southern Gothic with a toulousain brick belfry. Inside, in the first chapel on the left there is a renaissance triptych of the Crucifixion.
Musée cantonal – 🕘Open mid-Jul–

mid-Aug Tue–Sat 10.30am–12.30pm, 5.30–7.30pm, Sun am only; rest of the year by appointment. No charge. 🕿 05 62 67 71 66. The town museum contains fossile and Gallo-Roman and medieval pieces.
Petit musée de l'Oie et du Canard – In the same building as the restaurant and shop Ducs de Gascogne, Cahuzac roundabout. 🕘Open daily 10am–7pm. No charge. Everything you ever wanted to know about the raising and processing into food of ducks and geese is explained here through photographs, drawings and captions.
Conservatoire de la vie agricole et rurale d'autrefois – R. Pierre-Marcassus, Quartier St-Éloi. 🕘Open daily 10am–noon, 2–6pm by appointment only. 🕿 05 62 67 82 79. A 19C building containing a collection of 900 agricultural tools and other artefacts.

Take D 12 towards Saramon. Turn right towards Boulaur.

Abbaye Sainte Marie de Boulaur
Guided tours Wed–Mon 11am and 4pm. No charge. 🕿 05 62 65 40 07. www.boulaur.org.
This 13C Cistercian abbey has medieval facades, 14C frescoes and a 17C cloister. It's inhabited by nuns who sell homemade snacks and crafts in the shop.

The twisting D 626 leads to Castelnau-Barbarens.

The houses of 12C **Castelnau-Barbarens** radiate in concentric arcs from the church-topped hill.

Drive towards Auch.

On the plateau, D 626 offers a fine **panorama★** of the Pyrenees. The route crosses **Pessan**, an old *sauveté* (a rural township founded by a monastery as a sanctuary for fugitives), which developed around an abbey, founded in the 9C.

ADDRESSES

🛏 STAY

🛏 **Chambre d'hôte Le Castagné** – *Rte de Toulouse, 3200 Auch. ☎06 07 97 40 37. www.domainelecastagne.com. 4 rooms.* Quite a leisure spot with swimming, mini golf, fishing, pedalos; perfect for kids.

🛏 **Chambre d'hôte Le Hou Reste** – *32360 Jégun – 3km/1.8mi W of Jégun on D 103 rte de Vic-Fézensac. ☎05 62 64 51 96. 4 rooms.* This 19C house on a working farm offers small but well appointed guestrooms in a mini-chalet and old dovecot. Flower gardens, orchard and barnyard animals add to the charm.

🛏 **Chambre d'hôte Mme Mengelle** – *Au village, 32360 Jégun. ☎05 62 64 55 03. www.rolande-mengelle.com. Closed Nov–Mar. 5 rooms.* Lovely B&B decorated with tapestries, antique furniture and wallpaper in muted colours.

🛏 **Camping Les Chalets des Mousquetaires** – *32390 Mirepoix. ☎05 62 64 33 66. www.chalets-mousquetaires.com. ⚑. Reservations required; 11 chalets.* Comprising a group of chalets only; breakfast included.

🛏🛏 **Hôtel Le Robinson** – *Rte de Tarbes, 3200 Marciac. ☎05 62 05 02 83. www.hotel robinson.net. Closed Christmas period.* 🅿 *23 rooms.* 1960s hotel set back from the road; some rooms have balconies.

🍽 EAT

🍽🍽 **Le Café Gascon** – *5 r. Lamartine, 3200 Auch. ☎05 62 61 88 08. Closed Tue and Wed.* This small restaurant serves authentic local fare freshly prepared for your order. The speciality café gascon is prepared at table.

🍽🍽 **Le Papillon** – *Le Petit Guilhem, RN 21, 32810 Montaut-les-Crénaux. ☎05 62 65 51 29. www.restaurant-lepapillon.fr.* Offers a substantial and varied menu, a regional taster menu, and Gascon specialties; pleasurable dining experience.

🍽🍽 **La Table d'Oste** – *7 r. Lamartine, 32000 Auch. ☎05 62 05 55 62. www.table-oste-restaurant.com. Closed Sat evening in summer, Mon lunch and Sun.* In the old town, this rustic restaurant across from the covered market and cathedral, is a pleasant venue serving quality regional cuisine.

Marciac★

At any time of year except August, when its famous jazz festival takes over the entire place, Marciac is just another well-to-do bastide in bucolic countryside. The town was founded in the 13C and is distinguished from afar by the elegant spire of its 14C church, Notre-Dame de l'Assomption, pointing 90m into the air.

▶ **Population:** 1 333.
🖐 **Michelin Map:** 336: C8-D8.
🖼 **Info:** 21 pl de l'Hôtel de Ville. ☎05 62 08 26 60. www.marciactourisme.com.
▶ **Location:** 50km/31mi southwest of Auch by N 21 and then D 16.
🖐 **Don't Miss:** The Marciac Jazz Festival in August.

VISIT

The town is laid out on a regular plan around an exceptionally large (75m x 130m) square used to hold a weekly market. The town hall presides over this sqaure and shops, bars and restaurants shelter in its stone arcades. A short walk from the town itself brings you to the shore of the Lac de Marciac, a lake which is used for leisure boating and also has a floating restaurant.

Les Territoires du Jazz

Pl. du Chevalier-d'Antras. 🕐*Open Jul–Aug daily 10am–6pm (7pm during jazz festival); rest of the year by arrangement.* 🎫*€6 (children under 18 €3). ☎05 62 08 26 60.*
Permanent proof of Marciac's association with jazz is provided by this museum which pays homage to the music in all its forms in sound and vision and more static displays.

Jazz in Marciac

For the two weeks in August Marciac is internationally famous. Every night top jazz musicians perform in a marquee. There are free concerts in the square, which is packed with craft stalls and cafe tables, and impromptu performances by wannabes on street corners. The trumpeter Wynton Marsalis has even written a 'Marciac Suite' in honour of the town's contribution to music. *www. jazzinmarciac.com.*

🚗 DRIVING TOUR

BASTIDES AND CASTELNAUX★
77km/48mi. Allow half a day.

This tour explores the bastides and castelnaux typical of the Astarac and the Pardiac, former counties of the duchy of Gascony.

▷ Leave Marciac on D 3 towards Tillac. The château de Pallanne on the left has been transformed into a hotel and golf course.

Tillac★
This small *castelnau* has picturesque half-timbered houses and a fortified tower with a 14C **church**.

▷ Return to Mirande along D 16 and N 21.

Mirande
The lively town of Mirande is one of France's most characteristic south-western **bastides**, founded in 1281 by the Abbé de Berdoues Bernard VII, Comte d'Astarac, and Eustache de Beaumarchés. The village retains its chessboard symmetry, at the centre of which is a covered market 'place à couverts'. Stroll through the **place d'Astarac** and **rue de l'Évêché** to see period half-timbered houses. The turreted belfry of early 15C **Église Sainte-Marie** sanc-

tuary provided shelter to *bastide* defenders. Its tower is pierced by openwork Gothic bays. The **Musée des Beaux-Arts★** *(13 ru de l'Évêché; ℘05 62 66 52 87; &open Mon–Fri 9am–noon, 2–6pm; Sat 10am–noon, 3–6pm),* founded by Joseph Delort, contains antique ceramics, 17C–19C glazed earthenware and porcelain from such renowned centres as Moustiers, Samadet, Dax and Nevers, plus 15C–19C paintings.

▷ Take D 943 on the right.

The route crosses **L'Isle-de-Noé** village and its 18C château.

▷ Take the D 943 jon the right towards Barran.

Barran
This *bastide* on the site of an earlier ecclesiastical settlement has a church with an ingeniously spiralling spire.

▷ Return to L'Isle-de-Noé; continue W.

Montesquiou
This *castelnau* rises on a spur high above the vallée de l'Osse. A gateway on the main street is all that remains of the 13C outer wall. Close by is a picturesque row of half-timbered houses.

Bassoues★
The 14C **keep★** (open daily Jul–Aug 10am–7pm; Mar–Apr and Oct 1.30–6pm; May–Jun and Sept 10.30am–noon, 2–6pm; closed Nov–Feb; ℘05 62 70 97 34; www.bassoues.net) is a magnificent example of military architecture, and its rooms contain exhibitions tracing the evolution of Gascon villages.
The top-floor platform, where round watchtowers rise between the terrace and the top of the buttresses, offers a good **view★** to the northeast.
The village **church** was remodelled in the 16C and 19C and contains a fine 15C stone pulpit. D 946 now descends, via a 12km/7mi **crest route★**, to the Rivière Basse depression, with views through the Adour gap to the Pyrenees.

St-Christaud

The village **church** facing the distant Pyrenees features square windows, between buttresses, set in a diamond shape.

▷ The D 159 and D 943 lead to Marciac.

LOWER RIVER REGION
45km/28mi. Allow around 2h.

▷ Leave Mariac to the NW via the D 3.

Beaumarchés

This royal *bastide* was founded in 1288 as the result of a *contrat de paréage*, requiring that a lesser noble hands over part of his revenue to a greater noble in return for protection. The Gothic church has a striking massive appearance and 15C porch. A frieze of carved male and female heads runs around the upper gallery.

▷ Drive to Plaisance, turn left onto D 946 to Préhac-sur-Adour then left again onto D 173.

Mazères

Note the Romanesque **church** with gable belfry flanked by buttresses. The chancel retains its Romanesque capitals and a special marble reliquary (1342) for pilgrims.

▷ Take the D 935 again and turn right on the D 58 towards Madiran.

Madiran

The main grape variety used to make the strong dark red wines of the Madiran appellation is tannat, a black grape which is high in tannin. The town of Madiran holds a fete du vin in August and on one weekend after the harvest. The 11C–12C church has carved capitals around the altar and a crypt below.

▷ Rejoin D 935 and head towards Maubourguet.

Maubourguet

This town stands astride the Adour river and its tributary the Echez. It is a stop on the long distance footpath GR 653, part of the Road to Santiago de Compostela from Arles in Provence. The Romanesque church was built in the 11C and its portal dates from the following century. A new museum houses a Roman mosaic of the God of the Oceans unearthed in a villa nearby.

▷ From Maubourguet return to Marciac on D 943.

THE LAND OF THE MUSKETEERS
72km/45mi. Allow 2h.
🔾*See regional map.*

▷ Leave Marciac to the NW on the D 3.

Termes d'Armagnac

Only the keep remains from the castle built by Thibaut de Termes (1405–67), companion of arms of Joan of Arc at the siege of Orleans

▷ Take D 48 NE. Turn left on D 111.

Sabazan

The Romanesque church with a stout square tower dates from the 11C–12C.

▷ Continue on the D 48 to Aignan.

Aignan

An ancient town which was the seat of the Gascon parliament. It is now a wine town. Parts of the church are 12C.

▷ Leave Aignan on D 20 turn right on D 174. Join D 102, turning right.

Lupiac

The supposed true-life d'Artagnan came from this village. An interesting museum recounts his life and puts it in context. Outside the village is a lake with a sandy beach which serves as an indoor swimming resort.

▷ Take D 37 towards Plaisance and turn left on D 3 to return to Marciac.

Eauze

The ancient Roman town of Elusa – the inhabitants of Eauze are still called Elusates – and capital of the Bas Armagnac region made the headlines in 1985 when a remarkable treasure was found which is now displayed in the archaeological museum. The old town is contained within a ring of small boulevards. One unusual sight beyond the centre is the chateau d'eau imperial (down Avenue des Pyrénées), a monumental water deposit built under Napoleon III.

▶ **Population:** 3 956.
Michelin Map: 336: C6.
Info: 2 rue Felix Soulès.
℘ 05 62 09 85 62.
www.tourisme-eauze.fr.
▶ **Location:** 58km/36mi northwest of Auch on N 124.
Don't Miss: Treasure of Eaux in Musée Archéologique.

VISIT
Place d'Armagnac

This picturesque square is the heart of the town. On it stands two half-timbered buildings. One is the tourist information office. The other is the Maison de Jeanne d'Albret, its façade raised on wooden pillars, where king Henri IV and his queen Marguerite de Valois stayed as guests in 1579. Today it is a café–restaurant.

Cathédrale Saint-Luperc

A fine example of the southern Gothic style, Eauze's cathedral dedicated to Saint Luperculus was built over the site of a Cluniac monastery in the 15C. Inside, its structure can be seen in its bare walls which mix stone and brick. Some of the materials are believed to have been recycled from Roman buildings. Eauze is a halt on the Vie Podensis pilgrimage route to Santiago de Compostela.

Musée Archéologique ★

Pl. de la République. ⚓🕐*Open Mar– Nov daily 10am–noon, 2–6pm (Jul–Aug daily 10am–7pm).* ⊕€4.50.
℘05 62 09 71 38.
The highlight of the museum is the **Treasure of Eauze**. In 261, the Libo family, well to do Gallo-roman possibly of Etruscan origin, worried about the insecurity of the region at time hid their treasure (jewellery, bronze, silver and gold coins) in leather sacks. It is presented as it was discovered in the ground. Particular highlights

include golden necklaces set with precious stones (emeralds, garnets, saphires) pearls, bracelets rings and a knife with an ivory handle sculpted to represent the god Bacchus.

Itinéraire à Grand Gabarit

⊕*For details of convoys see www.igg.fr.*
Outside the town to the south, on the D 931 towards Nogaro, there is a large fenced and gated compound beside the road. This is a lorry park for Airbus convoys which transport massive pieces of aircraft fuselage and wings from the Garonne at Langon to the assembly plant in Toulouse. The convoys move on a specially adapted route, the *itinéraire à grand gabarit* or (Wide Vehicle Route, IGG) overnight at designated times.

EXCURSIONS
Barbotan-les-Thermes

23km/14mi NW of Eauze by D 626.
Unlike other spas, this one specialises in a 'vegeto-mineral' rich mud.
The 12C church has an arched gateway through which passes the avenue des Thermes.

Nogaro

17km/10.5mi SW of Eauze on D931.
Nogaro is best known for three sporting facilities: the Paul-Armagnac motor racing circuit; an aerodrome used by gliders; and the bull ring. The 12C Romanesque Église Saint-Nicolas has murals inside showing scenes from the life of St Lawrence and Christ in majesty.

Condom★

*Wine country, Vallée de l'Ossé,
Vallée d'Auzoue*

Condom is the main town in the Armagnac region, an area with many attractive rural churches and manor houses. The old mansions of Condom itself give the town a typically Gascon appearance. Its economic activities – selling grain and Armagnac, flour-milling and the timber industry – are also the traditional activities of the region. The River Baïse, stretching alongside the old quays, was channelled long ago to transport brandy to Bordeaux.

▶ **Population:** 7 296.
⏱ **Michelin Map:** 336: E-6.
🅘 **Info:** 5 Place Saint-Pierre. ℘05 62 28 00 80. www.tourisme-condom.com.
◗ **Location:** 45km/28mi N of d'Auch.
👁 **Don't Miss:** La cathédrale Saint-Pierre, Fourcès, Larresingle.
👪 **Kids:** La Cité des machines du Moyen Age in Larresingle.

🐾WALKING TOUR

1h30. Start by visiting the cathedral on place St-Pierre.

Cathédrale St-Pierre★

The belfry rises majestically above the cathedral, one of the last in the Gers region built (1507–31) in the Gothic style of South-West France. The Flamboyant Gothic south door still has 24 small statues in the niches of the archivolt. The nave is illuminated by windows with Flamboyant tracery, and the **cloisters★** feature attractive keystones on the polychrome vaulting.

Chapelle des Évêques

The chapel built in Gothic style has a Renaissance doorway surmounted by a baldaquin window.

◗ Walk along rue Lannelongue to rue Jules-Ferry.

On the right stand the former bishop's stables, now the Musée de l'Armagnac.

Musée de l'Armagnac

2 r Jules-Ferry. ◷Open Apr–Oct Mon, Wed–Sat 3–6pm. ◷Closed 1 Jan, 1 May, 25 Dec. ☜€2.20. ℘05 62 28 47 17. www.condom.org.
This museum contains rare vine-growers' tools and machinery – an 18t press and a grape-crushing roller, cooper's tools and bottle samples produced by Gascon gentlemen-glassmakers and various stills.

◗ Continue down rue Jules-Ferry.

Hôtel de Polignac

This 18C building now houses a school It has a classical facade of columns, tall windows and ornate wrought ironwork.

◗ Turn round and take the rue Gaichies. From place du Lion-d'Or, take rue Honoré-Cazaubon.

Rue Honoré-Cazaubon

There are several handsome mansions (hôtels particuliers) along this road. No. 11 is Empire style. The Hôtel de Galard (No. 10) is from the time of Louis XV.

◗ Turn left off rue Honoré-Cazaubon down rue Saint Exupéry.

College Salvandy

A the end of the street on the right, step into the courtyard of the **collège Salvandy** to see its handsome Gothic staircase tower and the doors to the classrooms marked with inscriptions: 'rhetoric', 'philosophy' and so on.

◗ At the end of the rue Saint-Exupéry, turn right on the street known as le 'Cours' (avenue du Général-de-Gaulle the prolongatation of rue Jean-Jaurès).

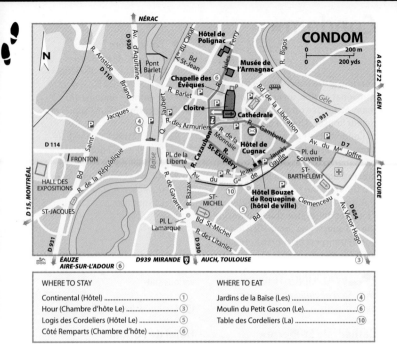

WHERE TO STAY		WHERE TO EAT	
Continental (Hôtel)	①	Jardins de la Baïse (Les)	④
Hour (Chambre d'hôte Le)	③	Moulin du Petit Gascon (Le)	⑥
Logis des Cordeliers (Hôtel Le)	⑤	Table des Cordeliers (La)	⑩
Côté Remparts (Chambre d'hôte)	⑥		

Le Cours

Avenue du Général-de-Gaulle and rue Jean-Jaurès.

After the noble **hôtel de Cugnac** comes the **hôtel Bouzet de Roquepine**, both from the 18C, the latter housing Condom's town hall.

Maison Ryst-Dupeyron (Hôtel de Cugnac)

In the hôtel de Cugnac, 1 rue Daunou. ♿ ☞Guided visits (1hr) Mon–Fri: 9am–12 noon, 2–5pm (Jul–Aug daily). ☞No charge. ℘05 62 28 08 08. http://maisonrystdupeyron.com.

Armagnacs and other fine wines are made by this prestigious Condom company. Its cellars, dating from the 18C, can be visited. There is also an audiovisual show.

▶ To return to your starting point at the cathedral continue along Avenue du Général de Gaulle/rue Jean Jaurès to the place du Souvenir and turn left down rue Léon-Gambetta. (The tourist information office is a short way beyond place du Souvenir.)

As you enter the place St-Pierre you have a splendid view of the apse and the cloister of the cathedral. Go across the square to the start of rue Charron.

Hôtel de Bourran

This beautiful hôtel on rue Charron was built in the 18C. It has an elegant balcony.

EXCURSION
La Romieu★

11km/6.6mi E on D 931 and D 41.

The entrance to the late 12C to early 13C **collegiate church★** is through the cloisters, with their interesting (though damaged) decorative motifs and through a doorway beneath a machicolated arch. The octagonal **eastern tower** stands apart. 14C murals may still be seen in the sacristy – 16 angels adorn the vaulting. A spiral staircase (153 steps) leads up to the platform which provides good views of the rooftops of the village, the belfry-tower and the cloisters.

Condom with Cathédrale St-Pierre

© C. Goupi/age fotostock

🚗 DRIVING TOURS

VALLÉES DE L'OSSÉ AND D'AUZOUE
Round trip 40km/25mi W of Condom. Allow half a day.

▶ Leave Condom via D 15 towards Montréal.

Larressingle★
The walls of this 13C fortified village surround a ruined three-storey keep, a Romanesque church and a few restored houses. The **Cité des machines du Moyen-Âge** reconstructs a 13C siege camp with machines like the trebuchet which fired cannon balls weighing over 100kg at a target 220m away.

Montréal-du-Gers
One of the earliest to be built in Gascony (1256), this *bastide* over the River Auzoue valley has a fortified Gothic church and a main square bordered by houses with arcades. The **Musée archéologique** exhibits pottery, iron objects, and Merovingian buckles found at Séviac (&🕓 *open Jun–Sep Wed–Mon 10am–12.30pm, 2–6pm, Feb–May and Oct–Dec 2–5pm;* 🕓 *closed Jan and public holidays;* ✆ *05 62 29 52 00).*

▶ Follow signs W of Montréal to reach Séviac.

Séviac, Gallo-Roman villa★
🕓 *Closed for renovation. Re-opens 2018. www.elusa.fr.*
Archaeological excavations here reveal the foundations of a fabulous 4C Gallo-Roman villa with pool and baths richly decorated with coloured marble and ornate mosaics, and vestiges of paleo-Christian and Merovingian buildings, indicating permanent occupation from the 2C to the 7C.

▶ D 29, N out of Montréal, follows the course of the River Auzoue.

Fourcès★
A small bridge across the Auzoue, bordered by a 15C and 16C castle, leads to this picturesque *bastide* founded by

Armagnac
Armagnac is always served after a meal, at room temperature, in special glasses which allow the elixir to be warmed with the palms to release the bouquet.
Three main grades are determined by age: the 3-star or 3-crown Armagnac spends at least 18 months in a cask; the VO (Very Old) and VSOP (Very Superior Old Pale) a minimum of four and a half years and the XO, Hors d'âge, Napoléon and Extra must be over five and a half years old.

the English in the 13C. The unusual village with its circular ground plan still has half-timbered houses with stone or wood arcades, around a large shaded main square with a stone cross in the centre.

▶ Return to Condom via D 114.

WINE COUNTRY

Round trip 50km/31mi. Allow half a day. Leave Condom via D 931 SW.

This tour, best in autumn when vines are golden brown, encompasses Armagnac's wine country and châteaux where visitors can taste and buy.

Mouchan

The village's Romanesque **church** dates back to the 10C.

▶ Go to Cassaigne Château via D 208.

Château de Cassaigne

♿ *Guided visits: mid-Jun–mid-Sept 9am–noon, 2–7pm; rest of year daily except Mon, 9am–noon, 2–6pm. Closed Dec 25, 1 Jan. ℘05 62 28 04 02. www.chateaudecassaigne.com.*

This 13C castle was the country residence of the bishops of Condom. Visit cellars where Armagnac is aged in oak barrels, the 16C kitchen filled with tin and copper kitchen utensils, earthenware and solid wood furniture and enjoy an Armagnac tasting session.

▶ Take D 229 towards Lagardère, then turn right after 4.5km/3mi.

Château du Busca-Maniban

Apr–Oct: guided tours (45min) daily except Sun and public holidays 2–6pm. ☞€6. ℘05 62 28 40 38. www.buscamaniban.com.

This two-storey castle features a remarkably majestic hall, monumental staircase, Italian Room with fine furniture and 15C chapel. From the terrace you can gaze across to the Pyrenees.

▶ Return to Cassaigne.

On the way down, vine-covered hillsides overlook the Mansecôme Castle ruins.

▶ At Cassaigne, turn right on D 142.

Abbaye de Flaran★

Open Jul–Aug 9.30am–7pm; rest of year 9.30am–12.30pm, 2–6pm. Closed 1 Jan, 2 weeks in Jan, 1 May and 25 Dec. ☞€5 (no charge 1st Sunday in the month Nov–Mar). ℘05 62 28 50 19. www.patrimoine-musees-gers.fr.

The abbey on the outskirts of Valence-sur-Baïse was founded in 1151 as the Cistercian Order expanded throughout Gascony. It is now a **cultural centre** hosting concerts, exhibitions and seminars.

The abbey's façade contains a lovely rose window. The 18C **living quarters** of the Prior have the charm of a small Gascon château. The **abbey church** built between 1180 and 1210 comprises a nave surmounted by broken-barrel vaulting. Of the four original cloister galleries, only that on the west side (early 14C) remains today. The **monastic buildings** extend from the northern arm of the transept. The **armarium** or library is entered via the **chapter-house** containing columns of beautiful Pyrenees marble. The **monks' common room** and **storeroom** contain an exhibition on the Santiago de Compostela pilgrimage with maps, sculptures, and pilgrims' funerary crosses. A stone staircase leads to the **monks' dormitory**, which was converted into separate cells in the 17C. Enjoy the French formal **garden** and garden of medicinal and aromatic plants.

Valence-sur-Baïse

This *bastide* resulted from a 1274 feudal contract giving equal rights to the Abbot of Flaran and Comte Géraud V d'Armagnac. At the confluence of the River Baïse and River Auzoue, the town square contains a 14C church.

▶ Leave Valence via D 232 N to visit the ruins of Château de Tauzia on a small road to the left.

Château de Tauzia

This modest 13C fortress with two side towers is now in ruins.

▶ Go back to D 142 via Maignaut-Tauzia. Turn left on D 42 to St-Puy.

Château Monluc

Guided tours (1hr): Feb–Jun and mid-Sept–Dec Tue–Sat 10am–noon, 3–7pm; Jul–mid-Sept Mon–Sat 10am–noon, 3–7pm, Sun and public holidays 3–7pm. ⏱*Closed Jan, 1 May, 25 Dec.* *No charge.* ☎*05 62 28 94 00. www.monluc.fr.*

For centuries France and England fought over the medieval fortress of St-Puy, once owned by the illustrious Maréchal Blaïse de Monluc. Château Monluc originated **pousse-rapière** (rapier thrust), a precious liqueur made by soaking fruit in Armagnac. Tour the vaulted cellars to learn how the drink is made.

▶ Follow D 654 towards Condom then turn right onto D 232 to St-Orens.

St-Orens-Pouy-Petit

St-Orens is a fortified village perched on a hill. A ramparts gateway leads to the promontory and castle.

▶ Return to Condom via D 654.

Béraut

Musée d'Art naïf – *Château d'Ensoulès.* ⏱*Open daily except Mon–Tue: May–Oct 10am–1pm, 2–7pm; Nov–Dec, and Feb–Apr 10am–1pm, 2–5pm.* ⏱*Closed Jan.* €5. ☎*05 62 68 49 87. www.123musees.fr.* A vast collection of naïve paintings by international artists is displayed in the Château d'Ensoulès.

ADDRESSES

🛏STAY

🛏 **Hôtel Continental** – *20 r. du Mar.-Foch, 32100 Condom.* ☎*05 62 68 37 00. www.le continental.net. Closed 20–27 Dec. 25 rooms. Restaurant*🍴. Early 20C hotel, close to la Baïse, completely renovated

modern rooms, soundproofing and air conditioning.

🛏 **Chambre d'hôte le Hour** – *32100 Béraut.* ☎*05 62 68 48 33 or 06 85 63 96 03. www.le-hour.com. 5 rooms. Restaurant* 🍴🛏. The rooms are decorated with an astute collection of old things; swimming pool and games for children.

🛏🛏 **Chambre d'hôte Côté Remparts** – *7 r. Jules Ferry.* ☎*05 62 28 38 97 or 06 70 95 36 22. http://cote-remparts.com. 2 rooms.* Visitors can choose between a romantic room and a family-sized suite in the old town. Pretty and comfortable, with a garden and swimming pool.

🛏🛏 **Hôtel Le Logis des Cordeliers** – *R. de la Paix, 32100 Condom.* ☎*05 62 28 03 68. www.logisdescordeliers.com. Closed 2 Jan–3 Feb.* 🅿. *21 rooms.* Located in a quiet part of the town centre; some rooms have balconies overlooking the swimming pool.

🍴EAT

🍴🛏 **La Table des Cordeliers** – *1 r. des Cordeliers, 32000 Condom.* ☎*05 62 68 43 82. www.latabledescordeliers.com. Closed Sun eve and Mon.* Close to the Logis des Cordeliers (*see above*), the restaurant occupies a 14C chapel. A lovely place to eat in summer, under majestic Gothic arches, illuminated by stained glass windows. Cuisine is based on what is available at the market; menu changes daily.

🍴🛏 **Les Jardins de la Baïse** – *20 r. du Mar.-Foch, 32000 Condom.* ☎*05 62 68 37 00. www.lecontinental.net. Closed Sat lunch, Sun eve and Mon.* The Hotel Continental's restaurant has a large dining room with views over the Baïse. It serves a wide selection of regional specialities.

🍴🛏 **Le Moulin du Petit Gascon** – *Rte d'Eauze, chemin de l'Argenté.* ☎*05 62 28 28 42. Closed Thu mid-Jul–Aug, Sun eve and Mon off season and Nov–Mar.* Nestling alongside the Baïse, this old mill serves lovely, appetising food in the charming original building.

ACTIVITIES

👥 **Gascogne Navigation***Quai de la Bouquerie, 32000 Condom.* ☎*05 62 28 46 46. www.gascogne-navigation.com. Cruises Jul–Aug daily 3pm; Apr–Jun and Sept–Oct Sun 3pm. Lunch on board available by previous booking.* Leisurely cruises (some with dining included) on the green and peaceful river Baïse on board the *Artagnan.*

Lectoure★

On the site of an ancient Gaulish settlement, the former principal residence of the counts of Armagnache and now capital of the Lomagne region occupies a remarkable site★ on a promontory overlooking the Gers valley. It has a number of handsome 18C *hôtels particulars* along its streets which can be visited on a guided tour by arrangement with the tourist information office.
On the outskirts of town is a shop selling products made from the traditional blue dye of woad.

- **Population:** 4 139.
- **Michelin Map:** 336 F6.
- **Info:** Place du Général de Gaulle. ℘05 62 68 76 98. www.tourisme-lectoure.fr.
- **Location:** 37km/23mi north of Auch.
- **Don't Miss:** Musée Archeologique.

SIGHTS
Cathédrale St Gervais-St Protais

Built in the 13C, essentially in southern Gothic style, the cathedral was damaged in a siege of the town by Louis XI in 1473. It now contains a museum of sacred art. The 240 steps up the 45 m tower can be ascended on a 30min guided tour *(by arrangement with the tourist information office)* for a superb view.

Ancien Palais Episcopal and Musée Archeologique E. Camoreyt ★

Guided tours (1hr) by arrangement with Lectoure town hall. ℘05 62 68 70 22.

The former bishop's palace (17C) on the main square of Lectoure contains an archeological museum, a reproduction 19C chemist's shop and the 'Ill Salles': three rooms dedicated to the memory of local celebrities produced by the town. The museum is renowned for its collection of 20 taurobolia.
These pagan altars, carved with the heads of bulls and rams date from the 2C or 3C and are believed to have been used in the cult of Mithra and Cybele. They had been incorporated into the ramparts of the town and were discovered in 1540 beneath the cathedral.

Fontaine Diane

The ancient rue Fontélie lined with ochre-coloured houses, runs down to the 13C Fontaine Diane enclosed by a 15C wrought-iron railing.

EXCURSIONS
Fleurance

10km/6mi south on N21.

A 13C bastide named after the city of Florence. The Eglise Saint Laurent is a beautiful example of southern Gothic, the façade dominated by an octagonal belfry rising through three storeys from the top of a square tower. There are three Renaissance stained glass windos in the apse. The work of Arnaud de Moles (responsible for the windows in Auch cathedral) who made them between 1507 and 1513. A little way from Fleurance is the Ferme des Etoiles a rural astronomical observatory.

🚗 DRIVING TOUR

CHÂTEAUX AND VILLAGES DE LOMAGNE

79km/49mi. Allow 2h.
See regional map.

Leave Lectoure north on N 21. After 7km/5mi turn left for St-Avit-Frandat.

Château de Lacassagne

A fine 17C country house (with some older parts) standing in English-style grounds.

From St-Avit-Frandat, take the little road to Frandat. Cross over N 21 and continue E to Castet-Arrouy. Turn N on D 23 to Miradoux, a 13C castelnau with a large church. Take D 953 N towards Flamerens.

Flamerens
The old château fort here has been restored.

Continue on D 953 N. Turn right on D 3 to Mansonville and left on D 11 at Caubel passing La Motte chateau at Bardigues and passing under the motorway.

Auvillar★
The old town is entered through an arched gateway. In the centre is a circular corn exchange.

Retrace your steps S on D 11 but continue to Lachappelle.

Beaumont-de-Lomagne

The capital of white garlic – a festival is held here in July – Beaumont-de-Lomagne, like other bastides, is built on a geometric plan centering on a large square in which stands an immense market hall. It has an imposing brick church and several half-timbered houses. Beaumont was the birthplace of Pierre de Fermat (1601–65), the mathematician whose famous last theorem, written in the margin of a book, took 385 years to solve.

EXCURSIONS
Mauvezin
20km/12mi SW.
Because of its strong leanings towards Protestantism, Mauvezin was once dubbed 'the Little Geneva'. It has an upper and lower town, the former built around a large square and 14C market

Lachappelle
It is worth stopping to see the Baroque church with its wooden galleries.

Continue S down D 11, passing a château at Marsac, then D 18. Saint-Creac is just to the right of the road.

Saint-Creac
The church here contains Greco-Byzantine mosaics.

Continue on D 18 then D 13.

Saint-Clar
A combination of old town (12C) and bastide (13C) each with its arcaded square and church.

Take 953 to L'Isle Bouzon where there is a circular dovecote then D 7, heading back to Lectoure and rejoining N 21 S just before the town.

- **Population:** 3 997.
- **Michelin Map:** 337 B8.
- **Info:** 5 rue Fermat (Maison Fermat) 82500 Beaumont-de-Lomagne. 05 63 02 42 32. www.tourisme.malomagne.com.
- **Location:** 52km/32mi northeast of Auch by N124 and D928.
- **Don't Miss:** The excursion to Cologne.

hall, being the more interesting. There is also an austere Protestant church dating from the 17C.

Cologne
29km/18mi S by D 928 and D 654.
Although only a small place, this 13C bastide has an exquisite central square, possibly the prettiest of the Gers, with half-timbered houses looking onto a quaint market hall.

MONTAUBAN *and Around*

At first sight, what best defines the department of Tarn-et-Garonne is speedy communication links. It straddles the all-important corridor of the Garonne river which carries a canal, a motorway and a railway main line between Toulouse and Bordeaux, between the Midi and the Atlantic. A north–south motorway forks off at Montauban, the department's capital and third city of the southwest, to Orléans and ultimately Paris. All of which gives the impression of modernity and movement. But step away from the river and you are soon deep in countryside. To the south (the Lomagne) and north (Quercy Blanc) are low hills with barely a sizeable town to be seen. In the west, meanwhile, the river Aveyron approaches its confluence with the Tarn through a magnificent wooded gorge.

Highlights

1 Walk around the old town of **Montauban** (p458)

2 Check out the Romanesque art in **Moissac** (p462)

3 Visit the château in **Bruniquel** (p464)

4 Make time to see **Saint Antonin-Noble-Val** (p465)

5 Explore the **gorges de l'Aveyron** (p467)

Rightful Due

Unlike most of the other French departments which were created in 1790 by the National Assembly, Tarn-et-Garonne wasn't constituted until 1808. Napoleon I was on his way back from Toulouse with Josephine and he spent most of 29 July in Montauban, sightseeing on horseback. He was given a triumphal reception and on his departure he declared 'I am pleased with the love shown to me by loyal subjects of Montauban. I have seen the loss you have suffered and I will restore your rights. You will become the capital of a department and I will put you in the top rank of the cities of my empire'. Four months later an imperial decree created the Tarn-et-Garonne out of bits of the neighbouring *départements*.

Old and New

The two aspects of the department – rurality cut through by a modern transport artery – can be pleasing and jarring in turns. Coming down from the tranquilty of hills into the Garonne valley you are greeted by the sight of the cooling towers of the Golfech Nuclear Power Station. The building of an extension of the TGV network from Bordeaux to Toulouse via Montauban will bring a further dose of modernity to the region. Yet always within a short hop are fruit orchards and vineyards – some of them, near Moissac, producing the renowned Chasselas table grapes.

Château de Bruniquel.

©Yvann K/Fotolia.com

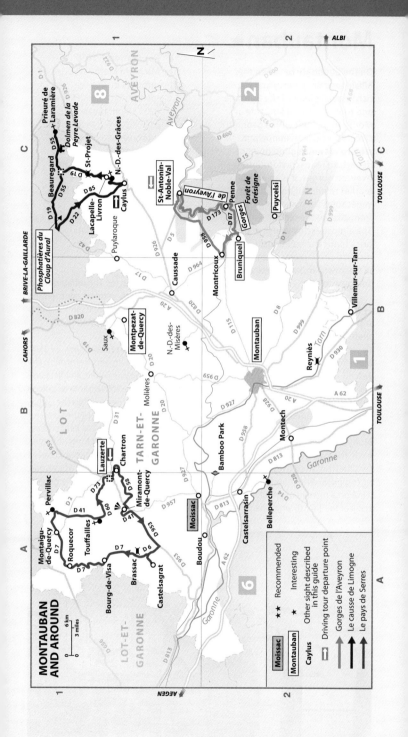

MONTAUBAN AND AROUND

0   3 miles
0   6 km

Moissac — Recommended
Montauban — Interesting
Caylus — Other sight described in this guide
— Driving tour departure point

Gorges de l'Aveyron
Le causse de Limogne
Le pays de Serres

N↗

ALBI

TOULOUSE

AEGEN

TOULOUSE

CAHORS

BRIVE-LA-GAILLARDE

AVEYRON

TARN

LOT

TARN-ET-GARONNE

LOT-ET-GARONNE

Prieuré de Laramière
Dolmen de la Peyre Levade
Beauregard
St-Projet
N.-D.-des-Grâces
Phosphatières du Cloup d'Aural
Lacapelle-Livron
Puylaroque
Caylus
St-Antonin-Noble-Val
Penne
Forêt de Grésigne
Puycelsi
Gorges de l'Aveyron
Caussade
Montricoux
Bruniquel
Villemur-sur-Tarn
Saux
Montpezat-de-Quercy
N.-D.-des-Misères
Montauban
Reyniès
Montech
Bamboo Park
Garonne
Lauzerte
Chartron
Miramont-de-Quercy
Molières
Moissac
Boudou
Castelsarrasin
Belleperche
Pervillac
Montaigu-de-Quercy
Roquecor
Touffailles
Brassac
Bourg-de-Visa
Castelsagrat

8

2

1

6

Montauban★

On the boundary between the hillsides of Bas Quercy and the rich alluvial plains of the Garonne and the Tarn, the old bastide of Montauban, built with a geometric street layout, is an important crossroads and a good point of departure for excursions into the Aveyron gorges. It is an active market town, selling fruit and vegetables from market gardens from all over the region.
The almost exclusive use of pink brick lends the buildings here a distinctive character, found in most of the towns in Bas Quercy and the Toulouse area.

- **Population:** 59 630.
- **Michelin Map:** 337: E-7.
- **Info:** 4 R. du Collège (pedestrian access Pl. Prax), 82002 Montauban. ☎05 63 63 60 60. www.montauban-tourisme.com.
- **Location:** Administrative headquarters of the Tarn-et-Garonne *département*, Montauban is served by the A 20.
- **Don't Miss:** The Musée Ingres; La place Nationale.

A BIT OF HISTORY

A powerful stronghold – In the 8C, there were already several communities on the site of the modern suburb of Moustier, on a hillside overlooking the Tescou. A Benedictine monastery was later established, around which a village called Montauriol grew up. The present town was founded in the 12C. Fed up with being exploited by the Abbot of Montauriol and the neighbouring feudal lords, the town's inhabitants sought protection from their overlord, the Count of Toulouse, who founded a bastide in 1144 on a plateau overlooking the east bank of the Tarn to which he accorded a liberal town charter. The inhabitants of Montauriol flocked there, contributing to its rapid expansion. Its name, *Mons albanus*, later became Montauban.

A Citadel of Protestantism – By 1561, most of the town was Reformist; the two town consuls were Calvinists and encouraged the inhabitants to pillage churches and convents, while the Catholic reaction failed to check the surge for reform. By the time of the Peace Treaty of St-Germain in 1570, Montauban was a safe refuge for Protestants. Henri of Navarre reinforced its fortifications, and it was on this site that the general meeting of all the reformed churches in France was held on three occasions.

Montauban by the River Tarn

©nougaro/Fotolia.com

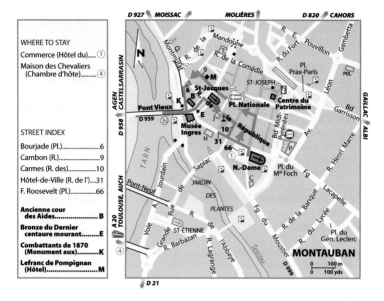

The accession of Louis XIII heralded a 'Catholic reconquest'. In 1621, Montauban was besieged by 20 000 men, under the direct command of the king and his favourite, De Luynes. The townspeople resisted, repelling three assaults. Success was short-lived, and when La Rochelle fell in 1628, Montauban, the last bastion of Protestantism, saw Louis XIII's army marching on it again. This time, the town acquiesced peacefully.

☙WALKING TOUR

OLD TOWN★

Restorations have made the historic centre a pleasure to stroll through. At the heart of the town is **Place Nationale★**, the starting point for this walk. Every morning the square comes to life with a busy, colourful market. The arcades were rebuilt in brick in the 17C to replace the wooden *couverts* destroyed by fires in 1614 and 1649. The pink-brick houses surrounding this beautiful square have high façades divided into bays by pilasters. On the corner of rue Malcousinat is a drapers' measure on the first pillar.

▷ Head W towards Rue Cambon.

Famous Local Artists

Born in 1780, **Jean Auguste Dominique Ingres,** son of a minor painter and craftsman, attended the studio of the Toulouse painter Roques. He spent nearly 20 years in Italy before opening a studio and founding a school in Paris. **Ingres** achieved a purity of line verging on technical perfection, while imbuing his works with personality and sensuality. Ingres won considerable recognition and glory before his death aged 87, when a major part of his work was bequeathed to his home town (*see Musée Ingres*).

Also born in Montauban, **Antoine Bourdelle** (1861–1929) owes much to his master, Rodin. His busts and sculpted groups combine strong energetic poses with simplicity of line and noble sentiment.

Rue Cambon

Hôtel Lefranc de Pompignan boasts a handsome brick **doorway★**. In the courtyard of No. 12 is an elegant wooden gallery supported by a stone colonnade.

▷ Turn left at the end of the street, then left again.

Place Léon-Bourjade

The brasserie terrace offers a good view of the **Pont-Vieux** spanning the Tarn.

Pont-Vieux

Built in the 14C by architects Étienne de Ferrières and Mathieu de Verdun, the 205m long Pont-Vieux spans the Tarn in seven arches resting on piers protected by cutwaters. Like the Pont Valentré in Cahors, it was also fortified.

Musée Ingres★

19 r. de l'Hôtel-de-Ville. ◑*Open Jul–Sept daily 10am–6pm; Nov–Mar Tue–Sat 10am–noon, 2–6pm, Sun 2–6pm; Apr–Jun daily except Mon 10am–noon, 2–6pm; Oct daily 10am–noon, 2–6pm.* ◑*Closed 1 Jan, 1 May, 1 Nov, 25 Dec.* ◉€7. ℘05 63 22 12 91.

The museum is housed in what used to be the bishops' palace, built in 1664 on the site of two castles. The first castle, called the 'Château-bas,' was built in the 12C by the Count of Toulouse. Demolished in 1229, it was replaced a century later by another fortress, built on the orders of the Black Prince, of which a few rooms still remain. The current palace was bought by the municipality when the diocese was suppressed at the time of the Revolution and converted to a museum in 1843. It is an imposing, sober pink-brick edifice.

The **works** of Ingres are the museum's main attraction. His admirable canvas *Jesus among the Doctors* was completed when he was 82. There are numerous sketches, academic studies, **portraits** – of Gilbert, Madame Gonse, Belvèze – and *Ossian's Dream*, executed in 1812 for Napoleon's bedchamber in Rome. A glass display contains the master's paintbox and famous violin, and 4 000 of his **drawings** in rotation.

Other museum highlights are works by primitive schools and **paintings from the 14C to 18C**, 15C Italian works, 17C Flemish paintings (Jordaens, Van Dyck), Dutch and Spanish (José de Ribera)

schools and the sculptures of **Bourdelle**. In the surviving part of the 14C castle, vaulted rooms display **regional archaeology**, **local history**, **applied arts** and temporary exhibitions.

Opposite the Musée Ingres stands the admirable bronze **The Last of the Centaurs Dies★** by Bourdelle (1914) and on quai de Montmurat, the 1870 War Memorial showing Bourdelle's architectural capacities.

Ancienne Cour des Aides

This beautiful 17C building which once housed the Court of Excise Taxes contains the museum of natural history. **Musée Victor Brown** – *First floor, 2 pl. Antoine-Bourdelle.* ◑*Open daily except Mon 10am–noon, 2–6pm (Sun 2–6pm).* ◑*Closed public holidays.* ◉*2.50€, no charge 1st Sunday in the month.* ℘05 63 22 13 85. Several rooms contain a variety of zoological exhibits and a huge ornithological collection including exotic parrots, humming birds and birds of Paradise.

Église St-Jacques

The tower façade of this fortified church dedicated to St James still bears traces of cannonballs fired during the 1621 siege. The **belfry** resting on a machicolated square tower dates from the late 13C. It is built of brick on an octagonal plan with three rows of windows. The nave was renovated in the 15C and rib vaulting was added in the 18C.

▷ Continue along Rue de la République as far as Rue des Carmes and turn right.

Rue des Carmes

At No. 24, the **Hôtel Mila de Cabarieu** features an interesting red-brick portico with surbased arcades.

▷ Turn right on rue de l'Hôtel-de-Ville.

Rue de l'Hôtel de Ville

Note the late 18C Hôtel Sermet-Deymie with an entrance doorway flanked by four Ionic columns.

◗ Retrace your steps; follow Rue du Dr-Lacaze.

Cathédrale Notre-Dame-de-l'Assomption

The cathedral is a classical building of vast proportions. The façade, framed by two square towers, has an imposing peristyle supporting colossal statues of the four Evangelists.

Place Franklin-Roosevelt

Next to a handsome building decorated with caryatids, the Passage du Vieux-Palais links two Renaissance courtyards and leads to **Rue de la République**, emerging at No. 25. At No. 23 there is an attractive courtyard with arcades.

◗ Turn right on rue de la République and first left up rue de la Résistance. Take the third right, rue du Collège.

Centre du Patrimoine

2, rue du Collège. ◷*Open Mon–Sat 9.30am–12.30pm, 2–6pm.* ℘*05 63 63 03 50. www.montauban.com.*
Montauban's Heritage Centre occupies a former Jesuit college. Two rooms contain a permanent collection of objects illustrating the development of the city. Temporary exhibitions look at particular local neighbourhoods or contemporary restoration projects.

◗ Return to Place Nationale.

EXCURSIONS
Montech
14 km/8.5mi SW on D 928.
Water is made to flow up a slope at the Pente d'eau on the Canal de Garonne. Two adapted diesel locomotives are used to push a boat trapped in a pool of water between them up to a higher level of the canal, thus avoiding the need to contend with a flight of five locks.
It takes 20 minutes to ascend the 443m ramp at a speed of 2km/hour (just over 1mph), a saving of 45 minutes against the time normally needed for the closing, filling and opening of locks.

Abbaye de Belleperche

Cordes-Tolosannes. From Montech, cross the Garonne river and take the D 26 to the right. ◷*Open May–Sept Tue–Sat 10am–6pm, Sun 2–6pm; Oct–Apr Tue–Fri 2–5pm.* ◎€1. ℘*05 63 95 62 75. www.musee-arts-de-la-table.fr.*
Built in the 12C, this Cistercian abbey was once a wealthy religious establishment. The abbey houses the Musée d'Arts de le Table, a collection of accoutrements for fine dining.

Château de Reyniès

Leave Montauban travelling S on D 21 towards Villemur-sur-Tarn. ◓*Guided tours of the exterior only: Jul–Sept daily except Wed 10am-6pm.* ℘*05 63 64 04 02.*
Built in 1289 then destroyed during the Wars of Religion after the Latour family converted to Protestantism.

Villemur-sur-Tarn

23 km/14mi SE.
Standing on the Tarn river, in the midst of the Frontonnais vineyards, Villemur conserves some traces of its past. By the waterside is the 17C Tour de Défense with a watermill attached to it. Two other buildings to see are the red-brick Greniers du Roy (17C) and the Eglise Saint Michel which has inside it frescoes by the 19C Toulouse artist Bernard Bénézet.

ADDRESSES

⌂ STAY

◉◉ **Hôtel du Commerce** – *9 pl. Roosevelt.* ℘*05 63 66 31 32. www.hotel-commerce-montauban.com. Closed at Christmas. 27 rooms.* A large 18C building in the centre of the city. Its public rooms are furnished with antiques.

◉◉◉ **Chambre d'hôte Maison des Chevaliers** – *Pl. de la Mairie, 82700 Escatalens.* ℘*05 63 68 71 23.* ▣◿ *5 rooms.* It is hard to resist the charm of this 18C building. The brightly painted rooms are equipped with old-fashioned baths.

Moissac★★

The town of Moissac lies clustered around the ancient abbey of St-Pierre (a site of major interest for lovers of Romanesque art), in a fresh and pretty setting on the north bank of the Tarn and either side of the Garonne branch canal. A jazz festival brings life to the town in July and classical music concerts are given throughout July and August. The surrounding hillsides are covered with orchards and vineyards which produce the reputed Chasselas grape variety (a white grape).

▶ **Population:** 12 980.
◔ **Michelin Map:** 337: C-7.
▯ **Info:** Pl. Durand-de-Bredon, 82200 Moissac. 𝄢05 63 04 01 85. www.tourisme-moissac.fr.
◑ **Location:** 72km/45mi NW of Toulouse. To get to the abbey by car, follow the signs and big orange arrows pointing the way.
⊘ **Don't Miss:** Tasting the famed Chasselas grape.

A BIT OF HISTORY

The golden age of the abbey – It was during the 11C and 12C that Moissac abbey was at its most influential. Probably founded in the 7C by a Benedictine monk from the Norman abbey of St-Wandrille, the young abbey of Moissac did not escape from the pillage and destruction wrought by Arabs, Norsemen and Hungarians.

It was struggling to right itself again when, in 1047, an event occurred which was to change its destiny. On his way through Quercy, St Odilon, the famous and influential abbot of Cluny, who had just laid down the rules at the monastery at Carennac, affiliated the abbey of Moissac to that of Cluny. This marked the beginning of a period of prosperity. With the support of Cluny, Moissac Abbey set up priories throughout the region, extending its influence as far as Catalonia.

A series of misfortunes – The Hundred Years War, during which Moissac was occupied twice by the English, and then the Wars of Religion dealt the abbey some fearsome blows. It was secularised in 1628 and then suppressed altogether during the Revolution. In 1793, during the Reign of Terror, the archives were dispersed, the art treasures pillaged and numerous sculptures disfigured. In the mid-19C, it narrowly escaped complete destruction when there was

Decorations on the capitals of the cloisters, Abbaye de Moissac

© Julien Garcia/age fotostock

question of demolishing the monastery buildings and cloisters to make way for the railway line from Bordeaux to Sète. The intervention of the Beaux-Arts commission saved it from ruin.

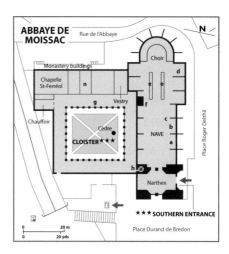

ABBEY★★
Église St-Pierre★

All that remains of the original 11C abbey church is the belfry porch, fortified c.1180 with a watch-path, crenellated parapet, loopholes and machicolated gallery. The nave is partly Romanesque and partly 15C French Gothic. The majestic tympanum above this **South portal ★★★** doorway, executed c.1130, is one of the finest Romanesque sculptures in France. The nave contains an Our Lady of Pity from 1476 (**a**), a Flight into Egypt from the late 15C (**b**), a magnificent Romanesque **Crucifix★** (12C) (**c**) and an Entombment (**d**) from 1485. The chancel is enclosed by a 16C carved stone screen and the choir stalls (**e**) date from the 17C. In an alcove beneath the organ is a white Pyrenean marble Merovingian sarcophagus (**f**).

Cloisters★★★

Entrance through the tourist office.
&. Open Jul–Aug 9am–7pm; *Sept 9am–6pm; Apr–Jun and Oct 9am–noon, 2–6pm (Sat–Sun and public holidays 10am–noon, 2–6pm); Nov–Mar 10am–noon, 2–5pm (Sat–Sun and public holidays 2–5pm).* Closed *1 Jan and 25 Dec.* €5.
℘05 63 04 01 85.

These late 11C cloisters have delicate arcades in harmonious tones of white, pink, green and grey marble, and sculpted decoration featuring animal, botanical, geometric and historiated motifs. A staircase in the south-west corner (**h**) leads to the first floor of the narthex and roof views of the cloisters, town and Tarn Valley beyond.

The conventual buildings include the calefactory, St-Ferréol Chapel containing some 12C capitals, a room (**k**) illustrating Moissac's influence on sculpture in the Quercy region, and another (**n**) housing religious art and liturgical vestments.

Musée Marguerite-Vidal

&. Closed for renovation. Contact the tourist office for information.
℘05 63 04 01 85.

The museum housed in the original abbot's lodgings celebrates the abbey's importance during the Middle Ages and its influence throughout the southwest France. The 17C stairwell displays religious items of historical interest. Collections show regional history and traditions with ceramics, furniture, Moissac headdresses, reconstructed 19C kitchen from the Bas Quercy region, and local craftwork and costumes.

ADDITIONAL SIGHTS
Centre d'art roman Marcel-Durliat

Bd Léon-Cladel. Visits by arrangement.
℘0899 236 018.

This archive has an important collecion of documents pertaining to medieval art. It also has a collection of illuminated manuscripts.

Pont-Canal du Cacor

Approximately 30min on foot from *the centre of Moissac going towards the swimming pool (piscine).*

This stone aqueduct, built in 1867, carries the Canal de Garonne over the Tarn. It has 15 arches and stretches 356m, making it one of the longest canal-carrying bridges in France. it resisted a serious flood in 1930 which swept away the railway bridge.

EXCURSIONS
Boudou
7km/4.5mi W of Moissac. Leave by the D 813 in the direction of Agen.
From a promontory, to the south of the church there is a fine **panorama★** of the Garonne valley. The river passes below a range of low hills covered with vines.

Bruniquel★

With the bold outline of its castle rising like a crown above the town, Bruniquel lies in a picturesque setting★ at the mouth of the great gorges that the Aveyron has cut through the limestone of the Causse de Limogne.

A BIT OF HISTORY

According to Gregory of Tours (bishop, theologian and historian, 538–594), Bruniquel has its origins in the founding of a fortress on this site by Brunhilda, daughter of the king of the Visigoths and wife of Sigebert, King of Austrasia. The memory of this princess is perpetuated by the castle tower that bears her name. The bitter rivalry between her and her sister-in-law Fredegund caused war to break out between Austrasia and Neustria in the 6C.

The brutality of Brunhilda's own death is legendary; she was bound by her hair, an arm and a leg to the tail of an unbroken horse and smashed to pieces.

OLD TOWN★

Stroll past the ruined fortifications and town gateways, along narrow streets lined with pantile roofed houses. Especially pretty are rue du Mazel, rue Droite-de-Trauc and rue Droite-de-la-Peyre.

Castelsarrasin
7km/4.5mi S on D 813.
This ancient town, today a sub-prefecture of Tarn-et-Garonne sits in the middle of the Lavilledieu vineyards. Over the centuries it has withstood the upheavals of the Albigensian crusaed in the 13C and the Wars of Religion from 1560 when Catholic Castelsarrasin was pitted against Protestant Montauban. The **Eglise Saint-Sauveur**, rebuilt in 1254, is in southern Gothic style. inside it has Baroque wood fittings. There are pleasant walks beside the Canal de Garonne. A 'green way' cycle track runs along the canal between Montech and Lamagistère.

▶ **Population:** 637.
Michelin Map: 337: F-7.
Info: Prom. du Ravelin, 82800 Bruniquel. ℘05 63 67 29 84. www.bruniquel.fr.
Location: 28km/17mi northeast of Montauban.
Don't Miss: The old town and painted murals in the Maison Payrol.

Château
Open Jul–Aug 10am–7pm; Mar and 1st 2 wks of Nov 10am–5pm; Apr–Jun and Sept–Oct 10am–6pm. ⊛€3.50 (Guided tours. ⊛€4.50). ℘05 63 67 27 67.
Although the castle's foundations probably date from the 6C, most of it was built from the 12C to 18C. The barbican, which defended the approaches to the castle from the side of the village, stands on the esplanade in front of the main buildings. Inside, the decor of the 12C-13C Knights' Hall features colonnettes with capitals. Stairs lead to the first floor where the guard-room boasts a beautiful 17C chimney-piece. In the seigneurial wing of the castle, a Renaissance loggia overlooks the sheer cliff, in which numerous rock shelters have been hol-

lowed out, giving an open **view**★ of the bend in the river below.

Maison Payrol

🕐Open 3–7pm: Jul–Aug daily; May–Jun and Sept–Oct Sat–Sun. ✆€3 (children under 14, €2). ✆05 63 67 25 23. www.maisoin-payrol.fr.
This town house owned by the influential Payrols family was built between the 13C and 17C. The 13C **murals**★ and imposing Renaissance ceiling are outstanding.

EXCURSIONS
Puycelsi★

13 km/8mi SE of Bruniquel, W of the forêt de Grésigne.
Standing on a rocky outcrop overlooking the wooded valley of the Vère, this fortified village (also spelled 'Puycelci') still has ramparts punctuated by seven towers (two from the 14C and 15C) and two ancient gateways.

Wandering the streets you come across some interesting buildings such as the château du Petit Saint-Roch, flanked by two towers; the Maison Féral with a 15C–16C façade.

Puycelsi is inseparable from the woods around it. A signposted footpath, the Sentier du Patrimoine (various permutations possible from 2km/1mi to 14km/8.5mi) leads down from Puycelsi into the **Foret de Grésigne**, a magnificent expanse of chestnuts and sessile oaks inhabited by deer and wild boar.

Saint-Antonin-Noble-Val★

and Aveyron gorges

The town's houses, with virtually flat roofs covered in half-cylindrical tiles faded by the sun, are built in gentle tiers on the north bank of the river.

A BIT OF HISTORY

So delightful was the setting of the Gallo-Roman settlement on this site that it was given the name 'glorious valley' (noble val). An oratory founded by Saint Antonin, who came to convert this part of the Rouergue, was replaced in the 8C by an abbey. The viscount of Saint Antonin, Ramon Jordan, born in 1150, was one of the most gifted troubadours of his age.

🐾WALKING TOUR

The town developed rapidly during the Middle Ages, due to trade in cloth, fur and leather, as can be seen by the 13C, 14C and 15C houses which were once the residences of wealthy merchants.

▶ **Population:** 1 928.
⚙ **Michelin Map:** 337: G-7.
🛈 **Info:** 10 rue de la pelisserie, 82140 St-Antonin-Noble-Val. ✆05 63 30 63 47. www.tourisme-saint-antonin-noble-val.com.
◗ **Location:** 24km/15mi W of Caussade D 926 then the D 5 and 31km/19.5mi NW of Cordes-sur-Ciel on the D 600 then the D 115.
🅿 **Parking:** Place des Tilleuls.
⊘ **Don't Miss:** The Ancien Hôtel de Ville and the Musée Marcel-Lenoir.

Ancien hôtel de ville★

This mansion was built in 1125 for a rich, newly ennobled townsman, Pons de Granholet, and is one of the oldest examples of civil architecture in France. In the 14C, it was the consuls' residence. Viollet-le-Duc restored it in the 19C, adding a square belfry crowned by a machicolated loggia in the Tuscan style, based on a project of 1845. The façade is

St-Antonin-Noble-Val with River Aveyron

© Pasticcio/iStockphoto.com

composed of two storeys. The gallery of colonnettes on the first storey is decorated with two pillars bearing statues of King Solomon and Adam and Eve. The building houses a **museum** (*open Jul–Aug daily except Tue 10am–1pm and 3–6pm; rest of the year by appointment at the tourist office*) of prehistory and local traditions.

Rue Guilhem-Peyre

This street leading from beneath the belfry of the old town hall was once a route taken by processions. On the right there is what used to be the Royal Barracks and a splendid 13C–16C mansion.

▷ Walk down the street towards Place de Payrols then turn right.

Rue des Grandes-Boucheries

The Maison du Roy situated on the corner of rue de l'Église, has five large pointed arches looking in at ground-floor level, and the same number of twin windows on the first floor, with youthful faces adorning the capitals.

▷ Walk up Rue de l'Église towards the new town hall.

Ancien Couvent des Génovéfains

Built in 1751, this convent of the Order of St Genevieve is now home to the town hall and the tourist office.

▷ Walk to Place de la Halle via Rue Saint-Angel and Place du Buoc.

Croix de la Halle

In front of the pillars of the covered market, there is a lollipop-shaped 14C **Cross**, carved on both sides which would once have stood at the entrance to or in the middle of the town graveyard.

Rue de la Pélisserie

There are 13C–14C houses redolent of the former wealth of master tanners and furriers all along this street.

▷ Turn left onto Rue des Banhs.

Rue Rive-Valat

A little canal spanned by bridges flows along this street; it is one of many tributaries of the River Bonnière which were dug during the Middle Ages to provide a main drainage system and water for the tanneries. These have open top floors, which are used to store and dry skins.

▷ Rue Rive-Valat leads back to Place de la Halle via Rue Droite.

Rue Droite

Two houses stand out because of their carved keystones: the late-15C **Maison de l'Amour** (House of Love) on which a man and woman are depicted touching lips, and the **Maison du Repentir** (House of Repentance) where, in contrast, two faces are shown turned away from one another. About halfway along the street there is a double-corbelled façade, decorated with half-timbering interspersed with slightly golden porous limestone and wooden mullions.

▶ Walk left to Place des Capucins then along Rue du Pont-des-Vierges.

Rue du Pont-des-Vierges
An old walnut-oil press can be visited (*apply to the museum*).

🚗 DRIVING TOUR

GORGES DE L'AVEYRON★
Round trip of 49km/30mi. Allow 3h.

▶ Leave St-Antonin S, crossing the bridge over the Aveyron and turning right onto D 115 which runs alongside the river. After 2.5km/1.5mi turn left onto a steeply climbing, narrow road up to the top of the cliffs (signposted 'corniche').

This picturesque **scenic route★★** leads through the hamlet of Viel-Four with its pantiled roofs. As the road drops back towards the river, the picturesque hamlet of **Brousses** comes into sight.

▶ At Cazals, cross the river and turn left.

The road (D 173) begins to climb again immediately, heading through farming country, giving good views of the Aveyron's meanders and the valley floor covered with peach and apple orchards.

▶ Cross back to the south bank.

Penne
This old village, overlooked by its castle ruins, occupies the most remarkable **site★**, perched on the tip of a bulbous rocky outcrop rising sheer from the south bank of the Aveyron.

▶ Park the car by the side of the road (D 9), at the entrance to the village.

From the belfry, a pretty little street lined with old houses leads up to the castle, then down to Peyrière gate on the opposite side of the village. The 17C plague cross marks the beginning of the steep footpath that leads up the rockface to the **castle** ruins. From the tip of the promontory, there is a good **view★** of the towers and jagged walls of the castle, the village of Penne and the Aveyron valley.

▶ Leave Penne S on D 9.

There are excellent **views★** of the village. The road edges along the plateau before dropping into the valley once more.

▶ D 1E on the left leads to Bruniquel.

Bruniquel★
👍*See BRUNIQUEL.*

▶ Cross the Aveyron following the road along the north bank to Montricoux.

Montricoux
Montricoux is built on terraces above the north bank of the Aveyron. The town's old curtain walls are still standing. Place Marcel-Lenoir and some of the streets contain picturesque medieval half-timbered houses with over-hanging upper floors (13C–16C).
Inside the château at Montricoux is the **Musée Marcel-Lenoir★** (👍🕐 *open May–Sept daily except Tue 10am–6pm;* 👁*guided visit possible (45 mins);* 💶€5; 📞05 63 67 26 48; www.marcel-lenoir.com), an exhibition the work of painter Marcel Lenoir, born in 1872 in Montauban.

▶ Take D 958 back to St-Antonin.

This road runs through the forest of La Garrigue, giving glimpses of the Aveyron below and to the right. The final stretch before St-Antonin is a spectacular cliff road overlooking the river.

Caylus

This little town has some medieval streets and half-timbered houses, but it is best known for a mansion that stands on the main street opposite the tourist information office and the 18C church.

THE TOWN

The 13C **Maison aux Loups** (House of the Wolves) is so-called beacause of the 'gargoyles' in the form of animal heads that protrude from its walls. The house stands on Rue Droite, the 'straight street' laid out in the reconstruction of the town after the Albigensian Crusade. At the other end of the street is a 15C–16C market hall. Bear left and you should find yourself in the rue de l'Ifernet. Turn left into rue des remparts. On the corner in front of is the Pavilion Gaulejac which has a polygonal corner tower. Turn left at the end of rue des remparts to return to your starting point.

🚗 DRIVING TOUR

LE CAUSSE DE LIMOGNE
Tour of 55km/34mi. Allow half a day.

▶ Leave Caylus on D 19 N. Stay on this road until Beauregard.

Nôtre-Dame-des-Grâces
This flamboyant Gothic chapel with a slate roof enjoys a good view over the valley.

Lacapelle-Livron
The remains of a Templar commandery have been incorporated into a fortified manor house.

Château de St-Projet
In 1595, Queen Marguerite de Valois is said to have taken refuge in this 13C château with her lover from the armies of her husband Henry IV.

Beauregard
In the middle of the village stands a market hall dating from the 14C.

▶ **Population:** 1 518.
◔ **Michelin Map:** 337: G6.
🏠 **Info:** Mairie, 82160 Caylus.
   📞 05 63 67 06 17.
   www.caylus.com.
▶ **Location:** 11km/7mi north of St-Antonin-Noble Val on D 19.
👁 **Don't Miss:** Maison aux Loups and Phosphatières du Cloup d'Aural.

▶ In Beauregard, turn right on D55. Beside the road stands one of the main prehistoric monuments in this part of France, the Dolmen de la Peyre Levade.

Prieuré de Laramière
A halt on the pilgrimage route to Santiago de Compostela, this priory was founded in 1148 by an itinerant Augustinian monk.

▶ Return to Beauregard and go through the town still on the D 55 heading W through Varaire. Turn left before reaching Bach.

Phosphatières du Cloup d'Aural★
The causse de Limogne suddenly gives way to luxuriant vegetation in this pothole from which phosphate-rich clay was extracted in the 19C to be used as a natural fertiliser. The visit gives a rare glimpse into the climate and fauna of Quercy 30 million years ago.

EXCURSIONS
Caussade
22km/13.5mi SW by D 926.
Every town has its speciality and for Caussade, since 1796, it is the straw hat which its workshops turn out in prodigious quantity. The main historical sight to see is the Tour d'Arles (13C).

Montpezat-de-Quercy★

This bastide built around an arcaded square in the has a number of half timbered houses and other fine buildings. The main sight, however, is in the church: a collection of prized Flemish tapestries.

▸ **Population:** 1 544.
Michelin Map: 337: E6.
Info: Bvd des Fossés, 82270 Montpezat-de-Quercy. ℘05 63 02 05 55. www.tourisme-montpezat-de-quercy.com.
Location: 42km/26mi NE of Montauban on N 20 then D 820 then D 20.
Don't Miss: Flemish Tapestries.

THE TOWN

The **Collégiale St-Martin**, built in southern Gothic style in the 16C, is renowned for the 15 large Flemish tapestries that hang on the walls of the choir. Made especially for the church, they are in five groups and are well preserved, having been restored three times. They tell the story of the legend and life of St Martin of Tours to whom the church is dedicated. Among the tombs in the church is that of Pierre des Prés born in Montpezat in around 1280. A brilliant and ambitous man he became a cardinal and vice-chancellor of the Cartholic church during the Avignon papacy. He died of the plague in 1361.

The 15C Collège des Chanoine is a residence for the canons of the church. Another fine building is the Couvent des Ursulines (17C) which has a cloister. It is now a school and municipal library. Little remains of the town's fortifications except one of its five gates, the porte de l'hôpital, next to the tourist information office. But there are many pleasant streets to stroll around.

Lauzerte★

Situated on a hilltop in the Quercy Blanc, between the valleys of the Lot and the Tarn, Lauzerte is classified as among the *plus beaux villages* – the most beautiful villages in France. It is a well to do bastide founded in the 13C by the count of Toulouse.

▸ **Population:** 1 511.
Michelin Map: 337: C/E6/7.
Info: Pl des Cornières, 82110 Lauzerte. ℘05 63 94 61 94. www.lauzerte-tourisme.fr.
Location: 24km/15mi northeast of Moissac on D957 and D953.
Don't Miss: Jardin du Pèlerin.

THE TOWN

The upper town (ville haute) is arranged around the 13C church, the **Eglise St-Barthélemy**, which has a Gothic doorway giving on to the square.

The promenade de l'Eveillé is the once fashionable quarter where the wealthiest and most respectable citizens had their residences. Some of the basements of the 13C and 14C buildings along the rue de la Garrigue and rue de la Gendarmerie have been turned into shops. Lauzerte is on the Via Podensis route to Santiago de Compostela and the Jardin du Pèlerin celebrates this fact and is also equipped with a large-scale set of the jeu de l'oie (Game of the Goose) which is associated with the pilgrimage. To play, ask at the tourist information office.

🚘 DRIVING TOUR

LE PAYS DE SERRES
A tour of 70 km/42mi. Allow one day.

Eglise St-Barthélemy, Lauzerte

◐ Leave Lauzerte heading S on D 2. Turn left on D 953, then right on D 81. After 2km/1.2mi, turn right towards Ste-Amans-de-Pellagal.

Chartron
This village has a beautiful **dovecote** mounted on pillars.

◐ Continue a little further and turn left and quick right. After Ste-Amans, follow the signs for Miramont de Quercy, from where there is a good view over the valley. Leaving Miramont de Quercy, turn left on D 41 then right on D 953. After 8km/5mi, turn right on D 7 then left on D 28.

Castelsagrat
Picturesque *bastide* with arcaded square, old well, houses roofed with round tiles. The façade of the 14C church conceals a fine Gothic nave at the heart of which is a large and unexpected gilt-wood altarpiece. The village is quiet and full of charm.

◐ Return to D 7 and turn left.

Château de Brassac
◷*Open Jul–mid-Sept Wed, Sat–Sun 11am–6pm, Thu–Sat noon–6pm.* ✍€4. ☎07 86 50 58 90.
Dominating the valley of the Séoune, this square fortress with four round towers was built in the 12C and remodelled in the 16C. During the Hundred Years

War it passed alternately from the English the French before finally ending up in the hands of Hector Galard, chamberlain of Louis XI who is said to be the model for the Jack in a French deck of playing cards. The castle was besieged by the Protestants during the Wars of Religion and set on fire during the Revolution. It was abandoned during the 19C but restoration work began in 1891.

◐ Continue on D 7.

Bourg-de-Visa
In the place de la Mairie stands an iron market hall surrounded by arcades. There is a dovecote-tower near the church.

◐ Continue on D 7 and after 10km/6mi turn left.

Roquecor
Perched on a rocky outcrop, the village overhangs the Petite Séoune. Below it are caves once occupied by troglodytes.

◐ Leave Roquecor heading N and turn right on D 7.

Montaigu-de-Quercy
Wrapped around a hillside, Montaigu has some pleasant streets to explore such as the rue des Frères-Quémeré which leads up to the place de la Mairie with its **washhouse** and church.

◐ Leave Montaigu going NE (D 24), After 2km/1mi, turn left.

Pervillac
The Romanesque church in this hamlet has 15C murals in good condition showing hell, purgatory and the virtues.

◐ Turn right towards Montaigu. Take first left (D 41) towards Touffailles.

Touffailles
The vault of the nave in the **église St-Georges** (15C) is painted with scenes of the childhood and passion of Christ.

◐ From D 41, turn left on D 60, and right on D 73 that leads to Lauzerte.

France's fifth largest department is also one of its least spoilt and most beautiful. With little industry, and not on the way from anywhere to anywhere, it has been barely touched by motorway and other signs of modernity. Most of it consists of plateau (accounting for two thirds of its surface area) and mountains of modest altitude (reaching a high point of 1 463m in the Monts d'Aubrac). It is an immensely green upland landscape trisected by three of the principal rivers of southwest France, the Tarn, Aveyron and Lot which each meanders through its own deep and beautiful valley from east to west. The Aveyron is stuffed with sights in great variety. It has more classified 'plus beaux villages' (most beautiful villages) than any other department except the Dordogne. It is estimated to have more dolmens than the whole of Brittany. It also has a significant number of bastide towns, chiefly in the west, castles and abbeys.

Say Cheese

This is not the first region to choose to visit if you are primarily interested in eating and drinking. The Aveyron has some excellent markets selling fresh local produce but doesn't have a great cuisine of its own. It does, however, excel in cheeses.

Its signature dish is *aligot*, a delicious, stringy, filling dish made of mashed potatoes and melted Tomme cheese.

To wash down the aligot, the Aveyron produces its own robust appelation d'origine controlée red and rosé wines in the vineyards of Marcillac. The monks of Conques are said to have been the first to realise that the red soils and gentle climate were suitable for the cultivation of vines.

Highlights

1. Take in the views from the top of **Najac castle** (p474)
2. Spend time strolling around the cathedral city of **Rodez** (p480)
3. See the delightful pilgrimage town of **Conques** (p485)
4. Meander along the beautiful green **valley of the Lot** (p488)
5. Try the local dish of aligot made in **Aubrac** (p493)

Laguiole

Since 1829, the town of Laguiole has been synonymous with pocket knives and corkscrews. They are on sale everywhere but there's still a certain caché about buying them in situ.

Najac and the fortress

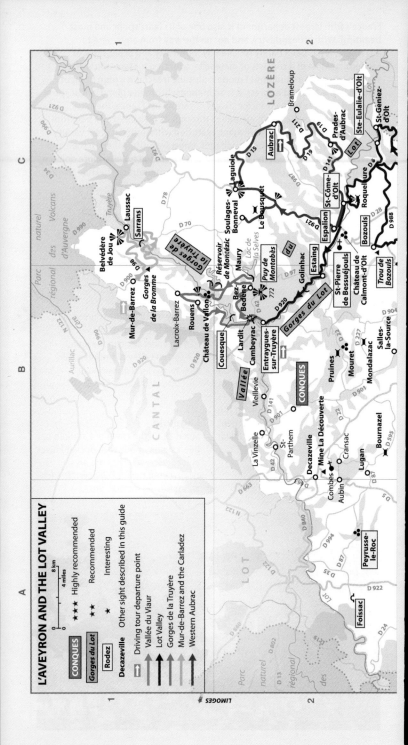

L'AVEYRON AND THE LOT VALLEY

CONQUES	★★★	Highly recommended
Gorges du Lot	★★	Recommended
Rodez	★	Interesting

Decazeville Other sight described in this guide

Driving tour departure point

Vallée du Viaur
Lot Valley
Gorges de la Truyère
Mur-de-Barrez and the Carladez
Western Aubrac

0   4 miles
0   8 km

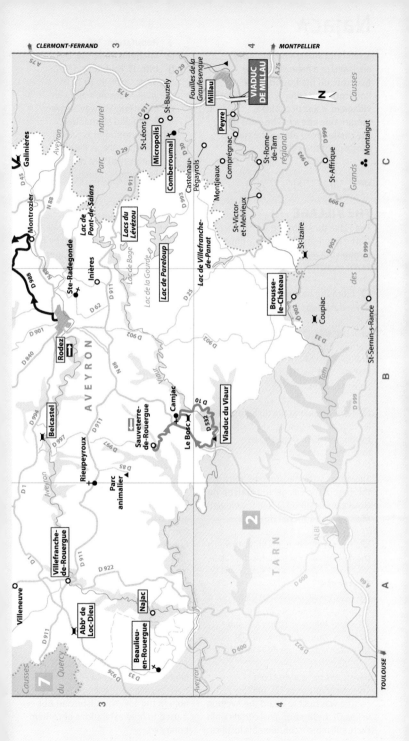

VIADUC DE MILLAU

Galinières
Montrozier
Ste-Radegonde
Iniès

St-Léons
Micropolis
Comberoumal
Castelnau-Pégayrols
Montjaux
Compeyre
St-Bauzely
Foussilles de la Graufesenque
Millau
Peyre
St-Rome-de-Tarm
St-Victor-et-Melvieux
St-Izaire
St-Affrique
Montaigut

Lac de Pont-de-Salars
Lacs du Lévézou
Lac de Pareloup
Lac de Bage
Lac de la Gourde
Lac de Villefranche-de-Panat

Parc naturel

Rodez
Belcastel
Sauveterre-de-Rouergue
Camjac
Le Bosc
Viaduc du Viaur
Rieupeyroux
Parc animalier

Brousse-le-Château
Couplac
St-Sernin-s-Rance

AVEYRON

TARN

Villeneuve
Villefranche-de-Rouergue
Abb° de Loc-Dieu
Najac
Beaulieu-en-Rouergue

Causses du Quercy

7

Najac★

Stretching along a promontory enclosed in a meander of the Aveyron, on the boundary of Rouergue and Quercy, the ancient village of Najac occupies a remarkable site★★. The ruins of the castle tower above the slate rooftops of the village.

▶ **Population:** 740.
♿ **Michelin Map:** 338: D-5.
ℹ **Info:** Pl. Faubourg, 12270 Najac. ℘05 65 29 72 05. www.tourisme-najac.com.
◐ **Location:** Midway between Rodez and Montauban.
🅿 **Parking:** Traffic is barred from the village. Park in or near the Place du Faubourg.

🐾WALKING TOUR

THE VILLAGE

The Place du Faubourg is the place to start exploring. There is only one road through the village between this square and the castle.

◐ From the bottom of the square go down the steep street of rue du Barriou.

Near the town hall, a fountain, carved from an enormous monolithic slab of granite dated 1344, bears the arms of Blanche de Castille, King Louis IX's (St Louis') mother.

◐ Continue along rue du Bourguet, leaving rue des Comtes-de-Toulouse to your left. Bear right and left through a gateway.

There are two fine aristocratic houses in this part of the village: the **Maison du Gouverneur** (13–15C), and the elegant **Maison du Sénéchal** (15–16C).

◐ The rue du chateau climbs towards the mound on which stands the castle.

Fortress★

◔*Open Apr–May and Sept–Oct 10.30am–1pm, 3–5.30pm; Jun 10.30am–1pm, 3–6.30pm; Jul–Aug 10.30am–7pm (9pm on Wed).* ◔*Closed Nov–Mar.* ⊜€5.50 (child 7–16, €4). ℘05 65 29 71 65. www.tourisme-aveyron.com.*
This masterpiece of 13C military architecture was built to guard the Aveyron valley. Of the three original curtain walls there still remain considerable fortifications flanked by large round towers. The castle itself, built partly from pale-coloured sandstone, is protected by thick walls and is shaped like a trapezium. The most impregnable of the towers, on the southeast, was the keep. Kids will enjoy the 'secret' passage on the first floor which leads to a viewpoint over the church.

◐ A pleasant path from beneath the walls of the castle leads down the hill to meet the road.

The 13C **Porte de Pique** is the only one left of the 10 original gates.

Eglise Saint-Jean

This Gothic building has a west front adorned with a rose window. Inside, the single nave ends with a flat chevet.

◐ To vary the return route, go around the church and take La Caminade and then rue Basse des Comtes-de-Toulouse which emerges near the fountain.

EXCURSION
Abbaye de Beaulieu-en-Rouergue ★

20km/12mi W of Najac. ◔*Open Jul–Aug daily 10am–noon, 2–6pm; Apr–Jun and Sept–Oct Wed–Mon 10am–noon, 2–6pm.* ◔*Closed Nov–Mar.* ⊜€5.50 (under 26, free). ℘05 63 24 50 10. www.beaulieu-en-rouergue.fr.*
Built in the 13C, this Cistercian Abbey is used to hold exhibitions of contemporary art.

Villefranche-de-Rouergue★

On the border of the Rouergue and Quercy regions, the ancient bastide of Villefranche-de-Rouergue, with its rooftops clustered round the foot of the massive tower of the church of Notre-Dame, lies in the bottom of a valley surrounded by green hills, at the confluence of the Aveyron and the Alzou.

A BIT OF HISTORY

Trade and prosperity – Villefranche was founded in 1099 by Raymond IV de Saint-Gilles, Count of Toulouse, on the south bank of the Aveyron.

The town enjoyed a new phase of expansion when, in 1252, Alphonse de Poitiers, brother of St Louis, decided to build a new town on the north bank of the river. This was built with the geometric layout typical of a bastide and completed in 1256. Despite the disagreement between the founder and the bishop of Rodez, who went so far as to excommunicate any newcomers, the town's population soon grew. Its situation near the Causses and the Ségala region, at the crossroads of major routes used since the days of Antiquity, made Villefranche an important trade centre during the Middle Ages. It was also a stopping place for pilgrims on their way to Santiago de Compostela. In the 15C, Charles V granted the town the right to mint money, and silver and copper mines added to the town's wealth, as it prospered in its function as seat of the Rouergue Seneschal and capital of Haute Guyenne. The Wars of Religion halted the town's expansion. Villefranche is now a centre of the farm-produce and metallurgy (bolts) industries.

THE BASTIDE★

With the destruction of its moats, its ramparts and its fortified gates, Villefranche has lost some of its medieval appearance, although it has kept many

▶ **Population:** 12 775.
🛈 **Info:** Prom. du Guiraudet, 12200 Villefranche-De-Rouergue. ☎05 65 45 13 18. www.villefranche.com.
⊙ **Location:** Villefranche is on the right bank of the Aveyron at the entrance to the Gorges, 40km/25mi W of Rodez.
🅿 **Parking:** Arriving by the D 922, there is parking on the Promenade St-Jean on the riverbank. Also the Place de la Liberté and the Prom. de Languedoc.
🕭 **Don't Miss:** A guided tour of the town – the tourist office organises commented tours of the town (1h) Jul–Aug, Mon–Fri at 3pm.

of the features of a bastide with its main square and its grid street plan.

Place Notre-Dame★

This fine square, in the heart of the town and always buzzing with life on market days *(Thursday)*, is framed by houses with covered arcades, some of which have retained their mullioned windows and stone turrets. On one side of the square the tall, solid shape of the old collegiate church can be seen.

Go round the arcades *(avoiding the cars)* to take a closer look at the arches and old sculpted doorways. In front of the terrace overlooking the square to the north stands a large ironwork figure of Christ. The whole scene is reminiscent of Spain, which inspired André Malraux to shoot some scenes from his film *L'Espoir (Hope)* here.

At the corner of rue Marcellin-Fabre and the square, there is a lovely 15C half-timbered house facing the street; the central section, which is seven storeys high, houses a staircase lit through mullioned windows. This staircase can be entered through a fine **stone door** on which the

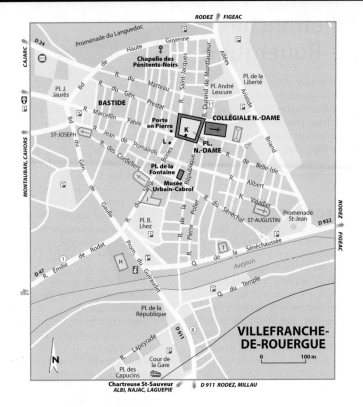

VILLEFRANCHE-DE-ROUERGUE

lower part of the canopy is adorned with sculpted scrolls and foliage.

On rue du Sergent-Boriès, south of the square, the first **house** on the right features another fine staircase tower (late 15C), with pilasters and a carved tympanum.

Maison du Président Raynal

This has a fine 15C façade with adjoining windows, on three storeys, in the Romanesque tradition.

Maison Dardennes-Bernays

Next to the Maison du Président Raynal. At the far end of the courtyard, a Renaissance staircase tower features two galleries adorned with sculpted portraits.

Église Notre-Dame★

The construction of this church, which began with the apse in 1260, lasted for over 300 years. The belfry-porch bears witness to the rivalry between Villefranche-de-Rouergue and Rodez, with each town intending their cathedral spire to be the highest.

Chapelle des Pénitents Noirs

Bd de Haute-Guyenne.
This chapel, surmounted by a curious double turret, was built in the 17C.

Musée Urbain-Cabrol

Rue du Sénéchal. ◷*Open Jul–Aug Tue–Sat 10am–noon, 2–7pm; Apr–Jun and Sept Tue–Sat 2–6pm.* ◷*Closed Oct–Mar, and public holidays.* ⌨*No charge.* ℘*05 65 45 44 37.*
The collections of Urbain Cabrol on archaeology, history, and the popular traditions of Villefranche and the region are on display in a Louis XV mansion.

Ancienne Chartreuse St-Sauveur★

Take D 922 towards Najac and Laguépie. ◷*Open Apr–May Tue–Sat 2–5pm; Jun and Sept daily 2–6pm; 1–mid Jul and 1–mid Sept daily 10.30am–*

Place Notre-Dame on a market day, Villefranche-de-Rouergue

© ChrisAt/iStockphoto.com

noon, 2–6pm; mid-Jul–Aug daily 10.30am–1pm, 2–6pm; Oct Thu–Sat 2–5pm. ⊘Closed Nov–Mar. ⊛€5 (children €3). ℘05 65 45 13 18.

This charter house, founded in 1451 by Vézian-Valette, a wealthy local merchant, was built in eight years of continuous effort, which resulted in an almost perfectly consistent Gothic style. The **Chapelle des Étrangers** used to stand outside the charter house wall, and It housed pilgrims on their way to Santiago de Compostela. The **great cloisters** are some of the largest in France (66m x 44m) while the **small cloisters** are the only authentic 'cloisters', in the strictly monastic sense (gallery with communal buildings opening onto it). Don't miss the 16C stained-glass windows in the **Chapter house** which depict, in the centre, the Shepherds being told of the Birth of Christ, and the founders on either side.

EXCURSIONS
Abbaye de Loc-Dieu★

10km/6mi W by D 926 and D 115. ⊘Open Jul–mid Sept daily except Tue and Sun morning 10am–noon, 2–6pm. ⊘Closed Mon and Sun am. Park open all year. ⊛€5.50 (children under 13, €3.50); park €2.50. ♿ ℘05 65 29 51 18. www.abbayedelocdieu.com.

Thirteen Cisterican monks founded this abbey in the 12C. At the time the woods in which it stands were infested with brigands preying on travellers on the road between Rodez and Cahors for which the location was known as 'locus diaboli', the devil's domain. It was thus decided to baptise the new religious house as 'locus dei', the 'place of God'. In 1409, during the Hundred Years' War, the abbey was burnt by partisans of the king of England. It was rebuilt as a château and still today it is both abbey and private house standing in beautiful grounds. In the first chapel on the right in the chevet is a 15C triptych of carved and painted wood. In the summer concerts are held in the church.

The abbey has one small claim to fame. As the German army advanced on Paris in the early summer of 1940, several treasures from the Louvre were spirited away for safe-keeping. Among them was the Mona Lisa which found a temporary refuge at Loc-Dieu.

Villeneuve

12 km/7.5mi N by D 922.
A neat oval of boulevards circles the old town centre of this 11C town granted the privileges of a bastide by charter from the count of Toulouse in 1231. It centres on the Romanesque Eglise Saint-

Sepulcre which has frescoes of pilgrims in the bays of the apse. The old streets are entered through medieval gateways, the most impressive being the Porte Cardalhac.

Grotte de Foissac★

22 km/13.5mi N by D 922. Open Jul–Aug daily 10am–6pm; Jun and Sept daily 10–11.30am, 2–6pm; Apr–May and Oct Sun–Fri 2–5pm. Closed Nov–Mar. 8.20€ (children 6.20€). 05 65 64 60 52. http://grotte-de-foissac.fr/en.
The visit to the cave takes in both spectacular rock formations and archeological findings from the Copper Age.

Peyrusse-le-Roc★

28km/17mi NE on D 1 to Lanéjouls, then D 635 to La Pagésie then D 87.
Situated on the basalt plateaux separating the Aveyron and Lot valleys, Peyrusse-le-Roc was handed over to England in 1152 after the divorce of Louis VII and Eleanor of Aquitaine. It prospered from its silver mines until these became redundant in the 18C because of trade with America. Having lost its raison d'être, the fortified lower town was abandoned and the present village of grew up on the plateau.

Medieval Ruins

The site is open all the time. The information centre is open Jul–Aug 10am–noon, 2.30–6.30pm; rest of year Mon–Sat, 10am–noon. Closed 1 Jan, 1 May. No charge. 05 65 80 49 33.
Walk across **place St-Georges** and through **Porte du Château**, the gate forming part of the curtain wall, to reach **place des Treize-Vents**. In the Middle Ages, this square was the site of the castle of the lords of Peyrusse. All that is left of it is a room that was used as a prison, and a tower (the church bell-tower), which houses a small **archaeological museum** (05 65 80 49 33).

Go through the Porte Neuve and the fortifications to the left of the church. The footpath on the left leads to the medieval site; beyond the graveyard, bear right (stairway).

Metal steps (*particular care needed on some sections*) lead to the **Roc del Thaluc**. From here it is easy to understand the important role played by Peyrusse as a strategic look-out post during troubled medieval times.

Follow the footpath to the bottom.

A small chapel houses the Tombeau du Roi, a richly sculpted royal mausoleum probably dating from the 14C.

Turn back then right to the **Hôpital des Anglais** (13C) with a fine round exterior chimney. On the way back to the village, stop by the **Beffroi** (belfry), a tall square tower, which, together with the **Porte de la Barbacane**, protected the town to the northwest.

Sauveterre-de-Rouergue

Sauveterre likes to celebrate its royal connections, having been founded in 1281 by the king's Senechal in Rouergue, Guillaume de Mâcon. The large and harmonious place des Arcades is a highlight but it also has some streets of delightful houses.

EXCURSION
Parc animalier de Pradinas

6km/3.7mi NW via D 71 then D 85. La Riale, 12240 Pradinas. ◷*Open Jul–Aug daily 10am–7pm; Apr–Jun, Sept and mid-end Oct daily 10am–6pm; 1st 2 wks in Oct Sat–Sun 10am–6pm.* ⊗*€13 (child 3–11, €7).* ℘*09 52 62 01 52. www.parcanimalierdepradinas.com.*
This wildlife park specialises in the fauna of Europe. Animals to see include bears, lynxes, marmots, wild boar, deer and birds of prey.

▶ **Population:** 808.
◷ **Michelin Map:** 338: F-5
🛈 **Info:** Espace Lapérousse, 12800 Sauveterre-de-Rouergue. ℘05 65 72 02 52. www.sauveterre-de-rouergue.fr.
▶ **Location:** 41km/25.5mi southwest of Rodez.
👁 **Don't Miss:** Place des Arcades.

🚗DRIVING TOUR

VALLÉE DU VIAUR

60km/36mi. Allow 3h. From Sauveterre go S on D 997. ◷*See regional map.*
Take D 10 and the first road on the left to see the murals in the **Eglise de Camjac**. Return to the D 10 and follow signs to Toulouse Lautrec's holiday home, the **Chateau du Bosc**. Continue on D 10 to Castelpers and take the D 532 to the Viaduc de Viaur (◷*see ALBI, Excursion*). Follow the D 532 back to Sauveterre.

Belcastel★

This pretty village climbs up the side of the Aveyron valley in terraces to reach an impressive castle with five round towers and a square keep.

CHÂTEAU
The castle was founded in 1040 but abandoned in the 16C. It was restored in the 1970s by an architect and now doubles as a historical monument and a gallery of modern art.

EXCURSIONS
Château de Bournazel

14.4km/8.9mi N. 12390 Bournazel. ◷*Open 2–7pm: Jul–3rd Sun in Sept Wed–Mon; May–Jun Fri–Sun and public holidays.* ⊗*€7.50 (children under 12, free).* ℘*06 85 10 46 52. www.chateau-bournazel.fr.*
This magnificent Renaissance chateau stands on the site of a medieval building of which vestiges remain. It has notable stone carvings rich in symbolism.

▶ **Population:** 207.
◷ **Michelin Map:** 338: G-4.
🛈 **Info:** 12390 Belcastel. ℘05 65 64 46 11. www.mairie-belcastel.fr.
▶ **Location:** 25km/15.5mi W of Rodez.
👁 **Don't Miss:** The Château.

Commanderie des Hospitaliers de Lugan

12220 Lugan. ◷*Open Jul–Aug Wed–Mon 3–7pm.* ℘*05 65 80 46 59. www.seigneurs-du-rouergue.fr.*
The Knights Hospitallers created this commandery in the 12C from which to administer their domains. It continued to function until the Revolution when it was sold. It is the only commandery in France to be given a social purpose as a retirement home for the elderly. The visit includes the church, kitchen and a small museum.

Rodez★

Once the capital of the Rouergue, Rodez is situated on the borders of two very different regions, the dry Causses plateaus and the well-watered Ségala hills.

A BIT OF HISTORY

Divided loyalties – In the Middle Ages, the town was shared between two masters. The bishops, who for a long time were the more powerful, occupied the Cité; the counts ruled the Bourg. These two adjacent areas were separated by tall fortifications and for many centuries the rivalry prompted endless fighting between the inhabitants.

The two main squares, place de la Cité and place du Bourg, reflect the former duality. When Henri IV became king, the Comté de Rodez joined the French crown and the bishops took contol of the town.

WALKING TOURS

OLD TOWN

The old town, which formed part of the bishops' estate, lies around the cathedral. Several interesting houses and mansions still remain.

▶ **Population:** 25 690.

Michelin Map: 338: H-4.

Info: Place Foch, 12005 Rodez. ℰ05 65 75 76 77. www.tourisme.grand-rodez.com.

Location: 66km/41mi NW of Albi on the N 88 and 63km/39.5mi SE of Figeac on the D 840.

Parking: Boulevard Galy near the Place Foch.

Don't Miss: The Bell Tower of the cathedral and the Musée Fenaille.

Timing: Allow one full day.

▶ Start from the north side of the cathedral. Cross Rue Frayssinous and enter the courtyard of the bishops' palace.

Cathédrale Notre-Dame★★

The red-sandstone cathedral was begun in 1277 after the collapse, a year earlier, of the choir and bell-tower of the previous building.

Exterior – The west front overlooking place d'Armes has a forbidding, fortress-like appearance. The lower half of the wall is quite bare, with no porch and only

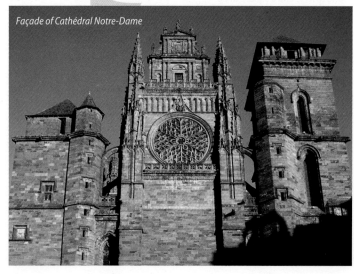

Façade of Cathédral Notre-Dame

©Flô/Fotolia.com

the occasional arrow slit. This austere façade, built outside the city wall, acted as an advance bastion to defend the city. Go round the church to the left. The late-15C north door, known as the Portail de l'Évêché (bishops' doorway), opens beneath three rows of archivolts and a pointed arch. The magnificent **bell-tower★★★**, which interestingly stands apart from the cathedral, comprises six tiers (*guided visits only, by request at the tourist office, Jul–Aug 3pm;* 05 65 75 76 77). The third tier, built in the 16C, is decorated with large window openings with distinctive tracery; the fourth, octagonal in shape, has statues of the Apostles adorning the niches in between the window openings; the fifth is elaborately decorated.

Interior – The elegance of the Gothic style is apparent in the soaring elevation of the chancel with its delicate lancet windows and in the height of the great arches surmounted by a triforium which reproduces the same pattern as that of the upper windows.

Palais épiscopal

The courtyard of the bishops' palace offers the best **view** of the bell-tower of Notre-Dame.

Tour Corbières, Tour Raynalde

These two 15C towers are the vestiges of the walls and the 30 towers that once fortified the town.

 Opposite the portal of the church of Sacré-Cœur, take the stairway leading to impasse Cambon.

Hôtel Delauro

This 16C and 17C mansion, once a canon's residence, now belongs to an association – the Compagnons du Devoir – who restored it.

 Return to Rue Frayssinous and carry on to Place de la Cité.

Place de la Cité

At the east end stands the bronze statue of an illustrious local hero, Monseigneur Affre, Archbishop of Paris, who was killed on the barricades of Faubourg St-Antoine on 25 June 1848 whilst attempting to make peace. Take rue de Bonald then rue de l'Embergue past beautiful old houses, antique shops and craft workshops.

 Cross place de la Cité diagonally and follow Rue du Touat, until it intersects with Rue Bosc.

Tour des Anglais

This 14C house (also known as the Tower of the English) features a massive forti-fied tower and fine gemel windows. The Guitards were rich bankers in the 14C.

Maison de Benoît

Place d'Estaing.
A Gothic gallery runs along two sides of the courtyard (*private*) of this Renais-sance house.

Maison Molinier

2 Rue Penavayre.
This old 15C canon's house stands behind an enclosing wall surmounted by a gallery and two Gothic loggias.

 Continue on Rue Penavayre; turn right.

Chapelle des Jésuites

This 17C Baroque chapel is known as the 'Chapelle Foch', because the future Maréchal Foch went to school at the *lycée* next to it.

 Walk along Rue Louis-Blanc and round the handsome 18C mansion that now houses the Préfecture.

Place du Bourg

This square, once the centre of the old town known as the Bourg, frequented by counts and merchants alike, is still a busy shopping area surrounded by pedestrian precincts lined with shops.

Maison de l'Annonciation

This 16C house is named after the low relief of the Annunciation on the corner turret.

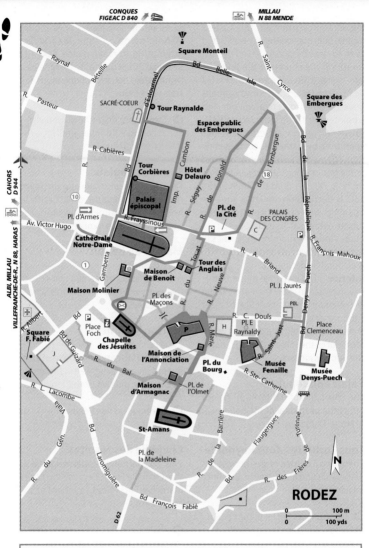

RODEZ

WHERE TO STAY		WHERE TO EAT	
Biney (Hôtel)	①	Taverne (La)	⑱
Midi (Hôtel du)	⑩		

Maison dite d'Armagnac

4 Place de l'Olmet.

The façade of this fine 16C mansion is adorned with charming medallions depicting the counts and countesses of Rodez. From place de l'Olmet, a 16C house that now houses a chemist's can be seen in rue d'Armagnac.

Église St-Amans

This church was built in the 12C, but the exterior was completely restored in the 18C. Inside, it has some of the original fine Romanesque capitals.

NEW TOWN

From its site on a hill, Rodez offers numerous points of view of the surrounding countryside. The boulevards built on the line of the old ramparts render it possible to make a round tour of the town by car (*outside peak times*).

▶ Leave from Place d'Armes and take Boulevard Estourmel.

To the right, the remains of the ramparts (16C) and terraces of the bishops' palace lead to Corbières tower (14C).

Square Monteil

View of the Causse de Comtal and the Aubrac and Cantal mountains.

Square des Embergues

Views to the north and west of town (*viewing table*).

Musée Denys-Puech

Boulevard Denys-Puech. ⚹🕐*Open Jul–Aug daily except Mon 2–7pm; Sept–Jun Wed–Sun 2–6pm.* 🕐*Closed 1 Jan, 1 May, 1 Nov and 25 Dec.* 🎫*No charge.* 📞*05 65 77 89 60.* *www.tourisme.grand-rodez.com.* Founded in 1910 by the sculptor **Denys Puech** (1854–1942), born in the Aveyron, this museum contains both permanent collections of 19C and 20C art and temporary exhibitions on contemporary art.

Musée Fenaille★★

14 place Raynaldy. 🕐⚹*Open Apr–Jun and Sept Tue–Sat 11am–7pm, Sun 2–7pm; Jul–Aug Mon 2–7pm, Tue–Sun 10am–7pm; Oct–early Apr Tue–Fri 10am–noon, 2–6pm, Sat 11am–6pm, Sun 2–6pm.* 🕐*Closed 1 Jan, 1 May, 1 Nov, 25 Dec.* 🎫€9, *ticket also gives entry to Musée Soulages.* 📞*05 65 73 84 30. www.musee-fenaille.com.* The museum is housed partly in the oldest mansion in Rodez and partly in an adjacent modern building which blends harmoniously with its neighbour. Inside are the most extensive collections concerning the Rouergue region, each section displaying a time scale for easy reference. In order to follow the exhibition's chronological order, start on the third floor in the modern building devoted to prehistory. Note in particular the menhir-statues from the south of Aveyron.

Musée Soulages

Jardin du Foirail, Avenue Victor-Hugo. ⚹🕐*Open Apr–Jun and Sept Tue–Sun 11am–7pm; Jul–Aug Mon 2–7pm, Tue–Sun 10am–7pm; Oct–early Apr Tue–Fri 10am–noon, 2–6pm, Sat–Sun 11am–6pm.* 🕐*Closed 1 Jan, 1 May, 1 Nov and 25 Dec.* 🎫€9, *ticket also gives entry to Musée Fenaille.* 📞*05 65 73 82 60.* *www.tourisme.grand-rodez.com.* Internationally renowned contemporary painter **Pierre Soulages** was born in Rodez in 1919. This new museum is dedicated to the artist, and houses works by him and reflects the multitude of techniques he used.

Square François-Fabié

Memorial to the local poet of this name. View of the Ségala region.

EXCURSIONS

Salles-la-Source

12 km/7.5mi NW of Rodez by D 901.
Built on the slopes of the Causse de Comtal, Salles-la-Source consists of three hamlets of beautiful stone houses superimposed on each other. The 'source' (spring) in the name refers to the resurgence of a subterranean river which comes out of the ground as a series of waterfalls. The water now drives a hydroelectric power station.
On the Causse de Comtal there are 200 tumuli, 67 dolmens and 3 menhirs dating from the Chalcolithic era (3 500–2 200 BCE). Several dolmens can be reached on walks from the town including those of Pérignagols (on the N 140), Nauquiès and Peyrelebade.
Musée des Arts et Métiers (Musée du Rouergue)★ – 🕐*Open Apr and Oct Wed–Thu and Sun 2–6pm; May–Jun and Sept daily except Tue 2–6pm; Jul–Aug Tue–Fri 10am–12.30pm, 1.30–6.30pm,*

Sat–Sun 1.30–6.30pm. ⊙Closed Nov–Mar. ⊚€4 (under 26, free). ℘05 65 67 28 96. www.musees.aveyron.fr. This museum of trades and skills typical of the Rouergue in earlier times occupies a former textile mill. On the ground floor is a large workshop in the form of an upturned boat, its ceiling supported by stout columns. It contains a collection of old machines including presses, oil and flour mills and saws. The displays on the upper floors look at mankind's relationship with the mineral world and with the vegetable kingdom.

🚹🚺 Château du Colombier

Mondalazac 20 km/12mi N of Rodez on D 988, D 904 and D 227.
⊙Open Apr Mon–Sat 10.30am–5pm, Sun 10.30am–6pm; May–Jun Mon–Tue and Thu–Sat 10.30am–5pm, Sun 10.30am–6pm; Jul–Aug daily 10.30am–7.30pm; Sept Tue–Thu 1–5pm, Sat 10.30am–5pm, Sun 10.30am–6pm; 1–mid-Octr Wed, Sat–Sun 1–5pm; mid-end Oct daily 10.30am–5pm. ⊙Closed Nov–Mar. ⊚€14.50 (child 3–13, €9.50). ♿℘05 65 74 99 79.
www.chateau-du-colombier.fr.
The grounds of this 13C–14C chateau have in them a garden planted with 350 species of flowers, vegetables, trees and shrubs known to have been cultivated in Europe between 800 and 1440. It is divided into various zones, some with evocative names such as The Garden of Curiosities, the Tapestry of a Thousand Flowers and the Labyrinth of Courtly Love. Other highlights of the garden include a tunnel of wisteria; an apothecary garden in which simples (herbs with medicinal properties) are grown; a rockery; a rose garden containing 150 varieties from France, Britain and China; an orchard and a games area where even the climbing frame is a wooden medieval castle.
Also in the grounds of the château is a zoo is intended to be a 'living bestiary' of the animals known about in the Middle Ages, notably lions, monkeys, bears and wolves. Children can help feed the lions. There is also a small farm with goats, chickens, swans and peacocks.

Château de la Servayrie

Mouret, 24km/15mi NW of Rodez by D 988, D 904, D 13 and D 548.
⊶ Closed to the public. ℘05 65 72 82 97. www.chateau-servayrie.fr.
Begun in the 12C, remodelled in the 17C and more recently restored, this château is a compendium of architectural styles and contains some period furniture. In the grounds the garden is planted with forgotten varieties of fruit and vegetables. The property is now used as a B&B.

Sainte-Radegonde

6km/4mi SW of Rodez by D 12.
This village of large stone houses is dominated by the imposing belfry-keep and defensive towers of its church. Built in the 13C, it was fortified at the end of the 14C to shelter the population in times of conflict. The sixty rooms inside were 'rented' to the villagers who would occupy them with their animals, supplies of fodder and provisions for themselves.

Inières

From Ste-Radegonde, take D 12 S, then D 112.
The tall square tower with a battlement and chemin de ronde at the top hides a small church with a splendid 15C **Annunciation★** in painted stone. Above it, as in Ste-Radegonde, are rooms prepared for the beleaguered population.

Lacs du Lévézou★

24km/15mi SE of Rodez by N 88 and D 911 as far as Pont-de-Salars.
🛈 For information on the lakes contact the Pareloup-Lévézou tourist office at Place de la Mairie, 12290 Pont-de-Salars. ℘05 65 46 89 90.
www.levezou-aveyron.com.
The Lévézou is a plateau between the valleys of the Aveyron and Tarn on which five large reservoirs have been created to supply hydrolectric power stations.
🚹🚺 At an altitude of 805m, the reservoir of **lac de Pareloup★**, indented with peninsulas, offers 120km of lakeside for anglers, walkers, picnickers and

practitioners of watersports. There are beaches at Arvieu and Salles-Curan. Two smaller lakes are also good for swimming, those of **Villefranche-de-Panat** and **Pont-de-Salars.**

ADDRESSES

🛏STAY

🍽🍽 **Hôtel du Midi** – *1 R. Béteille.* ℘*05 65 68 02 07. www.hotel-du-midi.net.* 🅿 *34 rooms. Restaurant🍽🍽.* A hotel with well-kept and well-lit rooms facing the cathedral.

🍽🍽🍽 **Hotel Biney** – *R. Victoire-Massol.* ℘*05 65 68 01 24. www.hotel-biney.com. 28 rooms.* This modern hotel near the centre of town is part of a building complex surrounding a quiet green park.

🍽🍽🍽 **Mercure Rodez Cathédrale Hotel** – *1 avenue Victor Hugo.* ℘*05 65 68 55 19. www.mercure.com. 28 rooms.* Centrally placed, opposite the cathedral, this beautiful art-deco building has comfortable and modern rooms. Limited parking – be sure to reserve a place.

🍴EAT

🍽🍽 **Les Arômes** – *5 Rue Sainte-Catherine.* ℘*05 65 87 24 41. www.lesaromes-restaurant.fr. Closed Sun evening, and Mon and Tue.* It's well worth tracking down this back street eatery – but, be advised, make a reservation, it is very popular. The owners bustle about and somehow manage to cook and serve everything very efficiently.

🍽🍽🍽 **Café Bras** – *7 rue Planard, Jardin du Forail.* ℘*05 65 68 06 70. www.cafebras.fr. Closed Tue in Feb–Mar, and Mon.* Adjoining the Musée Soulages this is a remarkable place, operated by the owners of the 3-star Sébastien Bras restaurant in Laguiole. It is a perfect place to dine; bright, modern and serving fine dishes that won't break the bank. Reservations strongly advised.

🍽🍽🍽🍽 **Goûts et Couleurs** – *38 rue de Bonald.* ℘*05 65 42 75 10. www.goutsetcouleurs.com.* Tucked away in a side street, this Michelin-starred restaurant is a place where fine dining and art combine not least because chef Jean Luc Fau is also an artist of some renown.

Conques★★★

This little village beautifully set on the steep slopes of the Ouche gorge crowds around a splendid Romanesque abbey church, a stop on the pilgrimage route to Santiago de Compostela.

A BIT OF HISTORY

The abbey became famous after it acquired the relics of St Faith (Sainte Foy in French), a 13-year-old Christian girl martyred around the year 303 in Agen. In the 9C, the legend goes, a monk from Conques went to Agen where St Faith's relics were guarded, with the intent of stealing them. After 10 years, he managed to win the confidence of the community and was placed in charge of guarding the relics, whereupon he promptly stole them and took them back with him to Conques. Once there, the saint doubled the number of miracles performed, called the 'japes and

▸ **Population:** 263.
⊙ **Michelin Map:** 338: G-3.
🅸 **Info:** Office de tourisme de Conques, R. du Chanoine-Benazech, 12320 Conques. ℘05 65 72 85 00. www.tourisme-conques.fr.
▶ **Location:** 39km/24mi N of Rodez.
◉ **Don't Miss:** The tympanum and the treasury.

jests of St Faith'. Thus Conques began to atract pilgrims on their way between Le Puy and Moissac.
Conques enjoued a Golden Age between the 11C to the 13C. Subsequently, the abbey was converted into a collegiate church and, in 1561, was reduced to ruins by the Protestants. It was only saved from further degradation by the impassioned plea of the writer Prosper Mérimée.

ABBATIALE STE-FOY★★

Allow half a day.
This magnificent Romanesque abbey church was built between the mid-11C and 12C.

Tympanum★★★

The tympanum depicting the Last Judgement in elaborate detail is a masterpiece of 12C Romanesque sculpture. It must have made a strong impression on medieval pilgrims with its clear separation of saints and sinners to their respective everlasting fates. Originally the tympanum was coloured, with Heaven predominantly blue and Hell in shades of red. As if to prove their skill, the stone carvers added tiny faces peering over the rim of the tympanum as if wondering what to make of the viewer below.

Interior

The church's inside makes a striking impression because of its enormous height (22m) and simplicity of line, verging on the austere. As in other pilgrimage churches, the chancel is wide and surrounded by an ambulatory to allow the faithful to see the relics of St Faith, once displayed there.
The sacristy walls show traces of 15C frescoes depicting the martyrdom of St Faith. Above the passage connecting the galleries is a beautiful sculpture group of the Annunciation.

Cloisters

In 1975, the ground plan was reconstructed with paving stones. All that remains of the cloisters are arcades opening onto what was the refectory and a beautiful serpentine marble basin, once part of the monks' lavabo.

Treasury★★★

🕐*Open Apr–Sept 9.30am–12.30pm, 2–6.30pm; rest of year 10am–noon, 2–6pm.* 🕐*Closed 1 Jan, 25 Dec.* ⊘€6.50 (child 7–16, €2). ℘05 65 72 85 00.
The treasury of the abbey of Conques houses an extensive collection of silver and gold plate from the 9C to the 16C. A particularly interesting set of reliquaries was produced by a goldsmithing workshop set up in the abbey in the 11C. Listed below, in chronological order, are the most important exhibits.
9C – Reliquary of Pepin, gold leaves embossed on a wooden core and inlaid with numerous precious stones, including an antique intaglio depicting the god Apollo.
10C – Reliquary statue of St Faith **(Statue-reliquaire de Sainte Foy ★★★)**,

Tympanum, Abbatiale Ste-Foy

© A. de Valroger/Michelin

Village of Conques with Abbatiale Ste-Foy

the main piece in the collection, gold and silver gilt plating on a wooden core. Over the years the statue has had numerous precious stones added to it, as well as the 14C monstrance through which the relic can be seen (in the middle of her chest, just behind the head of the little figure in her lap). It is also adorned with cameos and antique intaglios.

11C – Autel de Sainte Foy, a portable alabaster altar with embossed silver and enamel work.

12C – St Faith's reliquary chest – this leather chest decorated with 31 enamel medallions still contains the remains of the saint.

13C – Arm reliquary thought to be of St George, in silver on a wooden core, the hand making a sign of blessing.

14C – Head-reliquaries of St Liberate and St Marse, silver and painted canvas.

16C – Gilt gospel bookbinding; processional cross, made from embossed silver leaf on a wooden core with a relic of the true cross beneath the figure of Christ.

Trésor II (Musée Joseph-Fau)

Entrance through the tourist office.

This old house, located opposite the pilgrims' fountain, contains 17C furniture, statues, neo-Gothic reliquaries and Felletin tapestries from the abbey (*ground and first floors*). The basement contains a lapidary museum with a beautiful collection of Romanesque capitals and abaci, which are remains of the old cloisters.

VILLAGE★

The steep little streets are lined with lovely old houses in red stone which harmonises with their limestone roof slabs (*lauzes*). From rue Charlemagne, a rocky path leads to a hillock topped by the chapel of St-Roch from where there is a good view over the clustered rooftops and abbey of Conques.

EXCURSION
Decazeville

26km/16.5mi SW by D 901, D 22 and D 840.

In complete contrast to Conques is this nearby town which sits on a coalfield exploited from its foudation in the 19C by the duc Decazes until 2001. At the 'decouverte' de Lassalle just outside the town there is a viewpoint over a now disused open-cast mine (**Mine la Decouverte**).

Lot Valley★★

France's seventh longest river, the Lot rises in the Lozère and flows westward forming a deep green valley which its often just as beautiful – both for its scenery and its villlages – as the more famous Dordogne to the north. In Aveyron, the most appealing stretch of the Lot is its passage through the Pays d'Olt, a string of charming towns and villages.

> **Don't Miss:** The portal of the Persea Romanesque church in Espalion, and the Gorges du Lot.
> **Kids:** Château de Calmont d'Olt.

12.30pm, 1.30–6.30pm; €3, under 26, free; 05 65 70 75 00) offers thematic temporary exhibitions and audio-visual presentations on the region's past.

> Return to D 988 and head for Bozouls.

🚗 DRIVING TOURS

LOT VALLEY★★
50km/30mi. Allow half a day.
See regional map.

> Leave Rodez on D 988 heading NE towards Espalion. Fork right on D 27.

Montrozier
On the banks of the Aveyron is the picturesque village of Montrozier, with an old Gothic bridge spanning the river. The 15C–16C castle (*closed to the public*) has a five-storey round keep.
The **Espace archéologique départamental de Montrozier** (*open Apr and Oct Tue–Fri 2–6pm, May–Jun and Sept Tue–Sun 2–6pm; Jul–Aug Tue–Sun 10am–*

Bozouls★
Bozouls is distinguished from afar by its modern church (1964). Its sanctuary in the shape of a ship's prow houses a statue of the Virgin Mary by local sculptor Denys Puech.
Trou de Bozouls★ – The terrace next to the war memorial has a view of this canyon, hollowed out of the Causse de Comtal by the River Dourdou.
From the town hall, walk round the south side of the 'Trou' to see the **Ancienne Église Ste-Fauste**. The church's 12C nave, with its raised, semicircular barrel vaulting, was originally roofed with heavy limestone slabs (lauzes). Under this enormous weight, the pillars sagged

Trou de Bozouls

Sainte-Eulalie-d'Olt

© alfa_t/iStockphoto.com

and the old roof was replaced by a timber-frame one in the 17C. There is a view of the Dourdou gorge from the shady terrace to the left of the church.

▶ Leave Bozouls on D 988, heading E, passing the square keep of the Chateau de Thôlet. After Cruejouls turn right on D 64 for Galinières.

Château de Galinières

🕐 *Open for guided visits, for groups only by appointment.* ☎05 65 70 75 11. More than a chateau, this is a fortified Cistercian farmhouse established by the order in one of its agricultural domains. In the 15C a more comfortable residential wing was added.

▶ Continue towards St Geniez-d'Olt on D 45 then D 95.

Saint-Geniez-d'Olt

The town is in two halves facing each other across the river. On the right bank is the older medieval quarter which also has the church (originally 12C but mostly 17C). The buildings on the left bank mostly testify to the wealth of the town in the 17C and 18C although among them is the 14C **chapelle des Pénitents**, a remnant of an Augustine monastery flanked by a cloister (17C).

▶ Take D 988 downriver along the Lot.

Sainte-Eulalie-d'Olt★

Leave the car at the entrance to this beautiful village and explore its narrow winding streets on foot. On them are handsome buildings from the 15C to 18C. Note the old school, with its pepper pot tower, now used as an art gallery; the Hôtel Renaissance (16C); and the chateau de Curières de Castelnau (15C). There is also a Romanesque-Gothic church and an old mill.

▶ Continue on D 988 in the direction of Bozouls and turn right on D 6 for Saint-Côme-d'Olt.

St-Côme-d'Olt★

The houses of this small fortified town have spread beyond the limits of the old curtain wall, with 15C and 16C houses lining its narrow streets. The village church has a Flamboyant (16C) spiral bell-tower and Renaissance sculpted and panelled door.

▶ From St-Côme-d'Olt, a little road leads on a detour to the Chateau de Roquelaure.

Château de Roquelaure

Not open to the public.
From the terrace there isa good **view**★ over the Lot valley to the north. Below the chateau is a Romanesque chapel.

▶ Continue down the valley on D988.

Espalion★

Espalion lies in a pleasant fertile basin crossed by the River Lot. The feudal ruins of **Château de Calmont-d'Olt** (👥👤 ⏱ *open Apr and Sept–Oct daily except Thu 2–6pm; May–Jun daily except Thu 10am–6pm; Jul–Aug daily 10am–7pm;* €5.50, child 5–12, €4, but €8 and €6 in Jul–Aug; ✆05 65 44 15 89; www.chateaucalmont.org) are above the town.

Vieux pont (*spanning the Lot*) – The most famous monument in town, the 11C bridge frames a lovely tableau of the old tanneries lining the river banks.

Vieux palais – This 16C palace was the residence of the governors of Espalion.

Église de Perse★ – *1km/0.6mi SE along avenue de la Gare.* This 11C Romanesque church is dedicated to St Hilarian, Charlemagne's confessor, who legend says retired to Espalion and was beheaded by Moors. A south side **portal**★ includes a tympanum depicting Pentecost.

Musée Joseph-Vaylet et musée du Scaphandre – *38 r Droite.* ⏱*Open Jun–Sept Tue–Sun 10am–12.30pm, 2–6pm.* ⏱*Closed rest of year.* Combined ticket €4 (children €2.50). ✆05 65 44 09 18. The museum displays traditional weaponry, furniture, glassware, religious artefacts and pottery. Adjacent is a diving **museum** honouring the three Espalion men who invented the aqualung and the depressuriser (gas regulator) in 1860.

Musée du Rouergue – *Pl.Frontin.* ⏱*Open Jun–Sept Tue–Sun 10am–12.30pm, 2–6pm.* ⏱*Closed the rest of the year.* €4, under 26, free. ✆05 65 44 19 91. Former prison cells house exhibits on local life and customs and a costume collection.

A detour can be made from Estaing to visit the 11C **Romanesque chapel**★ of **St-Pierre-de-Bessuéjouls** which is decorated with knotwork, palmettes, Maltese crosses and historiated capitals.

▶ Leave Espalion S via D 920 and follow the signs to the Château de Calmont d'Olt. Return to Espalion and continue down the valley, now on D 920.

Estaing★

Old houses in Estaing huddle around the castle named after the family whose fame and fortune spanned several centuries until the 1789 Revolution.

Château – ⏱*Open May–Jun and 1st 2 wks in Oct Tue–Sat 9.30am–12.30pm, 2–6pm; Jul–Aug Tue–Sun 10.30am–12.30pm, 2–7pm; Sept Tue–Sun 9.30am–12.30pm, 2–6pm.* ⏱*Closed 1 May.* €6 (child 12–17, €3). Guided visits available €10 (child 12–17, €6. ✆05 65 44 72 24. Built between 15C–16C with a variety of materials, the castle shows a curious mix of architectural styles. Great view of the old town and River Lot from the west terrace.

Church – *opposite the chateau.* Fine Gothic crosses enhance the front of this 15C church containing the relics of St Fleuret.

The **Gothic bridge** features a statue of François d'Estaing who had the superb bell-tower built on the town's cathedral.

Maison Cayron in the old town retains its Renaissance windows and houses the town hall (*mairie*).

▶ Continue on D 920.

Gorges du Lot★★

After Estaing the valley narrows into rugged a gorge 300m deep and 1 500m across at the top of the valley walls, jagged rocky silhouettes rise up from the woods covering the sides of the gorges.

Entraygues-sur-Truyère★

See ENTRAYGUES-SUR-TRUYÈRE.

Entraygues-sur-Truyère★

and Gorges de la Truyère

This small town at the confluence of the Lot and Truyère was founded in the 13C by the Count of Rodez.

SIGHTS

Gothic bridge★

One-way traffic in summer.
The bridge across the Truyère dates from the end of the 13C.

Old town

To see the covered passageways known as *'cantous'* and houses with overhanging upper storeys, start from the place Albert-Castanié and walk down Rue Droite. On the right is a 16C entrance with a knocker placed above the door so that riders did not have to dismount. Turn left on Rue du Collège and follow **Rue Basse★**, Entraygues' best preserved street. Continue along the water's edge (quai des Gabares) to a fine view of the castle dating from the 13C (⊶*not open to the public*).

EXCURSION

Puy de Montabès★

11km/6.8mi NE along D 34 then right on D 652.
🚶 *15min on foot round-trip.*
Superb **panoramic view★** over the mountains of Cantal, Aubrac and Rouergue (and the cathedral in Rodez in clear weather).

Entraygues-sur-Truyère

©Hervé Lenain/Photoshot

- ▶ **Population:** 1 083.
- 🖊 **Michelin Map:** 338: H-3.
- 🛈 **Info:** Office du tourisme du Pays d'Entraygues-sur-Truyère, Pl. de la Republique. ✆05 65 44 56 10. www.tourisme-entraygues.com.
- ☺ **Don't Miss:** The old town with its Gothic bridge and covered passageways.
- 👥 **Kids:** A fairytale visit to the Valon château.

🚗 DRIVING TOURS

LOT VALLEY

50km/30mi. 🖊See THE LOT VALLEY.

GORGES DE LA TRUYÈRE★

80km/50mi round-trip. Allow 3h.

▷ Leave Entraygues heading N along D 34.

Barrage de Cambeyrac

The 14.5m-high Cambeyrac dam is the last Truyère valley hydroelectric installation before the river flows into the Lot. Farther upstream is the Lardit hydroelectric power station.

▷ In the hamlet of Banhars, turn left onto D 34. Beyond the bridge over the Selves, continue right along D 34.

The road winds through the Selves valley before reaching the Volonzac plateau.

▷ In Volonzac, turn right onto a narrow road leading to Bez-Bedène.

Bez-Bedène

This typical Rouergue-style village occupies a harsh, isolated setting and consists of a few houses strung out along a rocky ridge enclosed within a meander of the Selves. Of note are the small 12C church with a bellcote, and the 14C bridge.

▶ Continue to the crossroads with D 34 and turn right towards St-Amans-des-Cots. A detour, the D 97 leads to and from the **Maury dam.** Continue towards St-Amans-des-Cots on D97 NW.

Another detour is to the **Réservoir de Montézic.**

▶ Still on D 97, cross the Phalip suspension bridge over Couesque reservoir. The road skirts the ruined castle and hamlet of Vallon where there is a view over the Truyère gorges. Turn left on D 904. The road winds to Rouens. Downhill from its church is a scenic view of Couesque reservoir. The road continues to the valley floor, with views of the Truyère gorges and Couesque. Before the bridge over the Goul, take a road to the left which leads to the Couesque plant and dam.

Couesque dam★

The reservoir of this dam stretches as far as the confluence of the Bromme and the Truyère, where the tail-race from the Brommat underground plant emerges.

▶ The valley gradually offers a landscape of meadows, vineyards and orchards. Ahead, Lardit power station uses water from the Selves and the Selvet. Turn right on D 34 to return to Entraygues.

MUR-DE-BARREZ AND THE CARLADEZ

35km/22mi round tour. Allow 2h.

▶ Leave Mur-de-Barrez on D 900 SE.

Mur-de-Barrez

This small town is an anomaly. In its architecture and traditions, it has more in common with the Auvergne than the Aveyron. Its church is dedicated to the Thomas à Becket, a reminder of the English occupation during the Hundred Years' War. Its medieval gateway is called the Tour de Monaco because for 148 years, until 1791, the region was under the rule of the prince of Monaco.

Gorges de la Bromme

The road follows the course of the Bromme along a deep rugged gorge. Farther on, the River Truyère comes into view. Its flow is diverted by the **Barthe dam** and forms part of the Sarrans-Brommat complex.

▶ After negotiating several hairpin bends, turn left onto D 537, then D 98 towards the Sarrans dam; 1.5km/0.9mi before reaching the dam are fine views of the Sarrans installations.

Sarrans dam★

This dam, one of the most important hydroelectric installations in the Massif Central, is 220m long, 105m high and 75m thick at its base.

▶ Having passed the crest of the dam, D 98 runs alongside the reservoir as far as the outskirts of the village of Laussac, which is reached along D 537.

Laussac

The village is built on a promontory which, owing to the flooding of the valley, has become a peninsula.

▶ Rejoin D 98 and turn right.

Continue 1.5km/1mi on from the junction for a fine view of the reservoir.

▶ Carry on along D 98 as far as a crossroads and turn right onto D 139.

Belvédère de Jou

Beyond the hamlet of Jou, there is a panorama of Laussac peninsula, Devèze hospice and Sarrans reservoir.

▶ Return to Laussac along D 98 to the left, and then take D 166 towards Albinhac and Brommat.

The road offers views of the Barrez, the Cantal and the hills of Aubrac.

▶ Beyond Brommat, D 900 leads back to Mur-de-Barrez.

Aubrac★

The Aubrac plateau is the most southerly of the volcanic uplands of the Auvergne. It is a region of ponderous, rolling hills, with vast stretches of countryside covered in pastureland on which herds of cattle, named after the region, graze during the summer (Fête de la Transhumance in late May). The milk from the cows is used to make tomme cheese – the chief ingredient of aligot. In winter, cross-country skiers arrive at the resorts of the Espace Nordique des Monts d'Aubrac, set up in 1985 (Aubrac, Bonnecombe, Brameloup, Lacalm, Laguiole, Nasbinals, St-Urcize).

VISIT

Situated at 1 300m above sea level, Aubrac is a small inland holiday resort. A square tower, Romanesque church and 16C building (now a forester's lodge) are all that remain of the estate of the Brothers Hospitaller of Aubrac, monastic knights who, from the 12C to the 17C, escorted pilgrims to Rocamadour or Santiago de Compostela.

Jardin botanique d'Aubrac

Open Jul–Aug daily 9am–7pm; mid-May–Jun and Sept Tue–Sun 9am–6pm. €4 (child 12–18, €3). www.aubrac-jardin.org.
The Aubrac plateau has a rich variety of flora as can be seen in this botanical garden with 500 species of plant.

🚗 DRIVING TOUR

WESTERN AUBRAC
Round-trip of 117km/73mi leaving from Aubrac. Allow 4h.

Take D 533 to St-Chély d'Aubrac. Turn left on D 19 to Bonnefon. A spur, D 211, leads to the ski resort of Brameloup.

- **Location:** 57km/34.5mi NE of Rodez.
- **Michelin Map:** 338: J-3.
- **Info:** Maison de l'Aubrac 12470 Aubrac. 05 65 44 67 90. www.maisondelaubrac.com. Open Apr–Nov.
- **Don't Miss:** Jardin Botanique.

Prades-d'Aubrac
Note the octagonal bell tower on this village's 16C church. The road descends towards the Lot with views over the Rouergue plateaux of moorlands, meadows, fields of crops, groves of chestnuts, and luscious orchards.

Continue on D 19 and turn right on D 557.

Saint-Côme-d'Olt.
See THE LOT VALLEY, Driving Tour.

Espalion★
See THE LOT VALLEY, Driving Tour.

Take D 921 N.

A short detour leads to **Château du Bousquet,** an austere 14C castle built of volcanic basalt.

Soulages-Bonneval
Le grenier de Capou is a idiosyncratic and eclectic barn-cum-museum of objects mostly made from wood, some of which are sure to prompt guessing games.

Take D 541 to Laguiole.

Laguiole
Laguiole (pronounced Laïole) is famous for its elegant pocket knives with distinctive handles made of horn or wood; it also produces an excellent cheese from cows' milk.

Take D 15 back to Aubrac .

INDEX

INDEX

INDEX

INDEX

INDEX

INDEX

INDEX

W

STAY

INDEX

♀/EAT

INDEX

MAPS AND PLANS

MAP LEGEND

	Sight	Seaside resort	Winter sports resort	Spa
Highly recommended ★★★				
Recommended ★★				
Interesting ★				

Additional symbols

🄳		Tourist information
═══	═══	Motorway or other primary route
❶	❶	Junction: complete, limited
⊨═══	═══	Pedestrian street
I═══I	----	Unsuitable for traffic, street subject to restrictions
ɪɪɪɪɪ	----	Steps – Footpath
🚂	🚃	Train station – Auto-train station
🚌	SNCF	Coach (bus) station
•—•—•		Tram
Ⓜ		Metro, underground
🅿		Park-and-Ride
🕭		Access for the disabled
✉		Post office
☏		Telephone
⊠		Covered market
•✕•		Barracks
△		Drawbridge
ʊ		Quarry
✕		Mine
🅱	🄵	Car ferry (river or lake)
⛴		Ferry service: cars and passengers
⛵		Foot passengers only
③		Access route number common to Michelin maps and town plans
Bert (R.)...		Main shopping street
AZ B		Map co-ordinates

Selected monuments and sights

◉	⇨	Tour - Departure point
♟ ♟		Catholic church
♟ ♟		Protestant church, other temple
▦ ▦ ▥		Synagogue - Mosque
▬▬		Building
■		Statue, small building
♱		Calvary, wayside cross
◎		Fountain
•—•—•▪		Rampart - Tower - Gate
✕		Château, castle, historic house
•.•		Ruins
ᴗ		Dam
✿		Factory, power plant
☆		Fort
⋒		Cave
▣		Troglodyte dwelling
ⅲ		Prehistoric site
▼		Viewing table
Ⱳ		Viewpoint
▲		Other place of interest

Special symbol

⠿	Fortified town (bastide): in southwest France, a new town built in the 13-14C and typified by a geometrical layout.

Abbreviations

A	Agricultural office (Chambre d'agriculture)
C	Chamber of Commerce (Chambre de commerce)
H	Town hall (Hôtel de ville)
J	Law courts (Palais de justice)
M	Museum (Musée)
P	Local authority offices (Préfecture, sous-préfecture)
POL.	Police station (Police)
⚜	Police station (Gendarmerie)
T	Theatre (Théâtre)
U	University (Université)

Sports and recreation

	Racecourse
	Skating rink
	Outdoor, indoor swimming pool
	Multiplex Cinema
	Marina, sailing centre
	Trail refuge hut
▫—▪—▪—▫	Cable cars, gondolas
▫+++++▫	Funicular, rack railway
	Tourist train
◆	Recreation area, park
	Theme, amusement park
	Wildlife park, zoo
	Gardens, park, arboretum
	Bird sanctuary, aviary
	Walking tour, footpath
	Of special interest to children

COMPANION PUBLICATIONS

MICHELIN MAPS

Motorists who plan ahead will always have the appropriate maps at hand. Michelin products are complementary: for each of the sights listed in The Green Guide, map references are indicated which help you find your location on our maps.

To travel the roads in this region, you may use any of the following:

♦ the series of **Local maps** at a scale of 1:150 000 include useful symbols for identifying tourist attractions, town plans and an index. The diagram opposite indicates which maps you need to travel in Languedoc-Roussillon-Tarn Gorges.

♦ the **Regional maps** at a scale of 1:200 000 **nos 526, and 527** cover the main roads and secondary roads and show castles, churches and other religious edifices, scenic view points, megalithic monuments, swimming beaches on lakes and rivers, swimming pools, golf courses, race tracks, air fields, and more.

And remember to travel with the latest edition of the **map of France 721**, which gives an overall view of the region, and the main access roads that connect it to the rest of France. Also available in atlas and mini-atlas formats.

INTERNET

Michelin is pleased to offer a route-planning service on the Internet:
www.travelguide.michelin.com
www.viamichelin.com

Choose the shortest route, a route without tolls, or the Michelin recommended route to your destination; you can also access information about hotels and restaurants from The Michelin Guide, and tourist sites from The Green Guide.

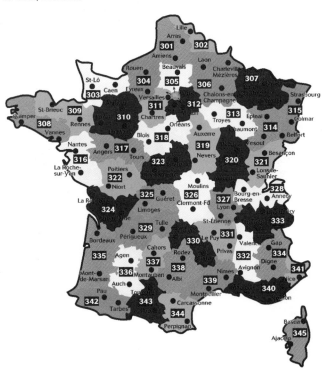

MICHELIN IS CONTINUALLY INNOVATING FOR SAFER, CLEANER, MORE ECONOMICAL, MORE CONNECTED... BETTER ALL-ROUND MOBILITY.

Tyres wear more quickly on short urban journeys.

TRUE!

You tend to accelerate and brake more often when driving around town so your tyres work harder!
If you are stuck in traffic, keep calm and drive slowly.

Tyre pressure only affects your car's safety.

FALSE!

Driving with underinflated tyres (0.5 bar below recommended pressure) doesn't just impact handling and fuel consumption, it will shave 8,000 km off tyre lifespan.
Make sure you check tyre pressure about once a month and before you go on holiday or a long journey.

Fitting **2 winter tyres** on my car guarantees maximum safety.

FALSE!

In the winter, especially when temperatures drop below 7°C, to ensure better road holding, all four tyres should be identical and fitted at the same time.

2 WINTER TYRES ONLY =
risk of compromised road holding.

4 WINTER TYRES =
safer handling when cornering, driving downhill and braking.

If you regularly encounter rain, snow or black ice, choose a **MICHELIN Alpin tyre**. This range offers you sharp handling plus a comfortable ride to safely face the challenge of winter driving.

MICHELIN

MICHELIN IS COMMITTED

▶ MICHELIN IS **GLOBAL LEADER IN FUEL-EFFICIENT TYRES** FOR LIGHT VEHICLES.

▶ **EDUCATING OF YOUNGSTERS IN ROAD SAFETY,** NOT FORGETTING TWO-WHEELERS. LOCAL ROAD SAFETY CAMPAIGNS WERE RUN IN **16 COUNTRIES** IN 2015.

QUIZ

1. TYRES ARE BLACK SO WHY IS THE MICHELIN MAN WHITE?

Back in 1898 when the Michelin Man was first created from a stack of tyres, they were made of natural rubber, cotton and sulphur and were therefore light-coloured. The composition of tyres did not change until after the First World War when carbon black was introduced. But the Michelin Man kept his colour!

2. FOR HOW LONG HAS MICHELIN BEEN GUIDING TRAVELLERS?

Since 1900. When the MICHELIN guide was published at the turn of the century, it was claimed that it would last for a hundred years. It's still around today and remains a reference with new editions and online restaurant listings in a number of countries.

3. WHEN WAS THE "BIB GOURMAND" INTRODUCED IN THE MICHELIN GUIDE?

The symbol was created in 1997 but as early as 1954 the MICHELIN guide was recommending "exceptional good food at moderate prices". Today, it features on the MICHELIN Restaurants website and app.

If you want to enjoy a fun day out and find out more about Michelin, why not visit the l'Aventure Michelin museum and shop in Clermont-Ferrand, France:
www.laventuremichelin.com

MICHELIN
A better way forward

Michelin Travel Partner

Société par actions simplifiées au capital de 11 288 880 EUR
27 cours de l'Ile Seguin - 92100 Boulogne Billancourt (France)
R.C.S. Nanterre 433 677 721

© Michelin Travel Partner
ISBN 978-2-067220-52-2
Printed: October 2016
Printed and bound in France : Imprimerie CHIRAT, 42540 Saint-Just-la-Pendue - N° 201610.0366